AUGUSTUS

By the same author

AUGUSTUS

First Emperor of Rome

ADRIAN GOLDSWORTHY

Yale

UNIVERSITY PRESS

New Haven & London

First published 2014 in the United States by Yale University
Press and in Great Britain by Weidenfeld & Nicolson.

Copyright © 2014 by Adrian Goldsworthy.

Yale University Press books may be purchased in quantity for
educational, business, or promotional use. For information,
please e-mail sales.press@yale.edu (U.S. office)
or sales@yaleup.co.uk (U.K. office).

Typeset by Input Data Services Ltd, Bridgwater, Somerset.
Printed in the United States of America.

Library of Congress Control Number: 2014940657
ISBN 978-0-300-17872-2 (cloth: alk. paper)

A catalogue record for this book is
available from the British Library.

This paper meets the requirements of
ANSI/NISO Z39.48-1992 (Permanence of Paper).

10 9 8 7 6 5 4 3 2 1

CONTENTS

ACKNOWLEDGEMENTS

Many of the ideas in this book have developed over many years. At the end of my first year at Oxford back in 1988, I took a course on Augustan Rome, which was wonderfully taught by my tutor Nicholas Purcell, who first brought me into contact with Platner and Ashby's hefty *A Topographical Dictionary of Ancient Rome* (1929). In the years that followed there were lectures, seminars and tutorials given by the likes of Alan Bowman, Miriam Griffin, Fergus Millar, Barbara Levick, Andrew Lintott and David Stockton, all helping to shape my understanding of the ancient world and Augustus and his era in particular. You will find works by all of these in the notes at the end of this book, and I should also acknowledge the great debt to the many other scholars whose books and articles I have consulted.

More specifically, I must thank those who have helped during the writing of this biography. Philip Matyszak is a friend made during those years at Oxford, whose ideas about the inner workings of the Roman Senate have always been inspirational. Once again he has taken time off from his own writing to read this manuscript and provide many useful comments. Similarly Ian Hughes took a look at a large chunk of the book and provided comments blending an understanding of the history with something of a copy-editor's eye. Kevin Powell read the entire book with his accustomed eye for detail and ability to retain sight of the broader picture. Another great friend, Dorothy King, listened to many of the ideas as they developed, invariably commenting with both insight and wit, and also helped by providing some of the pictures. Thanks should also go to my mother for her proof-reading skills, and my wife for taking a look at some sections. They and all the other family and friends have had to live with Augustus in their lives for the last few years, and I am very grateful for their support.

As always, I must thank my agent, Georgina Capel, for creating the situation allowing me to take the time to write this book properly, and for her unfailing enthusiasm for the project. Thanks must also go to my editors, Alan Samson in the UK and Christopher Rogers in the USA, and their teams for producing so handsome a volume.

Finally, I owe a great debt to David Breeze for producing the family trees in this book. Inspired by the tables in M. Cooley (ed.), *The Age of Augustus. Lactor 17* (2003), he not only suggested the idea of having more specific tables looking at the family at different stages, but then went to considerable trouble to produce them for me. The family connections of Augustus' relatives and their contemporaries are complicated in the extreme, but these diagrams go a long way to making them seem simple.

MAPS

INTRODUCTION

'And it came to pass in those days, that there went out a decree from Caesar Augustus, that all the world should be taxed. (And this taxing was first made when Cyrenius was governor of Syria.) And all went to be taxed, every one into his own city.' *The Gospel according to Luke, later first century* AD.[1]

This brief mention in the Christmas story must have been the first time I heard of Augustus, and although it is hard to be precise with such early memories I must have been very young. Like most people who hear or read these words, I doubt that I thought much of them, and it was only later that my love of history grew and I developed a particular fascination for everything about ancient Rome. You cannot study Roman history without coming across Augustus and his legacy. He was the first emperor, the man who finally replaced a Republic which had lasted for almost half a millennium with a veiled monarchy. The system he created gave the empire some 250 years of stability, when it was both larger and more prosperous than at any other time. In the third century AD it faced decades of crisis and survived only after extensive reform, but even so the 'Roman' emperors who ruled from Constantinople until the fifteenth century felt themselves to be rightful successors to the power and authority of Augustus.

Unquestionably important, his story is at the same time intensely dramatic. When teaching students about Augustus, I have always stopped to remind them that he was not quite nineteen when he thrust himself into Rome's extremely violent politics – hence almost always younger than anyone in the class. It is often hard to remember this when recounting what he did, skilfully and unscrupulously manoeuvring his way through the twisting allegiances of these years of civil war. The great-nephew of the murdered Julius Caesar, he was made the principal heir in his will and given his name, which

he took to mean full adoption. Power was not supposed to be inherited at Rome, but armed with this name he rallied the dead
dictator's supporters and proclaimed his intention to assume all of
his father's offices and status. He then proceeded to achieve precisely that, against all the odds and opposed by far more experienced
rivals. Mark Antony was the last of these, and he was defeated and
dead by 30 BC. The young, murderous warlord of the civil wars
then managed to reinvent himself as the beloved guardian of the
state, took the name Augustus with its religious overtones, and was
eventually dubbed 'the father of his country', an inclusive rather
than divisive figure. He held supreme power for forty-four years –
a very long time for any monarch – and when he died of old age,
there was no question that his nominated successor would follow
him.

Yet in spite of his remarkable story and profound influence on the
history of an empire which has shaped the culture of the western
world, Caesar Augustus has slipped from the wider consciousness.
For most people he is a name mentioned in Christmas services or
school Nativity plays and nothing more than that. Hardly anybody
stops to think that the month of July is named after Julius Caesar,
but I suspect even fewer are aware that August is named after Augustus. Julius Caesar is famous, and so are Antony and Cleopatra,
Nero, Alexander the Great, Hannibal, perhaps Hadrian, and a few
of the philosophers – but Augustus is not. One of the reasons is that
Shakespeare never wrote a play about him, perhaps because there
is little natural tragedy in a man who lives to a ripe old age and dies
in his bed. He appears as Octavius in *Julius Caesar* and as Caesar in
Antony and Cleopatra, but in neither play is his character particularly
engaging, unlike Brutus, Antony – or even lesser players like Eno-
barbus. His fate is principally to serve as a foil to Antony, weak, even
cowardly, but cold and manipulative where the latter is brave, intensely physical, simple and passionate. The contrast was already
there in the ancient sources, and had its roots in the propaganda war
waged at the time; it has only tended to become even more pro-
nounced in modern treatments of the story – think for instance of

the glacially cold performance with just hints of sadism given by Roddy McDowall in the famous 1963 epic movie *Cleopatra*.[2]

Calculating, devious and utterly ruthless, such an Augustus encourages the audience to sympathise with Antony and Cleopatra, and thus makes their deaths all the more tragic, for in the end these stories are about them. No play, film or novel with Augustus at its heart has ever captured the popular imagination. In Robert Graves' novel, *I Claudius* – and the wonderful BBC dramatisation which is now at least as well known – he is once again no more than prominent among the supporting cast. This treatment is much more sympathetic, and he plays a different role as the simple, emotional – and only occasionally menacing – old man being outmanoeuvred by Livia, his manipulative and murderous wife. Such stories are involving and entertaining, but on their own give no real understanding of why Augustus was so important, making it hard to connect the young schemer to the ageing and often outwitted emperor.

There is far more to Augustus' life than this, and this bigger story is far from dull. One of the great dangers is to assume an inevitability about his success, whether based on his genius for politics or – and this is an older view – wider trends which made the creation of a monarchy at Rome little more than a matter of time. Augustus' longevity surprised everyone, as did his success, especially in the early years. Much of the time the gambler is more obvious than the careful planner. Augustus took risks, especially during the civil wars, and not all of these risks paid off. There was more of Julius Caesar about him than is sometimes appreciated, not least in his ability to extricate himself from scrapes of his own making. Nor is there any real evidence of a long-nurtured plan for creating his new regime; instead the picture is one of improvisation and experimentation, creating the system by trial and error, with chance events playing almost as big a role as design. The image of the icy manipulator also quickly vanishes as we look at a man who struggled, and often failed, to restrain his passions and hot temper. This is the Augustus who had an affair with the married and pregnant Livia, made her husband divorce her and then had the man preside over their wedding mere days after she had given birth. It is an episode you might expect more of Antony – or perhaps even more of Nero, great-grandson of Mark Antony and Augustus' sister.

Alongside the passion came a good deal of savagery. Augustus, Antony and their fellow triumvir Lepidus were all guilty of mass murder, famously during the proscriptions – 'these many, then, shall die, their names are pricked' in Shakespeare's version – and on plenty of other occasions. That the other warlords of this era rarely behaved any better does not absolve them of such cruelty. It is often diffi-cult to like the young Augustus, in spite of his moderation in later life, and the struggle to reconcile two apparently different men has troubled most of his modern biographers. Often the solution is ef-fectively to divide his life into two. His initial rise up until the victory at Actium readily lends itself to narrative, packed as it is with bat-tles and intrigue, and such well-known characters as Cicero, Brutus, Sextus Pompeius and Cleopatra. Then many biographers will jump to his later years and turn to the alleged intrigue surrounding his choice of successors – and it is no coincidence that these two distinct stories mirror the themes chosen respectively by Shakespeare and Graves. Other authors, especially those from the academic world, also usually end their narrative in 30 BC, and for the rest of his life discuss broader topics – for instance 'Augustus and the Senate', 'Au-gustus and the provinces', 'Augustus and religion'.[3]

Biography has few champions in the academic world, in spite of – perhaps in part because of – its immense appeal for more general readers. I wrote my biography of Julius Caesar because none of the more recent books about him were entirely satisfying – either they lacked detail or they only covered one aspect of his life. Each looked at either his political or his military career, but never at both – a dis-tinction which would have baffled the Romans. It was while working on that book that I knew I had one day to write one on a similar scale about Augustus because no one has yet written the one he deserves. There are good treatments of aspects of his life, some excellent brief overviews, but nothing that deals with all of his life in any real detail. The great weakness of the thematic approach is that the man tends to be lost in discussion of policy, ideas, or the imagery employed by the regime. It far too readily becomes as disjointed as the leap from the young to the elderly Augustus, which loses any real sense of how the one turned into the other. As with *Caesar: The Life of a Colossus*, the aim is to write as if this were the biography of a modern states-man, asking the same questions even if our sources make it difficult to answer them, and trying as far as is possible to understand the real man.[4]

THE CHANGING FACE OF AN EMPEROR

Yet the real Augustus is very hard to pin down, not least because he took great care to reinvent himself during his lifetime. In the middle of the fourth century AD the Emperor Julian – himself lately having seized by force the supreme title of Augustus after several years as a junior Caesar in the imperial system of those years – wrote a satire imagining a banquet where the gods welcomed Rome's deified em-perors. Augustus is there, but is depicted as a strange, unnatural figure, constantly changing colour to blend with his surroundings like a chameleon. Only when instructed by philosophy is he turned into a good and wise ruler.[5]

Augustus was aware of his public image, but then all Roman politicians advertised their own and their families' merits and achievements at every opportunity. Mark Antony still has a reputa-tion as an experienced and capable general that has far more to do with his own propaganda than his actual military experience and abilities. The big difference with Augustus was that he had so much longer to develop and spread his message, as well as vastly greater re-sources than anyone else. More images survive of Augustus than any other human being from the ancient world. Especially after Actium, it is even harder to see past this façade and understand the real man. Even so we have plenty of stories about his domestic life and habits, a lot of anecdotes about everyday incidents and even a collection of jokes told by him or at his expense. There is far more material of this sort about Augustus than Julius Caesar or almost any other major figure in Roman history. Yet we need to be careful, for such apparently 'natural' moments were also opportunities to perform, and public life at Rome was highly theatrical. Roman politicians lived their lives in public, and Augustus in particular wanted to appear a model of proper behaviour in private life as well as when performing his official duties. Little about him was ever entirely straightforward.

Perhaps we should begin with the basic problem of what to call him, having noted that even Shakespeare uses a different name in each play. Born Caius Octavius, when he became Julius Caesar's heir he took his name and became Caius Julius Caesar. He could have added Octavianus to this as a reminder of his real – rather obscure – family, but deliberately did not, and only his enemies ever called him Octavianus. As the years passed he modified his name, dropping the first name Caius and replacing it with the highly unorthodox Imperator – victorious general or generalissimo. After Julius Caesar was deified he became the son of the divine Julius, and finally in 27 BC the name Augustus was awarded to him by the vote of the Senate and People of Rome, no doubt carefully prepared to know that this would please him.

Thus we have a man with three very distinct names at different stages of his life, and a fair bit of variation in form and detail even with these. The modern convention is to call him Octavian until 27 BC and after that to call him Augustus, avoiding the name Caesar altogether and with it the risk of confusion with Julius Caesar. While being clear, this is also deeply misleading and helps to reinforce the false division between the bloodstained triumvir and the distinguished statesman and ruler. Names mattered a good deal in the Roman world – and more recently, since we need only think of the longevity of Caesar or Kaiser or Tsar as a title of power. Mark Antony dubbed the young Augustus 'a boy who owes everything to name' precisely because being called Caesar gave the teenager a significance he could not otherwise have had. That was why Augustus never called himself Octavian, and if we call him this, rather than Caesar, then it makes it much harder to understand the events of these years. It is important to know what he called himself at each stage of his life, and so in the chapters to follow I shall always refer to him in this way, and have organised the book into sections accordingly. The dictator will always be named as Julius Caesar, and if ever the text mentions Caesar then it refers to Augustus.

It is not only his name that proves problematic. *Imperator* is the Latin word from which we get our word emperor, but it did not have this sense in Augustus' day. He called himself *princeps*, which means 'first' or 'leading' citizen, and this was how other Romans referred to him. If we call him emperor, then we are imposing a different concept onto his regime, one shaped by hindsight and the knowledge that Rome would be a monarchy for many centuries to come. Therefore outside the Introduction and Conclusion I will never refer to him as emperor, although I have sometimes used the term for his successors. Similarly I refer to the regime he created not as the empire – since the Republic also possessed an overseas empire – but as the principate, a term familiar to scholars but rarely used outside the academic world.

Another difficult word with Latin origins is precisely this Republic, which comes from *res publica*, the 'public thing' or 'commonwealth'. This was how the Romans referred to their state, but it did not have the specific institutional definition of our term 'republic'. It is too useful to avoid altogether – how else can we easily speak of the political system that had governed Rome for so long until it broke down in the first century BC? However, I have tried to avoid the modern tendency to refer to opponents of Julius Caesar and the triumvirs as Republicans, since this imposes a false coherence on what were in truth disparate groups with a wide range of attitudes and aims. The term also gives a legitimacy that many do not deserve – in much the same way that using the name Octavian gives a posthumous victory to Mark Antony. (There are limits to the quest for precision, and I have used July and August even before these names were introduced since few readers would be familiar with the months of Quinctilis and Sextilis.)

Throughout the discussion I will strive to be independent, which

may seem an odd thing to say when talking of 2,000-year-old conflicts and disputes, but history readily excites emotions and even
the most sober and serious of scholars is not immune. Julius Caesar
has often attracted fawning adulation and bitter loathing, and the
same is almost as true of Augustus. Throughout the nineteenth century and beyond he was widely praised for curing the malaise of
a broken Republic, giving the Romans peace, stability and prosperity as a benevolent monarch. In an era when kings and empires still
dominated Europe and much of the world, such an understanding
came readily. This would change during the twentieth century as
the world convulsed and old certainties vanished: the most influential treatment of Augustus came with Sir Ronald Syme's magisterial
book *The Roman Revolution*, first released just before the Second
World War. Deliberately provocative in its willingness not to assume
that the rise of Augustus was a good thing, and innovatively employing the developing field of prosopography – the study of families and
relationships among the aristocracy – it depicted the era as the rise
of the leader and his faction supplanting the old elite. Behind it all
was the spectre of contemporary dictators – most of all Mussolini,
who styled himself *Il Duce* in conscious emulation of the *dux* Augustus, and called his supporters fascists after the symbol of the *fasces*,
the bundle of rods surrounding an axe which marked the power of
a Roman magistrate. Today, a reader of the book is more likely to
think of the rise of the even more sinister National Socialism of Germany or the totalitarian control of Stalin.[6]

The modern world has grown very suspicious of dictators of
whatever political hue, and less willing to pardon the murderous
nature of Augustus' rise as being justified by the peace he eventually
created. Yet we need to be careful not to paint the past in simple
shades, or automatically to assume that all dictators or all empires,
or indeed all states, are essentially alike. Augustus killed a lot of
people, but he inflicted on the world nothing like the misery of a
Hitler or a Stalin, and, as ever, we should view his behaviour in the
context of the times. In his willingness to kill his enemies he was no
better or worse than the other warlords to appear at that time. Julius

Caesar had been different, and had pardoned Brutus, Cassius and several of the other men who later stabbed him to death – a point Augustus, Antony and Lepidus made when they posted death lists of their enemies.

To be not as bad as Hitler is scarcely a ringing endorsement, while to say that someone was no worse than his rivals is only a little better; but an awareness that a successful leader was flawed should not cause us to be blind to the failings of his rivals. Syme was too good a scholar to fall prey to this, although he was extremely charitable in his judgements of Antony and deliberately harsh in his comments on Augustus' supporters, especially the majority who came from outside the established aristocracy. He was also aware that family connections among Rome's elite were complicated, and did not in themselves dictate allegiances, which might rapidly shift or depend on many other considerations. Although three-quarters of a century old, *The Roman Revolution* – combined with Syme's considerable wider body of work and his influence on others – continues to set the tone of much discussion of Augustus and his age, especially in scholarship in the English-speaking world. There have been many new approaches and changes of emphasis, but on the whole these have looked at particular themes or details. There has been no other overarching study of the period with anything like as much influence, and so in many ways the era – as I studied it as a student and later taught it as a lecturer – remained one shaped by perceptions from the middle of the twentieth century.

The structuring inevitable in formal teaching always risks distorting the past. Courses on the late Republic tend to end with Julius Caesar. The Augustan age usually begins with Actium and is either kept separate or rolled into a study of the principate, while the triumviral years from 44–31 BC get little attention at all – helping to reinforce the distinction between Octavian and Augustus. More rarely is Augustus and his career looked at as a continuation of the Republic, and instead the attention falls on the apparent differences. Augustus did not know that he was creating a new system that would last for centuries, and studying it in this way exaggerates the change between the Republic and the principate that was certainly much less apparent at the time. It also feeds the modern usage of terms like Republic and Republicanism, and can extend to the portrayal of a senatorial opposition allegedly forcing Augustus to hide the reality of his power behind a Republican façade.

Attitudes to Julius Caesar also shape our perception of his successor. The dictator was murdered because he held supreme permanent power, while Augustus gained this and survived to old age. The natural logic for most scholars is therefore that Augustus must have behaved in a fundamentally different way to his 'father', softening and hiding his power where the latter had wielded it blatantly. This underlying assumption reinforces the unwillingness to call Augustus by the name Caesar in modern accounts. As we shall see, many scholars follow Syme and take this much further, asserting that Augustus very deliberately distanced himself from Julius Caesar the man – as opposed to the divine Julius – once he had beaten Antony and become master of the state.

The idea is convenient, at a glance seems to explain their differing fates, and is repeated again and again, making it unfortunate that there is no evidence to support it. In the first place the comparison is flawed, since it is inevitably drawn to the situations of Julius Caesar at the end of 45 BC and Augustus after Actium. No one seems to notice that the former had only just completed his victory in a hard-fought civil war and during the last five years of his life had spent very little time in Rome. For all his energy, there were limits to what Julius Caesar could achieve during such a brief and frequently interrupted period of supremacy. In contrast, by the time he had beaten Antony, Augustus had held unfettered power as triumvir for over a decade – and for the bulk of that time was in Rome and Italy without either of his colleagues. To begin after Actium ignores these long years when he cemented his control by a combination of force and the advancement of men loyal to him. Those years had also greatly thinned the ranks of the old aristocratic families, and the failure of Brutus and Cassius was hardly an inspiration for others to follow in their footsteps. Thus the assumption that since Julius Caesar faced

– and failed to placate – the resistance of a hard core of traditional senatorial opinion then Augustus must have faced and overcome similar opposition, is unfounded. Their situations differed in far too many ways. There really is no convincing evidence for the senatorial opposition to Augustus so beloved of many modern scholars. In fact academics have shown a far deeper loyalty to the Republican system than was ever displayed by the aristocracy of Rome. A closer look reveals far less difference between Julius Caesar and Caesar Augustus.

It is well worth stepping back from the accumulated generations of scholarly debate in an effort to tell Augustus' story afresh. This is not a history of the times, but a biography, and thus, although wider events are considered, our attention is fixed on Augustus himself. It is important to know where he was – and if possible what he was doing – at each point in his life. One thing this reveals is the amount of time he spent travelling in Italy or the provinces, something that few of his successors would choose to do until Hadrian in the second century AD. It also makes clear the heavy workload he maintained even as an old man. His career was based on more than simply reforms and legislation, and relied on attention to detail and day-to-day conduct which can all too readily be lost in rapid surveys of what he did and achieved. The changes that occurred, whether institutional, social, economic, or the physical transformation of Rome itself and the wider empire, assume their true importance if we gain a sense of the pace at which they came about.

This is a long book, but could easily have been twice or three times the size. I have tried to give glimpses of the impact of Augustus on Italy and the wider empire so that we do not simply look at the fate of the aristocratic families in Rome, but space prevents the inclusion of more detail. Whole books could be written about this and many of the other topics touched on lightly – there is something deeply frustrating in summing up Virgil's *Aeneid* in a couple of pages, and barely getting the chance to talk about Ovid and some of the other poets. One of the great joys of writing this book has been the chance to reread the poetry and other literature of this era – in many cases for the first time since I was a student. I have done my best to give a flavour of such things without losing sight of the central figure of Augustus, since this is a book about him. For those whose interest is sparked by the man and his times, there are the endnotes and a long bibliography which will give access to the truly vast literature on these subjects.

TELLING THE TALE: SOURCES FOR THE LIFE OF AUGUSTUS

Only a tiny fraction of the literature, official documents and private correspondence from the Roman world has survived into the present day. This was a time before printing presses, when everything had to be copied by hand – which, apart from being laborious, and thus expensive, ran the risk of introducing an ever-growing number of errors. Many things were lost because no one troubled to make sufficient copies. Far more vanished with the collapse of the Roman Empire and the change to a world where literacy was far less common and there was less of the wealth needed to promote the copying of books. In the Middle Ages, the Church preserved some ancient texts, but was selective in its choice and then these selections suffered further substantial losses to fire, accident and neglect. This always means that there is much we cannot know about the ancient world, and at every stage we must balance the probability of partial and often contradictory sources.

The fullest narratives of these years were written long after the events. Appian, whose *Civil Wars* extend down to the defeat of Sextus Pompeius in 36 BC, wrote in the early second century AD. Dio, whose history covers the entire period in greatest detail and survives with only a few missing fragments for Augustus' life, wrote in the early third century. Both men were Greeks – although Dio was also a Roman senator and senior magistrate – and wrote in their own language, which sometimes makes it harder to be sure of the Latin terms they translated. Both wrote at a time when the principate was firmly established and the rule of emperors unremarkable, and are inclined to transfer the attitudes of their own day to the earlier periods. Velleius Paterculus began his public career under Augustus, and his brief narrative has the advantage of being written much closer to the events, but also suffers from his determined adulation of the Emperor Tiberius. These are our fullest narrative accounts and do not cover everything, making it sometimes necessary to draw on later surveys by authors like Florus and Orosius, especially for events in the provinces and on the frontiers. While better than nothing, such sources must be used with extreme caution. The historian Livy was a contemporary, but the relevant books of his account, which went down to 9 BC, only survive in very brief summaries compiled at a much later date.

Until his execution on the orders of Augustus, Antony, and Lepidus in 43 BC, the letters and speeches of Cicero give us immediate and highly detailed – if obviously also highly partisan – descriptions of events. These are all the more fascinating for including letters written to him by others, as well as the often unfounded rumours that circulated in these desperate times and could have as much an influence on someone's actions as the truth. Sadly, we only have some of Cicero's works, and we know of others, including more correspondence between the orator and Augustus, that were available to ancient authors but which have since been lost.

Augustus' own autobiography covered the years down to 25 BC, but has not survived, although some of the information from it is preserved in the short biography written by the contemporary Nicolaus of Damascus. We do have the *Deeds of the Divine Augustus (Res Gestae)*, a text prepared in the last years of his life and set up outside his Mausoleum – and copied elsewhere – after his death. This mainly lists achievements and honours and so tells us what he wanted to be the official record of his career. More complete, and far more personal, is the biography written by Suetonius at the end of the first and beginning of the second centuries AD. Clearly drawn from a range of sources, some deeply hostile to him and most likely originating in the propaganda wars in the years from 44–30 BC, this provides a wealth of information. Especially interesting are the extracts from private letters written to family members, some of which also appear in his biographies of Tiberius and Claudius. More frustrating is the lack of any fixed dates or other reference points for many of the incidents.

Other sources provide snippets of comparable material. There is some in Plutarch's *Lives* of Brutus, Cicero and Mark Antony and elsewhere in his wider works, which have a similar date to Suetonius and Appian. Tacitus was their contemporary, and a senior Roman senator, but he did not cover Augustus in his historical works, and only indirectly conveys information about him. Both the older and younger Seneca, who were active a little earlier in the first century AD, also provide some fascinating details. Much later, but clearly drawing on earlier sources, the early-fifth-century-AD writer Macrobius provides the collection of jokes involving Augustus already mentioned. In all of these works we usually cannot know where the authors found their information, making it impossible to verify. Yet perhaps the most significant feature is that there are so many personal anecdotes about Augustus, telling us something about how people thought of him and how he in turn wanted to be seen.[7]

Inscriptions, whether carved on stone or the slogans on coins, also offer very deliberate statements from the time, just as images and sculptures carry conscious messages. Many have the advantage of being very immediate, especially when the dating is clear, and so may reflect short-term priorities as well as wider messages. Excavation of buildings and other structures can also reveal changing priorities, although here more caution is needed since the remains revealed by excavation require careful interpretation and are seldom so complete or so fully understood as to make this interpretation absolutely certain. Context means a good deal with all such physical evidence, but is almost never as clear as we would like, and older excavations were often carried out with less care and sophistication than more recent ones. Especially with works of art and architecture we can find it difficult to remain subjective, and struggle even more not to read too little or too much into minor details. How much time did the Romans really spend considering the pictures and slogans on the money they used? Yet, unlike the literary sources, ongoing work continues to augment the physical evidence for Augustus' era, and it adds greatly to our understanding of his world.

Understanding Augustus is not easy, and care needs to be taken with each type of evidence. It is also very important to be open about the limitations of our sources. There are some things that we simply cannot know, and probably never shall. There are plenty more where we are left to guess, and again we must be open about the basis of such guesswork. We must never pretend certainty where none is possible. Absolute truth is elusive, perhaps impossible, but that does not mean that we should not do our best to get as close to it as we can. We can say a lot about Augustus, and we can marshal all the different types of evidence as we attempt to understand the man and his world.

PART ONE

CAIUS OCTAVIUS (THURINUS)
63–44 BC

'As a child he was given the *cognomen* Thurinus, either in memory of the origins of his ancestors or because it was shortly after his birth that his father Octavius won a victory over fugitive slaves in Thurina . . . He is often called Thurinus as an insult in the letters of Mark Antony, to which he merely replied that he was surprised using his old name was thought to be an insult.'
Suetonius, *Augustus* 7. 1.

I

'FATHER OF HIS COUNTRY'

'On the day he was born, the question of the Catilinarian conspiracy was before the Senate, and Octavius was late because of his wife's confinement, when as is often told, Publius Nigidius, finding out why he was late and learning the hour of the birth, stated that the master of all the world had been born.' *Suetonius, early second century* AD.[1]

In 63 BC Rome was by far the largest city in the known world. Its population numbered at least three-quarters of a million and would rise to more than a million by the end of the century. Most lived in squalid, overcrowded tenement blocks or *insulae* (literally 'islands'), prone to fire and rife with disease. With so many people in one place, inevitably there were many births and deaths every day. So there was nothing especially remarkable when a woman named Atia went into labour and just before dawn on 23 September presented her husband with a son.

Atia was luckier than most mothers, for she was an aristocrat, and her husband Caius Octavius was a senator able to afford the best available care as well as a comfortable house on the eastern side of the Palatine Hill. When her time came, she was attended by female family members, slaves and freedwomen from her household, and an experienced midwife. Custom excluded men from the room chosen for the delivery, and a male doctor would only be summoned if things went badly wrong, although in truth there was little he could do in such circumstances. Atia knew what to expect, for she had already given her husband a daughter several years earlier.

Neither experience nor comfort and care made Atia safe. Childbirth was dangerous both for mother and child, and quite a few of the babies delivered on that day were stillborn or would perish in the ays to come. So would quite a few of the mothers. Nine years later Atia's first cousin Julia would die during labour, followed within a few days by her baby – this in spite of the fact that her husband was then the richest and most powerful man in Rome. The childbearing years were probably the most dangerous of a woman's life.

Things went well for Atia. She was unharmed and her son was born healthy. When the midwife laid him down on the floor for inspection there were no signs of deformities or other problems. The child was then taken to his father. Tradition gave the Roman father, the *paterfamilias*, power of life and death over the entire household, although such strict authority was rarely imposed with rigour by this era. Even so, it was up to Caius Octavius whether or not to accept the new child into the family. He did so readily, showing the boy to the relatives and friends who had gathered to wait with him or who called to visit as soon as the news of the birth spread. Caius Octavius already had two daughters – the older girl being from an earlier marriage. Girls were useful for an ambitious man, since marriage alliances helped to win and hold political friends. Yet only a son could follow a career in public life, matching or surpassing his father and so adding to the glory of the family name.

Fires were lit on the altars in the house, and offerings made to the gods of the household and hearth, the *lares* and *penates*, and to any other deities especially revered by the family. When the guests returned to their own homes they performed the same ritual. One of the visitors was no doubt Atia's thirty-seven-year-old uncle, Caius Julius Caesar, an ambitious senator who was already making a name for himself. Recently he had won a fiercely competitive election to become Rome's most senior and prestigious priest, the *pontifex maximus*. The post was primarily political, and Julius Caesar gave little indication of deep religious beliefs. Even so, like other Romans, he set great store by the traditional rites. Ritual surrounded all Roman aristocrats throughout their lives, and a successful birth was a happy occasion for a senatorial family and their connections.[2]

Otherwise there was no reason for the wider community to pay much attention, for Caius Octavius was a very minor senator. Only much later, long after the child had grown up to become Augustus, did stories begin to circulate of omens and even open predictions of the child's future greatness. Suetonius supplies a long string of these, many of which are improbable and some patently absurd. Among the latter is a claim that prophecy predicted the birth of a king of Rome, prompting the Senate to decree that no boy born between set dates should be allowed to live. The law was supposedly blocked on a technicality by a group of senators whose wives were pregnant. Not only was this not how legislation worked under the Republic, but it would be surprising if Cicero did not mention such a grim and controversial measure and it can easily be dismissed as romantic invention. The same is true of stories clearly drawn from the myths surrounding Alexander the Great and other heroes, for whom a human father was felt insufficient. Thus it was claimed that Atia had attended a night-time rite in the Temple of Apollo, and had fallen asleep in her litter. A snake appeared and slithered over her, leaving behind a mark like snakeskin on her thigh. She woke, feeling the need to cleanse herself ritually as if she had just had sex, for only the physically purified were fit to enter the precincts of the gods. Unable to remove the mark on her skin, she ceased to attend public baths. Nine months later she gave birth to her son.[3]

Caius Octavius had no need of such mystical experiences to feel happy. Birthdays were important in Roman culture, and were celebrated throughout an individual's life. September was the seventh of the ten named months in Rome's lunar calendar, for in archaic times the year began in March, the month of the war god Mars, when the legions used to set out on campaign. September 23 was for the Romans the ninth day before the Kalends of October, for they used a system based on days before or after three monthly festivals, the Kalends on the 1st, the Nones on the 7th, and the Ides on either the 13th or the 15th depending on the month. Lacking the number zero, the Kalends itself counted as one, and 23 September itself was included, hence the total of nine days.

For the Romans the year was the six-hundred-and-ninety-first since the foundation of the City (*ab urbe condita*) by Romulus. More immediately it was the consulship of Marcus Tullius Cicero and Caius Antonius. The two consuls were Rome's most senior magistrates, with equal authority and holding office for twelve months. The Republican system was intended to prevent any one man gaining supreme or permanent power, for no one could seek re-election until a decade had passed. The man who was first in the electoral ballot was listed first when the consuls gave their name to each year. Consuls tended to come overwhelmingly from a small number of well-established families, like the Antonii. Cicero was unusual, for he was the first of his family to enter politics at Rome and no other 'new man' (*novus homo*) had reached the consulship for more than a generation. Caius Octavius was also a new man, and surely hoped to copy Cicero's success.[4]

The consuls took precedence on alternate months, and so it was Cicero who presided over a meeting of the Senate on 23 September. Suetonius claims that Caius Octavius arrived late because of the birth of his son, although since this provides the setting for another story where the birth of the 'ruler of the globe' is predicted, we need to be cautious. Perhaps the incident is wholly invented, although there is nothing inherently improbable in Caius Octavius' late arrival or in the claim that the senators debated the rumours of conspiracy surrounding one of their members, Lucius Sergius Catiline. Whispers of revolution were rife, and many focused on Catiline, who had failed to win the consulship for the next year in the summer's elections. If the Senate did indeed discuss such matters, then no action was taken for the moment and it would be a while before matters came to a head.[5]

In the meantime normal life continued, and on the night of 30 September Caius Octavius and Atia held a night-time vigil in their house. Rituals were performed, culminating in sacrifices and a formal purification ceremony or *lustratio* on the next day, the Kalends of October and nine days after their son's birth. The purpose was to rid the baby of any malign spirits or other supernatural influences that might have entered him during the birth process. He was given a charm or *bulla*, usually of gold and worn around the neck, until he formally became a man. Afterwards, the flight of birds was observed by one of the priestly college known as augurs to gain some sense of the child's future. Probably the parents were told that the signs were good.[6]

Only now was the boy formally named, and in due course registered in the list of citizens. In this case he was named after his father, and so became Caius Octavius, son of Caius. Families tended to use the same names generation after generation, although some of the most powerful aristocratic families were starting to break such conventions during these years, setting themselves even further apart from the rest of the senatorial class. The family name or *nomen* – in this case Octavius – was automatic, and choice only exercised in the first name or *praenomen*. Most important men possessed the full three names or *tria nomina*. Therefore Atia's uncle was Caius Julius Caesar. The Julii were an extensive clan, and the third name or *cognomen* was held only by that particular branch. The system was not universal, even among the great families, in some cases because they were not especially numerous or simply because they were confident in being recognised. The Octavii had not yet seen any need to distinguish specific branches of their family.

Nor did the Romans feel it necessary to identify women so precisely, since they could neither vote nor stand for office. Atia had just this single name, the feminine form of her father Marcus Atius Balbus' *nomen*. The identity of her father and association with his family was what mattered. Roman women kept their name throughout their lives, and did not change it on marriage. Atia's daughter was called Octavia, as was her stepdaughter, the child from her husband's earlier marriage. If there had been any other daughters then these would also have been named Octavia. In some cases families numbered their girls for official purposes.[7]

Babies required a great deal of care, but Atia's role in this was most likely one of more or less distant supervision. She had much to do in overseeing the household, and supporting her husband in his career. Some voices advocated that a mother should breastfeed her children, but in practice this was rare and instead a slave wet-nurse was provided. This woman, or another slave, served as the child's nurse more generally. (One of the reasons some philosophers argued that a mother should feed her own offspring was the fear that they would otherwise somehow imbibe slavish characteristics along with the milk.) The amount of time either parent spent with their children was no doubt a matter of personal choice. In some cases it was very little, although there were exceptions. In the second century BC we are told that Cato the Elder, famous for his stern, old-fashioned and loudly proclaimed virtue, only let the most important public business prevent him from being present when his infant son was bathed. Cato's wife was one of those women who did breastfeed her own baby, and even sometimes suckled slave children from the household.[8]

Our sources tell us almost nothing about the early years of the young Octavius, although yet another of Suetonius' stories of signs predicting his rise to greatness is less dramatic than most and may just contain a germ of truth. In this, his nurse put him down for the night in a room on the ground floor. The boy, presumably now old enough to crawl, then went missing, prompting an urgent search. He was found at dawn the next morning, watching the rising sun from the highest room in the house.[9]

A TROUBLED WORLD

If this happened at all it was later, but in the closing months of 63 BC there was plenty to worry the boy's parents, for the mood in Rome was nervous. The Roman Republic had dominated the Mediterranean world since the middle of the second century BC. Carthage was destroyed, and the kingdoms of the east either conquered, or so weak and dependent on Roman goodwill that they presented no threat. Mithridates VI of Pontus in Asia Minor had waged war persistently for a generation, but was now soundly crushed by Rome's most successful and popular general, Pompey the Great. The king, finding that repeated doses of antidotes during the course of his life had rendered him immune to poison, ordered one of his own body-guards to kill him before the year was out. In October Pompey's legions stormed Jerusalem after a three-month siege, backing one side in a civil war between rival members of the Jewish royal family. It seemed no one could match the military might of the Republic.[10]

Rome was far stronger than any of its neighbours and potential enemies, but the immense profits of conquest and empire threatened delicate balances within politics, society and the economy. Competition among the aristocracy for high office and status had always been intense, but in the past was kept within strict confines of convention and law. Now many of the props of this system came under threat as senators spent ever-increasing sums to win popularity, and significant groups emerged within the population who felt their plight was desperate and readily rallied to anyone who championed their cause. There were opportunities for a few men to rise far higher than had ever been possible in the past and their peers resented and resisted this.

In 133 BC an aristocrat named Tiberius Sempronius Gracchus became one of the ten annually elected tribunes of the plebs and introduced a programme of legislation aimed at helping the rural poor. He won considerable acclaim, but was accused of aspiring to the dominance of a monarch and was bludgeoned to death by a gang of other senators led by his own cousin. In 122 BC Tiberius' younger brother Caius was killed along with hundreds of followers after he embarked on an even more radical set of reforms. This time the fighting was clearly premeditated and between organised forces. Political competition had become violent, and such scenes were repeated in 100 BC. A decade later discontent among the peoples of Italy exploded into rebellion when the tribune who proposed granting them Roman citizenship was murdered. The Romans won the war after a hard struggle, to a great extent because they finally and grudgingly gave the Italian communities what they wanted. The number of citizens was greatly expanded, giving politicians new voters to cultivate, and again shifting the political balance.

Almost immediately another dispute revolving around a tribune

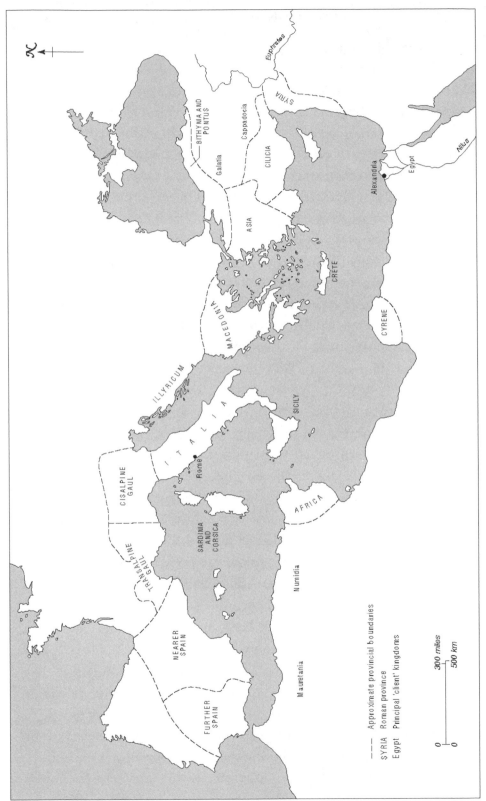

The Roman Empire in the first century BC

BITHYNIA AND PONTUS
Galatia
Cappadocia
CILICIA
Euphrates
SYRIA
Nilus
Egypt
Alexandria
ASIA
CRETE
CYRENE
MACEDONIA
ILLYRICUM
I T A L I A
SICILY
AFRICA
Rome
CISALPINE GAUL
TRANSALPINE GAUL
SARDINIA AND CORSICA
Numidia
NEARER SPAIN
FURTHER SPAIN
Mauretania

N

---- Approximate provincial boundaries
SYRIA Roman province
Egypt Principal 'client' kingdoms

0   300 miles
0   500 km

of the people became so bitter that in 88 BC for the very first time a Roman general led his army against the City of Rome. His name was Sulla, and rivalry between him and an ageing popular hero named Marius lay behind the conflict. Massacre followed massacre in an ever-worsening spiral of atrocity before Sulla won the Civil War and made himself dictator, turning a rarely used and temporary emergency measure into a position of permanent supreme power for himself. After a few years he retired to private life, only to die of natural causes within a matter of months. The Republic was already troubled by a new civil war, when Marcus Aemilius Lepidus, one of the consuls of 78 BC, raised an army and tried to seize control of the state. He was defeated and he and his partisans executed, but many opponents of Sulla fought on for years from bases in Spain.

The spectre of civil strife still lay heavily over the Republic in 63 BC. Every senator had lived through the brutal conflict between Sulla and the Marians, and most had lost close relatives or friends in the course of it. Julius Caesar's aunt was married to Marius and his first wife had been the daughter of one of the latter's closest allies, and it was probably only his youth that saved him from execution at the hands of the victorious Sullans. Even so, for a while he had been a hunted fugitive until his mother's Sullan connections saved his life. Descendants of men executed by Sulla were barred from politics and lobbied hard for a restoration of their rights. Sulla was gone, but all senior senators were men chosen – or at the very least, not rejected – by him. There was no obvious reason why a new civil war could not break out at any time, and with it would come chaos, danger and opportunities. Many of Sulla's supporters had made their fortunes from the spoils of his dead enemies. The prospect of a new revolution appealed to those failing under the current system.

Catiline was one of these Sullan partisans, but his new-found wealth had proved insufficient to match his flamboyant lifestyle and the political ambition that made him generous in gifts to potential supporters. Sulla had doubled the size of the Senate and increased the number of praetors – the next most senior magistracy to the consulship – to eight, but there were still only two consuls each year and so the contests for this supreme honour became even more fiercely contested. Added to the number of candidates seeking office were dozens of men expelled from the Senate in 70 BC during a sudden and rather uncharacteristic purge of the staggeringly corrupt and blatantly unfit. Several of these had both the money and ambition to rehabilitate themselves by winning office again.

Rising up the political ladder had become extremely expensive. Senators needed to possess substantial landed estates simply to qualify for membership of the order, and men borrowed ever-greater sums to spend in fighting the elections. Catiline did this on a spectacular scale, and so did Julius Caesar. At the election for the post of *pontifex maximus* his main opponent was an older and far more distinguished statesman, and both sides deluged the voting tribes with bribes. If Julius Caesar lost, then he knew that there was no prospect of repaying his creditors. Instead he gambled on winning, trusting that this would convince them that he remained a good investment whose rise would continue, making him both a useful connection and in the long run able to pay them back. As he left his house on the morning of the election Julius Caesar told his mother that he would return as a victor or he would not come back at all. In the event he won, and for the moment his creditors were willing to continue their support.[11]

Catiline was less fortunate. Like Julius Caesar he was a patrician, his family part of Rome's most ancient aristocracy. Plebeians, including Caius Octavius and thus his son, were far more numerous, and over the centuries many of these forced their way into the elite. Several of the patrician families were eclipsed and dwindled to obscurity. Neither Catiline's nor Julius Caesar's ancestors had enjoyed much electoral success for several centuries. Both men were determined to change this, and each was charismatic, talented and had acquired reputations as rakes that at least kept their names in the public mind, if only as subjects for gossip. Yet Julius Caesar kept succeeding while Catiline's career began to stall.[12]

A prosecution for his conduct while governor of the African province prevented Catiline from standing for the consulship for 65 BC

and 64 BC. In the next contest his increasingly wild comments al-
ienated too many influential people and he was beaten by a skilful
campaign managed by Cicero. Defeat at the hands of a 'new man'
was especially humiliating for the aristocrat of ancient lineage.
Catiline dubbed Cicero a mere 'resident alien' in Rome. The other
winner was Caius Antonius, one of the men expelled from the Senate
in 70 BC and now working his way back up the political ladder. Although he and Catiline had supported each other in their campaigns,
Antonius was won over to neutrality when Cicero voluntarily gave
him his own province of Macedonia, the command allocated to him
by lot for the year after his consulship. It was a lucrative region where
an unscrupulous governor could readily restore his fortunes.[13]

Yet Catiline tried again in July 63 BC at elections presided over by
Cicero as consul. Bribery was once more rampant on all sides, and
the candidates were backed by gangs of supporters, so that Cicero
arrived with his own followers and wore a breastplate under his toga,
which he 'accidentally' revealed to show his determination. There
was intimidation, but no serious violence, and Catiline was defeated
for a second time.[14]

Catiline was desperate, as were quite a few other ambitious men.
If a senator sold his lands to pay his debts, then he would probably
do so at a loss for the market was poor; but, more importantly, he
would lose this essential requirement of rank and any chance of a
political future. For some, the choice seemed either political extinction or revolution. In the countryside of Etruria an associate called
Manlius who had served in Sulla's legions as a centurion was raising
a disparate army from the poor and desperate. Sullan veterans who
had failed to make a go of the farms given to them when they left
the army – because the land was poor, the economy bad, or simply
through their own mistakes – joined former Marians, and others
who felt revolution was their only hope. They would march carrying
an eagle once borne by one of Marius' legions – not from the Civil
War, but from the great campaigns when he had saved Italy from a
barbarian horde. Yet at first it was not clear if or when it would come
to open rebellion.[15]

On 21 October the Senate passed its ultimate decree, the *senatus consultum ultimum*, which called upon the consuls to take any measures necessary to protect the *res publica*. Effectively it declared a state of emergency, but opinion was divided over how far this meant laws could be suspended. The same measure had been used against Caius Gracchus in 122 BC, and again in 100 BC, 88 BC and 78 BC. In many ways it was an admission that the traditional mechanisms of the Republic were inadequate when there was a threat of serious internal upheaval.

Catiline was still in Rome, and continued to attend meetings of the Senate, even after Manlius openly rebelled at the end of October. Cicero's public accusations became ever more virulent, but an attempt by the conspirators to assassinate him failed. Finally, on the night of 8 November, Catiline fled to join Manlius. His confederates left behind in Rome proved quite staggeringly incompetent, clumsily approaching the ambassadors of a Gaulish tribe, the Allobroges, in the hope of securing cavalry for the rebel army. The Gauls instead went to the authorities, and the conspirators were caught red-handed and arrested.

Four senators were taken prisoner, the most senior being Publius Cornelius Lentulus, currently praetor and one of the men expelled from the Senate in 70 BC. His wife was a Julia, third cousin to Julius Caesar and already widowed once before. For a while Lentulus and the others protested their innocence when brought before the Senate. Yet as the evidence piled up their determination crumbled and each confessed, leaving the question of what should be done with them. Their fate was decided at a meeting held in the Temple of Concord on 5 December – a location no doubt chosen as a deliberate plea for unity, but perhaps also as a reminder of strong action taken in the past, for it had been built by the man who led the suppression of Caius Gracchus.

In the debate that followed, speaker after speaker advocated the death penalty. Caius Octavius was too junior a senator for his opinion to be asked, but Julius Caesar was praetor-elect for the following year as well as *pontifex maximus,* and Cicero soon called on him for his opinion. People were claiming that Atia's flamboyant uncle was part of the conspiracy, and yet, rather than prove his loyalty to the Republic by agreeing with the rest, Julius Caesar boldly argued against execution. He was right to say that it was unconstitutional to do this without trial, although his own suggestion of sending each man to a different town in Italy to be held in custody lacked any precedent at all. The Romans had no prisons to hold criminals for any length of time, let alone permanently.

The consensus began to weaken, and for a moment it looked as if the ambitious Julius Caesar would win great fame for single-handedly changing the mind of the Senate. Then another up-and-coming man, the tribune-elect Cato the Younger, gave a powerful speech urging immediate execution. Others repeated the same belief and serious doubts were expressed at the practicality of imprisonment. When called, the vote was overwhelmingly in favour of the death penalty. We do not know how Caius Octavius voted, but it is quite possible that he followed the consensus rather than siding with Julius Caesar. One of the oldest and most respected statesmen in the Senate hailed Cicero as the 'father of his country' (*parentem patriae*).[16]

Lentulus was stripped of his praetorship, but given the courtesy of being personally led away by Cicero to the place of execution, where the prisoners were strangled. Afterwards Cicero announced laconically: 'They have lived' – in Latin the single word *vixerunt*. There had been talk in Rome of massacres and the starting of fires in the City to spread chaos, and for the moment public opinion was relieved to see this danger removed. The Republic had survived an immediate threat, although Catiline and his army remained at large. It was harder to predict the long-term consequences of this willingness to suspend the laws. Although Rome dominated the world, its politics remained dangerously competitive, with the threat of violence and instability never far away. Yet if the risks were high, so were the rewards, and as the year ended Caius Octavius was determined to pursue his own career.[17]

2

'A MAN OF WEALTH AND GOOD REPUTATION'

'Caius Octavius, his father, though not of patrician birth, was descended from a very prominent equestrian family, and was himself a man of dignity, of upright and blameless life, and of great wealth.'
Velleius Paterculus, c.AD 30.[1]

We do not know too much about Atia's husband, Caius Octavius. Our sources speak of his considerable wealth, although at no point do they give any indication of the scale of his fortune compared to other senators. He owned the house in the area of the Palatine known as the 'Ox heads', and had another house in Nola, a town some twenty miles east of Naples which had been turned into a colony for his veterans by Sulla. There was also a substantial family estate in and around the Volscian town of Velitrae, which lay to the south of the Alban Hills outside Rome. Formerly a persistent enemy, the Volsci had been conquered and absorbed by the Romans in the fourth century BC.[2]

Caius Octavius' wealth was inherited, and that was the best sort of wealth as far as the Romans were concerned. The Octavii were part of the local gentry in Velitrae, where one of the oldest streets in the town was named after them. There was also a story of an Octavius who hastily finished a sacrifice to Mars so that he could lead the town's warriors to repel the attack of a neighbouring community. That was evidently before the Roman conquest, and used to explain a local peculiarity in the manner of sacrifices to Mars. More recently, in 205 BC, a time of rather better records, Caius Octavius' grandfather served as a military tribune in the Roman army during the war against Hannibal. He made no attempt to seek public office when the war was over, suggesting that like many he simply joined to fight at a time when the Republic faced an unprecedented threat.[3]

His son, Caius Octavius' father, remained content with local politics throughout his long life and only held office in Velitrae itself. The family was already prosperous, but he built on this by shrewd investment and establishing himself as a banker, loaning money at interest – a far less honourable source of riches than the income from landed estates. In later years Mark Antony derided him as a squalid money-changer, and others claimed that Caius Octavius followed the same trade as his father, helping to distribute gifts and outright bribes to the voting tribes in Roman elections. Personal abuse was the common coin of Roman political exchanges, and such claims need to be taken with more than a pinch of salt. Even Suetonius, who happily reports plenty of scurrilous stories about Augustus, doubted this last claim.[4]

The son of a local aristocrat and a successful businessman, Caius Octavius was not simply a citizen, but a member of the equestrian order, the highest class registered in the Roman census. Equestrians had to possess property valued at more than 400,000 sesterces, although by the first century BC this was a comparatively modest sum and it was common for them to own far more. In earlier centuries the Roman army was recruited from those wealthy enough to buy their own arms and armour. The richest were able to afford horses and so formed the cavalry or *equites*. Although this military role had ceased – and the legions were now drawn from the poorest and equipped by the state – the name was preserved. Senatorial status was not based on a set property qualification, and came when a man was elected to a magistracy or simply enrolled in the Senate, but all had to be equestrians. There were some 600 senators, but thousands of equestrians, and, according to the most recent census figures from the start of the decade, some 900,000 Roman citizens.[5]

Probably the richest senator in these years was Pompey the Great, and the profits of his victories in the east were currently making him even wealthier. His closest rival in the Senate, who had shared the consulship with him in 70 BC, was Marcus Licinius Crassus, sometimes

known as 'the rich' (*dives*). Both men had served Sulla and done well
from the confiscated property of his executed enemies. Crassus was
also a shrewd and energetic businessman. He maintained a substantial number of slave craftsmen and builders, as well as others trained
to control fires. One of his tricks was to buy property cheaply when
it lay in the path of one of Rome's frequent blazes. Only then would
he send in his slaves, knocking down buildings to create a firebreak.
In time Crassus would rebuild and rent out the property, and eventually came to own substantial parts of the City. At one stage his
estates elsewhere were valued at 200 million sesterces – enough to
give 500 men the minimum equestrian census. He claimed that no
one could call himself rich unless he could afford to pay for his own
army. Pompey had actually done just this in the Civil War, recruiting
and funding three legions from his own estates.[6]

Caius Octavius is unlikely to have been in the same league as Crassus or Pompey, but will have been aware of how the former used
money. Crassus did not wish to be rich simply for the sake of it, but
made his wealth work to his political advantage, loaning money to
many senators either interest-free or at a very low rate. It was rumoured that a majority in the Senate owed Crassus money. When he
was accused of involvement with Catiline, fear of sudden demands
for repayment of these debts ensured that the matter was quickly
dropped. He also had wide business interests and connections with
the companies of *publicani* (the publicans of the King James Bible)
who undertook state contracts, such as collecting taxes in the provinces. Much of this was done behind the scenes, since senators were
not supposed to involve themselves in commerce, although many
did. Crassus was probably the most successful. As well as money,
he traded in favours. A capable and successful advocate, he worked
hard representing others in legal cases to put them under obligation
to him.[7]

With a banker for a father, Caius Octavius no doubt found that
quite a few prominent men were either in debt to him, or grateful
for earlier loans. In this respect it is quite possible that he did continue the family business, as a useful aid to his political ambitions.

Unlike many senators, the bulk of his fortune was not tied up in estates and so was readily disposable for political advantage. It was probably to a large extent because of his wealth that he secured Atia as his second wife. We do not know whether his first marriage to a woman named Anchaia ended in her death, or divorce when he saw the chance of making a more useful connection. For the Roman elite, marriage was a political tool.[8]

Julius Caesar, himself originally betrothed to the daughter of a wealthy equestrian, married one of his sisters to Marcus Atius Balbus, another local aristocrat from a family very like the Octavii. He came from Aricia, slightly closer to Rome in the Alban Hills, and was of substantial means, being related on his mother's side to Pompey. His father had clearly married into an established senatorial line, which helped foster his son's ambition to hold office at Rome. Julius Caesar's other sister married in turn two more of these minor gentry whose ambitions led them towards a career at Rome itself. Through this network of marriage alliances, Julius Caesar gained loyal allies eager to be associated with a patrician from such an ancient family, and quite possibly practical aid with funding his own career.[9]

In 62 BC Caius Octavius was probably in his early forties and felt ready to seek election as one of the eight praetors for the following year. Public careers were tied closely to age at Rome, and Sulla had sought to make this more clear by once again setting down in law a minimum age for each post. (For more detail on the public career or *cursus honorum*, see Appendix One.) Praetors had to be at least thirty-nine. It was a point of pride for an ambitious man to win office at the first opportunity, and especially to become consul in 'his year' (*suo anno*). Cicero had managed to achieve this last distinction, but good fortune, combined with a spectacular career in the courts, had helped him. We do not hear of Caius Octavius appearing as advocate and his talents may not have lain in this direction.[10]

He did serve twice as military tribune, some time in the seventies BC, and so at least at the beginning he may have done his best to acquire a military reputation, which generally went down well with the voters. There were twenty-four elected military tribunes every year, a legacy of the old days when the army consisted of only four legions, each led by six tribunes. By the first century there were usually dozens of legions at any one time, and the bulk of their tribunes were directly chosen and commissioned by provincial governors. We do not know where Caius Octavius served, but two terms – each at least a year in length – suggest some enthusiasm for the post. In the earlier Republic any candidate seeking office had to have served for ten years or campaigns. The rule was considerably relaxed by the first century, although even the unmilitary Cicero spent some time with the legions. Young men served as *contubernales* (literally 'tent-companions') to governors, acting effectively as junior staff officers to gain experience.[11]

Caius Octavius was then elected to the most junior of the Roman magistracies, the quaestorship, taking the first formal step in a political career. Since Sulla's reforms, becoming quaestor automatically led to a man's enrolment as a senator. There were twenty quaestors each year, and one of the others for 73 BC was Caius Toranius, with whom Caius Octavius was later associated, so it was also probably in this year that he held the office. The duties of these magistrates were primarily financial. Some served in Rome, while others were sent to assist provincial governors by overseeing the finances of their provinces. We do not know the duties assigned to Caius Octavius. In contrast Toranius found himself leading troops against the slave rebellion of Spartacus and was soundly beaten.[12]

In 64 BC – again the date is partly guesswork, but seems likely – Caius Octavius and Toranius were the two plebeian aediles. There were four aediles each year, two plebeian and two curule – the latter post open to patricians. Their tasks ranged from organising public festivals – specifically the *ludi Ceriales* celebrating the goddess of the harvest and the Plebeian Games – to regulating traffic and public works within Rome itself. It was a good opportunity to be highly visible to the electorate, especially for a man able to supplement the official funds with his own money. The games included processions, feasting and public entertainments such as beast fights. At this stage in Rome's history gladiatorial contests remained the preserve of funeral games. With so few posts available each year, it was not a compulsory magistracy. For Toranius it helped to rehabilitate him after his defeat. For Caius Octavius it was a way of winning more political friends and making himself known to voters.[13]

He was not a high-flyer like Atia's uncle. Julius Caesar's family had drifted a long way from the heart of politics since the early Republic, but their fortunes began to recover when he was a child. A different branch of the wider family started this rise, at least getting the name known once again. Caesar's father, aided by his sister's marriage to the popular hero Caius Marius, easily reached the praetorship and only his sudden death – he collapsed and died putting on his shoes one morning – prevented him from going further.

Julius Caesar himself was awarded Rome's highest decoration for bravery when he was still in his late teens, winning the civic crown (corona civica) traditionally given to a man who saved the life of a fellow citizen in battle. It may well have been this, possibly combined with an encouragement of patricians, that led to a dispensation permitting him to hold each magistracy two years before the normal minimum age. Julius Caesar was highly active in the courts, flamboyant in his dress and lifestyle, and conscientious in office, supplementing official funds with borrowed money. He was also the hero of colourful encounters with pirates and enemy invaders, and a fruitful source of gossip for his numerous affairs with other men's wives. Then as in so many periods, notoriety was more desirable for a politician than obscurity. For all that, Julius Caesar's career remained broadly conventional.[14]

Caius Octavius' rise was slower and less spectacular, but continued steadily. A man seeking office formally donned a specially whitened toga known as the toga candidata, from which we get our word candidate. It was important to be conspicuous during a campaign. There were no political parties at Rome as we would understand them, nor were elections primarily contests about policy. Quite openly, voters selected on the basis of perceived character and past behaviour rather than the views a candidate expressed. Where an individual's nature was not obvious, the Roman people tended to be drawn to a

famous name, for there was a sense that virtue and ability were inherited. Therefore, if a man's father and grandfather had served with
distinction – or at least avoided utter ignominy – then it was assumed
that he would possess comparable talent. He also tended to inherit
the networks of past favours, obligations and friendships built up
by previous generations. The established aristocratic families lost no
opportunity to advertise their achievements. Porches of houses were
decorated with the symbols of past victories, and as someone went
in they would pass busts of ancestors, each shown with the insignia
of their magistracies.[15]

The Octavii were not well known. Even so it was important for
friends, well-wishers and petitioners to visit Caius Octavius each
morning. Such was the daily routine of all senators, beginning with
this formal salute from those in their debt, those hoping for favours,
and others tied to him or wanting to be. It was especially important
for a candidate's house to be busy in these hours just before dawn
as the working day got under way. In 64 BC Quintus Cicero wrote a
pamphlet on electioneering presented as advice for his brother's consular campaign – something which Cicero himself scarcely needed,
but a convenient literary device. He notes that quite a few people
will choose to visit several of the candidates, hedging their bets on
who will win. Quintus advises the candidate to show great pleasure
at such visits, in the hope of flattering them into becoming genuine
supporters.[16]

A candidate could not have too many political friends, and this
was an opportunity to make new ones. As Quintus Cicero puts it:
'. . . you can make friends of any people you wish without disgrace,
which you cannot do in the rest of life. If at some other time you
were to exert yourself to court friendship with them, you would
seem to act in bad taste; but in a canvass you would be thought a
very poor candidate if you did not so act and with vigour too in connection with many such people.'[17]

It was a good opportunity to let people do a candidate a favour by
showing support and so put him under obligation to them for the
future. There were very obvious ways of displaying commitment

to a candidate, most notably walking with him through the Forum. It was important to be attended by as many and as distinguished a following as possible so that friendships could be noted. The Roman electorate tended to favour a perceived winner, and so big followings readily grew as more people wanted to join the winning side.

When a candidate proceeded through the heart of the City in this way, he would greet passers-by, and again wish to be seen to be associated with as many prominent people as possible. A special type of slave, known as a *nomenclator*, had the job of whispering in his master's ear the names of people so that they could be greeted properly. Too obvious a dependence on this assistant was seen as vulgar, but Cato the Younger was unusual in very publicly dispensing with one, and then attempting to ban other candidates from using them. Under pressure he relented, and *nomenclatores* continued to be an essential part of a politician's staff.[18]

There were certain big causes that helped to make a man popular with some sections of the community. Julius Caesar consistently backed legislation to redistribute publicly owned land to the urban poor and discharged soldiers, following in the footsteps of the Gracchi and other reformers. He also fought in the courts and Senate for the rights of the inhabitants of the provinces. An issue with even greater resonance with many at Rome was the question of whether there were limits to the actions of magistrates when the Senate invoked the *senatus consultum ultimum*. In 63 BC Julius Caesar was involved in the show trial of a man accused of killing prisoners taken during the disturbances of 100 BC, thirty-seven years earlier. The whole episode was about making political points, followed archaic procedure, and ended without a verdict. It was directed not at the need to kill citizens taking up arms against the Republic, but questioned whether such men could still be denied the right of formal trial after they had surrendered and were no longer a direct threat to the state. It was the same issue raised in the debate over the Catilinarians, and before the year was out Cicero was being attacked for his execution of these men.[19]

Caius Octavius is unlikely to have involved himself too closely in such controversial issues. In the early months of 62 BC, Catiline's army remained at large, threatening a prolonged bout of civil war. In the event his supporters began to drift away and the revolt failed to gain momentum. An army under the nominal command of Caius Antonius, but in fact led by a more experienced subordinate, soon cornered the rebels. Heavily outnumbered, the rebel cause was already lost. Even so Catiline and several thousand diehards went down fighting, preferring death in battle to surrender and subsequent execution.[20]

Probably the greatest concern in public life for most of 62 BC was the impending return of Pompey the Great from his eastern campaigns. Mithridates was dead, the war over, and although engaged for some months in reorganising the provinces and allied kingdoms in that region, the general and his legions were on their way home. No one was quite sure what they would do when they arrived. Some feared another Sulla. More hated the thought of one man with vast wealth and immense prestige coming to dominate the state. Pompey had already broken almost every rule of public life, raising a private army in the Civil War, and then refusing to disband it, so the senators decided to confer legal powers on him and employ him to fight rebels rather than turn him into one. He held no elected office until on 1 January 70 BC he became consul and a senator simultaneously at the age of thirty-six. In the Civil War he had earned the nickname of the 'young butcher' (*adulescentulus carnifex*) for the enthusiasm he showed for executing prominent noblemen. More recently men accused him of stealing the glory of others, taking over commands when wars were already won.[21]

Senators as different as Crassus and Cato resented Pompey's success, but to most of the population he was Rome's greatest hero. Julius Caesar willingly supported proposals in his favour, while retaining his political independence. Early in 62 BC he became involved with a tribune of the plebs wanting to recall the general and his army to deal with Catiline's rebels. Opposition was strong, so the tribune fled and Julius Caesar was briefly deprived of the praetorship until he made public penance. Caius Octavius most likely steered well clear of such disturbances, while still ensuring that he expressed appropriate opinions to strike a chord with his current audience.[22]

A wise candidate did his best to please as many people as possible. He and his friends were expected to entertain and praise both individuals and groups – the equestrian order, the *publicani*, the less well-off classes, and members of the various guilds in the City and voting divisions in the Assemblies. It was vital to be seen as generous and willing to help, particularly in return for support. As Quintus Cicero put it: 'people want not only promises . . . but promises made in a lavish and complimentary way'. They were also bound to ask for favours. 'Whatever you cannot perform, decline gracefully or, better yet, don't decline. A good man will do the former, a good candidate the latter.' Better to promise wherever possible, since 'if you refuse you are sure to rouse antagonism at once, and in more people. . . . Especially as they are much angrier with those who refuse them than with a man who . . . has a reason for not fulfilling his promise, although he would do so if he possibly could.'[23] Election pledges were just as impermanent in the first century BC as they are today, and voters similarly inclined to let optimism triumph over experience.

Caius Octavius had plenty of money to spend on entertainment, or to use as gifts and loans to preserve existing friendships and win new ones. There were no doubt also prior connections from his family's commercial activities, in addition to relatives such as Julius Caesar visibly attending him and showing support. Favour could be purchased, and most presents or favours would not infringe the laws intended to stamp out corruption. It was a fine line to tread, but for all the money he lavished on voters it is worth noting that Julius Caesar was never charged with bribery. These matters could be handled delicately and only the most blatant offenders ended up in court.[24]

There were eight praetorships, and so inevitably a dozen of each year's college of twenty quaestors would not win the higher office. Even so the odds were considerably better than in the competitions for the consulship. Praetors were elected after the consuls, in a meeting of the same Popular Assembly, the *Comitia centuriata*. In this the

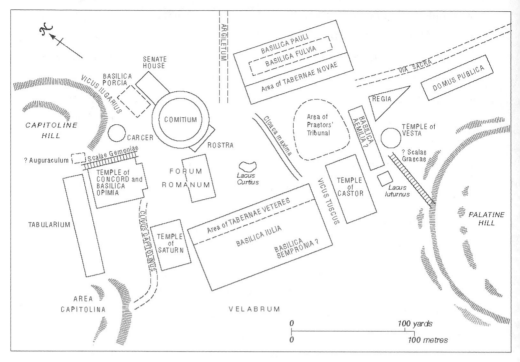

The centre of Rome around 63 BC

thirty-five tribes of Roman citizens were divided into different voting groups or centuries, based on property and derived from the ancient structure of the Roman army. Since armed bodies of citizens were not permitted within the sacred boundary of the City (the *pomerium*), they met outside, on the Campus Martius, in an area fenced off to reflect the voting divisions and known as the *saepta* or sheep pens.

The centuries of the better-off contained fewer people and got to vote first, filing across the wooden walkways or 'bridges' (*pontes*) to drop a tablet marked with the initials of their chosen candidates into a basket. The majority decision of each century determined the vote of the whole group. Candidates may have had the chance to make speeches at informal meetings before the *Comitia centuriata* was officially convened, but after that simply waited and watched from a platform outside, each wearing his bright white toga. The first man to win enough centuries to constitute a bare majority – 97 out of a total of 193 – was elected, and then the next and so on. The process was cumbersome and took time, and there were occasions when eight praetors had not been selected by sunset, so the Assembly broke up and the elections had to be restaged on the next legal date.[25]

Caius Octavius was the first to win a majority at this election. His father-in-law, Marcus Atius Balbus, would also soon reach the praetorship, probably in the following year, which may suggest that Julius Caesar's influence and name was an important asset to his relations. For their year of office the principal task of the praetors was to act as judges. Seven of them presided over the seven courts or *quaestiones* established by Sulla, while the other man had the prestigious and wider-ranging post of *praetor urbanus*, with authority second only to the consuls. Caius Octavius was allocated the supervision of one of the courts.[26]

Trials were conducted on raised platforms in the Forum, where crowds could gather to watch a case if it was important, entertaining, or simply scandalous. The presiding praetor sat on his chair of office, attended by six lictors carrying the *fasces*, the bundle of rods around an axe symbolising his power to inflict corporal or capital punishment. Staff like the lictors were professionals, unlike the praetors, who changed each year, and in some cases this experience gave them considerable influence over the conduct of a trial. Presiding over a court was another good opportunity for a man to become well known. He could also make more political connections, by dealing courteously and sympathetically with both accuser and accused, their advocates, and jurors who were senators, equestrians and other men of substance. In the Roman system there was no equivalent of the Crown or the State versus the accused and some private citizen or citizens had to bring a charge. Usually the accusers were young men, ambitious to make a name for themselves, while defence counsels were more distinguished. It was seen as more honourable to help another senator – even if patently guilty – than to seek to end his career. Thus once again the system favoured the established elite. Many trials had a political dimension. All were important to those involved, and were a way of bestowing favours.

Late in 60 BC, Cicero spoke highly of Caius Octavius' conduct as praetor, advising Quintus to emulate him during his spell as governor of Asia, for:

> . . . there must be civility in hearing, clemency in deciding a case, and careful discrimination in the satisfactory settlement of disputes. It was by acting thus that C. Octavius lately made himself most popular; it was in his court, for the first time, that the lictor made no fuss, and the *accensus* [another of the magistrate's attendants] held his tongue, while everyone spoke as often as he pleased, and as long as he pleased. It is possible that by so doing he gave one the impression of being too gentle, were it not that this very gentleness served to counteract such an instance of severity as the following: certain 'men of Sulla' were compelled to restore what they had carried off by violence and intimidation, and those who, when in office, had passed unjust decrees, were themselves, when private citizens, obliged to bow to the same rulings. This severity on his part might seem a bitter pill to swallow, were it not coated with the honey of many a kindness.[27]

Finding against particularly greedy or vicious former henchmen of Sulla was a popular cause, espoused at different times by both Julius Caesar and Cato. Caius Octavius seems to have been the ideal Roman judge, harsh against a few, while generally kind and understanding to those who deserved it – essentially the well born and well connected. When a senator saw that a guilty verdict was inevitable, he was permitted to give up his case and his rights as a citizen, fleeing from Rome with the bulk of his wealth intact to live on in comfortable exile. This was one reason why Cicero was reluctant to give the Catilinarian conspirators a formal trial, since they would inevitably have chosen exile over execution.[28]

Caius Octavius performed well by the standards of the senatorial class. With the growth in the number of provinces, most praetors followed their year of office with a spell as provincial governor. Postings were selected by the Senate, and then awarded to individuals by lot. Caius Octavius received the rich and militarily important province of Macedonia with the rank of proconsul. Proconsuls and propraetors were not directly elected, but given their power to command (*imperium*) by the Senate. On the way to his province Caius Octavius was sent to deal with a band of outlaws causing trouble in the area of Thurii near Tarentum in southern Italy. Suetonius says these were a mixture of survivors from Spartacus' slave rebellion and stragglers from Catiline's army, and were rapidly dispersed by Caius Octavius.[29]

A governor had plenty of opportunities for profit and most Romans associated foreign service with enrichment. Around this time the poet Catullus claimed that the first question a friend asked him on returning from serving on the staff of the governor of Bithynia was 'How much did you make?' One especially notorious governor of Sicily proclaimed that a man needed three years in office – the first to pay off his debts, the second to make himself rich, and the third to gather the funds needed to bribe judge and jury at the inevitable trial for corruption when he returned to Rome. Most were less blatant, but in his province the proconsul held supreme military and judicial authority and there were always plenty of people eager to gain his goodwill. Governors were not paid a salary, although they were given expenses for themselves and a modest staff.[30]

Once again, Caius Octavius appears to have won the approval of other senators for his conduct. Internally the province was peaceful, and trouble on the frontier with the Bessi and other Thracian peoples gave him the opportunity for military glory. He won a battle, and afterwards his enthusiastic soldiers hailed him as *imperator* or victorious general. Such acclamation was the necessary prelude to being awarded the honour of a triumph by the Senate. The law stipulated that a victory needed to be on a grand scale, resulting in at least 5,000 enemy dead, but in practice it is unlikely that anyone was bothered to count with such precision. Whether or not a man received a triumph often had more to do with the influence of his friends in the Senate.[31]

Caius Octavius' career was going well. A triumph would certainly help his campaign for the consulship. Julius Caesar was also riding high, holding the consulship in 59 BC, and there was every prospect that his niece's husband would soon follow him into the supreme magistracy. Then, on his way back to Rome from Macedonia, Caius fell ill and died in his house at Nola.[32]

THE CONSULSHIP OF JULIUS AND CAESAR

'"What if," someone else said, "he wants to be consul and still retain his army?" To this Pompey responded mildly, "What if my son wants to attack me with a stick?" These words have made people suspect that Pompey is having a row with Caesar.' *Letter from Caelius Rufus to Cicero, October 51 BC.*[1]

The young Octavius was only four when his father died, bequeathing the bulk of his fortune to his only son. Family wealth was intended to support the careers of future generations. Aristocratic marriage was usually a question of immediate political or financial advantage, and divorce and remarriage were common. Julius Caesar was betrothed in his youth, and then married three times. Pompey married four times. Just as Atia did not take her husband's name when she married Caius Octavius, her property remained separate, and, apart from the dowry, was controlled for her benefit by her father. It was unusual for a wife to inherit her husband's property and instead the expectation was always that any children, and especially sons, would be the principal heirs.

Guardians were appointed in the will to oversee the boy's property until he came of age. One of them was Caius Toranius, the man who had been aedile – and perhaps also quaestor – with the child's father. Property needed to be managed and money invested to protect and ideally expand the inheritance. Toranius was later accused of spending much of Caius Octavius' fortune for his own ends. There is always the possibility that it was misjudgement more than deliberate abuse of his position, but as an adult Octavius would not see it that way and would in due course exact grim retribution.[2]

Atia was a valuable asset to her father. Still young – she was probably in her twenties – and capable of bearing more children, it would
have been abnormal for her not to remarry. Roman law imposed a
ten-month period before it was acceptable for a widow or divorced
woman to take another husband, since this ought to make clear the
paternity of any child. Marcus Atius Balbus had done well through
his marriage to Julius Caesar's sister, and the alliance with Caius Octavius. This did not mean that he was not free to seek a fresh alliance
with another aristocratic line and win himself new connections. Atia
married again, this time to Lucius Marcius Philippus, who went on
to win the consulship for 56 BC. Philippus was no great friend of
Julius Caesar, but his family was very well established and politically
successful, making this a good match on both sides. For him the
new marriage may also have brought a welcome injection of funds.
Philippus already had an adult son starting out on a political career
as well as a daughter, and if he hoped for more children from his new
marriage then he was to be disappointed.[3]

Octavius did not accompany his mother to her new home.
Instead he – and, presumably for the moment, his sister – went to
live with Atia's parents, who took over the task of supervising their
care and early education. In time a *paedogogus* would be added to the
nurse; in Octavius' case his main attendant was called Sphaerus. A
paedogogus was usually a slave of Greek extraction, and part of his
task was to begin teaching the child this language as well as Latin.
Aristocratic Romans in the first century BC were fluently bilingual.
Apart from reading, writing and basic arithmetic, there was also a
heavy emphasis on the customs and history of the Roman Republic.
As Cicero put it, 'For what is the life of a man, if it is not interwoven
with the life of former generations by a sense of history?' Within
the wider history of the state, the greatest emphasis was always on
the part played in it by the family. Atia would no doubt have made
sure that Octavius learned of the great deeds and immense antiquity of the Julii in general and the Caesares in particular. No doubt
there was also a gentler pride in the less spectacular history of Caius
Octavius' family. In later years Octavius simply wrote that they

were 'an old and prosperous equestrian family' and went into no more detail.[4]

'THE THREE-HEADED MONSTER'[5]

Pompey the Great returned to Italy with his army at the end of 62 BC. Granted unprecedentedly large commands and resources by the Popular Assembly, his victories dwarfed those of past Roman generals. Pompey had served the Republic well, his experience and natural talent for organisation and planning first sweeping the Mediterranean clear of pirates, before finally crushing Mithridates of Pontus and carrying out the wholesale reorganisation of the Near East. Plenty of senators wondered whether a man grown accustomed to such power would be content to become just another senator once again. Many feared that he would use his legions to dominate the Republic by force as Sulla had done.[6]

Pompey was no Sulla, and on top of that the situation was utterly different, for Sulla had faced Roman enemies already in arms against him when he came back from his war against Mithridates. The unfinished civil war had simply continued when he returned from the east. As a grand gesture to allay people's fears, in 62 BC Pompey began demobilising his army as soon as he arrived in Italy. The political mood in Rome changed, as relief faded and was supplanted by a sense that the great conqueror was now vulnerable. Pompey no longer held formal power or controlled an army, although he would remain outside the formal boundary of the City and retain his *imperium* until he celebrated his triumph. Instead he had to rely on his wealth, his skill and that intangible thing the Romans called *auctoritas* – for which our English word authority is a poor translation. *Auctoritas* combined status and the respect due to an individual for his and his family's achievements and connections. In essence it was simply how important everyone else considered a man to be.[7]

No one doubted Pompey's importance, and no individual surpassed him in wealth or political connections, but he had no monopoly of these things and plenty of others possessed them to a lesser degree. Pompey had spent all of his youth and most of his adult years on campaign. He had little experience of the day-to-day manoeuvring of public life, of trading and exploiting political favours. On top of this he craved the adulation of the crowd and the willing approval of his senatorial colleagues, struggling to cope when this was not forthcoming. Practically he had three objectives. The first and simplest was the right to celebrate a triumph and parade his achievements through the heart of the City. The second was formal ratification of his reorganisation of the eastern provinces and kingdoms, confirming all his decisions. The last was a bill to grant plots of land to his discharged soldiers, setting them up on farms so that they could in future support themselves and their families.

These were all good things for the state. Pompey's eastern settlement was sensible, and when it was finally approved many of its provisions would remain in force for centuries. The legionaries had fought well and successfully, yet the Republic paid them a pauper's wage and most had no source of livelihood now that the army no longer required them. It was true that Pompey would gain the gratitude of these men and their future votes, swelling the great array of clients already obligated to support him. Roman aristocrats of this generation felt that the vast prestige of someone else diminished their own status. There were also plenty with grudges against Pompey, remembering relatives executed by the young butcher.[8]

Pompey got his triumph after a struggle. It was his third, and was celebrated with great splendour and an emphasis on the unmatched scale of his achievements. The crowds cheered the marching soldiers, the lines of captives and the floats bearing spoils of war, lists of conquests and paintings showing scenes from the campaigns. Pompey himself rode in a chariot, dressed in the purple robes of a triumphing general, wearing a laurel wreath and with his face painted terracotta-red so that he resembled the old statues of Jupiter Optimus Maximus, the chief of Rome's gods. For that day the general assumed the role of the god. The months and years that followed demonstrated all too clearly the limits of influence and wealth when faced with concerted opposition. As a private citizen Pompey had no power, and could not summon the Senate or present a bill to the People. In 61 and 60 BC his backing helped former subordinates to reach the consulship. Neither proved politically astute and they were readily blocked or marginalised by their respective colleagues.

Cato was prominent in the campaign to thwart Pompey, but many other members of distinguished families briefly set aside their habitual competition in the hope of cutting the great hero down to size. Such men liked to refer to themselves as 'the good men' (*boni*) or 'the best men' (*optimates*), and when they spoke of liberty and the Republic they understood both as the interests of their own class. For them it was better that a problem not be dealt with than to permit a rival to gain the credit for solving it. It was a recipe for inertia at the heart of public life. No bill to grant land to the veterans – or indeed to other poor citizens – became law, while the eastern settlement still waited for approval. Rulers and communities in the provinces and allied kingdoms remained in limbo, unsure whether the powers allocated to them would endure.

Crassus took part in many of the attacks on Pompey, but was soon equally frustrated. Several prominent companies of *publicani* had bid far above the odds to secure the right to collect taxes in Asia and other eastern provinces, and now found it impossible to cover their outlay. They pressed for a rebate of their original payment to the state. Crassus probably had investments in these companies and certainly close business connections with them. For all his network of indebted political friends, he was unable to prevent the matter from being blocked when it was raised in the Senate.[9]

It is a mistake to view these years purely from the perspective of Pompey, Crassus and their opponents. The annual cycle of elections continued to be hotly contested, often through bribery and intimidation, while politically motivated battles were fought out in the courts. Julius Caesar spent 61–60 BC as governor of Further Spain, although he was nearly stopped from going to his province when some of his creditors demanded immediate repayment of his staggering debts. Crassus intervened, paying some and standing surety

for the rest. A rebellion provided the new governor with the opportunity to fight a war, winning glory and gaining lots of plunder. By
the time he returned to Rome, Julius Caesar had eased his financial
situation and won the chance to triumph.

He was determined to round off this success by gaining the consulship for 59 BC, *suo anno*. To do this, he asked for exemption from
the law requiring a candidate to be physically present when he declared himself as standing. Cato blocked this by a filibuster, talking
incessantly when his opinion was asked in the senatorial debate, and
so preventing a vote from being called. The Senate was not permitted to continue a debate after sunset, and so anything unresolved by
then had to be abandoned. It was a technique he would use repeatedly, and one of the reasons why he had already come to be such a
formidable figure in the Senate in spite of his comparatively young
age. This time his success was fleeting. Julius Caesar came into the
City and appeared as a candidate, even though this meant dismissing
his troops and giving up his triumph.[10]

Some of Cato's hostility was based on sheer personal dislike,
not helped by a long-term affair between Julius Caesar and Cato's
half-sister, Servilia. His own son-in-law, Marcus Calpurnius Bibulus
– a man older than he was – was also standing for the consulship
and he may have hoped to secure both Bibulus' election and a less
flamboyant colleague. Perhaps he also hoped that a failure to win
the consulship would ruin Julius Caesar just as it had ruined Catiline, but if so then he badly misjudged. All the candidates spent
lavishly to win support. Julius Caesar was comfortably elected
first, and in the end Bibulus narrowly succeeded in becoming his
colleague.[11]

This was all public. Behind the scenes Julius Caesar had made an
arrangement with Crassus and Pompey, convincing them that the
only way to achieve what they wanted was to set aside their enmity
and work together through him. He also attempted to win Cicero
into a similarly close association, but failed to convince him. Modern
scholars term this alliance between the two wealthiest men in Rome
and the ambitious newcomer the 'first triumvirate'. At the time it

was a secret agreement, and only gradually during the course of 59 BC did it become public.[12]

In January, Julius Caesar began his year of office by bringing a land bill before the Senate. It was moderate in tone, and his attitude conciliatory, declaring that he was willing to modify any of the clauses if there was reasonable criticism. He had already decreed that all senatorial debates would be published so that opinions expressed there would now become public knowledge. Only Cato was willing to go on record as dissenting, and promptly began one of his familiar unending speeches. His anger flaring, Julius Caesar had him led off by his lictors, but Cato was very good at playing the part of a man victimised by a tyrant. At least one senator went with him, declaring that 'he would rather be with Cato in prison, than with Caesar here'. The meeting ended without a vote.[13]

This pattern was repeated as Cato, Bibulus and their supporters took every opportunity to obstruct Julius Caesar. They were less concerned with stopping him than with making him adopt more and more radical methods, casting doubt for the future on the legality of all that he did. The land bill was passed by the Popular Assembly, and so Pompey's veterans got their farms. A few months later this was supplemented by a second land bill, distributing more publicly owned land to former soldiers and to 20,000 married men with at least three children drawn from the urban poor. Twenty commissioners were appointed to oversee the distribution and one of these was Atia's father. Pompey's eastern settlement was finally ratified in its entirety. Around the same time, the *publicani* received a rebate for their overbidding, although this was accompanied by a warning for them to be more restrained in future.[14]

Pompey's and Crassus' backing had gradually become open as Julius Caesar resorted more and more to public meetings and the Popular Assembly to get his legislation through. Both sides employed gangs of followers and intimidation, but those of the triumvirate were more numerous and better organised. In a public meeting about the land bill, Bibulus' lictors had their *fasces* smashed and he had a basket of dung emptied over him. After that experience he retired to his house for the rest of the year, and declared that he was watching the skies for auspices and kept seeing lightning in the sky. If a presiding magistrate saw such a sign from Jupiter, then public business was suspended, but he was supposed to be present at the meeting or Assembly and not skulking in his house. Yet it served to muddy the waters over all of the legislation of this year.[15]

After his return from the east, Pompey had approached Cato in the hope of marrying one of his nieces and had been snubbed. Now he married Julius Caesar's daughter Julia, openly confirming their alliance. Julia's father was six years younger than Pompey, but in spite of the age difference the marriage was a great success, the older man basking in the adulation of his young and charming bride. Everyone now knew that Crassus and Pompey were allied to the ambitious consul, and men began talking of a 'three-headed monster' dominating the state. Others joked that they were living in the consulship of 'Julius and Caesar', since Bibulus was invisible and made no attempt to initiate any legislation or business of his own. However, apart from watching the skies, he was busily writing scurrilous attacks on his colleague, which he had posted up in the Forum for all to see. Others added to this flow of invective. Julius Caesar was dubbed 'a husband to women and a wife to men' as the old story that he had been seduced by the ageing king of Bithynia was dragged up.[16]

United, Pompey, Crassus and Julius Caesar were able to force through any piece of legislation, although often at the price of extreme methods. In spite of what their critics claimed, they were incapable of controlling every aspect of public business. They managed to secure the election of two friendly consuls for 58 BC – one of them Lucius Calpurnius Piso, Julius Caesar's new father-in-law. Yet they could not prevent far more hostile individuals winning other magistracies, or hope to control the elections in the long run. At the end of the year Julius Caesar departed for a five-year provincial command, giving him the chance to win glory and enough money to pay his debts and make his fortune. A bill brought before the Assembly by a tribune granted him the provinces of Cisalpine Gaul and Illyria. When the governor of Transalpine Gaul died, Pompey proposed in the Senate that this be given to him as well, and so Julius Caesar received a third province, this time by senatorial decree.[17]

'THEY WANTED THIS'

Alongside their formal education, senators' sons were supposed to learn by watching. From the age of seven they began to attend their father – or another male relative – as he went about his business, watching him receive and greet the clients who came to his house each day, and following him through the Forum to meetings of the Senate. Boys were not allowed inside the chamber, but the doors were left open and they and their attendants clustered outside to listen. They also exercised in public on the Campus Martius, in time learning to ride, throw a javelin and fight with shield and sword. Thus from an early age they were in the company of their generation, the men with whom they would compete for office and serve as colleagues.

We do not know when Atia's father, Marcus Atius Balbus, died, and his last known post was as land commissioner in 59 BC. It is possible that the young Octavius began to learn about public life by following his grandfather during the last years of Atius Balbus' life, but we have no direct evidence for this. His great-uncle was merely a distant presence, for Julius Caesar would be away from Rome for a decade. Around the same time that they began to observe public life, boys also started to receive formal tutoring from a *grammaticus* – a teacher of literature as well as language. There were something like twenty schools in Rome open to those whose parents could pay for such an education. The very wealthy usually had a *grammaticus* in their household, although they might allow the children of friends, relatives or clients to join their own offspring in the classes. At some stage during his education, Octavius began to forge friendships that would endure throughout his life.[18]

Young Romans read and memorised classic texts in Latin and Greek, so that they could comment on them as well as quote. They also learned by rote such things as the Twelve Tables, the ancient basis of Roman law. For all that, it was the practical observation of the workings of the Republic and the private business of a senator – or for girls the tasks of their mother in running a household – that most prepared them for adult life. Watching the public life of the Republic in the fifties BC was scarcely edifying. Without Julius Caesar as consul in Rome, Pompey and Crassus returned to wielding immense influence, but had even less control over day-to-day events than when he was present as senior magistrate. Many other senators had lesser influence than these great men, but some had power to make things happen. Political rivalries continued to rage that had nothing to do with Pompey, Crassus or Julius Caesar.

Publius Clodius Pulcher was charismatic, restless and a determined politician who became one of the central figures of this decade. The family name was Claudius Pulcher, but at an early stage he adopted the vulgar spelling of Clodius. He remained a patrician to his very core, with all the assurance of an ancient aristocratic family that had maintained its standing throughout the centuries. The family name Pulcher means beautiful, and well illustrates their own view of themselves; the Claudii were renowned for supreme self-confidence and sheer arrogance. In the First Punic War against Carthage, it was a Claudius Pulcher who grew tired of waiting for the sacred chickens to eat and show that the auspices were favourable for him to lead the fleet into the attack. Eventually he grabbed their cage and threw the birds over the side of his flagship, calling out that 'if the sacred chickens will not eat, then let them drink'. The Romans attacked and suffered their greatest defeat at sea in all the long wars with Carthage. A few years later Claudius Pulcher's sister was prosecuted because, when her litter was obstructed in the crowded streets of Rome, she loudly expressed a wish that 'her brother would go and drown more of the plebs' to clear her path.[19]

Clodius had a far better sense of the popular mood than such ancestors, but a similar lack of restraint when it came to doing or saying whatever he wished. As a patrician, he could not stand for the tribunate, and so made several attempts to become a plebeian. Clodius' deep hatred of Cicero was well known, and when in 59 BC the orator voiced public criticism of the triumvirate, the response was almost immediate. Within hours Julius Caesar as consul and Pompey as augur presided over an adoption ceremony, where Clodius officially became the son of a plebeian, who was in fact younger than he was. The whole affair was purely symbolic, with more than a hint of farce, but was technically valid. Clodius still remained in all other respects an aristocrat with a great array of clients and political friendships supporting him, and was easily elected tribune. Plenty of other politicians had employed mobs of supporters to intimidate and even attack opponents. Clodius took this to a new level, using the traditional *collegia* or trade guilds as the basis for organised gangs. Dismissed as rabble by his opponents, it looks as if many of his henchmen were shopkeepers and craftsmen, a good few freed slaves like much of the urban population.[20]

Cicero soon came under attack, centring around his execution of the Catilinarians. Within months he was abandoned to his fate and went into exile. Clodius was not the agent of Julius Caesar or Crassus or anyone else, and co-operation with them lasted only so long as it suited his purposes. Soon he was threatening to bring the legislation of 59 BC into question, and his gangs turned on Pompey, so that for a while the great hero of the Republic was frightened to leave his house. In time, a senator named Milo recruited his own band of supporters – many of them gladiators – to contest the streets and public spaces with Clodius. Political violence intensified, and bribery at elections rose to even greater levels.[21]

The old hostility between Crassus and Pompey resurfaced, and for a while it looked as if the alliance of the triumvirate was over. A frantic round of negotiations, culminating in meetings at Luca in Cisalpine Gaul – since Julius Caesar could not leave his province – patched things together. Pompey and Crassus stood for election and became consuls for the second time in 55 BC. Each arranged to take an extraordinary provincial command as proconsul once their year of office was over, and at the same time awarded Julius Caesar an additional five-year term in the Gauls and Illyria. Crassus took Syria and from the beginning clearly planned an attack on Parthia, the last great kingdom of the east not yet under Rome's sway. Pompey had both of the Spanish provinces and the legions garrisoned there, but never bothered to travel to the region. Instead, he stayed in his villa in the Alban Hills, outside the formal boundary of Rome, so that he kept his *imperium*. He sent his legates – the subordinates serving a Roman governor who issued orders by virtue of delegated *imperium* – to govern the area, all the while knowing that he had legions to call upon if necessary.[22]

None of this was achieved without violence, and rioting at elections was now almost routine, with deaths more and more common. On one occasion Pompey returned home spattered with someone else's blood and so shocked his wife Julia that she suffered a miscarriage. They still could not prevent senators of independent mind, and often bitterly hostile to them, from winning high office in the years to come. When Crassus left for his province he was hounded by a tribune who formally called on the gods to curse the proconsul and the unjust war he planned. Personal hatreds and rivalry loomed larger in most senators' minds than the good of the Republic.[23]

Cursed or simply careless, Crassus' invasion was a disaster. His army was checked at Carrhae in 53 BC and all but a small remnant killed or captured when they tried to escape from the fast-moving Parthian cavalry. Crassus tried to negotiate a surrender and was killed and beheaded. His death seriously weakened the alliance between Pompey and Julius Caesar. An even worse blow came around the same time, when Julia died in childbirth. Her father hastily proposed new marriage connections, offering Octavius' sister Octavia to Pompey as a potential bride. The offer was not accepted. Soon Octavia was married to Marcus Claudius Marcellus, a member of one of the most prestigious families of plebeian aristocrats. He was no friend of Julius Caesar, who may not have had any say in the arrangement, but in political terms it was a very good catch for the girl's close relatives. Atia's husband Philippus was consul in 56 BC, and Marcellus would win the same office in 50 BC.[24]

Clodius and Milo continued their running battles, while other leaders took part on a smaller scale. The disturbances were so bad that 53 BC began with no consuls elected, and it was not until the summer that the elections were finally completed and two men chosen. If anything, the violence was worse in the autumn of that year, for this time Milo was a candidate, while his arch enemy Clodius was standing for the praetorship. Once again rioting prevented the *Comitia centuriata* from completing its task and another year began without consuls. In January 52 BC Clodius and Milo happened to bump into each other outside the City. Clodius was wounded in the initial fighting and carried into a tavern. Milo sent men who forced their way in and finished off his hated rival. Supporters and sympathisers turned the subsequent funeral into the sort of dramatic protest the former tribune would no doubt have approved of. Clodius' corpse was carried into the Senate House itself and cremated, burning the building down in the process. Rome seemed to be collapsing into anarchy. There was no significant policing force to control the mobs, and only troops could do the job. It was a question of who had both the *imperium* and *auctoritas* to bring the situation under control.[25]

Cato and the *boni* managed to stop Pompey being named dictator. Instead he became sole consul – an utterly unprecedented post. Later in the year he took a colleague – Quintus Cornelius Metellus Pius Scipio Nasica, whose lengthy name advertised a grand heritage unmatched by any natural talent. Pompey also married Scipio's daughter Cornelia to confirm a new alliance with one of the aristocratic establishment. Order was restored by force. Milo was put on trial in a court surrounded by soldiers and a hostile crowd, and went into exile before the inevitable verdict was announced. He was of course guilty, but the trial scarcely gave the impression of being fair and ignored normal processes. Rather more of Clodius' supporters found themselves condemned in similar circumstances, and fled north to find a ready welcome in Julius Caesar's camp. Pompey's provincial command was extended and at the end of the year he resumed his unorthodox stance, lurking just outside the City. At times the Senate chose to meet in temples outside the *pomerium* so that he could attend without laying down his *imperium* and the command of his army.[26]

By 51 BC Julius Caesar was completing mopping-up operations in Gaul. It is doubtful that anyone – save of course himself – would have expected him to prove quite such a gifted general. Exploiting the migration of a Gallic tribe that threatened first Transalpine Gaul and then Rome's allies beyond, he had intervened over an ever-widening area, conquering – the Romans used the euphemism of 'pacifying' – all the land from the Atlantic in the west to the Rhine in the east. His victories were spectacular, and celebrated in his own annually released accounts, the famous *Commentaries on the Gallic War* that even Cicero praised as one of the highest expressions of the Latin language. Pompey had been awarded ten days of public thanksgiving to celebrate his eastern victories – double the amount ever given to a Roman general. Julius Caesar was given fifteen days for his first successes, then twenty more when he raided the unknown and mysterious island of Britain, and again when he suppressed a rebellion by a great confederation of tribes. The Roman people had a new military hero.[27]

Julius Caesar wanted to come back from Gaul, celebrate a triumph and then immediately become consul for 48 BC, having waited the full ten years legally required between consulships. He had no desire to be a private citizen, when he would become vulnerable to prosecution. Several of his enemies were loudly talking of bringing him to trial like Milo, in a court surrounded by soldiers. To achieve his aim, he needed the right to present his candidature *in absentia*. It was a small concession compared to the recent flouting of the rules by Pompey. Julius Caesar also wanted to remain as proconsul with *imperium* until late 49 BC, and argued that he was entitled to this as part of the command granted to him by the Popular Assembly. Although worse had happened since then, his critics spoke of the intimidation and violence of his first consulship and forecast an even more turbulent second term. More importantly, they sensed that Julius Caesar had become vulnerable, and rushed to exploit this just as they had turned against Pompey in the late sixties.

Pompey's attitude was crucial, and for a long time no one was sure what this would be. Cicero had long since conceded that the 'Roman Alexander' was a hard man to read. Yet gradually there were signs that he was turning against his former father-in-law. His support became less and less convincing. To later generations it appeared obvious, as summed up by the poet Lucan almost a century later – 'Caesar cannot bear anyone above him, nor Pompey any equal'. Only by acknowledging his need for Pompey's help and support could the proconsul of Gaul return in the way he wanted. When questioned over what he would do if Julius Caesar refused to obey the Senate, Pompey complacently responded, 'What if my son wants to attack me with a stick?' Statements like this encouraged Julius Caesar's enemies.[28]

A succession of consuls took up the attack, pressing for Julius Caesar's immediate recall. The first was the cousin and namesake of Octavia's husband, who was consul in 51 BC. Marcellus himself was equally hostile to his wife's great-uncle during his own consulship in 50 BC. To counter this assault, the plunder of Gaul flowed to Rome to win supporters, particularly from the ranks of the tribunes. On 1 December 50 BC one forced a vote in the Senate, demanding that both Pompey and Julius Caesar lay down their commands simultaneously. Only 22 senators voted against the 370 who supported this measure. The overwhelming majority did not want to risk another civil war, even though many disliked Julius Caesar and his prominence.[29]

A rumour spread that the proconsul had already invaded Italy. Marcellus tried to persuade the Senate to act, but was thwarted by their reluctance and tribunician veto. Ignoring this, he and his colleague, escorted by friends, hurried out to Pompey's villa in the Alban Hills and presented him with a sword, calling on the proconsul to defend the Republic with his legions. Pompey showed no reluctance to take up arms against his former father-in-law and friend. Then the report was found to be false and nothing happened. On 1 January 49 BC another Marcellus became consul, this time the younger brother of the consul of 51 BC. Each side made proposals, but there was little trust and a tendency to perceive willingness to negotiate as a sign of weakness. On 7 January the Senate passed the *senatus consultum ultimum*, calling on the magistrates and the proconsuls near the City – an obvious reference to Pompey – to do whatever was necessary to see that the Republic suffered no harm. Mark Antony and another tribune who had been urging Julius Caesar's case were advised that their safety could no longer be assured. They fled the City and went north.[30]

A few days later – probably on 10 January – Julius Caesar led a single legion across the River Rubicon, crossing the line that separated his province, where he still legally held *imperium*, into Italy, where he did not. The man who had received successive votes of public thanksgiving during his command was now a rebel, who must win or suffer the fate of Catiline. We do not know whether or not he actually uttered the old gambler's tag – 'the die is cast' – as he embarked on civil war, but there is no doubt about the risk, or his belief that he was left with no alternative. Julius Caesar was willing to plunge the Republic into civil war to protect his own position and his *dignitas*. Pompey, as well as Cato and Julius Caesar's other opponents, was equally willing to fight a war to deprive him of both.[31]

4

A WAY OUT

'They wanted it; even after all my great deeds I, Caius Caesar, would
have been condemned, if I had not sought support from my army.'
*Julius Caesar's comment on seeing the enemy dead at Pharsalus, according
to eyewitness Asinius Pollio, late first century BC.*[1]

The details of the Civil War need not detain us for long, since
Octavius was only thirteen and too young to be involved. Julius
Caesar overran Italy quickly. Perhaps Pompey had still expected that
his former ally would back down, or was simply complacent in his
own strength. Months before, he had boasted that he had only 'to
stamp his foot for legions and cavalry to spring up from the soil of
Italy'. Instead his allies were dismayed to see him abandon Rome
without a fight, and retreat to Brundisium. One senator cynically
asked him whether it was about time to start stamping his foot. Instead he took them all across the Adriatic to northern Greece, and
there set about building up a great army and fleet, drawing on all
his connections in the eastern provinces and allied kingdoms. Nearing sixty, Pompey displayed his great skills as an organiser. 'Sulla
did it, why shouldn't I?' he said repeatedly, for Sulla had come back
from Greece to win a civil war. Yet it was not the happiest example.
Some of his allies muttered that they were fighting merely to choose
which dictator to have ruling them. Others openly criticised every
decision he made. Pompey, the man whose career had broken every
constitutional rule, had somehow become the champion of the free
Republic, commanding many of the *boni* who had been his bitterest
opponents for so many years. It was a grim irony and produced an
uneasy alliance.[2]

His enemies and the majority who wanted to remain neutral

feared that Julius Caesar would prove a truly savage master, slaugh-
tering his enemies like Marius and Sulla. Instead he paraded his
clemency, only fighting those who fought him and sparing all who
surrendered. In March 49 BC he proclaimed: 'Let us see if in this way
we can willingly win the support of all and gain a permanent victory, since through their cruelty others have been unable to escape
hatred or make their victory lasting – save for Lucius Sulla, and I do
not intend to imitate him. This is a new way of conquest, we grow
strong through pity and generosity.'[3]

After Italy he went to Spain, and in a rapid campaign outmanoeuvred the legions left there by Pompey and forced their surrender.
Wherever Julius Caesar went himself there were victories, but his
subordinates proved less capable and several marched off to defeat.
By the start of 48 BC he had gathered enough ships to transport
some of his legions to Macedonia, where Pompey was still preparing to copy Sulla. Numbers and resources were on Pompey's side,
but Julius Caesar's smaller army was hardened by years of war and
utterly devoted to their commander. He attacked, and came close
to blockading the more numerous enemy into submission at Dyrra-
chium, before Pompey managed to break his lines. The Caesareans
retreated and the Pompeians followed, prominent senators nagging
the general to win quickly and already bickering over the anticipated
spoils. At Pharsalus, on 9 August 48 BC, Pompey offered battle and
Julius Caesar gratefully accepted. Pompey's plan was sound, if un-
subtle, staking everything on a flanking attack by his cavalry, which
outnumbered their Caesarean counterparts by seven to one. Julius
Caesar guessed his intention, countered it, and after that his veterans cut to pieces the inexperienced Pompeians and their foreign
auxiliaries.[4]

Roman aristocrats could be pardoned for military incompetence
as long as they were brave, refusing to admit permanent defeat
and rallying their army for the next battle. Pompey's nerve went
and he fled before the battle was over, going eventually to Egypt,
where the advisers of the boy king Ptolemy XIII ordered his murder
in the hope of pleasing the victor. The death may well have been

convenient for Julius Caesar, but when he arrived in pursuit and was presented with his former son-in-law's head he showed revulsion and anger. Needing hard currency to pay his armies – now swollen in size by tens of thousands of captured Pompeians – he intervened in the affairs of the kingdom, and was soon embroiled in their own civil war as the young king fought for power with his sister Cleopatra. The small Roman army was soon besieged, and it was only after a hard struggle and the arrival of reinforcements that the enemy was defeated. Julius Caesar tarried longer than many felt necessary, cruising along the Nile with his lover Cleopatra. In the meantime the Pompeians regrouped, Cato's iron will helping to muster a new army in Africa. Finally leaving Egypt, Julius Caesar crushed an army led by Mithridates' son in Asia, returned fleetingly to Italy in the autumn, and then crossed to Africa. The Pompeians were defeated at Thapsus on 6 April 46 BC. Cato killed himself rather than surrender and accept his enemy's mercy. It was not quite the end of the war. Pompey's older son Cnaeus raised an army in Spain, and so once again Julius Caesar left Rome and set out for war. Munda, the final battle fought on 17 March 45 BC, was a savage and desperate struggle, but in the end the veterans of the Gallic war prevailed.[5]

A WORLD AT WAR

By the time of the Civil War Octavius was living with his mother in the house of his stepfather Philippus. His grandmother Julia had died in 51 BC – her husband presumably some time in the years before that. Although only twelve, Octavius delivered the oration at Julia's funeral and was praised for his performance. Aristocratic funerals were public events, commencing with a ceremony in the Forum, followed by a procession outside the City where the cremation itself would be carried out. It was an opportunity not simply to praise the deceased, but to parade the achievements of all their ancestors. In the grandest funerals, actors were hired to don the regalia and wear the funeral masks of all the men who in former generations had held high office, making them visible reminders of past glories. It was conventional for a young man of the next generation to deliver the eulogy, connecting him with the great deeds of the past and implicitly promising similar achievements from him in the future.[6]

This was the first formal occasion where the young Octavius was the centre of attention, bringing him a closer association with his famous – and currently highly controversial – great-uncle. In other respects he was simply one of the teenage aristocrats riding out and exercising in public, meeting and competing with others of his generation. Philippus is said to have taken an active role in the supervision of his stepson, and it is more than likely that Octavius began to accompany him when he went about his business and attended public meetings or the Senate. Both Philippus and Atia daily questioned his *paedogogus* and tutors about his activities and progress. In later years Atia in particular was held up as an example of the ideal Roman mother:

> In the good old days, every man's son, born in wedlock, was brought up not in the chamber of some hireling nurse, but in his mother's lap, and at her knee. And that mother could have no higher praise than that she managed the house and gave herself to her children . . . In the presence of such a one no base word could be uttered without grave offence, and no wrong deed done. Religiously and with the utmost diligence she regulated not only the serious tasks of her youthful charges, but their recreations also and their games. It was in this spirit, we are told, that Cornelia, the mother of the Gracchi, directed their upbringing, Aurelia that of Caesar, Atia of Augustus: thus it was that these mothers trained their princely children.[7]

Mothers could be distant, and were certainly supposed to be authoritative figures, whose approval needed to be earned, as the child conformed to the behaviour expected by family and state.[8] When the Civil War began Atia and Philippus felt that Rome might become dangerous and sent the teenage Octavius to stay in one of his step-father's villas – we know of at least two, one at Puteoli and the other near Astura (on the coast nearer Rome), but there may have been others. Philippus refused to commit himself to either side. So too did Octavia's husband Marcellus, the man who had handed the sword to Pompey just a few weeks before. Julius Caesar declared that he would respect such neutrality and only fight those who fought him. The Pompeians, boasting of their defence of law and the Republic, threatened to treat anyone who was not for them as an enemy.[9]

We do not know when it was felt safe for Octavius to return to Rome, but he was certainly there by late 47 BC, and on 18 October he formally became a man. There was no set age for this ceremony, which tended to occur somewhere between the ages of fourteen and sixteen. Octavius was a few weeks past his sixteenth birthday. The *bulla* charm placed around his neck as an infant was finally laid aside, and the youth was given his first shave. His hair was also cut. Boys were allowed long, fairly shaggy hair, but a shorter, neater style was appropriate for an adult citizen. Boys also wore the *toga prae-texta* with its purple border – otherwise only worn by magistrates. Octavius now marked his new status by donning instead the man's plain *toga virilis*. Yet another of Suetonius' stories of omens of future glory claims that, in the process of removing his child's toga, his tunic ripped and fell down around his ankles – signifying that mag-istrates and Senate would one day be subject to him. As usual it is impossible to know whether this accident happened or was a later invention. After ceremonies held in the family home, male relatives and family friends would escort the new adult through the heart of the City, passing through the Forum and then climbing the Capito-line Hill to the Temple of Jupiter, to sacrifice and make an offering to Iuventus, the god of youth.[10]

It is just possible that Julius Caesar witnessed this important stage in his great-nephew's life. He had reached Italy on his return from the east at the end of September, but then had to organise the coming expedition to Africa, quell a mutiny of legionaries who had grown frustrated during his long absence, hold elections, and then get to Sicily by the middle of December. Probably he was too preoccupied to attend, but he was already displaying an interest in the sixteen-year-old. The death of a leading Pompeian at the Battle of Pharsalus left a vacancy in the college of pontiffs. Julius Caesar formally recommended his great-nephew as candidate and the electorate duly obliged.[11]

Although now officially an adult and one of Rome's senior priests, Octavius continued to live under the roof of Philippus, while Atia still regulated her son's life and his education. He was considered an uncommonly handsome lad. His hair curled a little and was slightly blond (*subflavum*), although such descriptions of colour are hard to judge and may simply mean brown rather than black. He had small teeth, separated by more space than was common; in later life these decayed badly, but they were no doubt better in his youth. His complexion was neither notably dark nor fair, his movements were graceful and his body and limbs so well proportioned that he seemed taller than he was. One of his own freedmen later claimed that as an adult he was more than five foot six inches (five foot nine by the smaller Roman measurements), but this was probably a generous estimate. Octavius clearly saw himself as short, and for much of his life wore shoes with built-up soles in an effort to seem bigger.[12]

Julius Caesar was a tall man with piercing eyes, and if he could not match his height, his great-nephew liked to feel that his own gaze was powerful. Roman aristocrats were raised with a highly developed sense of their own and their family's importance. Octavius was especially self-confident, and is said to have gathered a circle of friends around him from an early age. His biographer Nicolaus of Damascus later claimed that he also attracted the attention of predatory older women. In the hope of hiding his charms, he appeared less often at busy times of day when he might be seen, even taking to attending temples only during the hours of darkness. As well educated as their brothers, but barred from public life and married off and divorced to cement or break political alliances, there were plenty of bored senators' wives with absent or uninterested husbands in Rome. Clodius' sisters were the frequent subject of gossip about their affairs and their wild lifestyle – one of them was the 'Lesbia' of whom the poet Catullus wrote in love, then hatred and longing after she left him. The mother of one of Julius Caesar's subordinates, Decimus Junius Brutus, was described by a fellow senator in colourful terms:

> Among these was Sempronia . . . well blessed by fortune in her birth and physical beauty, as well as her husband and children; well read in Greek and Latin literature, she played the lyre, danced more artfully than any honest woman should, and had many other gifts which fostered a luxurious life. Yet there was never anything she prized so little as her honour and chastity; it was hard to say whether she was less free with her money or her virtue; her lusts were so fierce that she more often pursued men than was pursued by them . . . She had often broken her word, failed to pay her debts, been party to murder; her lack of money but addiction to luxury set her on a wild course. Even so, she was a remarkable woman; able to write poetry, crack a joke, and converse modestly, tenderly or wantonly; all in all she had great gifts and a good many charms.[13]

The young Octavius is supposed to have resisted the lure of such well-born sirens. Yet aristocratic youths were granted considerable licence when it came to sexual exploits, unlike their sisters. Rome had plenty of brothels, and there were numerous high-class courtesans, who needed to be wooed and cared for in expensive style. Mark Antony was currently having an affair with a mime actress named Cytheris, and had paraded her quite publicly while Julius Caesar was away and he was serving as his deputy in Italy. This was also a slave-owning society, when human beings were property. A slave had no right to resist if his or her owner wished to have sexual intercourse with them.[14]

Octavius went to Spain for the campaign against Cnaeus Pompeius, but due to illness arrived too late for the fighting. Even so he was welcomed and treated with particular warmth by Julius Caesar. On his return to Rome he moved out of Philippus' house and took an apartment nearby. Many of the better-class *insulae* had large flats and it was common for wealthy young men to rent them in the years before they married and acquired a house of their own. The seventeen-year-old still spent a good deal of time with his parents, although occasionally he held dinner parties for his friends. Some of these later claimed that for a whole year he abstained from all sexual activity, seeing this as good for his general health and especially his voice. A man wanting to climb the political ladder needed to be at least a moderately good orator. Yet whatever the professed reason, it is very revealing that a whole year of sexual abstinence was seen as exceptional, not simply for young Roman aristocrats in general, but as an achievement for Octavius in particular.[15]

DICTATOR

Julius Caesar made himself dictator for just a few days in 49 BC so that he could hold consular elections. He became consul for 48 BC, and again in 46 BC, 45 BC (when initially he was sole consul just as Pompey had been in 52 BC), and 44 BC. When news of Pharsalus reached Rome, he was named dictator again, and held this office for twelve months, double the normal period of dictators in the past with the exception of Sulla. In 46 BC he was named dictator for ten years, although the post was to be formally renewed each year. In the early weeks of 44 BC his dictatorship was made perpetual. Other powers were added. He became overseer of customs/behaviour (*praefectura morum*), taking over tasks traditionally associated with the censorship which had struggled to be effective in recent decades. In 45 BC the dictator was granted the right to nominate consuls and half the lesser magistrates for the next three years, for he planned a major expedition against the Parthians and so expected to be away for much of this time.[16]

Yet, for all his power, it is important to remember just how short a time Julius Caesar actually spent in Rome: he fought campaigns in every year except 44 BC, and even then was about to set out for war when he was murdered. There was very little time, and in the years that followed his true intentions were clouded by rumour and propaganda. Even so, the dictator showed all his accustomed restless energy in a flurry of activity, legislation and reform, but it is often difficult to tell how much was actually done rather than simply announced or planned. There was certainly an extensive programme of land distribution to demobilised legionary veterans and the urban poor, following on from his actions as consul in 59 BC. Many were set up on farms in Italy, often taken from the estates of dead Pompeians or purchased with the spoils of war. There were also citizen colonies established in the provinces, most notably at Carthage and Corinth.

The number of magistrates, except for the consuls, was increased, so that there were now forty quaestors and twenty praetors each year. Some of this was motivated by the need to reward loyal followers or newly loyal former Pompeians, but there was also a practical element. With an ever-growing empire to run, there was simply more work for magistrates. Many more senators were nominated, a high proportion of them from the local aristocracies of the Italian towns, but a few from the citizen populations of the Spanish and Gallic provinces. The Senate grew in size to over 900 members, replenished each year when the newly elected quaestors were enrolled in its ranks.[17]

Pompey had given Rome its first stone theatre, part of a grand complex paid for by the spoils from his victories. Julius Caesar employed the money from Gaul to begin a remodelling of the voting precinct on the Campus Martius. The old *saepta* was to be paved and walled with marble, and awnings provided to give shade to the citizens as they waited. As dictator he continued this project, rebuilt the Senate House, and began a new forum, the Forum Julium, at an angle from the main Forum and including a temple to his divine ancestor Venus and more space for public business and commerce.

Building projects gave well-paid work to the unemployed, and celebrated the glory of the man behind them. Roman aristocrats had long embarked on such monuments to their achievements. It was simply the scale that had changed.[18]

New laws regulated life and business in Rome itself, Italy and the provinces, and brought some relief to those in debt. The Roman calendar was based on the lunar cycle with a year of 355 days, and required extra months to be inserted into some years by the college of pontiffs in an attempt to keep some connection with the actual seasons. This was subject to politically motivated manipulation and by the middle of the first century BC was badly out of kilter with nature. The Julian calendar is essentially the one we use today, slightly modified in the sixteenth century, and was based on the solar cycle with a year of 364 days and an extra day every fourth year. Three intercalary months were added to 46 BC by the pontiffs, including the young Octavius, so that the year had 446 days and 1 January in the new calendar would begin at something like its proper time. As an honour, the month of Julius Caesar's birth was renamed Julius – our July.[19]

This was only one of a flood of honours and privileges offered to the dictator. On his return from the war in Africa he had celebrated four triumphs – one more than Pompey and more than any past hero of the Republic. All of them, for Gaul, Egypt, Asia and Africa, were ostensibly victories over foreign enemies. Even so there were paintings carried in the African triumph showing the deaths of leading Pompeians. When he returned from Spain at the end of 45 BC Julius Caesar openly celebrated a fifth triumph that was blatantly won over fellow Romans in a civil war.[20]

Yet his policy of clemency remained. Despite some people's fears, victory did not cause Julius Caesar to unveil hidden cruelty and become a new Sulla. Nor were his supporters permitted free rein to plunder and murder at will. Loyal Caesareans certainly did well – Julius Caesar once said that he would reward even a bandit if the man had served him faithfully. Men gained senatorial rank, high office and provincial commands. Property was confiscated from the estates of dead enemies, but it was not simply given away to his own partisans. Auctions were held, and Mark Antony was one of those surprised to find that the dictator actually expected the high sums bid to be paid. Similarly those who had hoped for an abolition of existing debt – a popular cry in Roman politics was for 'new account books' (*novae tabulae*) – were disappointed by the moderate relief offered to them.[21]

Octavius received a share of the rewards. He was awarded token military decorations in the African triumph even though he had remained in Italy throughout the conflict. He was also made a patrician as Julius Caesar added to the ranks of the ancient aristocracy, greatly thinned by decay and more recently civil war. His great-nephew's requests to pardon friends' relatives who had fought on the Pompeian side were readily approved by the dictator. Octavius received several honorary posts, and a degree of public affection from Julius Caesar. As well as his great-nephew, the dictator had two nephews, the sons of his other sister Julia (not the mother of Atia). Quintus Pedius, the child of her first marriage, was the oldest and served with him in Gaul and the Civil War. Less is known of her son from her second marriage, Lucius Pinarius, and it may be that he was only starting his career. It is impossible to say whether later claims of the particular affection shown to Octavius are inventions. He was only eighteen by the end of 45 BC, too young to be felt particularly noteworthy in public life.[22]

It was not only the loyal Caesareans who did well in these years. Two of the new praetors to assume office on 1 January 44 BC were Marcus Junius Brutus and Caius Cassius Longinus, both of whom had served with Pompey and only surrendered after Pharsalus. Brutus was the son of Servilia, Cato's half-sister and Julius Caesar's long-time mistress, and now received the especially prestigious post of urban praetor. Both men were already probably marked down for the consulship when they became old enough. In most cases petitions to let other Pompeians return from exile were successful. Cicero gave an enthusiastic speech in 46 BC when Julius Caesar permitted the return from exile of Marcus Claudius Marcellus, cousin of Octavia's husband and the man who as consul in 51 BC had been especially vitriolic in his hostility.

THE IDES OF MARCH

The rule of the dictator was far from harsh, his reforms practical and generally for the wider good of the state. Yet no one should have such vast powers at all, let alone in perpetuity. Sulla had been far more brutal, but at least Sulla had resigned his dictatorship after a few years and retired to private life. Julius Caesar called him 'a political illiterate' for doing so, and showed no sign of willingness to give up his dominance of the state. He was in his fifty-sixth year and, although troubled with epilepsy, it was perfectly possible that he would live on for decades. The planned Parthian War would give him the clean glory of fighting a foreign enemy, and add even more to his prestige when he returned in three years or so.[23]

Julius Caesar had *regnum*, effectively royal power over the state. The honours given to him were extensions to those granted to the great men of the past – most notably Pompey – but far surpassed them all in scale. He sat on a golden chair of office, wore the triumphing general's toga and laurel wreath on all public occasions, and was given the right to sport the high boots and long-sleeved tunic which he claimed were the garb of his distant ancestors, the kings of Alba Longa – a city near Rome and a rival in its early history. A pediment, like those on a temple, was added to his house. Other honours brought Julius Caesar very close to divine status, although it is harder to say whether or not he was actually deified in his lifetime. The idea was anyway less shocking to the Romans with their polytheistic tradition than to us. Stories told of heroes who became gods through their deeds, and it was common enough to praise great achievements as 'god-like'.[24]

Some very wild stories circulated – Julius Caesar was planning to move the capital from Rome to Ilium, the site of Troy, from which rumour claimed the Romans had come after its destruction by the

Greeks; or he wanted to move it to Alexandria, presumably to rule and live with Cleopatra, another of his mistresses. She visited Rome twice between 46 and 44 BC, and stayed with her entourage in one of the dictator's villas outside the formal boundary of the City. She had given birth to a baby boy, who was probably Julius Caesar's child. Later the Alexandrians nicknamed him Caesarion. A bastard and a non-citizen, he could have no status in Roman law, and there is not a shred of evidence that the boy received any particular attention from the dictator himself, making modern ideas of Cleopatra's great influence over her Roman lover pure fantasy. That did not stop more rumours – a senator was supposed to be about to propose a law granting Julius Caesar the right to take as many wives as he wanted for the purpose of having children. Cicero was no friend of the dictator's, but even he did not believe that one. Sensible observers were no doubt sceptical of most of these tales, but that was not really the point. The mere fact that they circulated reveals the fears and worries of the time. They were just plausible enough to be worth repeating, and reflected the glum mood of Rome's elite.[25]

Many of the stories focused on kingship. 'I am not King [*rex*], but Caesar,' said the dictator in response to a crowd hailing him as king – *Rex* was a family name of another aristocratic line. The subject was delicate. When tribunes had coronets removed from one of his statues, Julius Caesar responded angrily, claiming they denied him the chance to refuse himself and wanted to blacken his name by drawing attention to the whole business. The most famous incident came at the Festival of the Lupercalia, celebrated on 15 February 44 BC, with teams of priests clad only in goatskin loincloths running through the heart of the City, gently flicking passers-by with their whips. The dictator presided on a tribunal, and the leader of the priests, Mark Antony, concluded by running up and offering a crown to him. Julius Caesar refused, to the delight of the crowd, repeating the gesture when Antony offered it again. The most likely interpretation of the affair is that it was a deliberate pantomime, intended to show once and for all that he did not want the title of king. If so, then it did not work. Soon people were saying that it was a test, and that Julius Caesar would have taken the crown if only the people had responded with enthusiasm. Another story circulated that the Senate would debate making him king everywhere apart from inside Rome itself.[26]

The truth scarcely mattered. Deep in their souls senators knew that this was not how things should be. King or not, god or not, and however kind and efficient personally, Julius Caesar possessed supreme power, effectively *regnum*, whatever he called himself, and that meant that there could be no *res publica* – no state. For a Roman aristocrat the true Republic only existed when the senatorial class shared control, guiding magistrates elected through open competition and changing them regularly, so that plenty of people won the chance for high command and profit. This was liberty, and even for quite a few Caesareans it was now clearly dead.

The dictator's attitude did not help. In Rome for such short periods of time when there was so much to do, tired by years of war but accustomed to issuing orders, and habitually prone to impatience with those less energetic than himself, Julius Caesar was often tactless. He resigned as consul in 45 BC and had two replacements elected. When one died on 31 December, he hastily turned a legislative assembly into a voting assembly and elected another of his henchmen as consul for the rest of the day. Cicero joked that 'in the consulship of Caninius nobody ate lunch. However, nothing bad occurred while he was consul – for his vigilance was so incredible that throughout his entire consulship he never went to sleep,' but privately said that it was enough to make anyone weep. Individually recipients of the additional posts of praetor and quaestor were grateful, while lamenting that the rank was being devalued.[27]

'The Republic is nothing, merely a name without body or shape,' the dictator is supposed to have said. Decisions were now being made in private, dealing with the great backlog of petitions and problems left from the disruption of the Civil War and the long years of administrative chaos before it. They were often sensible enough, but that was not the point. Usually they were dressed up in the proper procedures as if they were genuine senatorial decrees. Cicero found himself being thanked by provincial communities for the grant of privileges at fictional meetings of the Senate where he was listed as attending and voting. When a procession of senators led by Mark Antony, consul for 44 BC with Julius Caesar, arrived to tell him of fresh honours, the dictator was conducting public business and did not stand up to greet them. Technically, his rank probably meant that he was not required to do so, but even so many took great offence. At public games Julius Caesar also kept busy, dictating letters to several scribes at once in his accustomed manner, always pressing on with work. The crowd did not like it, wanting him to share their pleasure in the lavish spectacles he provided. Julius Caesar seemed to be always in a hurry, and lacked the time to flatter either senators or the wider population.[28]

The crowd's annoyance soon faded, but the resentment of many aristocrats did not. The dictator himself realised it. Cicero later recalled Julius Caesar sadly saying, 'Can I have any doubt that I am deeply loathed, when Marcus Cicero has to sit and wait and cannot simply come to see me as he wishes. If ever there is an easy-mannered man then it is he. Yet I have no doubt that he hates me.' There is a great sense of resigned weariness in another frequent comment – 'I have lived long enough for either nature or glory'. His determination to get Rome and the empire running efficiently remained unabated, and there seems to have been an expectation that others would recognise the need for him to do this. The dictator predicted renewed civil war if he died suddenly or was killed, and believed others would have the sense to realise this and see that it was for the greater good for him to live. Determined to show confidence, or perhaps simply complacent, he dismissed his bodyguard of Spanish warriors. The Senate voted him an escort of senators and equestrians, but it was never actually formed. Julius Caesar walked or was carried in a litter through the streets, conducted business in public and attended the Senate. He was far from inaccessible while he was in Rome, although once he left for the Parthian expedition this would change.[29]

It was this that prompted a group of senators led by Brutus and Cassius to act. We do not need to define Julius Caesar's power in these months precisely, still less to ask unanswerable questions about his plans for the future. His powers and position were incompatible with the *res publica*, and this could not be restored until he was removed. The conspirators included several distinguished Caesareans as well as former Pompeians. Caius Trebonius had held the consulship in 45 BC, while Decimus Brutus – cousin of Marcus Brutus – had served Julius Caesar in Gaul, was praetor in 45 BC and earmarked for the consulship during the dictator's absence. (He was also the son of the Sempronia whose character was so acidly drawn by Sallust.) The leading conspirators were doing well under the current regime, but resented the dominance of one man, whoever he was.

This political motive was paramount. It is also fair to say that the conspirators would do at least as well – and perhaps far better – as the leading men of the Republic when the dictator was dead. These were Roman aristocrats, raised to be ambitious, and some at least were stirred by celebrated Greek killers of tyrants. Marcus Junius Brutus was the nephew of Cato, and yet he had surrendered and done well from Julius Caesar. His uncle had stabbed himself with a sword rather than accept the victor's clemency. Such a suicide is not easy to perform, and Cato did not die, allowing his son to fetch doctors and bind up the wound. When left on his own, Cato ripped the stitches apart and dragged out his own entrails, dying in a spectacularly gruesome fashion well in keeping with his skill for painting his opponents as brutal oppressors. Personal guilt probably added to Brutus' great reverence for his dead uncle, for not only did he compose an adulatory biography, but also divorced his wife and married Cato's daughter, the widow of Bibulus.[30]

Julius Caesar responded to the book, and another more moderate one written by Cicero, with an extremely vitriolic *Anticato*, in the most lurid traditions of Roman invective, but did nothing more. At the start of 45 BC Cassius had referred to him as 'the old clement master' (*veterem et clementem dominum*), preferring him to the aggressive Cnaeus Pompeius. Clement or not, he was their 'master', and that in itself was wrong. The conspirators did not bind themselves to an oath. Secret oaths were viewed as inherently sinister – the Catilinarians had sworn oaths – and publicly, all senators had recently taken an oath to protect Julius Caesar.[31]

On the Ides of March, Julius Caesar went to a meeting of the Senate convened in one of the temples in Pompey's theatre complex. Decimus Brutus had a troop of gladiators hired for forthcoming games waiting nearby. The dictator was unguarded. Trebonius drew Mark Antony aside and kept him talking outside the building. As fellow consul he would sit next to Julius Caesar, and was a vigorous, bold man who might well choose to fight. At Marcus Brutus' urging, they planned to kill no one apart from the dictator.

Clustering around Julius Caesar under the pretext of making a petition, one of the conspirators suddenly stabbed him from behind. The response was surprise, and then anger, as the dictator drew his long stylus pen and stabbed at his attackers with its sharp point. Clustering around him, the conspirators struck wildly with their knives. Brutus was wounded in the thigh and another of them injured by their comrades' blades. Julius Caesar collapsed – although only one of his twenty-three wounds was later thought to have been fatal – and fell at the base of a statue of Pompey. He had just enough strength to pull his toga over his face in a last attempt at dignifying his appearance.[32]

The dictator was dead and so the *res publica* could be free. Brutus called out Cicero's name and the other conspirators shouted that liberty was restored. The watching senators – Cicero included – fled in panic, fearing more widespread violence. Guarded by Decimus Brutus' gladiators, the conspirators went up to the Capitoline Hill. The City was stunned by their action, but they may already have sensed that the mood of the people was not with them. Much of the wider population remained devoted to Julius Caesar, who had done more for their needs than generations of senators. The Republic the conspirators imagined and longed for had not truly functioned for a very long time.

A few weeks later a senator named Matius, who was a staunch Caesarean, even though he did not like the dictatorship, wrote gloomily to Cicero that if Julius Caesar 'with all his genius could not find a way out, then who will find a way?'[33]

PART TWO

CAIUS JULIUS CAESAR (OCTAVIANUS)
44–38 BC

'Later he assumed the name Caius Caesar . . . by the will of his great-uncle.' – Suetonius, *Augustus* 7. 2.

5

HEIR

'In Octavianus . . . there is plenty of sense and plenty of spirit, and it looks as if he will be as well disposed to our heroes [the conspirators] as we could wish. Yet how far can we trust anyone of such an age, such a name, such an inheritance, and such an upbringing. His stepfather, whom I saw at Astura, thinks he is not to be trusted at all. Even so we must keep an eye on him, and at the very least keep him away from Antony.' *Cicero, June 44 BC.*[1]

Julius Caesar's great-nephew was far from Rome on the Ides of March, for at the end of 45 BC the dictator had sent him abroad to further his education. It was common for young aristocrats to serve as 'tent-companions' to a relative or family friend given command of a province. They lived with the governor and his staff, observing what he did just as they accompanied relatives around the Forum at home. Julius Caesar planned to take Octavius with him on the Parthian expedition and so wanted him to prepare for the experience. The young man was duly despatched to Macedonia, where six legions and substantial auxiliary forces were getting ready for the eastern war. This was only one part of the great army that Julius Caesar was mustering to avenge Crassus, but it was the most conveniently placed to Italy, with the added advantage of being in Greece. While training for war, Octavius was not to neglect the skills of politics, for these were the twin pillars of public life. Greek teachers of rhetoric were the most highly regarded, and young aristocrats often went to Greece to study.[2]

For four months Octavius and a party of friends and attendants lived at Apollonia on the western coast of Macedonia. The city was strategically placed on the Via Egnatia, the great Roman road built in the second century BC to cross the Hellenic Peninsula all the way to the shores of the Aegean. Apollonia had benefited from Julius Caesar's generosity and so readily welcomed his great-nephew. During the winter Octavius underwent voice training, practised oratory, and watched and joined army units in their drills and exercises. Apart from the legions, he trained with the non-citizen cavalry, for it was common for young aristocrats to be given command of such units. Mounted troops were also likely to play a vital role in operations against the cavalry armies of the Parthian king.[3]

It took time for news to travel across the Adriatic, and so it was not until late in March that a letter arrived from Octavius' mother, carried most likely by a member of her household or someone connected to the family in some way. Atia had probably written on the Ides of March itself, for she reported only the bare facts of the assassination. The written word was only ever part of the message, and it was normal for the messenger to add both detail and interpretation, but in this case the man knew little more. He had left Rome immediately and travelled in haste, so had no knowledge of what had happened since the Ides. Like Atia, he could speak only of the shock and uncertainty, and fears of more violence to come in which the dead dictator's relatives might well be targets. His mother urged Octavius to return to Italy as soon and as quietly as possible.

The youth responded to the news in a properly Roman way and sought advice from his companions in an ad hoc council or *consilium* of the sort which advised magistrates and provincial governors. Two of those present are known by name, Quintus Salvidienus Rufus and Marcus Vipsanius Agrippa, and they would continue to be associated with him for some time. Both came from similar backgrounds to Octavius' father, belonging to the local gentry of Italian towns. Salvidienus may well have been somewhat older, but Agrippa was an almost exact contemporary of Octavius and was most likely educated with him from a young age.[4]

As word of the dictator's death spread, military tribunes and centurions from the legions camped nearby came to visit, expressing their sympathy, anger at the assassins, and offering general support.

Claims that they were willing to put themselves under his command and march on Rome are probably later exaggerations, but there is no reason to doubt their goodwill. All six legions in Macedonia had been formed by Julius Caesar after Pharsalus in 48 BC, and every single officer owed his original commission and/or one or more steps in promotion to the approval of the dictator. Some may have served under him in different legions before this. Past favours were reinforced by eager anticipation of lavish rewards in the future. Wars in the east were renowned for the immense hauls of plunder waiting to be snatched from the wealthy kingdoms of that region. Julius Caesar was known to be both a lucky general who had never lost a war and exceptionally generous when it came to sharing the spoils. Alongside the soldiers, representatives of the city came, expressing their sympathy and assuring Octavius of his safety.[5]

A Roman aristocrat was expected to seek advice from his *consilium*, but then to weigh up the issues in his own mind and make a decision. Octavius decided to sail across to Italy, rather than wait until more news arrived, and arranged for ships to carry his party and their attendants. He may have touched at a remote spot on the coast of Calabria, before landing properly at the great port of Brundisium (modern Brindisi). Soon a picture began to emerge of the situation in Rome.[6]

After the initial shock at the assassination, some senators had praised the conspirators, but there was little enthusiasm from the wider population. Speeches by Brutus and others fell flat, as did distributions of money – later the historian Appian tartly noted the paradox of expecting an electorate who could be bribed to rally to a cry of liberty. The conspirators failed to act and lost the initiative, so that on 17 March it was Antony as consul who summoned the Senate. Brutus, Cassius and the others did not feel it safe to attend and remained up on the Capitol. After a long debate a motion framed by Cicero was passed overwhelmingly, granting amnesty to the conspirators, but confirming all of Julius Caesar's decisions and acts. The compromise was as illogical as it was necessary. The dictator had appointed most of the magistrates and if his decisions were invalid then presumably none of these men legally held office – including Brutus, Cassius and Antony. Similarly no provincial command would be legitimate, no recent law in force, and the land allocated to veterans and other settlers no longer their property. The restored Republic risked plunging into immediate chaos until new elections could be held, and every decree and law decided upon all over again.

Julius Caesar was also granted a public funeral on a motion put forward by his father-in-law. This was held in the heart of the Forum, most probably on 20 March, with Antony presiding and delivering the eulogy. Our sources differ over how much and what he actually said, but not about the result. Antony showed the crowd the dictator's cloak, torn by knives and stained with his blood, while a wax effigy of his body was hoisted up on a crane of the type used in theatres and rotated to display all twenty-three wounds. He read out the dictator's will, which made his extensive gardens beside the Tiber into a public park, and left 75 denarii (or 300 sesterces) to every citizen, adding to his many benefactions in the past. There was revulsion when it was revealed that Decimus Brutus was named as a secondary heir. Anger quickly boiled over into attacks on the houses of the conspirators and their sympathisers. A tribune and close friend of Julius Caesar named Cinna was murdered by a mob who mistook him for one of the conspirators with the same name. Like that other popular hero, Clodius, Julius Caesar was cremated in the Forum itself, benches and anything else combustible being heaped up to form a pyre. Rome was no longer safe for the conspirators and in the coming days all of them would leave the City.[7]

The will also named Caius Octavius as the heir to three-quarters of the dictator's vast personal estate, with the fairly common proviso that as legatee he take Julius Caesar's name. It had been drawn up on 15 September 45 BC on the dictator's return from the Spanish campaign and there is no indication that Octavius or any of his immediate family knew of its contents. The young man was clearly favoured by his great-uncle, who no doubt saw more talent in him than either of his nephews. Yet it is vital to remember that Julius Caesar did not plan on dying so soon. Cicero later declared that the dictator would not have returned from his eastern wars, but there is no reason to believe that this view was widespread or likely. Nor was there any certainty that Octavius would outlive his great-uncle, for the youth had already suffered a serious bout of illness that delayed his arrival in Spain in 45 BC and did not seem to have a robust constitution. If the teenager survived the rigours of the campaign and the arrows of the Parthians, and continued to show promise, then perhaps Julius Caesar would have given him more open recognition. Once again we return to the impossibility of knowing the dictator's long-term plans.[8]

Adoption was taken very seriously by the Romans, and an adopted son became to all intents and purposes the same as a true son, keeping in addition any useful prior connections from his real family. Such full adoption could only occur in the father's lifetime and could not be posthumous. This has prompted a prolonged and highly technical scholarly debate on precisely what status Julius Caesar's will gave to Octavius. To a great extent this misses the point. Octavius was the principal heir to his great-uncle's property and was to take his name. Julius Caesar's powers, offices and honours were each awarded to him personally and not possessions to bequeath. Yet he was a senator, who had revived the prestige of his family and taken it to unprecedented levels. A young man who received Julius Caesar's wealth and name inevitably also took on the political expectations of continuing the family's success. This need not be instant, but in due course and at a suitable age it would only be appropriate for him to enter public life and seek fresh distinction for the name of Caesar.

If Octavius accepted the legacy – and this was not compulsory, but a matter of choice, for we hear of individuals refusing to accept some bequests – then he inherited these political expectations as well as a name. The distinction between main heir and son was blurred even if it was clearly not full adoption. Some technical matters did make a real difference. A true or adopted son inherited rights over all of his father's freedmen – and in Julius Caesar's case these were both very numerous and often wealthy – who were obliged to support him as patron, voting for him and willingly placing their resources at his disposal. Without formal adoption Octavius might find it hard to enforce this legal right, although that did not mean that some or all of the dictator's freedmen would not choose to see him as their patron.[9]

At Brundisium Octavius received a letter from Philippus and another from Atia, both of whom by this time knew of the terms of the will. They also saw that the popular anger against the conspirators persisted in spite of the amnesty and continued support of many senators. As yet there had been no bloodbath or vengeful attacks on Julius Caesar's family. This did not mean that it would be safe for a young man to enter public life as the dictator's heir. An eighteen-year-old was more than a decade too young to stand for office and enter the Senate, but the name Caesar would attract attention and probably hostility which he might struggle to cope with – or indeed merely survive. His stepfather was already thinking about his own son's campaign for the consulship for 41 BC, when he would be up against Brutus and Cassius, and was not keen to rush Octavius into a career. Philippus advised him to decline the legacy and keep his own name. His mother wavered a little, but was similarly cautious. Our sources may exaggerate, for all are later and most derive from Augustus' own memoirs. The figure of the youthful hero refusing to be held back by the advice of experienced elders had a long literary tradition, stretching from Achilles to Alexander the Great. Appian even has the youth quote to Atia Achilles' words to his mother Thetis from the *Iliad*.[10]

That does not mean that caution was not advisable, and at the very least the letters will have urged Octavius to do nothing hastily. Whatever the details of their advice, the decision was his, and nothing that followed makes any sense unless his own ambition, confidence and self-esteem were the prime movers. Perhaps from the beginning he was convinced that he would win through against any rivals, no matter how much older and more experienced, even though no sensible observer could have predicted the events of the next few years and his part in them.[11]

If Octavius hesitated to accept the legacy and the name then he did so only briefly. At eighteen he ceased to be Caius Octavius and instead became Caius Julius Caesar. Convention expected that a man would retain a trace of his own name and add Octavianus to this formula. He never did this, although at times his enemies called him Octavianus to stress that his real family was obscure. As stated in the Introduction, we will ignore the modern convention to call him Octavian and instead call him Caesar, for that is the name he used and how he is referred to in our sources. The power of this name had a lot to do with the course of events.[12]

ROME

The young Caesar and his party set out from Brundisium for Rome – a journey that under normal circumstances took nine days or more. His friends already addressed him by his new name and it may have been as early as this that he sent a messenger to the province of Asia to secure some of the war chest Julius Caesar had prepared for the Parthian expedition. The group reached Rome in the early part of April, no doubt having forced the pace. Cicero was away from the City and on 10 April wrote to ask about the 'arrival of Octavius, whether there was a rush to meet him, or any suspicion of revolution', but clearly did not expect that anything too significant would have happened. In the event his visit proved brief and had little impact. Antony made the young Caesar wait for some time before granting him a brief and chilly meeting in the gardens of his house on the Palatine – formerly the home of Pompey. The consul was genuinely very busy dealing with a stream of petitioners, and there was no reason for him to consider the teenager politically useful or even relevant. The boy's expectation of taking over all of Julius Caesar's estate was deeply inconvenient for Antony when there was so much to do and all available funds were vital for building up his own position. On 12 April Cicero casually dismissed the requested report about Caesar as unimportant.[13]

Leaving Rome, the eighteen-year-old now travelled through Campania, heading for Naples. On the way he took time to speak to some of the many veterans from the dictator's legions settled in the area. On 18 April he met Lucius Cornelius Balbus, a Spaniard from Gades (modern Cadiz) who had become a Roman citizen through his services to Pompey, before joining Julius Caesar's staff. He had served him in Spain and Gaul, but increasingly took on a role as a political agent in Rome itself, easing many behind-the-scenes deals and acting as adviser. It was an important connection to renew and recognition by such an influential and rich political operator would be a considerable asset. Later in the same day, Balbus told Cicero that the youth was determined to accept his inheritance.[14]

A few days later Cicero met the young Caesar, who was staying at his stepfather's villa at Puteoli in the Bay of Naples, adjacent to the orator's own country house. He wrote to his friend Atticus: 'Octavius is with us and behaving with respect and warm friendship. His companions call him Caesar, but Philippus does not and so neither do I.'

This was a minor point in a letter concerned far more with threats to the conspirators and scorn for Antony's decisions as consul. As yet Cicero simply did not see the eighteen-year-old as very important. Unlike her husband, Atia was calling her son Caesar. Philippus had never been one to take sides openly, but was certainly not actively hostile to his stepson's ambitions and may quietly have begun to help him. The same was perhaps true of Octavia's husband Marcellus, although he remained on good terms with the conspirators for the moment. Years of civil war had added to natural wastage – as had multiple consulships by Pompey and then Julius Caesar – so that there were only seventeen former consuls alive and several of these lacked the energy or desire for active politics. There were very few senior statesmen to guide the Republic and to control the networks of patronage that held the Roman world together. Julius Caesar's death made matters worse, for he had stood at the centre of an unprecedentedly vast web of patronage and no one could readily fill this void. His supporters were each tied to him individually and were not in any way a coherent party.[15]

Mark Antony was consul, although he was only forty and thus

technically too young for the post. Julius Caesar had named Publius Cornelius Dolabella as suffect, or replacement consul, to take his own place when he left for the Parthian War. Dolabella was only thirty or so, making it an even more flagrant example of the dictator's flouting of tradition. In spite of this no one quibbled when he appeared in his regalia and accompanied by lictors after the Ides. Both men had supported Julius Caesar, but then so had several of the conspirators. Both also had a reputation for reckless and extravagant behaviour. More significantly, they were known to loathe each other – in spite of Julius Caesar's wishes Antony had tried to block Dolabella's election, even resorting to manipulating the state religion and claiming that he had observed thunder during the process, rendering any vote invalid. In the past, rivalry and open hostility between magistrates helped to prevent anyone from gaining too much power in the Republic.[16]

Mark Antony has gone down in history as a bluff, simple soldier and loyal lieutenant of Julius Caesar, making it hard to pierce the caricature and understand the real man. He certainly presented himself as a very martial figure, boasting of his descent from the swaggering demigod Hercules just as Julius Caesar claimed descent from the goddess Venus. Antony often sported the thick beard of the hero – in contrast to the straggly growths of the 'unconventional' young aristocrats, many of whom had supported Catiline – girded his tunic up high to show off his muscular thighs, and wore a sword even inside the City where such things were not seen as appropriate. Coins show a bull-neck and heavy features, confirming descriptions of a burly individual doing his best to exude aggressive masculinity. His oratory was vigorous in the florid Asiatic style disliked by Cicero.[17]

The Antonii were a well-established family of plebeian nobles. Antony's grandfather was one of the most famous orators of his day, with a distinguished career that took him to the consulship and later the censorship. Eminence came at a price in that violent era, and he was murdered on Marius' orders during the Civil War. His son was less highly thought of, being considered at best a well-meaning fool and at worst an inveterate wastrel. The family name, and perhaps

the sense that he was harmless, prompted the Senate to give Antony's father a special command against the pirates in 73 BC, although
with nothing like the resources allocated to Pompey six years later.
The result was a predictable failure, and Antonius died before he returned home. His widow subsequently married Lentulus, one of the
Catilinarians executed in 63 BC, so Antony had lost both father and
stepfather by his early twenties. There was little to inspire him with
belief in the Republic.[18]

An aristocrat to his core, Antony knew in his soul that he deserved
honours and glory and felt no need to respect conventions of behaviour. His father had left huge debts, and some family property was
so heavily mortgaged that Antony refused these parts of his inheritance. Seeing no need to restrain his own extravagance, he spent his
youth in happy pursuit of wine and women, not curbing his flamboyant instincts because of something as mundane as lack of money.
Antony's own debts were soon colossal but, as we have seen, such a
lifestyle was not uncommon in this era. Entering public life unusually late, he saw some military service in Syria, Judaea and Egypt,
before going to join Julius Caesar in Gaul. He missed most of the
main campaigns there, but did serve in the latter part of the great
rebellion culminating in the bitter siege of Alesia in the summer
of 52 BC. Following Julius Caesar in the Civil War, Antony fought
in the Italian campaign, and the second phase of the Macedonian
campaign, commanding the left wing at Pharsalus. He saw no other
fighting in the Civil War.[19]

Antony's military record was not actually especially impressive.
Personally brave, he had little experience of independent command
on any large scale, and all in all he had spent less time than was typical with the legions. Yet he presented himself as a great soldier and
commander – Hercules led armies as well as performing his more
famous feats of strength – and this image has persisted until this day.
Julius Caesar preferred to use him in more political roles, leaving
him to administer Italy in 49 BC and again after Pharsalus. The outcome was not entirely happy. Antony was well connected, and from
a better family than many of Julius Caesar's other supporters, but

he lacked subtlety. He processed around Italy in a caravan that very visibly included his mother and his mime actress mistress, as well as all sorts of other people felt to be unsuitable for a Roman magistrate's entourage. Antony liked the company of actors and actresses, who no doubt possessed all the passion and open enthusiasms of their more recent counterparts, and yet remained his clear social inferiors, whatever he might choose to pretend. A senator was not supposed to spend time with such people – many of them, including his mistress, former slaves – but once again Antony did not care about convention. On one occasion he took up his official chair in the Forum to receive petitions, but was blatantly suffering from a colossal hangover. Part-way through the business, nausea overtook him and he vomited – into his lap by one account, although another says that a friend conveniently held out his own cloak for him. There were rumours that he even experimented with a chariot pulled by lions in place of horses.[20]

Perhaps more serious than such tactless flaunting of power won through civil war was the unrest leading to violence in Rome itself and in the countryside, as a number of ambitious men – including Dolabella – championed the cause of debtors. When Julius Caesar eventually returned to Rome he made no public use of Antony for some time – and kept a close eye on Dolabella, taking him with him on campaign. The dictator summoned Mark Antony to Spain at the end of the Munda campaign, and there were signs of a return to favour. Antony rode with him in his carriage, while the young Octavius and Decimus Brutus followed behind in a second one. By 44 BC, the choice of Antony as consular colleague and Dolabella as his replacement were clear signs of renewed favour and confidence.[21]

As consuls, the two had immediate power for the remainder of the year. They had supported Julius Caesar and done well as a result, but both of them were aristocrats from well-established families with ambitions of their own. It is wrong to see them as simply Julius Caesar's men, rather than as individuals seeking personal distinction who found it convenient to back him. It was said that Trebonius had sounded out Antony in the early days of the conspiracy.

The 'Liberators' killed the dictator to restore a Republic in which aristocratic competition for office and influence would once again flourish. The consuls were naturally part of this, and their behaviour revealed irrevocable changes in the way these contests were waged.[22]

The truce with the conspirators was always uneasy. Neither Antony nor Dolabella had anything to gain by siding strongly with them or improving the positions of Brutus, Cassius and the others. Regardless of what they thought about the dictator and the assassination, the leading conspirators were all now rivals for office and prestige. All sides looked to the future, for although an amnesty and acknowledgement of Julius Caesar's acts were necessary for the moment, this situation was unlikely to last. In time the conspirators and the dictator's acts were quite likely to come under attack in the Senate, Assemblies or courts. The Civil War began in 49 BC over threats of prosecution for actions a decade earlier. The Roman system meant that no decision was set in stone, and things could be made illegal retrospectively, making permanent security almost impossible. Legal attacks could easily end a career and violence was a real threat.

Chaos and immediate breakdown into conflict suited no one. Neither the consuls nor the conspirators had troops at their immediate command. Lepidus, the dictator's deputy or Master of Horse (*magister equitum*), had a legion on the edge of the City and brought some of his soldiers into the Forum in the days following the Ides, but he had neither the strength nor will to extend this to more permanent dominance – especially since his *imperium* had technically expired with the dictator's death. Antony arranged for Lepidus to replace Julius Caesar as *pontifex maximus*, before the former Master of Horse proceeded to Transalpine Gaul and command of a large army, giving him protection from any enemies for the moment.[23]

Almost as soon as Julius Caesar's funeral was over, an altar was erected on the site of his pyre by a group of enthusiasts. Their leader was called Amatius and claimed to be Marius' grandson and hence the dictator's relative by blood if not in law. Julius Caesar had not recognised him, and the man had no more success approaching members of his extended family, including the young Octavius. Neither Antony nor Dolabella were any more sympathetic, ordering the dispersal of Amatius' followers and the removal of the altar. Later in April, when Antony left Rome to rally support among Julius Caesar's veterans, there was a more direct confrontation. Dolabella had Amatius and many of his followers executed, earning Cicero's enthusiastic praise. Yet it was a sign that substantial parts of the population mourned the dictator and resented the lack of action taken against his murderers. Antony was willing to exploit this to unnerve the conspirators and to recruit veterans, especially former centurions, but did not wish the frustration to explode in ways outside his control. For the moment he had a strong position, helped by the fact that his two brothers were praetor and tribune in 44 BC, but this would not last. Antony, like everyone else, was preparing for the future and needed to protect himself and remain powerful in the longer run.[24]

Julius Caesar's decisions were confirmed on 17 March. Some had not yet been formally announced, but were widely known and still to be recognised. Antony as consul was supposed to consult with a council of senior senators before each such decision was confirmed. This did not prove practical, and probably he did not see it as desirable. So many decisions were pending, and many more petitioners from all over the empire queued for attention. Julius Caesar had not yet cleared the backlog of decision-making from years of senatorial inertia and the more recent upheaval of civil war. On a practical basis there was no doubt much that Antony felt was urgent. It was also a situation giving him a splendid opportunity to dole out favours and win the gratitude of the recipients, hopefully adding them to his supporters. In the aftermath of the murder Antony had taken possession of the dictator's papers. Now he announced a number of previously unknown decisions of Julius Caesar and insisted on their ratification. Some appeared to contradict things the dictator had actually done in his lifetime. Cicero claimed that Antony's wife Fulvia – the widow of Clodius – took bribes from King Deiotarus of Galatia so that her husband would confirm his rule. Later the orator would fulminate against the inventions of Antony in these months,

making it difficult to know precisely what he did. Yet even though
Cicero exaggerated, he cannot have entirely made up such stories.[25]

Antony was raising the funds and favours needed for future success – and indeed for personal safety. In the longer term this depended
most of all on the possession of a large and loyal army. Trebonius
and Decimus Brutus were allocated the provinces of Syria and Cisalpine Gaul respectively. Brutus and Cassius were eventually given
administration of the grain supply in Sicily and Asia – important for
the state, but seen as demeaning for their rank and more significantly
without military resources. Antony and Dolabella co-operated to
give the latter Syria, replacing Trebonius at the end of the year and
taking on responsibility for the planned Parthian War. Antony took
Macedonia with its six legions, although he agreed to give one to
his colleague. Then he decided that his brother Caius would govern
Macedonia in his place, and that he would instead replace Decimus
Brutus in Cisalpine Gaul, so conveniently placed to keep an eye on
Italy, and combine this with 'Long-Haired Gaul' – the region recently
conquered by Julius Caesar. The five legions and auxiliaries remaining in Macedonia would transfer with him, leaving his brother to
raise fresh troops. Although the dictator had restricted the term of
provincial governors to two years, Antony had the Popular Assembly
vote him this enlarged province for five years, just as Pompey and
Julius Caesar had received their extraordinary commands.[26]

In many ways the situation was similar to the build-up to 49 BC,
with trust in very short supply and the main leaders giving themselves the capacity to fight just in case this proved necessary. Brutus
and Cassius were unable to regain the initiative as they watched from
a distance. The former was urban praetor and so had responsibility
for holding the *ludi Apollinares* – the annual festival and games dedicated to the sun god Apollo. Brutus funded the events, and decided
the programme and some of the performers, but felt that it was
too dangerous for him to return to Rome so was not present. Mark
Antony's brother Caius presided at the games in his place, making it
less clear to whom the crowd should feel grateful. The games went
well, and some people were willing to cheer the name of Brutus,

although others may have demonstrated against the conspirators. Shortly afterwards Brutus and Cassius would leave Italy and go to the eastern Mediterranean and in time they too would raise armies. Brutus may have done so only reluctantly, but still encouraged mutiny in the legions of the Roman people and illegally assumed command. Cicero had come to see Antony as the greatest threat to them and to the restoration of something close to a true *res publica*. He continually lamented the conspirators' failure to kill him as well as the dictator. With hindsight, he felt that 'for although the courage was that of men, believe me, the strategy was that of infants'.[27]

Cicero was yet to call the young Caesar by his new name, and some of what the eighteen-year-old was beginning to do and say worried him, but it was Antony who filled his thoughts. He knew Dolabella to be a rogue, for the man had briefly been married to Cicero's beloved daughter Tullia and had failed to return the dowry after their divorce, but once he set out for his province he ceased to be the main problem. Antony was the threat as the man who more than anyone else prevented the revival of the *res publica*. Cicero longed for some means to break his power and allow the conspirators to return and thrive.[28]

6

PRAISE

'At the age of nineteen on my own responsibility and at my own
expense I raised an army, with which I successfully championed the
liberty of the republic when it was oppressed by the tyranny of a faction.' *Deeds of the Divine Augustus, published soon after his death in AD 14.*[1]

The young Caesar was back in Rome in May. In later years it was
said that a halo surrounded the sun on the day he arrived, in
another omen of future greatness. Antony's brother Lucius was currently tribune and permitted the youth to speak at a public meeting.
Cicero was unimpressed with reports of what he said, but continued
to see him as of minor importance. The eighteen-year-old wanted
formal recognition of his adoption and to gain his full inheritance.
Probably he did not as yet attack the conspirators directly, and instead concentrated on asserting his 'father's' reputation and honours.
On at least one occasion – perhaps the games devoted to Ceres, the
goddess of the harvest – he attempted to have the dictator's chair
of office and laurel wreath placed on display in accordance with a
senatorial decree from Julius Caesar's lifetime. The wreath was the
very one offered to him and rejected at the Lupercalia, but Antony
refused to permit this display.

He was similarly unhelpful when it came to Caesar's other requests, particularly regarding the dictator's estate, and little or none
of the hard coin was handed over. The consul gave every impression
of seeing the new Caesar as a nuisance. Others simply saw him as
vulnerable. There was probably also genuine confusion over precisely what had been Julius Caesar's personal property and what
were state-owned assets that he had controlled. A number of court
cases were brought, challenging ownership of individual properties,

sometimes on the basis of illegal seizure during the Civil War, and on the whole the cases went against his heir.[2]

The youth borrowed money. Much was supplied by Matius and another banker named Rabirius Postumus, often associated with Julius Caesar. Oppius and Balbus may also have contributed, and some of his own and the dictator's property was sold or mortgaged to raise hard cash. Philippus and Atia also assisted, while the dictator's nephews who had received the remaining quarter of his estate more or less willingly handed this over to the principal heir. It is unclear how soon the money gathered as Julius Caesar's war chest for the Parthian expedition arrived. With it came a year's taxation from the province of Asia, but the young Caesar claimed to have handed over this and all other state funds to the treasury, and only kept the dictator's private property.[3]

For the next months much of the youth's time was devoted to preparing for the games vowed to commemorate both Julius Caesar's victory at Pharsalus in the Civil War and his divine ancestor Venus Genetrix. This was another honour voted by the Senate during the dictator's rule. In this case no one tried to block it or prevent his heir from celebrating them. Caesar decided to combine them with funeral games, allowing him to stage gladiatorial fights as well as beast hunts, feasting and theatrical performances. Much of this would occur in the Forum itself, with temporary stands built onto some of the main public buildings. The celebrations were staged in lavish scale from 20 to 28 July and more borrowed money was used to begin paying the dictator's bequest to every Roman citizen.[4]

During the games a comet appeared in the skies. Such 'long-haired' stars were seen as dreadful omens of impending disaster. Caesar or one of his supporters came up with a better interpretation, claiming that the bright light was Julius Caesar ascending to heaven to join the gods, and a star was attached to the head of a statue of the dictator placed in the Temple of Venus at the heart of his Forum complex. The story caught on, especially with those still devoted to his memory. In many ways it built on the semi-divine honours awarded by the Senate during his lifetime, and the altar to him set up and later knocked down on the consuls' orders. This time there was no official attempt to suppress the honour.[5]

Staging public entertainments and celebrating ancestors were well-established and effective ways of winning popularity, although in this case the scale of the games and the claims of divinity far outstripped the honours given to any individual in the past. Becoming tribune of the plebs was another well-trodden path to popularity, and when an election was held early in July to fill the vacancy left by the murdered Cinna, there was serious talk of the young Caesar standing as candidate. Given that Julius Caesar had made him a patrician even before naming him his heir, this was illegal. The precise details of the incident are now impossible to reconstruct – some historians would prefer to see him as attempting and failing to get a friend elected to the post rather than seeking it himself – but the episode suggests a serious misjudgement in contrast to the skilful handling of the appearance of the comet. While it may be repetitive to refer to the eighteen-year-old, we do need to keep reminding ourselves of just how young and inexperienced Caesar was. The immense self-confidence that led him to enter public life in this way readily spilled over into recklessness. Privately he was convinced the comet was actually a sign of his own impending rise. The very public sale of assets and borrowing of funds also helped to win as much gratitude to the young Caesar for staging the games as they brought honour to the dead dictator.[6]

Relations with Antony continued to be bad, and the consul was growing more powerful – by the late summer he had recruited a strong bodyguard from the settled veterans. Many were former centurions, who in battle were expected to lead from the front and so were usually formidable fighters. Experienced leaders would also prove extremely useful if Antony decided to raise new legions, for they would be capable of organising, training and commanding new recruits. Even more important was their political significance. Some centurions were equestrians, but the vast majority belonged to the centuries of the highest class in the *Comitia centuriata*, making their votes as significant as their muscle. Probably in the hope of winning favour with this group, as well as manipulating the courts, Antony introduced a law making some or all of this class eligible to serve on juries, forming a third panel alongside the ones drawn from senators and equestrians.[7]

In contrast to the consul, Caesar held no office or powers, and as yet his open supporters were able to fund him but had no direct political power. Matius claimed to Cicero that he was only helping the boy out of his friendship with Julius Caesar. Money and a name were his only real assets and from early on he had used both to win favour with the dictator's former officers and soldiers. Quickly he began to offer a bounty of 500 denarii – more than two years' pay for an ordinary soldier – to those willing to serve him, and promises of much more in the future. No doubt the rewards offered to centurions or tribunes were substantially higher. He may also have spoken of revenge against the conspirators, although as yet he did not repeat this in public meetings. Men started to take his money and pledge support, but for the moment their numbers were far fewer than Antony's entourage. Loyalty to Julius Caesar's memory remained fervent in all of these veterans, whomever they followed, and for a while some of the former tribunes and centurions persuaded the consul to behave in a friendlier manner towards the dictator's heir. The young Caesar stood outside the partitions of the *saepta* encouraging the centuries to approve the law giving Antony control of Cisalpine Gaul in place of Decimus Brutus. Yet later the relationship turned sour once again, as Antony claimed that one of the veterans in his bodyguard had been bribed by Caesar to murder him. Quite a few Roman politicians – most notably Pompey – had a neurotic fear of assassination, and there may well have been no substance behind the accusation. Pragmatically, it is hard to see what the young Caesar would have gained from disposing of the consul. If he did plot the murder, then that would be another sign of his still-naive thinking at this stage.[8]

On 1 August Julius Caesar's father-in-law, Calpurnius Piso, dared to criticise Antony in the Senate. The tone he took was admonishing rather than vitriolic, and more importantly was widely spoken of beforehand. Cicero was on his way to Greece under the pretext of wanting to help in his son's education, but in reality from despair and fear about the political situation degenerating into violence. All of the conspirators and other key players like Lepidus had left Italy. Dolabella was soon to follow and no one remained with the *imperium* to contest Antony's dominance in Italy itself. Many sensed a gradual slide into civil war and, just as in the years leading to 49 BC, there was no great enthusiasm for this. Piso argued for a confirmation of the amnesty, so that the conspirators would be able to return, and neither they nor former Caesareans like Antony need suffer diminution of their prestige. There was no violent response from the consul, and Cicero was sufficiently inspired by this prospect of renewed compromise that he returned to Rome. A month later, on 2 September, he delivered a speech that came to be known as the *First Philippic*, after the series of orations delivered in the fourth century BC by the renowned orator Demosthenes to warn the Athenians of the threat of King Philip of Macedon. Although critical of Antony's recent actions, it urged him to return to the spirit of reconciliation he had shown in the days following the Ides of March.[9]

As consul Antony had the power to act, whereas even the most senior senators could merely exhort and advise. He also had the force of recalled veterans to back him, who may by this time have numbered as many as 6,000. The first of the Macedonian legions was disembarking at the port of Brundisium and the others were following close behind, so he would soon have a properly formed army at his disposal. He responded angrily to criticism, but made no attempt to use the force available, although Cicero privately wrote that he was sure the consul plotted a massacre. Once again the orator stayed away from Rome and public meetings for a while and began to write his *Second Philippic* – a vitriolic pamphlet never delivered as a speech – which tore Antony's character to shreds as well as damning his recent acts. For a while there was a lull, but preparations for war continued. At the start of October Antony headed south to Brundisium to review his newly arrived army.[10]

By September, when he would celebrate his nineteenth birthday,

Caesar was in Campania on a fresh recruiting drive in the veteran settlements of the dictator. In the weeks that followed he was able to raise the number of his followers to 3,000 men, but equipment was in short supply. There was considerable loyalty to their old corps, and by the end of the year these men would be divided into new versions of Julius Caesar's *Seventh* and *Eighth* legions. Much like Catiline's army, the structure of these units may well have been laid down even at this early stage, in the hope that more recruits would in time be found to fill the gaps. It also gave the opportunity to name as many as 120 centurions and a dozen tribunes, confirming former ranks or making promotions to higher grades and thus greater status and pay. These men rallied as much to the bounty as to the name Caesar at this stage, for the teenager remained an unknown quantity. Julius Caesar had led them to victory and rewarded them lavishly, gradually bonding them to him over the years. The full force of this link could not be instantly or simply assumed by his heir, but they were willing to give the boy and his money a chance. Realising the power of hard coin and promise of future reward, the young Caesar sent agents down to Brundisium to work on Antony's legions.[11]

In the meantime, at the head of his band of veterans – the existence of which was clearly illegal – the nineteen-year-old returned to Rome early in November, leading his armed followers into the City to compound the illegality. He had planned this move for some weeks, bombarding Cicero – and no doubt other prominent senators – with requests for their approval and ideally open support when he arrived in the City. Caesar flattered the old statesman, urging him to 'save the *res publica* a second time', just as he had in 63 BC. Cicero admitted that he was 'ashamed to say no, and yet afraid to say yes. However he has been and continues to act with vigour. He will come to Rome with a strong band of followers, but he is just a boy. He thinks he can summon a meeting of the Senate at once. Who will come? If anyone turns up, who will upset Antony in these uncertain times?' However, he conceded that 'the country towns are enthusiastic towards him'.[12]

Caesar assured Cicero that he wished to work legitimately via the

Senate, ignoring for the moment his unauthorised armed followers. However, always uncomfortable with the boy's name and his claim to prominence, Cicero was beginning to worry about the young Caesar's intentions, and especially his insistence on confirming all of the dictator's legislation and honours. Even so, he still felt that the youth could be dismissed as having 'plenty of confidence, but too little *auctoritas*'. The orator's correspondent, the wily equestrian Atticus, who avoided a career in public life but maintained very good relations with almost everyone of consequence at Rome, was a little more cautious, noting that 'while the boy is currently strong and holds Antony in check, still we must withhold judgement for the long run'. Caesar's name and money robbed Antony of a substantial number of likely supporters, especially among the veterans.[13]

Antony was still away from Rome when the young Caesar arrived. An aggressive tribune who had already begun to attack the consul openly now brought the young leader into the Forum and summoned a public meeting. He and Caesar stood on the steps of the Temple of Castor and Pollux, which looked out onto an open area often used for meetings and legislative assemblies. Veterans openly wearing their swords stood guard around their leader in a blatant display of illegal force. The tribune spoke first, once again lashing Antony and calling on the people to rally to Julius Caesar's heir against the consul. The youth himself then delivered a speech that was promptly circulated. Cicero soon had a copy and was depressed by its contents. Praising Julius Caesar and his achievements, his heir turned to gesture at a statue of the dictator and pledged that he hoped 'to win the honours of his father'. The attack on Antony for obstructing him in securing his inheritance and the consul's general hostility may have been more to the orator's taste, but struck the wrong note with many of the veterans. Loyal to Julius Caesar, they were angry that his murderers went unpunished. Those were the true villains, not Mark Antony.[14]

The consul was on his way back to Rome, escorted by his own guard of veterans. The first pair of legions brought across from Macedonia were marching north from Brundisium and could readily

be summoned if necessary. Antony was not the main enemy as far
as the veterans were concerned, and his forces were also far stronger
than Caesar's little band of partially equipped men. If it came to
fighting, then they were bound to lose. Individual veterans began to
abandon their young leader for the moment and slip away to their
homes. There had been no surge of wider public support, and in
particular no enthusiasm from important senators. Not one senator attended the meeting apart from the tribune himself. Cicero was
not even in the City, and many others kept a similarly low profile
in their country villas. Disappointed, Julius Caesar's heir sloped off,
taking his remaining followers to Etruria for a new recruiting drive
in another area heavily settled by the dictator's veterans. There were
others recruiting in the same region, as former officers of the dictator began raising soldiers for Antony.

At this stage the young Caesar remained a minor player in the political contest. He had armed followers, unlike anyone in Italy apart
from Antony, but these were too few in number to make him a real
power. That he was noticed at all at such a young age was remarkable. That he made several false steps politically should only surprise
us if we take for granted either the political genius of Augustus or
the assumed strength – even existence – of a coherent Caesarean faction. As yet he was only a little more significant than the fake Marius
executed earlier in the year – only his wealth and unambiguous link
with the dictator made him different – and might be almost as easily
eliminated. Antony planned to summon the Senate and have the boy
declared a public enemy.[15]

Then something happened that changed everything, and suddenly
made the young Caesar of immediate importance.

WARLORD

The first legion to arrive in Brundisium was the *Legio Martia*, named
after the war god Mars, soon followed by the *Fourth*. As they camped
outside the port city the young Caesar's agents appeared, mingling

with the many camp-followers and traders who inevitably tailed any Roman army, eager to relieve the legionaries of their pay. Promises were whispered and pamphlets handed round the tent-lines, offering the now-familiar 500-denarii bounty and this time a further 5,000 more on eventual discharge – almost twenty years' pay for a single campaign. As usual the rewards for centurions and tribunes will have been considerably higher.[16]

These legions, along with the *Second* and *Thirty-fifth*, one of which was already disembarking and the other soon to cross from Macedonia, had all been formed by Julius Caesar in the aftermath of his victory in 48 BC. At least some of the ordinary soldiers may well have originally served against him in Pompey's legions, although it is doubtful if they felt any particular emotional involvement with his cause. The officers were different. It was Julius Caesar's practice throughout his campaigns to promote junior centurions from experienced legions to higher grades in newly raised units. All of the tribunes and centurions in each of these legions were Julius Caesar's men, appointed by him and committed to him. Many of them were likely to have been highly experienced. As formations none of the legions had yet seen active service, but they were at close to full strength and well prepared by years of training.[17]

Mark Antony had no prior connection with these legions before he arrived to take command. He was a stranger to officers and men alike. Nor, contrary to the myth, could he boast of a great military record of past victories or indeed long experience of controlling soldiers in difficult situations. Until a few months before eagerly anticipating Parthian plunder, these legions now found themselves commanded by a man they did not know and on the brink of civil war. At the same time the young Caesar's name was being spoken and he was very generous in his promises. Some of the officers may already have known him from the months in Apollonia and perhaps this encouraged them to think seriously about his offer.

The consul arrived accompanied by his wife, Fulvia, and from the beginning Antony handled the situation badly, clearly expecting the soldiers to obey without question. The legionaries were unruly and jeered when he offered to pay them 100 denarii – five times less than the rival bid and equivalent to less than half a year's pay. The consul lost his temper and tried to bully the soldiers into obedience, angrily bawling out, 'You will learn to obey orders!' He demanded the officers supply him with a list of names of troublemakers. Men were arrested and executed. Some of the victims were centurions. Whether there is any truth in Cicero's claims of officers and men being brought to the house Antony occupied and slaughtered there, the blood spattering onto Fulvia, is deeply questionable, and does not really matter. When the *Legio Martia* and the *Fourth* marched out of Brundisium and began to head north up along the coast towards Cisalpine Gaul their mood was sullen.[18]

Legio Martia was in the lead and was the first to declare openly for Caesar. The *Fourth*, led in person by Antony's quaestor, followed their example soon afterwards. Both legions refused to back down, although the rapid distribution of 500 denarii per man allowed the consul to keep control of the *Second* and *Thirty-fifth*, apart from a few individuals who deserted to join Caesar. Antony had at last realised that he could not simply bully legionaries into obedience or expect devotion from strangers, but only after losing a large section of his army.[19]

On 28 November he summoned a night-time meeting of the Senate (which in itself was illegal, since they were not supposed to debate after dark) and attacked the young Caesar. On the following day he paraded his veterans outside the City and demanded that the senators attend. All who did were cajoled into joining the soldiers as they took an oath of loyalty to him. Then Antony left for Cisalpine Gaul, on the way uniting with his two legions, along with another raised from the veterans of Julius Caesar's *Legio V Alaudae* – the 'Larks', originally raised in Transalpine Gaul and later made citizens. This formation was probably drawn from among the 6,000 veterans he had raised earlier in the year, and Cicero referred to Antony's bodyguard as the *Alaudae* as early as November. He also had substantial auxiliary forces, including Moorish cavalry. Roman legions – like units of armies in all periods – rarely managed to remain at their full theoretical strength for very long, and so altogether Antony's troops mustered probably something like 15,000 men, all of them well trained and properly equipped. It was a small but formidable army.[20]

Caesar remained a private citizen, as yet too young to seek office or membership of the Senate, but now he too had a formally constituted army. Hurrying to meet the two legions where they had halted at Alba Fucens, he immediately distributed the promised 500 denarii. The *Fourth* and the *Martia* paraded and performed exercises culminating in a mock battle. Such drills were a standard part of Roman military training, and since these legions had spent the last years preparing for the Parthian War they no doubt put on a very good display. A century later the Jewish historian Josephus would with some exaggeration talk of the Roman army's 'drills as bloodless battles, and battles are bloody drills'. At full strength a legion consisted of ten cohorts, each of 480 men. All were heavy infantrymen, fighting in serried ranks, protected by a helmet (usually of bronze), mail armour and a long, semi-cylindrical body shield – in the past normally oval, although by this period the more familiar tile shape may have been becoming common. They carried the *pilum*, a heavy javelin with an effective range of ten to fifteen yards, thrown just before contact, but each legionary was primarily a swordsman. During Augustus' lifetime the classic short cut-and-thrust pattern less than two feet in length became standard, but at this stage blades tended to be up to a foot longer. It was a heavy blade of high-quality manufacture, suited to cutting, but especially devastating when used to thrust, its triangular point well able to punch through the rings of an opponent's mail cuirass.[21]

The legions from Macedonia were probably fairly close to their theoretical strength. They were also fully equipped, and had all the supporting paraphernalia of tents, slaves, baggage animals, pack saddles and transport wagons necessary to operate in the field. Well led by experienced officers and at the end of a long period of training, they were used to working together as a team and had a strong sense of their own identity. *Legio Martia* presumably had a number, but this had not survived, which in itself is an indication of their pride in their name. To support them, Caesar also had his reconstituted *Seventh* and *Eighth* legions. Most of these were veterans, although we should not ignore the possibility that they also included young men, possibly the sons of veterans, recruited from the main areas where former soldiers had been settled. Individually the men who had served under Julius Caesar's command had far more experience of fighting and winning battles than the Macedonian legions. Yet for the moment all types of equipment remained in short supply and the reconstituted legions were still in the process of re-forming. It would take some time to make them collectively and individually fit to go on campaign. The legions from Macedonia were ready, and it was these that gave the nineteen-year-old Caesar immediate importance. They were under his command, even though he had no legal right to issue any orders or pay them at all.

Caesar's army matched Mark Antony's forces in both numbers and quality. The two consuls for 43 BC were in the process of raising an army of four new legions. Recruits – it is hard to know whether they were volunteers or conscripts – were plentiful, but few if any had prior military experience. With so many of Julius Caesar's former officers already lured away, the tribunes and centurions appointed to oversee the formation and training of these units are unlikely to have been the most experienced or capable. Recalled veterans might shape up into newly effective legions in a matter of months or even weeks. It would take far longer for wholly new units to have any chance of matching them. The legions from Macedonia had a lead of some four years when it came to training and experience. No one had any doubt that the four consular legions would be utterly outclassed if they came up against Antony's men. If the latter was to be opposed on the battlefield, then other troops were needed and the only ones in Italy had declared for Caesar.

The consuls themselves, Aulus Hirtius and Caius Vibius Pansa, had both been chosen by the dictator and had served him loyally for some time. Neither came from a distinguished family, and both were probably older than was normal for consuls. In public, Cicero praised them effusively. Privately he found them lacking in energy and commitment, while his brother Quintus who had served beside them during Julius Caesar's Gallic campaigns dismissed them as worthless and corrupt. With Antony gone, the orator was once again in Rome, pressing the Senate to act against him. On 20 December he delivered his *Third Philippic* at a meeting of the Senate summoned by the tribunes – both consuls and many of the other magistrates having left for their provinces. Back in November the young Caesar's – or rather, as Cicero insisted, 'Octavius's' – speech had dismayed him. As so often in his letters he quoted a Greek tag – 'I'd rather not be saved, than saved by one like this!' Now Antony seemed not simply the far greater, but the only evil. Decimus Brutus had written stating his refusal to let the consul take over Cisalpine Gaul from him. In the circumstances a lesser evil was acceptable, and he finally brought himself to speak of Caesar and not Octavius or Octavianus. The Republic should accept the aid of a nineteen-year-old with an illegal army.[22]

Cicero's rhetoric as usual soared to the occasion:

> Caius Caesar, a young man, or rather almost a boy, but one of incredible, and, as it were, divine intelligence and courage, at the very time when Antony's frenzy was at its greatest heat, and when his cruel and deadly return from Brundisium was dreaded, while we were not asking for or thinking of assistance, nor even hoping for it, for it seemed impossible, collected a very stout army of the invincible class of veterans, and lavished his patrimony . . . in the salvation of the *Res Publica* . . . Had he not been born into the *Res Publica*, we should, by the crime of Antony, now possess no *Res Publica* . . .[23]

The young man's soldiers also received their share of praise:

> we cannot be silent regarding the *Legio Martia*. For what single person has ever been braver, who more friendly to the *Res Publica* than the whole of the *Legio Martia*. Having decided, as it did, that Mark Antony was an enemy of the Roman people, it refused to be

an ally of his madness; it abandoned a consul . . . whom it saw to be
aiming at . . . the slaughter of citizens and the destruction of the *Res
Publica* . . .[24]

The mutiny – for the refusal to obey the orders of a consul of
Rome could legally be nothing else – of two legions and their defection to swell the ranks of an illegal private army, and obey the orders
of a man lacking any proper authority to give them, was condoned.
Antony was not a consul at all, but a public enemy – a new Catiline
or worse yet a Spartacus – and thus everything could be justified.
This was Cicero's case, even though as yet it was hard to see what
Antony had actually done to deserve condemnation. Caesar had
broken far more laws.[25]

Opinion began to shift in Cicero's favour, but far less quickly than
he wanted. Caesar and his army were a reality that could not be
opposed. The four new legions raised by the consuls were just as
unprepared to face these as they were Antony's forces. Caesar could
not be suppressed, and so for the moment must be accepted, even
condoned – Sulla's use of the private army of the twenty-three-year-
old Pompey offered a precedent.

Antony was a different matter. He was consul – his claim to office
at least as legitimate as that of Hirtius and Pansa, or indeed Decimus Brutus – and a Popular Assembly had passed a law giving him
control of Cisalpine Gaul, the voters encouraged by the presence of
Caesar. The legality of that vote was questionable, with claims of
intimidation, and, ironically enough, for once there really had been a
thunderstorm during the meeting rather than merely a conveniently
imagined bad omen. Whether or not they liked or approved of the
consul, there was as yet little appetite to fight a civil war over the
issue. Antony had allies in the Senate, and his mother and wife did
their best to drum up support. The conspirators themselves had all
gone abroad, leaving behind only sympathisers, and there were few
strongly committed to helping Decimus Brutus. For the moment the
Senate refused to declare Antony a public enemy, and instead sent
an embassy of three senior senators as ambassadors to him. One of

them was Philippus, and there is no indication that he did not genu-inely hope for compromise.²⁶

Even so the talks came to nothing. Antony continued to attack Caesar, insulting his real family as a reminder that he was not truly the son of Julius Caesar. The 'so-called' Caesar was a provincial nobody descended from foreign slaves, a mere child who had pros-tituted himself to the ageing dictator in order to win favour. The remarks dripped with aristocratic hauteur, but were otherwise fairly conventional pieces of Roman political invective, taken with a pinch of salt even at the time.²⁷

However, some of the comments stuck, and remained well known long after the context had been forgotten. The young upstart was merely 'a boy who owes everything to a name' – to which we might add 'and his possession of an army'. Cicero wanted to use both, for in his mind Antony now seemed worse than Julius Caesar had ever been. Some of this was sheer personal dislike, and more a lack of respect. Not only had tyranny continued after the tyrant was killed, but the new tyrant had done far less than Julius Caesar to win his prominence. Far more important were the frustrations and disappointments of Cicero's long career, and a sense that for one last time he could serve – perhaps even save – the Rome and the *res publica* that he loved so much. From the beginning the young Caesar showed him deference and respect. It need not have been insincere. Cicero was a distinguished elder statesman, well worth courting by an ambitious newcomer. Nor in return need his affection for the youth have been wholly feigned. Political friendships, much like the marriages that often confirmed them, were for immediate advantage and everyone knew that they might prove temporary. For the moment each of them was useful to the other and neither could know what the future held in store. Cicero was willing to use the boy and his army, just as in 49 BC Cato and his allies were willing to use Pompey against Julius Caesar. Mutual benefit did not require abso-lute trust – and in the end Caesar was only nineteen and politically inexperienced. Surely he could not be truly dangerous in the long run?²⁸

Italy

When Hirtius and Pansa assumed the consulship on 1 January, Cicero renewed his onslaught against Antony. The *senatus consultum ultimum* was passed, but specific mention of Antony avoided. His uncle, Lucius Julius Caesar, managed to block a vote declaring him a public enemy, and other wording was watered down. A state of emergency or *tumultus* was announced, but this was not yet formally a war. That did not hinder preparations. Decimus Brutus was confirmed as governor of Cisalpine Gaul. Far more dramatically, Caesar was given propraetorian *imperium* so that at last he could legitimately command the army he had possessed for some time. He was also admitted to the Senate and graded as a quaestor, allowing him to seek the other magistracies ten years earlier than was normal – it would still be more than a decade before he would be eligible for the consulship. Like their leader, his soldiers were commended, and the state agreed to pay the discharge bonus promised to them when the young man had bid for their services.[29]

In a matter of months the teenage Caesar had raised an army, briefly occupied the Forum, but failed to win significant support and been forced to retreat, then bought the loyalty of two legions and so become a power to be reckoned with, forcing the Senate to choose between fighting or recognising him. They chose the latter, and soon he would wage war against Antony, in the process aiding Decimus Brutus, one of his 'father's' murderers – and the man with whom he had shared a carriage in Spain in 45 BC.

REWARD AND DISCARD

'Caesar, he says, makes no complaints about you to be sure, except for a remark which he attributed to you: "we must praise the young man, reward him, and discard him". He added that he has no intention of letting himself be discarded.' – *Decimus Brutus to Cicero, 24 May 43 BC.*[1]

The winter months passed in abortive negotiations. It was difficult to feed armies at this time of year and the consuls were still busy training the new legions and gathering supplies. Decimus Brutus took shelter in the city of Mutina, his legionaries living off the salted meat of his slaughtered baggage animals. Antony enclosed them in a blockade, but did not press too closely and made no attempt at an assault. Time was on his side, for if he waited long enough the defenders would begin to starve and be forced to surrender. It also did no harm to make his opponents take the first steps in more aggressive warfare. The sides were not yet clearly drawn, and it was uncertain how the governors with armies at their disposal would act. Cicero urged Caius Asinius Pollio in Spain, as well as Lepidus and Lucius Munatius Plancus in the Gallic provinces, to support Decimus Brutus with their legions. Assuring him of friendship and loyalty to the *res publica*, none of them took any concrete action.[2]

Elsewhere the other Brutus was now in command of the province of Macedonia and its garrison. Caius Antonius, sent by his brother to control this region, failed to win over the legions and soon saw his own troops defect before himself becoming a prisoner. Trebonius was dead, arrested and then killed – some claimed tortured first – by Dolabella. He was the first of the assassins to perish. Soon afterwards the legions turned against Dolabella. In the months to come he would rapidly be overwhelmed and eventually took his own life. Cassius assumed control of all the legions in Syria. The conspirators had acquired armies and began to extort money and other resources from the provinces. Cicero set to work persuading the Senate to legitimise what they had already done. Yet none of these armies were in any position to aid Decimus Brutus. Caesar and his soldiers remained critical to the outcome in Italy itself.[3]

The newly appointed propraetor willingly placed himself under the command of the two consuls and his relations with them were cordial. Both had good Caesarean credentials. It was probably late in 44 BC that Hirtius added an eighth book to Julius Caesar's *Commentaries on the Gallic War* and he may also be the author of the *Alexandrian War* and the *African War* which continued the dictator's own *Commentaries on the Civil War*. These celebrations of past victories no doubt went down very well with former officers from Julius Caesar's army.[4]

By March, the forces controlled by the Senate began to move. The propraetor's legions were the only truly battle-ready section of the army, and Caesar put the *Fourth* and the *Martia* under Hirtius' command, allowing the consul to set out for Cisalpine Gaul. The young general followed soon afterwards with the *Seventh* – it is possible that the *Eighth* did not join him until later. They were supported by some cavalry and light infantry – and probably the corps of war elephants brought with the legions when they defected from Antony. Hirtius and Caesar also each formed a praetorian cohort of hand-picked veterans to serve both as guard to the headquarters and a formidable force in battle. For the moment Pansa remained near Rome, hurrying on the training and preparations of the four new legions and presiding over meetings of the Senate. He attended a meeting on 19 March, but by the next day had left the City and was on his way north with the four legions of recruits.[5]

Hirtius and Caesar built two fortified camps near Antony's lines, but did not feel strong enough to attempt to break through to

Mutina until the rest of the army arrived. They lit beacons as sig-
nals to Decimus Brutus, but could not tell whether or not he knew
they were there until a messenger managed to sneak through the
enemy outposts, swim a river and get into the city. Communica-
tion between the besieged garrison and the relief column had to
rely on a precarious mixture of such brave men and messages taken
by carrier pigeons. For weeks the two sides skirmished. Some of
the auxiliary cavalry who had joined Caesar when the Macedonian
legions declared for him now decided to defect back to Antony.
Antony may also have received other reinforcements as his forces
seem to have grown to more than three legions. Inside Mutina,
Decimus Brutus' men were coming to the end of their food, but
until they too were reinforced Hirtius and Caesar were unable to
help him.[6]

By the second week in April Pansa and his men were getting close,
following the Via Aemilia towards Mutina. Antony could not afford
to let the enemy armies combine and so resolved to strike quickly
while they were still divided and vulnerable. Small forces were sent
to demonstrate against Hirtius' and Caesar's camps in the hope of
keeping their garrisons busy. Antony himself took two of the Macedonian legions, the *Second* and *Thirty-fifth*, along with much of his
cavalry and light infantry and hurried south to ambush Pansa's raw
soldiers. Hirtius sensed or received some reports of this move, and
during the night of 13–14 April sent the *Martia* and his and Caesar's
praetorian cohorts to join up with Pansa and escort his column. This
was a gamble, risking the destruction of this detachment if they
strayed and bumped into stronger Antonian forces, but the risk paid
off and they linked up without difficulty.

On the morning of 14 April Pansa's reinforced army approached
the little town of Forum Gallorum, some seven miles from Mutina.
Most of the Antonians were concealed in the houses or the marsh
and scrubland on either side of the road, but enough outposts
were visible to prompt a precipitate attack by the *Martia*, enraged
by memories of the executions at Brundisium. The result was a
confused and savage fight, the terrain breaking it up into several

smaller battles. Caesar's praetorian cohort suffered appalling losses as it came up against Antony's own guards on the road itself. To the rear, the raw legions began to withdraw to the marching camp they had built overnight and did their best to strengthen its defences.

For a while the *Martia* held its own, and even drove back the *Thirty-fifth* for half a mile, but in time Antony's superiority in cavalry began to tell, forcing them to withdraw. The steadiness of these well-trained soldiers and the leadership of Pansa and his officers just managed to prevent the retreat from turning into a rout. Most of the army made it back to the shelter of the camp's defences, although the consul was struck in the side by a missile and badly wounded. The Antonians attacked the low turf ramparts of the camp, but failed to break in. It was well into the afternoon, and Antony realised that his men were tired and hungry. Julius Caesar would no doubt have built his own fortified camp on the spot and brought food to them, keeping up the pressure on the enemy. Instead Antony marched his men back to their original camp.

By this time Hirtius and Caesar had realised that the probes against them were feints. The consul took the bulk of the *Fourth* and the *Seventh*, leaving his young colleague to defend the camps. Through luck or design Hirtius was able to attack Antony's men as they withdrew. The Antonians formed a hasty battle line in the evening light, but with the elation of victory fading into exhaustion they were physically and mentally unprepared for another battle. The *Second* and *Thirty-fifth* broke, suffering heavy casualties and each losing its precious eagle as well as half of its other standards. Most of the men were scattered, some reaching the shelter of Forum Gallorum and others hiding in the marshes. Antony's cavalry had escaped with few losses, and during the night patrols went out to round up and bring in as many of these stragglers as possible.[7]

Apart from these remnants Antony still had *Fifth Alaudae* and other forces in good enough order to maintain the blockade of Mutina. He also retained a distinct advantage in the numbers and quality of his cavalry, and so was able to do well in the skirmishing that occupied the next few days. Yet he was on the back foot, and Hirtius and Caesar increased the pressure on him, advancing to camp closer to the enemy lines and offering battle, which Antony declined. Such gestures were good ways of building up an army's confidence in their superiority. At the end of a week Antony was at last provoked to form up and fight. He was beaten and Hirtius and Caesar were able to turn this into a full-scale attack on his fortified lines. The nineteen-year-old had played a minor role in the earlier fighting – Antony subsequently alleged that he fled the battle, abandoning the red cloak that marked him as a general – and he may have gone out of his way to act heroically in this second engagement. Suetonius tells us that at one point he carried the eagle of one of his legions after the standard-bearer (or *aquilifer*) was wounded – a well-known gesture meant to inspire men to attack boldly or rally when they were wavering. Assaulting fortified positions was always a difficult operation, but numbers and confidence told. Hirtius broke into Antony's main camp, but was killed in the confused fighting among the tent-lines. By the end of the day the Antonians had been driven from several key positions. Antony abandoned his blockade and retreated, hoping to join up with subordinates bringing him fresh reinforcements.[8]

The pursuit was lacklustre. Hirtius was dead, while Pansa remained confined to his tent and succumbed to his wound before the month was out. Decimus Brutus was consul-elect for the next year – another of Julius Caesar's appointments – and so senior to Caesar, but his own men were in a bad state after months confined in Mutina eating poor rations. Their commander was also desperately short of money, which made it difficult to pay the troops and provide them with provisions. Before the siege the defenders had slaughtered all their pack animals and mounts and it was difficult to replace them. Decimus Brutus had no effective cavalry or baggage train to take the field. The strongest part of the relieving army remained the legions loyal to the young propraetor and Julius Caesar's veterans were not well disposed towards one of his murderers.[9]

Caesar effectively now controlled his own and the consuls' legions. Later, Caesar was accused of ordering the murder of Hirtius – or even of performing the act himself – and then of arranging Pansa's death in order to take over the army. It was claimed that the latter's personal doctor was arrested and interrogated because the consul's condition had taken a sudden turn for the worse. Hindsight and the propaganda needs of an ongoing civil war were no doubt behind such tales, and it is unlikely that there is any truth in them. Roman commanders led from close behind the fighting line and were conspicuous targets in their scarlet cloaks and fine armour, at risk from missiles or bold enemies wishing to make names for themselves. The confusion inevitable in a civil war fought between identically dressed armies placed them in even greater danger. At the First Battle of Forum Gallorum one of the commanders of the *Martia* was nearly killed by some of Pansa's raw recruits who only recognised him at the last moment.[10]

It was surely chance rather than design that removed the two consuls, but that did not alter the essential truth that Caesar was now left at the head of some seven or eight legions.

ROME AGAIN

The Senate heard rumours of an Antonian victory – perhaps the defeat of Pansa's men – before the full story of Forum Gallorum arrived. Both consuls and Caesar were lauded for their part in the success, although in truth the latter's role was marginal. Reports of the breaking of the siege of Mutina were welcomed with even more joy by Cicero and those who shared his fears of Antony. A public thanksgiving of fifty days was proclaimed – far outstripping even Julius Caesar's honours and quite clearly celebrating a victory in a civil war. Antony was finally declared a public enemy, and Brutus and Cassius were recognised as legitimately in charge of their armies and provinces. Not everyone was so inclined to exult. Asinius Pollio was governor of one of the Spanish provinces and an old Caesarean.

When he wrote to Cicero it was to lament the wasted deaths of so many of Italy's finest sons.[11]

Decimus Brutus did his best, but could not prevent Antony from escaping. At the start of May he complained that 'it is impossible to give orders to Caesar, and impossible for him to give orders to his army – both bad things'. The Senate sent instructions for him to be given the *Fourth* and the *Martia*. The soldiers refused to accept him, and a few weeks later Cicero had to admit to Brutus that nothing could be done to compel them. He probably received more or less permanent command of some of the legions of recruits, and with them and his own ragged army he set out after Antony. The latter soon joined up with three fresh legions raised by one of Julius Caesar's old staff officers, Publius Ventidius Bassus. The whole force then crossed into Transalpine Gaul. Lepidus and Plancus were urged to move against him, but all their best officers and troops were once again veterans of Julius Caesar. In May Antony's army camped next to Lepidus' main force. Former comrades in each army fraternised and it was soon clear that there was no enthusiasm to fight each other. Lepidus' legions declared for Antony, their commander soon following. One of his senatorial subordinates committed suicide, but his was the only death. Lepidus and Antony became allies, and were soon joined by Plancus and later Asinius Pollio as well. The public enemy was now far stronger than he had ever been.[12]

Decimus Brutus was voted a triumph in the Senate. Caesar was given the lesser honour of an ovation, where the recipient rode on horseback instead of in a chariot and did not receive as much prestige. Both men were excluded from a board of commissioners set up to demobilise the legions and provide the discharged soldiers with land, which would mean not only taking away his army, but depriving the young commander of winning their favour through rewarding them. Many senators were inclined to relax, feeling that the crisis was over, and they were slow to appreciate the scale of Antony's recovery. Unwisely, a meeting decided to halve the bounty promised to the legions when they defected.[13]

On 24 May Decimus Brutus wrote to Cicero reporting that the nineteen-year-old was repeating a phrase that one of his staff assured him had been uttered by Cicero – 'we must praise the young man, reward him, and discard him'. The orator did not deny saying this, and the rhythm of the Latin, *laudanum aduluscentum, ornandum, tollendum* – the last word having a double meaning of both exalt and toss aside – suggests that it was genuine.[14]

From the beginning Caesar had been a convenient means of fighting Antony. For the youth, accepting the Senate's orders had given legal confirmation to his raising of an army and helped him to become an important player in the enfolding struggle. Now the Senate was giving official approval to the growing military might of Brutus and Cassius, and even recognising Sextus Pompeius, the younger son of Pompey the Great who had raised rebellion in Spain and the Mediterranean islands. None of these were likely to be well disposed to Julius Caesar's heir. Earlier in the year, Antony had written to Hirtius and Caesar warning them that the only people to gain from conflict between them were the former Pompeians.[15]

Caesar had no intention of being discarded, and said as much openly. Like everyone else, he was concerned with preserving his position in the longer run. At the beginning of the month Decimus Brutus hinted that the youth had his eye on the consulship, left vacant by the deaths of Hirtius and Pansa. He may have approached Cicero suggesting that the two of them stand together. A rumour circulated that the old orator had already succeeded to one of the vacant posts. Brutus heard this story in Macedonia, and had from the beginning expressed concern at employing Caesar at all. In June Cicero wrote to assure him that he had spoken in the Senate against relatives of the young man who were working for his elevation to the supreme office. Most likely he referred to Philippus and Marcellus but, although he also told Caesar himself to abandon such a wild ambition, he nevertheless continued to speak highly of the youth. Brutus, whom Julius Caesar had noted tended to be obsessive in his beliefs, remained unconvinced, fearing that Cicero was too ready to take fright and too easily flattered by the boy. He saw only an unelected warlord, whose status was inherited along with the name and wealth of the same Julius Caesar that Brutus and his comrades had killed as a tyrant. Cicero in response kept urging the leader of the Liberators to return to Italy with his army. In the end, armies trumped ideals.[16]

In July a deputation arrived from Caesar's army. At 400 men it was roughly the size of a cohort, and so not an army in itself, but it included a significant number of centurions as well as representatives from the rank and file. They demanded the consulship for their commander and the full bounty promised to themselves. Suetonius claims that the spokesman was a centurion named Cornelius. Precedents from the mainly distant past were cited of men below the legal age being promoted to the supreme office when the state needed their talents. Centurions were men of some property and often came from the aristocracies of the country towns of Italy. The old view of them as sergeant majors promoted from the ranks is a sadly persistent myth. Even so, senators saw them as far inferior in social status and resented the forceful tone with which they presented their case. Their demands were angrily rejected. Cornelius is supposed to have brushed aside his military cloak to show the pommel and hilt of his sword, which centurions wore on the left hip, unlike ordinary soldiers. 'This will do it, if you do not,' he said.[17]

Such a blatant threat may be just a story, but soon became a reality. When the deputation returned to Caesar in Cisalpine Gaul the army 'demanded' that he lead them to Rome. With no sign of any reluctance he took his legions south. Once again a Caesar crossed the Rubicon with an army, although this time the little river made no formal difference to his *imperium* since his extraordinary grant of power had not been tied to any specific region. He had some eight legions. The Senate had only a single legion, a unit formed by Pansa and presumably seen then as unfit for active campaigning. A messenger was sent to the North African province summoning its three legions back to protect Rome itself.

Realising their mistake, the Senate voted to grant Caesar the right to stand for election *in absentia* – the very thing Julius Caesar had wanted in 49 BC – but he was no longer inclined to trust them and continued to advance. Before he reached Rome two of the African legions arrived. These men were better trained than the raw recruits left by Pansa, but there was no incentive for them to chance the arithmetic of three legions against eight. Nevertheless, under the command of one or more of the praetors, they set to work preparing defences. On a more sinister note, parties were sent to secure Atia and Octavia as hostages, but failed to find them, most likely because they had been warned or were shrewd enough to realise that the situation was dangerous.

Caesar arrived, and the Senate's legions prudently defected to join him. A praetor took his own life in shame or rage, but there was no actual fighting as the youth and his bodyguard marched into the City. Crowds, and a steady flow of senators, came to greet him. Cicero was the last to arrive, as the young Caesar icily observed. Then during the night a rumour spread that the *Martia* and the *Fourth* had mutinied against the commander. The Senate met before dawn – yet another violation of tradition – and briefly revelled in the news before discovering that it was untrue.

On 19 August 43 BC Caesar was elected consul at the age of nineteen years, ten months and twenty-six days. There was no precedent for anyone so young ever holding the office and the youth was proud of this claim to uniqueness. His colleague was Julius Caesar's nephew Quintus Pedius. It seems doubtful that there were any other candidates, but all the formality of a proper election was preserved as the Roman people filed through the *saepta*. Quite possibly the selection was genuinely popular, although his legions were camped on the Campus Martius itself to help clarify the voters' thoughts. After winning the vote, Caesar performed the traditional sacrifices and it was claimed that twelve vultures flew overhead – the same omen the myths said was seen by Romulus when he founded the City.

Soon afterwards the Roman people met again, this time to vote into law confirmation of his full adoption by Julius Caesar. Other laws followed, including one reversing the amnesty of 17 March

44 BC and declaring the dictator's murder a crime. Brutus and Cassius lost the official approval of their seizure of provinces, and they and the other conspirators were all found guilty in their absence in a specially formed tribunal which sat and judged them in a single day. The jurors were carefully chosen and as carefully watched – only one dared vote for acquittal. Since the conspirators had clearly killed the dictator and boasted of their deed, they were evidently guilty as long as his murder was considered to be a crime. It was more the haste, and obviously unconventional trial of men in their absence that caused concern, even though this was more of a trial than Cicero had given the Catilinarians in 63 BC. Another bill reversed the branding of Antony and Lepidus as public enemies. Dolabella was also turned from public enemy back to a legitimate promagistrate, although he was probably dead before the news arrived. Sextus Pompeius lost his briefly held legal power and became a rebel once again. A praetor was accused of plotting the assassination of the young Caesar and summarily deposed and condemned to death. Judgement could be swift and brutal, but for the moment this was an isolated case.

The remainder of the legacy to the Roman people from the dictator's will was finally paid by the man now formally his son as well as heir. Using funds from an almost empty treasury, Caesar also gave his legionaries 2,500 denarii apiece, with the promise that the remaining half of their bounty would follow in due course. It is likely that his newly acquired legions had some – perhaps even a full – share in his generosity, for in the end his power relied on them. He now had eleven legions, but Antony and Lepidus had twice as many. Probably most of these units were skeleton formations, at half or less of their theoretical strength. A commander's prestige relied more on the number of his legions than the precise total of soldiers under his command, so there was a tendency to raise lots of units, which in turn had the added advantage of giving plenty of opportunities to promote loyal followers to the senior ranks.[18]

Caesar and his legions were soon marching back north to Cisalpine Gaul. Antony and Lepidus were waiting for him. Decimus Brutus had shadowed them from a discreet distance, but could not hope to fight against such numbers. Munatius Plancus and his army had joined him for a while, before they defected to join Antony. His troops deserting in droves, he fled with a small escort of cavalry and took refuge with a Gallic chieftain. The man was known to him from his years on Julius Caesar's staff, but an old tie of hospitality crumbled in the face of immediate necessity. Perhaps on Antony's orders – and certainly with his subsequent approval – Decimus Brutus was killed and his head sent as proof of the deed.

All of the best officers and soldiers on both sides were men who had fought for Julius Caesar and remained as devoted to his memory as they were hostile to his murderers. They had no desire to fight each other, and so even though Caesar's army was markedly smaller – perhaps half the size – than the host following Lepidus and Antony he was able to approach with confidence. All three leaders realised that it would be difficult to turn on each other. More importantly, they had little to gain from such a struggle. Although Antony had been willing to coexist with the self-proclaimed Liberators in the previous year, this was solely from necessity on both sides. Brutus and Cassius, backed by the military strength of the eastern provinces, were unlikely to be as willing to compromise, or well disposed to him or Lepidus, let alone the young Caesar. It was certainly too great a risk to rely on their good faith – a sentiment felt with equal force by Brutus, Cassius and their allies.[19]

Antony, Lepidus and Caesar had exchanged letters and envoys and knew that each was willing to compromise. At the end of October they met near Bononia, just to the north of Mutina, and for two days the three principals and their staffs negotiated the details of their alliance. Each had brought five legions, and pickets of soldiers watched from opposite sides of a river as the leaders talked on a small island. The resulting agreement had no precedent in Rome's history – and indeed is hard to parallel in any era. Whereas Pompey, Crassus and Julius Caesar had agreed an informal co-operative pact, this alliance was to be ratified in law as soon as they reached Rome. The three men agreed to share supreme power of the type only ever given to a dictator. They would become *tresviri rei publicae constituendae* – triumvirs (literally a board of three) with power to restore the state. With such extensive powers, Caesar agreed to give up his briefly held consulship, resigning in favour of Ventidius, already a serving praetor and the man whose reinforcements had helped to save Antony after his defeat. Ventidius would hold the office for the few weeks left in the year, but even so this granted him the status of an ex-consul for the rest of his life.

Together the three led a large part of their combined armies to Rome. There were no forces left in Italy to oppose them at all, and their entry into the City was as peaceful as Caesar's arrival a few months before. On 27 November a tribune named Titius summoned the Popular Assembly, which duly ratified the triumvirate and gave them their powers for five years. It may also have formally granted them the provinces they had already shared between themselves. Lepidus got Transalpine Gaul and the Spanish provinces, while Antony took the rest of Gaul. Caesar was granted Sicily, Sardinia and the other smaller islands as well as North Africa. This was probably the weakest portion, since large parts of each were already or soon to be overrun by Sextus Pompeius. Like that young man's father, Pompey the Great, the triumvirs would control their provinces through legates, and had no obligation to visit them in person. The key thing was to control the legions stationed there. The twenty-year-old Caesar possessed a strong army and that was of far more immediate importance than the longer-term benefits of controlling extensive provinces.[20]

The triumvirs were blatantly warlords with armies loyal to them over the state. The same was by now true of Brutus and Cassius – and indeed Sextus Pompeius – all of whom lavished generous gifts on their soldiers to secure their loyalty. Caesar was no different, and yet his rise was far more rapid and spectacular than any of the others. He was now of an age when in ordinary circumstances he would either have been serving as a junior officer in the army or beginning to appear as an advocate in the courts. Instead he was one of the most powerful men in the world.

8

VENGEANCE AND DISCORD

'Marcus Lepidus, Marcus Antonius and Octavius Caesar, chosen by the people to set in order and regulate the Republic, do declare that, had not perfidious traitors begged for mercy and when they had obtained it become enemies of their benefactors and conspired against them, neither would Caius Caesar have been slain by those whom he saved by his clemency . . . ; nor should we have been . . . insulted and declared public enemies. Now . . . we prefer to anticipate our enemies rather than suffer at their hands . . .' *Appian's version of the proscription decree, early second century* AD.[1]

'One thing, however, demands comment, that toward the proscribed their wives showed greatest loyalty, their freedmen not a little, their slaves some, their sons none.' *Velleius Paterculus, early first century* AD.[2]

The dominance of the triumvirate began with mass murder. As they marched south from Bononia, Caesar, Antony and Lepidus sent soldiers on ahead to eliminate a dozen or so prominent men. No warning was given, although Cicero and some of the other victims guessed their peril and fled from the City. Four men were cut down, and searches began for the rest, starting an overnight panic among Rome's elite who feared that they too were at risk. The consul Pedius, Caesar's colleague in the office and his uncle, sent around heralds asking for calm and for people to wait until the morning when the list of men still wanted was announced. No longer a young man, and in poor health, the strain of this business was believed to have shattered Pedius' health and he died within a few days. The triumvirs rewarded another of their followers with the vacant consulship for the last few weeks of the year.[3]

Once they reached Rome, the murders became more open and formal as the Sullan practice of proscriptions was revived. Two boards listing names were posted in the Forum – allegedly one reserved solely for senators – and those on them lost all legal protection and so could be killed by the triumvirs' men or anyone else eager to claim the reward of a share of their property. This was paid on presentation of the severed head of the victim, which was then fastened to the Rostra. The rest of the corpse was to be left where it fell or just tossed into the River Tiber with the City's rubbish. Anyone, including close family, who dared to help one of them risked being proscribed themselves. The initial list of victims numbered in hundreds, and the total rose to more than 2,000 in the months to come. The formality of the process should not conceal the simple truth that this was illegal killing on a scale to dwarf Cicero's execution of the Catilinarians without trial. This time no tribunes – or indeed anyone else – raised their voices in protest. As one of Antony's commanders later drily commented, 'it isn't easy to write [scribere] criticism of someone who can proscribe you [proscribere]'. The triumvirs commanded the only armies left in Italy, and even if they had each brought only a single legion and praetorian cohort into Rome itself, there was no force capable of opposing their will.[4]

The new regime's veneer of legitimacy was thin – the lex Titia creating the triumvirate was rushed through on the same day that it was proposed, ignoring the legal requirement for a three-day period before a law was passed. The triumvirs presented the proscriptions as the necessary elimination of enemies of the state and its leaders. They declared that Julius Caesar had shown clemency only to be murdered by the very men he had spared. They did not intend to repeat that mistake, and so would kill without mercy anyone they considered to be an enemy, ignoring even ties of friendship and family. As they drew up their death lists, Caesar, Antony and Lepidus traded victims in a scene later brought chillingly to life by Shakespeare: 'these many, then, shall die, their names are pricked'. Antony allowed his mother's brother, Lucius Julius Caesar, to be included, while Lepidus gave up his own brother, Aemilius Paul-lus, both of them former consuls. The young Caesar lacked any prominent relative to sacrifice, and made do with Toranius, the former guardian accused of defrauding him of much of his father's estate.[5]

Aemilius Paullus escaped to Miletus to live on in exile, quite possibly warned of the danger by Lepidus himself who made no serious effort to have him pursued. Antony's mother Julia sheltered her brother in her house, blocking the door when the executioners arrived and according to Plutarch telling them, 'You shall not kill Lucius Caesar without first killing me, the mother of your com-mander!' Later she publicly accosted her son in the Forum and he 'reluctantly' granted his uncle a pardon. Toranius found no protec-tor and died. So did hundreds more over the course of the next year or so.[6]

Cicero might have escaped. He boarded a ship heading for the east, but it was blown back to shore by bad weather, and he seems to have lost the energy to persist in his efforts. In the meantime his brother Quintus and his nephew were caught and both killed. Cicero's own son was already safely studying in Athens and would soon fight as one of Brutus' officers in the war against the trium-virs. The orator himself met his death with dignity and resigned courage on 7 December 43 BC. He was by far the most prominent victim of the proscriptions, and the only former consul, and his death was a warning that even the most distinguished were not safe if they offended the triumvirate. Still the *novus homo* in spite of his success, Cicero was both an obvious target and vulnerable because he lacked the generations of inherited connections enjoyed by the established aristocracy. The same factors had made him vulnera-ble to Clodius and other ambitious attackers in the years after his consulship.[7]

Later it was claimed that the young Caesar remembered the old statesman's support for him and argued for mercy. Perhaps he did, and perhaps he was even sincere and not simply horse-trading, but whatever the truth of the matter he let himself be overruled.

Antony gave orders for Cicero's right hand to be brought to Rome along with his severed head and in due course both were nailed to the Rostra, taking vengeance on the hand that had written and the mouth that had uttered the *Philippics*. Before that, the grisly trophies were brought in for his inspection while he was dining with his wife Fulvia. People said Antony clutched the severed head and laughed in savage delight. Afterwards, Fulvia took the trophy and hurled abuse at the dead man, even drawing pins from her hair and stabbing them into his tongue. Both had reason enough to hate him, and perhaps Fulvia most of all, for her first husband Clodius had been Cicero's bitterest enemy – the orator had even defended his murderer Milo in court, albeit unsuccessfully. More recently she had watched as the orator convinced the Senate to turn against Antony, the rightful consul, and declare him a public enemy. Living in Rome, she found herself and her property under legal assault as ambitious men sensed that a wealthy family was vulnerable.[8]

Our sources contain stories depicting all three triumvirs exulting in the massacre, and it is very difficult to separate the truth from later propaganda, given the violent and imaginative abuse so normal in Roman political invective. Most of those tales written down under the rule of the young Caesar and his heirs portray him as a mild and reluctant collaborator, his two colleagues as mere brutes. Yet that is not the only version to survive. Suetonius claims that Caesar's initial reluctance quickly changed to an enthusiastic pursuit of victims. Lepidus and Antony were mature men, of an age to play a role in public affairs, and even senators who envied and loathed their dominance resented it less than the murderous power of a callow youth. Most Romans felt that Caesar, still only twenty, simply should not yet have made so many enemies.[9]

In truth it was not just confirmed opponents of the triumvirate who found themselves proscribed. At the head of some forty legions of soldiers accustomed to lavish bonuses, Antony, Lepidus and Caesar were in desperate need of hard currency to pay them, apart from meeting the other costs of running the state. Many of the proscribed found themselves on the list simply because they were wealthy and the triumvirs decided that they had no strong reason for keeping them alive. Their property was confiscated, their houses and country estates auctioned off to raise funds for the new regime. In such cases it really did not matter whether the men were actually killed or simply fled abroad, for either way their assets were seized. Both Caesar and Antony were accused of killing men simply to get their hands on fine collections of Corinthian bronze vases. Antony also ordered the death of Verres, a provincial governor who was spectacularly rapacious even by Roman standards and who had been in exile since his successful prosecution by Cicero in 70 BC. His wealth was still substantial, and his art collection especially fine, and so the aged criminal was killed for them. Individually and as a group the triumvirs were desperate for money. There were stories that Fulvia and Antony accepted bribes to kill or pardon men during the proscriptions, and that she added people to the lists simply because she desired their property. Antony was also said to have pardoned a man after his wife agreed to sleep with him.[10]

The proscriptions claimed many victims, even if by far the majority escaped and survived, in time returning to Italy and Rome itself. These purges provided a fund of stories of dramatic survivals, of heroic protection and treacherous betrayal by family, friends and slaves, and in the years to come numerous books were filled with these tales. There is one claim that a boy was killed on his way to school, and of another hastily added to the list as he was going through the ceremony to make him a man, but on the whole children were safe unless they owned substantial property in their own right. The threats of execution for those harbouring the proscribed were not consistently enforced. One woman begged to be killed along with her husband when his hiding place was found. The soldiers refused, as did the magistrate – perhaps one of the triumvirs or a senior subordinate – when she publicly declared that she was guilty of protecting him. In the end the widow was said to have starved herself to death.[11]

There is no specific story of a wife being killed for harbouring a husband, unlike fathers or sons. One infamous tale claimed that a woman arranged for her husband to be proscribed, betrayed him by locking him in their house until the soldiers came, and promptly married her lover within hours of the husband's execution. We also have an inscription set up as a memorial by a once-proscribed husband to his beloved wife. The man tells how she hid him, helped him to escape, and then eventually was able to persuade Caesar to grant a pardon. This proved difficult to enforce, and Lepidus ordered his attendants to beat the woman when she tried to make him take action and recall her husband.[12]

There is another story of Caesar granting a reprieve. In this case a woman managed to hide her husband in a large chest and have this brought into the triumvir's presence while he was presiding over public games. The deception was revealed, and the crowd so impressed by her boldness and loyalty to her husband that Caesar sensed their mood and granted him a pardon. Public opinion could not be wholly ignored even by warlords. The proscriptions permitted slaves to win their freedom by betraying their masters, but in a few publicised cases, where they exulted too much or continued to attack their former owner's family, the triumvirs had them executed or re-enslaved to reassure people that the social order was not seriously in jeopardy.[13]

Neither Caesar, Antony or Lepidus can escape guilt for their ruthlessness in ordering the proscriptions. From a purely utilitarian point of view, these murders were highly successful in spreading fear. However, the financial yield proved disappointing, for little enthusiasm was shown at the auctions of confiscated property. Too many potential buyers were nervous about showing that they were wealthy enough to purchase new assets, and others remembered the frequent attacks on those who had profited from the Sullan proscriptions. Desperate for more cash, the triumvirs introduced a range of levies, taxing the wealthy on the basis of their property – a thoroughly un-Roman measure. The announcement that the estates of the 1,400 wealthiest citizen women were to be assessed so that they too could pay tax was without any precedent. During the desperate war against Hannibal in the third century BC, aristocratic women had voluntarily given jewellery and other valuables to the Republic, but they had never been taxed. Led by Hortensia, the daughter of the man Cicero had supplanted as Rome's leading orator, a large group of women went first to the female relatives of the triumvirs, and then into the Forum to confront Caesar, Antony and Lepidus in person. Once again the wider crowd sympathised with this display of feminine courage, and the triumvirate judged that a concession was wise. Only 400 women were taxed, and more levies announced on men. Half of the agricultural yield was to be taken from farms, while communities in Italy were forced to provide free winter billets for soldiers, an imposition usual only in the provinces.[14]

PHILIPPI

On 1 January 42 BC Lepidus began a second consulship, just four years after holding the office with Julius Caesar. This time his colleague was Lucius Munatius Plancus, one of the army commanders who had joined Antony after Mutina. They began by taking an oath – willingly joined by Antony and Caesar and less freely by the rest of the Senate – that all deeds of the dead dictator were to be forever binding. Julius Caesar was now formally consecrated as a god, and work began on a temple to him near the site of his cremation – its remains still stand in the Forum today. His heir was now not simply Caesar in name, but the son of a god, although he did not immediately adopt this title.[15]

Family connections were never far from the mind of any Roman aristocrat. Late in 43 BC Atia had died, having lived long enough to see her son reach the consulship. She was honoured with a public funeral. By this time her son was already engaged to the daughter of an elderly aristocrat, but this arrangement was broken off when the triumvirate was formed. Neither Antony nor Lepidus had a daughter of suitable age, but the army was vocally eager for some means of cementing the new alliance and so the young Caesar married Fulvia's daughter from her first marriage. The girl – her name was Claudia and was not changed to the vulgar form Clodia when her father was adopted into the plebeian order – came from important aristocratic families on both sides and so was a suitable match. However, she was very young, still a few years short of the normal marriageable age, and although the couple were married they did not live as husband and wife; when the couple divorced two years later, Caesar took an oath stating that the girl remained a virgin.[16]

For the moment the marriage provided a very traditional bond between Antony and Caesar, who only a few months before had traded invective and then fought each other in battle. Now they would go east in joint command to deal with the powerful forces assembled by Brutus and Cassius. Lepidus remained in Italy with only a few legions. Regardless of age and experience, it was clear that Caesar must go with the army sent to punish the men who had murdered his father. This was far more important than the distribution of provinces between the triumvirs. Antony and Caesar would win glory – or perish in the attempt. If they won, then Lepidus would gain only an indirect share of the prestige and power. If they lost and did not return, then a man who had shared in the proscriptions was likely to find that he had plenty of enemies.[17]

Winning would not be easy. The Liberators had acquired and recruited more than twenty legions. Some of these had originally been raised by Julius Caesar, but none had seen extensive service under him or had reason to feel a close bond to his heir or to Mark Antony. Nor were they profoundly committed to defending the rights of the senatorial elite, and Brutus and Cassius were careful to offer their legionaries financial incentives every bit as generous as those given and promised by the triumvirate. The provinces of the eastern Mediterranean had little choice but to foot the bill for this, and were squeezed with heavy taxes and required to supply food, material and allied soldiers. Some did so willingly, but none could hope to resist the might of the Liberators' legions. Cassius invaded Rhodes when the island proved reluctant to meet his demands, and sold into slavery the populations of several communities in Judaea who were similarly recalcitrant. Around the same time, Brutus besieged and sacked Xanthus in Lycia, prompting the mass suicide of many of its inhabitants. Such grim warnings ensured that most communities readily gave them what they wanted. Brutus employed some of the silver he acquired to mint coin series with his head on the face – something first done by Julius Caesar, but now copied by the triumvirs – and a more appropriately Republican cap of liberty on the reverse.[18]

By the end of the summer of 42 BC the Liberators felt strong enough to concentrate their armies and cross the Hellespont from Asia Minor into Macedonia. Antony and Caesar had sent a force of eight legions across the Adriatic while they prepared their main body and gathered the ships needed to transport so many soldiers. Outnumbered and outmanoeuvred, this corps managed to retreat westwards along the Via Egnatia to Amphipolis. The Liberators did not pursue them all the way, but took up a strong position in front of the city of Philippi – founded by and named after Alexander the Great's father, Philip II, in the fourth century BC.

Antony's and Caesar's main armies did not set sail until September – very late in the year to begin campaigning, but matching Julius Caesar's determined prosecution of the earlier civil war. Like him they were short of transport ships and faced powerful enemy squadrons of warships determined to hinder their crossing. Antony had to fight off raids on the port of Brundisium itself as he prepared the expedition. Before he had even reached the Adriatic, Caesar engaged in some indecisive naval skirmishing with the growing power of Sextus Pompeius. When they finally set sail, it was with only part of their forces, and the transport ships would have to return to bring reinforcements. They managed to carry across a second convoy before the Liberators' warships closed off the sea route for some time.[19]

The triumvirs landed at Apollonia – more than two years since Caius Octavius had left for the uncertainties of Roman politics – but the familiar surroundings were little comfort because he had fallen seriously ill during the voyage. We do not know what the sickness was, but he was incapable of going any further for the moment.

Antony pressed on with his legions, marching to reinforce the vanguard at Amphipolis. He then went further, boldly pushing on to camp facing Brutus and Cassius at Philippi. This was a risk, since they outnumbered him by at least a third, but the Liberators were too cautious to exploit their advantage. There was a little skirmishing between the rival armies' outposts for the next ten days, until Caesar and his legions finally arrived to join his colleague. Close to his twenty-first birthday, the young commander had to be carried in a litter since he was incapable of riding a horse.[20]

The triumvirs had nineteen legions with them – as many as Pompey and Julius Caesar combined at the decisive Battle of Pharsalus in 48 BC – and faced seventeen legions under Brutus and Cassius. The Liberators had the advantage in cavalry, allegedly fielding 20,000 against the triumvirs' 13,000. If the legions were close to full theoretical strength then this would mean that more than 200,000 soldiers fought in the battles to come, but we need to be cautious. Probably all of the legions were substantially under-strength and the totals for cavalry also inflated. Horses were difficult to transport by ship, and it would have been immensely difficult to feed so many mounts, along with similar numbers of pack and draught animals, and all these soldiers and camp-followers for any length of time. Brutus and Cassius had amassed considerable stocks of food and fodder, and had ready access to supplies brought by sea – advantages denied to their opponents – but it is doubtful in the extreme that they could have supplied such a large force for the duration of the campaign.[21]

Even if the armies were in fact two-thirds or half the size claimed then they would still have been large. There were some veterans on both sides, but the overwhelming majority of soldiers and many officers had little prior experience of battle. This was also true of the commanders. Cassius had served as Crassus' quaestor in 53 BC and led a fragment of his defeated army to safety, but that was now twenty years ago. He and Brutus both served in the Macedonian campaign in 48 BC, but otherwise gained no more military experience until their small-scale punitive operations to raise funds for this war. It was scarcely thorough preparation for controlling one of the largest Roman armies ever put into the field. Antony had more experience of command, although as we have seen considerably less than is usually assumed; he was by no stretch of the imagination a Julius Caesar or a Pompey – and even they had never led so many legions into battle. This was a war fought by large and clumsy armies, where none of the senior officers had any experience of warfare on so grand a scale. On each side the armies remained to a great degree separate, loyal only to the leader who paid them. They formed up beside each other, but were not integrated into a single command.

Brutus and Cassius each held a distinct camp on the higher ground outside Philippi. Brutus was on the right, his flank resting on a line of hills. Cassius was on the left, beside a wide stretch of marshland. Lines of fortification joined the two camps together. They had good access to water, a ready supply line to the coast, and their plan was to wait for the enemy to attack at a disadvantage or to run out of food. It might have worked, but did give the initiative to the triumvirs and that was not really the Roman way. Caesar's legions camped opposite Brutus, with Antony's men in front of Cassius' position. For a while they were content to skirmish. Most days the rival armies marched out to deploy in battle order in front of their camps, but neither side advanced to force an action. Such challenges to battle were a common feature of warfare in this era.[22]

In an effort to break the stand-off, Antony decided that the marshland on the left of the enemy position was vulnerable, and set his men to making a fortified line through the marshes. His men built outwards from their own camp, and the idea was to create a position running past Cassius' flank and eventually threatening the enemy's supply lines. At first the work was concealed by the high reeds, and care was taken to continue the main deployment outside the camps each day and occupy the enemy's attention. Eventually Cassius realised what was happening, and set a detachment to build his own ditch and rampart at right angles to Antony's. He planned to cut across Antony's line, overpower any men at that spot and cut off all those in advance of it so that they could be mopped up later. On 3

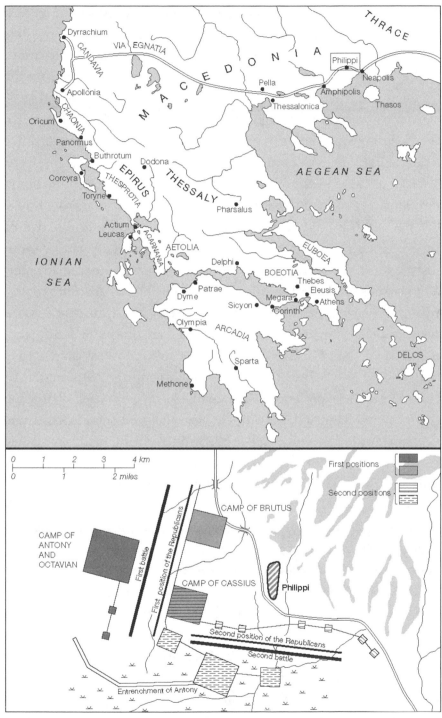

Greece and Macedonia, and the Battles of Philippi

October Antony's patrols discovered what the enemy were doing. As usual the rival armies were formed in battle-lines, and it is possible that the Liberators had decided to advance a little further forward or perhaps even to attack in order to distract their opponents from the building work.

Antony was at the far-right flank of his line and immediately led the closest troops into the marshes against Cassius' new line of fortification. Elsewhere a confused battle developed. Whether or not the attack was premeditated, Brutus' and Cassius' staff had difficulty in co-ordinating so many inexperienced legions. The orders to advance did not reach each unit at the same time, and on the initiative of local commanders some waited and others moved forward without instructions. The result was an enthusiastic but disordered advance. Things were even more confused on the other side. After days of posturing and facing the enemy without fighting, the triumvirs' legions were not expecting a full-scale battle. Brutus' line extended further to the right than Caesar's troops – probably more by chance than design. The *Fourth* held the post of honour on the extreme left of the line and the experienced Caesarean legion found itself charged in the front and flank and was quickly overwhelmed. Panic spread, and Caesar's entire left wing collapsed. Brutus' exultant troops surged forward into pursuit and broke into the enemy camp, where they quickly dispersed to plunder and forgot all about completing their victory.

In the meantime Antony's men had used ladders to scale and capture Cassius' new wall, and then kept going, urged on by their general. Antony was one of the first to break into Cassius' main camp. Most of the latter's legions were engaged to the front and not involved in the fighting in the marsh, but as rumour spread that their possessions were lost, the cohorts began to waver and retreat. Cassius himself despaired as his army dissolved around him. Short-sighted, he mistook some of Brutus' cavalry for the enemy and ordered his body servant to help him commit suicide rather than become a prisoner. (This man promptly disappeared, and some wondered if he had killed his master without waiting for the order.) Brutus was unable to get his men back under control and turn against Antony, and instead they began to drift back to their own camp, laden down with loot. Antony in turn had become too involved in the storming of Cassius' camp to influence the wider battle and was unable to exploit the disorder of Brutus' men. Caesar was simply nowhere to be seen.[23]

For the rest of his life controversy would surround the young triumvir's conduct on 3 October, and there is no doubt that he failed to perform as a Roman aristocrat should at the head of an army. He was still seriously ill, incapable of active command, and yet he does not seem to have appointed a subordinate to fulfil this role – no doubt because a warlord must avenge a dead father himself and not through a deputy. This leadership vacuum was the most important cause of the bad order and rapid collapse of his army under Brutus' attack. Caesar may have been with them, carried in his litter behind the battle lines. He was certainly not in his main camp when the Liberators' men broke in, although several of these came to Brutus boasting that they had killed the young triumvir. Caesar's own story was that his personal physician dreamed that it would be dangerous to stay in his tent, and so at some point his companions heeded the warning and he was carried away by his personal attendants. It was not clear whether this was before or during the fighting. They took him away from the battle, and hid in an area of marshland some distance to the rear. Perhaps they or he despaired of the battle, or he was simply too exhausted to move, but he remained there for three days before returning to the camp.[24]

Cumbersome and essentially amateur armies given poor leadership, or none at all, turned the First Battle of Philippi into a draw. Casualties were heaviest among Caesar's legions, which also lost a number of standards. Worse news came when a courier arrived to report that the latest convoy to come from Italy had been intercepted by enemy warships and destroyed. A large part of *Legio Martia*, along with another legion, perished by fire or drowning when the transport ships were burned. Brutus did not believe the report when it reached him, and seems to have sunk into depression following the death of his ally and brother-in-law. Cassius was dead, but the two armies remained fiercely separate, and so Brutus immediately gave his colleague's soldiers a generous gift of money to preserve their willingness to die for the Republic and liberty. Antony continued to extend his fortifications around the enemy left. Cassius had kept a garrison on one commanding hill but, whether through a simple mistake or a misplaced desire to assert his authority, Brutus withdrew them. Antony and Caesar spotted the error and immediately sent troops to the spot, who quickly built a strong fort there. Brutus' supply line was now in jeopardy. As the days and weeks passed his army grew frustrated, eager to end things by confronting the enemy again.

On 23 October Brutus reluctantly gave battle. This time the armies deployed at right angles to the first battlefield, which meant that Brutus' men no longer had the gentle slope in their favour. In spite of this the fighting was long and bitter, but steadily the triumvirs' men drove their opponents back 'like workmen pushing a heavy piece of machinery', and eventually they collapsed into rout. Brutus managed to keep a few legions together and retire in order. Then, inspired like so many of his generation by the example of Cato and others, he readily took his own life.[25]

Caesar was sufficiently recovered to play an active part in this second battle, although the chief credit for the campaign went to Antony. It was claimed that aristocratic prisoners jeered at the young triumvir and then hailed Antony as *imperator*. Certainly far more of those pardoned chose to join him, showing once again the preference for an older, more established man of unquestionably aristocratic blood. Antony was also praised for treating Brutus' corpse with respect, although Plutarch claims that Caesar was just as generous to the dead man's remains. The head was sent to Rome – under whose orders is unclear – to be laid at the feet of Julius Caesar's statue, but was lost when the ship carrying it foundered. The dictator's heir was accused of viciousness in his treatment of prisoners, for instance making a father and son gamble to determine who should be beheaded first.[26]

Antony took the lion's share of the prestige from defeating Brutus and Cassius, although in later years Caesar would declare simply: 'Those who slew my father I drove into exile, punishing their deed by due process of law, and afterwards when they waged war upon the republic I twice defeated them in battle.'[27]

For the moment it was enough that the main conspirators were defeated and dead and that he had at least taken part. A warlord needed to be successful and the war had been won. He and Antony also had to live up to the promises made to their soldiers, very many of whom were now due for discharge, either from length of service or because they had enlisted for the duration of the war. They had been promised land in Italy, and it was decided that Caesar would return to oversee the process. Antony would remain in the eastern Mediterranean, ensuring that the provinces were loyal and squeezing them for the vast sums of money the triumvirate needed to pay their troops and fund the land distribution. The provincial kingdoms and cities had no choice but to meet his demands, just as they had so recently met those of the Liberators, and only a few years before those of Pompey and then Julius Caesar. Kings and other leaders knew that if they failed to obey, the Romans would readily find ambitious rivals eager to replace them. Cleopatra was merely one of large numbers of eastern grandees desperate to win Antony's favour.[28]

Caesar fell seriously ill again before he could sail back to Italy. As before, we do not know the nature of the sickness, and whether it was something new or a resurgence of his previous ailment; for a while it was feared that he would die, and a false report spread that he had done so. As the months passed and his return was delayed, Rome grew ever more nervous. Rumours spread that he was plotting something terrible enough to make the proscriptions seem mild. During their absence, Caesar and Antony had become suspicious of Lepidus, suspecting that he had begun independent negotiations with Sextus Pompey. For the moment they divided Lepidus' provinces between themselves, although it seems that they held out the prospect of giving him the two African provinces at some point in the future. Although he remained formally a triumvir, he was clearly no longer the equal of the other two.[29]

When Caesar finally returned to Rome in 41 BC, he set about the task of finding land with great urgency and determination. Even before they left for the Macedonian campaign the triumvirs had named eighteen Italian cities which were to suffer confiscations of land to provide plots for discharged soldiers. The wealthy and well connected – especially senators and the most prosperous equestrians – protested whenever their estates were involved in the process. It was always dangerous to alienate the influential and most were granted exemptions. This meant that the confiscations fell disproportionately heavily on those of middling income and property who were less able to protest, although many still came to Rome in the attempt. In several cases the territory around the named cities was insufficient, and land was taken from neighbouring communities even though these had not been named by the triumvirate.

The soldiers had been promised farms. They had risked life and limb to fight their generals' wars and were conscious that the triumvirate only ruled through their support. This produced a surly determination to get what they considered to be a good deal. Notably they also wanted their relatives as well as the fathers and sons of fallen comrades to be protected from land confiscation. At the same time farms were being taken from families who had held them for generations, and who had committed no crime or act against the triumvirate. With the land went livestock, tools, buildings and houses, and the workforce of slaves. Feared, but never popular, the triumvirate had to walk a tightrope, satisfying the veterans without alienating too much of the rest of the population. At the same time Sextus Pompeius was harrying the sea lanes to Italy, so that fewer grain shipments were getting through than in normal times. Food became short, and as usual those most at risk of famine were the least well-off, already inclined to favour any change on the basis that their lot could scarcely be worse.[30]

Caesar was the man on the spot, and therefore the focus of resentment from so many disparate groups. Then an attack came suddenly from an unexpected direction. Brutus had executed Antony's brother Caius in reprisal for the killing of Decimus Brutus, but in 41 BC the remaining brother became consul. Lucius Antonius had all the self-confidence of a Roman noble and should not be seen as merely the tool of his older brother, but an ambitious man in his own right. As consul he took up the cause of the dispossessed farmers and discontented communities of Italy. As the months passed, his relationship with Caesar deteriorated. The truth of what happened next was difficult to establish even at the time, quickly becoming mired in propaganda. Fulvia joined Lucius at some point, doing her best to raise soldiers for him from Antony's veterans. Few were enthusiastic since, in spite of their fondness for their old general, they were reluctant to side with dispossessed farmers against the authority that was industriously giving the confiscated land to them as well as Caesar's discharged soldiers. Most of the troops to rally to the cause were raw recruits from the fertile regions of northern Italy and Campania most affected by the land redistribution.

Late in 41 BC Lucius marched on Rome with his newly raised legions. Lepidus was in the City, but his soldiers were heavily outnumbered and there was little enthusiasm for the triumvirate from the wider population. Rome fell quickly, Lepidus fleeing to join Caesar, but when the latter returned with a large and properly disciplined army, Lucius Antonius retreated even more quickly than he had arrived. He headed north, hoping to join up with several of Antony's generals who were in Italy with around thirteen experienced legions. Caesar's subordinate commanders blocked his path and he was cornered at Perusia (modern Perugia). The Caesareans surrounded the city with a ditch and wall strengthened with towers at close intervals and waited for hunger to bring the enemy to their knees. Over the winter months Lucius Antonius held out, waiting for Antony's generals to march to his rescue. They came close, at one point camping no more than twenty miles away, but there was a lack of purpose about their movements springing from a divided command and the absence of any instructions from Antony himself.

Probably they also realised that their soldiers did not sympathise with Lucius' rebels. None chose to force the issue with Caesar's commanders stationed to observe them, and these in turn were careful not to provoke a serious fight.[31]

Lead sling bullets have been found at Perusia with messages cast onto them revealing some of the propaganda and vulgar abuse hurled back and forth. Caesar's men mocked Lucius Antonius' baldness, or hoped that their missiles would strike Fulvia's *landica* – an especially crude piece of slang for the clitoris. In spite of the fact that she was not in Perusia, Antony's wife was clearly an object of hatred and mockery. The defenders replied with bullets which claimed to be aimed at Caesar's arse and depicted him as a degraded homosexual who permitted himself to be sodomised by others. Alongside this barrage of abuse there were frequent raids on the besieger's lines. On one occasion Caesar himself was surprised while conducting a sacrifice as army commander and only narrowly escaped being killed. More often the results were less spectacular, and at times a few men managed to break out and escape.[32]

His brother's commanders unable or unwilling to help, Lucius Antonius' food supplies eventually ran out and he surrendered in February 40 BC. Perusia was sacked and went up in flames, although there was doubt over whether the fire was started by the victors or some of the inhabitants. There were probably some executions of leading civilians and perhaps a few of Lucius Antonius' senatorial supporters. Rumour and hostile propaganda soon turned this into another ghastly massacre, with 300 leading citizens being sacrificed to Julius Caesar's spirit – an invention no doubt inspired by Achilles' killing of Trojan prisoners at the funeral of his comrade Patroclus in the *Iliad*. Suetonius claims that pleas for mercy and excuses were met by the young triumvir with a laconic 'He must die' or 'You must die' – *moriendum esse* in Latin. Yet on the whole reprisals were limited. The rebel soldiers were spared, and many no doubt were recruited into Caesar's legions. Lucius Antonius was not only left unharmed, but was sent to govern one of the Spanish provinces. Fulvia had already escaped to join her husband, and Antony's mother had similarly fled abroad, going first to Sextus Pompeius, who then had her conveyed eastwards to her son.[33]

Antony had not intervened in the Perusine War, either to support his brother and wife or to restrain them. By the spring of 40 BC he was on his way back to Italy, accompanied by a strong force of war-ships. No one knew whether this new civil war was truly over, or just beginning.

PART THREE

IMPERATOR CAESAR, *DIVI FILIUS*
38–27 BC

Imperator was the title given to a victorious general, but had never before been used as a permanent name. He became formally 'the son of a god' after the official deification of Julius Caesar in 42 BC, but did not always use the title until later.

9

SONS OF GODS

'Ah, shall I ever, long years hence, look again on my country's bounds, on my humble cottage with its turf-clad roof – shall I, long years hence, look amazed on a few ears of corn, once my kingdom? Is an impious soldier to hold these well-tilled fallows? A barbarian these crops? See where strife has brought our unhappy citizens!' *Virgil, early thirties* BC.[1]

'. . . the great line of centuries begins anew. Now divine Justice re-turns, the reign of Saturn returns; now a new generation descends from heaven on high. Only do you, pure Lucina, smile on the birth of a child, under whom the iron brood shall at last cease and a golden race spring up throughout the world! . . . And in your consulship, Pollio, yes, yours, shall this glorious age begin . . .' *Virgil predicting the start of a new golden age in 40* BC.[2]

At some point in 41 BC, as relations with Fulvia and Lucius An-tonius degenerated, Caesar was inspired to pen a short poem about his mother-in-law and Mark Antony's wife. 'Antony screws Glaphyra, so Fulvia as revenge wants to nail <u>me</u>! What, should I screw Fulvia? What then if Manius pleads with me to bugger him, should I? I don't think so, if I've an ounce of sense. "Either shag or fight," she says. Well, my prick is dearer to me than my very life. Let battle commence!'[3]

The poet Martial quoted these lines over a century later – and so preserved them for posterity – claiming cheekily that if Rome's first emperor could write filthy poetry then so could he. The Latin is especially crude, more than matching anything his soldiers cast into their lead missiles at Perusia. Glaphyra was the well-born mistress of the client ruler of Cappadocia, and became Antony's lover in the hope of convincing him to let her son succeed to the throne as the triumvir reorganised the eastern provinces. (At the time he gave power to someone else, but a few years later the lad was installed as king, so ultimately her efforts were not in vain.) Gossip of their affair had obviously reached Rome months before Antony met Cleopatra and provided a new and plentiful theme. Manius was an important agent of Antony's in Italy, and was later blamed for inflaming the situation and playing a major part in causing the Perusine War.[4]

Even by the standards of Roman political invective these half-dozen lines were crude stuff, the work of a very young man revelling in vulgarity and brimming with bullish self-confidence. In just a few years Caesar had become one of the two most powerful men in the world – within sight of claiming his 'father's' honours and status as supreme in the state. So rapid a rise speaks of immense and highly focused ambition, and of great political skill, but also of luck. Like almost any successful statesman, Caesar was an opportunist. If Julius Caesar had not been murdered his career would have been very different and considerably slower, although perhaps in the end as distinguished. He had the chance to grow in power and gain legitimacy thanks to a Senate led by Cicero, turning himself into an attractive ally for Antony and Lepidus when the leaders of the Senate chose to 'discard' him. There had been failures, such as the first march into Rome, and his ignominious role in the First Battle of Philippi. There had also been a lot of risks. He might have lost the battles, or fallen in action. He had survived two bouts of very serious illness, and faced mobs of angry citizens and mutinous veterans – the latter on one occasion murdering a centurion sent to calm them down and dumping his body in the path of Caesar's entourage to make sure that he saw it. In each case the young Caesar survived, and got what he wanted in the end. The omens reported in ancient sources were often later inventions, but it would have been surprising if the triumvir had not become convinced of his own luck and destiny to win.[5]

Before the Perusine War began, he divorced Claudia. Some claimed the failure to consummate the marriage was a deliberate act, in expectation that the union – and the political alliance it represented – was to be short-lived. Probably this was simply because the girl was so very young, since even the existence of children rarely hindered the ending of a politically inconvenient marriage. Caesar and his commanders defeated Lucius Antonius, helped by the ineffective support offered by Antony's generals. Yet again Caesar had won, and emerged stronger after an apparent setback. Then luck played into his hand once more. In the redistribution of provinces after Philippi, Cisalpine Gaul became part of Italy, and the remaining Gallic provinces were allotted to Antony, who controlled them through his subordinate Quintus Fufius Calenus. In the summer of 40 BC, Calenus fell ill and died, leaving his young son in charge. Caesar – probably marginally, if at all, older – hurried to the province and dragooned the younger Calenus into giving him command of his army. At a stroke eleven legions changed hands.[6]

While he was away, Antony returned to Italy. He had a large fleet of warships, having been joined by Cnaeus Domitius Ahenobarbus, former admiral of Brutus and Cassius. Until recently Ahenobarbus had raided the Italian coast, and when the combined fleet reached Brundisium the garrison recognised his warships and closed the harbour. Antony saw this as deliberate hostility on Caesar's part and besieged the city. Most probably it was a mistake, although in the heated atmosphere created by the Perusine War no doubt the partisans on both sides were nervous. Caesar returned from Gaul and certainly prepared for war, mustering his legions and once again trying to drum up volunteers from the recently settled veterans. Grateful for their land, the response was good, until the word spread that they were to fight Antony and plenty of their former comrades. Some turned back and went home at the news, and those that remained followed reluctantly.[7]

Modern scholars usually see Antony as being in the stronger position. Sextus Pompeius had already approached him and offered alliance against Caesar. Antony's mother Julia fled to Sicily and Sextus' care in the aftermath of the Perusine War. Perhaps she was genuinely afraid, but in truth it is doubtful that she was in any real

danger and more probably this was a public gesture of hostility to
Caesar. He certainly chose to interpret it this way. Sextus welcomed
the fugitive and had her escorted eastwards to meet her son. Antony
was grateful, but for the moment was unwilling to commit himself
firmly to war with his fellow triumvir. There were sound reasons for
such caution. He had spent the winter of 41–40 BC in pleasant leisure
at Cleopatra's capital of Alexandria – and by the time he left she was
pregnant and would in due course give birth to twins, a boy and a
girl. During these months the Parthians invaded Syria, supporting a
Roman force led by Titus Labienus, a diehard Republican who had
missed the Philippi campaign. His father was Julius Caesar's best
legate in Gaul, but chose to fight for Pompey in the Civil War and
killed himself after the defeat at Munda in 45 BC. Exhausted by years
of supplying both sides in Roman civil wars, the eastern provinces
were poorly garrisoned and in no state to resist the attack. Meeting
only feeble resistance, the Parthians took Syria, and then sent smaller
forces to overrun Judaea and much of Asia Minor.[8]

When Antony arrived off Brundisium he had a fleet, but only a
small land army. Some of his commanders still had legions in the
field in Italy and the west, but with the loss of Calenus' legions these
were heavily outnumbered by Caesar's armies. Given the state of
the eastern provinces, it would be difficult and politically damaging to draw troops from there and at best this would take months.
An alliance with Sextus Pompeius offered the prospect of gaining
many more well-crewed warships, but few soldiers. For the moment,
the military advantage was clearly with Caesar whatever the longer-
term balance of power. That did not mean that the outcome of the
war was certain, or that destroying the other was really to either
man's advantage at present.

In the event they were not given the choice. As the rival sides concentrated around Brundisium, veterans of Julius Caesar's campaigns
recognised each other and began to fraternise. At first they joked,
and then the talk became more serious. Officers and men alike were
unwilling to fight against former comrades. This was not the first
time the soldiery had tried to avoid a new war: in the build-up to

the Perusine War they had forced Caesar and Lucius Antonius into last-minute negotiations, although in that case mutual suspicion and misunderstanding provoked a skirmish before the meeting had started and it came to nothing. This time the soldiers were more determined and the rival leaders genuinely eager for compromise.[9]

They did not negotiate in person. Antony was represented by Asinius Pollio, and Caesar by a young equestrian named Caius Maecenas, one of his chief confidants – probably a close contemporary and perhaps one of the youths who was educated with him. Also in attendance was Lucius Coccius Nerva, an experienced senior officer trusted by the army who seems to have been considered a neutral. No one was there to speak on behalf of Lepidus, although he was confirmed as governor of North Africa, a responsibility that came with the command of a modest army by the standards of these years. Caesar kept Gaul and was allotted all of the other western provinces up to Scodra in Illyria. Antony received all of the empire to the east of this. Ahenobarbus and a few others were pardoned. Antony informed Caesar that Salvidienus Rufus, one of his most trusted commanders, had secretly begun negotiations with him. Rufus was arrested and executed, Caesar getting the Senate to pass its ultimate decree to give some legitimacy to the process. Antony in turn executed his agent Manius amid stories that he had forged documents inciting Lucius and Fulvia to rebel in the triumvir's name.[10]

Chance helped the deal along. Fulvia had received the frostiest of welcomes from her husband when she fled to Greece. Exhausted and deeply depressed, she soon fell ill and died, which meant that the chief blame for the recent war could most conveniently be assigned to her. With all the vitriolic propaganda surrounding her, it is now very difficult to judge Fulvia's real character and role fairly, but she was certainly one of the most politically visible women of her generation. Her death also left Antony single once again. By chance Octavia's husband Marcellus had also died during the year and so a marriage was swiftly arranged between Caesar's sister and his newly confirmed ally. Since Roman law decreed a ten-month interval before a widow was supposed to re-marry, Caesar and Antony made a show of seeking priestly rulings to permit the wedding before this time had elapsed, and the decision was duly given in their favour.[11]

Octavia was about thirty and already had a son by Marcellus. Aristocratic women rarely had much choice in their marriages, but in the years to come she did her best to be a good and loyal wife, and indeed at the beginning the couple seem to have been genuinely happy. News of the confirmation of the alliance between Antony and Caesar was well received throughout Italy and Rome itself, principally because it meant that there would not be a renewal of civil war. It was a message that the triumvirs were happy to reinforce. Octavia appeared alongside her husband on coins – the first woman to appear on Roman currency. Asinius Pollio was one of the consuls this year, and the poet Virgil wrote predicting that his magistracy would mark the beginning of a new golden age, augured in by the birth of a wonderful baby boy. Although the child is not named, it is clear that he meant the anticipated offspring of Antony and Octavia. The latter was indeed soon pregnant, although the child proved to be a girl and predictions of peace and widespread prosperity more than a little premature.[12]

Caesar had remarried before the reconciliation. His new bride was Scribonia, some ten years his senior, and already married more than once, but the sister of Sextus Pompeius' father-in-law, Lucius Scribonius Libo. Probably he hoped to increase his chances of dealing with Sextus, although Scribonius Libo was important in his own right and was one of Sextus' leading allies. The new marriage may at the very least have blurred the brothers' loyalties.[13]

THE SON OF NEPTUNE

Sextus Pompeius was far too strong to ignore. He had secured Sicily by 42 BC and in due course occupied Sardinia and Corsica. From these bases his strong and well-manned fleet was able to raid the coasts of Italy and disrupt the trade routes so seriously that food supplies to Italy and especially the metropolis of Rome were running short. Excluded from the peace settlement at Brundisium apart from vague talk of future negotiations, Sextus stepped up his raiding in the months that followed. Sicily provided a lot of the capital's grain supply in normal times. Without this, and with shipments from further afield often intercepted, food prices rose alarmingly and the state struggled to find sufficient quantities for the official dole confirmed by Julius Caesar. Rome, for more than a year the scene of periodic rioting between disgruntled veterans, dispossessed Italian farmers, and the urban poor resenting the presence and demands of both groups, now became even more volatile.[14]

Sextus Pompeius kept up the pressure. He was young, even in an era of young warlords, probably no more than three or four years older than Caesar. Considered too young to serve in the Pharsalus campaign, he had seen his father murdered in Egypt, and then watched his older brother raise an army to fight against Julius Caesar, only to be defeated and killed. Sextus escaped, and began a new rebellion in Spain. Family connections and his own charisma brought rapid success. His men seized or built ships and launched raids over an ever-expanding area of the western Mediterranean. In the spring of 43 BC Cicero convinced the Senate to legitimise the power he had assumed simply because he was the son of Pompey the Great, and Sextus was formally named 'Prefect of the fleet and the Maritime shores' (*praefectus classis et orae maritimae*). The abrupt shift of power at the end of the year turned him from legally appointed magistrate to outlaw as he was condemned by the *lex Pedia* along with the conspirators, even though he had not been involved in the assassination of the dictator. Although mutually hostile to the triumvirs, there was no active co-operation between Sextus and the Liberators – Cassius had earlier expressed a very low opinion of Cnaeus Pompeius and may well have had similar reservations about his brother. Both he and Brutus may also have been uncomfortable with a man who presumed to inherit his father's power.[15]

Like Caesar, Sextus paraded his respect for his father as the basis for his own right to command. Piety (*pietas* in Latin), the honour owed to gods, country and especially parents, was a profound and very Roman duty. Caesar proclaimed his own *pietas* as he avenged his murdered father. Lucius Antonius added the word *Pietas* to his name and rank as consul when he raised rebellion on behalf of his older brother. Sextus Pompeius called himself *Pius*, and then assumed his father's nickname Magnus and so appears on coins simply as the thoroughly unconventional Magnus Pius.[16]

Caesar and Sextus Pompeius were alike in many ways. Depictions of the latter on the face of his coins show him as bearded, a mark of mourning in honour of a dead father and brother. Caesar is shown the same way, even for a few years after he made a great show of shaving to mark the deaths of the Liberators. Yet Sextus followed a father who had been defeated in war and killed as a fugitive rather than murdered at the height of his success. His power was inevitably based away from Italy and drew on his own and his family's prestige rather than the traditional institutions of the state. Caesar was able to work his way into the heart of the state at the centre of the Republic's political life. There was one other great difference which must forever resound to the credit of Sextus. When the proscriptions began he offered sanctuary to all the victims and anyone else fleeing the rule of the triumvirate. His warships cruised the coastlines of Italy ready to rescue fugitives, and Sextus paid double the bounty offered for the heads of the proscribed to anyone who brought them to safety. Hundreds owed their lives to his efforts. Politically this was to his advantage, but even so such actions stand out in stark contrast to the murderousness of these brutal years.[17]

Yet Sextus also cut much of the food supply to Italy and Rome. His strategy was directed against the triumvirs, but inevitably it was the wider population, and especially the poorest, who suffered as a consequence. By the end of 40 BC both Antony and Caesar were in Rome, where they celebrated ovations for the victory in Macedonia. Neither man was popular, and so the crowds blamed them for the shortages because it was felt that they should be negotiating with Sextus. Like the veterans, the bulk of the wider population wanted peace, and, copying the veterans, they staged increasingly violent protests to force their leaders to deliver this. Early in 39 BC Caesar was confronted by an angry mob while he was conducting business in the Forum. Missiles were thrown, and the small entourage he had with him struggled to protect their leader.

Antony came to the rescue, leading a formed body of soldiers along the Via Sacra. At first a crowd blocked his path, without making any hostile moves, for he was seen as more favourably inclined to Sextus. Yet when Antony ordered his soldiers to force their way through, the civilians responded angrily, bombarding his men with stones and driving them back. The troops regrouped and were reinforced. Then they pushed into the Forum itself from two directions, cutting down those who opposed them. Antony's men hacked their way in to rescue Caesar and brought him out, but for some hours the crowd remained in possession of the heart of the City and only gradually dispersed.[18]

Antony and Caesar approached Sextus' mother and other connections and through them were able to begin negotiations in the spring. Trust was in short supply, and so the first meeting was held near the shore at Baiae on the Bay of Naples, the rival leaders and their staffs standing on separate wooden platforms built over the sea. No agreement was reached, but talks were resumed later in the summer at nearby Cape Misenum, and this time met with success. Sextus was once again to be given legitimate power to control his forces. He was enrolled in the Senate and granted as a provincial command Sicily, Sardinia, and Corsica – all of which he controlled – and also the Peloponnese in Greece. Antony, already an augur, oversaw Sextus' admission to this college of priests, and Pompey's son was scheduled to be consul in 33 BC in elections controlled by the triumvirate.

The Treaty of Misenum brought an end to the blockade of Italy, but the gains to Sextus were modest, since in the main it simply confirmed the status quo. However, he insisted that the triumvirs pardon all of the proscribed and others forced into exile and permit them to return to Italy and claim a quarter of their confiscated property. Only the remaining murderers of Julius Caesar and a handful of others were excluded from this amnesty. It is possible that the many aristocrats who had fled to Sicily put pressure on Sextus to make peace in the hope of returning home – it is interesting that Caesar's brother-in-law Scribonius was marked down for the consulship of 34 BC.

Sextus could not return to Rome without giving up command of the navy and its bases and he was just as reluctant to do this as Caesar and Antony would have been to disband all their legions. Only through force did any of the warlords retain importance and the chance of long-term security. Antony had bought at auction Pompey the Great's houses and estates, notably the grand house in the fashionable Carinae on the slopes of the Palatine. The name literally meant keels, and when Sextus entertained Caesar and Antony on his flagship he joked that the keels of his fleet provided him with his only home these days. It was during this feast, following on from ones given onshore by Antony and Caesar, that one of Sextus' admirals is supposed to have said that he could make his commander the master of the world by cutting the cable and disposing of their guests. Sextus was unwilling to order such treachery, and ruefully commented that it would have been better if the admiral had simply acted without consulting him.[19]

THE LOVERS

When the proscribed returned home, Sextus stayed in Sicily, and it is doubtful that he ever formally took control of the Peloponnese. Antony and Octavia travelled east to spend the winter of 39–38 BC in Athens, where he entered into the spirit of Greek city life with great enthusiasm. The Athenians named the couple the 'beneficent gods'; they styled Antony the 'new god Dionysius' and staged a ceremonial marriage between him and Athena, the goddess of the city. Such honours did not prevent him from demanding from the Athenians a new tax in the form of a 'dowry', but perhaps the locals' enthusiastic reception of the triumvir and his wife reduced the amount they might have had to pay. When spring came, Antony formally took off his Greek civilian clothes and dressed again as a Roman commander. His general Ventidius had already driven the Parthian invaders out of the Roman provinces. It would be Antony's great task in the years to come to punish them properly and finally gain vengeance for Crassus.[20]

Caesar remained in Italy, and embarked on a ship-building programme to create a strong navy. The only obvious target for such a force was Sextus, but for a while the fragile peace held, and the mood in Rome was generally cheerful now that food supplies were plentiful once again, and as the exiles came home. One of these was Tiberius Claudius Nero, who had been praetor in 42 BC, and then somewhat quixotically refused to lay down the office at the end of the year. A man of shifting allegiances – he had supported Julius Caesar in the Civil War and then eagerly praised his murderers after the Ides of March – he joined Lucius Antonius during the Perusine War and began raising troops from among those dispossessed by the veteran settlement. When the rebellion failed he was proscribed and followed the familiar path of flight to Sicily, but does not seem to have felt that Sextus Pompeius' reception was sufficiently generous and went from there to Greece. Trouble seems to have followed him for at one point he had to flee from Sparta, and his party got caught up in a forest fire and narrowly escaped harm.[21]

Claudius Nero's wife was a far more remarkable individual in every way than her husband. Her name was Livia, although she was often known by the nickname Drusilla, and she was also a Claudian by blood, descended from the other, far more distinguished branch of the great patrician clan. This heritage was reinforced when her father was adopted by Marcus Livius Drusus, scion of one of the oldest and most important families of plebeian aristocrats. Livius Drusus served as tribune of the plebs in 91 BC, championing the cause of Rome's Italian allies. He was murdered, and soon afterwards the allies rebelled in the Social War, forcing the Republic to start granting them Roman citizenship as they tried to control the crisis. Many remembered the tribune with great fondness. Livia's father was proscribed, fought with the Liberators, and took his own life after Philippi. By this time his daughter was already married, and in November 42 BC presented her husband with a son, whom they named Tiberius Claudius Nero.[22]

When the husband rebelled, his wife – aged about seventeen – journeyed to join him. She followed him during the rebellion and into exile, avoiding pursuers and living rough. Twice the infant Tiberius' crying was said to have threatened to give them away. In their escape from Sparta, Livia's hair and dress were scorched by the flames. When the family returned to Rome they were short of money, like many finding it difficult to recover even the quarter share of confiscated property promised to them as part of the Treaty of Misenum. They arranged for Tiberius to be adopted by a wealthy senator eager for a connection with an ancient patrician clan. Politically this may not have been an astute move. Not long before, the man's brother was suspected of plotting against Caesar. He was arrested and then died in somewhat mysterious circumstances.[23]

Livia's aristocratic pedigree was impeccable both through blood and adoption. She was also young and very attractive. Her mind was extremely sharp – much later her great-grandson the Emperor Caligula dubbed her *Ulixes stolatus*, or 'Ulysses in a frock' – and cleverness and wit no doubt reinforced her natural beauty. In January 38 BC she would present her husband with a second son, so that she must already have been a few months into this new pregnancy when she returned to Rome. This did not prevent her from catching the eye of Caesar, perhaps even at the feast he arranged on or close to his twenty-fourth birthday to celebrate the shaving-off of his beard.[24]

Caesar's year of self-imposed celibacy was a distant memory. Scribonia was pregnant and late in 39 BC gave birth to a daughter – inevitably named Julia – but the political convenience of that marriage was no longer so acute and the couple do not seem to have been at all close. The husband enthusiastically pursued other women. Antony viewed such things indulgently for the moment. In later years Caesar's friends excused his womanising by claiming that he often seduced senators' wives to find out what their husbands were thinking and doing. Antony later spread a story of Caesar 'hustling the wife of an ex-consul from the dining room into a bedroom in front of his very eyes, and returning her to the dinner with dishevelled hair and blushing to the ears'. In spite of her condition, Livia Drusilla soon became his latest lover, but this was more than a quick fling or a piece of political espionage.[25]

Caesar fell in love with both her beauty and her mind and Livia probably returned the love with enthusiasm. She is unlikely to have been much impressed by her husband's career so far or his future prospects. Power is famously an aphrodisiac, and the young Caesar's spectacular rise had given him great power and confirmed his immense self-satisfaction and confidence. Her aristocratic background and connections were valuable politically, but this was a long-term advantage and there was no immediate political gain sufficient to justify the scandal of the bizarre episode that followed. It makes sense only in the context of a Caesar used to getting his own way in everything, and of lovers utterly determined to do what they want without delay. Caesar was still just twenty-four and Livia not yet twenty. It may even be that she feared waiting in case her lover's fickle attention wandered.[26]

Caesar divorced Scribonia as soon as she had given birth to Julia. At the most basic level a Roman husband had only to utter the phrase 'take your things for yourself' (*tuas res tibi habeto*) to separate from his wife. In this case Caesar added as reason that he could 'no longer stand her bitter personality' and it is impossible to know whether this was true or simply a piece of gratuitous spite. Claudius Nero obligingly divorced Livia and around the beginning of October 39 BC Caesar and Livia were betrothed. A ruling was sought about this from the college of pontiffs to which he belonged, and seems to have involved the official confirmation that Livia was pregnant and Claudius Nero the father, firmly establishing paternity. This did not prevent rumours from circulating that the child was Caesar's, and there was a joke about how a lucky a couple was to have a child in just three months; but since he must have been conceived while Claudius Nero and Livia were in Greece this is impossible. For the moment Livia moved to live in Caesar's house as his betrothed, and it was there on 14 January 38 BC that she was delivered of a baby boy, Drusus Claudius Nero. The boy was sent to his father to be raised.[27]

On 17 January Caesar and Livia married, a mere three days after she had given birth. The bride's father was dead, and she seems to have had few close male relatives, and so her former husband accompanied her at the ceremony. It was a grand occasion, and the banquet that followed had an Olympian theme with the six men and six women attending all dressed as Greek gods and goddesses. Caesar took on the role of Apollo. Food and drink were on an extravagant scale, as the young couple revelled in their wealth and power. It was the fashion at the time for aristocratic ladies to be attended by *deliciae*, scantily dressed slave boys – perhaps on this occasion appearing as cupids – who whispered biting comments about those around them. The humour was acidic, camp, often crude, and was enjoyed by the sophisticated. In this case, one boy is supposed to have pointed at Claudius Nero reclining on the other side of the table and said to Livia, 'Why are you over here, lady, when your husband is over there?'

In later years critics spoke of Caesar abducting another man's wife – just the sort of thing tyrants were supposed to do. They exaggerated in the way of political abuse, for Claudius Nero was compliant, although admittedly he probably had little choice in the matter. It is difficult to believe that Livia was not an enthusiastic participant who agreed to, and perhaps even suggested, the rapid marriage. At the time, food was again running short in Rome, and the rumoured splendour of what was dubbed the 'feast of the twelve gods' was widely resented. People said that Caesar was Apollo indeed, but Apollo the Tormentor, one of the less pleasant aspects of the god. A rhyme circulated which spoke of 'Caesar playing the false role of Apollo and feasting amid novel debaucheries of the gods; then shall all the deities turn their faces from the earth and Jupiter himself fled from his golden throne.'[28]

IMPERATOR

Food was short in Rome because of renewed friction with Sextus Pompeius. Piratical raids had occurred, and Caesar claimed that captured raiders revealed under torture that they were sent by Sextus. Whether or not this was true – and it is possible that Pompeius was unable to control all of the men drawn to his cause – Caesar believed that he was fully prepared to fight and win a naval war. One of Pompeius' trusted admirals, a freedman named Menas, had defected to Caesar, bringing with him some ships and giving him control of Corsica and Sardinia. In the civil wars of these years there was great emphasis on mass, on simply fielding more legions than the opposition. There was also a well-entrenched Roman belief that throwing numbers and resources at a problem ought to bring success. Few Roman commanders, including Julius Caesar, fully adapted their thinking to see naval warfare as fundamentally different to warfare on land, and his heir was no different. There is every sign of complacency and a lack of respect for the unpredictability and power of the sea in the plans for the invasion of Sicily in 38 BC.[29]

The western coast of Italy lacks natural harbours all the way from the Straits of Messana (modern Messina) up to the Bay of Naples. This, combined with the ability of Sextus' men to raid any port within range of their bases on the islands, meant that the forces had to be prepared a considerable distance away from their objectives. The plan was for the two Caesarean fleets to unite at sea and co-ordinate their attack on Sicily, but this never happened and instead they fought separately. The ships were new, their crews inexperienced, and their commanders just as raw, with the exception of Menas. Sextus' experienced squadrons came off the better in the clash with one of the Caesarean fleets, and heavily defeated the other. The weather then finished the job. Exceptionally bad storms, even for the unpredictable seas off the west coast of Italy, blew up. Menas' ships knew how to cope, but most of the other captains had no idea what to do and their ships were dashed to pieces on the shore. By the next day Caesar was left with less than half of his fleet and the campaign was over. There were riots in Rome, and Maecenas was sent to calm the situation, but there was little that could be done about the food shortages.[30]

Sextus could barely believe his good fortune, for the bad weather had come at just the right moment. Later he took to wearing a sea-blue cloak and calling himself the son of Neptune. Caesar is supposed to have boasted that he would have the victory in spite of Neptune, and ordered that statues of the sea god were not to be carried in the procession at the next games in Rome. Most Romans blamed the triumvir rather than the god for the shortages of food and an unnecessary and disastrous war. Knowing that Caesar was addicted to dice games and gambling, some wag came up with the following verse around this time: 'When he has twice been beaten in sea battles and lost his fleet, then he plays with dice – hoping he can win one victory!'[31]

Caesar had asked Antony to come to Brundisium for a meeting at the start of the summer, but then failed to turn up as arranged. Antony grew tired of waiting and sailed back to the east. After the disasters of the summer Caesar sent Maecenas to him, and eventually a fresh conference was arranged and was held at Tarentum in 37 BC. Antony came with an escort of 300 warships, and as part of the new deal loaned 120 of these to his brother-in-law. The latter promised to send him soldiers for his Parthian War. Octavia was believed to have helped the negotiations, persuading her husband to add an additional ten small ships, while her brother gave Antony 1,000 elite praetorian guardsmen. More formally the triumvirate was renewed, since the five years of office originally given to them by law in 43 BC had now elapsed. The details of this constitutional façade elude modern scholars, and may well have been a little vague at the time, for there was no real precedent for such extended power. Antyllus, Antony's ten-year-old son by Fulvia, was betrothed to Caesar's infant daughter Julia to provide the now almost routine marriage bond to round off the deal.[32]

A new war was planned against Sextus, and all of 37 BC and the first half of the next year was spent in preparations. In charge was Agrippa, the old friend and contemporary who had been with

Caesar at Apollonia in 44 BC, and seems to have served him ever since in increasingly senior roles. He had missed the first conflict with Sextus because he had been in Gaul, where he suppressed a rebellion in Aquitania and emulated Julius Caesar by bridging the Rhine and leading an expedition against the German tribes. Skill and competence, whether as a general, engineer or administrator, would be the hallmark of Agrippa throughout his life, combined with absolute loyalty to Caesar and a studied modesty. Justifiably awarded a triumph, he chose not to celebrate it rather than highlight the failures of his chief. Instead he oversaw the creation of a new, more powerful fleet. Behind Cumae on the Bay of Naples he excavated a canal connecting Lake Avernus via a smaller lake to the sea, providing an extensive port and a safe expanse of water for training the crews.

Teams of rowers began practising on land, sitting in specially constructed tiers of seats to simulate the inside of a warship. Many of these men were former slaves, given their freedom in return for serving – one of the rare occasions when slaves were enlisted. The Hollywood image of galley slaves chained to their oars is a myth, and warships were always crewed by free and salaried sailors and rowers. The warships themselves were built to be large and strong, their decks covered to protect the rowers, and many were equipped with a new type of collapsible tower so that missiles could be flung or shot down onto the enemy vessels. There was also a secret weapon called the *harpax*, a hook with rope attached fired by catapult and intended to stick hard into an enemy vessel, grappling it so that it could be held fast and boarded.[33]

Sextus was also busy, and the opposing sides now each mustered more than 300 ships, each warlord hoping to overwhelm the enemy. Some of the problems were the same as in 38 BC, for Caesar's fleets had had to be prepared in separate places and his three-pronged attack on Sicily was difficult to co-ordinate when the campaign began at the start of July. Once again Neptune seemed ill-disposed, and Agrippa lost ships to bad weather. At the first attempt only Lepidus, crossing from North Africa, was able to land legions on the island, and even then a convoy of reinforcements was intercepted and destroyed by the enemy.

Agrippa won a battle off Cape Mylae – his large, heavily constructed ships proving difficult for the more manoeuvrable but smaller enemy warships to damage. Soon afterwards, Caesar was in turn beaten by Sextus off Tauromenium (modern Taormina), losing most of his ships and having to flee ashore. For a while he was attended by only a single bodyguard and was close to exhaustion by the time they met friendly forces. Yet over the days to come more and more soldiers were landed on Sicily until there were some twenty-one legions and supporting troops on the island. The Pompeians severely harassed a few of these detachments, but lacked the numbers and determination to destroy any of them. The odds were turning ever more decisively against them, as Sextus' bases were besieged and taken one by one. He was left with little choice but to fight a major fleet action.

On 3 September the battle was fought off Naulochus – there is even a chance that the time and location were mutually agreed before the battle. Agrippa commanded from his flagship, while Caesar watched from the shore. It was said that he had fallen into an exhausted sleep and could only be woken with difficulty so that he could give the signal to engage. Antony later taunted him with falling into a terrified stupor and being unable even to look at the enemy, let alone fight them. His presence proved unnecessary. Agrippa's growing skill as an admiral and his bigger ships crewed by newly confident and experienced men smashed the enemy fleet, destroying most of it as the Pompeians tried to flee. Caesar rewarded him with a special blue flag or *vexillum* and a newly created gold crown shaped like the prows of warships, the *corona navalis*.[34]

Caesar had won again, although the war with Sextus Pompeius had proved one of the sternest trials of his life. It was fortunate that Pompeius always lacked the land forces to carry the war to Italy for he never acquired the good recruiting grounds to raise many legions. Caesar took risks in this conflict, and suffered heavily when things went wrong. It is interesting that several stories are preserved of his personal escapades, and narrow avoidance of death – very similar in flavour to the tales of the escapes of victims of the proscriptions that clearly captured the Romans' imagination. Most of these probably derive from his memoirs, suggesting a style very different to Julius Caesar's dispassionate accounts of his campaigns, where little is said of the general's exploits. The genre was different, but more importantly the dictator was modestly telling stories of his own victories. His heir instead had to shed a personally heroic light on his failures and the battles won by his subordinates. Shrewd enough by 36 BC to admit that he needed to rely on the talents of men like Agrippa to do the actual fighting, he was skilful in securing the main credit for himself and painting his own involvement in the most exciting light possible.

RIVALS

'Wars, both civil and foreign, I undertook throughout the world, on sea and land, and when victorious I spared all citizens who sued for pardon.' *Deeds of the Divine Augustus.*[1]

'At last he broke off his alliance with Mark Antony, which was always doubtful and uncertain, and with difficulty kept alive by various reconciliations; and better to show that his rival had fallen away from conduct becoming a citizen, he had the will which Antony had left in Rome, naming his children by Cleopatra among his heirs, opened and read before the people.' *Suetonius, early second century* AD.[2]

C aesar was given an opportunity for fresh heroism almost immediately, this time at the expense of an ally. The capture of Sicily had given Lepidus an important role for the first time in years. Understandably resentful at his marginalisation since Philippi, the oldest member of the triumvirate now expected to regain some of his lost power. Bypassing Caesar's generals on the island, Lepidus arranged for the strongest Pompeian army to surrender to him and serve under his command, increasing his army to more than twenty legions – a prestigious total even if many were greatly understrength. He let the former Pompeians join his own men as they sacked Messana in an effort to win their goodwill. His own soldiers may have been less enthusiastic to share the spoils with recent enemies, but obeyed orders. For the moment Lepidus felt strong, and was determined to add Sicily to his African provinces and retain control of his enlarged army. There were angry exchanges with Caesar and his local commanders as he asserted his right to command on the island, and his troops were drawn away to camp on their own.

Legions were the ultimate basis of power in these years, and a man with a strong and loyal army could not be ignored. Yet loyalty was often negotiable, and Caesar's agents were soon at work among the soldiers, just as they had once courted the *Fourth* and *Martia* at Brundisium in 43 BC.

Imperator Caesar followed, riding at the head of his cavalry. He left these outside, and boldly went into the camp accompanied by just a few officers and guards. There was an echo of Julius Caesar's ice-cool confrontation of the mutinous *Tenth*, when he broke their spirits by calling them *quirites* – citizens or civilians – rather than the usual *commilitones* – comrades or fellow soldiers. His heir lacked something of the dictator's charisma and had no long association with the men he now faced. The latter were mainly strangers, some until very recently enemies, although no doubt there were a few officers who had served under Julius Caesar and perhaps this helped. Lepidus and those loyal to him tried to stop the bold young commander. Caesar was jostled, and narrowly missed by a javelin aimed at him, but he and his party were not massacred as they must surely have been if Lepidus' army had been at all determined.

Caesar spoke to the soldiers, urging them to join him. He personally grabbed a legionary eagle – just as he had done at Mutina – and began to march out of camp trusting that the men of that unit would follow. Some did, and some of these were standard-bearers themselves who in turn led more men with them. It was not an instant defection. For the moment the bulk of the troops were unsure what to do. The arrival of more of Caesar's men outside their camp may have helped many to make up their minds. More important was Lepidus' failure to ignite their passion on his behalf, and his soldiers left him – at first in dribs and drabs, and finally en masse. The abandoned commander took off his armour and military cloak and went to surrender clad in the civilian toga.

Julius Caesar paraded his clemency, but the triumvirs had openly followed a different path. Now his heir decided it was both practical and worthwhile to emulate his 'father'. Lepidus was expelled from the triumvirate and stripped of all power, but his life was spared and he was sent to live in comfortable captivity in Italy. Caesar's legal right to do this was unclear and in the conditions of these years unimportant. Lepidus remained *pontifex maximus* until his death many years later. He was spared because he presented no danger. There was a hint of cruelty within the judgement – made worse because for Roman aristocrats the admission that someone else possessed the power to decide their fate was a humiliation in itself – and over the years Caesar would occasionally bring Lepidus to Rome to take part in a ceremony or meeting of the Senate. Even so, this was still far more mercy than had been granted to the proscribed. Lepidus lived to a ripe old age.[3]

Sextus Pompeius was not so fortunate. With his few remaining ships and men he sailed east, preferring to deal with Antony rather than with Caesar. That was not unreasonable, and his initial welcome was encouraging, until he sensed a chance to revive his fortunes and negotiate from more strength and so began raising a new army. One of Antony's commanders quickly defeated him and soon afterwards had Sextus executed. It was unclear even at the time whether or not his death was on Antony's orders.[4]

The triumvir – for thus he continued to style himself even if now there were only two members of the board – had greater problems than the fate of Pompey the Great's son. In the summer of 36 BC, Mark Antony had finally launched the great attack on Parthia, intended to restore the Roman pride humbled by the defeat of Crassus and the more recent invasion of the eastern provinces. Caesar had failed to send his colleague the soldiers promised the year before, but even so Antony's forces were extremely large – with some fifteen to eighteen legions, supported by auxiliaries and strong allied contingents provided by client rulers. An exuberant Plutarch later claimed that rulers as far away as India trembled at the news of this mighty horde.[5]

Yet Antony was no Alexander the Great, and neither were the Parthians as ready to collapse as the Persians had been in the fourth century BC. A deception plan achieved little at great cost of valuable time, and then impatience led him to leave his slow-moving siege and baggage train behind with inadequate guard. The mobile Parthians promptly pounced and wiped them out, so that Antony's main column was stranded deep in enemy territory without equipment or much food as winter approached. The treachery of his Armenian allies made the situation worse, but the mistakes were Antony's alone. With no choice save retreat, the Romans withdrew and were mercilessly harried by the Parthians for four long weeks. Antony showed personal courage, and his men often fought bravely, but during one night-time panic in the Roman camp he despaired and contemplated suicide. Only the news that it was a false alarm prevented him from acting. In fact, the enemy soon afterwards gave up the pursuit, and the Roman army eventually made its way to safety. At least a quarter of the legionaries never returned; the losses were even higher among the camp-followers and allies, and inevitably higher still among the cavalry mounts and transport animals. The survivors are unlikely to have been in good health after their ordeal and would take time to recover. Fortunately for Antony, the Parthians were not inclined to launch a counter-invasion. He would be in no state to repeat his own attack for many years, if ever.

A great success in Parthia would have brought Antony military glory to match any Roman leader living or dead, and plunder to surpass Caesar or any other rival. Instead he failed utterly. Many modern scholars have underplayed the importance of this disaster, impressed because Antony did not lose his entire army and life. Hindsight tells us that the Romans would never conquer the Parthians – or indeed their Persian successors – but the Romans themselves did not know this and were not prone to doubts about their ultimate success. The greatest service to the Republic was to defeat a foreign enemy. Antony presented himself as a great soldier – as Hercules the great hero, and often as Dionysius who in the east was god of victory as well as wine. It is more than likely that he believed his own propaganda. As we have seen, in fact he had limited military experience, less still of high command, and the bulk of his previous campaigns had been civil wars. Antony's failure should not surprise us so very much. To him it was astounding, and personally and politically devastating.[6]

GLORY AND PROMISE

Imperator Caesar's unorthodox name proclaimed him to be a victorious commander and this was constantly reinforced by his propaganda. By this time he was aware of his limited personal talent as a general, and willing to rely heavily on gifted subordinates like Agrippa. At the end of 36 BC the defeat of Sextus was unequivocal, and contrasted strongly with the confused reports from the east as Antony made a futile effort to present his defeat as something more like success. Caesar returned to Rome and held an ovation to commemorate the victory in Sicily. Celebrating success in civil war was now almost as routine as it had once been taboo, but the enemy was also branded as a pirate and leader of runaway slaves to make his defeat more clearly deserved and certainly for the good of the state. Caesar's use of thousands of slaves freed solely to serve in his own fleet was conveniently ignored, and any former slave found among the prisoners returned to his owner. Some 6,000 captives whose owners were not speedily located were executed – most probably in a deliberate evocation of the mass crucifixion of the same number of survivors from Spartacus' slave army by Crassus in 71 BC. The Senate voted Caesar the honour of placing an heroically nude statue of himself atop a column decorated with the prows of warships. It stood in the Forum, next to a similar monument commemorating Rome's first great naval victory, also fought at Mylae, but in 260 BC against the formidable navy of Carthage.[7]

It did no harm to evoke memories of past victories over dangerous foreign enemies. It was better yet to win new victories in person, and so for the next three years Caesar spent the bulk of his time campaigning against the tribal peoples in and outside the province of Illyricum. Julius Caesar had planned a Balkan campaign as a prelude to his Parthian expedition. Two of the dictator's subordinate commanders had suffered defeats in the region during the forties, losing a number of the precious military standards in the process. The losses were small compared to those suffered at the hands of the Parthians, who had taken from Crassus and now Antony a far more impressive collection of trophies; nevertheless, Illyria offered the chance to avenge former defeats and recapture symbols of lost Roman pride.

In 35 BC Caesar operated in the north, driving as far as Segesta on the River Sava (modern-day Sisak in Croatia) and installing a garrison of two and a half legions to winter there. It is possible that he was contemplating a major expedition towards the Danube and Dacia, whose king had been seen as a real threat in recent years, and was most probably the ultimate target of Julius Caesar's planned offensive. If the idea was now considered, it was swiftly abandoned, at least for the moment. In 34 BC the focus was more to the south in Dalmatia. These were operations against many small tribes and clans – Caesar would list no fewer than thirty different peoples when he reported to the Senate at the end of these campaigns. The terrain was difficult, and in the past more than one Roman army had found itself bottled up, with the enemy holding all the passes into and out of the high-sided valleys. Caesar campaigned with care, sending flanking detachments along the tops of the hills on either side – a practice known on the North-West Frontier of India in the nineteenth century as crowning the heights. The aim was the same in the first century BC. Any enemy trying to attack the main column on the valley floor would in turn be charged from uphill by the Roman flankers. There were no pitched battles, but plenty of raids and ambushes, and many sieges of the tribes' hilltop strongholds.[8]

Once again there was an emphasis on Imperator Caesar's personal exploits in accounts which must surely go back to his own memoirs. At the siege of Metulus – a small place, scarcely a household name even in Roman times and now impossible to locate – he began by watching the main assault from the vantage point of a high tower. His soldiers had constructed a ramp facing the enemy wall, but not quite reaching it. On top of this were four drawbridges to drop onto the enemy rampart so that the Romans could reach it. The defenders fought fiercely and first one, then a second and finally a third bridge

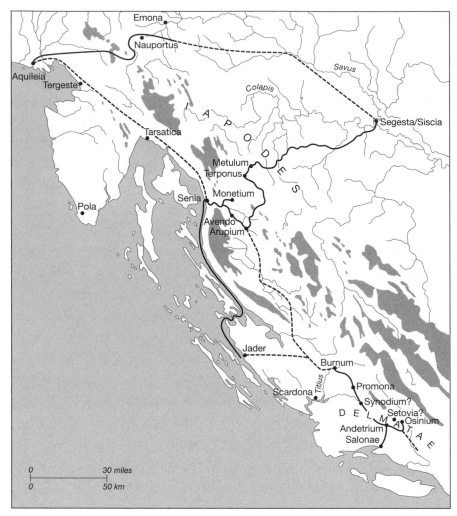

Augustus' campaigns in Illyricum, 35–33 BC

was toppled or fell under the shifting weight of the attackers, so that the legionaries grew understandably reluctant to set foot on the last remaining crossing.

Caesar hurried down from his observation post and shouted at his men, urging them to advance. When this failed, he decided to set a personal example, grabbed a shield from a soldier – something famously done by Julius Caesar in another moment of crisis – and rushed onto the last remaining bridge, accompanied only by Agrippa and some other members of his staff. Inspired or shamed, a flood of legionaries followed them – too many in fact, for their combined weight caused the bridge to collapse into the deep hollow between the ramp and wall. Some of the attackers were killed by the fall, and Caesar was lucky to escape with injuries to his right leg and both arms. He quickly went – presumably with more than a little assistance – back up to the top of the observation tower, so that the army would see that he survived and was still able to command (and in future years reward his soldiers). Legionaries were set to build new drawbridges so that the assault would be renewed. Dismayed by such stubborn – and very Roman – determination, Metulus surrendered soon afterwards.[9]

A year later, in fighting outside another obscure stronghold, Imperator Caesar was wounded in the knee by a stone – whether thrown or flung by a sling is unclear – and left unable to walk for a few days. These operations were fairly small-scale, but the fighting itself could be both serious and difficult. At another siege one cohort panicked and fled when the enemy launched a night-time sally. Caesar ordered their decimation, one man in ten being beaten to death and the remainder symbolically shamed by receiving barley – the food for animals and slaves – instead of wheat as their ration for the remainder of the campaign. More unusually, we are told that two centurions were also executed. Since there were at most six of these officers in a cohort, this suggests that they were held chiefly responsible. Antony decimated one of his cohorts in 36 BC after a similar panic in Armenia, and we hear of another general doing the same in Spain during these years. It was a traditional punishment, but in recent generations a rare one, seen as a piece of almost archaic sternness.[10]

Imperator Caesar clearly wanted to be seen as a great Roman general in the traditional mould, just like his murdered father. More than anything else, such leaders were expected to be successful, and even if his Illyrian campaigns were less important than Antony's struggle with the Parthians, they ended in victory and not failure. Caesar returned to Rome in the summer of 33 BC bringing spoils captured from defeated and suppliant enemies and, best of all, Roman standards

lost in earlier defeats. These were displayed in the newly rebuilt Porticus of Octavia. The Senate readily awarded him a triumph to add
to his two ovations, although he decided to defer this for celebration
at a later date. The world had changed a lot since Julius Caesar had
been faced with the choice between remaining outside Rome until
he had triumphed, or giving up the honour and entering the City so
that he could stand for the consulship. His heir came and went as he
pleased, with no change whatsoever to his power.[11]

He had returned on several occasions during the Illyrian campaigns, and on 1 January 33 BC became consul for the second time.
It was almost a decade since his first consulship, but as Caesar was
still only twenty-nine such conventions no longer had any significance. He resigned the magistracy before the day was out, allowing
him to appoint an immediate replacement. Antony had done the
same thing the previous year, and had not even left his provinces
to come to Rome to assume the post. The triumvirs far surpassed
Julius Caesar's casual treatment of Rome's senior magistracies. No
pair of consuls served for a full year any more, instead resigning
and allowing replacement or suffect consuls to assume their places.
These in turn might resign to give other men their chance, and there
were no fewer than six suffect consuls in 33 BC, although that in turn
was nothing compared to the sixty-seven praetors appointed back
in 38 BC, all of whom served simultaneously. Each gained the permanent distinction of having held the rank, with the corresponding
rights to precedence in senatorial meetings.[12]

Similar generosity was extended to triumphs, and several senior
commanders of both Caesar and Antony celebrated them during the
thirties BC – there were six in 34–33 BC alone. Many chose to create
permanent memorials to their victory by building or restoring major
monuments in the City. Asinius Pollio triumphed in 39 BC and proceeded to restore the Hall of Liberty used by the censors, adding to
it a public library with Greek books in one wing and Latin works in
the other. It was the first such library opened in Rome, since Julius
Caesar's planned project had been abandoned after his death. Titus
Statilius Taurus triumphed in 34 BC and began work on Rome's

first stone amphitheatre; in the past temporary seating was used, often built against the side of large public buildings. In the same year Caius Sosius celebrated his triumph for the recapture of Jerusalem and the restoration of Herod the Great to power in Judaea, and chose to construct a temple to Apollo – subsequently known after him as Apollo Sosianus (and visible today near the Theatre of Marcellus).[13]

Victories over foreign enemies were properly Roman things to celebrate. It is a mistake to look at these ceremonies and their accompanying building projects as a competition between the supporters of Antony and those of Caesar. Each of these men was a proud Roman in his own right, and even in an age when two triumvirs divided rule of the Republic and its provinces between them they did not lead fixed parties. If anything, the successes of Antony's lieutenants highlighted his own failure just as much as the triumphs of men associated with Caesar. More important was the feeling that wars were now being fought against real enemies and not fellow Romans. Construction work in the heart of Rome itself added to the City's bustling mood, encouraging optimism even before the amenities were finished. It also brought paid work to many, whether craftsmen or labourers, and good business to the suppliers of materials.

Imperator Caesar continued the construction of many of the dictator's grand projects, most notably his Forum with the rebuilt Senate House and new temple to Venus as its centrepieces. However spectacular other individual monuments were, none could match the collective grandeur and sheer scale of the projects he was building. In 33 BC Agrippa assumed the office of aedile – a magistracy rather neglected as the triumvirs' supporters were lavished with more senior posts. It was an extraordinary choice for a former consul – he had held that supreme magistracy in 37 BC – although perhaps we should remember that in the past it would have been extraordinary indeed to have a former consul who was barely thirty. The young man who had campaigned in Gaul, driven Sextus Pompeius from the seas, and been last seen with Caesar leading the charge over the precarious drawbridge at Metelus threw himself into the task of supervising the City's public amenities with all his accustomed energy and competence.[14]

A new aqueduct, the Aqua Julia – as usual the chief credit for Agrippa's efforts was tactfully given to his chief – was constructed, and others heavily restored or repaired. It was not just a question of grand building: good access to flowing water was provided throughout Rome, with 700 new cisterns, 500 fountain-heads, and 130 water towers. The sewers were surveyed, repaired and improved. It is possible to grab the popular attention while performing necessary but mundane tasks, and people long remembered how the spectacular aedile was rowed in a boat along the length of the Cloaca Maxima, Rome's main sewer. As well as such practical amenities, Agrippa treated the City to fifty-nine days of games, where prizes were distributed to the crowd, and arranged 170 times when the public baths were free, also providing barbers to shave citizens free of charge. The aesthetic was not neglected. Many of his fountains were decorated with statues or columns, and there were grand displays of art collections in public parks.

Life in Rome was made more comfortable for everyone, not simply the wealthy. Conditions in Italy were at the same time beginning to feel more stable after the chaotic years of civil war, proscriptions, land confiscations and colonisation. Imperator Caesar was guilty of all these things and many hated him accordingly. Yet now they appeared to have stopped, and no one wanted to return to those days. Few were inclined to love him, but there was gratitude for the return of internal peace and growing confidence that this might last. Some may have sensed that there was one more act left to play, for no one knew when or how Antony would return.

ACTIAN APOLLO

It is now time to speak of Cleopatra, and readers may be surprised that she has appeared so little up to this point. For all her fame and great appeal as a romantic figure, a symbol of the east, or as an independent woman in a male-dominated world, the simple truth is that she had little power and importance in a Mediterranean world overwhelmingly dominated by Rome. Cleopatra was one of many client rulers, ultimately dependent on Roman backing to remain in power and protect them from rivals. Julius Caesar restored her to power and disposed of her brother and co-ruler Ptolemy XIII. Cleopatra made two visits to Rome during the dictator's lifetime, no doubt concerned that the wandering eye of her lover did not make his support for her weaken. The idea that he installed her as permanent mistress, and was guided by her in his policies, is a modern myth. Their child, nicknamed Ptolemy Caesarion, came with his mother, but was not a citizen or legitimate and had no real significance in Roman politics. After the Ides of March, Cleopatra lingered in Rome for almost a month, doing her best to secure recognition from whatever new regime emerged now that the dictator was dead. Other client rulers and states were doing the same thing in person or via agents, and one faction was lobbying to give some or all of her realm to her sister, Arsinoe. Cicero mentions Cleopatra in an often-quoted passage, but her handful of brief appearances in his vast correspondence is a clearer indication of her overall lack of importance. When the queen returned to her realm, she promptly murdered her second brother, Ptolemy XIV, made co-ruler by Julius Caesar, and replaced him as king with Caesarion. An infant son was far easier to control than a teenage brother.[15]

Cleopatra and Antony became lovers in the autumn and winter of 41–40 BC. He left her pregnant and secure on the throne, and obligingly had Arsinoe killed, removing the last real adult rival to her rule – at least until her own children were old enough to be viable alternatives. The couple did not see each other again for three and a half years, and Antony married Octavia and had two daughters with her. In the winter of 37–36 BC he brought Cleopatra to Antioch, saw their twin children – a boy, Alexander Helios, and a girl, Cleopatra Selene, the sun and the moon – and renewed the affair while arranging for Egyptian grain to help feed his army and silver to pay them. By the time he set out for the Parthian expedition, the queen was pregnant once again. She gave birth to a boy, Ptolemy Philadelphus, before Antony returned in failure from the war. After summoning his lover to come and console him in a minor city on the coast of what is now Lebanon, the lovers were rarely apart for any length of time.[16]

In 35 BC Octavia travelled to Athens, bringing a contingent of elite praetorians, some cavalry and mundane but vital baggage animals to replace those lost by her husband. Antony took the supplies, but did not go to see her and sent instructions for her to return to Rome. Octavia had never journeyed further than Greece when she accompanied him in previous years, and it was not normal for a magistrate to take his wife to his province, let alone on campaign. Yet nor was it normal to keep a royal mistress so very publicly. Caesar was quick to contrast the curt rejection of an honourable, Roman wife with Antony's shameful parading of Cleopatra. Some wondered whether he had inspired the whole episode, encouraging his sister to go in order to make Antony look bad. There was certainly already a barely veiled cooling in the relationship between the two remaining triumvirs.[17]

Caesar was able to visit Rome during these years. Antony could not. Octavia continued to act as a dutiful wife, welcoming men who came from her husband and doing her best to gain them offices and honours. Yet in the main she had to go to her brother to secure these. It was said that she refused his suggestion that she separate from her husband, and instead continued to speak on his behalf. Caesar gained at least some of the credit for every favour done to Antony's men, and was in a far better position than Antony to win new supporters by his generosity, simply because he was in or near Italy. Concessions to victims of land confiscations now seemed like kindness rather than the mere mitigation of former harsh and arbitrary use of power. Caesar was successful in his Illyrian wars, Sextus Pompeius' blockade for ever broken and his threat removed, and Rome and Italy moving to something close to a normal, stable existence. On the spot, more honours came to Caesar than to his distant colleague. Late in 36 BC his person was made sacrosanct as if he were one of the tribunes of the plebs, but in his case this privilege was permanent and not simply held for a year of office. A year later, the same honour was given to both Octavia and Livia, who were also granted statues in their honour and the legal right to conduct their own financial affairs free from guardians. The person of Caesar was to be special, and so were his close family.[18]

In 34 BC Antony took the field again, capturing through subterfuge his former ally, the king of Armenia. It was a success of sorts, but little to set against the failure of his attack on Parthia. Returning to Alexandria, he staged a grand victory procession, the king walking in gold (or, in another source, silver) chains with other royal captives, followed by a chariot in which Antony was dressed as Dionysius. The culmination was his reception by Cleopatra, seated on a throne perched atop an ornately decorated platform. The whole thing smacked too much of a Roman triumph, but played out in a foreign city and not in Rome, and for the benefit of a foreign queen rather than citizens. Whatever the truth, Caesar and his allies happily portrayed it as such.[19]

Later in the year Antony and Cleopatra presided at another ceremony, celebrated in the spectacularly lavish style beloved of the Ptolemies. The so-called 'Donations of Alexandria' confirmed the queen's power and that of Caesarion as her co-ruler, and granted large swathes of the eastern provinces to the couple's three children – Alexander Helios was given Parthia and Media, neither of which were under Antony's or Rome's control. Cleopatra was named 'Queen of kings, whose sons are kings', and no doubt this was intended to confirm her rule and her dominance over her children, the oldest now a teenager, which would soon make him a potential rival. There was no actual change to the administration of the east, and it is hard to know what Antony intended as the truth swiftly became buried under a mass of hostile propaganda. Antony's closest allies suppressed his own report of the event because it was so damaging.[20]

Criticism of Antony grew steadily – if not from Caesar himself then from those close to him. Antony was in thrall to a sinister eastern queen and her decadent courtiers. A poem written by Horace a few years later captured the mood of this criticism:

'The shame of it! A Roman enslaved to a woman (you future generations will refuse to believe it) carries a stake and weapons, and in spite of being a soldier can bear to serve a lot of shrivelled eunuchs, while the sun gazes down on the degenerate mosquito net among the army's standards.'[21]

Antony was depicted as a drunk, perhaps even drugged or controlled by magic potions given to him by Cleopatra. He had ceased to behave like a Roman, or remember that he was a servant of the Republic. The contrast with Caesar, victorious, working for the good of the state, celebrated by the Senate and People of Rome, and living with his Roman wife, was emphasised at every turn. Antony claimed descent from Hercules, and so the story of the demigod being duped by Omphale into wearing a dress and spinning wool, while she carried his club and wore his lion skin, was revived in literature and art.[22]

The exchange was not one-sided. Antony wrote an open letter, attacking Caesar for his double standards in criticising the affair with Cleopatra: 'Why have you changed? Is it because I'm screwing the queen? Is she my wife? *(Of course not!)* Have I just started this or has it been going on for nine years? How about you – is it only *(Livia)* Drusilla you screw? Congratulations, if when you read this letter you have not been inside Tertulla or Terentilla, Rufilla or Salvia Titiseniam, or all of them. Does it really matter where or in whom you dip your wick?'[23]

Caesar's womanising was well known, but it was one thing to have numerous affairs with Romans and quite another to appear tied to one foreign mistress. Cleopatra was a Greek, and the Romans had a complex relationship of admiration mingled with a sense of their own cultural inferiority and contempt for a conquered people. Worse, she was ruler of Egypt, and there were plenty of ancient stereotypes of Egyptian barbarians with their animal-headed gods. Caesar and his allies had plenty of material with which to work. Antony's own conduct did little to help his cause. In his only published work, entitled *On His Drunkenness (de sua ebrietate)*, he defended himself against criticism of his drinking, perhaps by implying that he was never incapacitated or under the influence while performing official duties – we cannot know the details as the work has not survived. Simply having to justify his conduct showed that the damage had been done.[24]

Antony attacked more than he defended, and the mud slung on both sides was well within the tradition of Roman political invective and rarely troubled by any concern for the truth. The slurs of Caesar's conduct at Philippi were revived, and reinforced with stories of his defeat by Sextus Pompey and apparent cowardice. Caesar was a vile degenerate, who had prostituted himself to Julius Caesar to gain the dictator's favour. Since then, he had planned to wed the infant Julia to the king of some tiny Illyrian tribe, and even considered marrying the king's daughter – surely more damning than any dalliance with Cleopatra and it did not matter if it was not true. The aristocratic Antony naturally returned to his contempt for the obscurity of his rival's real – rather than adopted – family. It was only at this late stage that Caesarion began to assume some importance. This was not in his own right, but simply because a natural son of Julius Caesar showed that the self-proclaimed Imperator Caesar, son of the god, was no blood descendant at all. Caesar commissioned Oppius, one of the dictator's old subordinates, to write a pamphlet 'proving' that Caesarion was not the dictator's child at all. Antony replied by claiming that he had heard Julius Caesar acknowledge the boy.[25]

It is easy to blame Caesar entirely for the slide into conflict. He ultimately won, and therefore is readily seen as the driving force behind events, but in truth both of the triumvirs were jealous of power and neither showed much reluctance for a final confrontation. In the summer of 33 BC Antony's legions were concentrated on the Euphrates. Any thought of another attack on Parthia was swiftly abandoned, if it was ever seriously contemplated, and instead he ordered them to begin the long march of more than 1,000 miles to the coast of Asia Minor. The only possible enemy to the west was Caesar.[26]

Two of Antony's senior subordinates, Cnaeus Domitius Ahenobarbus – former admiral of Brutus and Cassius – and Caius Sosius
became consuls on 1 January 32 BC. The renewed five-year term of
the triumvirate had probably expired at the end of the previous
year, leaving Caesar and Antony with command of armies and provinces in spite of their lack of formal power. Domitius Ahenobarbus
praised Antony, and criticised Caesar indirectly. Sosius followed up
with a bitter personal attack, and presented a motion to the Senate
condemning Caesar which was blocked by a tribune's veto before a
vote could be taken. Tactfully absent from meetings up to this point,
at the next session Caesar arrived escorted by troops, and accompanied by friends who took care to reveal that they were carrying
'concealed' daggers. Whether or not he still held any legal *imperium*,
he calmly sat on his chair between the two consuls to show his *de
facto* power. Ahenobarbus and Sosius took the hint and left Rome,
travelling unmolested to meet Antony in Greece. Some others began
to follow them.[27]

Not all the traffic was one-way. Soon afterwards the former consul
Lucius Munatius Plancus arrived in Rome, along with his nephew,
Marcus Titius, consul designate for the next year and the man who
had actually ordered the execution of Sextus Pompeius. Plancus had
an unenviable reputation as a turncoat, but his decision was seen as
an indication of the way the wind was blowing. Until recently he
was an active participant in the revels of Antony and Cleopatra. It
was he who held the stakes when she famously bet her lover that she
would present them with the most expensive of meals, and declared
the queen the winner when she dissolved a fabulously expensive
pearl earring in wine and swallowed it. There was a story that he
had played the part of the sea god Glaukon at another feast with an
Olympian theme, and the former consul donned an artificial fishtail,
painted his skin and danced in the nude. Now he had abandoned
Antony. As one cynical senator put it, 'Antony must have done a
great many things to make you leave him!'[28]

Munatius Plancus had knowledge to trade as well as his simple
presence. As a witness to Antony's will, he was aware of the

damaging nature of some of its clauses. The document was stored in the Temple of Vesta in Rome, and although the Chief Vestal Virgin refused to hand over the will, Caesar went in and took it, having extracts read out at a public meeting in the Forum. The contents – or at least those Caesar chose to reveal – were inflammatory. Antony formally acknowledged Caesarion as Julius Caesar's son – an odd thing to include in his will – and gave legacies to his own children by Cleopatra. There must also have been proper legacies to his legitimate Roman children, but that was ignored. More damning was his wish that his body be interred in Alexandria with Cleopatra, even if he should die in Italy.[29]

None of our ancient sources suggest that the will was a forgery and they were surely right. Instead Caesar carefully distorted and worsened the impression made by an already embarrassing document which should never have been made public. His own behaviour was in deliberate contrast. Only thirty, he had already begun work on an immense tomb for himself and his family. Aristocratic monuments had in the past been intended to promote the glory of their families and to be noticed, but this project dwarfed anything that had gone before. It soon became known as the Mausoleum, after the famous tomb of the Carian king Mausolos, one of the Seven Wonders of the World.

Three hundred Roman feet in diameter, with a forty-foot-high wall topped in a dome-shaped mound and with a colossal statue of Caesar at its crown, the scale was blatantly monarchic, once again emphasising that Imperator Caesar was different from other men. Even more importantly it was in Rome, although on the Campus Martius outside the formal boundary of the City, as befitted a tomb. Caesar was a Roman through and through, and unlike Antony had no thought of being interred anywhere save in Rome itself. Rumours spread that the latter wanted to move the capital to Alexandria – matching an earlier rumour that Julius Caesar had planned the same thing. Another tale claimed that Cleopatra's favourite oath was 'as surely as I will dispense justice on the Capitol'; it did not matter that the stories conflicted, for the message was that Antony took her orders and no longer had Rome's interests at heart.[30]

Cleopatra was the enemy. That was the constant theme of the propaganda campaign, because it was easier for people to pretend that they fought a foreign threat to Rome than that yet another civil war between rival Roman warlords was about to break out. Ostensibly it was not to be a choice between Caesar and Antony, but a rallying cry to protect Rome. All of Italy – *tota Italia* – took an oath to serve under Caesar's leadership in this war in a carefully managed gesture of solidarity. Colonies of Antony's veterans were given the freedom to refuse if they chose, although very few took up this offer, and none at all showed any inclination to muster to fight for him. Some senators – perhaps numbering in hundreds – fled to join Antony, and modern historians tend to be impressed by this. Some were under obligation to him, and perhaps others simply judged him most likely to win, or were desperate enough to hope for revolution. The last few surviving conspirators rallied to Antony since they had little prospect of welcome by Julius Caesar's heir. Caesar boasted that over 700 senators took an oath to serve under his command, and even if this was a generous estimate it was still by far the majority of the senatorial order. A few remained openly neutral, the most famous being Asinius Pollio, who commented that he would 'stand apart from your quarrel and be a spoil of the victor'.[31]

In the summer of 32 BC Caesar led the Roman Republic as it formally declared war on Cleopatra. In the distant past, the college of priests known as *fetiales* oversaw the declaration of war and peace. Archaic ritual was revived – or just possibly invented in a plausibly traditional guise – so that Caesar could preside as a fetial in a sacrifice made in the Temple of Bellona, god of war. A spear was dipped in the victim's blood, grievances recited, and then the spear was flung into a patch of earth symbolically representative of Cleopatra's Egyptian kingdom.[32]

Antony's army and fleet were already mustering on Greece's western coast. It was too late in the season for either side to strike, but it seems that Antony's plan was to wait and fight the war in Greece. It was the same plan adopted unsuccessfully by Pompey in 48 BC, and

Brutus and Cassius in 42 BC. Yet Sulla was the only Roman based in Greece ever to win a civil war, and he did so by crossing to Italy and fighting the war there. Antony was relying on the sheer size of his armies and fleet, and trusting that the enemy would make a mistake and be crushed. Like other recent wars, this one would be fought on an immense scale. Cleopatra was at Antony's side, and her presence caused friction with some of his senior subordinates. It would certainly have been deeply damaging had he crossed to Italy, and perhaps this was one more reason why he was reluctant to do so. The result was to hand the initiative over to the enemy.[33]

Agrippa began the attack – and it was probably he who masterminded the entire campaign and certainly led at all the key moments, systematically smashing Antony's cause. In a series of lightning attacks he raided and destroyed several of Antony's bases, threatening his supply lines. As the enemy reeled from these blows, Caesar – consul for the third time in this year – himself sailed with the main army and landed in Epirus, occupying a town called Torone or 'ladle'. Cleopatra joked that they should not worry if Caesar 'sat on a ladle' – the word was a slang term for penis – but the truth was that the enemy was across the Adriatic and Antony had not yet concentrated sufficient of his forces to face them. Caesar closed on Antony's main base at Actium on the Gulf of Ambracia, beginning a blockade that was soon pressed by land and sea. From the end of spring throughout the summer Antony's men failed to break this stranglehold or draw the enemy into a battle on their own terms. All the while their ranks were thinned by disease, for their camp lay in an unhealthy spot, and malaria and dysentery were rife. Caesar's men watched and waited as their enemy grew weaker and as the months passed the Caesareans won numerous small victories, on one occasion coming close to taking Antony himself. Deserters – some of them ordinary soldiers or auxiliaries, and others senators like Domitius Ahenobarbus – slipped quietly away from Antony's camp to be welcomed by Caesar. No one went in the other direction.[34]

On 2 September 31 BC Antony's fleet sailed out to challenge the enemy. At least some of the vessels carried masts and sails on their

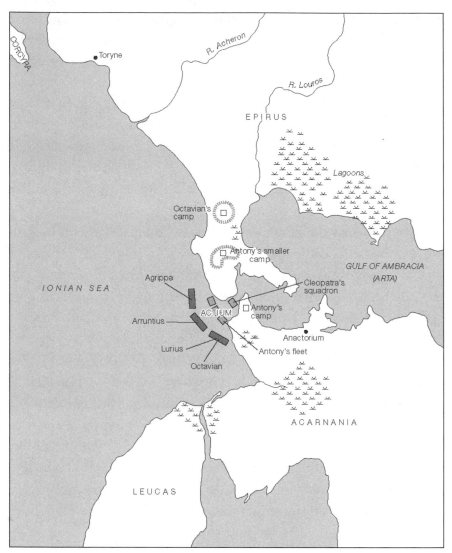

The Battle of Actium

decks, when it was normal to dispense with these cumbersome objects for battle. Warships manoeuvred exclusively by rowing when fighting, and the decision is a clear sign that Antony contemplated breaking out with some or all of the fleet. Perhaps he still hoped to change his fortunes by winning a naval battle, but was also planning for failure – scarcely an optimistic frame of mind for a commander. It took hours for the fleets to form in battle lines, and then more time passed as they faced each other, neither side wanting to fight too close inshore. When Antony's men eventually resumed their advance, Agrippa had his ships back water for some distance to give more sea room. Then they tried to outflank the enemy – Caesar's fleet was probably a little more numerous, and its captains and crews were certainly far more skilful after the bitter war against Sextus Pompey. Both fleets included many big warships, and when the fighting began it proved hard to cripple these with ramming. Instead, much of the fighting was with missiles and by grappling and boarding the enemy. As individual ships manoeuvred for advantage, the neat lines broke up and gaps appeared.

Taking advantage of the wind from the north-north-west, which usually picks up as the day goes on, Cleopatra and a squadron of ships under her command suddenly hoisted their sails and came from behind the main fleet to sail right for a big gap opened in the centre of the battle. Ignoring the fighting warships, they kept going, while Antony left his flagship and caught up with them in a lighter vessel. Some seventy to eighty ships escaped, carrying with them a good deal of Cleopatra's treasury, but this represented at most a quarter of the fleet and probably less. The rest were left to fight, and some of them continued to do so with great determination. Eventually, the survivors withdrew sullenly back into the harbour. Antony's fleet had lost some 5,000 men and a number of ships. Antony himself had lost the war, even if he and his lover had escaped with much of their money. His legions resisted the attempts of his commander, Publius Canidius, to march them away. Instead they negotiated a good deal before defecting to join Caesar. The remnants of the fleet surrendered with them.[35]

Antony survived, but all the money in the world would not buy him an army and navy to replace the ones he had lost, nor repair the damage to his reputation. A Roman aristocrat should never admit defeat, and certainly should not abandon his men to flee with his mistress. Caesar had more immediate problems than hunting down his rival. He had left Maecenas to control Italy and Rome itself – a job the latter performed with subtlety and skill, in spite of the fact that he remained an equestrian with no official office and had not

become a senator. Now there was pressure from time-served legionaries for immediate demobilisation and instant delivery of the
bounties and farms promised to them. Former Antonians added to
his own men in pressing for their rewards. It was no simple task to
supervise the movements and partial demobilisation of some forty
legions. Agrippa was sent to help deal with the problem, and Caesar
himself followed before the end of the year. Faced with threats of
mutiny or rebellion, he made generous promises. On the other hand
he wanted to avoid a return to the upheaval which had fed rebellion
at the time of the Perusine War. No land in Italy was to be found
through confiscation, which meant that money was needed to fund
purchases. Caesar headed east again, looking for plentiful supplies
of hard coin.[36]

The enthusiasm of the many client rulers and communities now
wishing to transfer their loyalty from Antony to him helped to provide what he needed. All were happy to pay to convince him of their
loyalty. Cleopatra approached him with the same hope in mind. In
spite of his propaganda she had always been a loyal ally of Rome,
and would no doubt exploit her subjects just as enthusiastically
for his benefit as she had in the past for Julius Caesar and Antony.
Antony could not be saved, and whatever her feelings for him, Cleopatra was a survivor who had reached the age of thirty-nine in spite
of the murderous competition among her family and court and
the repeated power struggles at Rome. Caesar cynically offered her
some encouragement, and perhaps she incited defections among her
forces as his legions pressed into Egypt.[37]

Antony decided to commit suicide, aping Brutus and Cassius
and so many aristocrats of his generation. Cleopatra may well have
engineered his death, but her lover did not do the job cleanly and
lived long enough for one last emotional reunion. For more than
a week the queen lived on, hoping to make a deal with Caesar. His
envoys managed to trick her out of the tomb – filled with her movable wealth and piled high with combustible material so that she
could threaten to destroy it. We do not know whether the young
Caesar and Cleopatra had met during her visits to Rome. Otherwise

their only face-to-face encounter came now, as she pleaded with the victor. The details vary in our accounts, but there is no reason not to believe that she did everything she could to win his pity and sympathy – dressing to look like a suppliant without hiding her beauty, and invoking her deep love for Julius Caesar and the latter's affection for her.

It was not to be. She had become too great a rallying cry during the build-up to war to be left in power, and the same was true of her children. Caesar needed her treasury to fund the new round of veteran settlement. He would have liked her as an ornament for his triumph, but it was hard to know how the Roman plebs would react to a woman marching in the procession – when Julius Caesar had included a teenage Arsinoe in his Egyptian triumph the crowd had shown sympathy for her – and this was far from vital. Probably, he did give orders for the queen to be kept alive, and sent for physicians and specialists in dealing with snake venom when she was found to have taken her own life. Yet a dead Cleopatra was almost as useful as a live one, and her effigy could be carried in his triumph with no risk that it would win sympathy. Caesar had her money, and would keep her kingdom as a largely private possession, with revenue going to his personal funds.[38]

Caesarion was betrayed by his tutor and executed as an embarrassment. Antony's oldest son Antyllus was also caught and killed. Both had gone through coming-of-age ceremonies just a few months before and so were formally adults, and this was probably enough to ensure their deaths. A few of Antony's key Roman supporters took their own lives or were killed, but most managed the transition to the new regime. Cleopatra's subjects were expected to pay heavy taxes, but that had been their fate under her regime and the rule of her family. Priests came and offered a voluntary contribution if they were allowed to maintain the queen's images on their temples. It was a sign less of affection than of reluctance to damage the buildings and of their enthusiasm to be seen as loyal to their new master. Caesar addressed an assembly of Alexandrians via an interpreter, conscious that his Greek was not as highly polished as it might be.

His life so far had been unusual in almost every way, and he had not had time to train in rhetoric as Cicero, Julius Caesar, Antony and most young aristocrats had done.[39]

At the end of 30 BC Caesar was thirty-three years old and for the moment had no serious rival for mastery of Rome and the entire Mediterranean world.

TRIUMPH

'When the killing of Brutus and Cassius had disarmed the state; when [*Sextus*] Pompeius had been crushed in Sicily, and with Lepidus thrown aside and Antony slain, even the Julian party was leaderless but for Caesar.' *Tacitus, early second century AD.*[1]

'Wars, both civil and foreign, I undertook throughout the world, on sea and land, and when victorious I spared all citizens who sued for pardon . . . Twice I triumphed with an ovation, and thrice I celebrated curule triumphs, and was saluted as imperator twenty-one times.' *Deeds of the Divine Augustus.*[2]

Nunc est bibendum sang the poet Horace on hearing the news that Cleopatra was dead – 'Now let the drinking begin! Now let us thump the ground with unfettered feet! Now is the time, my friends, to load the couches of the gods with a feast fit for the Salii.' Not too long before, the queen had threatened Italy – 'a woman so out of control that she could hope for anything at all, drunk, as she was, on the sweet wine of success'. Thankfully her success had proved short-lived when she fled from her burning fleet at Actium, and 'Caesar pursued her as she flew away from Italy . . . like a hawk after a gentle dove or a speedy hunter after a hare . . .' Yet the queen 'showed no womanly fear of the sword . . . She had the strength of mind to gaze on her ruined palace with calm countenance, and the courage to handle the sharp-toothed serpents, letting her body drink in their black venom . . . She would not be stripped of her royalty and conveyed to face a jeering triumph: no humble woman she.'[3]

Now defeated and dead, a once-feared enemy was easier to admire, and Cleopatra's courage and dignity in death added lustre to Caesar's victory. Yet it was not her suicide in itself, but the victorious end to the war that really mattered and brought the poet such joy. Elsewhere he had written of Antony 'enslaved' to the Egyptian queen, and Horace and everyone else knew that this had been another civil war. Most of the men left behind to perish in the burning ships at Actium were Romans. The war had been declared against Cleopatra, and the poets like everyone else spoke again and again of Antony's eastern allies, but they did not hide the fact that the triumvir had led the enemy. This was yet another civil war, if a just one, as Virgil made clear a few years later:

> On one side Augustus Caesar stands on the lofty stern, leading Italians to strife, with Senate and People, the gods of the households and the state . . . and on his head dawns his father's star . . . On the other side comes Antony with barbaric might . . . bringing in his train Egypt and the strength of the East . . . and there follows him (oh the shame of it!) his Egyptian wife . . . In the midst the queen calls on her hosts with their native sistrum [a rattle used in the cult of the Egyptian goddess Isis] . . . Monstrous gods of every form and barking Anubis wield weapons against Neptune and Venus and Minerva.[4]

This Actium was a victory for the virtues and traditions of a united Italy supported by wholesome deities and led by the son of the divine Julius. The enemy were the chaotic forces of the east with their weird gods – the jackal-headed Anubis, god of the underworld, is singled out even though Cleopatra and her Greek ancestors showed no real interest in such ancient cults. The right side had won an overwhelming and necessary victory, glorious because it brought the promise of peace.[5]

Virgil, Horace and the other poets had seen enough of civil war, which brought only slaughter and the theft of land and property. In the *Epodes*, a collection of poems published in 29 BC, but written in the preceding years as tension grew between Caesar and Antony, Horace was stirred by fear of a new struggle pitting Roman against Roman: 'Where, where are you rushing in this evil madness? Why are you drawing swords that have only just been sheathed? Has too little Latin blood been shed on land and sea – not to enable the Roman to burn the arrogant stronghold of jealous Carthage, or to make the Briton, so long beyond our reach, walk down the Via Sacra in chains, but to ensure in answer to the Parthians' prayers this city shall perish by its own hand?'[6]

Around the same time Horace lamented that 'another generation is crushed by civil war, and this city collapses under its own power!' Neither Italian enemies, the slave army of Spartacus, nor Hannibal and his Carthaginians had managed to defeat Rome, but now it 'will be destroyed by us, an unholy generation whose blood is accursed'. In spite of such dire warnings, the poet concludes that there is no choice but to fight, and gives a rallying cry for all Italians to join in the war.[7]

Men like Horace craved peace, but not at any price. For the Romans, true peace was the product of victory, ideally so complete that the same enemy need never be fought again. Julius Caesar had happily written of 'pacifying' (the Latin verb is *pacare*) the tribes he conquered in Gaul. Conflicts ended with absolute victory, the Romans dictating the terms, and not in compromise and conces-sion. The same attitude had spilled into the Romans' civil wars and left little chance that they could be settled by negotiation, at least in the long run. Horace had fought and fled at Philippi and knew something of real warfare. It is unclear whether or not he obeyed his own call to arms and took part in the Actium campaign. He spoke of following his patron Maecenas in a warship, but since it is un-clear whether the latter ever left the shores of Italy it makes it all the harder to know whether or not Horace actually did join the fleet in his desire for victory to bring an end to civil war.[8]

The poets reflected an almost universal desire for a return to peace and stability after so many long years of upheaval and violence. Ideology had played only a small role in these conflicts. Brutus and Cassius claimed to be fighting for liberty, but behaved no differently from the other warlords of the era. As importantly, they had lost and died. The last conspirators died as partisans of Antony, fighting for one triumvir against another. Such dramatic changes of allegiance were common at all levels. The vast majority of people now hoped only to survive with their lives and property intact. Men remembered how readily the young Caesar had condemned prisoners to death after Philippi or Perusia, but the truth was that far more were spared than died. In later years it was said that many of his closest friends and allies had followed Antony against him but managed to change sides before or after Actium.[9]

The 'liberty' of the conspirators no longer held so deep an 'attraction' even to the aristocrats who hoped to enjoy it. Its appeal would revive to be cherished as a romantic dream by senators like the historian Tacitus, who lived under the rule of emperors and never let nostalgia for the 'free' politics of earlier centuries alter their acceptance of this reality. He at least had few illusions about the brutality of the final decades of the 'free' Republic. In 30 BC no one could have had any illusions at all about this because too many had died for choosing the wrong side or no side at all.[10]

The Republic had been wracked by violence and disorder since the Social War and then Sulla's march on Rome, events still on the edge of living memory, and in Caesar's own lifetime the blood-letting had been even more savage and prolonged. No one could remember a period when politics had been free of the threat or reality of violence. It is easy to concentrate solely on the great aristocratic houses, and the casualties among these had been appalling, but the same was also true of the less prestigious lines which had long bolstered the numbers of the Senate. So much conflict and death had battered their political ideals, dislocated old ties of friendship and alliance, and even curbed the aristocrats' instinctive ambition. The senators, like the rest of the population, wanted peace more than they wanted anything else.

News of Antony's death was read out in a meeting of the Senate presided over by the suffect consul Marcus Tullius Cicero. Only son and namesake of the famous orator, the younger Cicero had fought for Pompey against Julius Caesar at Pharsalus, for Brutus against the triumvirs at Philippi, and subsequently joined Sextus Pompeius.

He had returned to Rome in 39 BC when the proscribed were pardoned, and had subsequently found sufficient favour with Caesar to
be named as a replacement when the consuls of 30 BC stepped down
from their office. He was only thirty-five, but such things meant little
during these years. One of the other consuls of that year was the
similarly youthful Marcus Licinius Crassus, the grandson of Julius
Caesar's ally, the Crassus who had led his army to disaster at Carrhae
in 53 BC. Until recently the grandson was a supporter of Antony, but
had managed to switch allegiance successfully. Both he and Cicero
went on to govern provinces, and Crassus fought a highly successful
war during his spell as governor of Macedonia. The old names were
returning, but it was not quite business as usual. Caesar was consul
for the fourth time in 30 BC and for the fifth time in 29 BC.

It was ironic that Cicero was there to hear of the suicide of the
man who had ordered his father's death. Caesar had agreed to the
order, but Antony was more widely blamed in this case, and it was
certainly he who had ordered the public display of the orator's severed head and hand. The news of Actium had prompted the Senate
to award Caesar a triumph, and now the death of Antony and Cleopatra and the occupation of Egypt moved them to give him another.
These were just a few of the honours showered on the absent victor.
Rams taken from Antonian ships were to be erected as trophies in
several key locations in the Forum, and an arch was to be built in further celebration of the victory, also commemorated by new festivals.
Caesar was inserted into the prayers of all Rome's priesthoods as
well as the Vestal Virgins, while even at private meals a libation was
to be poured in his name. The readiness with which this last, surely
unenforceable, custom became established is another indication of
the desperate longing for peace and the hope that Caesar would provide it.[11]

Other votes granted the victor new powers, including some form
of judicial responsibilities. Caesar refused some of the honours
awarded to him, and was said to cherish most of all a ritual performed
on 11 January 29 BC. This involved the small, arch-like Temple of
Janus Geminus in the Forum. This ancient god of the door and gate

was depicted with two faces, one looking forwards and the other backwards, and was associated with beginnings of things, so that he was often invoked when the year began in January. The narrow ends of the temple took the form of bronze doors, which were left open whenever the state was at war. Since the Romans were nearly always fighting someone, somewhere, the doors had not been closed for many years.

Now the Senate ordered a ceremony in which the temple was formally shut as a sign that Caesar's victories had at last restored peace. They announced that a ritual known as the *augurium salutis* was to be held, although this may not have occurred until 28 BC. It was performed only in times of peace, and sought favourable signs from the gods that it was appropriate to make prayers for the safety of the Roman people. Both rituals, rather like the fetial rite used to declare war on Egypt, were archaic, perhaps partly invented, at least in the details of the ceremonies. Yet this added to the sense of connection with the distant past, a time of Roman prosperity and success untainted by civil war.[12]

Senators shared the overwhelming majority's desire for peace, so much so that they conveniently ignored ongoing campaigns in Gaul and Spain when they ordered the rituals to be performed. If there was a good share of sycophancy in the votes of these and all the other honours showered on Caesar – just as there had been when the Senate deluged Julius Caesar with awards – there was a genuine hope for stability. The idea of one man holding supreme power could not be as shocking in 29 BC as it had been almost twenty years before when Julius Caesar had defeated Pompey. Then many aristocrats had found the dictator's dominance intolerable. Julius Caesar's peace following his final victory in Spain in 45 BC had proved short-lived, as had subsequent periods of hope in 40 and 36 BC. If the longing for stability was far stronger than in the past, so was the knowledge that it might prove fleeting. So much depended on the young Caesar and what he would do. For the moment he remained in the east, and would not return to Italy until late summer 29 BC. All the senators and the rest of the population could do was wait and hope.

THE VICTOR

It is worth pausing to consider what sort of man the young Caesar now was. So far we have followed his career, tracing his rise to supremacy. His ambition was clear from the start, and his political skill – along with a fair degree of the good luck the Romans felt was vital to any successful man – was also obvious. It is a mistake to exaggerate this into a perfect sense of political pragmatism, or assume that he was always the great and successful statesman he would become, his ideas fixed at an early age. Caesar had made mistakes, but had also shown a willingness to learn from them. As always with the ancient world, it is easier to say what he did than it is to understand the man's inner thoughts and character.

There are some glimpses of the man behind the politician, and surely the most interesting is the indecently hurried marriage to Livia. Some of this betrays the impatience of a youth who had risen so rapidly to wield great power. Yet the marriage endured for the remainder of his long life. At some point, most probably in the thirties BC, Livia became pregnant. The child was stillborn, and perhaps the birth was a difficult or unusually dangerous one. For whatever reason the couple never had any children and it is more than possible that she never again fell pregnant. The rumours that Caesar pursued numerous affairs with other women, some allegedly selected for him by his wife, may or may not be an indication that he found most or all of his physical pleasure elsewhere. Roman senators routinely married several times, divorcing wives when they ceased to be convenient. Yet Caesar did not divorce Livia, and there was no political necessity preventing this. Her family associations were good, but not so important that divorce would have damaged him, and other women were as well connected. Instead it speaks of a continuing deep love, as well as mutual respect and reliance. There was more to Caesar than simple political pragmatism, and we would do well to remember this when we trace the life of his wider family.[13]

He had shown passion of another sort in the obvious pleasure he had taken in issuing death sentences back in the days of the proscriptions and the victories at Philippi and Perusia. Caesar was aware that he was prone to outbursts of angry severity. One of his tutors, the Greek teacher of rhetoric Athenodorus, gave this advice: 'When you are angry, recite the alphabet before you speak.' It was said that Maecenas was almost the only one able to soften his friend when he was in such a mood, and Dio tells a story to illustrate this: 'Maecenas once came upon him as he was holding court, and seeing that he was on the point of condemning many people to death, he attempted to push his way through the bystanders and get near him. When he was unable to do this, he wrote on a tablet, "Pray rise at last, executioner!"'

He threw the note into his friend's lap, prompting Caesar to close the court without imposing any sentences. Dio tells us that Caesar was very grateful for Maecenas' frankness in pointing out that his anger was about to cause him to make a mistake. This was earlier in his career, and the victories over Sextus Pompeius and Antony were marked with a far greater willingness to spare his enemies, following the *clementia* of Julius Caesar. It was perhaps a sign of a mellowing disposition, although as yet no one could know whether or not the change would prove permanent.[14]

For all his rapid and violent rise to power, the young Caesar remained in many ways typical of his class. Some scholars like to see him as mixing the sensibilities of being born into the local gentry with the tastes of the senatorial elite, but this remains largely conjecture and we should admit that it is often hard to know the moral, spiritual and political attitudes of anyone outside the Senate. It is clear that he shared the literary interests of most of the Roman elite, dabbling in poetry – if at times of a very bawdy nature – and reading widely both Latin and Greek works.[15]

During the thirties BC, if not before, he regularly corresponded with Atticus, Cicero's schoolfellow and lifelong friend. A biography written shortly after Atticus' death claims that even when in Rome, if not able to visit in person, Caesar wrote to him almost every day 'now asking some question about ancient history, now putting before him some difficult passage in the poets, sometimes in jesting fashion trying to induce him to write longer letters'. Such themes were common topics of conversation among the aristocracy. Atticus, although he had chosen not to embark on a political career and remained an equestrian, was extremely wealthy and even better connected, having managed to be on good terms with almost all the key figures in public life. Avoiding politics made him a rare survivor of the generation born around the turn of the century. Pompey and Julius Caesar had written to him regularly, as had Brutus. Close to the conspirators, he had nevertheless aided and protected Antony's wife Fulvia when he was condemned in 44–43 BC. Later a grateful Antony saved him from the proscriptions, and also corresponded with him. Atticus was well established and widely admired, and friendship with him was no doubt a subtle mark of status, but that is not to say the interest was not genuine on both sides. Agrippa married Atticus' daughter in what was surely a good match and certainly a clear sign of closeness to Caesar. The marriage produced a daughter, Vipsania, who as an infant was betrothed to Livia's older son Tiberius.[16]

Atticus wrote several works, including a celebration of Cicero's consulship in 63 BC, but more famous was his *Liber Annalis*, a chronological history, primarily of Rome. He had a deep interest in the distant past, the origins of institutions, rituals and practices, and the achievements of past generations. He and Cicero were sometimes shocked by the ignorance of their contemporaries about the careers and offices of even their own ancestors. A fascination with the past was common at this time, both for its own sake and perhaps as an escape from the turbulence of the first century BC. The most industrious scholar to explore such things in these years was the polymath Marcus Terentius Varro, although like Atticus' works most of his books have perished. The Romans had not begun to write history until the turn of the third to second centuries BC, and although there were some records of earlier times these were frequently confusing and incomplete. Thus when Julius Caesar claimed to ape the long-sleeved tunic and boots of the kings of ancient Alba Longa, no one could know with certainty whether or not there was any real basis for such styles.[17]

His heir appears to have had a deep interest in Rome's traditions from a young age. There is no reason to doubt that this was not genuine, even if it was a useful enthusiasm for cultivating Atticus' friendship – and no doubt that of many other similarly inclined aristocrats. Politically it could be advantageous, although it is hard to say whether such things as the revival of the fetial ritual were inspired by his interests and genuine enthusiasm or were useful symbols that these interests made it easier to adopt. Atticus suggested another means of showing a worthy respect for tradition when he encouraged Caesar to restore the Temple of Jupiter Feretrius. The young warlord himself went into the semi-ruined building, examining the relics housed there, some claimed to be many centuries old.[18]

Atticus died in Rome in 32 BC, not quite surviving to see the end of civil war. Seriously ill, he decided to starve himself to death and perished at the grand old age of seventy-seven. This meant that he avoided having to choose between Caesar and Antony in the civil war, although no doubt his age and accustomed skill for such things would have allowed him to survive the war and retain the friendship of the victors without losing that of the surviving losers. Agrippa visited him in the last days, and although his funeral was simple it was attended by all of the *boni*. We do not know whether Caesar was present, but it is certainly probable if he was in Rome at the time.[19]

Respect for history and tradition represented a softer side to Caesar's character, albeit one that could be turned to political advantage. It offered little guide to his likely behaviour when he at last returned to Rome. For the moment there could be no doubt about his overwhelming military might. By 30 BC Caesar commanded around sixty legions, more even than Julius Caesar at the height of his power. In the immediate future there was nothing to stop him from doing as he wished, and so the Senate and everyone else praised him and hoped for peace. The prayers and offerings for his health may well have been genuine. Should he succumb to one of the bouts of illness that periodically afflicted him, then the result would surely be more chaos as new leaders appeared and fought to fill the resulting power vacuum. Whether or not they liked him, everyone knew that the future depended for the moment on Caesar, and so they waited for him to come back and reveal his plans.

RETURN

The wait proved a long one, and it was a whole year after the suicides of Antony and Cleopatra before Caesar returned to Italy. He remained in Egypt for several months, for there was much to do there. Money was the most pressing need, its importance brought home by the disturbances among the legions in Italy in the months after Actium. Caesar intended to give his own men – and those of Antony's who had defected – the promised farms without causing too much hardship to the communities of Italy. Land was to be bought where possible, and even when confiscated the former owners were to be compensated in cash or given new property, usually in one of the provinces. All of this required a plentiful supply of coinage. Cleopatra's desperate attempts to stockpile the kingdom's wealth while she still hoped to escape or make a bargain was a good start, but more needed to be extracted from the various communities.

Egypt's exceptional agricultural productivity and burgeoning trade routes had long excited Roman greed, and the kingdom's annexation as a province was only prevented by the jealousy of politicians unwilling to let any rival senator profit from the process. Caesar's supremacy removed this obstacle, and the country was now to be formally part of Rome's empire. A garrison of three legions and auxiliaries was to remain there, although since Roman troops had been present almost continuously since 58 BC this in itself was no great change. The imposition of a Roman governor was new, and when Caesar left this man would exercise full military and civil authority in his place, taking over control of the administrative system of the Ptolemies.

The first governor was Caius Cornelius Gallus, who had played a key role in the attack on Antony and Cleopatra. Gallus was a highly literate man, widely respected as a poet, and had been on friendly terms with both Cicero and Atticus. He was probably in his early thirties, but this was nothing unusual in this age of ambitious young men. More surprisingly, he was an equestrian and for whatever reason had not been adlected into the swollen Senate as a reward for loyalty. All his successors as governor (the office was titled *praefectus* in this case) were also equestrians and in time Caesar would formally ban any senator from visiting Egypt. It is impossible to say whether he had this in mind from the start or whether the loyalty and talent of Gallus was more important in his selection than his status. Caesar took substantial personal estates in Egypt, but it is an exaggeration to claim that the province was somehow uniquely his private property. There were imperial estates in other provinces as well.[20]

In due course Gallus' men would be deployed to deal with outbreaks of rebellion in the Thebaid, the old Upper Kingdom of ancient Egypt. The unrest may perhaps be a sign of lingering loyalty for the Ptolemies, resentment at the newly arrived conquerors, or simply the new levies imposed and forcibly raised by the Romans – or indeed any combination of these. The trouble was quickly suppressed. However, before they embarked on these operations, Caesar set his legionaries to work repairing and improving the irrigation system which helped control the water of the annual inundation and so made best use of the bounty of the Nile. At the height of their power, the Ptolemies had taken great care of these canals and drainage ditches, but in later years they were neglected as the family spent its strength squabbling for the throne. Modern claims that Egypt prospered under Cleopatra's rule ignore the long periods of chaos and disturbance throughout her reign, which clearly meant that a good deal of work had to be undertaken by Caesar's soldiers. The motive was not altruism. Caesar wanted the new province to produce a reliable stream of grain and other revenue as a permanent Roman asset.[21]

The time spent in Egypt was not solely devoted to work. Caesar made a well-publicised visit to the tomb of Alexander the Great, whose funeral cortège had been intercepted on its way home to Macedonia and taken to Egypt by the first Ptolemy. It was eventually installed in a grand tomb, known as the *sema* or *soma*, in Alexandria. The sarcophagus was originally gold, until a later impoverished Ptolemy had this melted down and replaced with one of crystal.[22]

Alexander was by far the greatest hero of well-recorded times. Pompey had cultivated an image as the Roman Alexander, while a maturing Julius Caesar was said to have wept when confronted with a bust of the great conqueror, lamenting the fact that by comparison he had so far achieved very little in his life. The parallels with Caesar – youthful, restlessly energetic and miraculously successful – were obvious, and it was no coincidence that in many images of him from this period his hair was styled like that of the Macedonian king. He decided to view the remains of the great conqueror, and had them brought out of the tomb, decorating the corpse with flowers and laying on it a golden crown. Perhaps his enthusiasm got the better of him for, when he reached out and touched the face, he accidentally snapped a piece off the corpse's nose.[23]

Caesar had touched the past – and if he was too forceful, then perhaps there was something of the spirit of the hero who had cut the Gordian knot in his impatience. His own grandiose tomb was under construction on the Campus Martius outside the formal boundary of Rome. The scale of this monument, and the conscious association with Alexander, show no desire to hide his power at this stage in his life. While he was in Alexandria, Caesar also gave orders for Antony and Cleopatra to be interred in the tomb she had prepared. The gesture was generous, while at the same time conveniently reminding everyone that here was a Roman who had fallen from his loyalty to his own country and wished to be buried abroad with his foreign lover. As the Senate back in Rome showered honours on Caesar, they also had Antony's statues and monuments pulled down, and even gave orders that his family should never again use the name Marcus Antonius. It was not an effort to remove him from history so much as to ensure a permanent and well-remembered disgrace.[24]

When Caesar left Egypt he moved to Syria. As on his earlier brief visit, he was faced with the need to confirm arrangements for the administration of the eastern Mediterranean. There, just as in Rome and Italy, the rulers and communities wanted stability and continuity more than anything else after over twenty years of Parthian invasions and being forced to fund Roman civil wars. A few client rulers were replaced, and some communities gained and others lost privileges. This quick statement conceals the long and laborious round of petitions, delegations and meetings at which Caesar made and then announced his decisions. Generosity on his part encouraged loyalty. No one in the area had had any real choice about whether or not to support Antony, or before him Brutus and Cassius and all the others.[25]

After Philippi, Antony had written to the Jewish high priest and king Hyrcanus, telling him that Brutus and Cassius had held no legitimate authority, that their brutality was an offence against the gods and that their defeat gave him the chance 'to let our allies also participate in the peace given us by God; and so, owing to our victory, the body of Asia is now recovering, as it were, from a serious illness'. The same spirit of relief was promoted now. The war was over and the best side had won, allowing particular rewards to communities whose citizens had fought for Caesar. As with past conquerors, communities were eager to parade their loyalty by worshipping the Roman leader himself. Ephesus and Nicaea were permitted to raise temples to the divine Julius and to the goddess Roma. Roman citizens were told to restrict their worship to these deities, but permission was given to provincials to offer Caesar divine honours, and major shrines were established in Pergamum in the province of Asia and Nicomedia in Bithynia. It was a distinction that would last for centuries.[26]

All in all, it was far simpler and more practical to change as little as possible, keeping things as they were and confirming the power of most client rulers. This in itself was likely to win the gratitude of men desperate for acceptance by the new regime. In the longer run stability was needed for the region to recover and so become once again fully profitable to the Romans. In the short term, as in Egypt, the rulers and city leaders eager to win Caesar's favour enthusiastically brought him gifts and further swelled his now very healthy financial position. In the course of a single year, Caesar went from a desperate shortage of money to enjoying a vast surplus. When he did return, interest rates fell dramatically – Dio says from twelve per cent to four per cent – as so much cash was injected into the economy.[27]

We know most of the efforts of Herod in Judaea to win Caesar's permanent support. Appearing as a suppliant he was confirmed as king before the invasion of Egypt, during which he again joined Caesar and brought with him supplies and money for the army. Another visit and further gifts followed when Caesar left Egypt, and in return he regained territory taken from him by Antony to give to Cleopatra. The queen's bodyguard of several hundred Gauls – another gift from Antony – was also presented by Caesar to the king of Judaea. Yet Herod's nervousness and increasing paranoia were shown by the instructions he had left behind. His wife Mariamme, the granddaughter of Hyrcanus and so of genuinely royal blood unlike the Idumaean Herod, was sent along with her mother to a fortress to await his return from the first nervous journey to Caesar. Ostensibly for their protection, he left instructions that his wife be killed if he failed to win favour and did not return. His own mother and sister, whose hatred for the wife and mother-in-law were both obvious and strongly reciprocated, were installed in the stronghold of Masada because neither side could stand living next to the other.

Herod came back successfully, but his wife was unimpressed on hearing of his secret orders and failed to see them – as he wanted – as a sign of so fervent a passion that he could not abide the thought of anyone else having her. Given that he was strongly suspected of arranging the 'accident' in which her brother had drowned several years before, the relationship had long been an uneasy one and soon became worse. There were accusations of a plot to poison him, eventually supported by her mother, who had decided that her daughter was already doomed. Mariamme was executed in 29 BC. At some point – most probably in 30 BC – Herod also killed her grandfather, the elderly Hyrcanus, still considering him a threat even though he had long since been mutilated and so rendered unfit to be priest or king. The old man, who for some years was held prisoner by the Parthians, was accused of negotiating with the eastern empire and condemned.[28]

To Caesar's great relief, the Parthians were currently preoccupied with their own civil war as rival members of the royal family fought for power. For the moment there was no prospect of any attack on the Roman provinces. Poets like Horace spoke of the need for vengeance for the loss of lives and precious standards at Carrhae and Antony's great defeat, but Caesar was as yet in no mood to gratify such opinions. An invasion of Parthia was a daunting prospect. At best, a victory would take years to achieve and any setback could shatter his reputation just as it had done to Antony. Moreover it is doubtful that the eastern provinces were sufficiently recovered to fund, supply and support such a major conflict, and certain that Caesar was in no hurry to spend so much time so far from Rome on so difficult a venture. Instead he permitted a defeated brother of the king to live in Syria. At the same time there were official assurances of friendship with the winner, King Phraates IV, who sent one of his numerous sons as a hostage to Rome. This diplomatic success was hailed as a great victory.[29]

With the eastern provinces for the moment settled and secure and his coffers now swollen with fresh levies from Egypt and the other provinces and kingdoms, Caesar began his return to Italy in the summer of 29 BC, pausing en route for a tour of Greece. The welcome he received in Italy was rapturous, helped by his generosity. The communities of Italy had offered him the conventional gold crowns awarded to a victor, although the award was nominal and it had long since become the custom to give the equivalent sum of gold. His substantial outstanding debts already paid, his expenses met, and still left with an immense surplus, Caesar announced that he would not accept the crowns. He had also refused the Senate's order for all classes and all priesthoods, including the Vestal Virgins, to greet him when he approached the City. The Temple of Vesta with its sacred flame should not be left untended, and so the Vestals stayed behind. Even without a formal order, all major cults and many individuals made public sacrifice to thank the gods for his return, and a great crowd voluntarily was waiting to cheer him.[30]

The welcoming people were not kept at bay, and it was not simply the most distinguished who were able to get close to Caesar. One man who approached the victorious warlord had a raven on his arm, which he had trained to call out 'Hail Caesar, *victor imperator!*' Impressed and flattered, Caesar bought the bird for 5,000 denarii. Soon afterwards another man approached him. This time it was the business partner of the bird trainer, who proved to be angry because he had not had a share in the money. He claimed that there was a second bird, and soon returned with another raven. This one had a less appropriate cry of 'Hail Antony, *victor imperator!*' Amused rather than angry, Caesar ordered the first man to share the 5,000 denarii with his colleague. No doubt a similar crowd of cheering citizens would have been there to welcome Antony should he have won. The greatest cause for joy was simply that the latest civil war was over and there was a chance that this victory would bring a lasting peace. News of the victor's generosity prompted someone else to produce a magpie trained to say the same phrase, which Caesar duly bought. An impoverished shoemaker was inspired to get another raven and try to teach it. All his efforts failed, until the bird began to copy his exasperated owner's cry of 'all my work and all my money wasted'. Caesar is supposed to have heard the creature croaking the phrase from the crowd of onlookers eager for his attention. Highly amused, he bought the bird for an even larger sum than the original 5,000 denarii.[31]

On 13 August 29 BC the young Caesar at long last celebrated the triumph he had been awarded back in 34 BC for his campaigns against the Illyrians. On the next day another triumph followed, this time marking the victory at Actium, and including rams taken from the prows of enemy warships as well as all the usual weaponry, captives and floats carrying painted scenes from the war. The parades were spectacular, with the plunder of Egypt liberally displayed on both days. A third triumph followed on 15 August, this time formally for the conquest of Egypt, and it was no doubt the most splendid of all. The Ptolemies were famed for their elaborate, fabulously expensive ceremonies and processions, where everything was made from gold or precious metals, encrusted with gems and draped in silks from the Far East, and now their finery was paraded through Rome. Among the trophies on this final day were the twins Alexander Helios and Cleopatra Selene, who were barely in their teens. Their mother appeared as an effigy, and also featured in at least one painting, showing her holding a snake as she prepared to take her own life. Seven other kings and princes or their sons were paraded through the heart of the City over the course of the three days, including the ruler of Galatia and other allies of Antony. A few were executed, although most were spared.[32]

Caesar himself does not seem to have taken part until the third triumph, and only then did he enter the City and ride in a chariot along the Via Sacra, clad in the purple robes of a triumphing general and with his face painted red. The car was pulled by a team of four horses as was usual. On the left trace horse sat Livia's son Tiberius Claudius Nero, while the right – always felt to be the place of higher honour – was ridden by Octavia's son Marcus Claudius Marcellus. Both boys were about eleven years old, and it was common for the sons and relatives of triumphing generals to take part in the procession so that there was nothing in itself dynastic about the gesture. Behind the car came not simply those senators who had served in the campaign, as was the normal custom, but also Caesar's fellow consul and many other magistrates of the year. It was more usual for these men to lead the procession and perhaps the gesture was intended to emphasise the involvement of the whole state in the victory.[33]

Just over a month short of his thirty-fourth birthday, Caesar had returned to Rome. Consul for the fifth time, he would begin a sixth consulship on 1 January 28 BC, this time with Agrippa as colleague. The Senate granted them the powers – though not the office – of censors, and their stated intention was to carry out the first proper census of the citizen body since 70 BC. Their wider plans were harder to judge. Caesar had for the moment defeated all of his rivals. It remained to be seen whether victory in this latest civil war would really bring a lasting peace.[34]

PART FOUR

IMPERATOR CAESAR AUGUSTUS,
DIVI FILIUS 27–2 BC

'For this service I was given the name of Augustus by vote of
the Senate'. *Deeds of the Divine Augustus 34.*★

★ The precise wording varied, and he might still be referred to as
Caesar or Augustus. The order was sometimes Augustus Caesar or
Caesar Augustus.

RENEWAL AND RESTORATION

'In my sixth and seventh consulships, when I had extinguished the flames of civil war, after receiving by universal consent the absolute control of affairs, I transferred the *res publica* from my own control to the will of the Senate and People of Rome.' *Deeds of the Divine Augustus.*[1]

The ancient and traditional form of the *res publica* was restored. *Velleius Paterculus, early first century* AD.[2]

A ugust 29 BC was a time of great celebration and lavish expenditure. Caesar gave 100 denarii (400 sesterces) to every adult male citizen, and then extended the largesse to boys, this time in the name of his nephew Marcellus. All this was announced as their share of the 'spoils of war'. At the same time a gift of 1,000 sesterces apiece went to the 120,000 or so veteran soldiers established in colonies in Italy and abroad. Sulla's veterans had received little attention once they had been settled on farms, and in the years that followed many had sold up or got into debt, and so become a source of militant support for men like Catiline. Caesar had settled far more soldiers and was determined that they should not be a cause of future disorder. It is unlikely that serving soldiers were neglected, although no source mentions the sum given to them. Agrippa and other officers received decorations for their part in the victories.[3]

Soon after the Egyptian triumph, ceremonies were held to dedicate two new monuments to victory and the glory of Caesar's family. In 42 BC the triumvirs had announced the construction of a Temple to the Divine Julius near the spot at the southern end of the Forum where the dictator had been cremated, and this was finally complete

and formally opened on 18 August 29 BC. The remains visible today
are all that was left after it was cannibalised for building material in
the Renaissance and give little hint of its original splendour. Attached
to the shrine was a new speaker's platform, the Rostra Julia, looking
across the Forum to the main Rostra. In 29 BC both were decorated
with rams taken from Antony's vessels and the shrine itself received
many of the trophies carried in the three triumphs.

Near the main Rostra was the new Senate House, the Curia Julia.
Julius Caesar had begun work on this building, shifting it from the
old site so that it would link the Forum Romanum with his own
planned Forum Julium. The present building dates to the late third
century AD, but used the foundations of the Curia Julia and probably conformed generally to its size and shape. There was originally
a colonnade in front, and the high roof – the one today is 104 feet
high and the original was probably similar – was topped by a winged
Victory perched on a globe. Inside was another statue of the goddess
Victory, this one taken from the Greek city of Tarentum (modern
Taranto) in southern Italy after its capture in the early third century BC. It was surrounded with a selection of ornate plunder from
Egypt. There was also a statue of Venus, ancestress of the Julian
family, made by the famous sculptor Apelles and purchased by Julius
Caesar.[4]

Alongside the formal ceremonies and triumphs were grand public
entertainments to enthral the inhabitants of the City. Professional
hunters slaughtered a variety of ferocious and exotic animals in a
series of beast fights and for the first time ever a rhino and a hippo-
potamus were displayed to the Roman crowd and killed for their
amusement. Athletic and other contests were staged to commemorate the dedication of the Temple of the Divine Julius, with patrician
boys riding in the competitive and often dangerous 'Trojan' Games,
whose name and alleged origins again invoked the ancient past
and the origins of the Julian family. These included horse races –
some where the rider handled a pair of mounts – as well as chariot
races. Several gladiatorial games were presented, the old association
of these with funeral rites now all but forgotten. Statilius Taurus

opened his newly constructed stone amphitheatre – the first to be built in Rome – with a series of fights. He was one of Caesar's most reliable subordinates and funded the monument with the profits from his African triumph in 34 BC. The games were a success, so much so that a popular vote granted Taurus the right to nominate one praetor for each year.

Caesar himself also staged gladiatorial fights around the same time, including one massed battle between captives, claimed to pitch German Suebi against Dacians from the Balkans. There were also fights between matched pairs of individuals, one of whom was the senator Quintus Vitellius, fighting voluntarily for the glamour of the thing. Not every gladiatorial contest was intended to be to the death. Some used blunt weapons, others were decided on points more like a modern fencing bout. There was still an element of danger, but many aristocrats were obsessed with weaponry and skill at arms and at times were keen to compete. The games lasted for many days, and continued even when Caesar fell ill and was unfit to attend them.[5]

A NEW START

On 1 January 28 BC, Caesar began his sixth consulship. On the last two occasions he had been away from Rome on the first day of the year, but this time he was in the City and able to perform the traditional ceremonies. It was a sign that this year would be different. Under the triumvirate, consuls were appointed and every year they resigned and were replaced by suffect consuls, most notoriously when Caesar and Antony had each held the magistracy for a single day. It was a good way of rewarding their many followers, but cheapened the dignity of the office. Times had changed, and this year Caesar and his chosen colleague Agrippa would serve until 31 December, when they formally laid down their office, taking an ancient oath to say that they had done nothing contrary to the laws and had served the state to the best of their ability.

Traditionally, each consul took precedence in alternate months. Under the triumvirate this was ignored, at least in the years when one of the triumvirs was consul. In 28 BC Caesar revived the proper practice and, after taking precedence in January as the senior consul, deferred to Agrippa in February. The change was symbolised by the behaviour of his attendants. In January the twelve lictors went ahead of Caesar, clearing a path for him. Each carried the full *fasces*. As triumvir Caesar and his colleagues had always been preceded by their lictors (although there is an argument over whether each had twenty-four of these like a dictator or the twelve usual for a consul). In February, and every other month when the precedence passed to his colleague, his lictors instead followed him, carrying a version of the *fasces* that was clearly different in appearance, although the details now elude us. The change demonstrated respect not simply for his colleague, but for the office itself. Similarly, the flood of praetorships doled out in the last decade was brought to an end, and there would only be eight or ten praetors in this and the following years.[6]

The Senate itself was also to be reformed and made more respectable. Julius Caesar had enrolled many senators, famously including Roman citizens from Gaul, prompting jokes of men taking off their trousers to don a toga and not being able to find their way to the Senate House. He added far more men from the local aristocracies of the towns of Italy and, in spite of the losses during the Civil War of 49–45 BC, the Senate had grown larger rather than smaller. In the confusion following the dictator's murder and under the rule of triumvirate the expansion was even more rapid as it was packed with their partisans, until it had swollen to more than 1,000 members. This was an era when a runaway slave could become praetor, and bribery help a man to climb far higher than would ever have been possible in the past.[7]

Caesar and Agrippa held the powers of the censorship and so began the process of performing the first proper census or *lustrum* of the Roman people for more than forty years. Since 71 BC, the censors elected every five years had failed to complete this central aspect of their role. When the task was complete, a grand total of 4,063,000 citizens had been registered and their property and status recorded. This was four times greater than the number listed in the last completed census. As part of the process the consuls reduced the size of the Senate. There is no hint that this was intended to remove recalcitrant Antonians or others hostile to Caesar. They announced their intention of restoring the former prestige of the Senate and Caesar made a speech, inviting each senator to look at his own reputation, wealth and ancestry and decide whether he was truly fit to belong to Rome's most prestigious body. Around fifty men voluntarily resigned in the days that followed, and another 140 were removed from the senatorial roll by the decision of the two consuls. All returned to private life, but were allowed to keep the privileges of senatorial dress and the right to sit in the seats reserved for senators at public games and entertainments. One of the men struck from the list was a tribune of the people, and was stripped of this office at the same time.

Only the names of the ones formally expelled were publicly posted as a mild rebuke for their failure to resign. Suetonius records a story that Caesar wore a sword and had a cuirass under his toga at the meeting where these men were expelled – just as Cicero had done at the elections in 63 BC – and surrounded himself with ten burly friends from among the remaining senators. If so, then no trouble occurred then or afterwards. Perhaps the tale is an invention, although we should be careful before assuming that the nervousness of the last decades had already vanished. It may simply have been a reminder of the fate of Julius Caesar, and a clear indication that, for all his generosity, his heir did not intend to fall victim to a similar plot. Yet in other respects the Senate as a body and senators as individuals were treated with scrupulous respect. In 29 BC Caesar had received and used the power to create new patricians. It was intended that the new, smaller Senate – albeit still far larger than the 600 of the Sullan Senate, let alone the 300 that was normal before Sulla's dictatorship – should regain much of its former dignity and be ornamented with famous names from families of high prestige. The first member listed on the senatorial roll, the *princeps senatus* who enjoyed considerable prestige if little formal power, was Caesar himself.[8]

Three senators celebrated triumphs in 28 BC, one each in May for a victory in Spain, in June for one in Gaul, and in October for one in Africa. The triumvirs lavished triumphs on their supporters, often on the slimmest of pretexts, making Agrippa's refusal to accept such honours for genuine victories all the more striking. Still, it was good to celebrate victories over foreign enemies, and there was no real question of these single processions competing with Caesar's victory celebrations. No one could match his prestige or the gold of Egypt, and no one could dream of staging three triumphs on consecutive days. In all of Rome's history, Romulus and Pompey were the only other men to win three triumphs. Julius Caesar had held four in total but, since his adopted son could boast two ovations as well, he could claim to have matched or even surpassed his father. It is doubtful that anyone thought of such things, as the heir had clearly lived up to the prestige of his ancestors, including the divine Julius. The boy who once 'owed everything to a name' now had won victories on the grandest of scales. For the moment at least, Caesar stood apart from other senators.[9]

During these years he held the rank and prestige of the consulship. The triumvirate had formally lapsed, and it was years since he had employed the title. However, it is quite possible that the powers he had been voted in 43 BC continued until they were formally laid down and so added an additional legal basis to his position. The triumvirs' full title named them a board of three 'to restore the commonwealth (or state)' – *rei publicae constituendae*. Antony had talked of formally resigning and challenged Caesar to do the same before the Civil War, and then announced that he would give up his own power after he had won. Returning stability to the state was tied up with the promise of permanent peace. Writing over a century later, Tacitus would characterise the years of civil war and triumvirate as an era when there was 'neither law, nor custom'. Basic institutions had broken down and were replaced with arbitrary power.[10]

In 28 BC Caesar named one of the praetors as the *praetor urbanus*, who had specific responsibilities for the City of Rome itself, including overseeing the major courts. It seems that no one had been appointed to this prestigious post for some time, and indeed there is no evidence for the traditional permanent courts (*quaestiones*) functioning under the triumvirate. The conspirators and their other enemies were all tried in specially created tribunals which operated swiftly and gave the desired result. Traditionally the appointment to this role was made by lot, although Julius Caesar had chosen the urban praetor – selecting Brutus over Cassius for 44 BC – and it may simply be that the choice of a suitable candidate was no longer seen as offensive. A gold coin issued in 28 BC carries the slogan 'he restored the laws and rights of the Roman people' – *Leges et Iura P(opulo) R(omano) Restituit*. Caesar's head is on the face of the coin, wearing the victor's laurel wreath, and on the reverse he is depicted sitting in a magistrate's chair of office, the curule chair of the consul. No one was to be left in any doubt who 'he' was.[11]

As well as re-establishing the courts, it was announced that proper elections would resume, employing the grandly refurbished and rebuilt Saepta, begun by the dictator and now completed by Agrippa. The Roman people could assemble in 'sheep pens' decorated with marble and works of art, and wait shaded from the sun by canopies. This end to the appointment of magistrates may not have begun until the autumn of 27 BC, but it is possible that it started the year before. Dio tells us that in 28 BC Caesar returned control of the state treasury to a pair of officials selected from the former praetors. Many debts owed by individuals to the state were cancelled, but the treasury was still left in a healthy condition, following the transfer to it of substantial quantities of wealth taken from Egypt and the eastern provinces after Actium. Stability in the provinces and allied kingdoms promised a steady flow of income in the years to come.[12]

Alongside the revival of traditional institutions – if sometimes in a modified form – came a physical renewal of the City of Rome itself as the concerted building activity of the late thirties BC continued and intensified. In 28 BC Caesar himself responded to a request from the Senate and ordered the restoration of eighty-two temples within Rome. Many were small, and in most cases the structures conformed to the simple traditional designs rather than the grander styles of the modern era. Structural restoration was accompanied by careful revival of the old rituals undertaken in each one. *Pietas* was a virtue central to Rome's sense of identity and the neglect of proper reverence due to the old gods of the Roman people was symptomatic of the moral decline of recent generations, so evident in the decades of discord and violence. Moral explanations for upheaval came most readily to the Roman mind, and so restoration must involve changes in behaviour, conduct and a reassertion of a good relationship with the gods who had guided Rome's rise to greatness. At the same time the Egyptian cult of Isis was banned from the City itself. The spirit of religious revival was strictly traditional and was led by Caesar personally.

The repair and restoration of temples went alongside the continuing construction of grand projects in the heart of the City and out on the Campus Martius. Agrippa remained busy, and senators who had triumphed continued to plough some of their spoils into monuments. All provided a lot of well-paid work for thousands – perhaps even tens of thousands – of men living in Rome. In 28 BC Caesar also gave out four times the normal allowance of grain to those citizens eligible to receive it from the state. An attempt to arrange distribution so that it would not interfere with work proved unsuccessful, but shows how important the creation of jobs was in the grand building projects of these years. The combination of good employment opportunities and some state assistance helped to spread confidence that a man could feed himself and his family, and left few inclined to riot.[13]

In September the Actian Games were celebrated for the first time and lasted for several days, providing yet another reminder of victory and the peace it had brought. There were gymnastic contests held in a temporary wooden stadium erected on the Campus Martius. Many of the participants were drawn from distinguished families and competed in various events to commemorate Caesar's great victory. At least one day was also devoted to gladiatorial fights between foreign prisoners of war. During the course of the festival Caesar once again fell ill, and was unable to attend the remaining days. Agrippa took his place, and as always behaved in a way that made clear the credit should go to his leader, who paid for the festival.[14]

A month later, on 9 October, the Temple of Apollo on the Palatine was opened. This had been vowed in 36 BC, after a lightning bolt struck part of a grand house recently acquired by Caesar. Unlike many of his restorations, the new temple was an opulent affair, built in gleaming white marble with gold decoration, and showing a strong Greek influence while being well within the Roman tradition. It was part of a larger complex, including a sacred grove and a library. Apollo was the deity given most credit for the victory at Actium, and this new temple, high up on the Palatine, was visible over a wide area, including from the Forum. It was also next to Caesar's house, which already seems to have combined more than one existing aristocratic residence. Around this time work was begun on a road which would have approached the main entrance of his home from the far side of the hill, coming from the Forum Boarium rather than up from the main Forum itself, which would have meant passing the houses of other aristocrats on the way. Caesar was marked out as special, favoured by the gods, and beyond rivalry with other senators. He ordered all the golden statues and other monuments depicting him to be melted down and offered as ritual tripods in Apollo's Temple. This was modesty intended to be celebrated, and as much an expression of power as the acceptance of such honours in the first place.[15]

Another magnificent temple to Apollo was completed during these years, although in this case it was a rebuilding of an earlier shrine. Paid for and supervised by Caius Sosius, who had captured Jerusalem in 34 BC and as one of the Antonian consuls in 32 BC had led the attack on Caesar, it was unusual in that it would take his name, and become known as the Temple of Apollo Sosianus. It incorporated classical Greek sculpture in its friezes, but the newly commissioned pieces depict defeated enemies who wear trousers and look more western than Judaean, and may be intended to represent some of the Illyrian barbarians conquered by Caesar in the Balkans. Sosius had managed to win pardon after Actium, and was permitted to complete his building work and take credit for it. Restoring an old temple and commemorating a victory of the legions were good things. Sosius had worked hard to win this pardon and his expensive building work may well have been a pledge of loyalty to the new regime. It should not be seen as competition. With Antony gone, along with all the other warlords of the civil wars, there was no one who could rival Caesar.[16]

It is in this light that we should view the episode of Marcus Licinius Crassus, who after his consulship had gone to govern Macedonia. Responding to raiding by hostile tribes in 29 BC, he counter-attacked aggressively and with considerable skill. In the first major battle he not only shattered an army of the Bastarnae tribe, but personally killed their leader, King Deldo, in hand-to-hand combat. Following up on this success, he expanded the scope of his campaigns and won a succession of victories in this and the next year. These operations have something of the feel of Julius Caesar's initial interventions in Gaul, with a bold, even ruthless exploitation of any opportunity to widen the conflict, and achieve the rapid destruction of each new enemy. Dio describes them in some detail, and it looks as if Livy did the same. Yet they lasted no more than two years and, just like Julius Caesar, Crassus did nothing that could not be presented as well within the wider interests of the Roman people.[17]

He probably returned to Rome at the end of 28 BC or early the following year and was awarded a triumph – one that was clearly far more deserved than many celebrated under the triumvirs. Dio claims that sacrifices honouring the success were made in both his name and Caesar's, and that the latter took the title of *imperator*, but Crassus did not. This is clearly a mistake. Crassus is granted the title on two inscriptions from Greece, and there is no reason to believe that these were cut before word was received that the honour was not to be granted. It is also clear that Caesar did not accept the title on this occasion.[18]

Dio also tells us that for the killing of Deldo Crassus would have been eligible to perform an additional honour as the culmination of his triumph if he had been fighting under his own auspices – he was a proconsul rather than still in the year of his consulship. This ritual was the *spolia opima*, the right to dedicate the armour and weapons of the dead enemy leader in the Temple of Jupiter Feretrius. Only three Roman commanders had ever performed this rite. The first was Romulus in the eighth century BC, the second Cornelius Cossus in the fifth century BC, and the last Marcus Claudius Marcellus in 222 BC. Romulus was a king and Marcellus consul when they won this honour. The status of Cossus was less clear, but the version recorded by Livy during these years had him serving as a subordinate rather than the supreme Roman commander. However, in what is clearly a later addition, Livy asserts that, 'contrary to what my predecessors and I have said, Cossus was consul' when he killed the king of Veii. His source was none other than Caesar himself, who 'had entered the shrine of Jupiter Feretrius, which he repaired when it had crumbled with age, and had himself read the inscription on the linen breastplate' allegedly dedicated by Cossus. Livy 'thought it would be almost sacrilege to rob Cossus of such a witness to his spoils as Caesar, the restorer of that very temple'. In spite of this insertion, Livy did not change the narrative in the main text, which states that Cossus was a military tribune, serving under a dictator.[19]

Modern scholarship has guessed an ulterior motive for Caesar's testimony, and turned the evidence for what appears little more than an antiquarian curiosity into signs of a nervous leader frightened of any competition. In this version Crassus, heir to his grandfather's fortune and possessing the heritage and prestige of an ancient patrician family, acted and behaved like a true Roman aristocrat, determined to win fame and compete for glory with all of his contemporaries, including Caesar. The first general in almost two centuries to kill the enemy commander with his own hand, it was natural to claim the ancient privilege of dedicating the *spolia opima*, adding to the glory of his family and himself. Caesar feared a rival and, jealous of others' distinction – especially when it involved grand, ancient rites like this or the closing of the gates of Janus – ensured that the Senate refused

Crassus the additional honour. The grounds were technical, and possibly spurious, based on what he claimed to have seen painted on an ancient cuirass in a crumbling temple. Caesar was desperate, frightened that more senators might rally to the head of such an established family, and so was willing to do anything to block the revival of such an ancient honour in case it helped to raise up a rival. Crassus was allowed his triumph, but no more, and disappears from the record afterwards, although the family line continued.[20]

Conspiracy theories are always appealing, and this one creates an attractive image of a Caesar under pressure from strong opposition among senators, nervously struggling to consolidate and protect his position. It is now routinely stated as fact in most accounts of these years – I have done as much myself elsewhere. Unfortunately, closer examination quickly collapses the whole structure. Dio does not say that Crassus claimed the right to dedicate the *spolia opima* and was refused – and no other source mentions the incident at all. He did triumph – scarcely an inconspicuous honour – and many other senators never again appear in our sources after they have held office, governed a province, and won a war, so there is no hint of anything suspicious in his subsequent absence from the record. Caesar's restoration of the temple was inspired by Atticus, and dated to several years earlier. It is impossible to say when he made public his inspection of the cuirass but, given his deep interest in ancient Roman ritual, it may have had nothing at all to do with Crassus. Livy mentions it as an honour, and the failure to revise his main text is a weak prop for suggestions that he was somehow critical of Caesar and his regime.

It is extremely unlikely that there was any public controversy when Crassus returned. If the idea of claiming the *spolia opima* ever occurred to him – and not simply to Dio writing centuries later – then a formal request, debate and refusal in a session of the Senate would surely have appeared more clearly in his account or another source. Crassus had served with Sextus Pompeius and Antony before managing to switch his allegiance to Caesar, which suggests considerable political tact. Even if the idea of claiming the honour occurred to him, it is most probable that he either gave it up himself or was privately dissuaded – perhaps by someone close to Caesar. Some perspective is worthwhile. There is not a shred of evidence for Crassus possessing a wide following in the Senate. He may well have been popular with the legions he had led to victory, but these represented a very small proportion of an army otherwise uniformly loyal to Caesar, who had been busily rewarding his soldiers and veterans in the last few years. Crassus could not hope to rival Caesar even if he wanted to do so, and in the meantime had won office and honours enough to satisfy the expectations of most aristocrats.[21]

For the moment, Caesar's military might was unassailable, and most classes were reasonably content, the commonest emotion being sheer relief at the return of peace. Italy was no longer full of recently dispossessed farmers, unruly discharged soldiers or debt-ridden citizens desperate enough to follow any leader promising them the hope of better fortune. There is no good evidence for the survival of determined Antonian or Pompeian partisans, and the slogans and allegiances of the decades of civil wars had worn thin. Caesar was supreme and faced no immediate threats. The future was harder to predict, and there was no obvious template to copy in creating a regime that would ensure both stability and his own security.

Dio devotes almost all of his fifty-second book to opposed speeches put into the mouths of Agrippa and Maecenas, the former arguing for a revival of a system based closely on the Republic and the latter advocating a veiled monarchy. The words are the historian's own, reflecting the empire that he knew in the early third century AD, and many of his own ideas may well have more to do with the politics of his own lifetime. Yet his claim that Caesar thought seriously about the problem matches Suetonius' claim that he considered restoring a Republican system during these years. Whether or not this would have included his own withdrawal from politics, matching Sulla's resignation of power and retirement, is harder to say. If he toyed with the idea, then he clearly decided against it.[22]

Modern historians readily invoke Julius Caesar's dictatorship and see this as an object lesson to his heir of what to avoid. No ancient source claims this. The dictator was dead less than a year after returning from the Munda campaign and had so little time to do anything that it is doubtful that there were many lessons to be drawn from his fate. Perhaps his assassination highlighted the importance of showing respect to the Senate and other institutions, but it is hard to see that Caesar's power was any less blatant in 28 BC, even if he did not call himself dictator. Circumstances had changed, and the Senate and its moods were very different compared to 44 BC.[23]

The work of restoration of something resembling normality filled 28 BC. It was a gradual process, and the new respect for magistracies and institutions did not diminish Caesar's power. In August there seems to have been a formal declaration of the end of civil war. He also announced that all of the illegal acts of his triumviral colleagues, as well perhaps as the powers and some of the extra honours granted to him as triumvir, should become invalid from the end of the year. It suggested the task of 'restoring the commonwealth' was well under way, the crisis largely over so that extraordinary magistracies were no longer needed. Everything about this indicates an ordered, deliberate process, and there is no hint of an unwilling Caesar being hustled into making concessions. At the end of the year when he and Agrippa took their oaths as they laid down the consulship, Caesar's power was undiminished.[24]

AUGUSTUS

On 1 January 27 BC Caesar began his seventh, and Agrippa his third, consulship. It is unclear whether formal elections had been held. If so, then his popularity would have ensured their success, whether or not other candidates came forward. On the Ides – the 13th in the case of January – the Senate convened with Caesar as presiding consul. Only a few of the assembled senators were warned that the meeting was to involve a major announcement rather than general debate. Caesar had with him a carefully prepared speech. Suetonius tells us that it was his practice to write out any important – and sometimes even fairly trivial – announcement in full, and read it out, to make sure that he expressed himself as clearly as possible and neither said anything he did not want to say nor omitted anything by mistake.[25]

It is impossible to say how far the speech given by Dio reflects what Caesar actually said beyond the central point. He announced that he was resigning his powers, and returning control of the provinces, armies and laws to the Senate. In Dio's version he begins by declaring that what he is about to say will amaze them, since he is at the height of well-earned success and could not be forced to give up power. It is only if they consider his virtuous life, and understand that he has acted out of duty to avenge his father and protect the state, that they will find his action now less surprising and more glorious.

> Who could be found more magnanimous than I – not to mention again my deceased father – who more nearly divine? For I – the gods be my witnesses! – who have so many gallant soldiers, both Romans and allies, who are devoted to me, I who am supreme over the entire sea within the pillars of Hercules except for a few tribes, I who possess both cities and provinces in every continent . . . when you are all at peace . . . and, greatest of all, are content to yield obedience, I in spite of all this, voluntarily and of my own motion resign so great a dominion and give up so vast a possession.[26]

Julius Caesar is constantly invoked, for his achievements, his own refusal to accept the crown and title of king and his undeserved murder. His heir now follows in his footsteps, perhaps winning even greater glory by laying down the power he wields. He has done what needed to be done, leaving the commonwealth strong and stable, so that the task of governing it can now safely be left to others.

Whether or not Dio's version is faithful to the original, his description of the senators' reaction seems highly plausible. Caesar's intimates knew what he was going to say and loudly applauded at appropriate moments. Of the rest, some suspected that the thirty-six-year-old consul was merely play-acting and had no intention of giving up his dominance, but did not dare to show this and accuse the young warlord of lying. Those who believed him were split between some who welcomed the thought of his resignation and others – probably a majority – who feared that this would simply bring on yet another civil war as new leaders emerged to squabble for supremacy. Neither group cheered – the former through fear and the latter in dismay. There were plenty of shouts begging him to change his mind and continue to control the state. Caesar presided over the meeting and therefore it was his task to choose who would speak. For some time he persisted in his request to be permitted to resign and be allowed to live in well-earned peace. As individuals and as a whole, the most senior council of the Republic pleaded with the consul to remain at the head of the state.[27]

With a great show of reluctance, Caesar eventually agreed. Dio saw the whole episode as a charade. With no intention of giving up his supremacy, Caesar simply wanted a public show of support, to appear a reluctant servant of the state forced to accept contin-ued responsibility by his own sense of duty and by universal consent – the Popular Assembly would meet and confirm the decision of the Senate in the next few days. It was a skilful piece of showman-ship, with the Senate and People enthusiastically approving, even if behind the scenes they did not really have any other choice.[28]

It is not clear whether the details of Caesar's future role were set-tled on 13 January or in the days to follow. One honour was definitely awarded to him on that first day, namely the right to display an oak wreath on the porch of his house above the door. This was identi-fied with the *corona civica*, Rome's highest award for bravery, given to someone who had saved the life of another citizen. Traditionally the rescued man made the wreath from oak leaves and presented it in person, acknowledging his debt to the rescuer and symbolising a permanent obligation to him. Julius Caesar had won this award during his early military service in his late teens. In 27 BC the symbol portrayed his heir as the saviour of all citizens and once again in-sisted that his victory was for the good of all. Around this time coins were minted bearing the oak wreath and the inscription 'for saving citizens' (*Ob Civis Servatos*). In a sense, all placed themselves in his debt. The laurels of a victor were also added as permanent decoration to the porch of his house.[29]

The Senate did not meet on 14 January, because it was a *dies nefas* – an unlucky or ill-omened day when it was not permitted to conduct public business. Such days came into the calendar after military disasters or dreadful occurrences. In this particular case the black mark placed on the day was recent, introduced by the Senate in 30 BC because it was the birthday of Mark Antony. There was a meeting on 15 January, although it was cut short because of the need to celebrate a religious festival, and then the senators convened for a full session on 16 January. We cannot allocate many of the decisions to specific days, but the end result is certain.

Under concerted 'pressure' from the senators, Caesar agreed to accept responsibility for some provinces, on the basis that these were most in need of protection from foreign enemies or internal disorder. As a result he took control of all of the Spanish Peninsula, where conquest was incomplete, all of Gaul, where the occupation was still fairly recent and stability threatened by the German tribes from across the Rhine, and Syria, so often disturbed in the civil wars and with Parthia as a neighbour. He also retained control of Egypt, perhaps on the basis that it was a very new province. The entire command was voted to him for ten years, although he stressed that he hoped to return some of the regions to senatorial control earlier than this, should he succeed in bringing the areas under full control more quickly. The remaining provinces were placed under the supervision of the Senate.

Caesar's provinces contained the greater part of the Roman army. There were legions in Macedonia, where Crassus' recent success suggested that there was no need to include the province among the regions felt most vulnerable and so in need of Caesar's direct supervision. Africa also contained several legions. Otherwise the senatorial provinces contained no significant military forces. The soldiers in Macedonia and Africa may well have continued to take an oath to Caesar, as was certainly the case within a few years.

Some details of the system were set down during these days, and others added in the future. Since Caesar could not be everywhere at once, legates were to be chosen to take responsibility for regions within his large province. They controlled areas equivalent in size and made decisions similar in every way to the provincial governors of the past, but held only delegated *imperium*. In contrast, senatorial provinces would be governed by proconsuls, chosen by lot from former magistrates who possessed *imperium* in their own right. With the probable exception of Macedonia and Africa in the early years, the dress and symbols of these men were overtly civilian, whereas the imperial legates wore swords and military cloaks. There were not separate careers in imperial and senatorial service, as men moved between the different classes of posts. Outside Egypt, Caesar chose senators to serve as his legates and command in his provinces. This ensured that there were plenty of opportunities for the senatorial class. Men could win honours to add to the reputation of their families, and if the honours and titles open to legates were slightly different to those of proconsular governors who held *imperium* in their own right, they were nevertheless still honours. The aristocratic urge to excel and win fame continued under the new system.[30]

Caesar was above such competition since he had no peers, and since he chose the legates he also controlled the men who were granted all the major military commands. The independence of proconsular governors of Macedonia and Africa was limited. It is doubtful that they were permitted to raise fresh troops, and neither had the capacity to oppose the man who controlled the rest of the army, even assuming they could win the loyalty of the legions under their command. A large part of every senator's career came to depend on winning Caesar's favour.

No one could have had any doubts about Caesar's supremacy. His ten-year command mirrored earlier extraordinary commands of the likes of Pompey and Julius Caesar. It helped to create the façade of a public servant, taking on heavy responsibilities for the common good. The wider population are unlikely to have felt any qualms about this. Extraordinary commands had a proven track record of getting things done far more effectively than the traditional pattern of frequent transfer of responsibilities from one ambitious magistrate to another. Some senators may have felt the same way, and even those who did not drew solace from the chance of participating in the system. There was no other realistic alternative for as long as Caesar controlled the overwhelming bulk of the army. Dio notes cynically that one of the first things Caesar did after he was 'persuaded' to accept a major role in the state was to get the Senate to pass a decree awarding a substantial payrise to his praetorian cohorts. The evidence is poor, but these probably received an annual salary of 375 denarii instead of the 225 denarii paid to legionaries. There were nine cohorts of praetorians, so they were kept just below the nominal strength of a ten-cohort legion, and several cohorts were routinely stationed in or near Rome itself. This was in contrast to Julius Caesar, who had dismissed his bodyguard early in 44 BC. Armed force remained the ultimate guarantee of Caesar's supremacy.[31]

Much of the senators' time in the meetings on 13 and especially 15 and 16 January was taken up with praising Caesar, and awarding him permanent honours. This may well have been an area where members could exercise genuine independence as regards detail, although no doubt the debate was shaped both by Caesar's selection of the order of speakers and by contributions made by men who had already been primed. Considerable momentum quickly gathered to grant Caesar an additional *cognomen* as a mark of his incredible past and future services to the state. Some speakers suggested that he be called Romulus, linking him for ever with the founder of Rome, since he had renewed and effectively refounded the City.

As well as founder, Romulus was also Rome's first king, and one tradition maintained that instead of dying he had been raised to the heavens to become a god. Yet some of the associations were less attractive. The foundation of Rome had begun with fratricide, Romulus' twin brother being killed with a spade, and that was an uncomfortable thought for a generation who had seen so much civil war. An alternative tradition explained the disappearance of Rome's first king less grandly, claiming that he had been torn to pieces by a mob of senators. After a while, opinion in the Senate shifted away from the idea of giving Caesar the name. Suetonius claims that he and his close advisers were keen, but if so they must have changed their minds at some point. That it was considered so openly and seriously tells us a good deal about the mood of the times. Senators were eager to vote honours to so powerful a man. Whether or not they liked him and what he had done, no one doubted the reality of his supremacy.[32]

Eventually a vote was taken on a proposal made by Munatius Plancus, the same man who had once painted himself blue and donned a fishtail to dance for Antony and Cleopatra, and who had later defected to Caesar, bringing news of his rival's will. Plancus proposed the name Augustus, and the resolution was passed with a sweeping – perhaps unanimous – vote as senators moved to show their acquiescence by standing beside him. The presiding consul now became formally Imperator Caesar Augustus *divi filius*. No Roman had ever had such a name, and it is easy for familiarity to make us forget just how novel it was. Augustus carried heavy religious overtones of the very Roman tradition of seeking divine guidance and approval through augury. Ennius, Rome's earliest and most revered poet, spoke of the City being founded with 'august augury' in a passage as familiar to Romans as the most famous Shakespearean quotes are to us today.

Caesar Augustus – sometimes the order was reversed to Augustus Caesar for added emphasis – was special, unlike anyone else, and, unlike the ten-year provincial command, the new name was a permanent honour. It was hard, perhaps impossible, to imagine Imperator Caesar Augustus, the son of a god, ever retiring to private life, or ever being approached in glory, *auctoritas*, and pre-eminence by anyone else. Earlier precedents – for instance, Pompey's extraordinary commands, and his distant supervision of the Spanish provinces from 54 BC onwards – fall far short of Caesar Augustus' position. Other men had won grand names in the past – Sulla was *Felix* (lucky / blessed) and Pompey *Magnus* (great), but none had held so grand and sacred a name as Augustus. The only person to wield comparable power and pre-eminence was Julius Caesar. The convention of referring to his heir as Augustus and not Caesar Augustus can conceal the great similarities between their places in the state.

At some point a further honour was awarded, this time by vote of the people, namely the setting-up of a golden 'shield of virtues' (*culpeus virtutis*) in the Curia Julia, praising his *virtus*, his justice, his clemency and his piety towards gods and country. The *Res Gestae* associate this with the granting of the name, but it is possible that the award came later, perhaps on the first anniversary of the award of the name. A copy of the shield survives from Arles in southern France and is expressly dated to his eighth consulship in 26 BC. Originally it was one of many set up throughout the provinces, and many coins carry the slogan *CL(upeus) V(irtutis)*. The virtues are strongly reminiscent of similar praise of Julius Caesar and there is no reason to think that this echo was anything other than deliberate.[33]

Caesar Augustus held a personal, permanent pre-eminence in the state, matched in the past only by his father. Like Julius Caesar he continued to hold the consulship every year. The charade of handing over power to the Senate and being handed it straight back was important – and more successful than the confused message given at the Lupercal in 44 BC. This should not make us focus so much on the few differences in Caesar Augustus' self-presentation and conduct that we are blind to the overwhelming – and very public – similarities between him and his father. In a sense, he had now fulfilled his teenage announcement of his intention to win the honours and offices of his father. Julius Caesar once dismissed the *res publica* as a 'mere name without form or substance', although we do not know when and in what context he expressed the view. His heir was more tactful, and avoided the abolished title of dictator, but the difference is more apparent than real. He was also *divi filius*, the 'son of a god', and both this and the name Caesar constantly paraded his connection with the murdered Julius Caesar. The monuments adorning Rome and associated with him already far surpassed the ones celebrating the dictator during his lifetime.[34]

There was another similarity in behaviour. Just as his father had planned to leave for major campaigns in 44 BC, Caesar Augustus, following the award of these honours, intended to leave Rome and go to his provinces in the west for several years. By the end of the year he was in Gaul, but we do not know when he actually left Rome. There is no reason to believe that he would particularly have wished to be absent when Crassus triumphed in July. This was not the only triumph celebrated that year, for another was staged by Marcus Valerius Messalla Corvinus in September. Caesar had been in the City for the triumphs in 28 BC. If he had already left before Crassus processed along the Via Sacra it was because he wanted to begin his work in the provinces before the year was out. With him went the teenage Marcellus and Tiberius to gain their first experience of the army by serving as military tribunes. It was normal for young men to learn in this way, by accompanying relatives to the provinces. More unusually, it is probable that Livia accompanied her husband, and this would certainly become her habit on his frequent journeys throughout the remainder of their marriage. Governors' wives had in the past stayed at home, so it had been surprising when Octavia accompanied Antony to Athens. Augustus Caesar was also willing to ignore this old convention.[35]

TO OVERCOME THE PROUD IN WAR

'. . . remember, Roman – for these are your arts – that you have to rule the nations by your power, to add good custom to peace, to spare the conquered and overcome the proud in war.' *Virgil, twenties BC.*[1]

Before Caesar Augustus left Rome the gates of the Temple of Janus were reopened, symbolising an end to the officially declared peace. The man who had accepted Spain, Gaul, Syria and Egypt as his province was going to war, beginning the task of restoring (Roman) order and stability to these regions. This was to be war fought in a distant land against a foreign enemy and so did not threaten a return to the upheaval and chaos of recent years. Instead it was part of the restoration of health to the *res publica* and the mood was enthusiastic, with excited talk of the conquest of Britain.

Julius Caesar had twice landed on the island, claiming that this was necessary for the security of Gaul since the Britons had sometimes sent warriors to aid chieftains on the continent. In 54 BC the major tribes of the south-east capitulated and agreed to pay tribute to Rome, but we do not know how often this was sent in years filled first with major rebellions in Gaul and then the long disruption of the civil wars. Markets which in the past were controlled by Gaulish middlemen were opened to Roman merchants as a result of Julius Caesar's activities, and by the end of the century such traders would establish a permanent settlement at Londinium on the Thames. Many Romans clearly expected more, and eagerly anticipated the formal reduction of the still-exotic island to become a permanent province. Poets readily ranked the Britons alongside the Parthians as existing enemies whose total defeat was both inevitable and richly deserved. A few years later Horace declared:

Augustus will be deemed a god,
on earth when the Britons and the
deadly Parthians have been added to our empire.

Sometimes the Indians were also included as another people destined to submit to Rome and its great leader, just as they had once succumbed to Alexander the Great. Victories over dangerous and exotic foreign races were unambiguously good things, and a fitting service to the state on the part of its greatest servant.[2]

Around this time, a power struggle among the tribes of southeastern Britain appeared to offer a tempting opportunity for intervention. In due course, this would lead to the domination of the wider region by a confederation of two tribes north of the Thames, the Catuvellauni and Trinovantes, allowing their kings to monopolise access to the luxury goods offered by Roman traders. On at least two occasions during Augustus' reign defeated British rulers fled to the Roman Empire and appealed to him to use his influence and army to restore them to their thrones. Such appeals to Senate or emperors were common throughout Roman history, and tended only to be granted when it was convenient for Rome's leaders.

Caesar Augustus may have considered a British expedition. A fleet of transport ships was gathered on the Aquitanian coast of Gaul, which suggests a degree of preparation. Perhaps it was merely contingency planning, or intended to reinforce active diplomacy. In the event this resolved the situation to Augustus' satisfaction. The details are obscure, and we have no real idea either of the problem or the mechanisms used to resolve it. On balance it seems unlikely that Augustus was genuinely keen to attack Britain. Julius Caesar's example suggested that it would take at the very least several years of campaigning, offered modest profits, and was a risky enterprise. In both 55 BC and 54 BC he had lost much of his fleet to storms and nearly been left stranded on the island to winter unsupplied and unsupported in the midst of hostile tribes. The scale of the challenge was also uncertain. It was another century before a squadron of Roman warships circumnavigated the north of Britain, confirming that it was an island and getting a clearer idea of its true size. Without more serious provocation, Augustus decided against conquest, displaying the same caution that deterred him from risking war with Parthia unless it became unavoidable. The poets would continue to sing of ultimate victory over both peoples, but for the moment Caesar Augustus had other things in mind.[3]

He went from Rome to Gaul, where he spent several months holding assizes, receiving petitions, and beginning the process of holding a census. It was barely a generation since Julius Caesar had conquered all the territory west of the Rhine and as far as the English Channel and Atlantic coasts, and the final shape of the settled provinces was not yet clear. Even so the visit was brief, and by the end of the year Augustus was at Tarraco (modern Tarragona), the capital of the province of Nearer Spain, which would soon be renamed Tarraconensis. It was there that he took up his eighth consulship on 1 January 26 BC, this time with Statilius Taurus as colleague, who was in Rome. Recent disturbances by some of the few remaining independent communities in the north-west were the immediate pretext for his visit to Spain, but there is a good chance that it had always been his planned destination and that it was there he planned to fight his war.[4]

Roman legions first came to the Spanish Peninsula during the long struggle with Hannibal and Carthage at the end of the third century BC. It was in Spain that the Republic first established permanent garrisons outside Italy and had its longest experience of a frontier zone. It proved a bruising one, and if a good few governors won triumphs, there were others whose exploits brought them only ignominy. In each case the methods employed were seldom edifying, and unwarranted aggression, treachery and massacre were all too common aspects of the frontier experience. Many of the inhabitants of the Peninsula were determined and skilful fighters. The Romans recruited them enthusiastically as allies, and early on adopted the famous *gladius hispaniensis* or Spanish sword as their own side arm.

Yet the Romans were united and the indigenous peoples were not, and over time the Roman provinces of Nearer and Further Spain expanded until they encompassed all of the Iberian Peninsula apart from the north-west, protected by the Cantabrian mountain range. The first century BC was not peaceful. There were still some wars between the Romans and the native communities, but far more disturbing were the Roman civil wars fought in the seventies and forties BC, when the locals found themselves swept up in the Republic's rivalries. At times this proved every bit as savage. Excavation at Valencia revealed skeletons of men tortured and executed during the fighting between Pompey and Sertorius, while one of Julius Caesar's officers wrote of how his men decorated a parapet with the severed heads of their enemies.[5]

In spite of such grim episodes, cities like Tarragona flourished. There was a long tradition of urban settlement along the Mediterranean coast, where Greek and Carthaginian colonies and trading posts had mingled with indigenous communities. Iberian settlements developed with ruling magistrates and council leading an administration which made at least some use of the written word in their own language although employing the Punic or Latin alphabet. Some Roman soldiers were settled in Spain at the end of the Second Punic War and over time more followed, particularly in the first century BC. Other Italians and Romans travelled to Spain seeking opportunities in trade, especially in the exploitation of the plentiful mineral resources including gold and silver. Large numbers of Spanish served as allies with Roman armies and some of these gained citizenship; one inscription from 89 BC records such a grant to a *turma* – a cavalry troop, usually of some thirty or so men – of horsemen who had fought for Pompey the Great's father. The son was even more generous in securing citizenship for the leading members of communities who supported his war against Sertorius. One of the beneficiaries in this case was Lucius Cornelius Balbus from Gades (modern Cadiz), who subsequently became one of Julius Caesar's most trusted agents and aided his heir with money, influence and advice after the Ides of March. He became Rome's first foreign-born consul in 40 BC when he was rewarded with a suffect consulship.

Gades was an exceptionally prosperous trading centre, and

landowners with ready access to the sea were already turning to the production of goods for the markets of Italy and elsewhere. Olive oil was to become a major export from the region, as were fermented fish sauces, such as the famous *garum*. A generation later the geographer Strabo recorded that Gades alone could boast 500 men who were not merely Roman citizens, but registered as equestrians. Scarcely a city in Italy – apart of course from Rome itself – could claim so many. A handful, like Balbus and his nephew and namesake who was granted consular status and made proconsul of Africa, made their way to Rome and sought careers in public life.

This did not mean severing their connections with their home community. The Younger Balbus in particular spent considerable sums staging entertainments and building monuments in Gades. Other cities would also acquire theatres and amphitheatres through the largesse of local aristocrats, provincial governors or Caesar Augustus himself, allowing them to share in the *res publica*'s culture of music and drama, and the violent taste for gladiatorial games. Such things were clearly popular and a sign of widespread aspiration to be Roman – or at least to take part in the lifestyle of the empire. Many adopted 'Roman' names before they gained citizenship, and especially in the south there was a fashion for wearing togas. During these years locally minted bronze coins ceased to carry slogans in the Iberian language and switched solely to Latin.[6]

Away from the Mediterranean coast, many communities had resisted the Roman advance far longer and this, combined with their location, slowed the pace at which they – or at the very least the local nobility – embraced the imperial system. Central Spain was dominated by the Celtiberians, a distinct group of nations who spoke a Celtic language akin to that of the Gauls and Britons, although the ancient belief that they represented a fusion of Iberians with Gallic invaders is now felt unlikely. Apart from language, their customs and artefacts seem to have had little in common with contemporary 'Celtic' societies on the far side of the Pyrenees. To the north of the Celtiberians lay the Asturians and Cantabrians, divided into many separate groupings often based around particular fortified hilltop communities. Few Roman armies had ever penetrated far into their lands and none had stayed for any length of time. Several of the numerous Spanish triumphs celebrated under the triumvirs were won in this area.[7]

There is no particularly good reason to doubt that some of these still-independent peoples were raiding the neighbouring more settled Celtiberians within the Roman province. Plundering raids were common in much of the ancient world in many periods. Weaponry was plentiful throughout the Spanish Peninsula long before either the Carthaginians or the Romans arrived, which suggests that neither invader introduced warfare to previously peaceful indigenous peoples. That is not to say that their interventions did not profoundly alter the type and intensity of local warfare, whether through direct conflict or their insatiable demands for mercenary and allied soldiers. The impact of over a century and a half of conquest, and more recently civil wars, inevitably disrupted all societies within the wider area, making worse the struggle for an at best meagre livelihood in the rugged Cantabrian mountains. All of this must have added to the temptation to plunder neighbours who seemed vulnerable.[8]

Augustus may well have planned from the beginning to complete the conquest of Spain by overrunning the north-west. The task had a clear limit, seemed achievable in the space of just a few years' campaigning and, while unlikely to be easy in such difficult terrain, it lacked the potential for disaster on the same scale as an attack on the Britons and especially the Parthians. That it was not a war against such exotic or famous opponents was perhaps another attraction, showing that Caesar Augustus was willing to undertake less glamorous tasks in the interests of the state, and to fulfil his promise of restoring order and security to the provinces placed under his command. By the spring he had left Tarragona and gone north to join the army mustering for the attack aimed at 'pacifying' the Cantabrians.

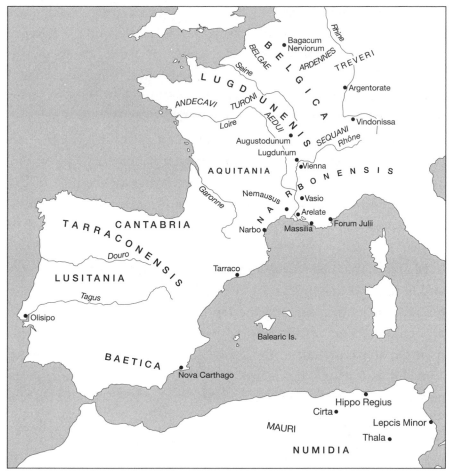

The western provinces, including Spain and Gaul

'BETTER A SAFE COMMANDER THAN A BOLD'

Imperator Caesar Augustus remained a warlord whose dominance of the state was based ultimately on his control of far greater military force than anyone else. By modern standards he was and would remain a military dictator, even if he always carefully avoided the title in its Roman sense. For all the display of resigning his powers and reluctant acceptance of the duties pressed on him by the Senate at the start of 27 BC, no one could compel him to do anything as long as he continued to monopolise military power. The legions were his, and the Senate had no real say in how they were run, nor did it any longer control the raising and disbanding of these and other army units. Although Augustus would present measures detailing soldiers' service conditions for the Senate's approval, there was no real discussion or prospect of the senators withholding their consent. In the past a good deal of the regulation of the legions, including most promotions to the rank of tribune and all commissioning and promotion of centurions, was delegated to individual governors. This remained the case, with the difference that for the bulk of the army that governor was and would remain Augustus himself. Ambitious officers needed his favour if they were to have a distinguished career.[9]

Military force had raised Augustus to his position of dominance, and in the end only military force had any real chance of breaking his hold on power, making the legions both essential to him and a potential threat. It was vital to prevent anyone following in his own footsteps, or indeed those of Marius, Sulla, Pompey and his sons, Julius Caesar, Mark Antony and all the other warlords great and small who had made the first century BC so turbulent an era. Soldiers' loyalty could not be taken for granted – Caesar Augustus had enough experience of mutinies to understand that. It was not simply a question of restricting the commands given to senators to just a few years at the head of only a small fraction of the army. The legions and their officers needed to be kept content and loyal.

After Actium and the final defeat of Antony, all of the sixty or so legions in existence came under Augustus' control. A good proportion of officers and soldiers alike had served more than one commander. Most of those old enough had at some point taken an oath to Julius Caesar, and this was a powerful emotional tie linking them to his heir; but in itself that was not enough, as the mutinies of men impatient for discharge quickly showed. Some of the legions were doubtless skeleton formations, and most significantly under-strength, but even so overall troop numbers were higher than they had ever been in the past, including during the bitter struggle with Carthage.

This was untenably expensive in the long run, as well as dangerous since it was likely to prove hard to keep so large a force of men content.[10]

Therefore it was up to Augustus and his advisers to decide on the size and shape of the army they would maintain. They needed to judge how many soldiers were necessary to secure his position against potential Roman rivals as well as how many were required to maintain the empire, defending and, where it was desired, expanding the provinces. The two were closely related. Imperator meant 'victorious commander' and it would be seriously damaging to Augustus' reputation and *auctoritas* if the empire appeared weak to its foreign neighbours and began to suffer reverses on the frontiers or within the provinces. In itself this might not be enough to break his power, but it was likely to create dissent, and thus give a chance for rivals to appear.

Balancing these factors, Augustus decided to keep a force of some twenty-six or twenty-seven legions – the number is uncertain as it is unclear when two of the units with higher numbers were raised, and at some point the total rose to twenty-eight. This reduction of more than half was eased by the renewal of veteran settlement in the aftermath of Actium. By 29 BC there were 120,000 discharged soldiers settled in colonies – the equivalent of some twenty-four full-strength legions. Probably, once the men due for discharge and unwilling to stay with the colours were released, the remaining soldiers comfortably provided sufficient manpower to make up twenty-six (or twenty-seven) more or less full-strength legions.[11]

The details of military service in the last decades of the Republic are elusive, but at least some men enlisted for a spell of six years or until the end of the war, so that many of those eligible for discharge were not necessarily especially old. Some chose the army as a career and extended their enlistment, and this was especially common for officers. During the turbulent decades of the first century the small existing group of effectively professional army officers rapidly expanded. Such men served mainly as tribunes, prefects and centurions, developing considerable experience and expertise. At least some were equestrians, or became members of that class through their share of the spoils. For some the army was a stepping stone to social advancement, and for others both a good living and an honourable career.

Ignoring such men was unwise, and we should not think solely of the need to offer senators some prospect of winning a military reputation, since other levels of society were just as keen in their own way. Many of these officers came from the local gentry of the Italian towns. Others had joined this class as a result of the veteran settlement, being given substantial estates commensurate with their army rank and so gaining access to local magistracies and town councils. Whether or not such men wanted to continue serving with the army, they and others like them were keen to see the opportunity to do so continue, whether for themselves or their sons. It may be no coincidence that we never hear of difficulty in filling vacancies in these ranks.

Twenty-six legions meant not simply employment for some 130,000 soldiers, but 156 posts as tribune and 1,560 commissions within the centurionate. Almost a legion's worth of praetorians added to the total – and at each grade their pay was commensurately higher – and even more opportunities were provided by the increasingly formal organisation of the auxiliary units raised from non-citizen soldiers. These came to be organised in cohorts of infantry and comparably sized *alae* of cavalry, and were generally commanded by Roman citizens, albeit sometimes drawn from the aristocracy of the people from which the unit was raised. At first it was common to give command of one of these units to a former senior centurion. For a while Augustus experimented with placing two young men from the senatorial class in joint command of a cavalry *ala*, hoping to give them experience of leading and caring for horsemen before they moved on to more senior posts in the legions. However, as the years passed he increasingly chose an equestrian prefect or tribune to lead each auxiliary unit. This represented a huge increase in the number of permanently available public posts open to *equites* – and involved them in taking an oath to the *princeps*, and receiving their rank, pay and future advancement and benefits from him.[12]

Maintaining a substantial standing army was an important way of meeting the aspirations of this important group, as well as keeping them and those inclined to enlist in the ranks busy. It was a former centurion of Sulla's who had raised an army for Catiline in 63 BC, and such men had played a major role in making the civil war armies effective. Dio, writing from the scathing perspective of a senator in the early third century AD, made Maecenas advise Augustus to re-cruit soldiers into the army to prevent unemployed young men from turning to banditry. A greater danger was that they might enlist in an army raised by a rival.[13]

Unit pride and existing interests played an important role in shap-ing the new army. In the earlier Republic, it was normal to renumber the legions every year, so that the consuls commanded the legions *First* to *Fourth*. The system had broken down in the first century BC, and Julius Caesar's legions in particular proved fiercely protec-tive of their identity, whether they subsequently fought for Lepidus, Antony or the young Caesar. Antony's legions readily switched alle-giance to Caesar after Actium, but in many cases refused to give up the numbers, names and traditions of their units. This meant that from the very start the newly reorganised army was not numbered in any logical sequence. There were two each of legions numbered *Fourth*, *Fifth*, *Sixth* and *Tenth*, and no less than three with the nu-meral *Third*. Several, like *Legio V Alaudae*, kept their identity in spite of close associations with Antony, perhaps because they had once fought loyally for Julius Caesar. This legion continued to use the ele-phant as a symbol, commemorating its defeat of the Pompeian war elephants at Thapsus in 46 BC.[14]

Legio V Alaudae was one of six legions preparing for the campaign in north-west Spain. There were also the *First* and *Second*, as well as *VI Victrix*, probably the *Ninth* (usually written in the archaic form *VIIII* by its members), which would earn the name *Hispana* during these years, and certainly *Legio X Gemina*. *Gemina* meant 'twin' and there was also a *XIII Gemina* and *XIV Gemina*, although neither took part in the operations in Spain. In each case these were legions formed by the amalgamation of two existing units. One of the units forming *X Gemina* had served under Antony and claimed descent from the old *Tenth* of Julius Caesar; for a while it kept its nickname of *Equestris* – dating back to 58 BC when the soldiers had briefly served on horseback and joked that their commander planned to make them equestrians. Amalgamation of two units presumably maintained the pride of both, and was clearly thought preferable to disbanding an established legion.[15]

Officers and soldiers alike were permitted their traditions, but the newly reorganised army was not to be pampered and indulged as generously as the legions from the Civil War years. Terms of service were extended for the men in the ranks, and before long these would be obliged to serve for the traditional maximum of sixteen years before becoming eligible for any grant of land on discharge. At some point an obligation to serve a further four years was added, during which men were classed as veterans and excused from some duties, but obliged to remain with the colours and under discipline. Promises of bounties and bonuses became occasional instead of a regular feature to secure loyalty, and were issued solely by Augustus himself or a member of his extended family. The change in attitude was marked by a change in speech. During the civil wars, the young Caesar had routinely aped his father and addressed his officers and soldiers as *commilitones* or 'comrades'. After 30 BC this familiarity ceased, and they were always simply *milites* or 'soldiers', a rule he insisted on being followed by every governor and commander, including members of his own family. In Spain he continued to impose the stern discipline he had practised in Illyria. We read of centurions symbolically humiliated by being made to stand to attention outside his tent, sometimes holding a square of turf of the type used to make ramparts, or without wearing their belt, so that the long military tunic hung down to the ankles like a woman's dress.[16]

The most senior officers were also to be kept on a tight rein. In his

youth, Caesar had often taken great risks, and although he had prevailed in the end there had been moments of great danger along the
way, most notably in the war with Sextus Pompeius. Now mature
– he was in his thirty-eighth year when the Cantabrian campaign
began – Imperator Caesar Augustus inclined more towards caution.
According to Suetonius:

> He thought nothing less appropriate in a competent leader than haste
> and recklessness, and so some of his favourite slogans were: 'Hurry
> slowly', 'Better a safe commander than a bold', and 'That is done fast
> enough which is done well enough'.
>
> He used to say that neither battle nor war should be initiated care-
> lessly, but only when the promise of gain clearly outweighed the cost
> of failure. For he compared those who risked heavy loss for slight
> gain to a man fishing with a golden hook, the loss of which could not
> be matched by any possible catch.[17]

The instincts of a Roman aristocrat placed at the head of an army
– knowing that his spell of command would be temporary, eager
to add to his own and his family's reputation, and complacently
convinced after centuries of Roman success that victory was almost
a matter of course – inclined him to bold, even rash action. Augustus did not want his legates, or the few senatorial proconsuls left
in charge of an army, to seek out unnecessary wars or to risk serious defeats simply for the sake of winning glory and plunder in the
style of Pompey or Julius Caesar and the many other commanders
of earlier generations. Defeats reflected badly on him, even if he
was far from the theatre of war. This was the price of his vast provincial responsibilities and the *auctoritas* of being the man who had
ended civil wars and brought peace to the state. Imperator Caesar
Augustus could not afford too many reverses, whether in person or
by proxy.[18]

Nor were too many spectacular and well-advertised successes
without a degree of peril if they were won by anyone other than
himself or men like Agrippa or Statilius Taurus, who came from his

inner circle and were so closely tied to him that he shared in the glory. As we have seen, it is doubtful that Augustus openly blocked Crassus in an attempt to celebrate the *spolia opima*, and like many others the aristocrat was allowed to triumph. From now on few men would get an opportunity to campaign on such a grand scale unless they were intimates of Caesar Augustus. Even then there were risks. It was probably in 26 BC that the man he had left to govern Egypt fell from grace. The equestrian Cornelius Gallus had campaigned with great success, putting down rebellion in Upper Egypt, and then winning victories and raiding the lands of the kingdom to the south after it had launched plundering attacks into the Roman province. However, he celebrated his victories rather too loudly; an inscription proclaiming them survives and according to Dio he had others inscribed on the Pyramids themselves. The historian also claims that he gossiped freely and unflatteringly about Augustus – something all the more dangerous because Dio knew him well. Gallus' judgement had proved questionable in the past, for instance admitting to his circle a teacher of rhetoric who while serving as tutor to Atticus' daughter had seduced the child. Such behaviour was particularly inappropriate for a freedman, and since the girl subsequently married Agrippa, Augustus was especially angry to hear of the welcome the man received from Gallus.[19]

As so often the details are impossible to unravel. Gallus' accuser was a certain Valerius Largus, previously an associate and so presumably another man enjoying at least a degree of favour from the *princeps*. Yet the situation is not clear, and Largus had a reputation for launching savage and often unjustified prosecutions. Dio tells a story of one man meeting Largus for the first time and asking him whether or not he recognised him. Largus said no, and the man made a show of having this written down just in case the accuser ever tried to bring charges for some imagined offence. He also tells us that another of Augustus' inner circle – himself as it happens an equestrian like Gallus – on one occasion clapped his hands over his mouth and nose as soon as he spotted Largus, hinting that it was unsafe even to breathe in the man's presence.[20]

Caesar Augustus withdrew his favour from Gallus and stripped him of his office. The specific charges are unknown, but were probably made under the laws dealing with corruption on the part of provincial governors – something to which equestrians had not formerly been subject. Yet in every respect of duties and powers Gallus had been a governor, and it was perhaps a consolation to the Senate that he was now held accountable to the same regulations as senators serving in this capacity. Egypt was an important source of revenue and grain kept very closely under Augustus' supervision, and excessive peculation by Gallus or the men under his command would not have been looked on favourably. It may simply be that the equestrian was behaving too blatantly, as so many senatorial governors had behaved in the past, but all this is conjecture.

Stripped of Augustus' friendship or *amicitia* – a gesture seen as a sign of direct hostility on Caesar's part – the Senate eagerly voted to condemn and exile the man. Gallus despaired and took his own life, something that Suetonius says prompted Augustus to burst into tears, complaining that 'only he was unable to set a limit to the wrath shown towards his friends'. Seeing the episode as a sign of concerted opposition in the Senate is unconvincing, and it may well have been an indication of the desperate enthusiasm of some senators to win favour by doing what they thought the *princeps* wanted. It is just possible that the attacks on Gallus were meant to show that even an equestrian governor appointed by Augustus was not above the law. If so, then this may well have had the approval of the *princeps*, or at least that of his representatives in Rome such as Agrippa, Statilius Taurus and Maecenas.[21]

THE FINAL BOOK OF AUTOBIOGRAPHY

Augustus divided the army into three columns which advanced, each using a different route, into the Cantabrian mountains. The aim seems to have been to seize the major passes and to subdue the main fortified settlements of the local peoples. Archaeology has confirmed that there was serious fighting and destruction in a number of these sites and has also located some temporary camps built by the Romans during these campaigns. Sadly it has so far proved impossible to connect any site to the places named in the brief (and almost certainly badly garbled) accounts in our ancient sources. Augustus concluded his own autobiography with his victory in these wars, but there is almost no trace of this lost work in the surviving narratives. No stories of personal exploits and perils survive from the campaign, but it seems the greatest personal danger he faced did not come from the enemy. Before the year was out, he once again fell seriously ill and returned to Tarragona, supervising operations from there until their conclusion in 25 BC.[22]

The Cantabrians and Asturians fought with considerable determination and there are stories of besieged warriors killing themselves rather than surrender. There is a strong and deeply misleading instinct to associate warfare in Spain at any period automatically with guerrilla warfare. In such mountainous terrain ambush certainly played a part, and we read of a surprise attack being betrayed by informers from an allied community, which allowed the Romans to move quickly to reinforce the threatened contingent and defeat the enemy. Yet it is clear that some of the fighting was fought on a large scale, and there were numerous sieges. Roman losses were significant, since not every engagement was successful and the storming of even a small walled village was highly dangerous for the attackers. At some point a fleet carrying a substantial force of soldiers sailed from Aquitania in Gaul, and made one or more landings on the northern coast of Spain, attacking while the enemy was distracted by the main columns.[23]

There were similarities with the operations in the mountains of Illyria, although how many men served in both is impossible to know. Nor is it clear how far lessons learned in one theatre were passed on to units elsewhere. The temporary camps built during these campaigns follow the traditions of the Republican army, exploiting the contours of the ground. Although the internal structures were no doubt laid out in an organised way – something which had attracted the admiration of Greek observers since the third century BC – they do not yet conform to the standard plan of playing-card shape and re-markably consistent template of internal layout that would become normal in the next few decades. Like conditions of service, the rou-tines and drills of the Roman army were not instantly devised and introduced, but developed gradually during Augustus' life as more and more regulation was imposed.[24]

As in the earlier campaigns, the Romans attempted to secure the high ground as their columns forced their way through the valleys and passes. One stronghold was surrounded by a fifteen-mile-long rampart so that the defenders were denied any chance of escape. It was grim, methodical and not especially glamorous warfare, but it gave the officers and soldiers a chance to win distinction and gain promotion or other rewards. The honorary title *Augusta* was awarded to both the *First* and *Second* legions, and the latter at least adopted the capricorn, Augustus' astrological symbol, as one of its emblems.[25]

It took two years of tough campaigning before victory was de-clared, and word sent to Rome for the gates of the Temple of Janus to be closed once more. Augustus was hailed as *imperator* and voted a triumph by the Senate. He took the salutation, but declined to celebrate the triumph and would in fact never again do so. The effec-tive declaration that he had no need of personal glory since he had already won so much was more powerful than yet another parade through the heart of Rome. Like Agrippa, he would labour unre-warded for the good of the state – at least in his case unrewarded by conventional honours. In the event, the declaration of final victory proved premature and the Cantabrians and Asturians renewed the fight soon after Augustus left Spain. There were more campaigns, culminating in a characteristically effective, if ruthless, operation by Agrippa in 19 BC. Even then, the fighting did not at first all go the Romans' way – *I Augusta* was stripped of its title for some failure. (It would later gain the name *Germanica* after prolonged service on that frontier.)[26]

Augustus assumed his ninth consulship at Tarragona on 1 January 25 BC. He may have left the city to go in person to receive the surrender of some of the Cantabrian leaders, but his sickness remained serious and it is unlikely that he travelled much. This did not mean that he was idle. We know of several embassies from the provinces which went to Rome and after being presented to the Senate travelled on to see Augustus at Tarragona, and it is highly unlikely that these were the only ones. Petitioners no doubt came from throughout the empire in the hope of being granted their requests.[27]

Only a minority of people living in the provinces would ever see Augustus in person. His image was another matter, and would become more common than that of any individual, whether human or divine. All gold and silver coinage was minted by the Romans and bore either his head or a symbol closely associated with him. His name was on monuments and his statues were erected throughout Italy and the provinces. This was an idealised Augustus, handsome, authoritative and tall. He was also forever young – or better, forever in his prime. There is not a single image of a middle-aged or elderly Augustus.

That did not mean that he was unaware of his mortality, especially in view of his repeated bouts of illness, and unconcerned with the future of his family. Marcellus and Tiberius had both adopted the toga of manhood and formally become men before they accompanied him to Spain. The campaigns had given them a taste of military life – something Livia's son would come to enjoy. For young aristocrats, marriage alliances were an important part of their ambitions. Given the role played by his adoption by Julius Caesar in his own rise, Augustus knew that any connection to his extended family was an important matter. If Livia was with him then no doubt the couple discussed these things in detail – something that clearly happened with regard to most family matters. Tiberius was betrothed to Agrippa's daughter Vipsania, while Marcellus received greater favour and was betrothed to Julia, Augustus' only child. The marriage of first cousins was rare even among the closely intermarrying aristocratic families of Rome. It was another sign that Caesar Augustus, for all his talk of tradition, was not bound by the old rules.[28]

THE 'TITLE OF GREATEST POWER'

'People of Rome! Caesar, who was reported but now to have sought a crown of bay at the cost of his life, comes home victorious like Hercules from the Spanish shore. Let the lady who rejoices in her incomparable husband come forth, performing due ritual to the righteous gods, and with her the sister of our dear leader . . .' *Horace, 24 BC, describing the return of Caesar Augustus from Spain.*[1]

The journey home from Spain took a long time. Augustus fell ill again, probably with a return of the same problem that had troubled him in recent years. The crowded metropolis of Rome was known to be an unhealthy place, and so he followed the normal aristocratic practice of staying away from the City while he recovered. He may have been in Italy by 1 January 24 BC, but was certainly not in Rome to assume his tenth consulship in person. This did not prevent the Senate from taking an oath to uphold all his formal deeds, and granting his 'request' to be permitted to present a gift of 400 sesterces to every citizen in Rome, repeating the largesse that accompanied his triumphs. The senators responded by voting further honours for the *princeps*, some of which were refused.[2]

As his consular colleague Augustus had Caius Norbanus Flaccus – married to the daughter of the Younger Balbus and the son of one of the senior commanders in the Philippi campaign. Agrippa and Statilius Taurus were still in Rome, as was Maecenas, so there was no shortage of loyal, immensely wealthy and powerful subordinates to ensure that matters were arranged to Augustus' satisfaction even when they did not formally hold office. Taurus maintained a strong force of burly German slaves in his household, although there is no evidence that these were ever actually used to coerce others. Some praetorians were doubtless also in the City, even if several cohorts at the very least will have accompanied the *princeps* to Spain, and so Caesar's supporters were not without some force at their immediate disposal.[3]

More importantly, Agrippa was busy with a series of great building projects, which provided plenty of well-paid employment as well as a constant advertisement for the glory of Augustus and the peace his victories brought. In 26 BC the Saepta – renamed the Saepta Julia in honour of Julius Caesar, but more especially his son – was fully completed and formally opened in the Campus Martius, the voting area paved in marble and bedecked with statues and paintings of high quality, with much of the enclosure richly canopied so that voters could enjoy the shade as well as admiring the works of art. Nearby and aligned with it were public baths and an exercise area, a basilica dedicated to Neptune – and thus a reminder of victories at Naulochus and Actium – and a magnificent temple which soon became known as the Pantheon, since it contained statues of all the great gods and goddesses. Originally Agrippa planned to place a statue of Augustus with them, and name the structure the Augusteum, but the *princeps* refused an honour which smacked strongly of deification. The story may simply have been a contrived opportunity to parade his modesty. A statue of the divine Julius Caesar was placed inside, while images of Augustus and Agrippa adorned the entrance porch, at a safe and respectful distance from those of the gods. It is more than likely that the pediment above the entrance was decorated with a carving of the *corona civica* wreath, providing yet another reminder of Augustus' service to his fellow citizens.

A century and a half later the Emperor Hadrian rebuilt the Pantheon, on the same spot, but with a different orientation, and it is this grander structure with its awe-inspiring domed roof that visitors can see today. Agrippa's building was more conventional in its design, although still monumental in scale. Hadrian left or renewed the original inscription, and thus Agrippa's name is carved onto the front of the building, providing a useful illustration of how for the Romans restoring a building rebounded to the glory of both creator and restorer. It was inevitably of most use to the latter, who was alive and well when the work was complete. Agrippa's developments on the Campus Martius provided plenty of employment for the people of Rome, and at the same time gave them practical and luxurious amenities, continuing the pattern begun in his extraordinary aedileship a decade earlier. In the coming years the bath-house would be expanded, the supply of water to it improved by the completion of a new aqueduct, the Aqua Virgo, in 19 BC. The basilica provided more space for public business, but, as with his other projects, the functional was combined with the aesthetic and it boasted among other ornaments a famous painting of the mythical Argonauts. Open display of famous artworks was a distinctly *popularis* move, like the public libraries in the Temple of Palatine Apollo, since they made available to the wider population things that only the rich could normally afford. Yet, unlike earlier politicians, Agrippa never paraded his own achievements in a way that did not attribute the greatest glory to Augustus. Instead they celebrated the peace brought by the latter through victories.[4]

The victories continued. When Janus' gates were closed for the second time in just a few years it was a public declaration of fresh success brought by the *princeps*. The ceremony had only been performed twice before in all the long centuries of the Republic, but it is hard to know how many people were aware of this, and they were yet to see that the declaration of peace in Spain was a little premature. The news from other provinces was also good, as Augustus' generals fought campaigns of their own. There was success in the Alps, on the Rhine, and if Cornelius Gallus' career had ended in disgrace there was no doubt that his victories were genuine. His successor Aelius Gallus was also an equestrian, and by now, if not earlier, Augustus appears to have decided to treat Egypt differently, and govern through an equestrian prefect rather than a senatorial legate.[5]

His instructions were also blatantly aggressive. Aelius Gallus launched an expedition to Arabia Felix, the north-west corner of the Arabian Peninsula, whose population did very well as middlemen in the luxury trade in spices, gems and silks. From the start, when many of his ships were lost in a storm on the Red Sea, the attack went badly. The Roman column struggled to cope with the desert conditions, losing only a handful of men to enemy action, but many more to thirst, heatstroke and disease. Aelius Gallus took the wrong route – an ally was blamed and later executed for this advice, but it is harder to say whether he was genuinely malicious or simply incompetent. They took several strongholds, but ran out of water and had to abandon the siege of the last one they reached. If they lacked skill, Aelius Gallus and his men showed stubborn determination, and managed their retreat rather better than their advance.

The invasion was an undoubted and costly failure, but was fought far away and on a fairly modest scale, involving at most parts of two legions along with auxiliaries and allies. Like Julius Caesar's expeditions to Britain which achieved so little, but were greeted with wild celebration, Arabia was exotic, mysterious and, best of all, a region never before reached by a Roman army. Victory was proclaimed by Augustus and no one was much concerned with the truth. No senator had gone with the expedition, nor would any accompany Aelius Gallus' successor Publius Petronius when he took a large part of the provincial army south down the Nile, winning victories between the First and Second Cataracts. One of the main cities of the Ethiopians was stormed and another victory declared over an exotic, far-flung people, this time with justification.[6]

Successes abroad, even if some were more imagined than real, reinforced the stability at home. The *princeps* appeared to be fulfilling his promise to bring order to the provinces allocated to him, whether he did it in person or through representatives. If there were difficulties in the day-to-day running of Rome resulting from the prolonged absence of one consul, then means were found for coping with them. The path was not always smooth. In 26 BC Marcus Valerius Messalla Corvinus, son of a consul and himself suffect consul in 32 BC, as well as a man who had in the past sided with the Liberators and then Antony, was appointed Prefect of the City (*praefectus urbis*). Julius Caesar had revived this archaic post, choosing several men to undertake tasks in the administration of Rome during his absence, but otherwise it belonged to the dimly known and distant years of the early Republic. Messalla resigned after a few days 'because he did not know how to exercise' his office. It is tempting to see this as being prompted by a realisation that his power was curbed and made to seem a sham by the behind-the-scenes manipulation of events by Augustus' close confederates, but this is pure conjecture, as is the modern idea that he was under pressure from other aristocrats who disapproved of the regime. In later years the office was revived and given to the reliable Statilius Taurus.[7]

AGE, ILLNESS AND DEATH

When Augustus finally returned to Rome it was late in the year, but he was able to travel along roads newly restored. He had himself paid for the repair of the Via Flaminia and encouraged other senators, and especially men who had triumphed, to undertake work on other major roads. A few followed his lead, but in the end the bulk of the task was performed by Caesar Augustus and Agrippa. Once again these projects combined the practical with a strong visual message. Milestones recorded the name of the restorer, while at prominent points, such as major bridges, there were statues of the *princeps*.[8]

The statues were elegant and showed a strong man whose face betrayed no sign of age or strain, in contrast to the heavily creased and jowly portraiture so common in Rome for the last few generations. Yet in truth Caesar Augustus was in his thirty-ninth year and beset by serious illness, so he was unable to attend the wedding of Marcellus to Julia. Agrippa stood in his place – a statement true of so many situations. No one, least of all Augustus himself, could be sure how much longer he was going to live. We do not know the cause of his repeated ill health, although Suetonius tells us that the problem was in the liver, so it seems safe to assume that it was at least something in that general area. Some scholars have wanted to depict the illnesses as feigned, intended to frighten the wider population with the prospect that the *princeps* might die and civil war return and so make them grateful for his continued life and accepting of his dominance as better than any alternative. Others have suggested that the condition was psychosomatic, although as one eminent scholar noted, this is always 'a suggestion popular among doctors for diseases they cannot diagnose'.[9]

Grooming the next generation for a public career was natural for Roman aristocrats. Both Marcellus and Tiberius publicly came of age before they left Rome to accompany Augustus to Spain. This was normal, as was the gaining of their first military and provincial experience on the staff of a relative, albeit they were a little young to be given the rank of military tribune. Yet the attention they continued to receive was far greater than normal. The two youths returned to Rome before Caesar, but in their last weeks with the army in Spain they presided over a series of games and entertainments staged for the legionaries at the end of the campaign. Then in 24 BC the Senate, under Augustus' encouragement, granted them accelerated careers. They were added to the senatorial roll, and Marcellus graded as an ex-praetor and given the right to hold each office, including the consulship, ten years before the normal age. Tiberius was permitted to hold office five years early.

In the autumn the two eighteen-year-olds first stood for office, certainly with Augustus' open support and quite possibly his physical presence during canvassing and at the election. The result was never in any doubt, as with any of his recommendations – Marcellus was elected aedile and Tiberius became quaestor. Although they were exceptionally young, we should never forget that each was also a member of an old and extremely prestigious noble family. In this sense they were highly acceptable to other senators, more so than someone like Agrippa.

Marcellus was especially favoured, receiving higher offices as well as the greatest honour of marriage to the *princeps'* only child. Yet the honours granted to Tiberius were still generous and highly exceptional, and his bride-to-be, Vipsania, was the daughter of a man who could boast three consulships, and the granddaughter of

Atticus. In 23 BC Augustus chose Livia's son as his own quaestor and gave him special responsibility for organising the grain shipments on the last stages of their journey to Rome. He also had a roving brief to investigate the slave barracks maintained on many of the great rural estates, some of which were rightly suspected of wrongfully imprisoning innocent travellers and forcing them to work. Both were useful tasks and, as importantly, ones that gave Tiberius a good opportunity to do prominent and popular public service. This was even more true of Marcellus, who as aedile was responsible for staging games, which he did in especially memorable style, aided by his uncle and father-in-law, the *princeps*. Canopies were erected over the temporary stands in the Forum to shade the audience, and among the performers was a dancer who held equestrian status and a young lady from one of the aristocratic families.[10]

Marcellus and Tiberius were both nineteen in 23 BC. Caesar Augustus was in his fortieth year and was consul for the eleventh time. His elected colleague was to be a certain Varro Murena, but he died either late in 24 BC or very early the next year. His replacement was Cnaeus Calpurnius Piso, who had served against him at Philippi. Piso's family was distinguished, but since the Civil War he had taken little active part in public life and was said to have refused encouragement to seek office in the past. This time he was persuaded; we cannot know what changed his mind, but it broke the succession of consular colleagues who were known as close associates of Augustus. It may have been meant as a sign of reconciliation, or at least as assurance that aristocrats from established families were able to enjoy the high honours they felt to be their due.[11]

The year did not go well, but that had nothing to do with either consul or their ability to work together and was instead due to natural disasters. A serious epidemic broke out, which caused heavy loss of life throughout Italy and flared up on several occasions in Rome during this and the following year. The River Tiber flooded, affecting lower-lying parts of the City, causing more disease, and bad harvests produced shortages of grain. Although Tiberius' efforts may have helped, the market was badly disrupted and prices soared. Augustus used his own funds to give twelve – presumably monthly – gifts of grain or flour to 250,000 citizens in Rome to relieve the hardship of the less well-off.[12]

Everyone expected Caesar Augustus to die. At some point in the first half of the year he was once more critically ill with the same liver problems that had dogged him for some time. The normal treatment involved warm compresses, but these failed to provide relief. Augustus summoned to his bedside the senior magistrates, prominent senators and representatives of the equestrian order and spoke to them about affairs of state. At the end of this session, he passed his signet ring to Agrippa, but gave a report of the current state of the army and the public accounts to his fellow consul Piso. No mention was made of Marcellus, and Caesar Augustus very deliberately did not name a successor. This would have been difficult, since his powers and *auctoritas* were personal and there was not a formal position of *princeps* to pass on to someone else. Apart from that, Marcellus was only nineteen and at the very start of his career, and even Augustus himself had assumed the position of his father over the course of time. If Caesar Augustus had died, then Agrippa was best placed to take control of the bulk of his legions, but his lack of political connections and past willingness to give the lion's share of credit to his friend were weaknesses. He was not a Caesar, nor indeed from a noble family at all, and the odds were that he would have had to fight to hold onto any power he was able to seize.

Caesar Augustus clung to life, although for a while he was incapable of coping with any further meetings, or even making important decisions. A new doctor was brought to attend him, the freedman Antonius Musa, who like many physicians probably hailed from the Hellenistic world. Reversing the normal treatment, he made use of cold, instead of warm, compresses and cold baths. The *princeps* responded and gradually regained his strength. Whether Musa's treatment was responsible or his body had simply recovered itself, he was never again to be so seriously ill or troubled with this liver problem. Other illnesses, including colds and a tendency to sickness at the start of spring and around the time of his birthday in September, struck most years, but the seemingly frail Augustus would in fact live on for three and a half more decades.

For his apparently miraculous cure Musa was richly rewarded by the recovering *princeps*. The Senate followed with its own public display of gratitude and promptly voted the physician an additional generous sum of money as well as the right to wear a golden ring. They also commissioned a statue of him and had it set up next to Aesculapius, the god of healing, while both he and his fellow doctors were made permanently exempt from taxation. As the news spread, individuals and communities offered public thanks for Caesar Augustus' recovery.[13]

Stability was – at least for the moment – assured, and even those not especially well disposed towards the *princeps* were glad of it. Yet concerns remained about the future, and there was gossip suggesting why Marcellus had been ignored, making it clear that at least some felt the favour shown to him was a sign of preparing an heir. Augustus was displeased by the talk, which marred his otherwise very proper and very public handover of responsibilities to his consular colleague and old friend. When well enough to begin attending meetings of the Senate, he publicly denied that there was any truth in the belief that Marcellus was being groomed to succeed him. As evidence, Caesar Augustus brought with him a document he claimed was his will and offered to read it to the senators to show that his nephew could expect nothing beyond normal legacies – an interesting echo of his release of Antony's will almost a decade earlier. Since accepting the offer would imply the need for the *princeps'* word to be backed up by proof, the senators quickly shouted out their refusal to let him to do any such thing.[14]

On 1 July Augustus left Rome itself for the nearby Alban Mount, where he resigned from the consulship. Outside the formal boundaries of the City and quite possibly with little prior warning to prevent demonstrations of 'loyalty' by senators or the wider population forcing him to reconsider, he probably also announced his intention not to hold the office again in the immediate future. The remaining consul, Piso, presided over the rapid election of a suffect consul to replace him. How many candidates appeared at such short notice is unclear, and Augustus may already have encouraged Lucius Sestius to stand. Sestius had been Brutus' quaestor and had fought for him against the young Caesar. Although he had surrendered after Philippi and been pardoned, he was still open and enthusiastic in his praise of the dead Liberator, keeping images of Brutus in his house and delivering regular eulogies. The choice of such a man who was most clearly not a crony of the *princeps* was widely admired, especially by the aristocracy. Like Piso, he was seen by the established families as a very suitable man to hold the supreme magistracy, and in fact over the course of the next decade many consuls would come from the aristocracy. It was a further gesture towards the restoration of at least a veneer of normality.[15]

Yet even though Augustus was no longer consul, he was less than halfway through his ten-year command of all the key military provinces of the empire. He continued to enjoy immense *auctoritas* and, even more importantly, a virtual monopoly of military force, so that his resignation of the consulship in no way weakened his supremacy. How this dominance was to be expressed legally required attention. The Senate quickly voted him permanent proconsular *imperium*, granting him the formal right to control his provinces and the legions within them now that he no longer possessed the *imperium* of a consul. This power to command and dispense justice normally lapsed when an individual returned from his province and crossed the *pomerium* to enter Rome – apart from the special dispensation given to a man on the day of his triumph. Augustus planned to leave and return to Rome frequently, and to avoid the need to renew the grant on every occasion he did this, the Senate and the Popular Assembly ratified an exemption.

Imperator Caesar Augustus was granted permanent proconsular *imperium* even when he came into Rome. It was also to be defined as superior (in later years expressed by the word *maius* or 'greater') to the *imperium* of any other proconsul. If Augustus ever found himself in any of the senatorial provinces, this prevented its governor from blocking or overruling his actions and decisions. The grant did not place him in command of these provinces as well as his own, or require him to issue regular instructions to the proconsuls. As before, he continued to receive and answer petitions from communities within these areas and his decisions were respected because of his overwhelming *auctoritas* as much as any formal power.

On several occasions in the past Caesar had received grants of some of the rights and powers of the tribunes of the plebs. In 23 BC these were either revived or granted more fully. As a patrician he could not legally hold the office itself, in spite of his attempt in the confusion of 44 BC to seek the post. Since 36 BC he – and subsequently Octavia and Livia as well – was held to possess the same *sacrosanctitas* as a tribune, making it an offence against the gods to harm him in any way. Now that he was no longer consul, he lacked the formal right to conduct business within the City, and the powers of the tribunate were introduced to permit this. As a magistrate, a tribune could summon a meeting of the Senate or the *Concilium plebis*. Augustus was given an additional right never possessed by the tribunes, which permitted him to propose one motion in every senatorial meeting.[16]

The precise details of these new powers and the reasons why they were introduced remain highly controversial, subject to ongoing scholarly debate. There are no simple answers and, as is almost always the case, we have no real idea what motivated Augustus and his advisers. The plan was surely the result of careful consideration, although it is harder to say whether this began before or after his illness. The consulship was convenient and an obvious expression of power that was traditional and distinguished. Yet 23 BC saw Augustus' ninth consecutive magistracy, and apart from the first two years he had always served a full term. Until that year, his colleagues had mainly been close associates. While useful as a means of holding power and acting in a legal and open way, this meant a decade when the pinnacle of the senatorial career was denied to all but the *princeps*' inner circle. Routine resignation and appointment of suffects diminished the dignity of the office, expressed the blatant dominance of Augustus since he controlled the system, and required frequent elections.[17]

Dio was probably right to say that Caesar Augustus wanted to give more senators the opportunity to win the supreme magistracy. After 23 BC there were no suffect consuls for a decade and even then this was an isolated break in the pattern. Most of the men who held the office came from aristocratic, often noble, families, but were too young to have served in anything other than a junior capacity in the civil wars, especially the increasingly distant Philippi campaign. Men like Piso and Sestius represented the old senatorial elite and might openly associate themselves with the cause of the Liberators and wish for an ideal *res publica* guided by the Senate and dominated by no one man or faction.[18]

Yet they were also all men who had now lived under the dominance of the triumvirate or of Caesar Augustus himself for more than twenty years. Whether willingly or not, they had no choice but to accept the reality of the new regime, at least for the moment. Their presence in the *fasti*, the official lists of consuls, and their public performance of the duties of their office were ornaments to a properly functioning commonwealth. Ironically, the reversion to a pattern of two consuls each year was not only traditional, but also prevented any individual from attaining too much or too permanent influence and power, just as it was supposed to do. However distinguished his name, none of the consuls could in any way compete with Caesar Augustus, eleven times consul, celebrant of three triumphs and formally credited with even more victories, still entrusted with control of all the most important provinces and with an active role in public life in Rome itself.

In spite of attempts to understand these years in terms of concerted opposition, there is not the slightest hint that Augustus was forced into this change of his formal position. Many senators were surely pleased to see the consulship once again opened to wider competition between suitable candidates. Not everyone shared that view. In the next few years the majority of voters in the *Comitia centuriata* routinely wrote Caesar Augustus' name on their ballots even though he was not standing as candidate. This was in spite of the fact that such elections were presided over by one or other of the aristocratic consuls of that year, and were fiercely contested – we hear of widespread bribery and some violent disturbances in the fullest tradition of earlier decades. Augustus always refused to accept re-election, but it is clear that many people only felt secure if he had open power to maintain stability and avoid the return of civil war. Voting in the *Comitia centuriata* was led, and often decided, by the centuries composed of the well-off, so this was not a question of the unruly and ill-educated poor simply wanting to keep in power the man who gave them entertainments and free grain.[19]

It was sensible to keep senators reasonably content, since they were the men through whom Augustus would work both in Italy and the provinces. Apart from in Egypt, senators provided all his provincial legates and the junior legates who commanded the legions. The system required a continuous supply of such men to serve willingly, taking the reward of honours, titles and opportunities to win reputations for themselves and their families. There was a lot that needed doing. In 23 BC Augustus also increased the number of praetors from the traditional eight to ten, using the extra two to help administer state finances. Having two new consuls every year, combined with his own new powers, provided additional senior executive officers and enabled more to be done. Holding the consulship continuously may also have been inconvenient for Augustus, and certainly placed a heavy burden on his colleague in the years when he was away from Rome. There were thus sound practical reasons for the change.[20]

Even more important was the question of how Caesar Augustus' power should be openly expressed for the future – a future that his recovery from illness now suggested might last some time. Tact was important. In later years great stress would be laid on the tribunician power and his reign would be dated according to the number of years he had held this, a pattern followed by his successors. Tacitus, writing at the start of the second century AD, would describe the *tribunicia potestas* as the 'title of greatest power' (*summi fastigii vocabulum*).

Yet the emphasis placed on this power was not immediate, and the system of dating was at first little more than a convenience now that it was no longer possible to measure time by the number of his consulships, which had been the case since 30 BC. Many Romans had a strong sentimental attachment to the tribunes of the plebs, seeing them as guardians of citizens' rights, and association with this was no doubt appealing. Even so, the repeated attempts to force the *princeps* to assume the consulship – and on one later occasion even the dictatorship – suggest that there was little satisfaction felt for Augustus' association with the tribunes in itself.[21]

There are some signs of a conscious effort to make his supremacy a little less blatant during these years. Thus the earlier plans for a grand approach to his house on the Palatine were abandoned. Instead, it would be reached by a route leading up from the Forum and passing the fronts of many of the grandest aristocratic houses, their porches decorated with trophies and symbols of their owners' and their ancestors' achievements. In this way the *princeps* stood not alone but as the culmination of the great men of the City. Even so there was no attempt to conceal his vastly greater glory and status. No one else lived in so grand a complex, which included within it the magnificent Temple of Apollo, or dwelled alongside so many of Rome's oldest and most sacred sites, such as the hut of Romulus or the Lupercal, the shrine marking the spot where he and his brother were found after being suckled by the she-wolf. This could not be the dwelling of just another senator, or even of one *princeps* or leading man among many. The Forum, where the walk up to the house began, was steadily filling with monuments to the glory of Imperator Caesar Augustus, the son of a god.[22]

As consul – and indeed as triumvir – Augustus held a formal magistracy and thus the powers that came with it, limited only by those of his colleagues in the emergency legislation which had created the triumvirate. This changed with his resignation from the consulship in 23 BC. From then on he only occasionally held any formal magistracy. Instead his powers were personal and not associated with any office. They were also permanent. Augustus possessed tribunician power and proconsular *imperium* as well as other rights because the Senate and People had given them to him. There was no time limit, and indeed no office from which to resign. His provincial command was for a set period, although it was readily renewed long before it came close to expiring, for periods of five or ten years. Caesar Augustus was the greatest servant of the *res publica* because he was Caesar Augustus and this would always remain true. In many ways his supremacy was more rather than less obvious after 23 BC and what is known conventionally as the Second Augustan Settlement. Although titles such as king or dictator were scrupulously avoided, his dominance was as clear, and by every indication intended to be as permanent, as that of Julius Caesar in 44 BC.

RIVALRIES AND PLOTS

Agrippa left Rome for the eastern Mediterranean at some point in the second half of 23 BC. He received a special grant of proconsular *imperium*, perhaps for a set period of five years. It is less clear whether he was given a specific command and if so what this was, although it certainly seems to have included responsibility for the imperial province of Syria. Yet Agrippa did not go there, and instead established himself on the island of Lesbos – itself normally administered by the proconsul of Asia – and from there exercised a general supervision of the wider region. He probably acted as Augustus' representative, receiving delegations from communities within the senatorial as well as imperial provinces and so saving the *princeps* some work. The Parthian king was currently nervous about his rival living within the Roman Empire and this had increased tension on the frontier. It was possible that the Parthians might launch an invasion just as they had done in 41–40 BC, and did no harm to have someone capable of co-ordinating a response. In itself, the despatch of Agrippa was a signal of preparedness and perhaps enough to deter the king from open hostility.[23]

At the time rumours abounded that there was more to it than

this. People spoke of rivalry between the nineteen-year-old Marcellus and the forty-year-old Agrippa. The older man was supposed to be jealous of the favour shown to Augustus' young and unproven nephew, or perhaps generously unwilling to stand in his way. It is possible that the relationship was a little uneasy. Agrippa was known to possess a temper and at times could be difficult. Already boasting a long string of victories and public works, he was now of the age when traditionally a Roman could expect to be at the peak of his career. Marcellus was young and may well have found his newly acquired eminence intoxicating. There are hints that his judgement and speech were both sometimes questionable. The powerful attracted clients and less formal hangers-on hoping to benefit from their association with them, and it is just possible that some of these saw advantage in diminishing the prestige of anyone felt to match or surpass their patron.[24]

There is unlikely to have been any more to it than this, and the stories of bitter rivalries were either grossly exaggerated or wholly invented. It is more than likely that it was always planned to send Agrippa to the provinces when Augustus was back in Rome, so that at any time one of them would be labouring to ensure that the empire was stable, secure and yielding a steady flow of revenue. It was still less than a decade since the eastern Mediterranean had been squeezed to support Antony's war effort and then fund Caesar's victorious army. Even if the Parthian threat proved illusory, there was much to be done in ensuring that the region continued to recover and remained under effective control. Caesar's illness probably delayed the departure and it was only after he recovered that his greatest subordinate set off for yet another mundane and unglamorous task. The gossip continued, but is unlikely to have shaped any of the important decisions.

Caesar Augustus was well and continued to enjoy good health even though food shortages, outbreaks of plague and other natural disasters ravaged Italy and Rome itself. Near the end of the year Marcellus fell ill. One source maintains that his symptoms were similar to those so recently suffered by Augustus, but with the epidemic

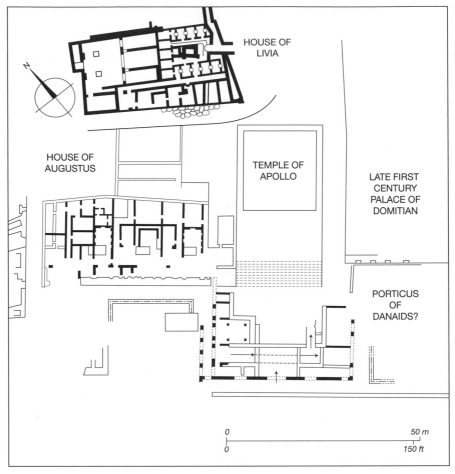

HOUSE OF
LIVIA

HOUSE OF
AUGUSTUS

TEMPLE OF
APOLLO

LATE FIRST
CENTURY
PALACE OF
DOMITIAN

PORTICUS
OF
DANAIDS?

0   50 m
0   150 ft

Plan of the Palantine quarter developed by Augustus

still raging it is equally possible that he was a victim of the plague
(whatever that may have been). Antonius Musa was summoned to
attend him in the hope that he could work a similar miracle to the
one he had performed on the young man's uncle. This time he failed.
Marcellus died, leaving the sixteen-year-old Julia a widow. The brief
marriage between these teenage first cousins had failed to produce
a child.[25]

Later there were rumours of foul play, claiming that the death
was not a natural one but the result of poison, the assassination engineered if not actually performed by Livia. While it is impossible
to prove with absolute certainty that Marcellus was not murdered,

it is extremely unlikely. At a time of plague there were many premature deaths, and the famous were not immune, while even in
ordinary years young people might well fall ill and die in Rome. In
a city crammed with almost a million inhabitants and constantly receiving goods and people from all over the world, germs had plenty
of opportunity to spread and claim victims. It is most probable that
Marcellus died of natural causes. At that moment his death was not
especially convenient for any potential rival. The *princeps* showed
every sign of continued health and his refusal to name Marcellus as
successor earlier in the year surely made it unlikely that he would
show more open favour to Tiberius or anyone else now that his
nephew was removed from the scene.[26]

Publicly there was great mourning. After his funeral Marcellus'
ashes were deposited in the great Mausoleum of Augustus out on
the Campus Martius, the first to occupy this still not quite complete
monument. Octavia constructed a public library as a memorial to
her son. Augustus added his own tribute, giving the name 'Theatre of Marcellus' to the stone theatre begun – or at least planned
– by Julius Caesar and now nearing completion. Propertius devoted
a poem to his memory, recalling the festival he had staged and the
canopies shading the crowd. A few years later Virgil depicted his
hero Aeneas visiting the underworld and seeing the images of great
Romans of the future, men yet to be given bodies and born into the
world. Among them he spotted a youth of 'surpassing beauty', but
sorrowed because the 'dark shadow of death' lay over him. His guide
explained that it was Marcellus and that:

> . . . only a glimpse of him will fate give the earth nor suffer him to
> stay too long. Too powerful, O gods above, you deemed the Roman
> people, had these gifts of yours been lasting. What sobbing of the
> brave will the famed Field waft to Mars' mighty city! What cortège
> will you behold, Father Tiber, as you glide past the new-built tomb!
> No youth of Trojan stock will ever raise his Latin ancestry so high in
> hope nor the land of Romulus ever boast of any son like this. Alas
> for his goodness, alas for his chivalrous honour and his sword arm

unconquerable in fight! In arms none would have faced him un-
scathed, marched he on foot against his foe or dug with spurs the
flank of his foaming steed.[27]

The natural disasters persisted into 22 BC, but the health of Augustus
himself continued to be good. There were two new consuls with
sound aristocratic pedigrees, if perhaps without any particular personal distinction, and the ongoing food shortage prompted cries for
the *princeps* to take direct charge, just as Pompey the Great had done
during a similar crisis in 56 BC. Caesar Augustus refused any additional powers or titles, but did turn his attention to the problem. By
placing informal pressure on some of the people who were hoarding
grain until the price reached its highest level, stocks were immediately released onto the market, providing some short-term relief. In
the longer term, provision was made for two former praetors to be
appointed each year as prefects to oversee the grain supplies to the
City.[28]

Augustus was able to make things happen. If he was not involved,
then the inertia which had characterised senatorial government for
so many years seemed to return. Many remained uncomfortable
with his resignation from the consulship and refusal to accept any
other magistracy. Some demanded that he become censor or take
on the powers of censorship permanently. On another occasion a
determined crowd surrounded a meeting of the Senate, closing the
doors of the Curia, and threatening to burn the place down with
the senators inside if they did not immediately vote to make Augustus dictator. Perhaps on the same occasion, a large group of people
either managed to seize the real *fasces* or made something resembling them and approached Caesar with the twenty-four that were
the symbol of dictatorship.

Imperator Caesar Augustus, the son of the divine Julius, made a
speech refusing the honour, and met their continuing pleas in the
same way. Yet the crowd was determined, prompting him to a histri-
onic display when he tore his garments in frustration. In later years
he boasted that he had twice refused the dictatorship and much of

the scene is reminiscent of Julius Caesar at the Lupercal, although curiously while some scholars remain inclined to doubt the latter's sincerity they do not in the case of Augustus. Similarly there is little debate over whether or not these demonstrations were orchestrated, and generally it is assumed that they were more or less spontaneous. At the very least they offer further important reminders that Caesar Augustus had to concern himself with opinion outside the senatorial and equestrian classes. It was not simply the elite who mattered, and long-term stability would only be preserved if other groups were also content. In this case it was enough to demonstrate his continued commitment to serving the state and dealing with crises. People were reassured that his resignation from the consulship did not mean his effective retirement or determination to focus solely on the provinces. Instead he used his existing power to do what he could.[29]

In addition, two censors were elected in another return to the appearance of traditional practices. One was Munatius Plancus, a man whose reputation no doubt made his appointment to oversee morals seem somewhat ironic, and the other a man who had survived being proscribed in 43 BC. Their term of office did not go well, and on one occasion a platform collapsed under them while they were presiding over a ceremony. Dio notes that Augustus actually arranged most of the tasks normally supervised by the censors. At a time of food shortages, some public feasts were cancelled and others celebrated on a more modest scale. Limits were placed on the sums spent on festivals, the magistrates responsible being permitted to use no more funds than their colleagues. Gladiatorial fights were only to be staged with formal approval from the Senate, and were limited to a maximum of two a year, each involving no more than 120 fighters. Other measures followed the censorial tradition by curbing behaviour as well as extravagance. The sons and grandsons (as long as they were still wealthy enough to be registered as equestrians) of senators were forbidden from appearing onstage – something Caesar Augustus had permitted during Marcellus' games. Some measures may have been passed into law on the motion of others, but it was clear that Augustus was behind them.[30]

Such dominance was obviously reassuring for many people, but in the early months of 22 BC the question of his power and status was raised in a less welcome context. First came the trial of Marcus Primus, lately returned from a spell as proconsul of the senatorial province of Macedonia. It was one of the few that still contained a legionary garrison, and Primus had made use of his army to wage war, winning glory and enriching himself with booty. Now he was charged under the *maiestas* law, dealing with actions considered to be damaging to the majesty or reputation of the Roman people. Both Sulla and Julius Caesar had confirmed existing legislation banning a governor from leading his army outside his province without the express permission of the Senate. In this case, one of the peoples attacked by Primus were the Odrysae, a tribe defeated just a few years before by Crassus who had then granted them allied status after their surrender to him. If he were still alive, it is more than likely that Crassus would have assisted the Odrysae in seeking redress, since it was normal for the conqueror of an enemy to become their patron. Others may also have taken an interest in the case, helping to mount the prosecution. No non-citizen individual or community could bring a case in a Roman court and so they needed to be represented.

Primus was defended by a senator generally considered to be a good man and in favour with Augustus. His name was Murena, although it is variously given as Licinius Murena or Varro Murena in our sources. He may well have been related to the man who had died before, or soon after, assuming the consulship for 23 BC, although how closely is impossible to say. His sister or half-sister was Terentia, the wife of Maecenas, and another sibling was the Caius Proculeius known to be an intimate of the *princeps*. There was no suspicion that Murena was hostile to Augustus, and it may be that as the leading advocate – there were most likely others speaking for the defence as well – his sole concern was to exonerate his client. A glance at Cicero's speeches is enough to show the readiness with which Roman advocates distorted the truth.

There was no doubt that Primus had attacked the Odrysae, or that the tribe were officially allies of the Roman people. It is possible that the defence argued that this was a sham, and the tribe were plotting or had committed hostile acts and so deserved punishment – Julius Caesar had offered a similar justification for attacking some German tribes during a truce. Yet in this case Primus went further, claiming that he had been given permission – perhaps even direct instructions – to launch the attack. Dio says that his testimony varied. At one point he claimed that Augustus had instructed him, and then later asserted that in fact Marcellus had done so. Perhaps the claim was that Marcellus had passed on a hint or direct command from Augustus.[31]

This was shocking on many levels – not least the implication that a proconsul could be ordered or encouraged to do something by a teenager only recently admitted to the Senate. It smacked of the earlier years of triumviral rule or of monarchy where no magistrate or governor possessed real independence and could be forced to do the bidding of one man or his inner circle. This was not the image carefully cultivated by Caesar Augustus in 27 BC, or by his more recent resignation from the consulship and dramatic refusal to accept the dictatorship.

Marcellus was dead and could not testify. Caesar Augustus was not summoned, since no one wished to challenge his *auctoritas* in any way. Murena and Primus probably hoped that invoking the name of the *princeps* might be enough to muddy the waters and aid his acquittal. In the past, Roman courts had routinely failed to convict many patently guilty men, and it is probable that quite a few of the jurors were well disposed towards Primus, or willing to be lenient for the promise of future friendship and favour.

Augustus arrived in court even though no one had either dared or wanted to request his presence. He made it clear that he was willing to give testimony, and when asked by the presiding praetor whether he had instructed Primus as claimed, the *princeps* denied it. He remained to be questioned by Murena, who was by now growing increasingly desperate since the presence and irresistible reputation of Caesar Augustus were adding to the pressure on his client. They had surely hoped to avoid this, and a mixture of anger and fear soon let the defence counsel adopt the aggressive and abusive tone common in Roman trials. Augustus remained infuriatingly impassive. When asked why he was there and who had summoned him, the *princeps* gave the laconic reply: 'The common good'.

Primus was found guilty, although a number of jurors voted for acquittal. Most probably they did so out of existing bonds with the accused, but perhaps some were also annoyed by the interference of Augustus in the trial. It is impossible to know whether or not the *princeps* spoke the truth – whether the whole truth or the carefully worded and intentionally misleading avoidance of a direct lie after the style of many modern politicians. That he wanted an attack on the Odrysae and arranged it in so crass a way does seem unlikely. Yet there are stories that he was sometimes disappointed in Marcellus' judgement and behaviour, which raises the intriguing possibility that his nephew had unwisely said something to Primus.[32]

While many admired the calm and dignified intervention of Augustus, at least a few suspected deceit. That Primus could claim to have been given orders and expect to be believed cast into high relief the reality of the dominance of the *princeps* instead of the façade of normality, and this was damaging whatever the facts of the case. Murena was certainly enraged, and a few months later was named as one of the members of a conspiracy to murder Augustus. This was the first talk of such a plot since the attempted coup by the younger Lepidus in the aftermath of Actium. The leader was Fannius Caepio, said to be a man of dubious reputation, although whether this should be interpreted as a 'Republican' sentiment is harder to say – he may have been as much a Catiline as a Brutus.

The aims of the conspirators are as obscure as the identity of most of them, but the majority were clearly senators or from senatorial families. They may have hoped to kill Caesar Augustus and restore traditional government just like the Liberators in 44 BC. Even if this was the case, like Brutus, Cassius and the others they also wanted the glory of the deed and political advantage in the future. On the other hand it is not impossible that they hoped to remove the 'tyrant' and replace him with one of their number. Such as it was, the plot did not get far. Julius Caesar had taken few precautions to protect himself. Caesar Augustus maintained the praetorians and other bodyguards, as well as a less visible, but clearly efficient, network of spies and informers, since he had no intention of suffering his uncle's fate.

Charges were brought and the conspirators fled either before or soon after their trials began. Their absence did not prevent the cases from being tried, with Tiberius one of those appearing as prosecuting counsels. Prosecution was generally left to the young, and had long provided an opportunity for youthful aristocrats to catch the public eye at an early stage in their careers. Flight was generally accepted as an admission of guilt. It was also the privilege of aristocrats just before or immediately after being convicted, and in the past many had taken their readily movable property and gone to live in comfortable retirement in an allied city. This meant the loss of rights as citizens and the end of their careers, but avoided the death penalty.

Such traditional leniency was denied to Caepio, Murena and the others. Soldiers – presumably praetorians – were sent after them and they were caught and executed. The father of one of the dead men subsequently praised a slave attendant who had tried to protect his son, but publicly executed another who had betrayed him. Murena was said to have been warned of their likely fate by Maecenas' wife. Since there were rumours of a long-running affair with Augustus it is unclear whether it was claimed that her husband or the *princeps* was her source. Gossip alleged that for a while Augustus was distant with his old friend, but since so much of Maecenas' influence was behind the scenes the claim is difficult to judge. On balance it was probably no more than a rumour, and as far as we can tell he remained close to Augustus.

The historian Dio lamented that it was harder to recount events after Augustus' victory in the Civil War than it was before, since so many key decisions were made in private and unrecorded, while much that was public was merely an empty ceremony. A century later the Emperor Domitian complained that the only way to prove that a conspiracy was genuine was to be murdered. Whatever the details, it is highly unlikely that the plot of 22 BC was invented. Scholarly attempts to move this and the trial of Primus to the year before and see them as forcing Augustus to step back from his annual consulships are unconvincing. It is far better to see Caepio and Murena as acting after that change, when in many ways the *princeps'* power was more blatant, and certainly suggested permanence, since his powers were personal and no longer presented as tied to a fixed-term magistracy.[33]

In 44 BC the Liberators had been surprised by the lack of enthusiasm for their action. There is even less sign of widespread hostility to Augustus in 22 BC, although the pressure for him to become dictator may have made those who were opponents fear that he would soon take far more obvious and permanent rule. The conspiracy does not give the impression of good organisation and may never have had any realistic chance of success. Allowing those involved to live on in exile was not something Cicero had been willing to permit to Catiline's conspirators in 63 BC. Augustus made the same choice. The provinces were in the process of becoming more settled, and may well have seemed less distant than they did to earlier generations. The civil wars had also offered quite a few instances of men who had fled from convictions at Rome only to return as partisans of one or other of the leaders. Augustus did not wish to take this risk, and may well have wanted to send a clear message to any others who contemplated attacks upon him. It was a reminder that he was the same man who had ordered proscriptions and executions so many times in the past, and that it was only through choice that this had stopped. Caesar Augustus held overwhelmingly greater power than anyone else in the state and had no intention of giving it up. His public emphasis on legality and tradition softened this, but did not attempt to hide it.

He continued to provide Romans and provincials alike with peace. Some of the aristocracy privately hated the fact that this was necessary, but nevertheless accepted the reality. If some of them resented the public declaration of victory, and the subsequent celebration of the defeat and execution of the conspirators, most of the population did not. Caesar Augustus remained immensely popular, and his death through illness or assassination was feared for its consequences. For the moment the regime was secure, even if with Marcellus gone he needed to look elsewhere for the longer-term future.

15

THE EAGLES

'The Parthians I compelled to restore to me the spoils and standards of three Roman armies, and to seek as suppliants the friendship of the Roman People.' *Deeds of the Divine Augustus.*[1]

'Phraates, on humbled knees, has accepted Caesar's imperial sway.' *Horace, c.19 BC.*[2]

Caesar Augustus spent less than two years in or near Rome before leaving for another tour of the provinces. This would remain his habit for most of his life, alternating between visits to Rome and longer periods spent in the provinces. He was away far more often than he was in Rome, and so the regime he created developed largely in his absence. It would be a very long time before any of his successors travelled so much – Hadrian was the first to match him. In the course of his life Augustus visited almost every province of the empire. In 22 BC he went first to Sicily, Rome's oldest overseas province and not one of the ones allocated to him. There was probably little or no chance of any confrontation with the senatorial proconsul, but his greater *imperium* ensured that the governor could not attempt to obstruct him in any way.

Sicily was an important source of grain for Rome, and his newly assumed responsibility for relieving the famine in the City doubtless offered an immediate reason for visiting, but probably none was necessary. In later years Augustus and his successors issued written *mandata* (instructions or guidelines) to the proconsuls going out to senatorial provinces, just as they did to their own legates in the imperial provinces. It is possible that he already did so – Murena's defence of Primus seems to have relied on the claim that there were additional informal orders rather than that there were no instructions at all. No one ever questioned the right of communities in the senatorial provinces to appeal to Augustus or for him to pass judgement on such petitions, since this was already routine. A one-year tenure quickly became standard for proconsuls, so it was both easier and more consistent for the *princeps* to set major precedents, and deal with larger issues or those having implications for other provinces. Caesar Augustus had both *imperium* and *auctoritas* wherever he was, and dealt with issues beyond the capacity of the governor of that province. The latter were still kept busy, dispensing justice and making decisions on a more local scale.[3]

In this case Augustus had little chance to begin work before he was called back to Rome. In his absence the *Comitia centuriata* chose him as colleague to the consul for the next year, even though he was not one of the candidates, and then refused to elect anyone else. The *princeps* would not be swayed and neither would he return to restore order. In the *Res Gestae* he claims to have refused the dictatorship on two occasions and it may be that the second refusal occurred at this point. On 1 January 21 BC a single consul assumed office and when he summoned the Assembly to elect a colleague the meeting broke down amid disturbances orchestrated by two rivals for the remaining post. Caesar Augustus still refused to return and instead summoned the fractious candidates to Sicily. The pair were admonished and barred from attending the next election. It did not prevent a repeat of the disorder, but in the end one of them was elected and the matter settled.[4]

Augustus remained in Sicily throughout the winter of 22–21 BC, his first visit since the war with Sextus Pompeius. Granted Latin rights by Julius Caesar, more recently the Sicilians had paid a heavy price for backing the wrong side in those years. When Sicily was invaded in 36 BC the young Caesar plundered cities, confiscated their land, executed many leading citizens and probably revoked the grant of Latin status. Agrippa was one of several of his supporters to be given extensive estates on the island from the spoils of war. In the longer run punishment of former enemies was less important than restoring stability and prosperity to the Sicilian communities. Although Egypt and North Africa now supplied the greater proportion of the grain and other crops that fed Italy and Rome, the contribution of Sicily remained a significant one. Augustus founded six new colonies, including Syracuse, Catina and Panormus (modern-day Catania and Palermo respectively). All were existing cities and blended the established population with discharged veterans and perhaps some civilian settlers. Several other communities were granted Latin rights, but this was not universal. The *princeps* himself ordered substantial building projects in Syracuse and Catina, and possibly in other cities as well, so that they would look both grand and Roman. The local elite no doubt followed his example, and cities gained amphitheatres, arches, basilicas and temples.[5]

The coastal communities, and particularly those on the northern and eastern coasts with best access to Italy, gained the greatest benefit from this development and rapidly booming trade. Most were originally Greek colonies – Syracuse was one of the greatest cities of the Hellenic world, and had defeated Athenian invasion and fought Carthage to a standstill before becoming in turn an ally, enemy and defeated subject of the Roman Republic. In time Sicily came to be seen as almost a part of Italy, and at some point it became one of only two provinces that a senator did not need imperial permission to visit. Becoming more Roman or Italian did not mean abandoning either Greek language or culture. Existing cults and customs remained, and although some older buildings were replaced, others were repaired or restored to stand alongside newer designs. Sicily remained part of greater Greece, and thus it seemed as natural to Augustus as to anyone else that in 21 BC he should go from there on a tour of other Greek-speaking provinces.[6]

RENDER UNTO CAESAR

Augustus had visited Greece in the months before Julius Caesar's murder, and later for the Philippi campaign, and again before and after Actium, when he had also gone to Asia, Syria and Egypt. The wider region had demonstrated consistent loyalty to Rome, and as a result three times found itself caught up on the losing side in a civil war. A decade after Actium, no one questioned the supremacy of Caesar Augustus, and the constitutional façade so important for Rome's elite mattered very little to provincials who from the beginning saw him as a monarch. The name of Caesar was already well known throughout the empire. Augustus was rendered in Greek as *Sebastos* – the reverend or august one – and his image soon became more common than that of any other human being. Local mints issued coins bearing his head or symbols of his rule, usually along with his name and title. Quite swiftly almost all new gold and silver coinage was produced by Roman-controlled mints, but local bronze coin issues flourished. Roman weights and denominations were adopted rather than imposed because they were convenient, not least for taxation and trade. In the east the silver denarius was called a drachma, but – with the exception of Egypt, which preserved its own slightly different system – it was the same coin with the same value.[7]

A generation later, when asked whether or not it was proper for Jews to pay taxes to Rome, Jesus told his questioners to bring him the silver coin used to pay tax, and then asked them: 'Whose is this image and superscription? They say unto him, Caesar's. Then saith he unto them, Render therefore unto Caesar the things which are Caesar's; and unto God the things that are God's.' Given the amount of currency produced during Augustus' long life, it is more than likely that the coin in question showed his portrait rather than that of the Emperor Tiberius. More importantly, the Gospel writer could tell this famous story knowing that any reader would immediately be familiar with such a coin, would expect it to depict the image of the emperor, and would automatically accept this as a sign of his power and supremacy.[8]

By name or image, Caesar Augustus reached far more of the provincial population than would ever actually see him. A papyrus written at the end of 26 BC in a village near Lake Moeris in Egypt records the ten-month lease of 'one red cow, whose name is Thayris'. It is dated to the 'fifth year of the domination of Caesar, son of the deified'. The Egyptian tradition was to number according to the rule of the monarch – or in some cases the monarch and consort – and so Augustus' years began with the end of Cleopatra's regime, which was officially extended for a few days after her death for administrative convenience. Thus in 30 BC the men who lit the oil lamps in the streets of Oxyrhyncus swore an oath to do their duty, dating it to the first year of Caesar as they had done the year before, which was the twenty-second and which was also the seventh – that is the twenty-second year since the start of Cleopatra's reign and the seventh of her rule with her son Caesarion as co-ruler.

The document arranging the transaction is written in Greek, although the cow was owned by a man called Pompeius who was most likely a Roman citizen. His side of the bargain was arranged with one of his slaves. The man hiring the animal was called Papus and his spelling of some Greek words strongly suggests a native Egyptian speaker. A Roman – presumably a landowner on a large or modest scale – his slave and a native Egyptian give a sense of the mixed population of the province. In Egypt the Romans were simply a new occupying power to replace the Greeks and all the other foreigners who had ruled the country in the past. Life, lamp-lighting and animal husbandry all went on just as they had done century after century in that truly ancient land. The whole transaction concerns a single cow, although given the duration of the lease it is more than likely that Papus hoped to breed the animal and keep any calf. He paid for the loan in grain, and stated that 'I shall return the cow in good condition and unharmed, and if I do not return [it], I shall pay back from my own resources 187 drachmas of silver money', pledging his property as surety.[9]

After a while, the use of Caesar's name as part of a date and his near-universal presence on public monuments and on coins doubtless became routine and unremarkable, in the same way that most people today spend little time thinking about the symbols and legends on the currency they use. Such familiarity is a mark of success, but as important is the speed at which the change occurred. Roman control had long been accepted as an unavoidable reality by the vast bulk of the population in the eastern provinces. Association of this power with a single leader, rather than constantly changing magistrates, made it easier to understand and to placate – perhaps even harness to local or personal advantage. In Matthew's Gospel Jesus' questioners readily accept the association of coinage and taxation with the emperor. In a technical sense this was not true. Taxes were paid to the Roman state and its treasury and not directly to Augustus or his successors. Yet for provincials the man on the coin was the clear head of that state, making the association natural. Since the *princeps* directly or indirectly disposed of state revenue it was also essentially true, in spite of the legal mechanisms designed to conceal this underlying reality. Once again, the population of the empire naturally perceived Augustus as a monarch and was either unaware or unconcerned by the careful avoidance in Rome of titles like king or dictator.

Since the power dominating their world was led by a supreme ruler, it was entirely natural for the inhabitants to wish that he would look with favour upon them. One common method was to honour Augustus publicly in their community. At Athens not long after 27 BC, a city magistrate dedicated a new building on the Acropolis. It seems to have been a *monopteros* or circle of columns – in this case nine – surrounding an altar erected by 'the people to the goddess Roma and Caesar Augustus'. The formula was the one permitted to the provincial population by Augustus in 29 BC, allowing cult offerings to him only if combined with the deity of Rome itself. Around the same time the council of the city of Miletus set up an altar to Rome and Augustus in the courtyard of their meeting place. At Ephesus another inscription dealing with a number of fairly routine civic duties mentions that one citizen had set up 'the *Sebastos*' and dedicated the shrine, suggesting a similar structure. Building something of this sort honoured the *princeps*. It also provided an admirable pretext for writing or sending an embassy to tell Augustus what they had done, and at the same time make other requests.[10]

Going to the *princeps* for an audience was the most effective method of gaining his attention and hopefully a favourable response. In 29 BC the geographer Strabo was on board a merchant ship which anchored off the fishing village of Gyaros, a tiny settlement on an obscure Greek island. One of the fishermen came on board and revealed that he was acting as ambassador for the whole community and hoped to see Caesar for a reduction in the tribute they owed to Rome because 'they were paying 150 drachmas when they could only with difficulty pay 100'. The ship carried the man to Corinth, where Augustus was pausing on his journey back to Italy to celebrate his triple triumph, but we do not know whether he managed to gain an audience and have the tribute reduced. Strabo only told the story to illustrate the poverty of this and the neighbouring islands, otherwise we would not hear of it at all. Although the Egyptian drachma was of slightly lower value, the entire sum paid as tax by the villagers was less than the worth of 'one red cow, whose name is Thayris'. The issue was understandably of critical importance to the villagers struggling to survive in a poor region. Clearly they felt that it was both possible and worthwhile to bring this matter to the attention of Augustus himself. It gives some idea of the hundreds – probably thousands – of petitioners who each year sought an audience with the *princeps* or with someone like Agrippa who acted in his stead.[11]

Inevitably the bigger, more important communities and wealthier individuals were better placed to gain attention and favour than the inhabitants of a fishing village, but this did not deter the latter from trying to reach the *princeps*. Sometimes the more prominent communities attracted attention that was unwelcome. Athens had been especially enthusiastic in the cause of Brutus and Cassius, and had welcomed Antony and Cleopatra in 32–31 BC, and as a result was aware that it could not automatically expect the goodwill of their victorious enemy. Like many other communities, it had faced demands for money and resources to fund Caesar's war effort after Actium, and the need to show loyalty no doubt encouraged the rapid construction of monuments to him.

The famous cities of Greece had an advantage since all Roman aristocrats so deeply revered their past history and cultural achievements. When Athens had backed Mithridates of Pontus in his war against Rome and fallen to Sulla's legions, the sack of the city was dreadful. Yet its consequences were less severe because of its past history, Sulla saying that he would spare the 'living for the sake of the dead', meaning their famous ancestors. Athens continued to flourish, at the cost of becoming little more than a museum to the past as visiting Roman aristocrats paid for statues or monuments. As always, Augustus and his inner circle followed the tradition, but acted on a far larger scale. Agrippa soon began construction of a great Odeion, a roofed theatre built in the middle of the old Agora or market place. It was lavish in its decoration and deliberately daunting in scale. Such a large roof unsupported by pillars was only possible through Roman techniques and the use of the concrete they had developed. Traditional Greek music and drama – and also formal declamation of speeches in Latin – were thus performed in a monument to Roman achievement, and most of all the glory of the *princeps* and his associates, their names carved upon the building and their images on display. At some point work began on a new market place, meaning that ordinary commerce would similarly go on surrounded by symbols of Caesar.[12]

As well as admiring the Hellenic past – or at least a version of it suited to their own needs and claim to be heirs to Greek civilisation – the Romans also understood and trusted the institution of the city state, and it was both natural and convenient for them to permit most day-to-day affairs and administration to occur at this level and be managed by locals. If anything, this became stronger under Augustus than in the years of the Republic. Relatively quickly the *publicani* lost their central role in collecting taxation and levies from the provinces. Responsibility passed to the cities and other communities in each area instead of the Roman contractors. Those who benefited most were the local aristocrats, the men with the influence and wealth to win office within their communities, which they could then exercise with considerable autonomy. As in Sicily, throughout the other provinces there were building projects paid for by local men alongside the gifts of Augustus and his associates.

The wealthy and aristocratic expected to be honoured and hold power within their communities, but in return there was a long tradition of using their fortunes to benefit the wider community by paying for festivals and entertainments or constructing more permanent monuments. On a smaller scale, it was the same ideology that had formed part of political competition at Rome itself. There it was increasingly restricted by the overwhelming largesse and prestige of the *princeps*. In the provinces it was not a threat to him, but was actively encouraged. Under Caesar Augustus the local elites throughout the Hellenic world built and spent with enthusiasm. Festivals and athletic competitions were revived, expanded or introduced, often with newly restored or constructed theatres and other facilities to house them. Actors, musicians and athletes all received new opportunities to perform and be rewarded, as such traditional and quintessentially Greek activities flourished with a renewed vigour.

Alongside them came new and alien elements, varying from styles and methods of construction to the brutal spectacles of gladiatorial games. In the second century BC a Seleucid king returned after a youth spent as a hostage at Rome and tried to introduce these blood sports to his homeland. Then his subjects were disgusted, but a century and a half later enthusiasm for gladiators spread rapidly throughout the Greek world. Some built amphitheatres, many more simply used their theatres or some temporary arena for staging these grim combats. In all forms of public service there was competition for reputation, whether between individuals in the same community or with neighbours. A city magistracy was an honour, but it was an expensive, sometimes even burdensome, one. Augustus encouraged men to spend in this way, offering the prospect not only of local prestige, but of a better chance of winning favour with him, gaining citizenship and the chance to have a career in imperial service.[13]

The greatest of the local elites were the client rulers, who between them controlled more of Asia Minor and the broader area of Syria than did Roman governors. These men – and occasionally women – relied on Roman favour for their power, but enjoyed considerable

freedom of action within their realms, taking care of local administration. At times some of them even fought small wars against each
other. This was risky, especially if they had not received approval in
advance, and relied upon keeping their ambitions on a small scale
and not doing anything that would upset Augustus. These were not
genuinely independent kingdoms, and were counted as under the
imperium of the Roman people. At any time the Romans – and in
all practical senses this meant Augustus – could strip them of their
office. While most of these rulers possessed small armies, none were
ever so deluded as to believe that they could stand up to the military
might of the legions.

It is unclear whether the client rulers paid a regular tribute to
Rome. Gifts, often on a lavish scale such as the gold crowns sent to
honour an imperial victory, are recorded frequently, as is the provision of food, resources and soldiers to support Roman campaigns;
Herod the Great sent 500 men to take part in Aelius Gallus' Arabian
expedition. Some scholars prefer to see the kingdoms as obliged to
meet Roman requests rather than subject to regular tribute, but it is
equally possible that money or services or goods of some sort were
delivered each year, even if they were tactfully represented as gifts.
In a very loose sense the client rulers were equivalent to provincial
governors, with the difference that their power was not temporary,
although it could be removed by Augustus at any moment and would
not automatically be transferred to their heir – Herod the Great was
granted the special privilege of choosing his own successor, but we
do not know of any other such case.[14]

Herod's career is better recorded than that of any other client
ruler from these years and reveals both his considerable freedom
of action and utter dependence on the Romans. During his life he
made several visits to Rome itself. Whenever Augustus, Agrippa or
any other senior family member or representative came to the east,
Herod went to seek an audience with them and pay his respects. In
20 BC this resulted in the grant of new territory to the Jewish king,
who around the same time sent several of his sons to be educated
in Rome. This was a common practice for client rulers. In part their

children were hostages, but more importantly they would be raised with a Roman education, and there was even a chance of judging their character and reliability since they spent most of their time with Augustus' extended family. Herod was trusted as reliable, but others were not. Most of the lands given to him on this occasion were stripped from another client ruler.[15]

The heartland of Herod's kingdom remained Judaea, Samaria, Galilee and his homeland of Idumaea. Within these areas were Samaritans and many Gentile communities, and the lands added to his realm by Augustus were also of mixed population. For his Jewish subjects, and especially while in Jerusalem itself, the king was careful to present himself as devoutly Jewish. Soon he would begin a grand reconstruction of the Great Temple and he took care to do this properly, using the finest materials and employing a workforce of priests for all the areas considered to be sacred. With the exception of Augustus and Agrippa themselves, Herod was probably the most prolific builder of the age, and paid for monuments throughout the neighbouring provinces as well as in his own lands. Some projects were practical, such as the construction of an artificial harbour at Caesarea Maritima because there were no natural ports along the coast. Its creation required vast quantities of the Romans' waterproof concrete made from volcanic sand, the *pozzolana* from the area around Vesuvius, which was formed into blocks some forty-five feet by twenty-five by thirteen and sunk onto the seabed to form a mole. The new port, with its extensive harbour and warehouse facilities, quickly attracted a good deal of trade, easing Herod's access to luxury goods and providing a steady revenue from levies made on commodities and business.[16]

The name Caesarea was one of the more obvious ways of flattering Caesar Augustus. Herod founded more than one city with this name, while the newly rebuilt capital of Samaria was renamed Sebastos and given a largely Gentile population, many of the colonists being discharged soldiers from Herod's army. It would remain a good recruiting ground, and when the kingdom was finally absorbed into a Roman province the Sebasteni were taken into the Roman army to become regular auxiliary cohorts under the governor's command. The soldiers who executed Jesus were almost certainly Sebasteni.[17]

All the cities named after Caesar appear to have included shrines to Rome and Augustus. These communities were overtly Gentile, even if they included a substantial Jewish minority, and were given other pagan temples and decorated with statues of gods and goddesses as well as the *princeps* and often his family and associates like Agrippa. There were no images of Herod himself, and in Jewish cities and especially Jerusalem there were no images of anyone at all with the exception of Roman coins. The Temple minted its own currency for offerings, hence the money-changers in the Temple court, and these were free of any symbol offensive to religious sensibilities. Like most of the elite, Herod himself spoke Greek, had some familiarity with Greek literature and philosophy, and admired many aspects of Greek culture, for instance donating generously to the Olympic Games. He gave Jerusalem a theatre and a hippodrome for horse and chariot racing and perhaps also an amphitheatre, although some historians believe that this and the hippodrome were one and the same, and that his gladiatorial games were staged there. Games were instituted in many of the Gentile cities in his realm, as was a major athletic and dramatic festival to be held in Jerusalem every fourth year. There was no pressure for his Jewish subjects to take part, and only a little for them to watch.[18]

Herod was eager to be seen as a man of importance in the wider Hellenic and Roman worlds as well as his own kingdom. Almost all of his senior advisers and officials were Greeks, and his army consisted mainly of Gentiles. Augustus had given him the Gallic bodyguard once given by Antony to Cleopatra, and we hear also of Germans and Thracians. The few Jewish soldiers were either Idumaeans like himself and thus not considered truly Jewish by the Judaeans, or Babylonians who had fled from Parthia and relied on him for land and livelihood. The king's reliance on such foreign assistance and his absolute dependence on Roman backing did little to endear him to many of his Jewish subjects. His senior governors and generals were usually Jewish, and mostly relatives, although this was not enough to save many of them from execution for real or suspected disloyalty. The male members of the Hasmonaean royal family were all gone, as were many of the women.

As long as he kept Roman support, Herod was simply too strong to be deposed by force. An assassination attempt was made by a group of young Jewish aristocrats in these years, but the conspirators were notable more for their courage and conviction than any real competence. Herod's spies exposed the plot and all involved confessed when summoned to the king. They were tortured before execution and many of their relatives were also killed. Herod remained exceptionally unpopular among his Jewish subjects. The attitude of Gentiles is harder to discover and they and the Samaritans had nothing to unite them in hostility to his rule. This, combined with his ruthless use of force against any sign of opposition, helped to keep him in power. From the Roman point of view, it did not matter whether or not Herod was popular as long as he remained loyal to them and able to control his subjects.[19]

Augustus was celebrated in the naming of cities and in the decoration of some of the new buildings. The hippodrome – assuming this was also referred to as the amphitheatre and was not a separate building – mounted trophies commemorating his victories and listing them by name. The trophies were to the traditional Roman design, representing a post and crossbeams bearing shields and topped by a helmet, all supposedly taken from the enemy. A crowd of Jerusalemites mistook the shapes for crude figures of men and immediately broke into an uproar. Meeting with leading men, they informed Herod that, while they were offended by the sight of gladiators fighting beasts or other men to the death, it was the graven images that could never be accepted. Repeated denial that they were statues failed to convince them and eventually the trophies had to be stripped of the spoils to prove that they were no more than wooden posts. The incident ended in laughter, and at no point does the anger seem to have been directed against the celebration of Augustus' achievements or indeed the influence of Roman culture except when it threatened to conflict with Jewish law.[20]

In later years Jewish resentment of Roman rule would build up and erupt into major rebellions under Nero, Trajan and Hadrian, but for the moment resentment was focused more directly on Herod himself. The king could be savage in his punishment of any perceived threat, and those closest to him knew that his moods were unpredictable and often homicidal. Yet under his rule the kingdom grew prosperous, benefiting from trade and the practical advantages and employment offered by his grand building projects. On several occasions he reduced the tax burden on his subjects, which does not of course tell us whether this remained oppressive or how evenly the new prosperity was shared. Probably the lot of the rural poor was a harsh one.

Even so, during years of bad harvests and food shortages in the late twenties BC, Herod requested assistance from Aelius Gallus' successor as the equestrian prefect of Egypt, offering as payment some of his own gold and silver ornaments melted down and turned into coin. The historian Josephus mentions that the prefect Petronius was a friend of the king, and now the latter permitted him to purchase substantial quantities of Egyptian grain and helped to arrange shipment to Judaea. It is inconceivable that this occurred without the knowledge – or at the very least subsequent approval – of Augustus, and helps to emphasise the degree to which the kingdoms were integrated with the formal provinces to form a single empire. Once the grain was delivered, care was taken to distribute flour and bread to those most in need. For a while at least, Herod's generous actions, conforming as they did to traditional Jewish concern for the poor, won him more favour with his subjects.[21]

Cities and other communities in the provinces and client states alike ran themselves for most of the time. Above them, Rome and Augustus offered a higher authority, capable of resolving difficulties, conferring benefits or bringing relief in times of need – and was of course also wielder of overwhelming military force that could be directed against any subject community. In the past Roman commanders had granted citizenship to loyal provincials, and this became more common as men like Pompey and Julius Caesar rose to power.

Augustus took it even further, although since anyone enfranchised by him or by the dictator took the name Julius it is often hard to be precise as to when an individual was rewarded in this way. More and more auxiliary soldiers were granted Roman citizenship on discharge from the army – something that under his successors became automatic – and it was a common reward for local dignitaries. This, combined with the influx of native Romans and Italians as part of the colonisation programme, created many more citizens who were permanently resident in the provinces. In the eastern provinces only a few colonies such as Berytus (modern-day Beirut) remained distinctively Roman for very long or in the longer term continued to employ Latin for most official business. Elsewhere Greek was too firmly entrenched and too widely admired. There was no pressure from the Romans to change this, although many ambitious men in the eastern Mediterranean chose to learn Latin.[22]

Large numbers of residents of provincial communities became Roman citizens, and one important issue faced by Augustus was deciding whether this meant that they were no longer obliged to hold magistracies in their home communities. His decision was that they were, unless he granted them an individual exemption. Thus a man could be a Roman, and if wealthy might perhaps serve as an officer in the army or perhaps as an imperial official, but when he returned home he would be expected to play his full part in the public life of his community. The Romans had always cultivated the aristocracies of conquered territories, and this practice was fostered even more strongly under Augustus and his successors. For all provincials, he was quite literally a personification of Roman power, and there was a very personal quality in the tone of his answers to their petitions, which were often set up as inscriptions in public places. Thus he could write to Ephesus about their ambassadors and say, 'On receiving them I found them to be good and patriotic men' and later promise that 'I will do my best to be of service to you and to preserve the privileges of the city.' Negative responses were rarely recorded, except by another community which had done better. Thus the people of Aphrodisias smugly set up an inscription recording Augustus' refusal to exempt Samos from tribute – something he had done for the Aphrodisians. Even so, the message is couched in affectionate terms: 'I am well disposed to you and should like to do a favour to my wife who is active on your behalf, but not to the point of breaking my custom. For I am not concerned for the money which you pay towards the tribute, but am not willing to give the most highly prized privileges to anyone without good cause.'[23]

Some documents record the formal senatorial decree granting the privilege or other benefit given by the *princeps*, and it is safe to assume that this occurred in all major grants so that matters were given a veneer of constitutional legitimacy. However, the impression is overwhelmingly one of autocratic rule, even if, at least openly, that rule was exercised for the good of the subjects. Embassies to the *princeps* were opportunities for oratory as well as gift-giving. Many speeches were in Greek, which enhanced the sense of a benevolent ruler and one who was sympathetic to provincial culture. The unashamed mention of Livia as an advocate for the Samians was a marked change from the days of the Republic and an open admission that anyone capable of influencing Augustus was worth cultivating. It was not unusual. There were generous grants to communities who had welcomed and helped Livia and her then husband after their flight from Italy.[24]

Once again it is quite possible that Augustus' wife accompanied him on some or all of his tour. From Sicily he went to Greece in 21 BC, wintered on the island of Samos, and then crossed to Asia in 20 BC, touring this province and Bithynia, before moving on to Syria. It was only at this point that he actually reached one of the provinces allocated to him and governed via his legates. This did not matter, and no doubt the proconsuls in each region kept on with their normal business of dispensing justice and handling appeals while he was there. The *princeps* dealt with bigger and more sensitive issues, and records of surviving embassies and petitions give some idea of the unending flow of questions waiting to be considered and answered. Perhaps some ambassadors were surprised when they came into the presence of Augustus, and saw not the flawlessly youthful image from sculpture but a man now in early middle age, with skin so sensitive that he wore a broad-brimmed floppy hat to shield himself from the sun.[25]

The imperfections of reality have never been a barrier to diplomacy and, day after day in city after city, business was carried on. Ambassadors waited for the chance to be presented, made their speeches – probably at considerable length – and were then either pleased or disappointed at the outcome. Some communities suffered. Athens lost territory from the region administered by the city while Sparta gained authority over a wider area. Cyzicus in Asia was severely punished for an outbreak of violent disorder during which several Romans were flogged and then executed. It lost civic status and some of its citizens were enslaved. This was an extreme punishment, and only a few others suffered similar penalties.[26]

While travelling, Augustus had to keep up with events in Rome itself, where there was more unrest in 21 BC. Wherever he was, petitioners travelled from other provinces to reach him, just as they had gone to Tarragona during his residence there. In Egypt the prefect Petronius had faced serious raids by the Ethiopians into the south of his province. He drove out the first attack, but the difficulty of keeping an army in the desert caused him to pull back most of his forces. The Ethiopian Queen Candace again sent her warriors to attack the Romans, prompting another campaign and Roman counter-attack, which this time a better-prepared Petronius extended further south. The British Museum houses the head from a statue of Augustus that was cut off and carried back home as a trophy by the Ethiopians. It was later buried beneath the entrance to one of their temples and was still there when excavated, having survived the destruction of the building by Petronius' vengeful soldiers. Eventually Candace sought terms, and Petronius referred their ambassadors to Augustus. Interestingly, Strabo tells us that the Ethiopians complained that they did not know 'who Caesar was or where they should have to go to find him' and so Petronius 'gave them escorts; and they went to Samos, since Caesar was there . . .'[27]

In 20 BC Agrippa was sent back to Rome to deal with the continuing disorder in the City, but he soon had to move on to suppress renewed rebellion in Spain. In the following year he fought a tough campaign and at long last brought to an end large-scale resistance among the Cantabrians and Asturians. In the meantime voters in the *Comitia centuriata* once again wrote Augustus' name on their ballots and refused to elect more than one consul. At the start of 19 BC this man, Caius Sentius Saturninus, still lacked a colleague. Another election was held, but was badly disrupted by the violence of one of the candidates. This was Marcus Egnatius Rufus, a man who had won popularity for himself serving as aedile a few years earlier. At a time of floods and fires, Rufus not only entertained the population but formed his slaves into a fire brigade which helped to protect their homes. Still below the legal age for the consulship, he nevertheless put himself forward and organised his household and supporters into the sort of intimidating band used in the past by men like Clodius and Milo. Perhaps he promised radical reforms if elected, or was simply seen as a threat to stability, for later sources felt that he conspired against Augustus himself. (This may reflect the same attitude that attributed military defeats to the *princeps* even when he was nowhere near the theatre of war.) Saturninus had the Senate pass the *senatus consultum ultimum* – the last time this was ever done – and Egnatius and some of his supporters were arrested and executed. Probably this was made easier by the assistance of whatever force of praetorians were in or near the City and the active support of men like Maecenas and Statilius Taurus. The episode was a reminder of the violent past, and a warning that such things could still happen, especially when the *princeps* was far away. Yet in many ways it was more a sign of the growing stability of Augustus' regime. Traditional mechanisms dealt with the problem, and Egnatius Rufus proved to be the last in the long succession of ambitious senators – often tribunes – willing and able to use force to get their way.[28]

RESTITUTION

Given the distances involved, Augustus may not have heard of these events until the affair was over. Before he left Rome envoys had come from the Parthian King Phraates IV, demanding the return of his rival Tiridates. The latter had fled to seek Augustus' protection and support, bringing as captive Phraates' son. Both were given comfortable accommodation in case they proved useful in the future, but in 23 BC a delegation was sent by Phraates asking for their return. The Parthian ambassadors went first to Augustus, who then brought them and Tiridates before a meeting of the Senate. Rather than make a decision on the matter, the senators promptly passed a vote asking the *princeps* to do so. Syria, the region closest to Parthia, was part of his province so there was perhaps a degree of justification for this, but more importantly it revealed the underlying truth of power in Rome.[29]

Augustus gave the king back his son, but refused to hand over Tiridates, and demanded the return of Roman standards and prisoners held by the Parthian king. Negotiations continued at a lesser distance when in 20 BC the *princeps* arrived in Syria. They were backed by a show of force. A rebellion in Armenia had overthrown and killed King Artaxias II. The kingdom lay between the greater powers of Parthia and Rome, and was culturally closer to the former, although on balance even more exposed to the military might of the latter. Artaxias had been backed by the Parthians, but now leading aristocrats offered the throne to his brother Tigranes, another exiled foreign prince who had sought and found sanctuary in Rome.

Augustus granted the request, and sent the twenty-one-year-old Tiberius at the head of an army to take him to his kingdom. It was an extraordinary command for someone so young, only matched in the recent past by the activities of Pompey and the young Caesar during the civil wars. In the event there was no fighting, and the advance was little more than a parade culminating in the enthronement of Tigranes as the new king. Such peaceful displays of Roman strength had a long tradition and were widely admired. No doubt

Tiberius was accompanied by older, experienced officers, but even so it gave the young man an opportunity to issue orders and control a large force in the field.[30]

The expedition to Armenia provided the background to the ongoing negotiations. Augustus did not want to fight Parthia any more than he had done in 29 BC. The risks were great, and the scale of the task daunting. At the very least it would have kept him away from Rome for two or three more years, during which time it would be harder to continue dealing with all the petitions and other problems brought before him. Phraates IV was no more enthusiastic for confrontation. He had other frontiers in addition to the one with Rome, as well as facing the more immediate threat posed by rival members of the royal family and an unruly nobility. In the last years Augustus had ensured the loyalty of the cities and client monarchs in and around Syria, making it very unlikely that the Parthians would get any support there, should they risk an invasion.

Neither side wanted war, and it was really a question of finding a peaceful way for both to claim success. Probably the Romans promised not to support Tiridates, although he was most likely permitted to live on in comfortable exile. In return Phraates IV pledged to keep the peace, and as a gesture returned the Roman standards captured from Crassus, Antony and during the invasion of the Roman provinces in 41–40 BC. With them came Roman prisoners, some of them held captive since Carrhae thirty years earlier.

The return of the lost legionary eagles and other standards was one of the most publicised of all Augustus' achievements, seen for instance on the breastplate of the famous *prima porta* statue of him, and it really did not matter that it came through diplomacy and not from a successful war. For the Romans it was an acknowledgement of their superiority, since the Parthian king recognised their strength and met Augustus' demands. The standards were reclaimed and, even if such tokens had far less significance for the Parthians than the Romans, the former must by now have been aware of their symbolic value. As far as we can tell, Phraates gave more than he received in this settlement. No doubt for a home audience he presented the arrangement as an agreement between equals. The Romans saw it differently: a proud and dangerous enemy had been humbled by the fear of Roman might at no cost in Roman lives. While Horace might declare that it was 'sweet and fitting to die for the native land' – *dulce et decorum est pro patria mori*, a phrase now perhaps most famous as Wilfred Owen's 'old lie' – the Romans never needed a victory to be costly to themselves in order to be glorious and never depicted their own fallen on any victory monument.[31]

Coins were soon minted depicting the standards and carrying slogans proclaiming their return – *signis receptis*. The Senate greeted the news with a flood of fresh honours, many of which Augustus ultimately rejected when the offers reached him. This did not prevent some of these awards appearing on coins minted in Spain and other provinces before the news arrived that he had turned them down. Thus some show a new temple on the Capitol to hold the standards, although as far as we can tell it was not actually built. Although Augustus accepted a formal thanksgiving for his victory he declined the offer of celebrating an ovation – or perhaps even a full triumph – on his return, but not before coins appeared depicting the symbols of this. One series shows the *princeps* riding in a chariot pulled by a pair of elephants, so presumably this rather bizarre honour was offered to him. Pompey had tried to celebrate a triumph in this way, only to be thwarted and forced to change to a conventional horse-drawn chariot when he discovered that an arch on the processional route was too narrow for such an unwieldy vehicle and team. Julius Caesar had had forty elephants as torch-bearers in a night-time ascent of the Capitoline Hill after his Gallic triumph. Clearly the idea of such flamboyant gestures, using these large and exotic animals, still stirred some aristocratic imaginations.[32]

Augustus refused almost all of the new honours. It still meant that he enjoyed the glory of being given them in the first place and the admiration for his modest refusal, carrying with it the confident assurance that his fame and reputation was already so immense that he had no need for any more. In due course the returned standards would be placed in the Temple of Mars Ultor

(Mars the avenger) which formed the centrepiece of his new complex, the Forum Augustum. He had vowed to build this temple after Philippi, having achieved vengeance over the murderers of his father, but the work had scarcely begun and now it would also happily serve to mark the avenging of defeats at the hands of the Parthians.

More immediately, the Senate voted him the right to construct a triumphal arch. It was the third time that he had received this honour, for similar awards were made after Naulochus and Actium. As far as we can tell, only one arch was ever built. This commemorated Actium and stood beside the Temple of the Divine Julius on the edge of the Forum Romanum. Instead of building another, Augustus seems to have decided to modify the Actian Arch, mounting larger-than-life statues of the *princeps* driving in a chariot with the goddess Victory behind him, while suppliant Parthians hand back Roman standards. Such imagery reminds us that even if he refused many honours, Augustus was still very obviously marked out as the greatest ever servant of the state. He was everywhere, his name, image or symbols on monuments in the heart of Rome, in the towns of Italy and throughout the provinces.[33]

On 27 March 19 BC the Younger Balbus celebrated a triumph for a victory achieved while proconsul of Africa, and he would spend some of the spoils building a new stone theatre. Augustus' legates did not receive triumphs since their victories were his. Instead they were given the symbols of triumph (*ornamenta triumphalia*). Opportunities for large-scale campaigning were denied to most senatorial proconsuls, and very rare for the governors of Africa and Macedonia who still commanded legions. It is unclear whether or not anyone realised this at the time, but Balbus' triumph would be the last after the old style. Augustus himself never celebrated another, and in the future only members of his family would be permitted the honour. Even for them the award was a rare one. Wars would continue and victories would come steadily, but all were now credited mainly to the *princeps*, who did not bother to commemorate them in the traditional manner. Perhaps a hint of this came when a list of all past triumphs was added to the Actian Arch. It ended with Balbus, and there was no space for anyone else.[34]

Augustus returned to Samos for the winter of 20–19 BC and the constant flow of embassies and petitioners continued throughout these months. Among them was a deputation from one of the Indian rulers, bringing some tigers as gifts and an unfortunate boy born without arms but able to grasp objects with his feet. Dio felt it worth remarking on these presents more than two centuries later. The animals were probably taken to Rome, displayed to the people and quite possibly slaughtered for their amusement, for that was the grim Roman way. The crippled boy was an object of curiosity rather than sympathy. The Indians stayed with the court for some time, following them when they proceeded to Athens. Dio also claimed that one of the ambassadors there committed suicide by throwing himself onto a specially prepared pyre. The historian was unsure whether the man did this out of extreme old age or 'to make a display for Augustus and the Athenians'.

India remained far distant and little known, reached by Alexander the Great but never by a Roman army. Even so, this was just one of several embassies from India known to have come to Augustus, and that in itself reveals some Indian leaders' recognition of Rome's wealth, power and reputation. The Romans and the inhabitants of the provinces had a voracious and ever-growing appetite for silks, spices and other luxuries from the Far East, and it is likely that the main aim of the envoys was to secure access to that market. At the same time such exchanges allowed Augustus to boast that Rome ruled virtually the entire world. The idea thrilled Roman and Greek alike and would seem more real as the victories continued to come. If Rome's honour and standards were regained without actual war, it was not a sign of slowing expansion.[35]

AN END AND A BEGINNING

'From this noble line shall be born the Trojan Caesar, who shall extend his empire to the ocean, his glory to the stars . . . Him, in days to come, shall you, anxious no more, welcome to heaven, laden with Eastern spoils; he, too, shall be invoked with vows. Then wars shall cease and savage ages soften . . .' *Virgil, late twenties* BC.[1]

Caesar Augustus appears to have spent several weeks in Athens, and his return to Italy was a slow progression, as he paused to give audiences in all the major communities along the route. Work continued and even such macabre distractions as the suicide of the Indian delegate were brief intervals between receiving petitioners and writing correspondence. More welcome was the appearance in Athens of the poet Virgil, who was travelling in Greece as a rest from working for more than a decade on his twelve-book epic, the *Aeneid*. A long-time intimate of Maecenas, through him the poet had been introduced to Augustus and it was widely – and no doubt correctly – believed that the *princeps* had urged him to embark on his great project. Certainly we know that Augustus took a keen interest in its progress, for instance writing from Spain to ask about it. Before leaving Rome for the east, he and some of his family attended when Virgil gave a public reading of a part of the *Aeneid*. The passage lamenting the recently dead Marcellus moved them all so deeply that Octavia fainted.[2]

Virgil was a perfectionist, choosing each word with such care that he rarely composed more than a couple of lines of the *Aeneid* in the course of a day. His friend Horace, another of Maecenas' circle, was at times even slower than this in his composition. Such dedication was not mere affectation or the mark of a dilettante, for these

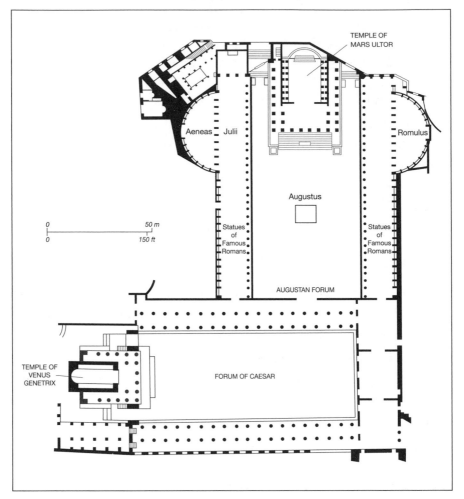

The Forum of Augustus

were serious artists of truly extraordinary talent. Horace was universally admired, while Virgil's poetry was already spoken of as probably the most beautiful expression of the Latin language. Maecenas chose well in selecting poets to join his circle of friends. All of them were probably equestrians, including Horace, the son of a successful freedman, and wealthy enough to possess the education and the leisure to devote themselves to verse. Even if some of them had lost land during the civil wars, they were not dependent on the patronage of Maecenas and Augustus for a livelihood, whose gifts merely added to their comfortable lifestyles. Probably in the aftermath of his illness, Augustus hoped to employ Horace and wrote to Maecenas accordingly: 'Before this I was able to write my letters to my friends with my own hand; now, overwhelmed with work and in poor health, I desire to take our friend Horace from you. He will come then from that parasitic table of yours to my imperial board, and help me write my letters.'[3]

In the event Horace declined the offer, but this did nothing to damage his continuing good relationship with Augustus. The informal, bantering style of this small fragment from the *princeps'* letter to his old friend Maecenas was extended to his correspondence with the poets themselves. Literature was an utterly respectable and highly fashionable leisure interest for the Roman elite – the mark of the truly civilised man. Julius Caesar's staff in Gaul were an especially literary bunch, and Augustus shared Maecenas' reverence for poets and writers. Such matters were useful – and conveniently neutral – topics of conversation for social meetings with other senators or men of importance. Alongside tradition, literature had formed a major theme in his friendship with Atticus. Both Augustus and Maecenas wrote on their own account, and the former joined Horace and the others in mocking the latter's efforts at poetry. He was also willing to denigrate his own efforts, joking when he abandoned an attempt at writing a tragedy that his hero had 'fallen on his sponge'.[4]

Like everyone else, the poets of Maecenas' circle cannot have failed to see the reality of Augustus' dominance or been unaware that it rested ultimately on his military might. Yet they were no more compelled to write than senators were to seek office or a public career. It is a great mistake to dismiss their work as propaganda, or even to suggest that its content and themes were carefully controlled by Maecenas and through him by Augustus. Equally misguided is the quest to reveal carefully veiled subversion or hinted criticism of the *princeps* and his regime. Augustus prided himself on association with only the finest writers. This was a matter of self-respect, but also good politics. Alexander the Great's reputation had suffered through accepting overblown praise from mediocre poets.

Men like Virgil, Horace and Propertius could be encouraged and cajoled into writing on certain topics, and would themselves be aware of what was likely to please the *princeps*. At times they joked of being 'pressed' to write, but this was a common enough literary device often combined with false modesty. Cicero, Atticus and their contemporaries often played the same game and urged each other to write on particular themes. Augustus once wrote to Horace gently chiding the poet for not addressing him in any of his works. 'Are you afraid that your reputation with posterity will suffer because it appears that you were my friend?' he remarked in his usual bantering tone, and it is hard to see an edge of real menace behind the words. The talk is of friendship – Horace is a *familiaris* – rather than politics, and although the two were often blurred at Rome, the implication is that any work would be an honour to both of them. Horace responded with the first poem of his second book of *Epistles*, which talked of the service to the state offered by poets like himself, and included the famous line telling of how 'captive Greece conquered the fierce victor, and brought the arts to rustic Latium'.[5]

Compulsion was slight, and most of the subjects congenial to the poets. Caesar's victory and the peace it brought was something almost anyone who had lived through the civil wars could easily celebrate. The restoration of religious rites, the return of stability and the defeat of dangerous foreign enemies were all unambiguously good things for all Romans, and especially members of the elite, and the poets would have been unusual indeed if they did not share these sentiments. There was no direct intervention in the words they wrote, still less any direct censorship. To have value, men like Virgil, Horace and the others needed to be left to compose in their own way and after their own style.

The result was an outpouring of works of the highest quality that continued to be admired for centuries; it included much that was congenial to the new regime, but also much that spoke more generally to the human experience. This was far more powerful than any controlled propaganda could ever have been, and helped feed the mood of restoration. Augustus' association with the poets added lustre to his dominance, since this was an entirely proper interest for

The Forum Romanum: Taken from the Palatine Hill, this view shows the western end of the main Forum. Most of the remains, including the triumphal arch and the Senate House in the centre of the picture, date to the centuries after Augustus. However the basic plan would have been familiar to him. The Rostra or speakers' platform is just to the left of the arch. (*Author's collection*)

Julius Caesar: This bust from Tusculum depicts the dictator with a receding hairline and heavily lined face. It may well have been produced in his lifetime and is less idealised than subsequent portraits. None of the images of Augustus were ever as realistic. (*W&N archive*)

Pompey the Great: One-time ally and son-in-law of Julius Caesar, Pompey's drift towards his opponents led to civil war in 49 BC. His career had begun in Rome's first civil war when he raised a private army and earned the nickname of the 'young butcher'. In many ways Augustus' early career followed his example. (*Author's collection*)

Coin showing the young Caesar: A refusal to shave was a display of mourning intended to show everyone that the heir of the dictator was determined to gain vengeance on his assassins. The inscription styles him 'Imperator Caesar, son of the god (Julius), triumvir to restore the Republic.' (*CNG*)

Mark Antony: From a well-established aristocratic family, Antony felt himself born to eminence. One of the few nobles to back Julius Caesar in the civil war, he was consul in 44 BC and so well-placed to make his own bid for permanent power in the aftermath of the dictator's assassination. (*National Trust/Simon Harris*)

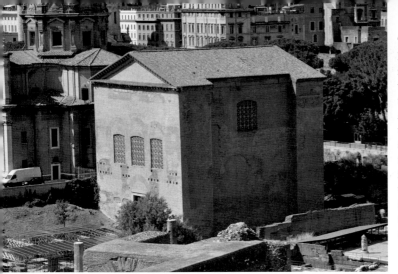

The Curia Julia or Senate House: Julius Caesar began the rebuilding of the Curia after it was burnt down in 51 BC, but the job was finished by Augustus. This building was later destroyed, and the structure seen today dates to the third century AD, surviving into the modern era because it was converted into a church. In size and plan it seems to follow closely the design of Julius Caesar. *(Author's collection)*

Livia: Well-born, intelligent and ambitious, Livia was also considered a great beauty and caught the eye of the young Caesar. His marriage to her was scandalous but enduring, even though it proved childless. *(Author's collection)*

The Rostra: Julius Caesar altered the position and shape of the old speakers' platform, but as with so many of his projects the work was actually completed by Augustus. Much of what is seen today is modern reconstruction. In its original form it was faced with marble and decorated with the prows of enemy warships. *(Author's collection)*

Octavia: The fate of aristocratic women was to be married in order to advance the careers of the men in the family. Antony's neglect of Octavia was an important part of the propaganda campaign directed against him. *(akg-images/Nimatallah)*

Cleopatra: The ruler of a client kingdom, Cleopatra was consistently loyal to Rome, realising that only Roman support would keep her alive and in power. Her misfortune was to live at a time when Rome was wracked by civil war and it was not easy to be on the winning side. *(Scala)*

Sextus Pompeius: The younger son of Pompey the Great, Sextus relied on the fame of his dead father to turn himself into a warlord. With strong fleets based in Sicily, he dominated the western Mediterranean, but lacked the soldiers to overrun Italy. Even so, he inflicted some of the worst defeats ever suffered by Augustus. *(Alinari/Topfoto)*

Marcus Vipsanius Agrippa: Close contemporary and friend from Augustus' youth, Agrippa proved consistently loyal and remarkably capable. His skill as an admiral and general defeated first Sextus Pompeius and then Mark Antony. In spite of the age difference, he later married Julia and sired five children with her. *(Author's collection)*

A war-galley: This sculpture from Praeneste depicts a heavily stylised warship of the type used at Naulochus and Actium. The crew are out of proportion to the vessel, but details such as the raised tower on the prow are realistic. The naval victories over Sextus Pompeius and Antony were common themes in Augustan literature and art. *(Scala)*

Puteoli: Sextus Pompeius was able to block many of the grain ships coming to Italy. Since Rome in particular relied heavily on imported food, this added to the unpopularity of the triumvirs. Some of the negotiations were carried out here, in the Bay of Puteoli (modern Pozzuoli). Cape Misenum is in the background. *(Author's collection)*

The victory monument at Actium: Augustus' victory over his last rival was celebrated time and again throughout the empire, but the first monument was planned and built near Actium itself. Little is now left, but it was originally decorated with the bronze rams taken from enemy warships. *(Erin Babnik/Alamy)*

The Bay at Actium: The losses were lower than in the battles against Sextus Pompeius, but Actium forever broke Antony's power as soon as he fled to follow his lover. Although they escaped with their treasury, the abandonment of his legions and most of his fleet forever discredited the Roman warlord. *(Harry Gouvas collection)*

The spoils of victory: Augustus had two ancient obelisks brought to Rome as part of the commemoration of his success in Egypt. Restored and moved to its current location in the Piazza di Montecitorio at the end of the eighteenth century, this one was used as the gnomon of Augustus' vast sundial. *(Author's collection)*

The new Latin inscription: Set up in 10 BC to celebrate the conquest of Egypt, the inscription styles him as 'Imperator Caesar Augustus, son of the divine (Julius), *pontifex maximus*, hailed as *imperator* twelve times, consul eleven times, in the fourteenth year of his tribunician power.' *(Author's collection)*

The Temple of the Divine Julius: The view from the Palatine down onto the eastern end of the Forum Romanum has the remains of the temple dedicated to the deified Julius Caesar just below the centre (marked by the semi-circular metal roof). It was erected near the spot where the murdered dictator was cremated. Originally faced with marble, it also boasted a speakers' platform looking towards the old Rostra. *(Author's collection)*

Copy from Arles of the 'shield of virtues': Awarded by vote of the Senate and People of Rome, the inscription is to Imperator Caesar Augustus, son of the divine (Julius) and praises his *virtus*, clemency, justice and piety. This is a marble copy of the gold original set up in Rome. *(Author's collection)*

The *imperator*: Probably the most famous image of Augustus, the *prima porta* statue depicts the ever-youthful Augustus as a great general. Even though he relied heavily on more capable subordinates, military glory was a cornerstone of his self-presentation. The style of the head and face represents the most common style of all the many portraits of Augustus. This image was paraded throughout the empire. *(Vatican Museums & Galleries/ Bridgeman)*

Lucius Caesar: Augustus adopted his two grandsons when they were infants and showed them great favour, especially when Tiberius' voluntary exile left him without close family members to send to the provinces. Almost all the portraits of Caius and Lucius Caesar are posthumous, set up during the grand display of public mourning throughout Italy and the provinces as communities wished to demonstrate that they shared Augustus' grief when both boys died very young. *(akg-images)*

Julia: The only child of Augustus, his daughter was married off for political reasons in the traditional manner of the Roman aristocracy. Five children were produced by her second marriage to Agrippa, but the third union with Tiberius proved deeply unhappy for both of them. Augustus later exiled her for repeated adulteries, refusing ever to recall her. *(Interfoto/Alamy)*

The face of the *princeps*: More images of Augustus survive from the ancient world than those of any other Roman emperor – or indeed any other human being. The idealised image of the ever-youthful leader was carried on coins and depicted on busts and statues while his name was equally ubiquitous. This larger-than-life head comes from Arles in Southern France. *(Author's collection)*

Augustus as *princeps*: An example of another common portrait type of Augustus; the faint lines around the mouth suggest maturity without changing the essentially youthful appearance of the great leader. He is often depicted wearing a triumphal wreath. *(Author's collection)*

The Mausoleum of Augustus: Construction of his own great tomb was Augustus' answer to the stories that Antony wanted to be buried in Egypt. Although in keeping with the style of earlier aristocratic funeral monuments, it dwarfed them in scale and soon acquired the name Mausoleum, after the famous tomb of King Mausolos, one of the Seven Wonders of the World. As it turned out, several of his family would be interred in the tomb before Augustus' ashes were deposited there. *(The Art Archive/Alamy)*

The Theatre at Merida: As well as the wholesale rebuilding of Rome, monuments began to appear throughout the provinces. Augusta Emerita (modern-day Merida) in Spain was established as a colony for discharged soldiers after the Spanish campaigns. Both Augustus and Agrippa built grand public buildings in the city, including this stone theatre. *(Author's collection)*

The Theatre of Marcellus: Like many other monuments, this stone theatre was planned by Julius Caesar, but the bulk of the work only occurred under Augustus. It was named in honour of his nephew Marcellus, and finally completed a decade after his death in 23 BC. In the Middle Ages it was converted into a fortress, changed into a palace during the Renaissance, and later divided into apartments. *(akg-images/Gerard Degeorge)*

Statue base from Athens: Agrippa constructed an Odeion or enclosed theatre at Athens, making full use of the possibilities offered by Roman concrete. In thanks, the city re-used an old statue base which had carried images of Hellenistic kings and then Antony and Cleopatra, and set up a statue to Agrippa, describing him as 'their own benefactor'. *(Dorothy Lobel King)*

The gate of Athena: In spite of showing enthusiasm for his enemies in the civil war, the fame of Athens ensured that it received its share of largesse. This is the western gate of the Roman Agora or market place, the inscription proclaiming that it was paid for with money provided by Augustus in 11–9 BC and dedicated to the goddess Athena. *(Dorothy Lobel King)*

The *princeps* and his family: The Ara Pacis or 'Altar of Peace' celebrated the end of civil war and the return of peace and prosperity thanks to the actions of Augustus. The *princeps* and his family feature prominently in the religious procession depicted on its sides, symbolising the harmony of the family and the assurance they offered for the future. Agrippa, with his head covered, is shown on the left, but was dead before the monument was completed. Livia stands behind him, then Tiberius, and further back Antonia and Drusus. *(Author's collection)*

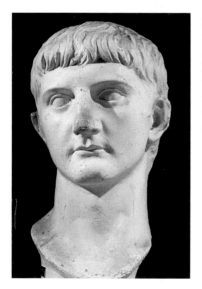

Drusus: The younger son of Livia and her first husband, Drusus was born immediately before her wedding with Augustus. More charismatic than his awkward older brother, Drusus proved just as capable a general and the two of them were given accelerated careers and a series of important commands. The *princeps* led the widespread public mourning when Drusus died in 9 BC from injuries suffered in a riding accident. *(De Agostini / A. Dagli Orti / Bridgeman)*

Antonia the Younger: Augustus employed marriage as a way of cementing the alliance between members of his extended family. The younger daughter of Octavia and Mark Antony, Antonia married Livia's younger son Drusus. The future emperors Caligula, Claudius and Nero were all descended from them. *(Author's collection)*

Roman legionaries: This sculpture from the headquarters building of the army base at Mainz dates to the middle of the first century AD, but gives a good idea of the appearance of the legions by the end of Augustus' life. The man on the right crouches for protection behind his shield and prepares to thrust with his sword. The man behind uses his shield to protect the other soldier, and holds a heavy throwing spear or *pilum*. Body armour would normally have been worn. *(De Agostini / akg-images)*

Battle scene: This relief from the Arch of Orange in southern France shows Romans fighting against Gauls and was carved in the early first century AD. After the Civil War, Augustus devoted immense resources to wars of conquest and consolidation in Europe. *(Nik Wheeler)*

The Pantheon of Agrippa: In the second century AD the Emperor Hadrian rebuilt the pantheon to his own design, creating the spectacular domed roof which still stands to this day. However, he kept or renewed the original building inscription, and so the name of Marcus Agrippa, consul for the third time, stands proudly over its entrance. Augustus similarly restored many existing buildings, and boasted that he kept the names of original builders in place. *(Author's collection)*

Imperial soldiers: Augustus' power was ultimately based on control of the army, although he was careful to veil this reality by posing as merely a servant of the Republic. The nine cohorts of his personal bodyguard, the praetorians, were the most visible reminder of this reality. This sculpture dates to the middle of the first century AD, by which time the guard had been concentrated in the City and given their own fortress. *(Author's collection)*

The Temple of Mars Ultor: A temple of Venus the ancestor was at the heart of Julius Caesar's Forum. The Augustan Forum more openly celebrated Rome's military might and past successes, and was centred around the temple to the war god Mars, in his guise as the avenger. On the left are the steps climbing up to the temple. It was here that the standards returned by the Parthians were placed amid much ceremony. *(Author's collection)*

The return of the eagles:
The breastplate of the *prima porta* statue carries many symbols of the successes of Augustus and the peace and prosperity they brought. In the centre, Tiberius in the uniform of a Roman commander is handed an eagle standard by a Parthian, depicted as a rather generic barbarian. Mother Earth reclines below holding a horn of plenty, while above the Sun god and Apollo and Diana preside. The imagery continued themes repeated time and again in art, poetry and ceremonies such as the Secular Games. *(Prisma Archivo / Alamy)*

The great harbour at Caesarea:
As well as the grand projects begun by Augustus and his family, many communities and client rulers throughout the empire embarked on building programmes in the stability of these years. Herod the Great's kingdom lacked a natural Mediterranean harbour, so this vast artificial one was built at Caesarea, formed from large stone blocks sunk to form a mole. *(Author's collection)*

Enemies: This larger-than-life head of Augustus was found in Sudan. It seems to have been plundered in a raid on Egypt by an army from Meroe. Later it was buried beneath the steps of a temple – perhaps as a symbolic humiliation and also to hide it from the reprisal raids launched by the Romans. *(De Agostini/Getty)*

Barbarians: This group of Germanic chieftains are depicted on Trajan's Column, set up a century after Augustus' death, but it is unlikely that the appearance of such leaders had changed much in the intervening years. Several wear their hair in the famous Suebian knot. *(Author's collection)*

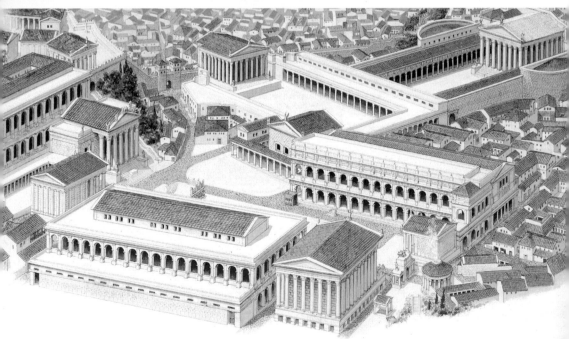

The centre of Rome: This Peter Connolly painting depicts the reshaped centre of the City after Augustus' building programme. It gives a good idea of its grandeur and the association of almost everything with Augustus and his family. In the centre is the Curia Julia, topped by the golden statue of Victory. In the foreground is the Forum Romanum, filled with monuments built or restored by the *princeps*. Behind the Curia is Julius Caesar's Forum with the Temple of Venus Genetrix at the far end. Extending at a right angle to the top right of our picture is the Forum of Augustus, and the great Temple of Mars Ultor. *(akg-images/Peter Connolly)*

any senator, and because the poetry produced was so obviously good he did not appear a tyrant nor did the poets seem sycophantic. When Propertius rejected the theme of war against the Parthians and other enemies and turned instead to speak of love it was not an attack on state policy, but a witty and charming device in poems designed to amuse, not to convince readers to abandon public life. Augustus' dominance created an environment where literature and the arts were encouraged to flourish and poets, writers and artists struggled to make their names, often reinventing well-established styles. There is no good reason to doubt that Virgil and the others were sincere in the views they expressed, even if the modern prejudice is to assume that all great artists must by nature be dissidents, especially if they live under a leader who has fought his way to power. As a comparison, we would do well to think of the many great works of music and art produced under the rule of, and often with the direct patronage of, absolute monarchs in the eighteenth and early nineteenth centuries.[6]

At one point Virgil talked of writing an epic about Augustus himself, before rejecting that idea. The *Aeneid* instead was set in the distant past and told the story of Aeneas, the Trojan hero who had escaped from the fall of his city and led a party of exiles to Italy where, several generations later, his descendant Romulus would found Rome. This was the world of Homer's *Iliad* and *Odyssey*, the oldest and greatest of Greek epics, and was a deliberate attempt to match their grandeur in the Latin language. Aeneas was also claimed as the ancestor of the Julii, their name being derived from his son Iulus, and since the Trojan hero was the son of Venus, this gave the aristocratic family their divine pedigree. Virgil devoted himself to the project, and even his trip to Greece was intended as a rest to inspire him to continue reworking and improving the poem. For all his effort and the favourable reception of early recitals of extracts, the poet was not satisfied – he was even known to alter lines during the course of a reading. Less gregarious than the *bon viveur* Horace, Virgil spent much of his time closeted away on one of his estates, tinkering with the poem and modifying or rejecting line after line.[7]

The *Aeneid* was not finished, but whether Greece proved less inspirational than he had hoped or he simply felt obliged to accompany Augustus, Virgil joined the *princeps* and his entourage as they returned to Italy. During the journey he fell ill, initially with sunstroke and then a bout of fever. Virgil reached Italy, but died at Brundisium on 21 September 19 BC, in his fifty-second year and just two days short of Caesar Augustus' forty-fourth birthday. Both the *princeps* and Maecenas were named as heirs in his will, as was Lucius Varius, another of the latter's circle of poets. Still dissatisfied with the state of the *Aeneid*, Virgil had begged Varius in the event of his death to burn the manuscripts. The latter refused, and in his final days Virgil implored his attendants to bring the scrolls to him so that he could set fire to them himself. Augustus made sure that they did not obey this command, and the *princeps* urged Varius and a colleague to tidy up the poem and quickly release it to the world.[8]

In spite of the wishes of the author, this disobedience was a great service to the world, saving one of the greatest achievements of Roman literature. There was the obvious appeal for Augustus of a grand and beautiful epic written by a famous author, telling inspiring stories of one of his Julian ancestors and of the origins of the Romans, which celebrated both their past and future. Thus his actions were not wholly selfless, although it is clear that he would not have wanted to circulate the poem unless it was substantially finished and of obviously exceptional quality. People soon began to ponder the changes Virgil may have planned – and this speculation continues among scholars to this day – but the *Aeneid* was universally hailed as a fitting rival to Homer. It quickly became a standard text in Roman education. (A century later two bored military clerks at opposite ends of the empire, in northern Britain and Judaea, scrawled a line from the poem on the back of routine documents which chance later preserved for archaeologists to discover.) The *Aeneid* was one of the most-quoted works of Latin literature, although it should be noted that these quotations are largely from the early books. Much like Shakespeare, a good deal of the epic was neglected as teachers concentrated on a few familiar selections.[9]

'I sing of arms and the man' (*arma virumque cano*) runs the first line of the first book – and the use of the first person by the poet was in itself a break with the Homeric tradition. The world of the *Aeneid* is interwoven with Homer's world, and many of the characters – most of all Aeneas – came from Homer. The first half mirrored the *Odyssey* as the Trojan refugees wander the Mediterranean, sometimes crossing the trail left by the Greek hero. Thus they find one of Odysseus' men who had been left behind when the others escaped from the cave of the cyclops Polyphemus, and then see the blinded monster blundering angrily around. Throughout the gods intervene, Juno vindictively pursuing the Trojans while Venus protects her son.

For all the echoes of Homer and the many allusions to other literature, there are hints alongside the myths of a more modern and complicated world. Aeneas is sometimes afraid, angry or confused, and able at times to feign confidence and enthusiasm to inspire his men while privately despairing. Homeric heroes were utterly self-confident and equally self-centred – the *Iliad* tells of the anger of Achilles over a personal slight, so that he sulks in his tent until the death of Patroclus moves him to return to the battle and wreak savage revenge. The wider fortunes of the Greek army are almost irrelevant to his personal motivation, as he chooses a short but glorious life instead of living to old age in obscurity. In the *Odyssey*, the hero Odysseus loses all of his followers during his journeys with little sign of regret, and dallies with nymphs and goddesses before returning home to slaughter his wife's suitors and any of the household who have accepted them. Personal honour and success are all that really matters to such heroes, which helps to explain why many generations of Greeks and Romans – and especially aristocrats – would see these epics as guides to their own behaviour.

Aeneas is different, for he is always aware of his wider duty. He is *pius* Aeneas, respectful to gods and his family, especially the father he carried from the ruin of Troy, and aware that he is charged with the destiny of his race, needing to lead them to Italy so that in time Rome may be founded and the Romans rise to the greatness of Virgil's day and even grander achievements to come. More than once he is shown glimpses of this future glory to inspire him. As well as open enemies he faces temptation, most famously when he and his followers are welcomed by Queen Dido of Carthage. Juno and Venus conspire to make her fall in love with the Trojan hero, and their love is consummated when they both take shelter in a cave during a storm-interrupted hunting excursion. The threat to the future is brief, as Aeneas soon afterwards leaves with all his people rather than settling among the Carthaginians – an alternative which would have led to them and not the Romans becoming the greatest people of the region. The heartbroken Dido kills herself, binding her people to undying hatred of Aeneas' descendants, and thus providing an ancient grudge for the real clash between Rome and Carthage in the third and second centuries BC.[10]

Virgil's epic is a mixture of existing tradition – sometimes choosing one version from several – and of Homer and other epics, as well as a good deal of invention. Allusions to his own day are numerous, but not heavy-handed. Sicily features heavily in the poem – Aeneas visits it twice – which is surely a reflection of its central role in the rise of Augustus. A despairing Dido regrets that her lover has not given her a 'little Aeneas' as consolation for his abandonment of her, which must have made contemporaries think of Julius Caesar, Cleopatra and Caesarion. The association of the Carthaginian queen of the epic with the Egyptian queen of recent history was natural, but is never forced. Dido is treated with great sympathy, manipulated by the gods into falling in love and then abandoned. The single appearance of Cleopatra herself later in the story is deeply hostile, but Dido appears more as victim than villain, and only as the poet describes her ghastly suicide is she depicted as unstable and dangerous – a change probably more jarring to modern than ancient sensibilities.[11]

Pius Aeneas puts the greater destiny of his people before his own feelings and abandons Dido. Later, when he visits the underworld and encounters her spirit, the queen refuses to acknowledge him in a scene more concerned with his sorrow and guilt than her feelings. Time and again Aeneas does the right thing for the future, but at great cost to himself and those around him. When they finally reach Italy, the welcome given by some local kings leads to war with their neighbours that foreshadows in many ways the civil wars of Virgil's day. Homer's battles are grim and savage, with detailed descriptions of wounds and death, and Virgil followed in the same tradition. It is tempting to see an even harder edge – one allied king trips over and falls onto an altar, and is killed there, his opponent mockingly calling out, 'He's had it [*hoc habet* – the cry crowds used at gladiatorial fights], this better offering given to the great gods,' while nearby another man has his beard set alight before he is knocked down and slaughtered. There is certainly more sense of the cost of war, and the sorrow felt by the families of the fallen, than in the *Iliad*.[12]

Yet we should not see in this a condemnation of war itself, for although Virgil depicts the fighting as terrible and full of sadness, he does not present it as unnecessary. Aeneas is as implacable in battle as anyone else, carving his way through a long succession of foes, including a man wearing the insignia of a priest. At the end of the story he confronts Turnus, king of the Rutulians, who has already cut down many of the Trojans and their allies, most notably Pallas, son of King Evander. Wounded by Aeneas, Turnus asks to be spared for the sake of his poor father, reminding the Trojan of his own beloved – and now dead – father, Anchises. For a moment the victor is moved and hesitates. Then he notices that Turnus is wearing a belt stripped from the corpse of Pallas, and pity turns into 'fury and terrible anger'. Calling out that this is just punishment for Pallas, Aeneas thrusts his sword deep into Turnus' chest, whose 'limbs fell slack and cold and with a sigh his life fled indignantly to the shadows below'.[13]

The poem ends with these words, and for all that Virgil had not finished refining his great work, it is doubtful that he planned to change the final scene so that the story culminated in mercy rather than retribution. Turnus had taken up arms against Aeneas, had exulted in the havoc he wrought on the enemy, showing them no mercy whatsoever, and in the final encounter he had broken a truce. He is not depicted as a monster without any virtues, and Virgil extends the same sympathy to him as he does to Dido and his other characters. Such a sympathetic understanding of the human condition is the mark of a great artist, but at no point does Virgil encourage the reader – and even more a first-century BC Roman reader – to equate the characters with Aeneas, or hint that they might be in the right. Many Romans were capable of admiring their enemies and of confessing that their wars of conquest often meant dreadful suffering for subject peoples. Such awareness never seriously challenged the deep-seated belief that Roman expansion was just. Enemies remained enemies, to be defeated and only then treated with kindness. In poetry as in real life, the joys of peace came only as a result of Roman victory.[14]

Aeneas reflected Augustus in many ways, albeit in the glamorous form of an overtly heroic, handsome and physically strong warrior, and suggestions that this was not a deliberate celebration of the *princeps* lack conviction. Both men placed duty and piety before their own comfort and interests, enduring great hardships and struggling for many years before the final victory was won and the wider community enjoyed peace and prosperity. At times it was necessary for them to do dreadful things for the greater good and destiny of the Roman – or in Aeneas' case the pre-Roman – people. Given such a high stake, all those who opposed them had to be destroyed, and calm *pietas* could give way to justified and passionate rage. Aeneas sometimes even mocked his enemies as he killed them, just as the young Caesar was said to have done after Philippi and at Perusia.[15]

Caesar Augustus is celebrated in the poem, and is shown at the moment of his great victory at Actium as the centrepiece of the ornate shield forged for Aeneas by the god Vulcan. Sometimes Virgil refers more vaguely to a Caesar – on one occasion a 'Trojan Caesar . . . laden with Eastern spoils' – and it is hard to know whether he means Augustus or Julius Caesar. Probably the vagueness is deliberate and he means both, the best of the father reinforcing the achievements and virtues of the son. Similarly when he has a Cato judging the dead in the underworld it is a generic Cato, as much the famous ancestor as the descendant who so bitterly opposed Julius Caesar. Virgil was keen to celebrate the great Romans of the past. The dead Catiline is consigned to terrible punishment, but otherwise there is little hint of political differences. In the description of Rome's future heroes waiting to be born are two 'gleaming in matching panoplies', clearly Pompey and Julius Caesar, who will 'alas ... cause battles and bloodshed', the 'bride's father' against 'her husband'. They are urged to restrain themselves from civil war. This is surely criticism, but it is mild and directed as much against Pompey the Great as the dictator, and the latter is urged to be first to 'spare', which is surely an approving reference to his famous clemency.[16]

The *Aeneid* was patriotic, filled with inspiring talk of past glories and the even greater destiny of a Rome led by the son of the divine Julius Caesar. For all the unflinching depiction of warfare and strife so familiar to Virgil's generation, there was optimism for the future, with Rome promised unlimited power. Like all great works it can be read on many levels and interpreted by different people at different times, often in ways that would surprise or dismay its creator. Such complex interpretations are unlikely to have occurred to Augustus; instead he was simply moved by the beauty of the verse, pleased both at the appearance of such a universally praised poem and by his close association with it.

FAMILIES AND POWER

It was late in the year by the time the *princeps* and his entourage reached Rome. There was still only a single serving consul after the disturbances associated with Egnatius Rufus and it was not until now that a senatorial delegation came to him and he chose one of them as the other consul. How this was done is unclear; Dio implies that Augustus did it on his own authority and without a formal election, but this may simply be because Dio described the essence of what he felt happened rather than the technical details. The man chosen had served Augustus loyally during the civil wars. Having made this arrangement, he once again refused the honour of a formal greeting by the assembled Senate and People. Discovering that a large deputation of senators was still determined to welcome him, he slipped quietly into the City under the cover of darkness. He did accept the vote of a Temple to Fortuna Redux – goddess of fortunate homecoming – to be erected near the Porta Capena, the gate from which he had come into Rome after journeying up the Appian Way. Annual sacrifices would be made there on 12 October, the newly created festival of Augustalia in commemoration of his return.[17]

Rome without Caesar Augustus had been uneasy, with only the direct supervision of Agrippa temporarily preventing the *Comitia centuriata* from electing him as consul every year. It may well have been on his return that he floated the idea of having three consuls, so that he could hold the office and still ensure that two others also got the opportunity. The suggestion was quickly dropped as too unorthodox, for there had never been more than two consuls in office simultaneously. Instead Dio claims that he was awarded permanent consular power, but scholarly opinion is divided over whether or not this is accurate and, if it was, then precisely what it meant. There is general consensus that Augustus was awarded the chief symbols of the consulship, so that he was from now on accompanied by a dozen lictors while he was in the City. He also would sit on his own magistrate's or curule chair between those of the two consuls at senatorial meetings. Whatever the details, the powers granted to him now were personal, just like those awarded in 23 BC, and not associated with any office. Symbols – and especially symbols of office – had a deep importance in Rome, and reinforced Augustus' control of the state.[18]

Some of the other new powers recorded by Dio as accepted at the time may actually have been refused or be garbled. The claim that Augustus was appointed as permanent 'overseer of public morals' was probably another temporary grant of the powers of the censorship, for in the following year the *princeps* again embarked on a purge of the Senate, hoping to reduce it in size and restore its dignity, something damaged by the recent disturbances at elections. When no one volunteered to step down, Augustus selected thirty senators, taking a public oath that he had chosen the best men. The thirty then took the same oath and each was asked to write down the names of five other senators, but were not permitted to include themselves or their relatives in their selection. One man from each batch of five was then chosen by lot to be included on the new senatorial roll, and the thirty thus selected repeated the process, each writing the names of another five. It was laborious, and open to behind-the-scenes horse-trading. Augustus was annoyed when Antistius Labeo included Lepidus among his five names and tried to get him to change his mind. Labeo refused, saying that he was entitled to his opinion and if the *princeps* permitted Lepidus to remain *pontifex maximus* then he could not be blamed for naming him as a senator as well. Augustus let the choice stand, and his old triumviral colleague must have been drawn by lot as he remained a member of the Senate.[19]

Frustrated, he abandoned this method and chose the remaining senators himself. There were still protests, for instance from a father excluded when his son was not, who made his point in a very Roman way, tearing his toga and pulling away his tunic to reveal the scars of honourable wounds earned in the service of his country. Another senator asked to resign in favour of his own father, who had lost his place. The expelled men were, as in the earlier expulsion, allowed to keep the insignia and prestige of their former rank and some were subsequently re-enrolled or won a place in the Senate through election to a magistracy. Augustus was once again said to have aimed at reducing the supreme council to 300 members, but was forced to give up the idea and be satisfied with double that number. Any fewer and it would prove difficult to fill all the necessary posts or have the quorum of 400 present at a meeting in order to vote on any issue.

Around this time, the *princeps* established a smaller and more convenient council, later known as the *consilium principis*, formed from representatives of all the colleges of magistrates along with fifteen senators chosen by lot and serving for six months. It was a useful sounding board for wider senatorial opinion and helped to tighten up any proposal before it was brought for discussion in the Senate. Augustus continued to treat the Senate with respect, attending every meeting whenever he was in Rome, and encouraging the members to speak their minds. Although angry, he did not act against Labeo, and when the Senate subsequently offered to take turns sleeping outside the *princeps'* bedchamber to ensure his safety, Labeo told them that he would have to be excluded because he snored too loudly. Suetonius tells us that on occasion Augustus' speeches in the Senate were interrupted by shouts of 'I do not understand' or 'I'd speak against you if I had the chance' – the last comment no doubt from men not called upon to contribute. Sometimes the bitter exchanges between angry senators made him so annoyed and exasperated that he left the meeting before it was finished, prompting calls that senators ought to have the right to say what they thought on important public affairs.[20]

In the past senators were registered with the wider equestrian order, and required its minimum property qualification of 400,000 sesterces. Now, in an effort to add to its dignity, Augustus formally separated the senators as a distinct class, required to possess property valued at at least 1,000,000 sesterces. Some of the men unable to meet this requirement lost their seats in the Senate, while others considered sufficiently worthy were given the necessary money by the *princeps*. At the same time he passed a new law to deal with bribery and intimidation at elections.

Such legislation had rarely proved effective, but Augustus possessed both power and prestige to enforce it more rigorously, and the problem was certainly reduced, if not eradicated altogether. The next decade saw the return of many well-established families to the consulship. These had suffered heavily in the civil wars, and they were men who were too young to have taken part, but were now willing to enter public life in a state dominated by Augustus. Honours such as the consulship were still worth pursuing. There is no evidence that these men were any more or less well disposed towards Augustus than the rest of the Senate. Dio claims that around this time several men were executed for plotting against the *princeps*, but gives no names.[21]

In 18 BC Livia's younger son, Drusus, was quaestor. He was only nineteen, and like his brother Tiberius was now granted the right to hold the praetorship and consulship five years before the normal age. Betrothed to Agrippa's daughter while she was an infant, Tiberius finally married Vipsania when he returned from the eastern campaign since she was now of marriageable age. Within a few years, his younger brother Drusus was married to Antonia the younger, daughter of Mark Antony and Octavia. An even more significant marriage had taken place during Augustus' absence in the east. In 21 BC, when Agrippa was sent back to Rome to deal with the disturbances, he was also charged with more personal matters. He divorced his second wife, the daughter of Octavia and Marcellus and thus the *princeps'* niece, and instead married Augustus' daughter, the widowed Julia. The bride was eighteen, her husband closer in age to her forty-two-year-old father, but such a gap was common in an aristocratic marriage. The alliance was a mark of great favour, uniting Augustus even more closely with his most trusted and consistently reliable deputy. Gossip implied some compulsion in the arrangement, Maecenas allegedly telling Caesar Augustus that he had made Agrippa so strong that he must either kill him or make him his son-in-law. In reality there were few other options. Augustus' feelings towards Tiberius are unclear, but severing the planned marriage to Vipsania would surely have appeared a snub to her father.[22]

Many aristocrats never forgave Agrippa for coming from outside the inner circle of the Senate, or for rising so far through his connection to Caesar Augustus. Like other new men, Agrippa seems to have paraded this difference, consciously associating more with the wider population and building them amenities while disdainfully refusing personal honours such as the triumphs so craved by other senators. He was an enthusiastic collector of artworks, but only for public rather than private display, and, unlike the rest of Augustus' circle and the aristocracy in general, he showed little interest in literature and did not befriend poets and writers. Energetic and efficient, Agrippa was as successful a husband – at least by Roman standards – as he was a general, administrator or builder. Before he left Rome in 20 BC Julia was pregnant, and later in the year she gave birth to a son, Caius. In 19 BC Agrippa stamped out the last serious rebellion in Spain, and on his return to Rome once again declined the award of a triumph. Julia was soon expecting another baby, and in 17 BC was delivered of another boy, who was named Lucius.[23]

As son-in-law to the *princeps* and a man who could boast so many great achievements, his *auctoritas* far outstripped that of any other senator. This was soon reinforced by formal powers. In 18 BC, a year before it was due to expire, Caesar Augustus was granted a five-year extension of his great provincial command. At the same time Agrippa was also given a five-year proconsulship, although this was probably not tied to specific provinces and would only later be made 'greater', or *maius,* than those of ordinary governors. At times in the past he must have held similar *imperium*, although the details of his status throughout the twenties BC are often hard to reconstruct. More conspicuously, in 18 BC he was also granted *tribunicia potestas* for five years. No one apart from Caesar Augustus had ever possessed this. The grant had a time limit, unlike the permanent award made to the *princeps*, but remained in essence a personal right, marking Agrippa out as distinct from other magistrates and prominent senators. All in all, his new status placed him second only to Augustus, and if the latter died in the next few years, Agrippa would surely have expected to step into his place.[24]

A dynasty was taking shape, an impression reinforced when, soon after the birth of Lucius, Augustus adopted both of Julia and Agrippa's sons. The form of this ceremony involved a symbolic purchase, Augustus tapping a low-value bronze coin known as an *as* three times on a balancing scales in the presence of a praetor. The infants, grandsons of the *princeps* and sons of his closest confederate, now became Caius and Lucius Caesar. It seems unlikely that by this stage anyone still expected Caesar Augustus to retire – and since so many of his powers were personal awards there was not really an office from which he could resign. Yet when he took the five-year extension of his province he claimed that this was sufficient time to bring order to those regions. Perhaps some people believed him, although there was to be no furore when after a while this term was increased to a decade. Some Romans may still have resented the holding of so much permanent power by one man, but few even of these wanted to risk a return to civil war – at least for the moment. As the years passed the new reality of a monarch in all but name became less and less remarkable. In the foreseeable future there was no chance of a rival warlord emerging for them to rally behind, and so, short of assassination, there was no means of removing the *princeps*. Augustus was far more careful to protect his personal security than Julius Caesar had been, making any plot against him a dangerous enterprise, while the events of 44 BC had shown everyone that even if the deed was done, there was a good chance that it would bring only a return of chaos and civil war.[25]

It would not have been impossible to murder Caesar Augustus, and the precautions he took should not be exaggerated. He attended senatorial meetings, and for this and other reasons often walked or was carried in a litter through the streets of Rome. At meetings of the Senate he greeted each senator in turn as he met them, and often bid them farewell in the same personal style. When presiding over meetings he was careful to know each member's name, and he called on them in this way to voice their opinions, relying on his excellent memory rather than a *nomenclator* to prompt him. The *princeps* was accessible to petitioners here as everywhere else, and took pains to demonstrate his willingness to listen, chiding one man who approached him nervously by saying that he looked like someone offering 'a coin to an elephant'. Another story is told of a Greek poet who took to waiting around outside the porch of Augustus' house on the Palatine – probably among a crowd of others wishing for his attention. He carried a poem he had written in praise of the emperor, and hoped to be rewarded for it. For a long time Augustus ignored him. Happy to be associated with talented men like Virgil and Horace, he had no desire to receive the mediocre efforts of an unsuccessful writer, and so he passed by without letting the man near him.²⁶

The Greek persisted, and eventually Augustus decided to play a joke on the man. On the next day the poet was there as usual, but this time the *princeps* went over to him and gave the man a piece of papyrus with a few verses of Augustus' own poetry. Unfazed, the Greek declaimed the little poems aloud, praised them for their quality, and then gave Imperator Caesar Augustus a few coins for his trouble, apologising because it was so little and saying in Greek, 'I swear by the good fortune of Augustus that if I had more I would give you more.' Amused, the *princeps* ordered one of his attendants to give the man 100,000 sesterces.²⁷

This and so many other anecdotes make it clear that Caesar Augustus was not a distant figure but one who could be approached, not just by the wealthy and important, but by almost anyone. It also confirms the impression that the overwhelming majority of Romans were content to accept his dominance as better than any likely alternative. In this context, the more public recognition of Agrippa and the adoption of his two sons were reassuring promises of future stability and security. This clearly mattered to Augustus himself, hence the adoption of the two infant boys. The wider future of the Roman race, and especially the elite, also became a great concern of his at this time. Civil wars and proscriptions had wrought havoc among senatorial and many equestrian families. Some lines died out altogether, and others had one or more generations cut down before or during the prime years of a political career. Raising children was expensive, especially if they chose to seek office, and there was a widespread belief that more and more men were choosing either to remain bachelors or marry but not have children.

Augustus decided to act, no doubt discussing the matter beforehand with the *consilium,* or smaller council, to prepare it for presentation to the Senate. His concern was moral only in the sense that he wanted Rome's elite to do their duty and keep on providing young men to follow a public career. It was also a proper thing to do, and in the past the censors had as part of their role a supervision of public morals and behaviour. On his return from the east, he had been voted the right to pass a *lex Augusta*, a decree that would become law without the formality of senatorial discussion and vote in the Assembly. It is not clear whether he accepted this right, but even if he did, the *princeps* chose not to make use of it. Instead his proposal was presented for senatorial approval and then voted on to become the *lex Julia de maritandis ordinibus*. Benefits were granted to the fathers of three or more children, with penalties for the unmarried and childless. Concerned as ever with the dignity of the senatorial class, senators were forbidden to marry freedwomen, but this was permitted to other citizens including equestrians because many people believed there were fewer women than men in the citizen population.[28]

Around the same time he also introduced a law, the *lex Julia de adulteriis*, punishing adultery and any sexual intercourse with freeborn women outside of wedlock. In this case the concern is said to have begun with the Senate, who felt that the habits of the younger generation were too wild and that this was preventing many from marrying and raising families. The law was passed, but when some wanted even stronger action Dio claims that Augustus was reluctant to intervene further, feeling that the new legislation was adequate. Such matters are inevitably difficult to regulate, and there is a fair chance that those involved will merely seem ridiculous. In the case of Augustus, his own reputation for affairs with other men's wives scarcely helped, and there was ironic talk during the debates implying that he was well qualified to discuss this topic. Facing mockery, and also still under pressure to do more, he advised them to control their wives better – 'You ought to rebuke and instruct your wives as you think fit. This is how I behave.' Even at 600 members, senators were part of the small aristocratic world that included the *princeps* and his family. Many knew Livia and all were aware of her formidable reputation, and thus this declaration prompted a good deal of surprise. Several speakers pressed Augustus for details of the sort of instructions he gave to his wife, and the best he could come up with were claims of suggestions about Livia's and Julia's deportment, dress and manners.[29]

Senators felt free to embarrass the *princeps* without fear of reprisal. Perhaps it damaged some men's careers, but many had already achieved all that they wanted in terms of office, honours and provincial commands, and were not deterred. The mockery was gentle, especially when compared with the often extremely vulgar abuse traditional in Roman politics, and stopped short of direct criticism of Augustus. In many ways such exchanges helped to preserve the façade that he was still no more than the most distinguished member of the Senate. His laws were passed without any difficulty. Enforcing them was another matter, but resistance to the new rules had little to do with formal opposition to him. Some men arranged betrothals with infants, gaining the benefits of marriage without the inconvenience of actually contracting one for a good few years. Augustus responded by modifying the legislation so that a betrothal was only recognised if the wedding took place within two years.[30]

The efforts to make these laws work created more uncomfortable moments, his temporary responsibilities for public morals meaning that individual cases were brought before him. One man was accused of marrying a woman with whom he had previously had an adulterous affair, something rather too close to home given Augustus' unorthodox courtship of Livia. In this instance the man's accuser brought many other charges about his character, and clearly bore a deep grudge against him. Augustus finally dismissed the case, vaguely declaring that they all ought to forget the fractious quarrels of the past. Aged forty-five at the start of 17 BC, the *princeps* was a mature man, less prone to the angry outbursts and sometimes clumsy statements of his youth. He coped with the ironic questioning of senators or the interruption of his speeches, and even when placed in awkward situations dealt with minor losses of dignity with good humour.[31]

His affability softened the hard reality of his control, and only occasionally was the steel of the former triumvir apparent. On one occasion Augustus dined with an equestrian called Vedius Pollio, who was known for his wealth, love of luxury and his cruelty. He was also an old friend, probably one of the wealthy backers who had supported the young Caesar when he thrust himself into politics in 44 BC. Like many of Cicero's generation, he owned extensive ornamental fish ponds, one of which was filled with carnivorous lampreys to which he would feed slaves who displeased him. During the meal, a slave accidentally broke one of a set of expensive drinking cups, and his master immediately ordered him to be thrown to the fish. Imperator Caesar Augustus gave an order of his own, telling one of his attendants to gather the rest of the set of cups and then smash them one by one in front of their owner until he released the slave. The story is told to illustrate his disapproval of the senator's viciousness and that was surely his motive. There is also something chilling about his absolute assurance, knowing that he could act in this way and that there was nothing his host could do about it. Later the man died and bequeathed one of his luxurious villas to the *princeps*. Augustus had it demolished so that no memorial would preserve Vedius' name. It was his property and so he was free to do with it whatever he pleased, but the disdainful erasure of someone's memory – however well justified – illustrated the utter dominance of Caesar Augustus.[32]

There was no force to oppose him, and whatever they pretended no one failed to understand this. People could voice criticism of him, but the very fact that this was so restrained confirms the fear as well as respect he commanded. In the past, the Romans had never been so reticent in voicing their opinions even of the greatest men in the state. Stronger sentiments were expressed in anonymous pamphlets left in public places including the Curia. Caesar Augustus spoke in the Senate to defend himself from these attacks and announced that in the future their authors would be sought out and held to account. Sometimes the most savage insults were directed against other senators, unconnected with him or his regime, and reflected older hatreds. As in any era, high politics occupied only a small part of the majority's time, efforts and interests. During these years Augustus recalled the actor Pylades from exile, a punishment awarded after rivalry between his fans and those of another actor named Bathyllus had grown too strong. Pylades humiliated one heckler by singling

him out and turning the abuse of the rest of the crowd onto the
man. Bathyllus was a favourite and at times the lover of Maecenas,
who had protected him. Now his rival returned to the stage and both
men continued to be very popular with audiences. Chided by Augustus for the past disturbances, Pylades confidently assured Caesar
that it was in his best interests for the people to devote their spare
time and enthusiasm to the theatre and its famous – or sometimes
notorious – stars.[33]

THE CYCLE OF YEARS

In 17 BC, with the newborn Lucius and his brother Caius adopted as
his sons, Caesar Augustus was looking to the long-term future. For
all the celebration of peace after decades of strife, for all the talk of
physical and spiritual renewal, and the deep interest in tradition and
past glories, the ethos of the regime was always far more about the
future than the past. The great achievements of the Romans under
the leadership of Caesar Augustus would be followed by far greater
things as he led them into the future. Renewal was an important
part of making them fit for this destiny, re-established in a proper
relationship with the gods who had guided the City's progress for
centuries, the citizens acting and behaving as Romans should, but
ultimately this was not about making things as they were in the past.
Instead it was about moving forward in the right way.

The Romans had several methods of measuring time. The year
was based on the natural passage of the seasons and tied closely to
the political world, its name derived from the consuls of each year.
Every five years or *lustrum*, the censors were supposed to review
the numbers, prosperity and rank of the entire citizen population.
Beyond this was a longer period, the *saeculum* or cycle, felt to be
more than the longest human lifetime. It had only definitely been
celebrated on a handful of occasions in the past, and there was some
doubt about its length, although most felt it came every hundredth
year or so. The last celebration was in 146 BC, but 100 years later

the turmoil of the civil wars ensured that no one was concerned with commemorating the new cycle. Augustus himself reported talk that the comet heralding Julius Caesar's ascent to join the gods also marked the start of a new *saeculum*. Yet the timing was inconvenient, and it took the concerted efforts of one of his supporters, the noted jurist Caius Ateius Capito, to 'discover' that the cycle was in fact every 110 years, and that if it was calculated from the origin of the City in this way then the festival was due in 17 BC. Not everyone was convinced – the Emperor Claudius went back to the traditional system so that he could commemorate the festival during his own reign – but this was of small concern to Augustus, eager to stage such a grand and appropriate event.[34]

Considerable effort went into planning the *ludi saeculares* or Secular Games – the modern transliteration is rather misleading since these were in every respect religious rites. Augustus was heavily involved at every stage, as was Agrippa, his role far more prominent since the grant of tribunician power. Both were members of the key ancient priestly college, the *quindecimviri sacris faciundis*, who were tasked with supervising these rituals. All of the other members – there were now several more than the traditional fifteen from which they took their title, for Augustus had enlarged all of the priestly colleges and was a member of them all – were senators, and the arrangements were brought before and approved by them. The Senate decreed that the details should be recorded on inscriptions on the site in marble and bronze, paid for by the state treasury. Everything was done in a traditional and proper way, but throughout the process the role of Augustus and Agrippa marked them out as far above priestly colleagues and other senators: 'Whereas the consul Caius Silanus reported that after a lapse of many years the Secular Games would be celebrated in the present year under the direction of the Imperator Caesar Augustus and Marcus Agrippa, holders of tribunician power . . .'

The recent law regulating marriage barred unmarried young men and women from watching public festivals, but in this case the event was too important and – since the whole idea was that the cycle was longer than any lifetime and this was their only chance of witnessing it – this ban was lifted.

On 31 May 17 BC the *ludi saeculares* began with a night-time sacrifice performed by Augustus on the Campus Martius near the River Tiber. In accordance with the rite established by the Sibylline Books, he sacrificed nine ewes and nine female goats to the Fates, called on this occasion *Moirae*, their Greek name. He prayed to them for good fortune for the Roman people – given their additional name of *Quirites* to make their identity absolutely clear to the divine powers – for continued success in war, for the safety of the state and their legions of soldiers. An archaic touch was added by prayer to keep the 'Latins obedient'. The Latin-speaking neighbours of Rome had been securely under Roman control since the fourth century BC, but Roman ritual was obsessively conservative and so survivals of the distant past were common enough, even to the extent of repeating words no one could understand. In this case it is unlikely that the ritual owed much to earlier celebrations and this was surely a deliberate attempt to make it seem ancient. Into this traditional façade was interwoven the modern: twice in the prayer Augustus asked for blessing to 'the Roman People, the *Quirites*, to the board of fifteen, to me, to my house and my household'.

That night there was a ritual feast for a carefully selected group of 110 married women, all of them mothers, at which the images of the goddesses Juno and Diana were seated at the table. There was also a dramatic performance, watched by crowds who stood in the traditional Roman way rather than being given seating in the style adopted from the Greeks. On the next day, 1 June, Augustus and Agrippa each went to the Capitol and killed a perfect sacrificial bull, offering the animals to Jupiter Best and Greatest, and then on 2 June each sacrificed a cow to Juno, again on the Capitol. Other members of the priestly college attended them, but the offerings were made only by these two men. Apart from addressing the particular god or goddess, each time they repeated the first prayer, asking for the Latins to be kept under control and adding the *princeps*, his house and his household to the safety and success of the Roman people, the *Quirites*. On the night of 1 June ritual cakes were offered to the Ilithyia, Greek goddesses of childbirth, and then on the night of 2 June Augustus slaughtered a pregnant sow in honour of Mother Earth beside the River Tiber. On the next day he and Agrippa were on the Palatine to offer sacrificial cakes to Apollo and Diana.

Animal sacrifice is very alien to us, and it is all too easy for scholars of the period to take these common rites for granted and forget how much care and preparation they required. The right animals had to be found, kept in good health and brought calmly to the altar so that they did not panic. The actual killing was normally done by highly trained specialists, since it needed to be neat and efficient. Augustus and Agrippa stood by, part of their togas draped over the tops of their heads as they recited the words of the prayer. There are many images of Augustus – and quite a few of Agrippa – shown with their heads covered in this way, and it is clear that the *princeps* wished to parade his *pietas* and his priestly role. Any mistake – whether in the rituals of preparation, the slaughter of the victim or the slightest error in the enunciation of the words of the prayer – invalidated the entire ritual, requiring it to be repeated.

The sacrifices were accompanied by more sacred feasts held by the 110 matrons, who at times also took part in public prayers. There were also more dramatic performances in Greek and Latin lasting for seven days after the rituals, some of them held in a temporary wooden theatre, others in the Theatre of Pompey, and the still not fully completed Theatre of Marcellus. There were also days with beast fights and chariot races, rounding off almost two weeks of pageantry and spectacle, throughout which the present and future greatness of Rome was inseparably linked with the leadership of Caesar Augustus and his confederate Agrippa.

On 3 June, on the Palatine and later on the Capitol, a specially commissioned poem was sung by a choir formed of twenty-seven boys and twenty-seven girls – three times nine was a combination of sacred numbers. The composer was Horace, although it seems more than likely that Virgil would have been preferred if he were still alive. The poem, the *Carmen Saeculare*, survives; it calls upon the

gods propitiated by sacrifices and on other deities to bless and protect the Romans, and speaks of the Trojan past celebrated in the
Aeneid. Many of Augustus' concerns are on display, such as the 'Fathers' [another term for senators who were traditionally fathers of
families] edicts on the yoking-together of men and women and on
the marriage law for raising a new crop of children'. The *princeps*
himself appears as 'the glorious descendant of Anchises and Venus
. . . may he be victorious in battle over his foes yet merciful once
they are down'. This emphasis on the Julian family was repeated in a
series of coins issued that year depicting Julius Caesar.[35]

The games were intended to be a sign of ongoing and already
well-established renewal and the promise of an even greater future.
The Romans would multiply, and the generations to come grow
even more in strength during this next cycle of history, and Caesar
Augustus was at the heart of everything. He could now boast sons,
for the bond of adoption was a strong one as his own career had
shown, apart from which adopted children were as costly to raise as
a man's own sons. In this way Augustus tried to live up to the ideal of
raising a new generation of Romans, just as he encouraged and tried
to compel the rest of the elite to do likewise. The same was true of
the early marriages of his stepchildren and wider family.

Others in the *princeps'* circle did not set such a good example.
Maecenas was married, but had no children and seems to have been
more interested in male lovers. Virgil does not appear to have married, and was rumoured to have felt passion only for boys. Horace
was enthusiastic in his pursuit of women, but restricted his activities
to professional courtesans and other prostitutes. He was said to have
mirrors covering the walls and ceiling of his bedchamber so that he
could watch while he made love to them – if true, this would have
been a highly expensive indulgence, for mirrors were very costly. Augustus did not seem to mind, playfully nicknaming the poet 'a most
lecherous little man' and 'a perfect penis' in letters to him. None of
these men embarked seriously on a public career – Maecenas had
influence and behind-the-scenes power but never held office.[36]

In a very Roman way, Caesar Augustus was far more concerned

with public appearances and practicality than with changing behaviour for its own sake. He needed the aristocracy to reproduce so that there would be another generation, and he needed them to behave with dignity in public, respecting the gods and tradition in general. His marriage laws were resented and ignored by many, but overall a majority probably conformed to them more or less willingly. If they did this, and behaved appropriately in public, neither he nor anyone else was much concerned with discreet private activity.

FAMILY AND COLLEAGUES

'Augustus Caesar . . . had become disliked by many as a result of his long stay in the capital.' *Dio, early third century* AD.[1]

'I pacified the Alps, from the area closest to the Adriatic Sea all the way to the Tuscan sea, without waging an unjust war against any tribe.' *Deeds of the Divine Augustus.*[2]

Late in 17 BC or early in 16 BC three Germanic tribes, the Usipetes, Tencteri and Sugambri, suddenly rounded up some Romans who were in their lands – presumably there as merchants – and crucified them. We do not know what prompted this outburst of hostility, but a large group of warriors then mustered and launched a plundering raid across the Rhine into Roman Gaul. The legate, Marcus Lollius, responded by gathering a force to deal with them – just as Julius Caesar, Agrippa and others had done in the past in much the same area. It seems that Lollius lacked their skill, and this time things did not go well. The auxiliary cavalry patrolling ahead of the army were ambushed and soundly beaten. Exultant German warriors chased the horsemen as they fled, and the whole mass fell back on the main force which was surprised and thrown into confusion. *Legio V Alaudae* broke and lost its precious eagle. For a time most of the Roman army was in flight, before order was restored and the enemy repulsed.

Lollius and his army survived their defeat, and the losses were probably not very high. Suetonius dubbed the reverse 'more infamous than serious', but still included it as one of only two serious defeats suffered by Augustus' armies after the civil wars. Lollius was his legate, and the soldiers were his soldiers, so their defeat was every bit as much his as their past successes. Imperator Caesar Augustus led the state because his victories brought peace and prosperity. Any reverse was damaging, and after the much-trumpeted return of the standards from Parthia and Illyria the loss of another eagle was embarrassing. Augustus announced that he would go to Gaul in person, and left Rome late in the spring. Before he arrived the campaign was over. Lollius gathered together a larger and better-prepared field force to invade the tribal heartlands in reprisal for the raid. News of this prompted the Germans to send ambassadors begging for peace, which was granted on Rome's terms. We do not know what happened to the eagle, but there was no fanfare surrounding its return and it is possible that the loss was temporary, and the precious standard had been recovered in the first encounter.[3]

Augustus continued on to Gaul, and most probably a tour of the western provinces was already planned before news arrived of Lollius' defeat. Agrippa had also left for the east, and neither he nor his father-in-law would return to Italy for more than three years, continuing the now-established pattern of alternating spells in Rome with longer visits to the provinces. Dio claims that Augustus was glad to leave the City behind, and used the news from Gaul as a pretext to hurry. The recently introduced marriage legislation continued to aggravate some senators and equestrians. The *princeps* was willing to grant exemptions or more lenient treatment to friends and supporters caught infringing the laws, and although this was understandable and very Roman, it only added to the resentment of his harsher treatment of others. There is no hint of concerted opposition, but Augustus' informal style, approachability and claims of wanting free and open debate in the Senate provided plenty of opportunities to embarrass him. The longer he stayed in Rome itself, the easier it was for those so inclined to test the limits of his tolerance, and there was little he could do if he wished to preserve the traditional and constitutional façade of his regime.[4]

Livia probably accompanied Augustus to Gaul, although Dio does report an absurd piece of gossip which claimed that he was leaving Italy so that he could carry on his affair with Maecenas' wife Terentia away from the public eye. Livia's son Tiberius soon joined them and both of Augustus' stepsons were to enjoy an especially prominent role in public affairs during the next few years. One of the reasons Tiberius tarried in Rome was so that he and Drusus could jointly preside over gladiatorial games to mark the opening of the rebuilt Temple of Quirinus, another of Rome's ancient cults now seen as the deified Romulus. It may not have been a coincidence that the brothers organised these games, for the new temple frieze depicted the brothers Romulus and Remus – not in strife, but sitting as augurs seeking the guidance of the gods before the foundation of the City. Such fraternal harmony – whether between brothers or simply all Romans – was the present and the future proclaimed by Augustus' regime.[5]

Tiberius was elected praetor for 16 BC, finally holding the office some years after being ranked among the former praetors on the senatorial roll. He was twenty-five, and permitted by senatorial decree to stand for each magistracy five years earlier than normal. At some point Augustus reduced the minimum age for all of the important posts, although it is not clear precisely when and whether this occurred in one sweeping reform or as a succession of smaller changes. The process seems to have been complete by the late twenties BC, and meant that posts could be held at a younger age than in the past, so that a praetor had normally to be just thirty and a consul thirty-three. It was a change that helped to replenish the ranks of the consulship and the magistracies in general with men bearing famous names, as the new generation of families devastated by civil war and proscriptions reached adulthood.[6]

On 1 January 16 BC the two new consuls were Lucius Domitius Ahenobarbus and Publius Cornelius Scipio. Both had impeccably aristocratic pedigrees – as indeed did Tiberius and Drusus. Ahenobarbus was also Augustus' great-nephew, being the son of the elder Antonia, daughter of Octavia and Mark Antony. The connection with Scipio was less close, although he was half-brother to Julia, being the child of Augustus' divorced wife Scribonia by another marriage. Such close inter-relation was a well-established feature of Roman public life and had never guaranteed political co-operation. In the event, Scipio did not serve for a full year, and was replaced by one of Augustus' old senior officers as suffect consul. We do not have any idea why this occurred, but the silence of our sources makes it unlikely that there was any sinister reason for the change.[7]

Before he left the City, Augustus once again reinstated the office of urban prefect and this time gave it to his experienced subordinate, Statilius Taurus. His earlier attempt to revive this old office had failed when Messalla resigned after a few days in 26 BC, but a decade later presumably its powers and role had been clarified. At some point three urban cohorts were formed and placed under the prefect's command to serve as a police force. Tiberius may well have received the prestigious post of urban praetor, but if so he was only able to perform his duties for a few months before he accompanied Augustus to Gaul. In his absence, Drusus acted for him, even though he had not yet held any formal office. Men like Statilius Taurus were old confederates, but the emphasis was more and more on the *princeps'* extended family. Agrippa, his son-in-law and fellow holder of tribunician power, was in the east. Tiberius was with him in Gaul, where he would soon replace Lollius as legate, while Drusus would be summoned from Rome to take on a more active role in the provinces in 15 BC. The brothers, and in the longer term the real sons of Agrippa and the adopted sons of Augustus, offered assurances of stability for the future. The *princeps'* death no longer threatened the immediate collapse of his regime and descent into civil war.[8]

COLONIES, COMMUNITIES AND ROADS

This was Augustus' fourth visit to Gaul, and that in itself is a testimony to the area's importance. It was the conquest of Gallia Comata or 'Long-Haired Gaul' that had given Julius Caesar the wealth, prestige and loyal army to match Pompey. In the years that followed, the region played a strategically vital role in the civil wars even if it saw little actual fighting. Recently conquered, and prey to raids from across the Rhine, the new Gallic provinces usually needed a substantial garrison, and those legions inevitably stood closer to Italy than any other Roman army. In addition, Gaul was a fertile recruiting ground for auxiliary soldiers, and was especially famed for its cavalrymen. Control of the army in Gaul had made Lepidus a real power in 43 BC, while Augustus' securing of the legions there in 40 BC had fundamentally undermined Antony's position.

Cisalpine Gaul was now part of Italy and was no longer garrisoned. Julius Caesar's main base had been Transalpine Gaul (modern Provence), and this area was included in the vast provincial command given to Augustus in 29 BC. In that year he had promised to transfer areas to senatorial control once he had made them secure from any threats, and Transalpine Gaul was presented as the first proof of his sincerity. At some point – 22 BC is the most likely date, but we cannot be sure – the province was handed back to the Senate's authority and from now on governed by a proconsul. Renamed Gallia Narbonensis after its capital city Narbo (modern Narbonne), it no longer contained a legionary garrison, although many discharged veterans were settled in numerous colonies established in the last few decades. Such men were grateful to Augustus, and this loyalty made it unlikely that they would rise in support of any rival. In the longer run the area proved a fertile recruiting ground, as the descendants of the colonists followed family traditions of military service.[9]

Gallia Narbonensis was already very Roman – a generation earlier Julius Caesar had found its aristocrats useful allies. Such men were fluent in Latin, familiar with Roman and sometimes Greek culture, and readily able to mix socially with his Roman officers and staff. Some already possessed citizenship, and many more would receive it as a reward during the years that followed. Julius was by far the most common name for citizens throughout all of Gaul, but especially in Narbonensis, and testifies to the largesse of Julius Caesar and later Augustus. The most favoured of these local aristocrats became equestrians or even senators. In many cases their home communities were already turning into something very close to the Roman model of a proper city, and the establishment of veteran colonies only accelerated the process. Many cities were planned around an ordered grid of streets, centred on a forum with a basilica for public business, space for commerce and usually a temple dedicated to an appropriately Roman deity. Most soon acquired theatres and amphitheatres, whether given by the *princeps* or the product of local largesse. Less than a century later Pliny the Elder could describe Gallia Narbonensis as virtually a part of Italy.[10]

The rest of Gaul was different, and here the Roman influence was far less advanced. In time Gallia Comata developed into three provinces: Aquitania in the south-east, Lugdunensis in northern and central Gaul, and Belgica in the north-east. These were roughly, but not exactly, equivalent to the *tres partes* or three parts into which Julius Caesar declared Gaul was divided at the start of his *Commentaries*. There is reference to 'the three Gauls' under Augustus, and the later provinces may already have been defined, although it looks as if a single legate governed the entire area. It was most definitely a military province, as Lollius' unfortunate encounter with German raiders had so recently demonstrated. There were also occasional problems in the area near the Alps, whose peoples remained free of Roman control, and in Aquitania. All in all it was reasonable for Augustus to present the three Gauls as difficult regions requiring his attention.[11]

There is no real trace of serious resistance among the tribes of Gaul itself, even though their conquest remained within living memory. Aquitania was the only exception to this, and now that northern Spain was fully subjugated there were no longer independent peoples on the far side of the Pyrenees ready to raid or assist the Gaulish tribes of that area. We hear of no more serious fighting there in the years to come. Yet for the moment the regions closest to the Alps and the long border with the Germanic tribes were exposed to attacks from outside Rome's empire. If the Romans failed to deal with these and offer protection, then some Gaulish aristocrats were likely to wonder whether alliance with Rome was worthwhile, and they or their rivals might instead seek support from German war leaders. This had been the situation in Julius Caesar's day, and he had seen it less as a problem than as providing plentiful opportunities for intervention.[12]

Augustus needed to find a more permanent solution. In many ways the Alps were easier to deal with, since they were already virtually surrounded by Roman provinces, although it was far from a straightforward task. The peoples living in the higher valleys were loosely organised, consisting of many distinct communities whose leaders only held sway over very small areas. Harsh living conditions produced tough and ferocious warriors, apt to raid down into the settled valleys and extort tolls from merchants and sometimes even Roman armies, wanting an unmolested passage through the passes. More recently there were reports of dreadful savagery which suggested that at least some of the communities had come to loathe the Romans. In a spate of raids it was claimed that they slaughtered any male Romans they captured, and murdered any pregnant women thought by their diviners to be carrying a baby boy.[13]

In recent years Augustus had ordered several Alpine campaigns, and now he resolved on completing the conquest of the area and gave the task to his stepsons. Drusus began operations in the spring of 15 BC, advancing with several columns from Italy into the Valley of the Inn. Tiberius then advanced from bases in Gaul, and this became a war of tough little skirmishes and the storming of walled villages. By a happy coincidence the two brothers joined forces to win a larger-scale action on 1 August – the fifteenth anniversary of Augustus' victory in Egypt. By the end of the year almost all of the Alps were under firm Roman control, and the few remaining areas were mopped up soon afterwards. Rome's possession of the mountains and their passes was never again to be challenged. To mark this success – and match a similar trophy set up by Pompey in the Pyrenees – a spectacular victory monument was erected in the Maritime Alps at La Turbie and listed forty-five peoples defeated during these campaigns. A good few of the names are barely attested anywhere else, reflecting the loose society of the region, and it seems there were other peoples who did not resist and chose to accept Roman rule. There was probably little fighting in Noricum, but at least some of the Rhaeti and Vindelici resisted fiercely even if they could not hope to stand up to the greater resources employed by the Romans. Horace devoted two poems to praising Tiberius' and Drusus' victories. Augustus boasted that he had just cause to fight against all of these peoples, but of course that was something that the Romans always liked to believe.[14]

Controlling the routes through the Alps greatly improved communications between Italy and Illyricum in the south and Gaul in the north, making Rome's empire a more coherent unit. In many ways it seems surprising that it took the Romans so long to achieve this, but it required the confidence and control of an Augustus to devote substantial resources to a grim series of campaigns that involved difficult, unglamorous fighting with little profit in terms of loot or slaves. In the past, it was simply easier and more economical to pay off the Alpine tribesmen. Much as he had conquered the mountainous north of Spain, Caesar Augustus was willing to undertake difficult but useful tasks – and as willing to celebrate his achievements.[15]

More than a decade before, Agrippa had begun work on an extensive road system in Gaul, ensuring good communications across the country, and in particular improving access to the Rhine in the north and east, and Aquitania and ultimately Spain in the west. The two main roads met at Lugdunum (modern-day Lyons), so that the street grid of the city was orientated on these major highways. As with all Roman roads, the initial concept was military, providing good, well-drained routes for the use of the army and, most importantly, its supply convoys throughout all the seasons of the year. The quantities of grain, meat and other materiel needed by the legions was substantial – even the coins required to pay the armies on time were heavy and bulky to transport. Wherever possible these goods were transported by water since it was so much easier and cheaper, and thus the new road system complemented the much-used waterways such as the Rivers Rhône and Garonne. Much of what the army consumed was supplied by levies of grain and animals within the province, but it took care and considerable effort to transport these to where they were needed. Over the next few years more and more legions were moved to the Rhine frontier, greatly increasing demand. Along with the convoys of essentials went an ever-growing flow of greater and lesser luxuries, feeding and creating markets all along the way, as civilians as well as soldiers discovered a taste for things like wine and fine tableware.[16]

None of this was entirely new. Julius Caesar had discovered Roman merchants living and trading in the native towns or *oppida* throughout Gaul, and archaeology testifies to the Gauls' enthusiasm for goods from the Mediterranean. The quantities of Italian wine shipped north to Gaul in the first century BC were truly staggering: one scholar estimates that some 40,000,000 amphorae went up the Rhône. Nor were roads entirely an innovation, for the Gauls had laid down major trackways along a number of routes, bridging rivers and building causeways through marshland. Many Gaulish towns reveal the presence of craftsmen, sometimes in substantial numbers and with a range of skills producing goods for sale over a wide area. Many of the tribes, especially in central Gaul, show signs of considerable political and economic sophistication.[17]

Yet even so the arrival of the Romans as occupiers brought profound changes beyond the – often dreadful – trauma of conquest itself. The existing tracks and roads, while functional enough for much of the year, fell far short of the new system of all-weather metalled roads in design and even further behind in the sheer scale of the network. If the flow of trade goods before the arrival of Julius Caesar had been on a grand scale, it had still focused very much on luxuries for the elite. The beneficiaries were almost exclusively the aristocracy, and control of trade confirmed their power. Among the Aedui, whose lands lay along the Rhône, a few chieftains gained immense wealth and dominance within the tribe through controlling levies on the wine trade. Under the Romans such monopolies were broken, and the native aristocracy could only seek local power through becoming part of the Roman system of government. A wider range of goods went north from Italy – and in time came from other provinces – aimed at a broader section of society. The locals also adapted to new-found tastes. Under Augustus widespread cultivation of vines and wine-making began in Gaul, while manufacturers of ceramics responded to the demands of a growing market by establishing workshops in Gaul itself. Use of coinage based on the Roman standard, already widespread in the south, extended over a wider area, fostered particularly wherever the army was based and legionaries inclined to spend their wages. An official Roman mint was set up at Lugdunum, producing gold and silver coinage which provided wages for the soldiers and funds for official projects and rapidly became more widely circulated. The economy soon became more and more monetised, at the same time circulating the image and symbols of Caesar Augustus.

Roman influences spread widely and quickly, but the process was neither instant nor so total that the area did not retain a distinctive character and some regional variation. The three Gauls were far less Roman than Narbonensis. Only three veteran colonies were established outside the latter, at Lugdunum, Noviodunum (modern Nyons), and Raurica (modern Augst in Switzerland) during the great phase of colonisation, and although towns were already an important feature of Gaulish society in many areas, they did not function in the way the Romans expected. For them a city was a political entity, administering the lands around it, but each city essentially independent from its neighbours. In Gaul the nation – or *civitas* – was more important, and most included several towns, all of which felt part of the wider entity, while many aristocrats might dwell on their own farmsteads and not in the *oppida*.[18]

Augustus followed what was probably the existing Roman approach of ignoring the details of this structure, and instead treating each *civitas* as if it were a city state, naming one of the towns as its capital – the true *civitas* centre, even if there were in fact other communities of similar size. Development in some of these centres was encouraged by the state, but the pattern was often a blending of styles. Many lacked the neat grids of planned Roman cities, although almost all quickly acquired a forum. Over time, most centres moved away from the hilltop sites favoured in pre-Roman times to locations on lower ground, and ideally with ready access to the road network. Roman institutions for local government were gradually adopted, even if once again these merged with local traditions. Old Gaulish names such as *vergobret* remained in use for the supreme magistrate of a *civitas*, while even when Roman titles such as praetor were adopted there was usually just one of these officials in the traditional way, rather than the two *duoviri* or some other college of magistrates.[19]

Roman citizens were less common in the three Gauls than in Narbonensis, although the number rose steadily over time. The local aristocracy were encouraged to give their sons a Roman education, and in due course rhetoric would flourish in Gaul. In the meantime there were opportunities to assist the Roman administration, to serve on its behalf as local magistrates, and most of all to find employment as officers in the Roman army. Around a third of the auxiliary units raised under Augustus came from Gaul. An aristocrat's power was no longer judged by the number of warriors in his train as it had been in Julius Caesar's day, but the opportunity was there for the descendants of these leaders to win glory fighting for Rome. Quite a few men were still buried with a sword or other weapon by their side in the last years of the first century BC as they had been for generations. Some things changed only gradually. The druidic cult, glimpsed in our sources but still poorly understood, provided some extra-national structure and arbitration in pre-Roman Gaul, and it did not vanish instantly. Practices such as human sacrifice were suppressed, as was the endemic raiding, head-hunting and warfare between the tribes which fed it. Augustus banned Roman citizens from participating in druidic rites, but did not outlaw the religion itself. Other Gaulish cults took on Roman names and associations, and increasingly became housed in stone temples, even if these were often still raised outside the towns on existing sacred sites.[20]

The persistence of tradition did not necessarily mean an active and deliberate rejection of Roman ways, and overall the impression is of widespread eagerness to become Roman, at least on the part of the better-off. In fact the Romans made little effort to impose their own culture, except where it served the purpose of administration. Thus the Roman calendar was introduced to divide up the year and show when festivals and taxes were due, in place of the traditional lunar calendar overseen by the druids. As with any new system, it was not always fully understood at first, and one of Augustus' financial officials chose to exploit the ignorance of the unfamiliar system. His name was Julius Licinus, and he was himself a Gaul, but had been captured and enslaved, quite possibly during Julius Caesar's campaigns. In due course he became part of the latter's household, and served him so well that he was eventually granted freedom. Loyal also to Augustus, he was made a procurator – a rank not yet fully defined, but increasingly associated with equestrian status and employed to assist imperial legates much like a quaestor assisted a proconsul – and given the task of collecting taxes owed to the state.

Licinus showed little sympathy for his fellow Gauls. Probably already rich when he arrived in the province, he was determined to become even richer before he left and took every opportunity to take more than was due and pocket the difference. December was the last month of the year in the old Roman calendar, which had only ten named months. When Julius Caesar reformed the calendar, he kept January as the first month and December as the last since both included important dates in the political and religious year. Licinus now pointed out to the provincials that the name December obviously meant 'tenth month' in Latin, and that the logical inference was surely that there must also be an eleventh and twelfth month before the year was complete. On this premise he extorted two more months' worth of tax from them.

Whether or not they were convinced by his reasoning, the Gauls had little choice but to pay if they were not to face the wrath – and ultimately forcible compulsion – of the imperial power. Yet many were suspicious, and when Augustus arrived in the province in 16 BC they complained to him. At first the *princeps* dismissed some of the claims, in part because he did not want to admit to having appointed such a venal representative, and only accepted some milder criticism of his procurator. Yet the weight of evidence and the clear hostility of so many important local aristocrats piled on the pressure against Licinus, who then came up with an even more imaginative scheme to avoid punishment. He invited Augustus to his house, and presented the *princeps* with all the extra money he had gathered, declaring that he had done so to prevent the aristocracy of Gaul being rich enough to rebel against Rome. This is a rare hint that the Romans even worried about the possibility of rebellion in Gaul, and should not be pushed too far. However, it does seem that Licinus went unpunished, so perhaps his excuse was credited.

It was often difficult for Augustus to know what his agents were doing in the provinces until he visited the region, and this was one of the reasons for his extensive tours. A measure of self-enrichment was expected and accepted, but the aim was to restrain the excesses of provincial government under the Republic, which too often had driven the provincials to the rebellions Licinus claimed to be preventing. Travelling to seek an audience with the *princeps* took time and was expensive, since it might involve a journey to Rome or wherever he happened to be at the time. The tours through the provinces made it possible for far more individuals and communities to speak to him. While Augustus was in Gaul, Agrippa was in Syria and the other eastern provinces, acting in the same way. It was not only a chance to resolve specific petitions, but offered a clearer statement of the attitudes and ideology of Roman government. This made it harder in the future for individual governors – whether proconsuls or legates – to adopt a markedly different approach in dealing with communities.

From Gaul Augustus moved on to Spain, making his third trip across the Pyrenees. The Iberian Peninsula was now peaceful since Agrippa's suppression of the last serious rebellion in 19 BC, its peace only sporadically interrupted by small-scale outbreaks of trouble. Of the three newly organised provinces, Baetica, made up of the most settled and prosperous areas of the south where Roman culture happily combined with a long tradition of urbanism, had passed over to senatorial control. This change probably occurred around the same time as the transfer of Narbonensis to a proconsul and offered further proof that Augustus was willing to give up power once he had discharged his duty to stabilise a region. The other two provinces remained under his control and were governed by his legates. In the west Lusitania – a somewhat larger area than modern Portugal – was generally settled and no longer contained a substantial garrison. Three legions were stationed in Hispania Citerior, which stretched from modern Galicia through central Spain to the Mediterranean coast, and included the peoples conquered in recent years. The other legions who had fought in those wars were already leaving Spain and being posted elsewhere – in most cases to Gaul or Illyricum.[21]

Some of the legionaries stayed. Augustus established two major veteran colonies during or after the wars in Cantabria, both of which took his name: Caesaraugusta (modern-day Zaragoza) on the River Ebro in Hispania Citerior and Augusta Emerita (modern-day Mérida) on the River Guadiana in Lusitania. Just as in Gaul, a grow-ing network of new roads combined with the rivers to provide good communications to these and other major cities. The colonies re-warded veterans for their loyalty, and at the same time were bastions of Roman rule, potentially being of military use in the unlikely event of serious problems. Augusta Emerita was certainly built to be impressive, surrounded by city walls more for show than defence, and was approached over the long, many-arched bridge across the Guadiana.

The colonies were also models of Roman life, and were precisely planned and organised, with a grand forum at their heart – perhaps two of these in the case of Augusta Emerita. Agrippa built the city an imposing stone theatre, decorated with statues of himself and Au-gustus and with inscriptions recording the years of their tribunician power. The *princeps* gave the colonists a similarly grand amphitheatre so that they could enjoy those most Roman of entertainments. Later generations would greatly embellish the city and add to its monu-ments, in many cases copying some of Augustus' great projects in Rome itself. Other colonies were established or given a new influx of discharged veterans in both Spain and Gaul, and urban growth in general flourished throughout most of the Spanish provinces, in the main through local aspiration. Most major communities acquired a Roman forum, and although the designs are not identical the similarities are striking. Size varied, but almost without exception they were laid down to the best principles of Roman architecture, employing a basic unit of measurement to dictate every other dimension, from the width and spacing of columns to the size of buildings and courts. The unit itself varied, but the concept did not and imposed a geometrical neatness that was the ideal of Roman design. As in Gaul, there were profound economic changes as new markets appeared, and locals or Roman landlords began to produce olive oil, fish sauce and wine for consumers in other provinces and Italy itself.[22]

OLD COMRADES AND OLD RIVALS

Soldiers remained vital to the Augustan regime, and it is worth reminding ourselves that, although it was only the second decade after Actium, it was already the longest period without civil war since 88 BC – or since 91 BC if the Social War is included. Legionaries needed to be controlled and kept loyal during their service, and provided with land on retirement in a way that made them content and did not cause too much of a disturbance to the people living in the area. Around this time – Dio dates the reform to 13 BC – Augustus introduced new regulations for the army, confirming the length of service for legionaries as sixteen years, and just twelve years for the more pampered nine cohorts of praetorian guards. The number of legions was fairly static, and less prone to the sudden rapid increase in numbers common during the civil wars, so it was easier to predict the number of veterans due for demobilisation each year.[23]

At the same time it seems that auxiliary units were becoming more permanent. Some were still named after their commander – such as the *ala Scaevae*, a cavalry regiment led probably by one of Julius Caesar's famous centurions – but increasingly they were numbered and named after the region of the nation from which they were raised. Gallic, Thracian and Spanish units were all common.

Professional officers, often equestrians or from the classes that produced most centurions, commanded such regiments as prefects, giving them honourable and profitable careers. The same was true of provincial aristocrats, for whom serving as an army officer offered the opportunity for citizenship and joining the hierarchy of the empire. In each case such opportunities came from the *princeps* and bound these men to him. After long or short spells in the army, former officers returned to prominent roles in their home community, whether this was a colony or a town in Italy or the provinces. Ideally they remained Augustus' men, content with their lot and so unlikely to rally to any rival who attempted to raise an army. The name Caesar mattered, for there were now surely many families for whom loyalty to the dictator and then his heir was already a well-established tradition.

It was a personal relationship. On one occasion a veteran – most probably a veteran officer or a praetorian, since the story is clearly set in Rome – was involved in a court case and went in person to ask Augustus to support him. The *princeps* sent his best wishes and offered a man to act as advocate on the veteran's behalf, but this was not enough, and prompted the man to pull back his tunic and show the scars of his wounds to the crowd. 'But I, Caesar,' the old soldier declared, 'did not send a substitute to serve in my stead when you were in danger at Actium, but I fought for you myself.' When he heard this Augustus blushed and duly appeared to support the man in person, 'for fear of appearing not simply haughty, but ungrateful'. Although he no longer called his soldiers 'comrades', Imperator Caesar Augustus wanted them to believe that he respected them for the dangers they had undergone under his leadership.[24]

He cared less about the feelings of another former comrade. Lepidus remained a senator, even though he was only ever brought to meetings on the order of the *princeps*, when Augustus did nothing to conceal his contempt for his former ally. Yet he remained *pontifex maximus* until he died in 13 BC. Rome's most senior priest had therefore been almost inactive for more than twenty years, and although this permitted Augustus quietly to assume guidance of state ritual at Rome, there were some things that he could not do. It surprised many that he did not strip the disgraced triumvir of the rank and take it himself, but he was later to boast of refusing to do this, having only 'accepted the office when he was at last dead who, taking advantage of a time of civil disturbance, had seized it for himself'.[25]

On 6 March 12 BC Augustus was duly installed as *pontifex maximus* – a post, he noted, formerly held by 'my father' Julius Caesar and never again held by anyone who was not emperor, until Rome had fallen and the pope took the title. It was a grand occasion, celebrated with great pomp and appropriate solemnity, and Augustus' own description makes clear that he saw it as both his right and inheritance. Tradition dictated that this most senior priest live in his official residence on the edge of the Forum Romanum next to the Temple of Vesta, which had recently been damaged by fire. Augustus gave the building to the Vestals and remained in his house on the Palatine, consecrating part of it as a temple and making it nominally public property so that he could fulfil his priestly role properly. This merely reinforced the distinctly religious overtones of a complex which joined onto the precinct of Palatine Apollo as well as several other less spectacular shrines.[26]

Augustus returned to Rome in the summer of 13 BC. Tiberius had preceded him, and began the year as consul with Publius Quinctilius Varus as his colleague – the latter a son-in-law of Agrippa. Rome was troubled again by flooding, with the Tiber overflowing its banks so badly that Balbus was only able to reach his newly completed theatre by boat, which did not prevent him from holding celebrations to mark its formal opening. In honour of the occasion, Tiberius called upon the Spanish former consul for his opinion about how to mark the return of the *princeps*. Fresh honours were awarded on Balbus' motion, and in due course politely declined by Augustus in a pattern that was now routine. Attempts to greet him formally were also thwarted when once again Imperator Caesar Augustus sneaked into Rome at night without fanfare. The next morning he received the crowd that gathered outside his house, and then climbed the Capitol, where he took the victor's laurels from the *fasces* of his attendants and hung them on the statue of Jupiter Optimus Maximus. Won by Tiberius and Drusus and attributed to Augustus, these marks of success were now presented to the god who protected Rome.

On that day Caesar Augustus arranged for the baths – chiefly the one built by Agrippa – to be free, as were the barbers who waited within them to shave or trim the hair of any fellow citizen who chose to attend. Later, at a meeting of the Senate, his voice was too hoarse to permit him to make a speech and so it was instead read for him by a quaestor. It was a time for festivals and celebration, for the Theatre of Marcellus was also now ready and was opened with great ceremony. His seven-year-old grandson Caius Caesar took part in the dramatic and sometimes dangerous riding exercises and mock fights of the so-called Trojan Games, at least nominally leading one of the teams of patrician boys. Beast fights were also part of the spectacle, with some 600 animals being slaughtered. In September there were more games and more killing of animals to mark the *princeps'* birthday, and ironically enough the ceremonies were arranged and presided over by Iulus, son of Mark Antony and Fulvia.[27]

There were some awkward moments. At another set of games, this time given by Tiberius as consul to commemorate Augustus' return to the City, the former permitted Caius to sit with the *princeps* in the place of honour. This was probably the occasion when the audience rose en masse to hail the boy, greeting him with cheers. Augustus was not pleased, and rebuked both his stepson and the people more generally. Although he would accept acclaim on such occasions for his own achievements, he felt it inappropriate for them to lavish it on a seven-year-old child who had not yet done anything or even come to formal manhood. More generally he would permit no one, whether family, senator or the crowd in general, to call him *dominus* – master or lord.[28]

The crowd's reaction suggests that many wished to celebrate all those associated with Augustus, and implies that they saw the boy as worthy of power because of his birth and adoption. Yet the *princeps* took great pains to deny the existence of any dynasty which would in turn imply monarchy. Some of this was for the benefit of the aristocracy and was intended to preserve the illusion that they lived in a *res publica* which was not ruled by a single man, even if it was well and deservedly guided by its leading citizen. This was clearly a concern for Augustus, even if the readiness with which senators voted him ever more grand and unprecedented honours suggests that many now cared little for the liberty so dear to Brutus and Cassius. On balance, his own self-image probably had more to do with it. Augustus' relentless pursuit of supremacy runs as a central thread throughout his life. This does not mean that his use of power was no more than a means to maintain it, since he worked very hard to use it well. There is every reason to believe that the *princeps* felt he deserved to win the civil wars, to gain supremacy and to hold onto it because it served the wider good – obviously as he perceived it. Thus he could really see himself as merely the first magistrate of the state, a servant rather than a ruler. Self-restraint, and the desire to live up to his own ideal, make far more sense as curbs on his behaviour than the opinions of the senatorial elite.

Now that he was back in Rome, there were opportunities both for unwelcome and inappropriate flattery and for uncomfortable moments during public debate. At one session of the Senate, a noble named Cornelius Sisenna was criticised for the behaviour of his wife. (It is possible that she was the daughter of Statilius Taurus, although since there was more than one Cornelius Sisenna active in these years we cannot be sure whether it was the same man.) In response, the husband denied that he was responsible for his spouse, since he had married her following the advice and active support of Augustus. Angry at being dragged into such an undignified dispute, and feeling in danger of saying or doing something he might later regret, the *princeps* got up and rushed from the Curia. He waited until he had calmed down before he returned to the chamber.[29]

The man who openly encouraged free debate did not always care for its content and tone. Nor, whatever he pretended, could anyone truly ignore his overwhelming prestige and patronage. In 13 BC Augustus made a fresh attempt to have senators who fitted his ideal of their role, but faced the problem that quite a few descendants of established senatorial families chose not to enter public life and contented themselves with equestrian status. There was a particular shortage of men seeking the tribunate – its major powers were now taken over by Augustus, but it still had a good deal of work to do as a means of appeal in minor issues for every citizen. To meet the vacancies, lots were drawn from a pool of former quaestors still aged under forty. Equestrians under thirty-five, and with the wealth and family making them eligible for the Senate, were also enrolled as senators unless they could prove in person to the *princeps* that they were physically unfit for their duties. The mask of a distinguished public servant in a free state sometimes sat uncomfortably on one who tried to compel others to do their duty. There were limits to how far even Augustus could make reality conform to his vision of how he wanted the world to be.[30]

Imperator Caesar Augustus was a monarch in all but name, and neither Senate nor people could deny him any power he wanted, even in the unlikely event that they should want to do so. In 13 BC his grand provincial command was renewed for another five years, while Agrippa was granted five more years of *tribunicia potestas* as well as – for the first time – *maius imperium proconsulare*, superior to everyone else's *imperium* with the probable exception of Augustus himself. Both men were about fifty, and Agrippa's status made him the closest thing to a colleague Augustus had had since the triumvirate. It stopped short of equality, whatever the precise definition of the two men's *imperium*. Agrippa was his son-in-law, which implied a political closeness but also conferred a degree of superiority in his relationship to Julia's father. More importantly Agrippa was not a Caesar, and lacked the *auctoritas*, let alone the network of client obligations owed to that name. If he was second only to Augustus, then he remained second and there was no effort to make him an equal.[31]

Although middle-aged, Marcus Vipsanius Agrippa remained both capable and vigorous, and utterly loyal to his old friend. His favourite proverb was, 'If peace makes small things grow, discord will tear down great things.' He returned to Rome in 13 BC, staying for a few months before leaving to deal with a military problem in the Balkans. By the time he left, Julia was pregnant for the fifth time – the couple already had two daughters as well as Caius and Lucius. A demonstration of force proved sufficient to quell the disturbances so that by 12 BC Agrippa returned to Italy, but fell ill and died before he reached Rome. The illness is unknown, but the unusual appointment of three suffect consuls during the year may hint at some kind of epidemic. Shortly afterwards Julia gave birth to a third son, who was named Agrippa Postumus.[32]

Augustus was not with his old friend when he died. Dio says that he was in Athens, presiding over the Panathenaic Games, but hurried back as soon as he heard of Agrippa's sickness. The body was carried in state to Rome, and given a public funeral at which the *princeps* himself delivered the eulogy. Then, for the second time, the ashes of another of his extended family were interred in the great Mausoleum Augustus had built for himself.[33]

18

AUGUSTAN PEACE

'The Senate voted in honour of my return the consecration of an altar to Pax Augusta.' *Deeds of the Divine Augustus.*[1]

'The course of my song has led me to the altar of Peace . . . Come, Peace, thy dainty tresses wreathed with Actian laurels, and let thy gentle presence abide in the whole world. So but there be neither foes nor food for triumphs, thou shalt be unto our chiefs a glory greater than war. May the soldier bear arms only to check the armed aggressor . . . ! May the world near and far dread the sons of Aeneas, and if there be land that feared not Rome, may it love Rome instead!' *Ovid, first decade of the first century* AD.[2]

Agrippa bequeathed extensive gardens and his bath complex on the Campus Martius to the Roman people, along with some of his estates to provide an income for their upkeep. Augustus made the announcement personally, and thus ensured that it happened, and also distributed 400 sesterces to every male citizen, or at least those in Rome, stating that this was another of his friend's wishes. The largesse was typical of Agrippa's activities for the last two decades, spending much of his newly acquired wealth on amenities and comforts for the people and leaving his mark on cities throughout the empire, but most of all in Rome. In sheer scale his activities far outstripped those of any other Roman aristocrat living or dead, apart from Caesar Augustus, and combined a taste for the monumental with the practical. When a crowd complained to the *princeps* about the high price of wine, he replied by saying that his son-in-law had already given them plenty of water to drink when he built them an aqueduct.[3]

Augustus was always the greatest beneficiary of Agrippa's industry and talent, and his will was no exception, for by far the largest
part of his property went to his old friend and father-in-law, including extensive estates in Italy and throughout the provinces – Dio
singles out one encompassing most of the Chersonese in Greece.
A great fortune, won through loyal service in the civil wars and afterwards, thus returned to the leader he had followed and whose
rise he had shared, and might eventually return to Caius and Lucius.
Political and familial loyalty are hard to separate, but that in itself
was nothing unusual at Rome. Men rose to high office through the
support of new or inherited friendships and bonds of patronage, and
by marriage alliances. Agrippa had done especially well from the
latter, marrying in turn Pomponia, the daughter of the very wealthy
and superbly well-connected Atticus, Caesar's niece Marcella, and
finally his daughter Julia. The closeness of the bond created by this
last wedding became even stronger with the adoption by Augustus
of the couple's two sons.[4]

Family mattered to Augustus. In many ways this was nothing
unusual, for in Rome relatives by blood, adoption or marriage traditionally aided one another in their careers, but the son of the divine
Julius developed the role of his family to an unprecedented degree.
In the past, power and office could not be shared, since both were
temporary and subject to competition and the whims of the electorate. Such restrictions did not apply to Imperator Caesar Augustus,
who was able to grant Agrippa effectively permanent office in one
form or another, eventually advancing him to the tribunician power
and *maius imperium proconsulare*. As early as 36 BC Augustus' wife and
sister were marked out as public figures by the unprecedented grant
of the sacrosanctity of the tribunate, while Marcellus, Tiberius and
Drusus, and in due course Caius and Lucius, received special recognition and accelerated careers which brought them post after post
as soon as they were adults. For all his disapproval of the crowd's
acclaim for the young Caius, Augustus consciously marked out his
family as worthy of more respect and a greater public role than
anyone else in Rome.

Nowhere is this more clear than on the Ara Pacis Augustae or altar of Augustan peace. Decreed by the Senate on 4 July 13 BC in honour of his victorious return from the provinces, it had been chosen by Augustus in preference to the initial award of an altar to him inside the Curia Julia itself. Instead it was built on the Campus Martius, continuing the process by which he and Agrippa turned this area into a giant monument to his glory. Set within a sacred precinct, the design had echoes of the Temple of Janus, with an entrance at each end, and on the inside the marble was delicately carved to resemble the wooden planking of a traditional shrine. The same exquisite craftsmanship decorated the outside walls, most notably with friezes on the north and south sides showing a religious procession. Its precise nature, and whether it represents a specific occasion or some imagined ceremony combining real and invented elements, remains fiercely debated by scholars to this day. One of the most convincing suggestions is that it shows the formal thanksgiving or *supplicatio* commemorating Augustus' victories in 13 BC – one of the fifty-five public thanksgivings awarded to him, which added up to a grand total of 890 days, dwarfing even those granted to Julius Caesar.[5]

What is not in doubt is the central role given to Augustus' extended family in the procession and on the friezes. Other senators do appear, for instance the priests known as *flamines* who wear their peculiar hats each topped with a spike. One of them must be the *flamen* of the divine Julius, created only in 44 BC, while the other priesthoods reached back to the ancient past. Caesar Augustus walks ahead of them, preceded in turn by his lictors. The *princeps* is shown as marginally taller than those around him, which given his modest stature is unlikely, but he does not tower over the rest in the manner of a great king or pharaoh. Agrippa, who follows the *flamines*, is also slightly bigger so that he stands out. He has a fold of his toga over his head, perhaps as a mark of prayer or some role in the ritual, although other scholars prefer to see this as a sign that he had died before the sculpture was complete. A small boy in a tunic tugs at his toga, but looks behind him upwards at Livia who pats the child's head, perhaps to calm or still him.

This informality is typical of the rest of the scene. Next to Livia stands Tiberius, while further back Antonia holds a child's hand and turns her head round to talk to her husband Drusus. The latter, recently returned from his command in Gaul, wears the distinctive military cloak (*sagum*), which in this case is clutched by another small boy, who in turn looks up at a slightly older girl. Identifying individuals on the Ara Pacis is difficult. Augustus and Agrippa are depicted clearly, but everyone else is shown in a stylised way, helping the two leading men to stand out all the more. The others look dignified, in all save a few cases youthful, and although their features are not identical, they are certainly similar to each other, and the differences points of detail. A contemporary would no doubt have recognised them instantly, understanding the subtle variations in the almost uniform faces, but for us it is much harder, especially with the less well-known personalities; all of this is made worse by successive and often heavy restorations of the sculptures which began in Late Antiquity and continued through to Mussolini in the twentieth century. It is probable that the figures include Mark Antony's son Iullus Antonius and Domitius Ahenobarbus, both married to daughters of Octavia, and other members of the *princeps'* extended family, and it is regrettable that these cannot be identified with confidence.[6]

The children are hardest of all to recognise, each of them given generic, chubby features emphasising their youth but making it impossible to age them precisely. Most are dressed as miniature adults in the togas or formal dresses of the men and women around them. In this the boy holding onto Agrippa's cloak is different, since he wears only a tunic and has a torque (a heavy gold, silver or bronze necklace originally Gallic in style) around his neck. This has led some to suggest that he is a barbarian prince, many of whom came as hostages to Rome and were raised in Augustus' household in the hope that they would grow up to be allies. Yet we also know that the boys riding in the Trojan Games wore torques, and so it is far more likely to be Caius Caesar. A smaller boy dressed in the same way appears elsewhere on the sculpture and is probably his brother Lucius.[7]

Material and craftsmanship on the Ara Pacis are of the highest

quality. The influence of Greek art is obvious, with especially striking
– and no doubt conscious – echoes of the friezes on the Parthenon.
Many scholars assume that the senior sculptor was Greek, but there
is no evidence for this one way or the other. There is also much that
is very Roman and specifically Augustan in concept, and this is far
from a simple copy. The informality of husbands and wives speaking
to each other and to children was unprecedented, as was the prominence of so many women and children in the procession. On the
wings of the precinct, separate from the processional friezes, are
scenes showing divine protectors of the Romans, Roma and Tellus,
and their mythical ancestors, Aeneas, Romulus and Remus. Smaller
details depict bulls being prepared for sacrifice. The distant past of
the Romans and the ancestors of the Julii and thus the *princeps* are
invoked and connected with a present overwhelmingly populated
by Augustus and his family. These are themes familiar from Virgil
and from so much of the art and literature of the age. Peace is celebrated, but it is a Roman peace following on from military victory
and most specifically a peace won by the successes of Augustus. A
few years later the poet Ovid, scarcely an unambiguous mouthpiece
of the regime, would sing of the Ara Pacis and hope for peace because foreign peoples either loved Rome or feared her. This peace
was to be the peace of unchallenged Roman dominance.[8]

Such a glorious future was assured by the leadership of Augustus,
supported by a family shown in such numbers – three generations
are on view on the Ara Pacis. The oldest and most distinguished
consists of Augustus and Livia, as well as Agrippa, even though he
did not live to see the completion and dedication of the altar early
in 9 BC. As usual, Augustus is ageless, shown as a mature and commanding figure, but scarcely as a man in his early fifties. Then comes
a generation led by Livia's sons, both of them still in their twenties,
and finally the youthful promise of Caius and Lucius and the other
children. A family line reaching back to Aeneas was bountifully provided with a future. Augustus was less troubled by severe illness than
in the past, but was not young and must one day die. Modern scholars invariably search for the *princeps'* heir at each stage of his life,

and the attention given first to Marcellus and then to others makes it clear that contemporaries were inclined to think in much the same way. Hindsight tells us – just as it did Suetonius, Tacitus and Dio – that after the death of Augustus, Rome would be ruled by one emperor or *princeps* after another for centuries to come.

This may not have been quite what Augustus planned, for certainly after the death of Marcellus he seems always to have searched not for one heir, but for several supporters for the moment and successors for the future. Agrippa shared his powers and a good deal of his workload and was a contemporary, but lacked his *auctoritas* and came from an obscure background. Tiberius and Drusus were the products of an aristocratic family, were given greatly accelerated careers and married to Agrippa's daughter and Augustus' niece respectively, but were not adopted. Caius and Lucius became Caesars and would in turn enjoy rapid promotion. Once adult, all five of these men shared the tasks of administrating the provinces, fighting campaigns and supervising much that occurred in Rome. They were colleagues, albeit all more or less inferior to the *princeps*.[9]

There is not the slightest hint that any one of them was ever marked out as his sole successor, and that the others were expected to stand aside and accept one man's pre-eminence. Not all were equal, but in theory all would be united and serve for the common good. Once again hindsight encourages us to accept as normal the high mortality rate among those closest to Augustus, instead of seeing it as exceptional even by the dangerous standards of the Roman world. Hence the prominence given to so many relatives by adoption, blood or marriage can be seen as allowing for inevitable losses. Nothing suggests that Augustus thought in this way. He led the state with the close assistance of men drawn from his family circle whose loyalty to him was certain, and seems to have expected this arrangement to continue after his death. There would not be one *princeps*, but several *principes*, able to share the arduous responsibilities and by their existence showing that the death of the most senior would not create a power vacuum and invite a return to civil war.

In a sense it was a very Roman concept – less a monarchy than

the rule of a small, informal college, each with monarchic power –
and under Augustus it worked. Subsequent attempts to revive the
system invariably failed, primarily because no one else ever enjoyed
the same prestige as Caesar Augustus. He was the son of the divine
Julius, consul more often than anyone else, awarded more public
thanksgivings and triumphs than anyone else. Not even Agrippa ever
matched this record, and even if he had actually done most of the
work, the credit had always gone to reinforce the prestige of Augustus. No other emperor would do so much or even – at least for
several centuries – rule for as long as Caesar Augustus was supreme
in the Roman state. Who he was, and what he had done, made it all
possible, since no one from within his family was likely to challenge
him, and no one from outside the circle was capable of doing so.

The loss of Agrippa was a blow, and no doubt deeply felt, since
he had supported Augustus for more than three decades, succeeding in every task given to him, but the virtue of the system meant
that others were ready to take on his duties. Inevitably the greatest
burden fell on Tiberius and Drusus, and both men would serve on
campaign with little break for the next few years. The former was
also required to divorce his wife, Vipsania, who had already given
him a son and would soon give birth to a daughter. By the standards of the Roman aristocracy it had proved a happy marriage, but
divorce and remarriage to suit the current political situation was so
well established an aspect of aristocratic life that it is unlikely their
separation caused much surprise. Twice widowed and the mother of
five children, Augustus' daughter was still only twenty-seven, and it
would have been unusual in the extreme for her not to remarry. For
a while he considered choosing her a husband from the equestrian
order, hoping to find a man who was rich and eminently respectable,
but unlike a senator not tempted by a career in public life. Yet such
a man would have received far more attention as son-in-law to the
princeps than as a private citizen, and it is doubtful that he could have
remained altogether free from political activity.

Julia was keen to marry Tiberius, and in many ways he was
the obvious choice, since choosing a son-in-law from outside the

extended family was bound to raise them to a position of eminence.
It was no longer important to retain Agrippa's loyalty, while Drusus
was married to Augustus' niece, someone less easy to discard, and
so Vipsania was divorced. In time she would remarry, and live on
for many years, giving at least five children to her senatorial husband; but since she did not carry the slightest hint of the Julian
bloodline this did not matter. Tiberius and Julia were betrothed,
but followed the proper legal requirement and waited for more
than ten months before they were married. It was an alliance intended to bring Tiberius even closer to Augustus and his adopted
sons, who would one day join him in helping the *princeps* to run the
empire.[10]

CONQUEST

In the meantime Tiberius was sent to the Balkans where trouble
had broken out again, encouraged by the news of Agrippa's death.
His brother Drusus went back to Gaul, and for the next three years
both would campaign aggressively on these frontiers. It was clearly
part of a concerted plan, although modern claims that Augustus was
striving to create defensible boundaries based on the Danube and
ultimately the Elbe do not convince. After years of tidying up the
existing provinces, completing the conquest of the Iberian Peninsula
and most recently occupying the Alps, Imperator Caesar Augustus
was determined on large-scale conquests in Europe. This was clean
glory, winning the victories that would fulfil the promise of peace
through strength celebrated in the Ara Pacis and justify his supervision of the provinces facing military problems. It was also a chance
for Tiberius and Drusus to add to their reputations and win further
experience of high command.[11]

These aggressive campaigns were premeditated, and in the last
few years troops and supplies had gathered on the Rhine and in the
Balkans to undertake them. That is not to say that they were unprovoked, and modern cynicism over claims that almost every Roman

war was fought in response to earlier raids is unnecessary. Raiding was common and often serious, but the Roman response to it was less predictable, varying from minor reprisals to heavy attacks or outright conquest. The coincidence of available resources and a commander with the freedom of action and the desire to win glory determined the scale and type of Roman response. These factors and the opportunity offered by the migration of the Helvetii in 58 BC had led to Julius Caesar's conquest of Gaul, rather than the Balkan war he had expected to wage.[12]

Untroubled by serious warfare elsewhere, and with a freedom of action unmatched by any Roman leader in the past, Augustus decided to add to Roman territory in both these areas. Like any Roman, he did not think so much in terms of physical as political geography, seeing the world as a network of peoples and states. It was these he would attack, and 'spare the conquered and overcome the proud in war'. Some would be added to the provinces while others would simply be forced to acknowledge Roman power. The Greeks and Romans had only a vague sense of the lands far from the Mediterranean, and certainly did not appreciate the sheer size of central Europe and the steppes beyond. It is quite possible that Augustus believed that he could conquer all of Europe as far as the ocean that was believed to encircle all three known continents, but such possibilities were for the future. At the moment his ambitions were more restrained. He would add to Rome's *imperium*, punishing the peoples who had attacked the provinces in the past and preventing them from doing this in the future.

Tiberius and Drusus would lead the legions in person, while Imperator Caesar Augustus supervised from a distance. In a change from the recent pattern of long tours of the provinces, over the next years he made short trips to be near the theatres of operations, stationing himself in Aquileia in northern Italy on the border with Illyricum or at Lugdunum in Gaul. Neither were so very far from Rome, and he returned to the City on several occasions, usually after the campaigning season was over. Suetonius provides a glimpse of these trips in an extract of a letter handwritten by Augustus himself,

telling his older stepson about the five-day festival celebrated between 20 and 25 March in honour of the goddess Minerva:

> We spent the *Quinquatria* very merrily, my dear Tiberius, for we
> played all day long and kept the gaming board warm. Your brother
> made a great outcry about his luck, but after all did not come out so
> far behind in the long run; for after losing heavily he unexpectedly
> and little by little got back a good deal. For my part, I lost 20,000 ses-
> terces, but because I was extravagantly generous in my play, as usual.
> If I had demanded of everyone the stakes which I let go, or had kept
> all that I gave away, I should have won fully 50,000. But I like that
> better, for my generosity will exalt me to immortal glory.[13]

The informal style is typical of surviving letters to family and friends,
and at least openly Augustus got on well with his stepsons. Drusus
was famous for his charm and affability, and had quickly become a
popular favourite. Tiberius was a reserved and complex character,
easier to respect than to like, but the fragments of letters written to
him contain repeated statements of affection and a gentle, bantering
tone and heavy use of irony, such as the talk of 'immortal glory'. In
another he describes a dinner where he and his guests 'gambled like
old men'. There are many echoes of Cicero's letters in Augustus'
correspondence, in the repeated statements of affection, the frequent quotations and jokes and perhaps also in false claims of deep
affection. Even so, at this stage there is no hint that the relationship
between the *princeps* and the man soon to become his son-in-law
were anything other than cordial.[14]

Early in 12 BC Drusus completed a formal census in the three Gauls,
no doubt helping to organise the provinces, recording property and
the taxation due to Rome, and ensuring that they would give him
plentiful supplies for the forthcoming campaigns. The process had
perhaps begun before Augustus left the provinces the previous year,
and the *princeps* had personally supervised the first such census held
in the region in 27 BC. Perhaps it was also intended to be fairer than
the existing system of levies which had been so recently exploited

by Licinus. Apart from Luke's Gospel, we have no other evidence claiming that at some point Augustus issued a single decree to hold a census in, and arrange the taxation due from, the entire empire. It is perfectly possible that there actually was such a single decree, effectively making clear what already happened in an ad hoc way, and that this – like so many other details – is simply not mentioned in our other sources. On the other hand, the Gospel writer may merely reflect the perspective of a provincial, for whom census and taxation were imposed by the Roman authorities with a regularity that must have seemed as if it was a system imposed by a single decision.[15]

Sometimes the holding of a census provoked resentment and even rebellion, especially in recently settled provinces – the prospect of paying tax is rarely a pleasant one, especially if it went to an occupying power. Livy claims that there was some trouble in Gaul in response to the census, and Dio hints that this was the case, but gives no details, and if there were disturbances then they were probably small-scale. There were advantages to individuals and communities in registering property and rights, since these were recorded in a form that had unimpeachable legal authority. Most areas quickly became used to the process, and Drusus efficiently suppressed whatever resistance did occur.[16]

As well as organising the finances of the Gallic provinces and keeping order, there was considerable activity preparing for the forthcoming advance across the Rhine. A series of large military bases were established to accommodate the troops mustering for the planned war. Numbers are difficult to establish, but probably at least eight legions were gathered, supported by substantial numbers of auxiliary troops and some naval squadrons manning both small war galleys and transport ships. One of the bases was at modern-day Nijmegen on the River Waal, and excavations suggest that it was constructed somewhere between 19 and 16 BC. Some forty-two hectares in size, and built of earth, turf and timber, it probably housed two complete legions as well as auxiliary units. Like most of the other forts built by the army in these years, whether on or to the east of the Rhine and in Spain, it does not quite conform to the neat, playing-card shape so familiar for Roman army bases in the first and second centuries AD. Augustus' legions exploited good natural positions and often sited forts on high ground, the ramparts roughly following the contours to produce six-, seven- or eight-sided shapes. Their internal layouts also vary, as does the design of individual building types, but in each case the variation is less marked than the very close similarities. If it lacks the greater uniformity of practice of the next century, it suggests the ongoing development of such regular planning, evolving from traditional methods. Many of the regulations for the army were set down by Augustus and would remain in force for over a century without significant change.[17]

Used to seeing the big stone forts of later years, it is all too easy for us to accept without remark the scale and organisation of these camps. Nijmegen was occupied for less than a decade, perhaps only for a few years, and yet for that time the soldiers lived in well-built, neatly ordered barrack blocks constructed to a standard design, with a pair of rooms for each tent group (or *contubernium*) of eight men. Some of the excavated barrack blocks are a little smaller and have been identified as auxiliary rather than legionary, but even these offered considerable comfort for men living through a north European winter. Far more generous are the headquarters building and the substantial houses built for the senator serving as legate in charge of a legion – or perhaps in such camps one man in charge of both legions – and for the equestrian and senatorial tribunes. All of these buildings are matched by similar structures in other forts built during these campaigns. In size and organisation, such army bases resembled well-ordered Mediterranean-style cities springing up on the fringes of the empire.

The winter months of 13–12 BC saw another raid by German warriors into the Roman provinces, but this was repulsed by Drusus. In the spring he launched the first of a series of attacks against the tribes living east of the Rhine. Some of the army advanced using land routes following the valleys feeding into the Rhine, while another part embarked on board ships and sailed around the North Sea to make landings on the coast. At one point he seriously misjudged local conditions, leaving many of his vessels aground when the tide went out further than he expected. Julius Caesar had similarly under-estimated the power and tidal range of the sea during his British expeditions. Fortunately the Frisii, a recently acquired local ally, arrived to protect and assist the stranded Romans. Yet on the whole the story was one of success. Tribal homelands were attacked, villages and farms burnt, animals rounded up and crops destroyed, and any warriors who gathered defeated in battle. A century or so later Tacitus would make a barbarian leader grimly joke that the Romans 'create a desolation and call it peace'. Faced with such displays of the price paid for resisting Rome, several tribes joined the Frisii in seeking alliance. Tiberius employed similar methods with similar success in Pannonia.[18]

Drusus returned to Rome at the end of the year for a brief visit which demonstrated how many of the old restrictions on provincial governors simply did not apply to those close to the *princeps*. He was elected praetor, given the prestigious post of urban praetor, but tarried for only a short time before hurrying back to the Rhine frontier to continue the war. Now aged twenty-seven, at the start of spring 11 BC the *princeps'* stepson attacked again, this time leading one of the columns making its way overland. Some of the tribes which had briefly capitulated may have decided to risk war once more. Florus tells a story of the Sugambri, Cherusci and Suebi seizing and cruci-fying twenty centurions who were in their territory, and this episode may date to that year. The most likely reason for their presence would have been either diplomatic activity as Roman representa-tives or more likely raising recruits promised by treaty for service in the auxiliary cohorts. However, as so often the Romans benefited from rivalries and disunity among the tribes. The Sugambri mus-tered an army and attacked the neighbouring Chatti because they refused to join them in alliance against Rome. While the warriors were occupied in this way, Drusus struck quickly, devastating their homeland.[19]

Such incidents are a valuable reminder that the area east of the Rhine was populated by many distinct and often mutually hostile communities. The Romans called them Germans, but it is unlikely that any of the inhabitants of the region thought of themselves in that way. Julius Caesar portrayed the Germans and the Gauls as clearly distinct, although even he admitted that there was some blurring with the Germanic peoples already settled in Gaul. The distinction was useful to him, since it helped to establish the Germans as a threat to Gaul, and also made it easier for him to stop his conquests at the Rhine. He and other ancient authors paint a gloomy picture of Germany and its peoples, making them more primitive and at the same time more ferocious than the inhabitants of Gaul. For them Germany was a land of bogs and thick forests, with few clear tracks, no substantial towns, no temples and a population that was semi-nomadic, who kept animals and hunted in the forests but did not farm. Many old stereotypes of barbarism, stretching back to Homer's portrait of the monstrous Cyclops in the *Odyssey*, fed this impression of peoples who were utterly uncivilised, and thus unpredictable and dangerous.

The archaeological evidence challenges much of this, while presenting problems and complexities of its own. Before Julius Caesar arrived in Gaul, a wide area of central Germany closely resembled the lands west of the Rhine, boasting large hilltop towns with similar signs of industry, trade and organisation as the Gaulish *oppida*. There was much contact between these areas, and whatever the political relationship the cultural similarities are striking, both belonging to what archaeologists call La Tène culture. During the first half of the first century BC, these towns in central Germany are all either abandoned or shrink dramatically in size and sophistication. In at least one case there is evidence for violent and bloody destruction of the town, and in general weaponry becomes far more common in the archaeological record. The destruction was not wrought by the Romans, who had yet to reach these lands, although it is possible that a contributing factor was the ripple effect caused by the impact of Rome's empire, whether through the shifting trade patterns or direct military action. It is unlikely that the Romans were ever aware of what was happening so far from their empire; they naturally assumed that the situation they encountered when they did reach the area was normal, and that the local peoples had always behaved in this way.

These German towns and the societies based around them had probably already collapsed before Julius Caesar arrived in Gaul. How this happened is impossible to know, and the evidence could equally be interpreted as internal upheaval causing destructive power struggles, or as the arrival of new, aggressive peoples. Migrations are often difficult to trace archaeologically, but the repeated talk in our sources of large groups moving in search of new land must at least in part reflect reality. Tribal and other groupings also frequently defy the best attempts to see them in the archaeological evidence, and are likely to have been complex, with recently formed and short-lived groups mingling with older ties of kinship. Linguistic analysis of surviving names based on later Celtic and Germanic languages does suggest real distinctions at the time, but still does not make it easy to establish the ethnic and cultural identity of particular peoples. There is a fair chance that the Romans did not fully understand the relationships between named groups like the Sugambri, Cherusci, Chatti, Chauci or Suebi, and it is more than likely that these changed fairly rapidly as leaders rose and fell.

At the higher levels of society, there was certainly enough instability and rapid change to justify some of the Romans' view of a population constantly on the move. Lower down this was less true. The towns had gone, but in most areas east of the Rhine farms, hamlets and small villages remained in occupation for long periods of time, spanning several generations. The overall population was probably large, even if there were no big settlements. Agriculture was widespread, albeit geared mainly to feeding the local population and producing no more surplus than was needed to cushion them against bad harvests. In the longer term the social and political structures of the tribes were in a state of flux, and substantial populations periodically on the move, but even so for decades at a time some tribal groups were settled on the same lands, and had clearly acknowledged leaders. The Romans could try to identify the tribes and know where their current homelands and chieftains were, at least in the immediate future.[20]

No doubt they misunderstood a good deal and made mistakes, but Drusus and his staff steadily added to their knowledge of the peoples they were fighting. The absence of good roads made movement of men and supplies difficult for them. The lack of large communities meant that it was hard to find large stores of food and fodder. In Gaul, Julius Caesar had frequently gone to one of the *oppida* and either demanded or taken the supplies needed by his army. It was far more difficult to go to hundreds of little settlements for such needs, and so in Germany the legions were forced to carry almost all that they needed. Where necessary, they built bridges over rivers and causeways through marshes and this inevitably took time. In most cases Drusus and his men followed the lines of rivers since this made it easier to carry some supplies by barge, and the difficulty of moving overland helps to explain the reliance upon sailing around the North Sea coast.[21]

In spite of such difficulties the second season of campaigning was successful, with the Roman columns penetrating deeper than ever before into Germany before running short of supplies. With summer drawing to a close, Drusus led his men back towards the Rhine – at this stage it would have been difficult to feed and impossible to support any garrison left deep in hostile territory over the winter months. German chieftains maintained bands of warriors who had no other job apart from fighting, but these were few in number. The army of a whole tribe or an alliance of tribes relied for numbers on every free tribesman able to equip himself with weapons and willing to fight, and inevitably it took a long time for such an army to muster. This meant that a Roman army was far more likely to encounter serious resistance when it retreated rather than in the initial attack. In this particular case men had also returned from the raid on the Chatti and joined the bands gathering to fight the enemy who had ravaged their lands. The Roman column was large and cumbersome with its supply train, and thus its route was predictable. The warriors were angry and they were confident, since a retreat on the part of the invader inevitably seemed like nervous flight.

Drusus' column marched into a succession of ambushes. The Romans steadily fought their way onwards, but even when they repulsed the attackers they were in no position to pursue them and inflict serious losses, and could not afford the time to halt and manoeuvre against this elusive enemy. Each success, however small, encouraged the warriors, and no doubt inspired more to join them. This culminated in a much larger-scale ambush, which bottled up the Roman column in a restrictive defile. The Romans were trapped and risked annihilation, but then the essential clumsiness of a tribal army saved them. German warriors did not carry enough food for a long campaign and thus wanted the fight to be over quickly so they could return home. There was no single leader able to control the army, but lots of chiefs with varying amounts of influence, while each warrior reserved the right to decide when and how he would fight. The Romans seemed to be at their mercy and so, instead of waiting and letting them starve or fight at a disadvantage, bands of Germans massed together and surged forward to wipe out the enemy and enjoy the plunder to be taken from their baggage train. Close combat of this sort played to the strengths of the legionaries, giving Drusus and his men the opportunity to strike at their opponents at last. Turning at bay, the Romans savaged the exultant warriors, whose over-confidence quickly turned to panicked flight. Drusus and his men marched the rest of the way back to the Rhine unimpeded.[22]

The campaign was declared a victory, as was the one waged by Tiberius near the Danube. Augustus was awarded a triumph, which as usual he chose not to celebrate, and his stepsons were granted the lesser honour of an ovation combined with the symbols of a triumph (*ornamenta triumphalia*). In the autumn both men returned to Rome, as did Augustus himself, and 400 sesterces were given to each male citizen in the City to celebrate the success of Livia's sons. His fifty-second birthday was marked by a series of beast fights and around this time Julia and Tiberius were married. Yet the news was not all good. Octavia died suddenly, and so the ashes of yet another family member were installed in the Mausoleum. The *princeps'* sister received the honour of a state funeral, with the principal oration delivered by her son-in-law Drusus.[23]

In spite of this personal loss the mood was confident, and the Senate decreed the closing of the doors on the Temple of Janus to signify the establishment of peace throughout the Roman world. News of a Dacian raid across the Danube prevented the rite from being performed, and in 10 BC the wars were resumed. Augustus and Livia accompanied Drusus and his family to Lugdunum in Gaul, where later in the year Antonia gave birth to their second son, the future emperor Claudius. This year most likely saw the dedication there of a lavishly built and decorated precinct enclosing an altar to Rome and Augustus. Tribal leaders were summoned from all over Gaul to attend the ceremony and take part in the rituals that would from then on be repeated annually. Julius Caesar had talked of regular meetings of all the tribes of Gaul, and it is quite likely that this new cult was intended to fill the gap left by the abolition of such potentially subversive gatherings.[24]

Tiberius spent the year campaigning in the Balkans, supported by at least one other army whose leader also received the insignia of a triumph. Drusus fought in Germany, and the brothers regularly wrote to each other, just as they did to Augustus and their mother. On one occasion Tiberius showed such a letter to the *princeps*, in which his brother talked of their combining to force Augustus to 'restore liberty'. Suetonius tells the story as the first sign of Tiberius' hatred of his kindred, but there is no other evidence for hostility between the brothers and every indication of deep affection. Perhaps the incident was an accident or a later invention. Modern scholars tend to assume that Drusus wanted the *princeps* to resign and the Republican system to be revived, and like to portray both brothers as aristocrats with highly traditional views of politics. Yet the phrase is vague, and may have meant no more than a dislike of some of the people given office and influence under Augustus, and a desire that these be replaced by better men – including themselves. Drusus was certainly ambitious. Elsewhere Suetonius tells us that he was desperate to win the *spolia opima*, even going so far as to chase German kings around the battlefield in the hope of cornering them and killing them in single combat. It is a great leap of the imagination to connect this with the incident involving Crassus in 29 BC, rather than seeing it as the eagerness of a young aristocrat to win one of the rarest and most prestigious of all honours.[25]

In January 9 BC Drusus became consul just over a week before his twenty-ninth birthday, and it may be that his hunt for the *spolia opima* came in this year, when as consul he fought under his own *imperium* and auspices. This was the year when he took his army to the River Elbe; a story soon circulated that he was there confronted with the apparition of a larger-than-life woman who warned him not to advance any further and prophesied that his life was almost at an end. It was late in the season, and Drusus returned to his bases on the Rhine, but was now able to leave some garrisons in Germany. In the course of the four campaigns the land between the Rhine and the Elbe had been overrun, and most of the peoples there claimed to acknowledge Roman rule. How permanent this would prove was not yet clear, but the achievement was certainly considerable. Then, on the way back to winter in Gaul, Drusus had a riding accident and badly injured his leg. The wound failed to heal and in September the young general died.[26]

Tiberius was soon at his brother's side, having rushed to join him in a journey that became famous for its speed. He arranged for the body to be embalmed and carried back to Rome with great ceremony. The first to bear it were tribunes and centurions from his legions. Later they passed this duty on to the leading citizens of Roman colonies and towns. On many of the stages Tiberius walked with the procession. The mourning was a genuine reflection of Drusus' popularity – Seneca later claimed the mood was almost that of a triumph as they marked the passing of the dashing young hero. The ceremonies culminated in a public funeral in Rome. Tiberius delivered a eulogy to his brother from the Rostra outside the Temple of the Divine Julius in the Forum. Augustus gave another – perhaps to an even bigger crowd – in the Circus Flaminius and outside the *pomerium*, the formal boundary of a city. (He was in mourning and this prevented him entering Rome and performing the rites required to mark his latest victory.) Actors wore the funeral masks and insignia of Drusus' ancestors in the traditional way. These were augmented by those of the ancestors of the Julii, even though Augustus had never adopted his stepson, before the body was cremated and the ashes added to those in the Mausoleum – association with the *princeps* clearly trumped the right to be commemorated as a member of the dead man's real family.[27]

Nearby was the Ara Pacis, which had been formally dedicated on 30 January 9 BC. Alongside that was a vast sundial, the gnomon an obelisk brought from Egypt, a reminder of the defeat of Antony and Cleopatra, and a demonstration that Julius Caesar's calendar was now functioning properly to mark the 365.25 days of the year. Raised on a pedestal, the obelisk towered about one hundred feet high, and at noon each day cast a slightly different shadow, which was to be measured by a grid marked out in bronze lines on the paving stones, using Greek letters to symbolise the signs of the zodiac and the solar year. For all its grandeur, either the calculations were wrong or the foundations of the obelisk shifted, so that by the middle of the first century AD Pliny noted that it had not been accurate for thirty years. (Heavily restored, the obelisk itself now stands at a different site in Rome's Piazza di Montecitorio.)[28]

Nature was hard even for Augustus to control. Five years earlier he had enjoyed the assistance of three active and capable men from within his family, with the promise of two more in the long-term future when Caius and Lucius came of age. Now Agrippa and Drusus were gone, and only Tiberius remained. The burden would fall heavily upon him in the next few years.

PART FIVE

IMPERATOR CAESAR AUGUSTUS, *DIVI FILIUS, PATER PATRIAE* 2 BC–AD 14

'While in my thirteenth consulship, the Senate and the equestrian order and the Roman people as a whole called me the father of my country.' *Deeds of the Divine Augustus* 35.

FATHER

Augustus 'said to his friends that he had two spoiled daughters, and was forced to put up with them – these were the res publica and Julia'. Macrobius, early fifth century AD.[1]

'Fortune has lifted you up to a high place of honour: Livia, carry this burden . . . remain upright, rise above your sorrows, and keep your spirit unbroken, if you are able. When we search for an ideal of virtue, it will be better when you are the first woman of the Romans [principis Romanae].' Anonymous, written probably in the early first century AD.[2]

Livia was distraught at the loss of her younger son – her pain perhaps made worse by a rumour that Augustus had had a hand in Drusus' death. Suetonius thought the story absurd, and was surely right, but it may already have been circulating. Privately Caesar's wife sought the advice of the Alexandrian philosopher Areus, a man who had enjoyed her husband's respect for some time. In an interestingly modern way, he encouraged the grieving mother to talk about her son at every opportunity and to display his images throughout the house. Drusus' widow Antonia, although only in her twenties, refused to remarry and moved with her children to live permanently with her mother-in-law. The couple's two sons were granted the name Germanicus in honour of their father's victories. Livia was honoured by the Senate with a number of statues in the City and also granted the status of a mother of three children (*ius trium liberorum*) – stillborn children like the one she had had with Augustus were not officially counted and so she had not already earned this status.[3]

The award reinforced the public image of Livia as the ideal

Roman matron. Her grief was genuine, but kept within acceptable limits which did not prevent her from continuing to fulfil her
public and private roles. This was in contrast to Octavia, who after
the death of Marcellus had largely withdrawn from public view. In
later years Livia's reputation would be blackened by innuendo and
direct accusation of intrigue and murder. All the accusations alleged
secret crimes, but not even her bitterest critics ever suggested that
her public conduct was less than impeccable. Praised for her great
beauty, her faithfulness to Augustus was never questioned, and all
depict her as chaste – in the Roman sense of a wife who only slept
with her husband. One story may suggest an arch humour. When
being carried past some men stripped naked and awaiting execution,
she is supposed to have claimed that she noticed them no more than
naked statues. Livia was seen as a loyal and a compliant wife – the
latter allegedly to a remarkable degree, so that she personally picked
out girls for her husband to bed.[4]

Portraits of Livia have similar ageless good looks to those of her
husband, and her hair, clothes and posture exude dignified elegance.
She is fashionable – indeed her look was widely copied – but always
within bounds appropriate for an aristocratic Roman lady. Her
household of slaves and freedmen and women was extremely large,
including many cosmetic specialists as well no doubt as the mischiev-
ous *deliciae* and dwarfs trained to be amusing and often given heroic
names. Livia delighted in them, and included in her household the
smallest woman in Rome. It was a taste probably shared with most
of the other aristocratic ladies in her circle of friends, but Augustus felt that midgets and anyone with a serious deformity was a bad
omen and did not care for them. On 30 January in either 9 or 8 BC,
Livia celebrated her fiftieth birthday. Her health seems always to
have been good, while her confidence and sharp intelligence were
certainly undiminished even by the sadness of losing her son.[5]

When Tiberius celebrated his ovation in 9 BC, the feast he gave
for senators was mirrored by a dinner given to prominent women
and presided over by Livia and Julia. This was another Augustan innovation, giving women a more active place in victory celebrations

conducted by his family. Livia wielded no formal power, but she and the other women of the imperial household often played a public role in a way utterly different from the wives of magistrates in the past. One source even spoke of Livia as a *princeps* to the women of Rome, extending this very male concept to suggest similar leadership for a woman over the wives and daughters of Romans.[6]

At first the marriage between Augustus' daughter and Livia's son showed every sign of success. Julia followed her husband when he left Rome for the Balkans, and supported him from the city of Aquileia on the border between northern Italy and Illyricum. She was pregnant again, but this time things did not go well and their son died soon after being born. Probably this disappointment soured the relationship, and as the years passed the couple drifted apart. There were rumours that Julia had had designs on Tiberius even while she was still married to Agrippa, and he came to believe this and resent her. Lingering affection for Vipsania remained, or grew as he became less and less comfortable with Julia. When he happened to encounter his former wife in Rome Tiberius followed her, his eyes glassy with tears and a look of desperate longing on his face. Care was taken by the family to ensure that they never again met.[7]

More and more Julia's and Tiberius' very different temperaments clashed rather than complemented each other. A complex man, who was no doubt able to remember the fear and flight of his boyhood years, he had a stern, rather old-fashioned view of behaviour combined with social awkwardness. For all the lineage of his family, Tiberius' father's line was undistinguished and he owed his present prominence solely to his mother's marriage to Augustus. In contrast Julia was born both a Caesar and the daughter of a triumvir, and before she entered her teens her father became sole master of the Roman world. As the rift between the couple widened, she grew openly contemptuous of her husband's background. Even so he, like Maecenas and Agrippa, was a man marked out by the *princeps* for favour and power, and the same was true of Julia's sons.[8]

Having dutifully played her role in her father's political plans, securing the loyalty of Marcellus, Agrippa and Tiberius in turn, and given him five grandchildren in the process, Julia saw no reason to hide her pride in being Augustus' daughter or her enjoyment of luxury and pleasure. When someone suggested that she might do better copying the sober and restrained lifestyle of her father, she replied: 'He forgets that he is Caesar, but I remember that I am Caesar's daughter.' As conscious as Livia of fashion, Julia was some twenty years younger, with a style that was far more flamboyant and a good deal racier. On one occasion she realised that her father disapproved of her appearance even though he said nothing. The next day she appeared in a considerably more modest outfit and his pleasure was obvious. 'Isn't this a more fitting style for the daughter of Augustus?' he said, to which Julia replied, 'Today I am dressed for the eyes of my father – yesterday for the eyes of my husband.' Augustus' daughter was witty, preferring to decide for herself how to behave rather than take instructions from others, and much of the time she was on her own while first Agrippa and then Tiberius went off on campaign. Her pride did not slip into arrogance and Julia was popular in Rome, both in her own right and through enthusiasm for her father, husbands and sons.[9]

THE MAN WHO WALKED AWAY

Augustus was concerned that Drusus' death might encourage the German tribes to renew the fight against Rome and so sent Tiberius there in 8 BC to replace his brother. The *princeps* waited for his formal mourning to be complete and then entered Rome and spent some months there before hurrying to Gaul to observe the operations of his armies beyond the Rhine. This display of Roman might and determination in spite of the death of the commander convinced the tribes to sue for peace. Envoys from all the Germans were summoned to meet Augustus at Lugdunum, but when the Sugambri failed to send anyone he announced that he would not deal with any of the others. Eventually, perhaps pressured by their neighbours, the Sugambri appeared, only to be placed under arrest. It was a breach of convention

– albeit scarcely a unique one on the part of the Romans – but in this case proved to be a serious miscalculation. The captives were split up and sent to different communities to be held as hostages, but all took their own lives at the first opportunity. For the moment their fellow tribesmen did not resort to open war, but this Roman act of treachery stored up hatred and mistrust for the future.[10]

The details of the operations that year are vague and these may have involved more demonstrations of force than real fighting. For the first time Caius Caesar was shown something of the life of the legions. Aged only twelve, and not yet formally a man, he took part in some exercises – and was depicted on coins minted to pay the army. It may well be that the loss of Agrippa and Drusus encouraged Augustus to give his older son some experience at an earlier age than was normal. More strikingly, and in spite of the modest results of the year's operations, Tiberius was granted a full triumph – the first awarded to anyone other than Augustus for more than a decade, and as usual the *princeps* chose not to celebrate the ones given to him. In the autumn Tiberius was also elected consul for the second time.[11]

If the scale of the victory was questionable, its celebration was not, and in many ways it was seen as the culmination of the harder campaigning in Germany and in the Balkans over the last few years. This had resulted in considerable conquests, with new provinces in Pannonia on the Danube and in Germany east of the Rhine. Augustus revived another ancient prerogative of the conqueror and formally enlarged the *pomerium*, although this change still left substantial suburbs technically outside the City, something that was often convenient. A census carried out under special consular powers given to the *princeps* was also completed in 8 BC, and 4,233,000 citizens and their property were registered. Augustus' grand provincial command, already held for twenty years, was extended for another ten. Although he had handed control of some regions back to the Senate, in recent years he had also assumed control of Illyricum, as well as the newly conquered territories. Augustus routinely complained to the senators of the burden of his office, but neither they nor he had any hesitation in extending this. Just like Julius Caesar, the *princeps* now received the honour of having a month renamed in his honour. Some were keen for this to be September to commemorate his birth, but instead he chose the preceding month when he had first become consul and won so many of his victories. Sextilis, the sixth month in Rome's old calendar and the eighth in Julius Caesar's, thus became August.[12]

There was sadness alongside the celebration, for at some point in the year Maecenas died. Augustus' two oldest friends were now gone, as indeed was the bulk of the generation which had fought in the civil wars, while even men who were young at Actium were now at least in their forties. The *princeps* was fifty-five and still imposed on himself a formidable workload. Maecenas' activities had always been largely behind the scenes, unmarked by formal rank or office. Perhaps his influence had diminished in the last few years, but as a source of advice and honest opinion he remained important. Like his life, his death passed without great fanfare, but Augustus was his principal heir, and received among other things a substantial and luxurious villa on the outskirts of Rome. Not long afterwards the poet Horace also died, and so Augustus lost his 'perfect penis', both a jovial correspondent and a man willing and able to praise him and his regime in words of great beauty. Younger poets, like younger politicians, were taking over, and Augustus did not always find them so easy to control or in tune with his own view of the world.[13]

In the last few years he had made several attempts to encourage more men to seek a career in public life, and to increase attendance at meetings of the Senate. Traditionally Rome's highest council met whenever convened by a senior magistrate, so meetings could occur at short notice. Although some emergency sessions would still be required, in 9 BC it was established that the Senate would meet twice every month on days set well in advance and kept free of court sessions or other business requiring some senators to be present. Fines for failure to attend without good reason were increased, although since so many were already guilty of this only a small fraction selected by lot were forced to pay. Augustus established a quorum needed for a formal vote on any issue which would produce a *senatus consultum*

– the official opinion of the Senate. If fewer members were present their decision was still to be registered, but had lesser status. Lists of senators were annually posted up, and the names and numbers of those attending a session were also recorded.

Augustus initiated these reforms, but had all of the proposals posted inside the Curia, and gave ample opportunity for the senators to read them before they came up for discussion. A few changes may have resulted from this, and he took care to appear open to reasoned and reasonable objections. At times public life took on a freedom that cannot have pleased him. Bribery occurred on so grand a scale in the consular elections for 8 BC that all of the candidates, including the victors, were found guilty. No one was punished since it seemed that everyone was involved, but in future Augustus insisted that candidates provide a deposit which would be forfeit if they were found guilty of corruption.[14]

When Tiberius returned to Italy late in 8 BC he remained outside the *pomerium* until he celebrated his triumph. Therefore, when he assumed the consulship on 1 January 7 BC, the Senate convened outside the formal boundary of the City, assembling in the Porticus of Octavia next to the Theatre of Marcellus. Augustus was away in the provinces, and so his eminence did not overshadow his son-in-law's great moment. In his first speech Tiberius announced that he would restore the Temple of Concord in the Forum in his own name and that of Drusus. First built by the man who had led the lynching of the radical tribune Caius Sempronius Gracchus in 121 BC, this was where Cicero had summoned the Senate to decide the fate of Catiline's conspirators in 63 BC. At some point in this or the preceding years, he also promised to repair another temple, this time that of Castor and Pollux, also in his own and his brother's name.[15]

The Dioscuri or 'Heavenly Twins', brothers of Helen of Troy, were famous both for their manly virtue and their deep love for each other. When one died, the other shared this with him so that the brothers were alive and dead on alternate days. The Dioscuri had appeared at notable moments in Roman history, supposedly arriving to announce the victory at the Battle of Regillus in 494 BC.

Livia's sons may well already have associated themselves with them while Drusus was alive, and in the years to come Tiberius would certainly promote this. In the past, the temple was often used as an impromptu speaker's platform for informal meetings of the Roman people, and witnessed many disturbances and controversial rallies during the last decades of the Republic. It is hard to say whether Tiberius was deliberately making some comment on these historically significant monuments – and if so, even harder to say what it was. Whether or not this was the case, he certainly was contributing to a restoration of the centre of Rome which made it grander and at the same time linked everything to Augustus and his extended family.[16]

Early in January Tiberius celebrated his triumph – the first the City had seen since Balbus' procession in 19 BC. Afterwards he presided over a feast for the senators on the Capitol, while Livia gave another for the leading women of Rome. Mother and son dedicated the newly built Porticus of Livia on the Esquiline Hill, constructed by Augustus in his wife's name. This was built on the site of the demolished house of Vedius Pollio, the man infamous for feeding his slaves to carnivorous fish. It was no doubt a popular gesture to remove the house, and with it some of the memory, of such an unpopular man. As importantly, the new structure was a vast hall, providing covered space for public business of all sorts, including some minor trials – something grand and useful for the wider community in place of a monument to the excessive wealth of an individual. Inside the building was an altar or shrine to Concordia, repeating the theme of harmony within state and family.[17]

Julia is not mentioned in any of these celebrations, and this is probably more than simply chance. There was no particular reason for her to have played a prominent role in the opening of the portico named after Tiberius' mother, but her absence from the feast marking his triumph suggests a clear change from his ovation a few years earlier. The private rift between husband and wife may have begun to spill over into their public roles. It is unlikely that either of them were displeased when Tiberius left Rome to return to Germany for the campaigning season of 7 BC. No doubt Julia was more visible when her father returned to Rome and Caius Caesar presided over the celebrations marking this and the opening of the Diribitorium, the covered hall for counting votes which formed part of Agrippa's lavish rebuilding of the Saepta and the area around it. It was a remarkable feat of engineering, with the largest roof unsupported by pillars ever built by the Romans. When it succumbed to fire almost a century later it was considered too difficult to replace and left open to the sky.[18]

Fire was also a problem in 7 BC, with a blaze causing serious damage to parts of the Forum and the adjacent areas. In this case the cause was thought to be arson rather than accident, and suspicion fell on a group of men heavily in debt and hoping to make false claims when their property was destroyed. In spite of this disruption to the heart of the City, funeral games were held in honour of Agrippa, with Caius and Lucius Caesar presiding alongside Augustus. The gladiatorial fights included clashes between matched pairs of fighters and large group battles, and were staged in the Saepta, presumably in temporary stands both for convenience and as a reminder of Agrippa's service and generosity to his fellow citizens. All of the *princeps'* party apart from Augustus himself donned the black clothes of mourning, and it was a further stage in introducing his sons to the public.[19]

The year saw a major administrative reorganisation of the City, in part prompted by the recent fire. Rome had traditionally been split into little regions known as *vici* (literally towns, but better rendered as wards or districts). Augustus now redrew the boundaries to create 265 of these, which were in turn grouped into fourteen larger regions. In each *vicus* local magistrates supervised the cults centred on crossroad shrines to the gods of the region, and these men were now given greater responsibility and enhanced prestige. On special occasions the magistrates were attended by a pair of lictors and allowed to wear official garb within their *vicus*. Most if not all of these men were freedmen, as was much of the City's population, and it gave this class opportunities to hold formal rank and enjoy local power and prestige. Augustus was generous in paying for the crossroad shrines throughout the City to be replaced in finer style, connecting his name with the local spirits and deities protecting each neighbourhood. The *princeps* was not simply present in all the monumental parts of the City, but everywhere in its maze of backstreets. People – freeborn and former slaves alike – made regular offerings as individuals and communities at altars where he was ranked alongside the gods. One set up in AD 1 bears a long inscription: 'To Mercury, to the eternal god Jupiter, to Juno the Queen, to Miverva, to the Sun, the Moon, Apollo and Diana, to Annona Ops, Isis and Pietas, to the divine fates, that it may go well, propitiously and prosperously for Imperator Caesar Augustus, for his [power] and that of the Senate and People of Rome, and for the Nations . . . Lucius Lucretius Zethus, Lucius' freedman, dedicated this Augustan Altar at the command of Jupiter. Victory to the People! Health in seed-sowing!'

Augustus was not worshipped directly, but those taking part in the cult on 'Augustan' altars worshipped on his behalf. Alongside the traditional gods and goddesses, the inclusion of Isis reflected changing beliefs – and perhaps the ever-changing ethnicity – of much of Rome's population. Periodic attempts by the state to repress this Hellenised Egyptian cult failed to check its steady progress and in the end it was embraced, joining the traditional pantheon of gods protecting the City.[20]

In 6 BC Tiberius returned to Rome and in June was granted fresh honours. When Augustus began a new year of his *tribunicia potestas*, this was also given to his son-in-law for five years, as was *maius imperium proconsulare*, at least over the eastern Mediterranean. Only Agrippa had ever shared the *princeps'* eminence in this way, and it was clear that Tiberius was now expected to fulfil the same role, sharing much of the workload and acting as an imperial fireman, going from one crisis or problem to the next. In this case a palace coup in Parthia threatened the stability of Armenia and Rome's interests in the east. Tiberius, who would celebrate his thirty-sixth birthday in November, was now a proven general and administrator, having spent almost half of his adult life in the provinces. With

Agrippa and Drusus gone, and Augustus' sons still children, there was every prospect that from now on he would almost permanently be kept busy in the empire. Eminence came at a cost.[21]

Late in the year, the Roman people assembled as the *Comitia centuriata* in the Saepta built on such a lavish scale by Agrippa and chose Caius Caesar as one of the consuls for the next year. Caius was not a candidate, and indeed was not formally a man, for although in his fourteenth year he had not yet assumed the toga of manhood; but the voters wrote his name on the ballots just as in the past they had insisted on choosing Augustus even when he was not a candidate. The *princeps'* two sons were very popular – the eleven-year-old Lucius had recently been cheered by the crowd when he attended the theatre without any distinguished attendants – and yet it is hard to believe that the election was entirely spontaneous. More than likely the idea was canvassed, probably by friends of Julia or at least those hoping to win her own and her sons' gratitude.

Augustus was not pleased, and acted quickly to restrain the popular enthusiasm. It was another occasion when he seemed more closely wedded to tradition than many other Romans. Although he had lowered the minimum age for the senior magistracy by ten years and had family members granted the right to stand when even younger than this, the election of a mere boy simply because he was his son could not fail to devalue the consulship. The *Comitia* – which was dominated by the wealthier citizens – had to be restrained, and afterwards at a public meeting Augustus refused to accept the vote; he openly prayed that never again would the needs of the state require a man younger than twenty to become consul, as he had done in 43 BC. It was probably at this point that the *princeps* put his own name forward for election instead of his son, and may have made promises to grant the boy honours once he had become a man. Then he would become a pontiff, receive the right to attend meetings of the Senate, and assume the consulship in AD I when he was finally twenty. Probably that was the age when his father planned to give the youth more of a public role, but the announcement of a consulship may well have forced his hand and reflected pressure from within his own family and some sections of the wider population to advance Julia's sons.[22]

Not long afterwards, Tiberius suddenly declared that he wanted to withdraw from public life, claiming that he was weary after years of exertion. Instead of supervising the eastern provinces and frontiers, he wished to live a private life and pursue his studies on Rhodes. At first he was not taken seriously, but persisted in spite of Augustus' refusals to consider letting him go. In the end Tiberius went on a hunger strike, refusing to eat anything for four days until the *princeps* relented. Augustus publicly condemned his son-in-law for fleeing from his duty to the state, and only grudgingly permitted him to do as he wished. Instead of setting out for the provinces with the pomp and ceremony of a Roman commander, Tiberius left Italy quietly and attended by only a few friends. News that Augustus was ill made him pause for a while. Perhaps this was genuine, or maybe the *princeps* feigned illness in the hope of bringing Livia's son to his senses. Yet the news did not get any worse, and feeling that it appeared suspicious for him to tarry almost as if hoping that his father-in-law would die, Tiberius eventually sailed on. He stopped en route, compelling the city of Paros to sell him a statue of Vesta which he announced would be placed in the Temple of Concord.[23]

Augustus made no attempt to hide his rage at what he saw as betrayal by the man he had made his son-in-law and raised to greatest eminence in the state after himself. Agrippa had never abandoned him in this way – although in later years attempts were made to interpret his eastern command as caused by rivalry with Marcellus – but Agrippa was dead, and so was Drusus, and now Tiberius had left him when Caius and Lucius were still too young to assist. At the age of fifty-seven Imperator Caesar Augustus had for the moment lost all the active colleagues he had taken such care to create. Anger at betrayal was matched by bafflement, as Augustus and everyone else struggled to understand why Tiberius had so suddenly turned his back on public life. This confusion is reflected in our sources and has puzzled scholars down to the present day. Various explanations were given: that Tiberius was jealous of Caius and Lucius, or that he

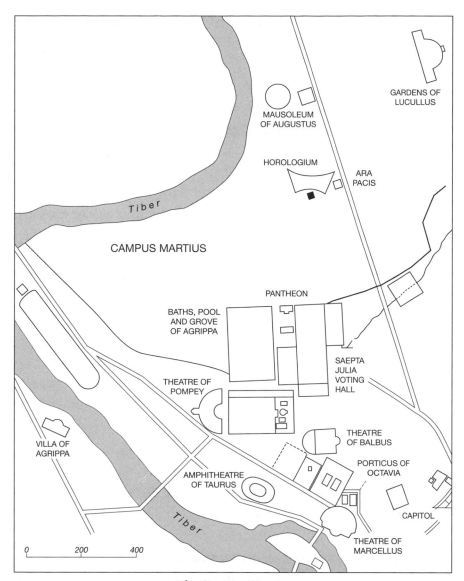

The Campus Martius

wished to give the boys a chance to make their way without being overshadowed by his own successes. Later, people claimed that he fled Rome because he could no longer bear to live with Julia.[24]

None of these reasons make much sense. Tiberius would have got away from his wife for years by touring the provinces and did not need to take such drastic action. Caius and Lucius were still too young to be serious rivals, and before he left Tiberius had opened his will to show Augustus and Livia that he had included the boys among his principal heirs. Modern scholars often interpret Tiberius' position as essentially a regent, who would help lead the state until the boys were old enough to take over. Augustus clearly did not think this way, and continued to plan for a college of men aiding him and after his death co-operating to guide the *res publica*. Even at the time, not everyone may have shared his view. If Julia and those around her were pushing for the rapid advance of her sons, then Tiberius may have felt that his longer-term position was precarious. Yet it is hard to see what further powers Augustus could have given him that he did not already enjoy. If the threat to retire was a bargaining position, it was at best misguided and badly backfired, leaving Tiberius politically isolated and stripped of all responsibilities, although he continued to hold the *tribunicia potestas* and *imperium* until these expired in 1 BC.

Sometimes the obvious may contain a good deal of truth. Tiberius claimed to be weary, and he had indeed spent eight of the last ten years on campaign, and faced the prospect of a future in which such activity would be normal. This was a big change from the traditional public career, where magistracies and provincial posts were interspersed with less active spells at home. Augustus, Agrippa and those they marked down to help them worked constantly and without any significant periods of rest. The prospect was daunting: a life of constant toil like the one that had worn out Agrippa and brought him to an early grave. For all his aristocratic sense of duty, Tiberius would spend much of his own time as *princeps* in seclusion away from Rome. Augustus complained of the burden of his office, but seems to have thrived on the activity and the constant encounters with people as individuals and crowds. Tiberius never showed any real enthusiasm for the task, instead working with a grim sense of obligation. Upset by the loss of his brother, unhappily married, tired and with a future composed of unending work and eventually sharing power with the as yet untried offspring of a wife he loathed, his retirement may have had little to do with politics. Weary and fed up,

Tiberius walked away from pressure, responsibility and – at least for the foreseeable future – any chance of resuming his career.[25]

FATHERS, CHILDREN AND TRUST

Augustus was left on his own to run the empire. He was consul for the twelfth time in 5 BC, eighteen years since he had last held the post, and in this capacity led out his older son on the day Caius first donned the *toga virilis* and formally became a man. Soon afterwards the lad was given the unprecedented title of *princeps iuventutis* (or leader of the youth) and made honorary head of the equestrian order – an equally unprecedented concept. None of this meant formal power or any real responsibility, but certainly raised the public profile of the boy. While he waited for his sons to mature, Caesar Augustus had no choice but to rely on others to command his armies in the field. Lucius Domitius Ahenobarbus, consul in 16 BC and married to the elder Antonia, so part of the *princeps'* extended family, was given command in Germany and fought a major campaign. So did Marcus Vinicius, his successor, a new man who had been consul in 19 BC. Not all the men chosen for these commands were related to Augustus, but all were trusted and most were given successive posts and sometimes rewarded with triumphal honours.[26]

Our sources for the years of Tiberius' retirement are poor and make it difficult to reconstruct events in any detail – Dio's narrative exists only in a summary which jumps straight from 5 BC to 2 BC. There may well have been more military activity on other frontiers, and perhaps some of the otherwise unknown victories listed in the *Res Gestae* belong to these years. As far as we can tell, Augustus travelled little, and does not appear to have made any visits to the provinces for some time. Without a senior colleague, it was better for the *princeps* to stay in Rome and let delegations come to him. The constant flow of petitions continued, and now only he could deal with most of them. Sometimes the issues were large. In 12 BC the communities of Asia had suffered severely from a spate of earthquakes and resulting fires and pleaded for relief from their taxes. Augustus rescinded the taxation for two years and paid the equivalent sum into the treasury with his own money to give the Asians time to recover.[27]

Other matters were smaller-scale and more personal. In 6 BC the Greek island community of Knidos sent an embassy to see the *princeps*. Two men are named – Dionysius son of Dionysius, and his colleague Dionysius son of Dionysius son of Dionysius – and they came to accuse a certain Euboulos, son of Anaxandridas, and his wife Typhera of the murder of one Euboulos, son of Chrysippos. If those in Knidos were less than imaginative when it came to names, the crime itself was unusual. The victim's brother and his followers had attacked the accused couple's house for three nights in succession, as described in Augustus' letter to the community: 'The householders Euboulos and Typhera, since they could not achieve safety in their own house, either by negotiating . . . or by barricading themselves against the attacks, ordered one of their household slaves not to kill, as perhaps someone might have been provoked to do by quite justifiable anger, but to force them back by pouring their excrement over them. But the household slave . . . let go of the chamber pot together with what was being poured down, and Euboulos fell under it . . .'

The local community, presumably influenced by the dead man's brother, had blamed the householders, and these had appealed to Augustus via the proconsul, Asinius Gallus. The latter had ordered their slaves to be interrogated under torture in the normal Roman way, and the one who had dropped the chamber pot was adamant that he had not intended to do so, although a measure of doubt was expressed about this. Augustus went on: 'I have sent to you the actual interrogations too. I would have been surprised at how much the defendants feared the examination of the slaves at your hands, had you not seemed to have been excessively harsh against them, and tough on crime in all the wrong respects, being angry not with those who deserved to suffer everything whatever, since they launched an attack against someone else's house at night with violence and force three times . . .'

In this case, the real victims both of an assault and a subsequent miscarriage of justice at the local level eventually received a fair verdict from the *princeps*, but it may well have taken a long time and involved considerable hardship and expense to achieve this. Euboulos the householder had died by the time Augustus issued his decision and instructed Knidos to alter 'the records in their public archive' to agree with his opinion.[28]

Individuals, communities and even entire provinces appealed to Caesar Augustus' judgement. So did monarchs. Herod the Great had no fewer than ten wives and a large number of children. Two of the most favoured were sent to Rome to be raised and educated in Augustus' household, but since these were sons of the executed Mariamme, trust was always in short supply. Years later Herod recalled them, and in 13 BC took them to Italy where father and sons appeared before the *princeps* and accused each other of treachery. Matters were temporarily resolved, but in 7 BC the king again accused them of plotting against him. This time he did not go to Rome in person, but sent ambassadors, and Augustus ordered that a special court including his legate in Syria and other Romans meet in Berytus to try the case. The sons were found guilty and swiftly executed, even though the Romans had advocated no more than imprisonment.[29]

Ageing and in poor health, Herod's final years witnessed a spate of executions of family members, as the king saw threats and treachery in every direction. Augustus commented drily that he would 'rather be Herod's pig than his son'. Yet the king of Judaea never for a moment wavered in his loyalty to Rome. In 4 BC, when it was clear that Herod's days were numbered, a group assembled and tore down the golden eagle he had erected over the main gate of the Temple – probably hated more as a graven image than a symbol of Rome. They acted too soon, and were swiftly arrested and brought before the king. He ordered the men who had done the deed to be burnt alive, and those who had inspired them were executed. In spite of his unpopularity, Herod's control of his kingdom was as strong as ever. He died soon afterwards, and Augustus formed a commission which included Caius Caesar to decide on the arrangements for the future, eventually dividing the kingdom into three and giving rule to three of his surviving sons. At some point in the last year or so of Herod's reign, Jesus was born – an event of obviously profound importance for future history, but not part of Augustus' story. (For discussion of the evidence see Appendix Two.) Within less than a year of the king's death, the legate of Syria twice marched his legions into Judaea to suppress violent disorders directed against his successors and their Roman backers.[30]

Actium was a long time ago, and since 30 BC the eastern provinces had been almost entirely free of warfare apart from a few small-scale campaigns on the fringes. Roman rule was accepted, and the peace and stability it was now providing were welcomed and valued. As long ago as 26–25 BC the assembly formed by the communities in Asia to take part in the cult of Rome and Augustus had offered a prize for anyone who could come up with an appropriate way of honouring Augustus, the man who had presided over this era of calm. This was finally awarded in 9 BC, and since the recipient was the Roman proconsul it strongly suggests that the *princeps'* approval had already been sought and given. From now on, all of the communities changed their calendars so that their year would begin on what had been 23 September, Augustus' birthday. This became the first day of the month called Caesar. In 4 BC he introduced a new procedure making it quicker for provincial communities to charge a governor with extortion or any other abuses of power which stopped short of unlawful killing. Augustus was visible throughout the provinces in image and name, and made some efforts to ensure good administration, although the new system may well have favoured corrupt administrators as they were to be tried by a jury solely consisting of other senators whose instincts were likely to be sympathetic.[31]

In 2 BC the sixty-year-old Caesar Augustus was consul for the thirteenth time, adding even greater honour to the ceremony when Lucius Caesar became a man. The fifteen-year-old was made an augur and joined his brother as joint *principes iuventutis*. He was also permitted to attend the Senate and marked down for a consulship in AD 4. On 5 February 2 BC the Senate and People voted to name Augustus *pater patriae* – the 'father of his country'. It was an honour mentioned more than once in the past, but declined up until this point. Cicero in 63 BC and Julius Caesar as dictator had each been named *parens patriae* – 'parent of his country' – although the title is uncertain and some believe that either or both were named 'father' rather than 'parent'. In Cicero's case the award was informal, whereas Julius Caesar was granted it by a formal vote of the Senate. The father, especially the *paterfamilias* who headed a household, was greatly revered in Roman culture, but it is doubtful that there was much difference in the title, save perhaps that the slightly different wording distinguished Augustus and emphasised his universal fatherhood. At first Augustus refused when offered the title by a deputation representing the wider population. It was conferred at a performance in the theatre, when to universal acclamation Valerius Messalla, acting as spokesman for the other senators, again approached him, declaring: 'Every blessing and divine favour be upon you and your family, Caesar Augustus! For in this way we also beseech perpetual good fortune on the *res publica* and lasting joy for our city. The Senate with the support of the entire Roman people acclaim you Father of your Country.'

Augustus was moved to tears as he replied: 'Having attained my deepest wish, Fathers of the Senate, for what else have I to pray to the immortal gods, except that I may keep this universal consent of you all until the end of my days.'[32]

The pattern of popular pressure overcoming modest reluctance on the part of the *princeps* was well established, and both sides no doubt understood the part they were playing. This does not alter the fact that Augustus only took the title at this stage. Had he wanted it, he could surely have received it earlier. This way flattered both sides, but the main restraint on his honours came from Augustus himself, and not from any putative senatorial opposition. Messalla was the consul of 31 BC, former ally of Brutus and Cassius, and then Antony, who had switched sides before Actium and gone on to enjoy a provincial command and a triumph. He was one of that ever-diminishing generation who had seen the horrors of civil war at first hand. Whatever else he had done, Augustus had already given the state stability and internal peace for almost three decades, and on this basis alone the acclamation of him was surely genuine. His pride was also genuine, and the award concludes the main text of his *Res Gestae*: 'In my thirteenth consulship . . . [the Senate], equestrian order and the entire Roman People declared me *pater patriae* and decreed that this should be inscribed on the porch of my house and in the Senate house'.[33]

In a career spanning more than forty years, Augustus had gone from the angry avenger of a murdered father to the unifying elder statesman and 'father' of the Roman world. His adopted sons shared his popularity and were being prepared for high office. His daughter – and only actual child – proved less willing to play the part given to her by her father.

Tiberius' retirement to Rhodes left Julia on her own again. Most likely the couple had not lived together for some time before this and so the change may not have been too dramatic when he left. Nor was it unusual in her experience, for Agrippa had spent most of their marriage away in the provinces, but Julia did not care for solitude. Lively, fond of the arts and especially poetry, she enjoyed the company of other bright, well-educated, attractive and aristo-cratic young people. Deeply aware of her own eminence, her circle consisted almost exclusively of young aristocrats with names reach-ing back far into Rome's history. All were too young to have taken part in the civil wars, surely the most profound experience to shape their parents' generation, and had grown up in times of peace and prosperity.[34]

The poet Ovid – Publius Ovidius Naso – was of a similar age and experience, and his verses have beauty and passion, as well as a sense of mischief – at times almost of flippancy. Their spirit lacks the dark undertones and seriousness of the earlier poets who had lived through the years of proscriptions, land confiscation and loss, and instead has an irrepressible sense of joy. Around 2 BC he was working on the three books of his *Art of Love* (*Ars Amatoria*), presented as a mock technical manual of how to find and win over a lover. It is far less about sex than seduction, and finds time to tour some of the monuments of Augustan Rome, and recount some famous myths such as the story of Icarus, while he gives his advice to both men and women. Several times he assures his readers that he is not celebrating adultery – his women were not wives but mistresses, many of them former slaves, and so no threat to proper Roman marriage and the production of children so keenly promoted by the Augustan regime. The tone is never serious, down to the last line of the second and third books, as he makes each group he has advised declare 'Naso was our teacher'.[35]

Sallust and Cicero had sometimes complained of the loose morals and casual affairs of the younger generation of Rome's elite, mixing truth with wild exaggeration. By the first century BC, many wealthy and well-born Roman women were no longer content to sit quietly at home waiting for husbands to return from the empire. Julius Caesar and Augustus had both pursued plenty of affairs with married women, and they were not alone. As always, rumour no doubt outstripped fact by a long way, but some aristocratic wives readily took lovers, and many more enjoyed the company of young aristocratic men and revelled in wine, feasting, dance and music.

Julia was one of these, and clearly enjoyed luxury and male companions. During her marriage to Agrippa, Augustus is said to have wondered whether she was unfaithful, only to be reassured when all her children resembled their father. Julia was said to have quipped that she never 'took a passenger on board, unless the ship's hold already has a full cargo'. On at least one occasion Augustus wrote to a senator instructing him not to call on his daughter, but he seems to have convinced himself that her conduct was more foolish than dangerous. The suggestion that she ought to copy her stepmother, whose friends were mature and sober in contrast to the faster set forming Julia's circle, unsurprisingly met with a frosty reception. Livia was some twenty years her senior, and his daughter assured the *princeps* that her friends would 'grow old with her' as well. By 2 BC Julia was thirty-seven and had given birth to six children. Many people struggle to cope with ageing, especially when they take pride in their good looks. Augustus surprised Julia when her slaves were plucking out her first few grey hairs, and later asked her whether she would prefer to be 'bald or grey'.[36]

Matters came to head late in 2 BC, when the *princeps* was confronted with clear evidence that Julia was conducting one or more adulterous affairs. We do not know how Augustus came to learn of this, nor is it possible to discover what really happened. None of our sources doubt that she took a number of lovers. Some are named, and include a Sempronius Gracchus, who was known as a poet, an Appius Claudius, a Scipio, Titus Quinctius Crispinus, who had been consul in 9 BC, and, most interesting of all, Iullus Antonius, the son of Mark Antony and Fulvia. Other more obscure lovers are claimed, but no names are given. The aristocratic pedigrees of the named lovers are unsurprising, and all were most likely of a broadly similar age to Julia.

Claims are made of outrageous behaviour on top of the affairs. There is talk of drunken parties held in public, and even on the Rostra, and of nightly gatherings where the statue of Marsyas – a satyr famed from his musical skill and associated with feasting and Bacchus, the god of wine – in the Forum was crowned with a garland. Wilder stories claim that Julia openly prostituted herself to passers-by in her craving for new thrills. Our instinct is to dismiss such tales as gossip and we are most probably right to do this, although the fact that people have done some remarkably stupid things throughout history should make us cautious about expressing absolute certainty. Yet this may be an indication that Julia and her circle were becoming increasingly indiscreet, and perhaps they did carry one or more of their parties out into the streets and public places. If so, it would be an ironic echo of Antony and Cleopatra's night-time forays in Alexandria. Perhaps everyone assumed that Augustus knew all about it and was willing to turn a blind eye and indulge his daughter.[37]

Given the distinguished names and family connections of the lovers, many scholars have assumed that politics lay behind everything, and that this was really a conspiracy to seize power. Pliny claims that there was a plot to murder Augustus, and Dio suggests Iullus was behind it, but no one else even hints at this, and it seems unlikely that Julia would have conspired to kill her father. A more plausible suggestion is that she hoped to be allowed to divorce Tiberius and marry Iullus, who would thus become the *princeps'* new son-in-law; as such, he could no doubt expect to be rewarded with ever-greater power and responsibility, joining him, and in time the young Caius and Lucius, as leaders of the state. If Augustus were to die in the next few years, Iullus and Julia would be in a position to guide her sons and share power with them. The election of Caius in 6 BC suggests concerted lobbying to promote the rapid rise of Julia's sons and it makes sense that she and others hoped to gain from this. Perhaps this was the plan, and perhaps there was also wild talk of liberty and restoring the dominance of the old aristocratic families – the statue of Marsyas and the fig tree that shaded it had a long association as symbols of popular liberty.[38]

Wild talk is likely, and perhaps Julia did hope to marry Iullus. Yet in spite of all the ingenious theories of historians, an organised conspiracy is highly unlikely. Augustus certainly did not deal with it in this way, and public condemnation of serial adultery by his daughter is a most unlikely smokescreen to cover a failed coup, especially from the man who had introduced strong – and widely resented – laws on marriage and adultery. The *princeps* had given his family a very public role, and held them up as *exempla* of proper Roman behaviour. Julia's adultery was a greater betrayal than Tiberius' retirement and Augustus clearly felt it deeply. This did not need to be a public matter, but he insisted on bringing it before the Senate, having a quaestor read out a letter since he did not feel capable of addressing them himself.

Iullus Antonius killed himself – perhaps in anticipation of a death sentence, since later sources say vaguely that he was killed – and all of the other lovers were sent into exile. One was a serving tribune, who was permitted to complete his term of office and then sent abroad. Iullus Antonius' young son was also exiled, and sent to live out his life in Massilia. All in all, this relative leniency is one of the strongest arguments against a political conspiracy. In the past Augustus had shown little hesitation in killing anyone who plotted against him. Yet most Romans clearly found the punishment unduly harsh for adultery – Tacitus later claimed the *princeps* treated it almost as if it was treason against the state, and this may get closest to the truth. Augustus was outraged, seeing his daughter's misbehaviour as a deep personal shame, and her lovers as deliberately insulting him and his household. This was a blow to his *auctoritas*, or in many ways worse, since wider opinion of him was not damaged anywhere near as much as his own self-image and pride. Imperator Caesar Augustus was more shamed and enraged than afraid.[39]

He refused to see Julia, and condemned her to exile on the tiny island of Pandateria. She was to be allowed no wine, no luxuries of any sort and virtually no male companionship – any man, whether slave or free, visiting the island on any duty was only permitted to go after Augustus had closely examined his appearance and character. Julia's freedwoman Phoebe committed suicide, presumably from shame at having been involved or fear of punishment. Augustus said that he would have 'preferred to be Phoebe's father'. However, Julia's mother Scribonia accompanied her daughter into exile. Some see this as a public refutation of the accusations of adultery, ignoring the simple possibility of a mother's continued affection for her daughter and a willingness to forgive that was markedly absent in her former husband.[40]

Caesar Augustus' response to the whole affair was one of rage, and he wanted all those involved to be punished and publicly shamed. In time his anger abated a little. After five years on the island Julia was allowed to move to a more comfortable villa on the mainland near Rhegium, but was still denied luxuries and male company. He was adamant in refusing to recall her in spite of several large demonstrations by crowds in Rome. In time he is said to have regretted his handling of the business, wishing that he had dealt with it privately. Seneca tells us that he complained that none of this would have happened if only Agrippa and Maecenas had still been alive to advise him. At the very least they would have told him the truth, and prevented the whole thing from happening – or at least stopped Julia's misbehaviour from getting as bad as it did. Yet his old friends had gone, and so had the younger ones, leaving Augustus feeling old and isolated. More and more his hopes focused on Caius and Lucius.[41]

20

THE 'SENTRY POST'

'Mars comes, and at his coming he gave the sign of war. The Avenger
descends himself from heaven to behold his own honours and his
splendid temple in the Forum of Augustus. The god is huge, and so
is the structure; not otherwise ought Mars to dwell in his son's city
. . . He beholds . . . the name of Augustus on the front of the temple;
and the building seems to him still greater, when he reads the name
of Caesar.' *Ovid, turn of the century* BC *to* AD.[1]

Caius and Lucius were not damaged by their mother's disgrace,
and Julia had probably had little to do with their upbringing
for some time. Both of the teenagers were now formally adults, and
began to assume a more and more public role. Although 2 BC ended
on a sour note of anger and betrayal for Augustus, the year was otherwise one of confident celebration and festivities, in which his sons
played a prominent part. On 12 May Caius and Lucius presided over
the games accompanying the inauguration of the Temple of Mars
Ultor, the centrepiece of the new Forum of Augustus. This lay at a
right angle to the Forum of Julius Caesar, which Augustus had largely
built, and this in turn joined onto the main Forum Romanum, which
he had transformed. In this way the public space at the heart of the
City more than doubled in size, providing far more covered and
open areas for administration, court sessions, ceremony and ritual.
The need for this was real – the porticoes of the Forum of Augustus
were put to use long before building work on the entire complex was
complete. Many of Augustus' own reforms created new officials and
new tasks, or revived long-neglected practices. Structural renewal of
this area was in many ways a physical sign of making the state function properly once again.[2]

Both Julius Caesar and Augustus purchased the land needed for their Forum projects, since almost none was in public hands. They paid for it from their own funds and then demolished houses, flats, shops and warehouses to create clear sites. Not all the owners were willing to sell, and none were compelled to do so – at least if the plot lay on the fringes of the planned complex. A young Caesar had vowed to build a temple to the avenging war god before Philippi, and it took forty years to fulfil this – some of the delay was no doubt due to the need to wait for land to become available. In the end he was unable to secure everything that he wanted; the Forum of Augustus is not symmetrical because one or two owners refused to sell, and so its north-eastern corner has an irregular shape. Perhaps it was frustrating for Augustus, but his willingness to accept this showed his respect for the rights of property and an unwillingness to override them even for the wider good of the state, let alone his own fame. In some ways the very imperfection of the new Forum was a more valuable symbol than perfect symmetry would have been.[3]

In every other respect no expense was spared. All of Augustus' building projects were grand in both design and execution, even when this involved the deceptively simple restoration of archaic shrines. The remodelled Forum Romanum and the neatly planned Forum Julium were magnificent, intended to reflect the grandeur of Rome's power and also as reminders that the current greatness and restoration was led by the *princeps*. The Forum Augustum outdid them both, and since it could only be accessed through two entrances its impact was enhanced. A high wall shut off all sight of the City streets beyond at the same time as it protected the monument from the risk of fire. The courtyard was paved in marble, arranged in colourful patterns. Modern ideas mixed with classical architecture in the design, and the porticoes included Caryatids – supporting pillars shaped like statues of women – which Agrippa had also employed in the Pantheon. Seeing these, an educated observer would immediately think of the Erechtheion, a temple built by Pericles in the fifth century BC on the Acropolis at Athens, invoking associations with the Athenians at their cultural and imperial height. Others might miss the reference, but would still see rows of elegant and delicately carved statues decorating the sides of the Forum – Pliny felt that the Forum of Augustus was one of the most beautiful buildings in the world. The invocation of a famous past was not rigid – the Caryatids in the Forum were in high relief, their backs flat and flush against the wall, unlike their models at Athens which were fully rounded, free-standing statues capable of bearing the weight of the roof.[4]

The Temple of Mars Ultor was faced in white Italian marble and approached by a wide flight of steps, with the main altar set into them. Roman temples were homes for the gods when they chose to visit the City rather than places of worship. Altars of all the main cults were almost invariably outside them – and certainly all animal sacrifices were made in the open air. At the front of the temple was a row of eight very high Corinthian columns, with matching rows down the left and right sides all supporting its tall pediment. The design mirrored the shape of the Temple of Venus in Julius Caesar's Forum, but was half as big again. Venus and Mars were traditional Roman deities, strong protectors of the res publica, and the goddess was claimed as ancestor by the Julii. The clan also boasted of descent from the kings of Alba Longa, and that dynasty produced Rhea Silvia, who bore the twins Romulus and Remus to the god Mars. The Julii did not pretend to belong to that line, but more recently Julius Caesar and Augustus had claimed an association with Rome's founder and his father the war god.

In the porticoes on either side of the courtyard were statues invoking the past. On the left stood Aeneas, and around him the kings of Alba Longa and the most notable of the Julii – the last not very numerous and no doubt including many men with modest records, for the family had enjoyed few periods of prominence. Opposite stood Romulus, surrounded by the 'most distinguished men' (summi viri) of Rome's history, some of whom bolstered the numbers on the other side as well. Inscriptions, which Augustus certainly approved but probably did not write, recorded each man's deeds. There were no foreigners, save the figures from the times before the foundation of Rome, and so far there is no direct evidence from the site for any women among their number. Julius Caesar was not included, since as the divine Julius he could not stand with mere mortals. Instead his statue was inside the temple with those of the gods.[5]

Aeneas was shown carrying his father Anchises from the wreck of Troy, and leading his son Iulus by the hand – an image common in private art of this era as well as official iconography. Scholarly opinion was divided over whether or not this Iulus was in truth the ancestor of the Julii and ultimately Rome's founder, but there was no certainty and at the very least the Julian version was felt to be plausible. Romulus' statue showed him carrying the *spolia opima* and unsurprisingly the focus was mainly on martial glory and especially on men who had triumphed.

It was intended as a parade of those who had helped to make Rome great, and was not overtly partisan, including both Sulla and Marius, as well as Pompey the Great. The inscriptions emphasised victories over foreign enemies, and seem to have kept any mention of involvement in civil war brief and neutral. In the case of Marius it told of the defeat of Jugurtha in Numidia, the wars against the Cimbri and Teutones and his successive consulships, and in approving tones of his suppression of the tribune Saturninus in 100 BC, before concluding more neutrally that 'at the age of seventy he was expelled from his country by civil war, and restored by force of arms. He became consul for the seventh time.'[6]

Augustus declared that the statues of the *summi viri* were there so that people could measure his own achievements and those of future *principes* against the heroes of the past. It was obvious from the design of the complex what conclusion he expected them to reach in his own case. Alone, in the centre of the courtyard leading up to the temple, was a bronze statue of Imperator Caesar Augustus riding in a four-horse chariot like a triumphing general. This was his Forum, and the newly awarded title of *pater patriae* was carved on the statue's base. This was also a view of Roman history placing him squarely in the centre, associated with gods and heroes from the origins of the City down to his own generation. Augustus identified himself with the success of Rome, as the worthy heir to such great men since he had led the state to its greatest achievements of power and prosperity. Indeed, he was the link between all these disparate figures, both human and divine, the son of one of the deities whose images stood in the temple.[7]

The Forum of Augustus celebrated his leadership and Rome's glory. Its porticoes would house court sessions, and the Temple of Mars Ultor would play a central role in the state's life. At long last the eagles recaptured from the Parthians were given a permanent home, while any other Roman military standards lost and recovered in the future would also be placed in the shrine. Whenever the Senate met to discuss the declaration of war or the award of a triumph they would convene in this temple. From here commanders would set out for their provinces and here they would return, and those who won triumphs would receive statues within the Forum. It was also decreed that from now on any aristocratic boy assuming the toga of manhood would do so at the temple, reminding him that this brought with it an obligation to serve the state in war if necessary.

Caius and Lucius were given some form of temporary authority to preside over the games, which included beast fights where 260 lions were killed in the Circus Maximus. A little later, the Circus Flaminius was flooded – or perhaps a section of it temporarily turned into a small lake – and the crowd treated to the sight of thirty-six crocodiles being slaughtered by professional hunters. Perhaps this was intended as commemoration of the victory in Egypt, but the killing of such exotic creatures was a common entertainment – just as the tiger presented to Augustus by the Indian ambassadors most probably ended up in the arena at Rome. Human beings also died to entertain the people, and grand gladiatorial games were once again staged in the Saepta. Not all the entertainments were intentionally lethal. Augustus' grandson, the ten-year-old Agrippa Postumus, rode in the Trojan Games – Suetonius says that Augustus felt this ritual was a good way for young noblemen to be introduced to the public. These were not serious fights, but even so were sometimes dangerous, and on one occasion the *princeps* presented a golden torque to

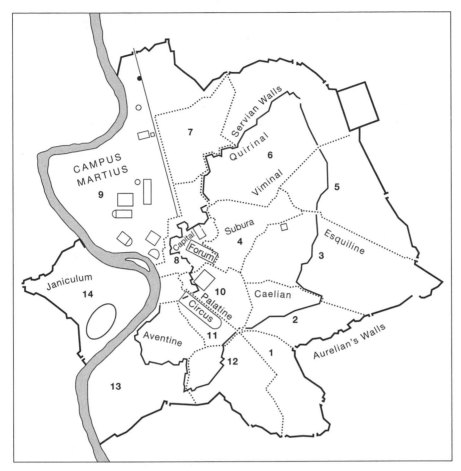

The fourteen administrative regions of Rome

a senator's son who was permanently lamed by a bad fall from his horse during the games. Asinius Pollio's grandson also broke a leg in this way – quite possibly in 2 BC – and his criticism of the sport in the Senate was so determined and well reasoned that Augustus soon ceased to celebrate them.[8]

PAST AND PRESENT

One of the longest-remembered aspects of this festival was grander and more expensive than any previous entertainment staged at Rome.

This was the *naumachia Augusti* – the naval battle of Augustus. An artificial lake measuring 1,800 by 1,200 Roman feet was dug on the west bank of the Tiber and filled with water supplied by a specially built aqueduct, the Aqua Alsietina, which ran for more than twenty miles. The theme was the Battle of Salamis in 480 BC, where the Greeks, led by the Athenians, had shattered the navy of the invading Persians, and if not quite so big as the real thing it was grand enough. Augustus later boasted that altogether 'thirty beaked warships, triremes or biremes, and many more smaller vessels fought. Around 3,000 men fought, not including the rowers.' It is unclear how this fight worked, and how far it was mock or real. Given the Romans' tastes, no doubt it was not wholly bloodless, but presumably it also involved considerable stage management. More than two centuries later, Dio says that you could still see some of the structures put up for this, while Velleius speaks of the Roman crowd's appetite for entertainment being 'sated' by the magnificence of these games.[9]

Dio also tells us that the Greeks won the fight, perhaps implying that the struggle was genuine and the outcome uncertain, although more than likely this was the hoped-for result. With echoes of the Acropolis in the new Forum, and the restaging of Athens' greatest victory, there was clearly a desire to be associated with the glories of the classical past and the heights of Greek culture so revered by educated Romans. In those years Athens was a democracy, led by elected leaders such as Pericles rather than tyrants or kings. Perhaps Augustus had a particular interest in invoking this, and thus presenting himself as such a leader, but we should not push this idea too far. It is unconvincing to claim that in earlier years he had thought more like a Hellenistic monarch from the age of Alexander the Great and his successors, and thus constructed gaudily decorated monuments like the Temple of Apollo, before turning to a more restrained architectural style befitting the leader of a free state.[10]

The clear distinction between the classical Greece of city states and the Hellenistic era of monarchies is largely an invention of modern scholarship. Romans fond of Greek culture saw no reason to restrict themselves to 'superior' styles and literature of the fifth and early fourth centuries and ignore later works. Also we should remember that the Forum of Augustus was every bit as spectacular as any monument built in earlier years, and as celebratory of the person of the *princeps*. Not only that, but two famous paintings of Alexander the Great were displayed within it, as were several statues, so the aim was clearly to invoke great victories and victors of the past without being tied too closely to their political context.[11]

The same building and the same symbols could be associated with more than one theme, and it is hard to believe that the sight of a grand naval spectacular did not evoke as many thoughts of Actium as it did of Salamis. Both could be portrayed as victories of civilisation over barbarism and of west over east, the recent triumph of Augustus worthily ranked alongside the greatest events of history, just as the *summi viri* added to the grandeur of his Forum. By association Caesar Augustus appropriated the glories of the past, taking all that was best. Thus he took men like Marius, Sulla and Pompey, stripped away the negative associations of the civil wars, and turned them into his predecessors, men who had added to Rome's power which culminated in his own achievements. It was much the same as Virgil's appropriation of an idealised Cato to act as judge in the underworld. Augustus openly expressed admiration for Cato the Younger, praising anyone who wanted to preserve the state as it was. The dead had no say over their use by the new regime, and such an inclusive view of history reinforced the sense that the partisanship of the civil wars was firmly in the past. Even former enemies – and others unlikely to have favoured Caesar Augustus and his permanent supremacy – provided examples of virtues admired and claimed by the *princeps*.[12]

The use of Julius Caesar's bitterest enemies stopped short of full rehabilitation. Pompey and Cato were employed as sanitised versions of the real men, and if their imperfections and bad decisions were remembered these served only to highlight the 'better' record of the *princeps*. Praising some of their deeds and characters should not be seen as tacit criticism of Julius Caesar. It is an article of faith among scholars that Augustus consciously distanced himself

from the dictator, repeated so often that it is never really questioned
even though it runs contrary to the evidence. The convention of
calling him Octavian and then Augustus has encouraged this, and
helps us to forget that for all his changes of name after 44 BC, he
was always called Caesar. It is true that he more often invoked his
father in the years of his rise to power than later on, but even this
was less marked than has been claimed. He was still Caesar Augustus, finished many of the dictator's projects, and in the new Forum
celebrated his Julian ancestry. Wider Roman history and its heroes
were added to this family and their associations, with Aeneas and
Venus, Romulus and Mars. This was private family history welded
to state history, just as the monument combined private and public
glory. The poet Ovid stressed that the Temple of Mars Ultor showed
the fulfilment of vengeance both for the murder of Julius Caesar
and the return of the lost standards by a humbled Parthia. Here as
elsewhere, Augustus elevated himself and his family to the centre of
public life, his personal achievements seamlessly interwoven with the
wider good.[13]

Julius Caesar was now a god, and could not be treated as simply
another Roman hero – hence his statue was inside the temple and
not with the rest of the Julii. There is no hint that any Roman would
have seen this as a conscious attempt to separate the god from some
of the more questionable actions of the man. A Roman aristocrat at
the beginning of his career talked a lot about his father and earlier
generations of his family, offering their achievements as proof of his
own worth. Yet once established – certainly once he reached any of
the senior magistracies – this faded away, for by that stage in his life
his own deeds were to speak for themselves. A man's ancestors were
not in competition with him, although it was clearly a good thing if
his achievements matched or surpassed theirs. It was only later, at
his public funeral, that the emphasis returned to the whole family
line, as the generations were paraded and used to show the promise
of sons and grandsons.

Augustus spoke less of Julius Caesar after the civil wars, but only
because this was natural – the same process on a bigger scale of any

Roman noble family. His own actions and victories were now far more important than those of his father and so were advertised. Julius Caesar was not forgotten, still less suppressed, and his reputation and glories continued to add to the *auctoritas* of his son, but they did not need to be paraded. Caesar Augustus had taken over and more than fulfilled the promise of his father's glory, but the latter's monuments were there, his statues numerous and prominent, and his image still sometimes useful for his son. Ultimately, it was only Julius Caesar who had raised the Julii from comparative obscurity, and made the name Caesar stand out as different from the family name of any other Roman aristocrat.

A century later Tacitus said that the writing of history withered under Augustus, not through active suppression but because of flattery. The Roman tradition was that history should only be written by the men involved in its making, by the senators who took part in debates, framed laws and led Rome's legions in the field. Only such men were supposed to be capable of understanding how great events occurred, but under Augustus such men were also dependent on the favour of the *princeps* if they wished to have a distinguished career. As the years passed, either senators did not write about the recent past or they did so in a fawning tone. It was not just a question of pleasing Augustus – the civil wars had seen plenty of men acting in ways that they would happily forget. Drusus' younger son Claudius announced a desire to write about the civil wars, and was quietly but firmly dissuaded from doing so by Livia and his mother Antonia.[14]

It was no coincidence that the most influential work of history written under Augustus was produced by Livy, a local aristocrat from northern Italy who never sought a career in public life. Here was a man without concerns about winning office – and also without direct experience of politics or war. Asinius Pollio felt that there was a strongly provincial tone to Livy's work, but no one could doubt the industry that eventually produced a history of Rome from the foundation of the City down to the death of Drusus in 142 books. It is unclear when the books were released and some may not have appeared until after Augustus' death. The tone of the introduction, written while civil war still raged, was markedly gloomy, but this may have changed as times improved. Livy was not part of Maecenas' circle, and although he was on friendly terms with Augustus, he was far from being an official mouthpiece. Yet the mood of his work chimed with many of the *princeps*' own views, and certainly the sense of Roman identity and culture his regime presented. Livy was fiercely patriotic, but also inclined to judge in moral terms – for him, Rome prospered when standards of morality were high and the Romans respected tradition and the gods, and behaved with virtue. Failures, outbreaks of disorder and ultimately civil war happened when all classes, and especially their senatorial leaders, failed to live up to proper standards.[15]

Only brief summaries survive of most of Livy's history, including all the books dealing with the final century and a half, so that it is largely guesswork to judge how he treated specific individuals. Surviving books do show considerable differences between his version of events and the epitaphs given to many of the *summi viri* in the Forum of Augustus. Sometimes these were on minor matters of detail – for instance, the precise number of days it took Aemilius Paullus to win the war against King Perseus in 168 BC. Others appear to represent wholly different traditions, and there are claims in the inscriptions from the Forum that are markedly at variance with all our other sources for some individuals. One summary makes it clear that Livy harshly criticised the final years of Marius and his bloody return to Rome at the end of 88 BC – a stark contrast to the inscription on his statue in the new Forum.[16]

Livy's account of Cornelius Cossus' winning the *spolia opima* included Augustus' interpretation but also conflicting traditions, just as he discussed the different accounts of whether Iulus was Aeneas' son by his Trojan wife or his subsequent marriage in Italy. It is probable that he was also generous in his treatment of Pompey the Great, since Tacitus says that Augustus gently chided the historian with being an unrepentant Pompeian. Since Pompey was included among the *summi viri* this was scarcely subversive, and it was more startling that Livy is said to have questioned whether or not it was a good thing that Julius Caesar was born in the light of his subsequent career. The passage is lost, making it harder to judge the tone or the conclusion, but the surviving summaries do not suggest an account deeply hostile to the dictator.[17]

Scholars who believe that Caesar Augustus played down his father would see this as confirmation, on the basis that Livy would not have dared to write such a thing unless he was confident that it would not provoke the *princeps'* anger. Yet, aside from the quiet pressure placed on the young Claudius to switch to a different theme, and a few cases in the final years of Augustus' life, there is no evidence for any suppression of literature by the *princeps*. On one occasion he wrote to Tiberius telling him not to 'take it too much to heart that anyone speak evil of me; we must be content if we can stop anyone from doing evil to us'. The official line was constantly promoted, in a lot of literature, in Augustus' and his family's speeches, decrees, Augustus' own autobiography and on monuments throughout Rome and the provinces. It was reinforced by every repetition, and given support by continuing success and prosperity – Livy's theme that success came from adherence to proper Roman virtues was a strong endorsement of the *princeps*.[18]

Augustus did not actively suppress alternative views or hide the past. Few chose to express such views and those few were lost in the deluge of opinion supporting and praising him. The fact that Julius Caesar had crossed the Rubicon and begun a civil war was as undeniable as Augustus' involvement in the proscriptions and the frequent executions and depredations of the years between 44 and 30 BC. This was still living memory and, even as that faded, all the records and propaganda of those years survived. Concealing them, let alone rewriting them, would not have been practical and it is doubtful that Augustus even considered it. His own version was clear, spreading the blame and shifting it far more onto others. We should note that Livy's willingness to ask whether Julius Caesar might have been wrong does not mean that he felt him wholly to blame and did not see others as also guilty. Livy deplored the death of Cicero while noting that the orator had been doing his very best to arrange the death of the triumvirs, and so was merely less successful rather than profoundly different to them.[19]

Literary sycophancy and adulation was transparent and in many ways self-defeating. Authors who appeared to offer their honest opinion, occasionally praising former – and invariably dead – opponents, or voice mild criticism of the *princeps* or those around him, reinforced their overall themes of praise for Rome and Augustus. Such works were likely to be of better quality, and just like the poetry of the age were an important part of creating a sense that there was once again a free and successful *res publica*. The boundaries were drawn as much or more by the authors themselves than by Augustus. Livy probably genuinely shared many of Augustus' opinions, as did a large proportion of society, especially property owners and the better-off throughout Italy. The historian was an enthusiastic reporter of victories over foreign enemies and of the expansion of Roman power, and the two decades from Actium down to 9 BC provided plenty for him to describe and to praise.

THE HOUSE OF AUGUSTUS

In 1 BC the nineteen-year-old Caius Caesar received his first command and left Rome for the Danube. Soon after he reached the legions there his mission was changed, and he was given *imperium* over the eastern provinces and sent to deal with a threat to the stability of Rome's eastern frontier. A power struggle within Armenia had led to Parthian intervention which placed their own nominee on the throne. As always, the prospect of a victorious war against the Parthians thrilled public opinion in Rome and inspired her poets. Ovid even worked such enthusiasm into the first book of his *Art of Love*: 'Lo! Caesar is preparing to add what was lacking to the conquered world.' The Parthians would pay the penalty for the massacre of Crassus' army in 53 BC. The age and lack of experience of the leader sent against them would be no impediment to this inevitable victory.

'Your avenger is at hand, and, though his years be few, proclaims his captaincy, and, though a boy, handles wars that no boy should handle . . . Valour falls early to the lot of Caesars . . . Father Mars and father Caesar, vouchsafe him your presence as he goes, for one of you is, and one of you will be, a god.' The poet, returning to his theme, then imagines picking up a woman while watching Caius Caesar triumph on his return, Ovid impressing the lady with a mixture of real and invented but confident commentary on the procession.[20]

Tiberius should have received this command, but he was still in Rhodes, and now that five years had passed both his *imperium* and his *tribunicia potestas* had expired. Augustus had not bothered to consult him, but had sent Julia notice of divorce on her husband's behalf when she was disgraced. Tiberius was simply informed that this had happened. He wrote, asking for leniency for his ex-wife, but was ignored. His frequent pleas to be allowed to return home as a private citizen were also refused, and so he remained on Rhodes, attending lectures and debates. Livia managed to secure him an un-defined rank as legate to give him some protection, and generally he was treated with respect, although he did have one philosopher arrested when the man followed him home after a debate, not only disagreeing with him but subjecting him to bitter abuse. There were moments of awkwardness and misunderstanding of the sort that dogged Tiberius throughout his life. When he expressed a desire to visit the sick, his attendants had the local magistrates gather all the invalids they could find and lay them out for his inspection by order of condition. Deeply embarrassed, Tiberius apologised to them all and had them returned home.[21]

As he was stepson of the *princeps* and until recently his son-in-law, it was difficult for all concerned to know how to handle Tiberius. There are signs that many dignitaries chose to visit him, as did most Roman officials travelling that way as they went to their provinces. When Caius and his entourage passed nearby, Tiberius left Rhodes to pay Caesar's son and the commander of the east his respects. Hostile sources later claimed that he prostrated himself before the youth, but this was probably a gross exaggeration. Yet his position was precarious. Communities throughout the east had to decide how to treat him, and how to treat those men whose local prominence owed a good deal to connections with him. In an effort to show that he was not plotting to build up a base of supporters or preparing to bid for power should the *princeps* die, Tiberius ceased wearing the garb of a Roman general and no longer practised such martial drills as riding and skill at arms. It was said that he dressed as a Greek, which if true was an echo of Antony's holiday in Athens when newly married to Octavia. One city in Gaul concluded that he was in disgrace and destroyed his statues.[22]

Caius did not linger on Rhodes, but was no doubt welcomed there as he was throughout the eastern provinces – after all, this was Augustus' son who had the power to answer petitions. Greek poets echoed the likes of Ovid: 'Be on your way to the Euphrates, son of Zeus. To you already the Parthians in the east are deserting apace. Be on your way, my prince; you shall find their bows unstrung through terror, Caesar. Rule in accord with your father's precepts. Be yourself the first to certify to the rising sun that Rome is bounded by the ocean on all sides.'[23]

Athens was one of many cities to honour the young prince, and at some point during these years moved an entire temple to Ares – the Greek war god equivalent to Mars – and rebuilt it stone by stone in the main Agora or market place. Yet for all the attention given to Caius Caesar, his father had taken care to send older and more experienced heads to advise the youth, and probably make many of the key decisions. His party was large, and included Lucius Domitius Ahenobarbus, who had recently done well in Germany, as well as Marcus Lollius, who had done less well and lost the eagle of *Legio V Alaudae* back in 16 BC. Another former consul, Publius Sulpicius Quirinius, may well have accompanied Caius from the beginning, for he was certainly on his staff in later years.[24]

Augustus remained in Rome, unwilling now to leave for long tours of the provinces. He was in his sixties, and probably feeling his age, especially since so few of his contemporaries remained. On his birthday in AD 2 he wrote to his elder son:

> Ninth day before the Kalends of October [i.e. 23 September]
>
> Greeting, my dear Caius, my dearest little donkey, whom, so help me, I constantly miss whenever you are away from me. But especially on such days as today my eyes are eager for my Caius, and whenever you have been today, I hope you have celebrated my sixty-fourth birthday in health and happiness . . . And I pray the gods that whatever time is left to me I may pass with you safe and well, with our country in a flourishing condition, while you both are playing the man and preparing to succeed to my sentry post.[25]

Sixty-three was considered a dangerous age in astrological terms, hence the joking relief to be past this. Talk of his 'sentry post' or 'station' – in Latin *stationem meam* – provides an insight into Augustus' view of himself as a guardian watching over the state, as well as his expectation that in time his sons would take over the duty. In spite of his age, the workload did not let up, especially since Caius and Lucius were still young and were only beginning to share the burden.

The *princeps* was close to his adopted sons, although sadly this is the only letter to survive from a published collection of letters to Caius. Most likely there were others written to Lucius. The style is similar to his correspondence with other family members, with its light tone and frequent use of Greek expressions. Augustus was fond of quotations, and often used them to illustrate examples of good behaviour in his correspondence with governors and subordinates as well as his relatives. Throughout their lives he wrote to his sons when he was not with them, and when present took a direct interest in their upbringing, teaching them to swim and ride. Around 10 BC he had selected the *grammaticus* Marcus Valerius Flaccus to teach the boys. Flaccus already ran a school in Rome, but for a salary of 100,000 sesterces a year happily moved all of his charges up onto the Palatine Hill, where he was installed in a house once owned by the famous *princeps senatus* Catulus and still named after him.²⁶

Augustus had purchased a number of houses on the Palatine and combined them to make up his own home. There was clearly a main entrance, the porch over which the *corona civica* was carved, but the various houses and the sacred spaces – notably the Temple of Apollo with its libraries and the shrine of Vesta which housed the *palladium*, supposedly originally brought from Troy by Aeneas – were probably separated by a network of narrow roads and alleys. The archaeology of the site remains unclear, and it has not proved easy to link the remains neatly to the literary record. The building known today as the House of Livia – her name was marked on a lead water pipe found there – was her residence after the death of Augustus, but it is impossible to know precisely where they lived before this. The site called the House of Augustus today is conventionally referred to in this way, but there is no clear evidence for its usage within the wider complex. Augustus adapted and modified existing buildings, and at least in the private areas does not appear to have altered the aristocratic houses in any drastic way.²⁷

The *princeps* claimed to live a simple life. Suetonius says that for more than forty years he 'stayed in the same bedroom in winter and summer', by which he probably means that he did not move to separate chambers in the cold and hot weather, rather than keeping the same bedroom for such a long time. Augustus was not a natural early riser, and whenever he needed to be in another part of the City first thing in the morning he usually stayed with a friend who lived conveniently close. Elsewhere we are told that in the heat of the summer he slept with the doors of his chamber open, or even had his couch moved into one of the inner courtyards and slept near an ornamental fountain. Augustus took no more than seven hours' rest each night, sleeping on a 'low and simply furnished bed', but if he woke he refused to lie there on his own and insisted on company. However, he often dozed after lunch or while being carried in his litter. He was moderate in his needs – the restlessly energetic Julius Caesar was satisfied with much less sleep – and also in his tastes, avoiding the conspicuous extravagance of many wealthy senators and equestrians, let alone the excesses of Mark Antony with his golden chamber pot. Couches and tables from Augustus' house survived a century later, and Suetonius noted that they were generally quite plain.[28]

Comfortable moderation was Augustus' hallmark. Such a comment should not be taken literally, but set against the taste for spectacular luxury already common in the first century BC, which would grow steadily and lead to the excesses of Caligula and Nero. Augustus lived in a way that he – and many of his peers – would have felt appropriate. Decorative wall paintings from the sites on the Palatine and others which may be associated with the *princeps* and his family are colourful, often elaborate, and conform to the latest fashions. His country villas – a frequent refuge from the bustle of Rome – were again not extravagant by aristocratic standards, and he only owned three of them, whereas even the moderately wealthy Cicero had maintained nine. Augustus did not own extensive art and sculpture collections kept only for private viewing, in contrast to some wealthy senators. Like Agrippa, his art was for display to the general population. Yet he did enjoy ornamental gardens, and had gathered all sorts of curiosities. His villa on Capreae (the island of Capri) displayed his 'bones of giants', the bones of huge animals and fish – presumably fossils of dinosaurs and the like – as well as ancient weapons claimed to have been wielded by famous heroes.[29]

Augustus lived in a fitting style for a leading senator – indeed it was clearly intended as a model for how these should behave – and the emphasis on modesty was relative. When at home, and not receiving guests or acting in any public capacity, he normally wore clothes made for him by Livia, Octavia or the other women of his family – no doubt assisted by their extensive household of slaves and freedwomen. Weaving was a traditional activity for the wives and daughters of the Roman elite, although by this era admired more than copied, and it is hard to know how far others followed the example set by the *princeps'* household in this respect. In winter he wore as many as four tunics over a vest and chest warmer, as well as leg wrappings around his thighs and calves – trousers were a barbaric custom, not to be adopted by Roman emperors for almost 300 years. In summer he dressed lightly, and invariably put on a broad-brimmed hat to protect against the sun, even when he was within the complex on the Palatine. Yet this was the informal garb. Whenever he appeared in an official capacity, Imperator Caesar Augustus dressed in a manner befitting his status. Appropriate official clothes were kept ever ready at home so that he could change into them if he suddenly needed to deal with any public business.[30]

Moderation also characterised Augustus' eating habits, and once again this was a mixture of personal inclination and living up to an ideal of proper behaviour for a leading Roman senator. Suetonius tells us that he was fond of simple bread rather than the finest loaves, and often ate moist cheese, figs and a little fish. On most days he happily nibbled at such things whenever the mood took him rather than waiting for a formal meal, and was inclined to eat while being carried in his litter or carriage. Quotes from his letters speak of his eating bread, dates and grapes in this way, and we are told that other favourites were cucumber, lettuce and flavoured apples – the last presumably dipped in or coated with something. He drank little wine, taking no more than a pint and vomiting up any excess. His feasts were generous and formal dinners frequent, although sometimes he took scant food himself, having already eaten beforehand or choosing to do so afterwards. As far as we can tell he took more pleasure in the company and conversation, or in playing dice or other games, such as making people bid for prizes without knowing what they were or their true value, mixing the genuinely valuable with the very ordinary – one trick was to show people only the backs of a set of paintings. At major festivals he liked giving out secret prizes, sometimes valuable, sometimes curiosities such as ancient coins, and sometimes joke gifts such as sponges or iron pokers, which he gave under punning names.[31]

Augustus frequently entertained guests at his house, and as frequently accepted invitations to dine with others, but these were always people considered appropriate by aristocratic standards. He never invited freedmen to share his table, but would on occasion have as guests freeborn men who were neither senators nor equestrians. Suetonius cites the example of a former *speculator* – originally a specialist scout, the term later came to mean intelligence operative and may already have had something of this sense – who was invited to a meal. Augustus had stayed in the man's villa, creating another acceptable debt of gratitude, and this suggests he was someone of at least moderate wealth. The *princeps* was careful to treat everyone with the respect suited to their rank and past service, just as he was patient in receiving petitioners. As we have seen, he had a lively sense of humour, with a particular – and very Roman – delight in puns and sarcasm. When one hunchbacked senator was advocate in a court case judged by Augustus, the man kept asking the *princeps* to 'set me straight if you spot a mistake'; Augustus finally quipped that 'I'll correct you, but I cannot set you straight!'[32]

A joke was often a gentle way out of an awkward situation, such as saying no to someone. They were also good stories that quickly circulated and added to the impression of Augustus as an ordinary man and not some distant tyrant. One merchant brought him a consignment of clothes dyed with Tyrian purple, but the *princeps* was unimpressed with the depth of the colour. The trader assured him that if he held it up to the light it would look better. 'What? You mean that I'll have to walk up and down on my balcony so that the Roman people can see that I am well dressed!' was the emperor's reply. At some point he owned a *nomenclator* who proved poor at remembering and recognising people in time to advise his master. One day as they were about to go down to the Forum the slave asked whether he had forgotten anything they needed. 'You had better take some letters of introduction,' Augustus said, 'since you don't know anyone there.'[33]

The jokes were sometimes biting, but never vicious by the standards of the day – the Romans were happy to mock physical deformities. More importantly they were never accompanied by cruel or arbitrary actions, and this was a marked change from his years as triumvir when he could execute men and joke that they would be 'food for the carrion birds'. Augustus neither paraded nor abused his power in his humour any more than he did in affairs of state. He was also ready to let himself be the butt of some stories and be laughed at. Once he is supposed to have encountered a man who looked uncannily like him, prompting the *princeps* to ask the man whether his mother had ever spent time in Rome. The man said no, before adding that his father was a frequent visitor. Moderation and courtesy in his dealings with others were probably reflections of Augustus' true character – at least at this stage in his life – as well as sensible policy. Acts of generosity and kindness were readily reported, for instance when he heard that a minor senator had gone blind and was planning to take his own life. Caesar Augustus barely knew the man, but still went to his bedside and after a long talk persuaded him to change his mind. Both the sympathy and the willingness to take trouble to help with another's problem carried over from his formal duties, but were important ways to convince people to accept – and often to like – his dominance.[34]

So much of what the *princeps* did was in public that many stories survive of his foibles and eccentricities. He generally held to Julius Caesar's recommendation that formal speeches and statements should be kept clear and in plain language, and mocked Maecenas and Tiberius for their fondness for obscure and over-complicated sentences. By contrast he used a few vulgar forms of words, and had a fondness for homespun sayings, such as 'As fast as you can cook asparagus', or 'They will pay up on the Greek Kalends' – since there was not such a day in the Greek calendar this meant that they would not pay. He was especially fond of the slogan 'Hurry slowly', which he seems to have employed in both Latin and Greek. Peculiarities of speech combined with a number of deep superstitions. Thunder and lightning frightened him – during a journey in Spain a lightning strike had killed the torch-bearer standing beside him – and so he always carried a piece of lucky sealskin with him as protection when travelling. If at home, he would flee to an underground room for safety. He would not travel on certain days, but was always pleased when he began a journey in a light rain as he believed this was a good omen – unlike finding that his slave had put out his shoes the wrong way round.[35]

Such things were inoffensive eccentricities, keeping well within the bounds of acceptable aristocratic behaviour. Similarly his care for his own health was not excessive, despite his record of poor health. He developed his own routine for bathing, which was less extreme than the conventional Roman bath with its exceptionally hot and cold temperatures, but left his skin scarred by over-rigorous use of the metal strigil when scraping off oil used as soap. He remained prone to serious illnesses, and at times suffered from rheumatism and weakness in his legs and hands – especially the right hand – sometimes making it impossible for him to hold a pen.

Up until Actium he publicly exercised with weapons both on foot and horseback in the normal aristocratic way. From 29 BC he switched to throwing and catching a ball, until advancing years made him content with simply riding and then taking a run, which he ended by leaping. Once again, this was normal for a senator of advancing years. Augustus' lifestyle, every bit as much as his manners and deliberate actions, cultivated the image of a normal, respectable Roman nobleman who did nothing to excess. Exercise, like so much of the *princeps*' life, was done in public, and his domestic lifestyle was meant as confirmation that he possessed the character necessary to lead the state. Somewhere in the complex of houses on the Palatine, Imperator Caesar Augustus gave himself a private refuge, and now and again he would go to this high room, which he nicknamed his 'workshop' or Syracuse after the great city in Sicily. It was a signal that he was not to be disturbed, and he would retire there for peace and quiet, or to plan legislation or other projects in detail. Another convenient hideaway was a villa owned by one of his freedmen just outside the *pomerium*.[36]

On 1 January AD 1, Caius Caesar became consul. He was far away on the border with Parthia, so the ceremonial burden fell on his colleague, Lucius Aemilius Paullus, the husband of Augustus' granddaughter Julia. It was the *princeps'* practice, when putting relatives forward for election to office, to recommend them to the voters 'should they be deserving'. Aided by his advisers, Caius was doing well, helped by the fact that the Parthians also had little appetite for open war with Rome. Augustus' son and the Parthian king met to negotiate, parading their armies for the other's inspection, and then held lavish feasts on either side of the Euphrates. Peace was confirmed and a Roman nominee placed on the throne of Armenia.[37]

In AD 2 the nineteen-year-old Lucius Caesar left Rome for his first provincial command, heading for Spain, where there was no longer any threat of war and he could gain experience in a safe environment. En route he passed through Gallia Narbonensis and stopped for a while at Massilia. No doubt at every stage there were formal welcoming ceremonies and a long line of petitioners as the young prince was prepared for his public role. Then fate took a hand, for the teenager fell ill and died at Massilia. Augustus was devastated, but for the moment took consolation in the continuing success of his remaining son. Yet there were problems in the east. Scandal rocked Caius' party when Lollius was accused of accepting bribes from foreign kings and took his own life. The initial success in Armenia turned sour when a large number of his subjects rebelled against the new king – probably unsurprisingly, since he was a Median rather than an Armenian and so was resented by the local aristocrats.

In AD 3 Caius led an army to suppress the rising, but at the siege of some obscure walled town he unwisely went in person to negotiate with the enemy leader and was treacherously wounded. The injury proved serious and did not heal. Throughout the autumn and winter he grew worse, and his behaviour started to become erratic. At one point he wrote to his father asking permission to retire from public life – a strange echo of Tiberius almost a decade before, but all the more bizarre for a youth in his early twenties. On 21 February AD 4, Caius Caesar died. Many communities throughout Italy and the provinces joined the *princeps* in public mourning, and honours were voted to the two young men outstripping even those given to Drusus as two more sets of ashes were interred in Augustus' Mausoleum. In his sixty-seventh year, Imperator Caesar Augustus was left alone at his sentry post.[38]

FOR THE SAKE OF THE *RES PUBLICA*

'But fortune, which had snatched away the hope of the great name [of Caesar], had already restored to the commonwealth her greatest bulwark . . . Caesar Augustus did not delay for any length of time; for he had no need to hunt for one to choose, but simply to choose one of obvious eminence.' *Velleius Paterculus, early first century* AD.[1]

Augustus 'accepted the death of family members with more resignation than their misbehaviour'. *Suetonius, late first century* AD.[2]

Rome heard of the death of Caius Caesar some time in the second half of March. Augustus' grief was genuine, but as he mourned he began to plan for the future, and within three months his decision was made public. As always he turned to his closest family, although the common belief among many scholars that he was obsessed with his own bloodline fails to convince. Yet his entire career had raised the *auctoritas* of the name Caesar to a level never before reached by any family name, constantly advertising it in every medium. Caesar Augustus had marked himself out as special, elevated far beyond anyone else, and from early on this mystique extended to his family. Whoever was to replace his lost sons would become a Caesar by name, but must clearly be felt to deserve that honour. In reality there were few options.[3]

One was Julia's sole remaining son, Agrippa Postumus, but he was only fifteen and had not yet formally assumed the toga of manhood. More viable – even if more distantly related since he was the *princeps'* great-nephew – was Germanicus, the oldest son of Drusus, who was now eighteen and showing a good deal of his father's charm and knack for winning over a crowd. Suetonius states that Augustus seriously considered choosing Germanicus as his main heir before deciding against it, probably because he could not be sure of living long enough for the youth to prove himself and be secure. As usual he does not seem to have considered raising the husbands of any of his nieces and great-nieces to higher eminence, and the same was true of his granddaughter's husband Lucius Aemilius Paullus.[4]

Yet there was also the forty-five-year-old Tiberius, twice consul, former son-in-law, former colleague in the *tribunicia potestas*, and probably the state's most distinguished living commander. After eight years spent on Rhodes, Augustus had finally softened his answers to his former son-in-law's pleas to return home. He did not grant permission, and instead had allowed Caius Caesar to decide the matter. The latter at first refused, but then eventually agreed – the change was said to have been due to the fall of Lollius, who cherished a long-standing and fully reciprocated hatred of Tiberius. That was in AD 2, and the 'exile', as he had become known, was back in Rome by the time news arrived of the death of Lucius Caesar, prompting him to write a public condolence to Augustus, full of shared grief and fulsome praise. Otherwise, apart from taking his son Drusus to the Temple of Mars Ultor so that he could assume the toga of manhood and be enrolled as an adult citizen, Tiberius took great care to avoid playing the slightest role in public life. He did not live in his own grand house, formerly owned by Pompey and then Antony, but instead moved to one of Maecenas' villas on the edge of the City.[5]

Once again Augustus was not looking for one successor, but for several – talk by modern scholars of regents or caretakers for the candidate he truly wanted is once again misguided. Augustus did not think in that way, and clearly expected close family members to be able to work as a team and share power – which was not to say that this belief was realistic. In the event, this was also the most complex and unorthodox of all his dynastic arrangements. As a first stage Tiberius adopted his nephew Germanicus. Then, on 26 May, Augustus adopted both Tiberius and Agrippa Postumus. There was nothing unusual about adopting a teenaged boy, but there was absolutely no precedent for the adoption of a forty-five-year-old former consul who now had two adult sons, Germanicus and the younger Drusus. In effect Augustus acquired not only two sons, but two grandsons as well. Marriages were soon arranged to confirm the bonds between this second generation. Germanicus was to marry Agrippina, daughter of Agrippa and Julia, while his sister Livilla – who seems formerly to have been marked down to wed Caius Caesar – would marry Drusus. Tiberius remained single, in part through inclination, but also because it was surely difficult to find a suitable match for someone who had been married to Caesar's only daughter.

Postumus was the odd one out, and not simply because he was the only one who was neither the son nor grandson of Livia. He was thirty years younger than Tiberius, far closer in age to the latter's sons, although still younger than they, and would seem to have had more in common with them than his new brother. Nor was there any attempt to accelerate his career and public profile. It was to be another year before Postumus underwent the ceremony to mark his coming of age as an adult. In the past, Augustus had chosen to become consul so that he could present his sons Caius and Lucius to the people in this way. He did not do this for Postumus, although since he never again held the consulship a reluctance to take on its ceremonial responsibilities at his advanced age may have had more to do with it than anything else. More significantly, Postumus was not granted the title of *princeps iuventutis* like his dead brothers, nor was any announcement made granting him admission to the Senate and early tenures in the magistracies. Similarly, there was no talk of marriage to another prominent member of Augustus' extended family. For the moment, the change from being the *princeps'* grandson to becoming his son granted Postumus the name of Caesar, but little other immediate advantage to the boy.[6]

Tiberius was also now Tiberius Julius Caesar, and when Augustus announced his adoption in the Senate he declared that 'I do this for the sake of the *res publica*' – a statement that the historian Velleius Paterculus clearly felt rebounded to the credit of Tiberius. Many have wanted to see either weary resignation or heavy irony in the words, but it is unlikely that such emotions were openly paraded. Augustus had clearly felt betrayed by his son-in-law when Tiberius retired from public life in 6 BC and this bitterness may never have gone away altogether. Yet Tiberius had not caused trouble while on Rhodes, and since his return had very carefully kept free of public life and behaved as inconspicuously as possible. Surviving letters from the years to come are almost indistinguishable in their affection, advice, quotations and bantering tone to Augustus' correspondence with the rest of his family. At the very least, and whatever his personal feelings towards Tiberius, in public he consistently showed respect, trust and fondness for his newly adopted son.[7]

It is obvious that Tiberius gained from the new arrangement, an assumption reinforced by hindsight since we know that he would succeed as *princeps* and rule for twenty-three years, outliving by a large margin both Germanicus and Drusus. Even without this knowledge, his situation changed from being a man whose career had ended a decade before – and showed no sign of resumption – into a leader of the state, second only to Augustus. Livia's son was the *princeps'* most senior assistant, and would be without doubt the most senior of his successors, who were in turn to include two of her grandchildren. Rumours soon circulated that she had schemed to achieve this, even arranging the deaths of Caius and Lucius so that Tiberius was the only viable choice left to Augustus. Such stories fed on the older tales of her supposed poisonings, and all would grow in time. None of this is probable – and indeed the practicalities of somehow arranging Caius' wounding during negotiations in Armenia make such claims fanciful in the extreme. We cannot ever truly know, but few, if any, scholars would give the slightest credence to such tales; it is considerably easier to believe that these and the earlier deaths were due to ill fortune – and far more likely. They are more inclined to talk of a power struggle between the Claudian and Julian families – the latter sometimes more specifically Julia's descendants or even those of her mother Scribonia. This can be almost as incredible.[8]

Augustus granted Tiberius *tribunicia potestas* for ten years in AD 4, and may well have done this before he adopted him – Augustus had received a decade-long extension of his provincial command

and *imperium* in the previous year. It was a renewal of Tiberius' earlier eminence, again raising him to a level only previously occupied by Agrippa, but this time the *princeps'* senior agent was his son rather than son-in-law. The distinction is vital, since not all of his new status was to Tiberius' advantage. In AD 4 he went from being the head of an old aristocratic family with full independence of action to becoming a junior member of another's family, accepting the supreme authority of his father. Instantly all Tiberius' property ceased to be his own, and instead became part of Augustus' fortune, to be disposed of as he wished. The same was true for Postumus, so that the remainder of Agrippa's great estates now passed to his old friend. Law and tradition gave considerable powers to a Roman father. He could repudiate an adopted son, whereas the son could not recant his adoption. Political independence was lost along with financial independence; it was almost unthinkable and certainly discreditable for a Roman son to oppose his father publicly.[9]

Tiberius made every show of taking his new status seriously, and for the rest of his life acted towards and spoke of his father Augustus with great reverence. Livia and her son – who was now of course also her husband's son – were no doubt highly satisfied with the new arrangement and more than likely had lobbied behind the scenes for the decision. Yet Augustus himself gained more than anyone else, and there is no reason to believe that he was manipulated into it. With a middle-aged son, another teenage son and two grandsons, the adoptions gave him close assistants for the immediate and longer-term future, their numbers surely providing protection against further blows of fortune like those that had robbed him of Caius and Lucius. Once again, he adapted to a new situation and created a group of close colleagues from his own family. Tiberius had expressed weariness at his constant employment up to 6 BC, but before the end of AD 4 he went to campaign in Germany and he would then remain on active service for the next decade. His long years of inactivity may have given him a renewed appetite for work, but even so Augustus could now command his son and be confident of his obedience, working him every bit as hard as he had once worked Agrippa.[10]

The new arrangement cost Tiberius a good deal of toil as well as his independence, and the surprising and unprecedented willingness of a mature and distinguished aristocrat to accept adoption by another – even one so prestigious as the *princeps* – probably does more than anything else to explain Augustus' comment that he acted 'for the sake of the *res publica*' in this matter. Such an act genuinely required explanation on both sides. Although the experienced Tiberius was the most convenient choice, his continued exclusion from public life was certainly an option, and one unlikely to pose a serious threat to stability. There may well have been voices urging other courses. Dio and Seneca present a confused and implausible account of an attempted conspiracy led by Cnaeus Cornelius Cinna. The plot was discovered, and Augustus was supposedly talked out of executing the man by Livia – allegedly so convincingly that instead he backed the man's candidature and ensured that he became one of the consuls for the next year.[11]

Dio also speaks of demonstrations in Rome calling for the recall of Julia, which leads us to suspect that these were orchestrated, or at least encouraged, by those hoping to do well from her rehabilitation. He dates them to AD 3, but some would place them in the next year or see them as part of wider agitation. In any event the *princeps* adamantly refused, declaring that fire and water would sooner mix than he would pardon his daughter, and so the crowd carried burning torches to the Tiber and hurled them into the river. Julia was finally permitted to return to the mainland of Italy in AD 3, and for the rest of her life lived near Rhegium, kept under an only slightly looser confinement. None of the sources even hint that she had sufficient freedom to be in touch with those asking for her recall. Similarly, there is no suggestion that the refusal to rehabilitate his daughter dented Augustus' own popularity in any way. Earlier in AD 3 his residence on the Palatine was badly damaged by fire, which led to a wave of offers of money from communities and individuals. Augustus took only a token sum from each so that they could share in the rebuilding, although it is unclear whether the rest was returned or instead used for public works.[12]

In AD 4 Augustus was given consular powers to hold a partial census. Poor citizens were not troubled, nor were those resident outside Italy, and instead he reregistered only those boasting of at least 200,000 sesterces' worth of property. At the same time there was another review of the senatorial roll, but there is no particular reason to believe that this was engineered to remove potential enemies of Tiberius – or indeed of Postumus. Probably it was simply a continuation of the earlier efforts, and examined men whose behaviour or status was in doubt. Some may have struggled to maintain the required property qualification. A decade later we hear of the grandson of the orator Hortensius, who raised four sons but only possessed property worth 1,200,000 sesterces and was thus unable to divide this so as to make all of them eligible for a senatorial career. In AD 4 the *princeps* gave money to eighty senators so that they could meet the property qualification for membership of the order. It is also sometimes claimed that Tiberius greatly influenced the choice of consuls from now until the end of Augustus' life. Most likely he played a part in promoting men, as Augustus continued to do, but none of the names are especially surprising and all are the sort of men who would most likely have reached this office anyway.[13]

The year did see the introduction of a law which reinforced other recent legislation and provided thorough regulation for the treatment of slaves, in particular for the granting of their freedom – notably by restricting the number that could be freed in a will, or by young owners, and also determining the precise obligations owed by a freedman or woman to their former owner. Augustus may well have had some concerns about too many freedmen swamping the numbers of Roman citizens, and certainly feared too many becoming eligible for the corn dole in Rome. Yet other measures protected freedmen, continued to grant them citizenship, if with a few limitations, and rewarded those who raised large families just as they did the rest of the citizen body. The ranks of freed slaves included many industrious and highly successful individuals, important in the *vici* of

Rome itself and sometimes rising to local prominence in towns else-where; and Augustus took care to cultivate their loyalty to him and to the state, just as he did with other groups within society. In terms of its laws and activities, AD 4 suggests not a radical shift of power or direction of government, but far more a sense of business as usual.[14]

THE GREATEST DANGER SINCE HANNIBAL

Before the year was out Tiberius was at the head of an army operat-ing east of the Rhine. He returned to Rome briefly during the winter months – something he would now do every year – before returning to lead another campaign the following spring, taking his legions at least as far as the Elbe. These were operations against leaders and tribes within the area already under Roman influence, reflecting continuing resistance or changed attitudes. Other communities in the region appeared to accept and perhaps even to welcome Roman dominance. Archaeology has provided clear evidence of at least one Roman-style town established around the turn of the first century AD at Waldgirmes, not far from an army base used during the wars of conquest, and there are hints of other similar communities. The urban lifestyle that was so quintessentially Roman still had little appeal for most of the peoples in this area, but that is not to say that the situation would not change in time, just as it had done in other provinces after their conquest.[15]

For AD 6 the Romans planned a grander operation, seeking to take new territory rather than simply consolidate their hold on existing conquests. The target was King Maroboduus, leader of the Marco-manni, a people belonging to a large sub-group of the Germanic peoples called the Suebi, who were famous for wearing their hair tied in a knot on the top or side of their heads – the Suebian knot. Clever, charismatic and no doubt a skilful war leader, he had carved out an empire for himself consisting of many groups as well as his own people, so that he controlled much of modern Bohemia, the area between the Rhine and the Danube. At least some of his youth

had been spent in Rome, probably as a hostage, and in the beginning
he may well have gone back to his homeland with Roman support.
Velleius dubbed him 'a barbarian by race, but not intelligence', and
speaks of an exceptionally large royal army, many of the troops
permanently maintained at the king's expense. No doubt he exaggerated when he claimed that they were trained almost to Roman
standards, but this was clearly a leader more powerful than any to
appear among the tribes for several generations. His lands bordered
on the provinces in Germany, Noricum and Pannonia, but although
he accepted refugees from those regions, even Velleius makes it clear
that he had taken no hostile action against the Romans. The most
he could say was that the king's envoys sometimes behaved with appropriate subservience, but at other times dared to speak 'as if they
represented an equal'.[16]

Such 'pride' in a foreign leader was sufficient to warrant at the
very least a display of Roman force. Mutual fear and suspicion fed
the situation, Maroboduus building up his strength as protection
and at the same time seeming to be more of a threat. A large force
was concentrated from the armies in Germany and placed under
the command of the legate Caius Sentius Saturninus, an experienced and mature former consul – he had held the office back in
19 BC – who had won the *ornamenta triumphalia* for his operations
in support of Tiberius the previous year. This force would advance
against Maroboduus from the north, while Tiberius came from
the south, leading another big column, this time drawn from the
armies of the Danube. In the spring of AD 6 the attack began, the
two Roman armies pushing through the territory of the tribes living
between Rome's provinces and Maroboduus' kingdom. There was
no fighting, and the German king made no aggressive move and held
back, until the Roman columns had almost joined together and were
just a few days' march away from his forces. Then, just before he
was forced to fight or submit, news came of serious rebellion in the
Romans' Balkan provinces and everything changed. Tiberius offered
Maroboduus terms for the restoration of peace. The king did not
want to risk fighting the Romans unless he had no other choice, and

was happy to accept, so the Roman armies turned around and with-drew to deal with the more pressing matter of the rebellion.[17]

The revolt of the Pannonians and Dalmatians spread rapidly through regions the Romans had complacently regarded as secure. Like many rebellions, this broke out just as a generation of younger men grew up who had never experienced defeat at the hands of the Romans. When auxiliaries were levied in Illyricum to support the war against Maroboduus, the local tribesmen are supposed to have looked at their own numbers and begun to realise their strength. Levies on the provincial population – whether of manpower, live-stock and crops to support the Roman military or straightforwardly in money – often fell heavily on the people, especially when those overseeing them were clumsy or corrupt or both. One of the leaders of the rebellion later claimed: 'You Romans are to blame for this; for you send as guardians to your flocks, not dogs or shepherds, but wolves.'[18]

Simmering discontent was fed by the sense of their own num-bers, especially when they saw the pick of the Roman forces in the region drawn off for the planned conquest of Bohemia. The out-break began with attacks on Roman merchants and other civilians in the provinces. Roman military doctrine was to confront any signs of rebellion as quickly as possible, attacking it with whatever troops could be quickly gathered. Inaction would be seen as weakness, and so encourage more and more people to rally to the rebel cause. Yet the risk of such rapid counter-attacks was that the forces involved were too weak to deal with any serious resistance. A Roman defeat, however small, was an even greater recruiter for the rebellion. De-tails are obscure, but at best there was a failure to crush the rebellion and probably there were a number of small reverses. At least one was more serious, and Velleius mentions the massacre of a force of legionary veterans.[19]

There were problems in other provinces as well. Around this time we hear of campaigning on the frontier in Africa – the last province with a legionary garrison entrusted to a senatorial proconsul – and of problems in Isauria in Asia. It was also in this year that Publius

Sulpicius Quirinius, the imperial legate in charge of Syria, intervened with the bulk of his field army in Judaea. Herod's son Archelaus had proved so woefully unpopular with his subjects that he was stripped of his throne and sent to live out his life in comfortable retirement in Gaul. Instead a large part of Herod the Great's former kingdom was taken under direct rule and turned into a Roman province. Unusually, it would be governed by an equestrian prefect rather than a man of senatorial rank – the first such province after Egypt, but an innovation that would later be repeated. As part of the process Quirinius began to hold a census. It was the first time that the population had been subject to registration and tax paid directly to the Romans rather than to a local king, and it soon prompted outbreaks of serious violence. The Roman response was characteristically brutal and quickly effective, just as it had been to the trouble following the death of Herod the Great in 4 BC.[20]

In his sixty-ninth year, Imperator Caesar Augustus was faced with serious problems on several fronts simultaneously and for a short time seems to have lost his nerve. Pliny claims that he fell into despair, refusing to eat for four days and declaring that he wished to die. The rebellion in Illyricum affected one of the closest provinces to Italy and from the beginning was clearly on a very large scale. Augustus had personal experience of the region, and so knew how tough its warriors were and how difficult the terrain made campaigning. At first he cannot have known what would happen in Bohemia, and if Maroboduus had chosen to fight rather than accept peace it would have been very difficult to draw troops away in the numbers needed to deal with the rebellion. His legions in the rest of the empire were either too far away to be quickly brought to the theatre of operations or already committed to dealing with other problems. In Italy, he had only the nine cohorts of praetorians, his small force of German bodyguards, the urban cohorts and the imperial fleets, and all of these combined could scarcely be seen as a viable field force.[21]

Ironically enough, the year had begun with a major reorganisation of military funding, aimed at setting it on a permanent and sustainable footing. To this end, Augustus created the Military Treasury (*aerarium militare*), priming it with 170,000,000 sesterses of his own money and setting three former praetors to serve as its supervisors for three-year terms of office. This would pay soldiers' salaries, and the bonus now normally given on discharge in lieu of a grant of land. By this time there were twenty-eight legions, and as a means of reducing costs by delaying the payment of the discharge bonus, the terms of service were now extended from sixteen to twenty years, with a further five years as a veteran – the type of soldier massacred during the early stages of the rebellion in Illyricum. Even so, this would in the longer run require a constant flow of funding, and to provide it Augustus introduced a levy of five per cent on inheritances going to anyone outside the immediate family. This was the first direct taxation of citizens living in Italy for more than a century and a half and was deeply resented from the start.[22]

Now, faced by a rapidly spreading rebellion, the priority suddenly became less long-term stability than the immediate raising of fresh troops to deal with the problem. Augustus announced in the Senate that unless something was done quickly the enemy could reach Rome within ten days, while others compared the danger to the great struggle with Carthage. A levy was held in Rome itself for the first time in decades, and when not enough volunteers appeared, resort was made to limited conscription as well as the acceptance of men normally considered unsuitable physically or because of their occupation. New cohorts were formed, although it is less clear whether these were intended ultimately to be absorbed by the legions or to remain as independent formations. At the same time slaves were demanded from the wealthy, and once handed over these men were given their freedom and citizenship, and then enrolled in special cohorts – the *cohortes voluntariorum civium romanorum* (volunteer cohorts of Roman citizens). The title, as well as different patterns of uniform and equipment, distinguished them from the freeborn citizens in the legions.[23]

The better-off were required to play their part as leaders, both for the armies already in existence and for the new levies. Augustus asked for volunteers, especially from young members of the senatorial and equestrian orders. Over the years he had encouraged a much stronger sense of identity among the *equites*, making Caius and Lucius their nominal leaders and reviving the annual parade of those traditionally eligible for military service as cavalrymen and re-stricting it to those of suitable age and physical fitness. These days they served not as horsemen but as commanders of auxiliary units and as tribunes in the legions, and in AD 6 some volunteered and most of the rest were willing to go if commanded by the state. A few were not, and one notorious case involved an equestrian father who cut off the thumbs of his sons to render them physically unfit for service. Augustus had him tried, condemned and punished by being sold as a slave, as well as auctioning off his property. The man belonged to one of the companies of *publicani* – the firms who con-tinued to take on many state contracts and levy some taxes – and when his colleagues began bidding for him, the *princeps* instead sold the man at a token price to one of his freedmen. The condemned man was to be sent to a country estate and held in servitude, but not otherwise mistreated.[24]

The reluctance of enough men of all classes to serve the state was part of wider problems. Fire continued to be a serious risk to all the inhabitants of Rome, and several recent outbreaks prompted Augustus to create seven cohorts of *vigiles*, each one responsible for two of the City's regions and acting as a fire brigade and night patrol. Most of the recruits were freedmen, reflecting not just the wider population of Rome, but also the shortage of manpower of all kinds at this time. A tax of two per cent on the sale price of slaves was created to fund the new service. There were also food shortages, presumably caused by bad harvests or problems in transporting the grain to Rome. Excess mouths – including gladiators and slaves for sale – were banned from coming within 100 miles of the City. At the same time some public business was suspended, senators were per-mitted to stay in the country and miss meetings of the Senate and an exemption was made so that votes would be valid even if a quorum was not present.[25]

Unsurprisingly, these worried times produced murmurs of

discontent. Anonymous pamphlets circulated, more or less openly hinting at revolution. It is hard to say whether they targeted the *princeps* or more those around him – or even other magistrates and senators who were held to blame or simply unpopular. Dio reports that people attributed much of the agitation to a certain Rufus – he calls him Publius while Suetonius names him Plautius – but that most believed he was too obscure and lacking in intelligence to be the real planner. Modern scholars are tempted to link some of this activity to those who felt that they would do better if Livia's descendants lost power in favour of Julia and her family. Dio does see the new inheritance tax as one of the sources of discontent and, given that this only affected those possessed of substantial property, historians suspect a degree of political manipulation by supporters of Julia's family hoping to focus wider discontents. However, such suggestions remain conjectural.[26]

Shortages continued for some months, prompting Augustus to refuse permission for public feasts to be held on his birthday. He set several former consuls to improve the grain supply system, and in the meantime gave at his own expense additional rations of food to those receiving the public dole in Rome. Gradually the food supply recovered to more normal levels, and the times became more suitable for celebration. Gladiatorial games were held in memory of Tiberius' brother Drusus and presided over by Germanicus and Claudius. The latter was physically weak, inclined to twitch and stammer, and clearly unfit for the military demands of any public career. His mother described him as a 'prodigy, left unfinished by nature' and was fond of insulting people by saying that they were 'as stupid as my son Claudius'. Yet at this stage he was considered capable of appearing in public, although at the games he was swathed in a heavy cloak rather than the usual toga, probably to conceal his appearance. Drusus was again invoked when Tiberius dedicated his rebuilt Temple of Castor and Pollux in the Forum, giving his name in this case as Tiberius Julius Caesar Claudianus to celebrate his former family as well as the name of Caesar.[27]

JULIA'S CHILDREN

It is hard to say much about Postumus' activities in the years following his adoption. He came of age in AD 5, publicly but without any great fanfare – although even this was better than the haste with which Claudius was stealthily whisked under cover of darkness to and from the Temple of Mars Ultor when he came of age. The family had yet to make up its mind how far Claudius was to be exposed to the public gaze. Postumus was still young, so perhaps his lack of any public role is unsurprising. Unlike Claudius he was strong and athletic, but our sources all claim that there were serious doubts about his character and intelligence, hinting vaguely at a violent temper and unspecified flaws of conduct. It may be worth remembering that he was not yet ten at the time of his mother's disgrace, and saw her exiled while his brothers were given rapid promotion and lavished with praise, but he was not. Perhaps he began to press for more recognition.[28]

In AD 5 Augustus reformed the voting of the *Comitia centuriata*, adding ten new centuries drawn from the highest classes and named in honour of Caius and Lucius. These would now vote first, setting an example that the rest of the centuries were likely to follow given the Roman electorate's fondness for backing winners. The change was probably coincidental and part of the longer-term efforts to make state institutions function more smoothly, but it would have done a lot to prevent a repeat of the incident in 6 BC, when the centuries had elected Caius Caesar as consul even though he was not a candidate. It is more than possible that ambitious individuals saw in Postumus an opportunity to aid their own rise. Perhaps the youth spoke or acted unwisely, and gradually he lost Augustus' confidence. In AD 7 it was expected that the seventeen-year-old would at last receive a public role and be given command of some of the newly raised troops, with instructions to march them to Pannonia and join the campaign. Instead the job was given to Germanicus.[29]

Postumus' disgrace seems to have come in stages. In the first he was reprimanded by being sent to Surrentum (modern Sorrento) on the Bay of Naples, where he spent most of his time fishing. Then

Augustus formally revoked his adoption, and instead of being a Caesar he returned to being a Vipsanius Agrippa. The property he had inherited from his father did not go with him, and Augustus used most of it to top up the *aerarium militare*. Postumus complained bitterly about this, and in particular attacked Livia, so that in the end he was exiled to the tiny Island of Planasia near Corsica and kept under strict guard. Suspicion that Tiberius and his mother were keen to dispose of a potential future rival was already circulating in the ancient world, and continues to attract scholars. There may be some truth in it, but more likely Postumus wrought his own destruction. Augustus may well have been guided by his wife in this, as in so many things, but he had watched the boy grow up and should have had a good idea of his nature. It is a mistake to claim that the family were willing to tolerate supposed mental as well as physical weakness in Claudius and thus would have permitted stupidity or worse in Postumus – Claudius was not Caesar's son or considered as one of his successors.[30]

As the *princeps'* only grandson, Postumus could not easily have been ignored in AD 4 unless he was put away somewhere. Augustus may already have doubted the boy's character, but hoped that he would learn and grow into a stable and capable man. The lack of any public role for him even after the adoption suggests general caution far more than the jealous suspicion of Tiberius or his mother. When Postumus failed to improve, Augustus rejected him. Tacitus later noted that the youth committed no actual crime, and it is hard to say whether any one act sparked his repudiation. Political rivalry no doubt played a part, but the judgement of our sources that his character and behaviour were behind his exile is probably right.[31]

Germanicus took the troops to Pannonia in AD 7 and so it was he who began to prove himself as a soldier. His role was still a junior one, and other contingents of recruits were marched to the area under separate command – the historian Velleius Paterculus proudly tells us that he led one of these, serving in the field instead of performing his tasks as quaestor for the year. Tiberius was in overall charge, having hurried to the front in the previous year. It was a

tough campaign, and attacks on nearby provinces by neighbouring peoples drew away some of the Roman forces sent to quell the
rising – another indication of just how fortunate the Romans were
that Maroboduus saw more advantage in keeping the peace than exploiting a temporary weakness. From this point on he remained a
staunch ally of Rome and bolstered his own position as a result.[32]

The fighting was on a grand scale and often bitter, especially since
many of the rebels had served in the past as auxiliaries with the
Romans. They understood Latin, knew how the legions operated,
and were themselves far more disciplined than most tribal armies.
On several occasions Roman field armies were checked and forced to
withdraw, or only prevailed after suffering heavy losses, while more
than one beleaguered garrison was relieved just in time to save it. At
one point Tiberius found himself at the head of the largest Roman
army concentrated since the civil wars, consisting of ten legions,
seventy auxiliary cohorts, fourteen auxiliary cavalry *alae*, 10,000 veterans – probably in this case including men recalled to the colours
and not simply those in the last phase of their military service – as
well as allies supplied by the Thracian king and other friendly leaders. This force represented more than a third of the entire Roman
army, and was larger than any of the armies ever led by Julius Caesar
in the course of his campaigns. Tiberius quickly realised that it was
too large to supply and control effectively, so after a short time split
it into several separate field forces. Even so it did not include all the
troops sent to deal with the rebellion. Altogether fifteen legions saw
service against the Pannonians and Dalmatians, along with comparable numbers of auxiliaries. Thus comfortably more than half of
the entire army took three years of tough campaigning to suppress
the rebellion in one province.[33]

It was the most serious war since Actium and a good deal harder
fought. Rhetoric about rebel armies marching on Rome was fanciful, but even so this was a conflict unlike all the other smaller wars
fought since 30 BC – far larger and much harder to win. For a while –
perhaps only a short while – it challenged the very basis of Augustus'
leadership, which boasted of constant, inevitable victory granted by

the gods to the Roman people and its *princeps* because their virtue and piety deserved it. Much of this was propaganda, but it is hard for such constantly repeated themes not to be absorbed even by those they were designed to serve. The prospect that they might lose a war and province was shocking, and readily implied that they no longer deserved to win. This as much as anything else helped to explain Imperator Caesar Augustus' near-collapse at the start of the war: everything he had created seemed under threat. Even after he recovered his nerve, there were still signs of fear which later expressed themselves as vocal impatience that Tiberius was not winning the war sufficiently quickly.[34]

Augustus celebrated his seventieth birthday in AD 7 and there were clear signs that age was catching up with him, and that his health was failing. In the following year he began to reduce his workload. Three former consuls were appointed to deal with the bulk of embassies from allied leaders and communities who constantly trooped to Rome to present petitions or simply give praise to the *princeps*. He attended the Senate far less often and, although he continued to preside over judicial hearings, these were now convened in part of his complex on the Palatine rather than in public buildings. At elections he no longer attended and showed his support for favoured candidates, but simply had his recommendations written out and displayed for the voters to see. Yet we should not exaggerate his frailty, and there were traces of the old determination. In AD 8 – and possibly in the other years – he travelled as far as Ariminum (now Rimini) on the border with Illyricum so that he could be near the theatre of operations.[35]

Food shortages occurred again in AD 7, leading to more disturbances. The following year's elections were so badly disrupted by riots that they could not be held, and so Augustus appointed all of the magistrates. As far as we can tell this was caused by rivalries between the candidates, independent of any factions supporting either Tiberius and his family or the discredited Postumus. Yet in AD 8 Julia, the daughter of Agrippa and Julia, was publicly condemned for adultery and, like her mother before her, exiled to an island. In this case only

one lover was named, Decimus Junius Silanus, and he was informed
that he had lost Caesar's friendship and told that he should go into
'voluntary' exile. The fate of Julia's husband is unclear, but since
adultery was the charge he was presumably still alive. In spite of a
consulship in AD 1, Lucius Aemilius Paullus received no senior command and is listed by Suetonius among the conspirators who plotted
against Augustus. No date is given, nor are the details of what he
did known, but if he was not already in exile then this would have
followed at the time of his wife's disgrace. Julia gave birth in the
months to follow, but Augustus refused to let the child be raised and
had it exposed – a grim reminder of the head of the household's
powers as well as those of the *princeps*.[36]

Caught up in the whole business was the poet Ovid, who faced
no formal charge or trial, and was simply instructed to take himself
off to the city of Tomi on the Black Sea and stay there until told
otherwise. This was the very fringe of the empire – and indeed of
Greco-Roman culture itself – and from there he wrote a succession
of poems pleading for pardon and recall. Sadly, but unsurprisingly
given the sensitive nature of the affair, these add frustratingly little to
our picture of the scandal. Ovid was blamed for some indiscretion,
probably seeing something he should not have, and more generally
for the corrupting influence of his *Ars Amatoria* – a poem now in
circulation for at least a decade and thus scarcely topical. The elderly
Augustus, failing in strength, recently frightened and now inclined to
quicker rages, may well have felt that this jovial celebration of affairs
outside marriage was a bad influence on the young, but the probability is that the other offence was more serious.[37]

All in all, the whole episode remains obscure, and it is understandably tempting for scholars to see a political plot concealed beneath
the sexual scandal, especially since Paullus is named as a conspirator.
Suggestions as to the nature of the intrigue have varied, depending
on whether or not he is assumed to be still in Rome; but invariably the episode is seen as an attempt to challenge the dominance
of Tiberius and his relations for the future leadership of the state.
An intriguing suggestion is that Julia and Silanus plotted to marry

– perhaps even held a ceremony which Ovid may have witnessed – and in some way force the *princeps* to advance his granddaughter's new husband to high office. Yet this is guesswork and, however appealing, other scenarios could equally well fit the meagre facts. If there was a plot, then it got nowhere and was probably naively conceived and executed from the very start. Julia may well have felt marginalised, but whether this led to her flinging herself into an affair or dangerous political talk – or both – is impossible to say. In later years, Augustus referred to the two Julias and Postumus as his 'three boils' or 'three ulcers', and perhaps their crimes really had more to do with their failure to live and act as he would wish than ambitious quests for power.[38]

The outcome was the same, and Livia's family line would dominate the succession, perhaps as much by chance as victory in a clandestine struggle for power. In AD 9 Tiberius returned to Rome and the award of a well-earned triumph for his defeat of the rebellion in the Balkans. He had done his job thoroughly if slowly, and in the later stages may have used as much conciliation as force. At least one of the senior rebel leaders was spared, and that was a rare thing in any war, let alone a rebellion. A surer proof is the fact that the risings were never again repeated, and that these regions remained stable and increasingly prosperous parts of the Roman Empire for centuries to come. The crisis seemed to be over, and peace through victory could reign again. Then news arrived of an appalling military catastrophe in Germany.

PAX AUGUSTA

'The pax augusta, which has spread to the regions of the east and of the west and to the bounds of the north and of the south, preserves every corner of the world safe from the fear of brigandage.' Velleius Paterculus, early first century AD.[1]

Arminius appeared to be a shining example of the Roman genius for absorbing conquered peoples and convincing them – or at least their leaders – that they were better off supporting Roman rule and joining the conquerors. Born somewhere around 18–15 BC, he belonged to the royal family of a Germanic people named the Cherusci, whose lands lay east of the Rhine near the River Weser. Quite a few other noblemen also carried the blood of kings, and in any case kingship played only a minor role in the loose social and political structures of the tribes, so royal birth did not guarantee supremacy. Arminius' father Segimer was simply one of the influential men vying for power among his people. It is possible that he fought against the Romans in the wars of the last years of the first century BC. If so, then he soon submitted to the invader, and it is equally possible that from the beginning Segimer saw an alliance with Rome as a means to gain advantage over his local rivals. Plenty of leaders throughout the world reacted in the same way, seeing the might of the legions as something to harness for their own ends rather than as a threat.

The young Arminius first appears as the leader of a force of auxiliary soldiers raised from his own people to fight alongside the Romans, and his younger brother Flavus soon followed him into service with the Roman army. It may be that both of them spent some time as hostages in Rome, living in Augustus' complex on the Palatine and receiving an education alongside the children of the *princeps'* family, although there is no direct evidence for this. Certainly both became fluent in Latin, which no doubt made it easier to grant them Roman citizenship, for Augustus preferred to restrict the franchise to those he felt deserved to be Roman. Arminius saw considerable service with the Roman army, campaigning probably in Germany as well as Illyricum during the great rebellion. At some point he was granted equestrian status and by AD 7 returned to his homeland to become one of the key leaders of the Cherusci – even the minimum equestrian property qualification of 400,000 sesterces was a great fortune by the standards of the new province of Germany. Wealthy, with a proven record as an ally, and used to the manners of Rome's elite, Arminius was a frequent dinner guest at the table of the imperial *legatus* in Germany, Publius Quinctilius Varus.[2]

Now in his fifties, Varus was an experienced governor who had served in Africa as proconsul and then in Syria as legate. Tiberius' colleague as consul in 13 BC, he had married in turn a daughter of Agrippa and then Augustus' great-niece, Claudia Pulchra, and was clearly seen by the *princeps* as loyal and reliable. In AD 7 he was given command of Germany, embracing the Rhine frontier and the developing province stretching to the Elbe; his task was to keep the area stable while the empire's attention and resources were devoted to dealing with the rebel Pannonians and Dalmatians. Varus had five legions and substantial auxiliary forces to back up his authority, although it is more than likely that these were depleted by detachments sent to Illyricum. In addition, the serious shortage of army recruits make it unlikely that any new drafts went to Germany. At the same time, no doubt, many ambitious and capable officers sought postings to the great war being waged in the Balkans in the hope of winning distinction. The fact that Varus was not also sent there, or to one of the provinces directly bordering on the troubled region, in turn suggests that Augustus considered him capable rather than exceptionally gifted, at least as a military commander. In 4 BC, while legate of Syria, he had marched into Judaea and put on a display of force which had crushed the disorders following the death of Herod the Great, but this operation involved little actual fighting, and as far as we can tell Varus had never taken part in a battle.[3]

Yet the signs in Germany were encouraging, not least because local noblemen like Arminius were embracing Roman rule. By this time his father seems to have died, but his uncle was another frequent guest at Varus' table, as was Segestes, a Cheruscan nobleman whose young son was a priest of the newly established cult of Rome and Augustus, based at the civic capital for the Ubii tribe (modern Cologne) founded by Agrippa. The last large-scale conflict had occurred in AD 5, and since then the peace of Germany had only been interrupted by minor outbreaks of rebellion against Rome and periodic inter-tribal violence. Under Varus, German chieftains started to settle disputes by appealing for the legate's judgement rather than raiding each other. The recently founded Romanised civilian settlements were growing, often on or near the sites of former army bases.[4]

In later years Varus was criticised for treating the province as already fully established and peaceful rather than in the process of being conquered, and for despising the inhabitants, seeing the Germans as 'human only in shape and speech, and that though they would not be subdued by the sword would nevertheless submit to law'. Yet this was very much the wisdom of hindsight, which does not mean that all of his actions were sensible or skilfully carried out. He began to impose a regular tax on the tribes, where most likely in the past they had only been subject to demands for cattle or crops when they submitted at the end of a conflict with Rome. The levy may or may not have been harsh, but it was new and inevitably resented as a sign that the Germans were not allies but subjects of Rome. Corruption was an all too frequent problem throughout the long history of Roman provincial administration, and may well have made things worse. Velleius claims that Varus was greedy, and that during his time in Syria he had gone 'to a rich province as a poor man, and left a poor province as a rich man'.[5]

Resentment of Roman rule grew, stoked by taxation, and as in Pannonia it was especially strong in the younger warriors who had never faced the legions in battle. At the same time, fear of Rome's might diminished in the face of their retreat from attacking Maroboduus and the long and difficult struggle to suppress the rebellion in Illyricum. It seemed that the Romans could be beaten, and even some of those who had done very well through allying with Rome began to wonder whether this was the wisest policy for the future. Arminius was one of them, and at some point the Roman *eques* decided to reject his new citizenship and rebel against the empire. We do not know when he made this decision or what triggered it. Anger at his own and the other tribes' loss of independence is likely enough, quite probably with distaste for their treatment by the conquering power. Although made a Roman, he may have found his fellow citizens patronising at best. His brother Flavus' name translates as 'Blond' or 'Blondie', and it is hard to tell whether this was meant as an insult or more affectionately, like such nicknames as Red, Ginger or Bluey. On the other hand we must also consider simple ambition. Arminius had risen high through association with the Romans, becoming one of the most important men in his tribe, but he may have decided that there was now little prospect of rising any further through continued loyalty. Recent events suggested that Rome was not invincible, and the man who led his own and other tribes to freedom would surely gain such immense prestige that he could win greater and more permanent power, with the prospect of becoming as strong a leader as Maroboduus. Personal ambition and desire for liberty are far from incompatible, and later events certainly suggested that Arminius yearned to rule.[6]

For the moment, though, he was cautious, planning a rebellion with care and in secrecy. In the spring and summer of AD 9 Varus began a tour of the province between the Rhine and the Elbe, taking with him three of his legions, the *Seventeenth, Eighteenth* and *Nineteenth*, supported by six cohorts of auxiliary infantry and three cavalry *alae*. It was a demonstration of Roman might rather than a campaign, since no serious resistance was expected. In response to local unrest, Varus sent small detachments to many of the villages and other communities who claimed to feel threatened and wanted protection. As he travelled he met with the noblemen in each area, listening to their petitions and arbitrating in their long and complex disputes in the normal manner of a Roman governor. By the end of the summer, the legate and his soldiers were preparing to return to winter quarters nearer the Rhine when news came of a rebellion further to the east. Arminius may well have told him of the outbreak, which he had secretly helped to arrange. Varus responded in the standard Roman way, just as he had done in Judaea in 4 BC, and immediately led his army against the rebels, and – again as in Judaea – open resistance crumbled as soon as the legions appeared.[7]

The problem apparently solved, in September Varus began the march back westwards, beginning later in the year and further away than he had planned. His supplies were surely running low, which meant that he needed to press on in some haste, but since there was no reason to expect further trouble this did not appear to be a serious problem. Given that his units were probably considerably under-strength, the column mustered at most some 10,000–15,000 fighting soldiers. There were also thousands of slaves, including those owned by the army and acting as grooms, muleteers and the like, as well as the slave and freed attendants of officers. Varus' army was travelling in some style – we know that at least one officer had an ornate couch with ivory inlay in his baggage – and so was encumbered with large numbers of pack mules and wagons. There were also civilians, some of them probably traders supplying the soldiers, others simply happy to enjoy their protection after a season spent among the tribes, and large numbers of women and children. At some point Augustus banned soldiers from marrying, but we do not know whether this occurred as part of the wider military reforms in 13 BC or AD 6 or in another year. The reason was most likely a reluctance to support families or to pay widows and orphans as much as the desire to keep the legions sufficiently mobile to be ready to be shifted from one end of the empire to another. Depending on the date of the reform, some soldiers may still have been in service with wives, having married before the ban. Others simply ignored it,

forming relationships and raising families even though it was illegal
– something to which the authorities turned a blind eye.[8]

There were no wide, properly paved Roman roads so far into
Germany, and the long column stretched for ten or more miles as
it snaked along old cart tracks through a mix of woodland, cultivated fields, meadows and marshes. Its route was predictable, for the
simple reason that it was forced to stay on the track. Local guides
provided by Arminius and other tribal leaders helped the Romans
find their way, and the column lumbered along with only the most
basic security, its commander confident that he was in friendly territory and intent mainly on making progress before the autumn rains
turned the path into a quagmire. Varus did not expect to face any
threat, and so did not look for one; he trusted the scouts provided
by the Cherusci and other tribes to give him plenty of warning in
the unlikely event of trouble. When Segestes suddenly told him that
Arminius was plotting rebellion, the imperial legate did nothing, no
doubt dismissing the story as an attempt by one ambitious chieftain
to discredit another. Arminius denied everything, and was after all a
Roman and an equestrian of proven loyalty. Most Romans – like the
leaders of most imperial powers – struggled to believe that anyone
would reject the obvious advantages of joining their conquerors and
enjoying the benefits of their 'superior' culture and dominance.[9]

A little later Arminius left the column, ostensibly going to fetch
more auxiliaries, guides or other aid. Instead he went to join the
army of warriors mustering to strike at the Romans. In the days that
followed, small parties of tribesmen began to harry vulnerable sections of the column, retreating before the Romans could muster any
sort of defence. Archaeological excavation at Kalkriese near Osnabrück revealed the site of what was probably the decisive ambush
in a series of attacks mounted over some twenty or so miles, and
shows Arminius' careful preparations. He selected a narrow pass as
a natural choke point, where the path ran through meadows with
wooded hills on one side and boggy ground on the other. Improving
on nature, the Germans felled trees to slow down the column, dug
a trench to prevent the Romans from turning off onto another track

and avoiding the ambush, and hemmed in the path on the other side
by raising a rampart for 500 yards on the slope amid the trees. This
was made partly from pieces of turf and partly from earth, and was
clearly inspired by the fieldworks routinely built by the legions.[10]

Arminius had learned a lot from his service with the Roman army,
and now employed his knowledge with ruthless skill. He had ensured
Varus would take this route, and the preparations for the ambush
must have taken days or more probably weeks. The odds were heavily stacked against the Romans, and became worse when heavy rain
started falling, slowing everything down by turning the track to mud
and making equipment awkward to handle. Varus did not cope well
with the crisis. Early on he ordered much of the baggage train to be
set on fire, a move likely to spread nervousness. Fast-moving attacks
nibbled away at the column, and the sense of desperation spread.
When they reached the carefully prepared ambush in the pass the
attacks became heavier – the Germans' wall had several sally ports
built into it to allow the warriors to surge forward and then retreat
to its shelter. Although no more than five feet high, it was enough
to take the momentum out of any charge, and gave the warriors
fighting from it a significant height advantage. Hemmed in along the
narrow path, and struck from several directions at once, the Romans
struggled to form any sort of co-ordinated fighting line.[11]

An exceptional commander might still have got them through,
bringing enough order to the chaos to mount a concerted attack
on the enemy. Varus was not such a man, and early on lost control. One of his subordinates led the cavalry off on their own, to
be surrounded and massacred on another path. Varus himself was
wounded – we do not know how badly – and soon afterwards committed suicide along with several other senior officers. His father had
similarly killed himself after Philippi, but while the Roman aristocracy could admire suicide when on the losing side in a civil war, this
was never acceptable for a commander leading an army against a foreign enemy. If their commander despaired, there was little incentive
for his men to fight on. Some, including several senior officers, surrendered, while others fled and were cut down without resistance by

the tribesmen. A few still fought, and mounted desperate attempts to break through the wall and escape the trap. Parts of the rampart collapsed during the struggle and the excavations provide cameos of the last bitter fights. The skeleton of a mule was found, the bell hanging from its collar stuffed full of grass freshly yanked up by the roots to muffle the sound, hinting at an attempt to attack in silence under cover of darkness. The remains of another mule were found where it had scrambled over the wall and then broken its neck as it fell down the other side.[12]

Efforts to break out failed, and one by one the men of Varus' army died. Many of the prisoners soon joined them, sacrificed by the jubilant Germans as thanks to the gods for their victory. Others were taken as slaves, and in the years to come some would escape or be ransomed and tell stories of the horror of those days. Varus had been given a hasty but ineffective cremation, and his buried remains were dug up and mistreated. The three legionary eagles were taken, as were many other standards and a great haul of armour, weapons and other equipment. Trophies of their success were distributed among the tribes, or sent to others encouraging them to join the rebellion. Varus' head was sent to Maroboduus, but the king of the Marcomanni preferred to keep the peace with Rome and feared Arminius as a rival, and so sent the grisly object to the Romans. It was eventually carried to Rome, properly cremated, and respectably buried.[13]

News of the catastrophe in Germany reached Rome only five days after the formal declaration of victory in Illyricum, and this at least meant that in time it should be possible to transfer troops from the Balkans to the Rhine frontier. Yet it was a far greater defeat than any of those suffered at the hands of the Pannonian and Dalmatian rebels, and drew parallels with disasters like Carrhae in 53 BC or even the great defeats inflicted by Hannibal. Three legions had been lost – more than a tenth of the entire army gone in a matter of days – and until more news arrived there was no knowing whether the other forces in Germany had also been wiped out and whether hordes of German warriors were across the Rhine and plundering Gaul.

Serious in itself, it was even more of a challenge to a *princeps* and his regime which prided itself on constant victory based on a proper relationship with the gods. Worse still, one of his armies had lost its precious eagles and created a new stain on Rome's honour, all the more damaging since recovery of standards lost in the past had been so trumpeted by Imperator Caesar Augustus. Fear and horror spread rapidly through Rome.[14]

Augustus was shocked, but seems this time to have felt more anger than despair; Dio claims some sources spoke of the *princeps* tearing his clothes in frustration. He increased patrols of the City's fourteen regions to prevent any disorder and particularly in case slaves of barbarian origin took it into their heads to riot. This was unlikely, but the visible presence of troops emphasised that the state was still in control, reassuring the nervous and intimidating the potentially unruly. An even less likely threat was posed by the Germans serving as a cavalry bodyguard to the *princeps* himself – a unit which at some point had replaced the Spanish bodyguards of his youth. These men were very publicly sent away from Rome. Another even more powerful gesture was the vowing of special games in honour of Jupiter Optimus Maximus 'if the state of the *res publica* should get better' – a typically Augustan revival of a ritual not used for more than a century. At the same time he extended the tenures of his provincial governors to ensure stability and the supervision of experienced men throughout the empire. A fresh recruiting campaign was ordered, but unsurprisingly found the well of recruits even drier than in AD 6. Conscription of citizens chosen by lot was introduced in spite of its unpopularity. Some men still tried to dodge the draft and a number were executed as warnings. In the meantime serving soldiers' terms were extended, more discharged veterans recalled, and once again slaves were purchased, given freedom and formed into special units.[15]

Tiberius was soon despatched to the Rhineland to take charge. In the meantime Augustus refused to be shaved or have his hair cut for several months, repeating the gesture of mourning he had adopted to honour the murdered Julius Caesar. This time no coin or other image showed his bearded face, and instead of the scruffy, wild-haired old man, his images continued to depict the ageless and imperturbable *princeps*. Privately he raged against Varus, and sometimes banged his head against the doors in his house, yelling, 'Quinctilius Varus, return my legions!' The dead commander was made a scapegoat, and the earliest sources also painted Arminius as a traitor. Neither view was altogether unfair, but each fell short of the whole story. In future the *princeps* marked the date of the disaster with a day of mourning. No legions were raised to replace the three lost, which in itself shows that there were barely enough recruits to top up existing units. Even in later years, when new legions were raised, the numbers seventeen, eighteen and nineteen were never revived.[16]

In the months that followed, slightly better news arrived from Germany. In the manner of irregular armies throughout history, Arminius' men had dispersed after their victory, taking their plunder home for the winter. For the moment only a few stayed in the field, joined by others inspired by their success and eager to win glory and loot for themselves. Most of the small detachments scattered around the country by Varus were lost, but when a force of warriors attacked the army base at Aliso – probably the excavated site at Haltern – their attacks were repulsed. After a gallant defence, the garrison and a large number of civilians slipped away under cover of darkness and managed a dramatic escape to the safety of the Rhine frontier. All the crossings of the river were held – and indeed do not seem to have faced a serious attack. Varus' two remaining legions and some auxiliaries were largely intact and their commanders doing their best to organise a coherent defence.[17]

THE LAST YEARS

Yet for the moment the province between the Rhine and the Elbe was lost – every excavated Roman garrison and civilian settlement in the area was abruptly abandoned at this time. Tiberius spent the next four campaigning seasons either on the Rhine or leading

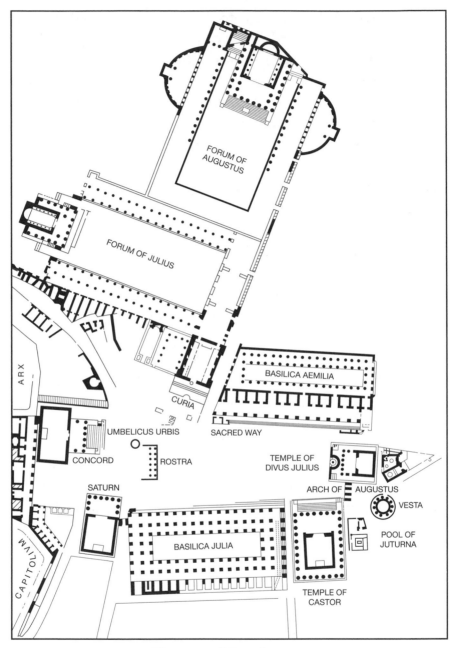

The centre of Rome by AD *14*

punitive expeditions to the east, and he was later joined by Germanicus. Few details survive of these campaigns, but they seem gradually
to have advanced further from the security of the Rhine, burning

villages, destroying crops, stealing herds and flocks, and killing or capturing anyone they could catch. The Romans called this *vastatio* – devastation – and were very good at it, but it is clear that they still faced serious opposition. As the man who had destroyed the legions, Arminius' power grew and he came to lead not only many of the Cherusci, but warriors from other tribes as well. The defeat of Varus had shattered the Romans' aura of invincibility as thoroughly as the rapid Japanese conquests of Hong Kong, Malaya and Burma in 1941–2 broke the reputation of the British Empire throughout the Far East. It is extremely difficult – perhaps impossible – to recover from such humiliating failures.[18]

The campaigns in Germany continued for the rest of Augustus' life, and it is clear that he still hoped to regain the lost province. Yet many of the achievements were more symbolic than practical. In AD 11 Tiberius and Germanicus combined their forces for the first major expedition across the Rhine, but little fighting resulted. Arminius and the other German leaders were too sensible to risk a battle on the Romans' terms, and the Roman commanders were equally cautious and so did not press the Germans too far. On 23 September, while still in enemy territory, they celebrated Augustus' birthday with a series of horse races organised by their centurions, before withdrawing to the Rhine. As yet there was no sign of winning vengeance for the defeat or recovering lost standards, but the confident advance of the Romans at least suggested that everything was under way to ensure that Rome eventually emerged victorious.[19]

An ongoing war offered Tiberius further opportunity to prove his worth and display his willingness to labour on behalf of the state. He continued to return to Rome each winter, and from either AD 9 or AD 10 he customarily took his place in the Senate or other public meetings sitting beside Augustus between the two consuls. It may well be that several of the letters written by the *princeps* to Tiberius, and later quoted by Suetonius, date to these years. His excerpts were designed to prove Augustus' affection, such as: 'I have nothing but praise for your conduct of the war, my dear Tiberius, and am sure no one could have acted more prudently in the face of so many difficulties and an army lacking in spirit.' 'When I hear and read that you are exhausted by constant labours, may the gods correct me if my own body doesn't ache in sympathy. I beg you to spare yourself, lest hearing of your illness slay your mother and me, and place the Roman people at peril . . .' 'It does not matter whether or not I am well, if you are not.' As usual, there were plenty of quotations and witty Greek tags intended to reinforce his points.[20]

In January AD 10 Tiberius dedicated the restored Temple of Concord in the Forum in his own and his brother Drusus' name, paying for the work with the profits of the wars in Germany – probably the earlier successful campaigns rather than the recent ones. The triumph awarded him for Illyricum was postponed until 12 October AD 12, and the occasion was marked by the extension of his proconsular *imperium* to cover the entire empire and not simply the western provinces where he was already running the war effort. Augustus had also been hailed as *imperator* for the defeat of the rebellion, but as usual chose not to celebrate a triumph. By the end of his life he had been hailed as *imperator* no fewer than twenty-one times – an utterly unprecedented total that was never matched in the future. Germanicus was awarded *ornamenta triumphalia* for the suppression of the Balkan rebellion and was consul for AD 12 at the age of twenty-six. He had skipped the praetorship, and Tiberius' actual son Drusus was quaestor in AD 11 and also marked down for an early consulship.[21]

Before the news of the disaster in Germany had reached Rome, one of Augustus' main concerns in AD 9 was an outburst of resentment at his legislation encouraging marriage and the raising of children. Although most agreed that this was an admirable ambition, they disliked the penalties imposed on the unmarried and the childless, which among other things restricted the ability to inherit estates from anyone outside the close family. In the past, rich childless men or women found it easy to win friends among those hoping to receive a bequest when they died. Not only was this made more difficult, but if there were no family members to inherit, then it was possible for the money and property to go to the state. Raising the three or more children encouraged by the laws was expensive, especially if funds were needed to give all of them equestrian or senatorial status, let alone provide for the expenses of a comfortable life.[22]

These laws were inevitably of most concern to the wealthy, and during the celebration of some games a group of *equites* were especially forceful in their demands for the laws to be repealed. Augustus responded with a public meeting, where he displayed Germanicus' growing family as an example, and then supposedly divided the assembled equestrians into those with children and – a far greater number – those without children. Either at this meeting or at another in the Senate he presented a speech, which was probably read out by someone else. For some time the quaestor allocated to him each year performed this task, and it is known that Germanicus also did this for him during these years. He repeated his arguments for the necessity of raising future generations, quoting at length from a famous speech delivered in the second century BC admonishing the senators of that age for failing to marry and raise enough children.[23]

The only concession Augustus made was a modified version of the law which was presented later in the year by the suffect consuls – both of whom ironically enough were single and had no children. The precise differences between the *lex Papia Poppaea* and the earlier law are difficult to understand, since later jurists conflated the two, but it is clear that it was still considered as harsh by the elite. In the long run it could not prevent the trend towards the extinction of the old aristocratic families, which ultimately had more to do with the high infant mortality rate than anything the state could control. The law did yield some revenue, and also emphasised what Augustus considered to be proper dutiful and moral behaviour for Romans – something probably especially relevant in the nervous months after the loss of Varus and his legions.[24]

These were difficult years, made worse by serious flooding in AD 12, which disrupted one of the major festivals. Caesar Augustus was old, and the prospect of a world without him loomed ever larger. Horoscopes, long an obsession of many Romans especially among the aristocracy, became even more popular. Augustus banned anyone from privately seeking forecasts from seers and astrologers, and even if a group went to consult one of these they were forbidden to ask about the end of anyone's life. At the same time the *princeps* published the details of his own birth and the star positions at the time, allowing those who were able to cast his horoscope if they chose. A year before, he also relaxed the ban on equestrians fighting as gladiators since several were ignoring it and appearing in the arena. The crowds seemed to like the appearances of wealthy men who chose to risk life and limb in this way, and even Augustus watched with every sign of enjoyment.[25]

Yet the *princeps* was not always inclined to such openness, generosity and willingness to ignore flouted laws. Around this time the books written by Titus Labienus were confiscated and publicly burnt. Grandson of the man who was Julius Caesar's lieutenant in Gaul, but had joined Pompey in 49 BC, he had the habit at public readings of his works of saying that he would skip the next passage and only permit it to be read after his death. Such dark hints seemed all the more sinister when compared to the virulent attacks he openly made on plenty of important public figures, although whether he slandered them or reminded them of past actions which now seemed indiscreet or inconvenient is harder to say. With that Roman fondness for punning, contemporaries nicknamed him Rabienus or 'rabid'. As far as we can tell he did not attack Augustus or his close family, but may well have written with favour of Pompey and other enemies of Julius Caesar. Labienus committed suicide in angry protest at the destruction of his work.[26]

The equally acerbic orator Cassius Severus boasted that he knew the destroyed works by heart. He was known for his determined and extremely aggressive prosecutions in court, but was also fond of writing pamphlets insulting prominent men and women in the fine old tradition of Roman rhetorical abuse. Once again, Augustus is unlikely to have been one of the targets, but around AD 12 he permitted a prosecution under the *maiestas* law remodelled in AD 6 and dealing with the vague concept of offences damaging the 'majesty' of the Roman state and people. It seems to have been the first time this was employed in answer to written and spoken attacks on individuals. Cassius was found guilty and sent into exile in the comparative luxury of Crete. Under Tiberius and his successors, *maiestas* became overwhelmingly concerned with perceived disloyalty to the emperor, and such trials became ever more common – as indeed did censorship. Such hindsight makes this seem a particularly sinister development, but perhaps more importantly we should note that the barrage of insults and abuse was also a sign of continuing enmities between members of the elite that had little or nothing to do with the *princeps*. Rivalry for office and honours also continued. In 11 BC the sixteen candidates for the praetorship were so closely tied that Augustus permitted all of them to hold the office, even though afterwards he reverted to the normal twelve in a year.[27]

Further measures were taken to lighten the burden of work and ceremony on the elderly Augustus. In AD 12 Germanicus read out a speech in the Senate in which the *princeps* asked that the senators no longer formally greet and bid him farewell when he arrived at and left the Forum. He also asked that they come to greet him less frequently when he was at home, and asked for their pardon if he was no longer able to dine at their homes as often as in the past. In the following year the *consilium principis*, which for so long had acted as a sounding board of senatorial opinion, was fundamentally altered. Instead of consisting of senators picked by lot and serving for six months, membership became permanent and all were selected by the *princeps*. It was also given greater authority, so that its decisions now counted as if they were decrees of the entire Senate. No doubt it was easier for the elderly Augustus to conduct a good deal of business in the comfort of his house – Dio notes that sometimes he would recline on a couch at meetings of this body.[28]

One other obvious consequence of this change was to further the influence of Tiberius and his sons, preparing the way for the succession when the *princeps* died. Yet it would be wrong to see Augustus as a mere puppet in all this. It is clear that he continued to undertake a considerable amount of work and make important decisions, even if guided by advisers and family. There were still traces of the experienced and wily politician. In AD 13 complaints grew about the five per cent inheritance tax levied to fund the *aerarium militare*. Augustus' response was to invite senators to suggest their own solutions for providing secure and steady funding for the Military Treasury – a vital thing at any time, but especially with the continuing war in Germany. Tiberius was away, and Germanicus and Drusus were instructed not to express any opinion on the matter in case this was seen as their grandfather's view. The Senate discussed the issue, and submitted a few proposals in writing to the *princeps*. None seemed practical and were essentially a hearty rejection of the current system without offering a viable alternative. Caesar Augustus then announced that he was favouring a levy on property, and sent men to begin the process of registering everyone for the new tax. A nervous Senate quickly agreed that they would be happier with the old inheritance tax rather than face so uncertain a prospect. The *princeps* declared himself equally happy to accept so sensible a decision.[29]

Also in AD 13 he was awarded another ten-year extension of his province and powers. At the same time Tiberius was finally granted these in full, and in the last years his head had begun to appear on the reverse side of coins which had Augustus on the face. The two colleagues were also granted consular powers to supervise a census which was completed by May AD 14 and enrolled 4,937,000 citizens – almost 900,000 more than were named in the first census the *princeps* had overseen in 28 BC. For Augustus, this growth was a visible sign of his success in restoring peace and prosperity to the Roman people. It was now forty-three years since the suicide of Antony, and Caesar Augustus was in his seventy-sixth year. Dio talks of omens that hinted that a change was coming. One occurred when a madman ran out to the procession of gods and symbols paraded at the games and sat in the chair of office of Julius Caesar; another when lightning struck the letter C of Caesar on the base of a statue of Augustus on the Capitoline Hill – AESAR was the Etruscan word for god and was taken to hint at impending deification. Suetonius claims that when the completion of the census was marked by the usual ceremony, an eagle flew several times above Augustus and then perched on a temple pediment just above the first letter in the name of Agrippa.

The *princeps* had been about to read out a formal vow for the welfare of the Roman people in the five years up to the next census, but instead he had Tiberius do this for him, commenting that he would not be there to see the promises through.[30]

THE FINAL JOURNEYS

At some point in the year, the *princeps* is supposed to have undertaken a long journey, sailing to the island off Sardinia where Postumus Agrippa was held. He was accompanied by only a single aristocratic attendant, the former consul Paullus Fabius Maximus, who died within the year. Many scholars dismiss the story as an invention intended to cast doubt over Augustus' true feelings over the succession. Yet it is hard to believe that tales could circulate claiming that he had left Rome for so long a period unless this was at least plausible, and so it may have occurred. It may also be true that Augustus and his grandson – once his son – had a tearful reunion. What is clear is that this made no difference to his plans. The *princeps* had drawn up his will the previous year and lodged it with the Vestals, and made no attempt to change it. Tiberius was primary heir to two-thirds of his estate, with Livia receiving the remaining third. Agrippa was not named other than to stipulate that he and the two Julias were not to be interred in Augustus' Mausoleum.[31]

The census had kept Tiberius in Italy for most of the year, but late in the summer he was to go to Illyricum on a brief tour to check that the province was still stable and secure. No doubt there were plenty of petitions and local disputes to answer, but there is no suggestion of any threat to the overall peace of the region. It was simply a convenient distance at which he could perform a useful and prestigious task and yet still be able to return to Rome for the winter. Augustus and Livia accompanied him on the start of his journey, planning to go as far as Beneventum in part because the *princeps* wanted to attend games in his honour to be held in Naples. The party travelled south-west to the port of Astura, where they took ship – breaking his habit of sailing only in the daytime because the wind was favourable. Overnight Caesar Augustus fell ill with stomach trouble that manifested itself as diarrhoea.[32]

It did not seem especially serious, and the ship sailed on southwards along the coast to Capri, where he kept a villa – the one with the collection of fossils. As they approached the major port of Puteoli, they were passed by a merchant ship from Alexandria, whose crew and passengers greeted him almost as worshippers. Clad in white, crowned with garlands, they burned incense – perhaps already engaged in an offering to mark their safe arrival. Enthusiastically they called out to Caesar Augustus that it was 'through him they lived, through him they sailed, and through him they enjoyed freedom and prosperity'. The *princeps* was delighted, and gave each of his party forty gold *aurei* (a sum equivalent to 1,000 denarii or 4,000 sesterces) with the instruction that they should spend it only on goods from Alexandria.[33]

He spent four days relaxing on Capri and seemed now to be recovering from his illness. His festive spirit and fondness for parties and jokes prompted him to give out Greek costume to his Roman companions, and Roman costume to his Greek friends. He would then bid them all to wear them. As part of the game, the Romans were to speak Greek and the Greeks were to speak Latin. During these days he watched with interest the exercises of the local *ephebes*, a legacy of the long-standing Greek settlement and influence in the area. These youths went through a vaguely military training of fitness and drills – the *ephebeia* – before they were acknowledged as fully adult citizens of their communities. Augustus gave them a feast, during which he threw tickets for prizes, such as fruit and delicacies, to the crowd, and encouraged them to joke, even at his expense. On another day he joked with one of Tiberius' entourage, asking the man to suggest the author of the couple of lines of poetry he had just composed as if they were quotes.

Still troubled by periodic attacks of diarrhoea, Augustus felt well enough to cross to Naples and watch the games honouring him. After that, he journeyed with Tiberius as far as Beneventum and there bade him farewell. Turning for home, Caesar Augustus had made only the short journey to his villa at Nola before the illness returned more severely. It was the country house where his father had died, and perhaps this coincidence more readily convinced him that the end was near. A message was sent recalling Tiberius, who most probably had followed the Appian Way towards the great port at Brundisium. Our sources disagree over whether or not the *princeps'* adopted son reached his father before he died, but Suetonius, who presents the most detailed and convincing account, claims that he did. They spent a long time alone together discussing affairs of state. Yet when Tiberius left, it was claimed that attendants heard Augustus mutter, 'Oh unlucky Roman People, to be masticated by such slow jaws.'[34]

After this meeting the *princeps* did not speak of any affairs of state, but did boast again that he had found Rome made of mud brick and left it in marble – no doubt reflecting the solidity of the peace and prosperity he had created as much as the physical rebuilding of the City. We do not know how many days he lingered. Dio says that he ate only figs from a tree he had cultivated in the garden – and also mentions the rumour that Livia smeared some with poison and gave them to Augustus, while she ate only unsullied ones. Such stories – much like his alleged jibe at Tiberius – are likely to date from the years when Tiberius was deeply unpopular, and make little sense. The death of a man who had never been robust and was now very elderly by the standards of the ancient world makes any explanation other than natural causes utterly unnecessary. Weakened by his inability to eat, most likely the *princeps'* heart simply gave out.[35]

Suetonius goes into some detail about his final day, 19 August AD 14, and although we do not know his ultimate source, his account has the ring of truth. At the very least, it represents how it was felt a good emperor should meet his end. Several times Caesar Augustus asked whether there were disturbances outside, apparently worried either about a display of affection or afraid of spreading unrest which might threaten the stability of the state and the ease of succession. Conscious of his appearance, he called for a mirror and instructed a slave to comb his hair into order and help him adjust his jaw – a more controlled version of the dying Julius Caesar pulling his toga up to cover his head. Thus composed, he told them to let in some of his friends, asking them whether they felt that he had played his part well in the mime or comedy of life. Then he slipped into Greek and spoke some lines which may have been a direct quote, or perhaps his own invention of the type of thing said by an actor leaving the stage at the end of a performance:

> Since well I've played my part, all clap your hands,
> And from the stage dismiss me with applause.[36]

The tone of the story makes it clear that Augustus expected approval and applause. There is no hint of last-minute doubt, but Dio may be right to see gentle irony and an admission that even the most successful life ends with the grave. Then he dismissed them, but before they left he asked some recent arrivals from Rome for news of Livilla, the wife of Tiberius' son Drusus, who had recently been ill.[37]

Left with Livia and his close attendants, there was a moment of agitation when Augustus called out that he was being carried off by forty young men. Suetonius notes that this was the number of praetorian guardsmen who would carry his corpse, but since the *princeps* had left detailed plans for his own funeral the idea may already have been in his head. He died at the ninth hour – that is nine hours after dawn, so late afternoon or early evening by our reckoning – held in Livia's arms and kissing her for the last time. His last words to her were: 'Livia, remember our married life, and farewell.'

Imperator Caesar Augustus, son of the divine Julius and 'father of his country', was dead. Livia may have delayed announcing his death until preparations for what followed were confirmed, although this claim may simply be part of the wider invention of a conspiracy surrounding the death of the *princeps*.[38]

There was one more journey for the body of the *princeps*, based on the funeral preparations for Agrippa, Drusus and all the others of

his family who had died while away from Rome. Beginning during
the night so that they could avoid the heat of an August day, the
town councillors of Nola carried the corpse in state at the start of its
journey to Rome. Each day it was laid to rest in the coolness of the
basilica of a town en route, whose leaders took over the task each
night of bearing it on to the next major community. Everywhere
there were public displays of mourning and respect – few people
could remember the times before Augustus had led the state. A
party of leading equestrians met the cortège at Bovillae, just south
of Rome and the old site of Alba Longa, and took it on into the City,
where it was placed in the vestibule of Augustus' complex on the
Palatine.[39]

The Senate debated how best to honour him, and as in the past
most of their proposals were rejected as excessive. Augustus' close
family made the few arrangements for his funeral that he had not already determined. It began, as aristocratic funerals had always done,
with a gathering in the Forum. A date of 8 September is a plausible
suggestion, but cannot be proved. Although it was a far more ordered affair than the funeral of Julius Caesar, his close association
with this spot was no doubt in everyone's minds as they came to pay
their respects to his son. Actors wore the funeral masks of Augustus'
ancestors as was the custom, but others wore the images and insignia of other unrelated great men from Rome's history. Pompey was
among them, and many – perhaps all – of the *summi viri* from the
precinct of the Forum Augustum were there to honour the passing
of the greatest Roman of them all. Caesar Augustus was more than
simply another aristocrat – he was the second founder of the City,
the man who had restored Rome to peace, prosperity and a proper
relationship with the gods, and so in death as in life he claimed association with all the great deeds and heroic leaders of the past.

Julius Caesar's image was not included, since he was a god now,
and no mere man, but that did not mean that he was neglected or
that his memory was suppressed. Tiberius mounted the Rostra outside the Temple of the Divine Julius to deliver the first eulogy. He
was dressed in a dark tunic and toga of mourning, as was his son

Drusus, who delivered a second eulogy, this time from the 'old' Rostra, which in turn had been remodelled by Julius Caesar and Augustus. All around in every direction were the symbols of Augustus on monuments and buildings. The Senate was present, and the magistrates-elect for the next year, wearing just their tunics and without togas, carried the body to the Campus Martius. All along the route were more reminders of the glory and building projects of the *princeps*. Augustus' body was concealed inside a coffin, no doubt because after several weeks in late summer it was not in the best condition; instead a neat and flawless wax effigy of him as a triumphing general was carried on top of it, reclining on a couch of ivory and gold. There were also two gold images of him in the procession, one brought by the senators from the Curia Julia which he had restored, and another carried in a triumphal chariot.[40]

A pyre was waiting on the Campus Martius, and the coffin placed upon it. Rome's senior priests then processed around it. After them, selected equestrians ran around the pyre, followed by praetorian guardsmen, some of whom threw their military decorations onto the coffin, just as Julius Caesar's soldiers had done at his funeral. Then praetorian centurions tossed lit torches onto the pile of wood, which was carefully prepared and quickly caught fire. At that moment an eagle was released from within the structure and flew away into the air, symbolising the ascent of the *princeps'* spirit to heaven to join his father among the gods. A former praetor later took a public oath to say that he had clearly seen Augustus' form ascending to the sky.[41]

For five days the elderly Livia remained near the spot – perhaps in some temporary shelter. She was attended by some of her household and by leading equestrians. At the end of that period these men, barefoot and with their tunics unbelted so that they hung down low around their ankles, gathered the ashes and remains of bone into an urn. This was carried to and placed within the Mausoleum, the monumental tomb that Augustus had begun building almost fifty years earlier.

CONCLUSION

HURRY SLOWLY

'Democracy, indeed, has a fair-appearing name . . . Monarchy . . . has an unpleasant sound, but is a most practical form of government to live under. For it is easier to find a single excellent man than many of them . . . for it does not belong to the majority of men to acquire virtue . . . Indeed, if ever there has been a prosperous democracy, it has in any case been at its best for only a brief period.' *Dio, early third century* AD.[1]

Augustus 'seduced the army by bounties, the people by the free corn dole, the whole world by the comfort of peace, and then gradually assumed the power of the Senate, the magistrates, and the making of law. There was no opposition, for the bravest men had fallen in the line of battle or to proscription lists . . .' *Tacitus, early second century* AD.[2]

Public business was largely suspended while the cortège moved towards Rome and during the funeral ceremonies themselves, although the Senate did convene to listen to Augustus' will. Tiberius and Livia were named as his principal heirs, although, in the normal Roman way, other more distant family members were named as secondary heirs in case they predeceased them. He also bequeathed the vast sum of forty-three million sesterces to the state, as well as individual bounties to every citizen and to the army. An ordinary soldier in the praetorian guard received 1,000 sesterces, the members of the paramilitary urban cohorts and *vigiles* each 500 sesterces, while legionaries and the freedmen soldiers raised during the emergencies of AD 6 and AD 9 each got 300 sesterces. In every case the scale for officers would have been much higher, and the generosity was a clear

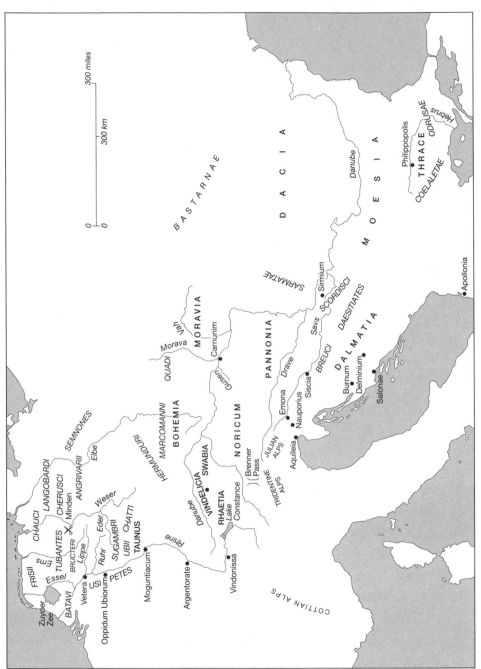

The Rhine and Danube frontiers

acknowledgement that supremacy ultimately relied on retaining the exclusive loyalty of the army. Augustus had never ceased to be the warlord he had become in his nineteenth year.[3]

Tiberius already possessed all of the important powers of Augustus, including the *maius imperium* and the *tribunicia potestas*. From the beginning he naturally issued orders to the praetorians and other units in Rome, and wrote to the commanders of the provincial armies. In practical terms the state had gone from having two *principes* to once again having a single *princeps*. It was not a question of inheriting Augustus' powers as adopted son or heir, since Tiberius had them in his own right. Yet appearances were important, and just as Augustus 'laid down' his powers in January 27 BC and resigned the consulship in July 23 BC only to be persuaded by the Senate to resume leadership of the commonwealth, so Tiberius wished to be called to his role. The two men were of very different characters, and this time the performance was less slick, or perhaps less well orchestrated. Tiberius' awkward manner and over-complicated rhetorical style confused many as to his real intentions, but in the end the senators were able to 'convince' him that he must assume all the responsibilities of his much-lamented father.

On 17 September the Senate had declared Augustus to be a god, so Tiberius was now properly Tiberius Julius Caesar Augustus *divi filius*. It was stipulated in the will that he must take the name Augustus, but the new *princeps* refused to let the Senate confirm this by a vote. Instead he maintained that he employed the name only in accordance with his father's wishes and to honour him. Similarly he refused an automatic award of the title *pater patriae*. Yet, just like his display of reluctance in the Senate, such modesty did little to hide his willingness to assume the supreme role, a decision already made when he was granted each individual power by Augustus.[4]

There was no serious alternative. News of the death of Augustus sparked mutinies among some of the legions on the Danube and afterwards on the Rhine. The causes were boredom, the long-delayed discharges for men well past their terms of service, and all the frustrations imposed by harsh discipline combined with the uncertainty of a world without the man who had paid them and to whom they had taken an oath of loyalty. In the main the mutineers wanted no more than improved conditions and other immediate privileges. On the Rhine there was briefly talk of proclaiming their commander Germanicus as *princeps* instead of Tiberius, but this quickly came to nothing. The adopted son was just as loyal as a Roman son should be, and there was no real enthusiasm for a return to civil war.

Almost as soon as Augustus had died a centurion of the praetorian guard set out for the island on which Agrippa Postumus was confined. Once there, the officer killed Augustus' grandson, although allegedly not without a struggle, for he was young and strong. When the centurion and his party returned to Rome and reported to Tiberius as his commander, the latter strenuously denied having given any such order. We cannot know whether or not the new *princeps* was telling the truth. Speculation at the time and ever since has sometimes claimed that he was lying, or has put the blame on Livia instead. Others have held Augustus responsible, so that almost his last order would have evoked the ruthless triumvir he had once been, with one last case of *moriendum esse*. Tacitus was sceptical, claiming that on no other occasion did he kill any of his close family. Tiberius obviously gained most immediate advantage from the death since it removed a potential rival, but we can never know who actually gave the order. Before the year was out his former wife Julia was also dead, her end hastened by living conditions made harsher on his instructions.[5]

The dreadfully high death toll among Augustus' extended family continued in the years that followed. Germanicus died in AD 19 while in the eastern provinces and, although there were rumours of poisoning by a jealous Tiberius or Livia, he was probably yet another victim of ill fortune. Drusus died in AD 23, and this time it was most likely murder and the culprits his wife (the sister of Germanicus and Claudius, and Drusus' first cousin) and her lover, the ambitious commander of the praetorian guard, Lucius Aelius Sejanus. The latter's machinations helped to discredit Germanicus' widow and sons. Agrippina – the last of Julia's children – and her two older sons were subsequently arrested and exiled, all dying in captivity. Livia survived her husband by fifteen years, although relations with her son became more and more difficult. She eventually died in AD 29 at the age of eighty-six, but received few honours from Tiberius and was not deified until the reign of her grandson Claudius.

In the early weeks Tiberius spoke a good deal of his desire for senators to play a greater role in aiding his leadership, but in practice his actions tended to centralise power even further. One of his first decisions was to transfer elections from the Popular Assemblies to the Senate, leaving the Saepta as no more than an ornamental park and venue for public entertainments. While it is true that Augustus had always been able to secure the election of his chosen candidates, the history of his principate showed plenty of occasions of genuine – and sometimes corrupt and even violent – competition for the remaining posts, as well as a tendency for the electorate to vote in ways he did not want. Yet there was no real public resistance to the change, and senators preferred having to win over only their peers instead of a larger electorate. The quality of magistrates does not appear to have altered for better or worse as a result of this reform.[6]

Unlike Augustus, Tiberius was unwilling to embark on tours of the provinces and in time he grew weary even of the day-to-day meetings with senators and others in Rome itself. In AD 26 he left Rome, retiring the next year to the villa on Capri and never returning to the City in the remaining ten years of his life. From AD 14–16 Germanicus continued to command on the Rhine but was then recalled and sent to the east. Drusus was mainly kept in Rome and, after the death of Germanicus, there was no attempt to use him for major tours of the provinces. Instead, these were left to the charge of their governors, many of whom remained in office for unusually long periods, but none of whom were instructed to fight aggressive wars. Augustus had left advice to keep the boundaries of the empire where they were and, even if he had not meant it to be more than a temporary pause to recover from the troubles of AD 6 and AD 9, Tiberius chose to follow this as a doctrine throughout his life. In contrast to Augustus' principate there were fewer campaigns and far fewer public celebrations of victory, nor were many new monuments built from spoils. Tiberius spent far less on building projects and entertainment in Rome than he had done while Augustus was alive.[7]

The principal sources for these years are Tacitus and Suetonius, both of whom portrayed him as vindictive and cruel, and implied secret perversions – in short, only marginally less of a monster than the likes of Caligula and Nero. Modern scholars have generally rejected this prejudice and, if a little inclined to be too generous to him, rightly point out that in the main Tiberius' supremacy was a time of peace and stability, especially in the provinces. If there were few aggressive wars, foreign affairs were generally successful. Arminius survived being defeated in battle by Germanicus, but when left alone turned his aggression against Maroboduus rather than the Romans. The king of the Marcomanni was defeated and fled to live as an exile within the empire, his own confederation of tribes breaking up. Around the time that Germanicus died, Arminius was murdered by some of his own chieftains who resented his power, and the peoples he had united once again fragmented into disunited and mutually hostile groups. It would be several generations before another such charismatic leader appeared on either the Rhine or Danubian frontier, and thus two perceived dangers were removed without the need for Roman action.

For twenty-three years the empire was generally stable, with problems on the frontiers and within a handful of provinces being kept under control, and in this respect Tiberius' decisions seem to have been sound. Most of his successors would follow his example and not tour the empire as Augustus had done, and, like Tiberius, they would not send senior family members to perform this task in their stead. For many, this was because they did not have anyone suitable – or at least any relative they were willing to trust. Augustus' concept of more than one *princeps* was only occasionally revived, and even more rarely successful. In itself this did not seem to matter, even if it did mean that in the future expansion was limited. Although this was a profound change from Rome's past, it is hard to say whether the impact on the political system, economy and society was good or bad.

Much more serious was Tiberius' gradual withdrawal from public life – he could only interact with senators and envoys from the empire and beyond if they came to him and waited their turn at Capri. Even while in Rome at the start of his reign he had become increasingly dependent on Sejanus, trusting him as he was unwilling to trust anyone else. In part this was because he was an equestrian and so not considered likely to harbour too much ambition. Agrippa had come from a similar background, but embarked on a senatorial career with the aid of Augustus and consistently proved himself as a highly successful general and administrator. Sejanus showed no interest in such things, but nevertheless his role rapidly grew from simple command of the praetorians to become the *princeps'* most important adviser. When Tiberius moved away from the City, Sejanus effectively controlled access to him. Drusus and the sons of Germanicus were removed, as were sufficient prominent men to discourage the others. Great use was made of the *maiestas* law, which was now liberally interpreted and rigorously enforced for the least apparent slight to the *princeps*. In AD 31 Tiberius held the consulship – although he did not come to Rome – and took Sejanus as colleague, subsequently awarding him proconsular *imperium* and thus giving every sign of advancing him to the status of fellow *princeps* and heir. At the last minute he changed his mind, and Sejanus was arrested and executed in a bloody purge which claimed many more victims among Rome's elite.

Tiberius' principate created a climate of fear among the senators and senior equestrians that evoked old memories of the civil wars and proscriptions and never really receded under his successors. The mood was very different from Augustus' day, and only in part because he had created enough fear during the triumvirate to deter all but the most bold or unwise conspirators. More importantly, Augustus took care to know the most important men in the state, mixing with them socially and treating them with respect. The unintentional consequence of Tiberius' social awkwardness and eventual retreat from the City was to make it harder and harder for later *principes* to cultivate the same easy style. Livia's son may or may not have been the bad man depicted in our sources, but in this respect at least he proved to be a bad *princeps*. Under him the monarchy became less veiled, and the aspect of a court and courtiers surrounding him became more obvious. Sejanus rose as high as he did purely through the favour of the *princeps* and without ever proving his talents as soldier or magistrate.[8]

OCTAVIUS, CAESAR AND AUGUSTUS

This is not a book about Augustus' successors, nor the changes they made to the nature of the principate, for these are big topics in their own right. The judgement of the Romans themselves was that he was superior to almost all of them, and much later it became the custom to hope that each emperor would be 'better [*melior*] than Trajan, and luckier [*felicior*] than Augustus' in reference to the premature loss of so many of his close family. In spite of a nostalgic fondness for the aristocratic leadership of the Republic, which most often manifested itself in praise of Brutus and Cassius, senators showed no resentment and certainly no serious opposition to the reality of the principate. Only following the murder of Caligula did the Senate briefly talk about a return to the Republic, but the idea was quickly dismissed and they instead turned to deciding who should be chosen as *princeps*. The acknowledgement that the principate worked was universal and only a little grudging. What mattered was whether or not the emperor was a good man and a good ruler, both of which were judged on a combination of domestic and foreign success, and that he treated the senatorial order with appropriate respect. Thus the Augustan system of government was unchallenged and Augustus himself became the foremost model of a good *princeps*. There could be few clearer indications of his success.[9]

Then and now the man himself was much harder to judge, for he was too many different things to permit an easy verdict. Ambition drove him throughout his life. At some point – perhaps not until the murder of Julius Caesar, but we cannot say – he determined to be first in the state, and everything he did was directed to this end. To achieve this he had no hesitation in resorting to violence, and so in the years that followed he killed and terrorised, switching alliances as it suited the moment. Ambition was in the blood of any Roman aristocrat, but never before had it been quite so untrammelled by convention nor so openly aimed at winning permanent unrivalled supremacy – but then never before had someone been heir to Julius Caesar, dictator for life and laden with honours greater than any Roman had ever received in the past. The situation in which the young Augustus found himself was as unprecedented as his actions, but his motivation at the very least had strong roots in the traditions of his social class.

Nakedly and unrestrainedly ambitious, Augustus became more generous to his enemies as his eventual success came closer. His clemency was more studied than that of Julius Caesar, but real nonetheless and especially during the war with Antony he killed opponents only when it seemed necessary (in his own judgement of course) and pardoned wherever he felt it was safe to do so. This does not seem to have been the case earlier, when he showed little or no mercy to any enemy. In a strange way, the restraint of a killer who stops killing can be more gratefully received than the automatic mercy of someone determined to pardon whenever possible – his opponents had not quite known what to make of the clemency of Julius Caesar. After Actium, Augustus largely stopped killing other Romans, with just a few exceptions following real or alleged con-spiracies, and even then there were no widespread purges. There is nothing to suggest that this restraint was imposed on him by anyone other than himself. It made good political sense, since it was surely easier to deal with a confident and well-disposed elite, but some of his successors executed far more readily than Augustus and still managed to stay in power for long periods. Pragmatic or not, his behaviour was ultimately his own choice, and we should admire Au-gustus for it just as much as we condemn him for the savagery of his earlier career.

There is no sense of any deeply held plans or projects in those early years, and certainly no hint that the idea for the regime he would one day create was already taking shape in his mind. Instead his activity was devoted solely to the immediate end of winning power and defeating his enemies, and probably left no time for anything else. During these years he advertised his connection with Julius Caesar, celebrated the latter's achievements, sought vengeance for his murder, and at the same time acquired power for himself. Later, in the thirties BC, he began to show more concern for the wider good, beginning to repair and add to the monuments and infrastructure of Rome, and to regulate the food supply of the City. Once again this was sensible politics, but the dedication with which he continued to act in this way after Actium suggests far more than the desire for immediate popularity. Augustus pursued power ruthlessly, but once he achieved it showed a great desire to make things work properly, whether it was the food or water supply, the road system, the various magistracies, or the administration of Rome itself, Italy and the provinces. The resources lavished on repairing old temples and building new ones were intended to restore a proper relationship with the gods who had once made Rome great and could do so again. Like so much of his innermost personality, we cannot know the real beliefs that underlay this concerted policy, but at the very least he wanted to be seen to be doing something about it, and more than likely the urge was genuine. Similarly the efforts to improve the conduct and morals of Rome's elite were based on the widely held belief that their bad behaviour had deserved as well as caused the turmoil of the late Republic, and that better conduct would accordingly bring better fortune for the state.

Augustus pursued power relentlessly and then clung to it, whatever he might pretend in public. Such ambition is surely the hallmark of any successful political leader – and no doubt plenty of less successful ones. Yet in his case he made use of that power for the common good. He worked hard to make the *res publica* function again, and we cannot deny that he succeeded, since the peace and stability he imposed brought ever greater levels of prosperity. At a basic level more people were better-off under his principate than they had been for several generations. The concerns he dealt with were traditional ones, even if some of his methods were innovative. Julius Caesar had tried to address several of these issues, as had others, but none had the chance to deal with them as thoroughly as Augustus. In the process he made sure that it was well known that he was working for the common good, but once again such advertising was what any Roman politician would have done. By doing favours for individuals and whole communities he placed them in his debt, and so, as so often, personal advantage was intertwined with the wider good. That does not alter the fact that he did rule well, whatever his motivation.

His own position developed gradually. From 30 BC he effectively monopolised the control of military force and so was in modern terms a military dictator, however carefully he avoided the title itself. The changes to his legal status do not seem to have formed part of any gradual plan. Each was carefully considered and skilfully prepared before it was implemented, but then modified by trial and error. At the same time, every year reinforced the infiltration of his name and image into every aspect of public, and a good deal of private, life. Augustus was everywhere in a way never before matched over an area the size of the Roman Empire. Alongside this prominence came the burden of receiving a constant stream of embassies and petitions from the provinces and beyond the frontiers. Dealing with so many of these in person, or through a close associate or relative, ensured that he received the loyalty of many individuals and communities, especially those granted a favour. The price he paid was spending hour after hour, day after day, working hard to understand and judge matters of often very local importance.

Caesar Augustus was a military dictator who seized control of the state, and his eventual popularity should never hide this truth. His career was only possible because of the chaos in the Roman commonwealth during the first century BC and would have been unimaginable in earlier times. There is little point in speculating about what might have happened if Brutus and Cassius had won at Philippi, or if Augustus had died fighting Sextus Pompey or Antony, or from one of his many bouts of illness. Such things may make entertaining after-dinner conversations for enthusiasts, but rely on far too many imponderables to have any historical worth. Augustus won, and lived into old age, and we can never know what might have been if he had not, or if he had chosen a very different style of rule to the one he adopted.

Similarly we should be careful before drawing hasty parallels with our own day and age. The apparent institutional inertia at the heart of many Western democracies has echoes of the last decades of the Republic, when the leaders of the Senate were too busy with their own rivalries to face the serious problems that all acknowledged existed. If aspects of this seem similar, then much more is very different: the Roman Republic was in a far worse state since its politics had become so violent. Its fate is a reminder that no system, even one that was successful for such a long time, is free from the danger of decay and collapse, but there is a long way to go before we plumb such depths. Although that fate is certainly possible, there is nothing to make us believe that it is inevitable; we have not yet come to a situation where a modern Julius Caesar or Augustus might appear, and for this we should be very glad. For all the talents of these men, each had given orders which led to the deaths of thousands in the civil wars, and unless we are willing to speak of ends justifying any means, then this cost must always be set against their achievements. They were also unusually efficient and benevolent by the standards of warlords and dictators, and most have proved far less pleasant.

Augustus was the man who signed the proscriptions and the man whose self-restraint turned down so many of the excessive honours voted to him by the Senate. He was the man who stole another's wife and whose lifelong faithfulness to her was marred by numerous adulteries, and also the man who proclaimed old-fashioned morality and the virtues of marriage. He was the man who exiled his daughter, granddaughter and grandson, and told others that they should raise families. As a youth he broke law and precedent to recruit a private army against a properly elected consul, and later made laws and agreed to be bound by them. If there is a theme, then it is that on the whole his conduct improved as he got older.

The contradictions remain, as does the simple fact that he was a warlord who fought his way to supremacy by killing fellow citizens and remained supreme because no one could ever match his military strength. The mature statesman hailed as 'father of his country', and the elderly *princeps* cheered by the Alexandrian sailors for letting them sail and live in peace, controlled the army and kept it loyal to him alone. Everything else he achieved in his life was based on his success as a warlord and we should never forget this, but nor should we deny that, as military dictators go, Caesar Augustus was not such a bad one, at least in the sense that, once established, he ruled well. For all the contradictions, to that extent his mime was surely deserving of applause.

APPENDIX ONE

The Senatorial Career or *Cursus Honorum*

A career in public life combined military and civilian responsibilities as a man undertook a series of elected magistracies. Augustus was to alter the responsibilities and their importance, and therefore it is useful to look at the career pattern at the time of his birth and his death.

The senatorial career in 63 BC

MINIMUM AGE	MAGISTRACY	NUMBER	RESPONSIBILITIES
			In theory ten years' military service. Usually this came through serving as a military tribune or on the staff of a governor who was a relative or family friend.
30	quaestor	20	Financial administration in Rome and the provinces. Each provincial governor was given a quaestor as his second-in-command. A quaestor was automatically enrolled as a senator.

MINIMUM AGE	MAGISTRACY	NUMBER	RESPONSIBILITIES
–	tribune of the plebs	10	Only open to plebeians and not compulsory. Tribunes were sacrosanct and charged with protecting the people. They could veto the act of any magistrate and could present legislation to the Popular Assembly (*Concilium plebis*).
36	aedile	4	Optional office, two of which were reserved for plebeians. Administrative role in Rome including supervision of some annual festivals, and overseeing the grain supply and public archives.
39	praetor	8	Judicial and administrative functions at Rome, where praetors presided over all the major courts. After their year of office usually sent as governor (propraetor or often proconsul) to a province.

MINIMUM AGE	MAGISTRACY	NUMBER	RESPONSIBILITIES
42	consul	2	Most senior executive officers of the Republic. They remained in Rome for their year of office, holding precedence on alternate months. Most presented legislation to the Popular Assemblies. After their year of office they would normally receive an important province as proconsuls.
–	censor	2 every five years	Usually former consuls, this was a prestigious post charged with overseeing the census of citizens and their property, as well as reviewing the senatorial roll.

Sulla had modified the *cursus* and restated the age requirements. The stated ages were the minimum needed to seek election to each magistracy. For all magistracies except the tribunes of the plebs, the year of office began on 1 January and ended on 31 December. Tribunes took up office on 10 December.

The senatorial career in AD 14

MINIMUM AGE	MAGISTRACY	NUMBER	RESPONSIBILITIES
Late teens	vigintivirate	20	Minor administrative duties in Rome.

MINIMUM AGE	MAGISTRACY	NUMBER	RESPONSIBILITIES
Early twenties	military tribune	24	One senior tribune from a senatorial family served in each legion except those stationed in Egypt. For a while Augustus also gave two such men joint command of a cavalry *ala*.
25	quaestor	20	Financial role reduced and now restricted to provinces governed by senatorial proconsuls. In Rome they assisted the consuls in organising senatorial sessions. Also oversaw public archives in Rome.
–	aedile*	6	Lost responsibilities for games, grain supply and public archives. Continued to perform other administrative functions.
–	tribune of the plebs*	10	These lost right of veto and of presenting legislation to the Popular Assembly. They continued to receive appeals from citizens and could become involved in legal cases.

* It was compulsory for plebeians to hold either the aedileship or tribunate. Patricians were permitted to omit these offices.

MINIMUM AGE	MAGISTRACY	NUMBER	RESPONSIBILITIES
30	praetor	12	Judicial role in charge of major courts. Now also responsible for festivals and games.
–	legionary legate	c.22	Command of each legion apart from those stationed in Egypt.
–	proconsul	c.10	Governor of one of the provinces overseen by the Senate.
42 (33)*	consul	2†	Senior executive officers of the state able to present legislation to the Popular Assembly and to preside over meetings of the Senate. In practice eclipsed by Augustus and Tiberius, who sat between them in the Senate.
–	provincial legate	c.9	Governors of the imperial provinces apart from Egypt and minor provinces such as Judaea. Each was garrisoned by one or more legions.

* Officially the Sullan minimum age of 42 remained a legal requirement. In practice, the lower limit of 33 appears often to have applied. It is not clear whether this was universal or due to specific exemptions.
† Occasionally supplemented by suffect consuls appointed to replace the elected consuls after these either died in office or resigned.

APPENDIX TWO

Date of the Birth of Jesus

The date and circumstances of the birth of Jesus of Nazareth rely entirely on the Gospel accounts. It is not mentioned by any other sources until much later, and these later accounts were certainly influenced by – and probably wholly dependent on – the Gospels. This is in contrast to the Crucifixion, which is mentioned in other early sources, but should not surprise us in any way, as there was no reason for Greek or Roman accounts to mention the birth of anyone in the provinces. Information about even famous Romans is also often wholly absent or vague. We cannot be sure of the date of birth of Julius Caesar. It was probably in 100 BC, but since the opening sections are missing from both the biographies written by Suetonius and Plutarch, this is a best guess, and some scholars have suggested 102 BC. The stories associated with Augustus' birth were all written down much later, after his subsequent importance was known.[1]

Of the Gospels, only Matthew and Luke describe the Nativity. These works are conventionally dated to the final quarter of the first century AD, although there is little direct evidence for this. It is fair to say that they could not be later, but it is possible that they are earlier. Mark is believed to be earlier – perhaps by a decade – and does not describe Jesus' birth, and neither does John, which is accepted as the last of the four accounts to be written. It is important to remember that the Gospels were not intended as histories of the times, but to convey a theological message. Thus they described those aspects of Jesus' life that were important in that respect, and only mention other events to serve that purpose – for instance there is very little in total about his childhood, and nothing at all about his adult life until he began his ministry. An historian – or a biographer – craves details of this sort, as well as as much context and background as possible, but this was simply not the focus of the Gospels. By comparison, we should note that we rarely know much about the lives of leading Romans until they became politically significant. For the moment it is worth noting that we should be careful before basing rigid theories on asides made by the Gospel writers which were probably never meant to be precise.

Matthew 2: 1 firmly dates the Nativity to the reign of Herod the Great. Luke 1: 5 specifically dates the birth of John the Baptist to Herod's lifetime, and by implication dates the birth of Jesus to the same period. Herod died in 4 BC, making it likely that Jesus was born some time in the preceding year or two, around 6–5 BC, or in the early months of 4 BC. It has also been suggested that the position of the stars in 7 BC would have had particular significance for Zoroastrian astrologers – the most probable identification of Matthew's wise men from the east – and so this year has been suggested. I do not feel sufficiently qualified in such matters to judge this claim, but any of these years would tie in with the Crucifixion occurring some time during the prefecture of Pontius Pilate, from AD 26–36.

Luke 2: 1–2 poses a problem, since it famously asserts that 'there went out a decree from Caesar Augustus, that all the world should be taxed. (And this taxing was first made when Cyrenius was governor of Syria).' As stated earlier, no other source mentions a single decree imposing a census and levy throughout the provinces. This does not mean that we can say with absolute certainty that Augustus never issued such a decree, but does mean that we should be cautious about accepting this purely on one piece of evidence. There was no reason for Luke to be careful in precisely describing the administrative mechanisms of taxation within the Roman Empire, even assuming that he understood such things, given how few people today really understand all aspects of the taxation systems in their own countries. What is clear is that under Augustus the taxation system of the empire was tidied up – much like many other aspects of government. As part of this process most – perhaps all – provinces were subjected to one or more censuses which assessed liability for taxation. In many cases it was for the first time, at least under direct Roman rule. Such assessments were distinct from the traditional Roman census, which dealt exclusively with Roman citizens and their property.

The census overseen by Publius Sulpicius Quirinius – the Cyrenius of the Authorised Bible – was long remembered and deeply resented by the population of Judaea, provoking outbreaks of resistance. For our present purpose, what is more significant is that it began in AD 6, when Herod's son Archelaus was deposed and Judaea became a directly administered Roman province, a process overseen by Quirinius as legate of Syria. Thus we appear to have a direct contradiction between Matthew's dating and Luke's – and indeed between Luke 1: 5 and Luke 2: 1–2. Many elaborate theories have been proposed to reconcile these passages, but none have proved entirely satisfactory. Suggestions that there was a census carried out a decade or so before, while Herod was still alive and when Quirinius was appointed to an earlier, otherwise unconfirmed, legateship of Syria, rely on many conjectures. Publius Quinctilius Varus was legate of Syria when Herod died, and was already in office in 6 BC, succeeding Caius Sentius Saturninus who had been there since 9 BC. These dates seem fixed even though they partly fall during the poorly documented years of Tiberius' sojourn in Rhodes. While it was not impossible under Augustus for a man to hold the same command twice – something that would later become very rare – it is hard to see how Quirinius could have been legate of Syria during the lifetime of Herod the Great, unless it was for a tenure of just a few months, which seems unlikely. He was probably in the wider area around this time – a spell as legate of Galatia seems possible, and he was certainly with the entourage of Caius Caesar a little later – but there is no evidence for his involvement in any census.[2]

For the Jewish historian Josephus, the AD 6 census overseen by Quirinius was the first Roman census in Judaea and was remembered as a traumatic event. An earlier one directly imposed by the Romans seems unlikely. We know of several censuses in Gaul during Augustus' principate, for instance in 27 BC, 12 BC and AD 14, but Gaul was a directly ruled province and not a client kingdom. Unfortunately, we really know very little about how client kingdoms in general and

Judaea in particular worked in terms of their taxation systems and the relationship these had to Rome. Herod was able to regulate the amount of taxation he levied, which implies a system of assessment of people and property, most likely based on some sort of census. How often these were carried out and how they worked – for instance whether people were required to be registered in their home communities – is unknown.[3]

Luke 2: 3–5 gives the need to be registered in the census as the reason why Joseph and his betrothed travelled from Nazareth in Galilee to Bethlehem in Judaea, where Mary gave birth to a son. It was important for the Messiah to be born in Bethlehem, and Matthew 2: 1 simply states that Jesus was born there, without explaining whether or not this was Joseph's and Mary's normal place of residence or making any mention of a census. This need not be a contradiction since, as mentioned earlier, the Gospel writers were not providing fully detailed historical contexts for the events they described, but telling their readers what they felt was important. It is possible that Joseph and Mary were required to be in Bethlehem to register for some form of census carried out by officials of Herod the Great's kingdom and tied to taxation. It is equally possible that people at the time may have felt that in some way they were ultimately paying a tax ordered by Caesar Augustus, who had after all installed King Herod over them and who kept him in power. Whatever the precise nature of the legal relationship between the Roman state, the *princeps* and a client ruler like Herod – a topic over which vast amounts of scholarly ink have been shed to little real gain, since the evidence is simply not there – it would not have been unreasonable to think in this way, especially a generation or more after the events.[4]

All this is possible, but it remains conjecture. It is quite likely that from the perspective of the later first century the mention of *a* census automatically invoked *the* famous census of Quirinius. It is much harder to believe that there really was any direct connection between any earlier census and the one in AD 6, other than that the latter almost certainly drew on already established structures of taxation set up in the Herodian period, which in turn drew on the system of the Hasmoneans and so on. In Roman Egypt there was considerable continuity between the Roman and Ptolemaic periods and it is unlikely that this was unique. That both Gospel writers believe that Jesus was born during Herod's last years does bring us back to an estimate of somewhere around 6–5 BC. Joseph may have gone to Bethlehem to be registered in a census held at this time and may have been forced – or chosen – to take his bride with him. Matthew's account seems to suggest that they were there for some time. The appearance of the wise men from the east – which suggests from outside the empire and probably the heartland of the Parthian kingdom – is perfectly possible, since plenty of traders made that journey. Similarly Matthew's claim that the family fled from Judaea to Egypt makes sense. Egypt, and especially Alexandria, had a very large Jewish community.[5]

Plausible does not mean certain, and ultimately we have only the meagre details of the two short Gospel accounts and not enough supporting information about Judaea in these years, and its relationship with Rome, either to prove or disprove them. It is important to remember this and unwise to be dogmatic, but a subject of this sort inevitably provokes a far more emotional response than mere details of the life of someone like Augustus, and different standards of proof tend to be applied to biblical accounts. Thus it is frequently stated that the massacre of the innocents – Herod's instructions to kill boy children in Bethlehem in Matthew 2: 16–18 – is an invention. More accurately we should say that there is no mention of this in any other source. Luke does not recount the episode, nor does Josephus, writing in the seventies and eighties AD, even though the latter is generally quite detailed about Herod's reign. Josephus does record plenty of homicidal episodes in the king's career, many involving members of his own family or of the Jerusalem aristocracy. In that sense the story in Matthew would not have been out of character, but others prefer to see it as inspired by the actual executions of his own sons on the charge of conspiring against him. These theories, much like others noting such things as the theological importance of Bethlehem as birthplace, warrant consideration, but fall well short of proof. Similarly, a statement that something is plausible does not mean that we can say that it definitely happened. As in the rest of this book, it is important to acknowledge the limits of our evidence, and there is no harm in reminding ourselves that there are similarly many aspects of Augustus' life, and of ancient history in general, that cannot be established with confident – let alone absolute – certainty.[6]

GLOSSARY

Aedile: The aediles were magistrates responsible for aspects of the day-to-day life of the City of Rome, including the staging of a number of annual festivals. The aedileship was usually held between the quaestorship and the praetorship. There were fewer aediles than praetors and the post was not a compulsory part of the *cursus honorum*.

Aeneid: The twelve-book epic poem composed by the poet Virgil and released after his death. It was immediately acknowledged as one of the greatest achievements of Latin verse and became a standard text for education. It tells of the journeys of the Trojan Aeneas after the fall of his homeland until he and his people settle in Italy, so that his descendants could subsequently found Rome.

Aerarium militare: The Military Treasury established by Augustus in AD 6 to fund the army and in particular arrange for the pay and discharge bonuses of soldiers. Although he provided the bulk of the initial money from his own fortune, an unpopular inheritance tax was set up to support it in the future.

Aquilifer: The standard-bearer who carried the legion's standard (*aquila*), a silver or gilded statuette of an eagle mounted on a staff.

Ala: An *ala* was a unit of auxiliary cavalry roughly equivalent in size to an infantry cohort.

Ara Pacis Augustae: The Altar of Peace is one of the great expressions of Augustan art. It was voted as an honour to commemorate his return to Rome in 13 BC and dedicated in 9 BC. The theme of peace celebrated both the end of civil strife and the peace achieved by victories over foreign enemies.

Auctoritas: The prestige and influence of a Roman senator. *Auctoritas* was greatly boosted by military achievements.

Augur: Members of one of the most important priestly colleges at Rome, the fifteen augurs were appointed for life. Their most important responsibility was the supervision of the correct observation and interpretation of the auspices, taken regularly as part of Roman public life. During his dictatorship Julius Caesar added a sixteenth member to the college.

Auxilia (auxiliaries): The non-citizen soldiers recruited into the army during the late Republic were known generally as auxiliaries or supporting troops.

Ballista: A two-armed torsion catapult capable of firing bolts or stones with considerable accuracy. These were built in various sizes and most often used in sieges.

Candidatus: A man seeking election wore an especially whitened (*candidatus*) toga to signal his intention to his fellow citizens, giving us our word 'candidate'.

Cataphract: Heavily armoured cavalryman often riding an armoured horse. These formed an important component of the Parthian army.

Centurion: An important grade of officers in the Roman army for most of its history, centurions originally commanded a century of eighty men. The most senior centurion of a legion was the *primus pilus*, a post of enormous status held only for a year.

Century (*centuria*): The basic sub-unit of the Roman army, the century was commanded by a centurion and usually consisted of eighty men.

Cohort (*cohors*): The basic tactical unit of the legion, consisting of six centuries of eighty soldiers with a total strength of 480.

Comitia centuriata: The Assembly of the Roman people which elected the most senior magistrates including the consuls and praetors. It was divided into 193 voting groups of centuries, membership of which was based on property registered in the census. The wealthier members of society had a highly disproportionate influence on the outcome. Its structure was believed to be based on the organisation of the early Roman army.

Comitia tributa: The Assembly of the entire Roman people including both patricians and plebeians. It was divided into thirty-five voting tribes, membership of which was based on ancestry. It had power to legislate and was presided over by a consul, praetor or curule aedile. It also elected men to a number of posts including the quaestorship and curule aedileship.

Concilium plebis: The Assembly of the Roman plebs, whether meeting to legislate or elect certain magistrates such as the tribunes of the plebs. Patricians were not allowed to take part. The people voted in thirty-five tribes, membership of which was based on ancestry. This Assembly was presided over by the tribunes of the plebs.

Consul: The year's two consuls were the senior elected magistrates of the Roman Republic, and held command in important campaigns. Sometimes the Senate extended their power after their year of office, in which case they were known as **proconsuls**.

Curia (and Curia Julia): The Curia or Senate House building stood on the north side of the Forum Romanum and had traditionally been built by one of the kings. Sulla restored it, but it was burnt down during the funeral of Clodius. As dictator, Julius Caesar began work on a new Curia, and this was completed by Augustus. Even when the building was in good condition, on some occasions the Senate could be summoned to meet in other buildings for specific debates.

Cursus honorum: The term given to the career pattern regulating public life. Existing legislation dealing with age and other qualifications for elected magistracies was restated and reinforced by Sulla during his dictatorship, and subsequently modified by Augustus.

Dictator: In times of extreme crisis a dictator was appointed for a six-month period during which he exercised supreme civil and military power. Later victors in civil wars, such as Sulla and Julius Caesar, used the title as a basis for more permanent power.

Ephebe: Adolescent males in Greek cities underwent a process of state-supervised training at the gymnasium. This was mainly concerned with physical fitness, but often included elements of more specifically military training.

Equites (**sing.** *eques*): The equestrians or 'knights' were the group with the highest property qualification registered by the census. From the time of the Gracchi they were given a more formal public role as jurors in the courts, an issue that became extremely contentious. Only under Augustus was a separate senatorial order created as a distinct class.

Fasces (**sing.** *fascis*): An ornamental bundle of rods some five feet long, in the middle of which was an axe. They were carried by **lictors** and were the most visible symbols of a magistrate's power and status.

Forum Augustum: The Forum constructed by Augustus with the Temple of Mars Ultor at its centre.

Forum Julium (or Forum Caesaris): The Forum planned and begun by Julius Caesar and completed by Augustus. It had the Temple of Venus Genetrix at its centre.

Forum Romanum: The political and economic heart of the City of Rome, which lay between the Capitoline, Palatine, Quirinal and Velian hills. Public meetings were often held either around the **Rostra**, or at the eastern end of the Forum. The *Concilium plebis* and *Comitia tributa* also usually met in the Forum to legislate.

Gladius: A Latin word meaning sword, *gladius* is conventionally used to describe the *gladius hispaniensis*, the Spanish sword which was the standard Roman side arm until well into the third century AD. Made from high-quality steel, this weapon could be used for cutting, but was primarily intended for thrusting.

Hasmonaean: In the second century BC, Judaea successfully rebelled against the Seleucids. An independent kingdom was created, ruled by the Hasmonaean dynasty. Antony and Octavian eventually installed Herod the Great in place of the old royal family.

Imperium: The power of military command held by magistrates and pro-magistrates during their term of office. Augustus was granted what was later termed *maius imperium proconsulare* – i.e. proconsular power that was superior to all other proconsuls. This would subsequently be granted to Agrippa and Tiberius.

Legatus (pl. ***legati***)**:** A subordinate officer who held delegated *imperium* rather than exercising power in his own right. *Legati* were chosen by a magistrate rather than elected. Under Augustus they were divided into two main grades, later known as the *legatus legionis* who commanded a legion, and the *legatus Augusti* who commanded a province.

Legion (*legio*): Originally a term meaning levy, the legions became the main unit of the Roman army for much of its history. In Augustus' day the theoretical strength of a legion was around 4,800–5,000 men in ten cohorts, each of 480 men. The effective strength of a legion on campaign was often much lower than this, especially during the civil wars.

Lictor: The official attendants of a magistrate who carried the *fasces* which symbolised his right to dispense justice and inflict capital and corporal punishment. Twelve lictors attended a consul, while a dictator was normally given twenty-four.

Magister equitum: Second-in-command to the Republican dictator, the Master of Horse traditionally commanded the cavalry, since the dictator was forbidden to ride a horse.

Mausoleum: The monumental tomb of Augustus begun before

Actium and named after the famous tomb of the Carian King Mausolus, one of the Seven Wonders of the World.

Naumachia Augusti: The *naumachia* was the famous naval battle staged as entertainment by Augustus in 2 BC. It involved some thirty warships and thousands of crewmen in a specially excavated lake.

Nomenclator: A specially trained slave whose task was to whisper the names of approaching citizens, permitting his master to greet them in a familiar way. Such a slave normally accompanied a canvassing politician.

Ornamenta triumphalia: Augustus introduced the 'ornaments' of a triumph given as a reward in place of a triumph itself. After 19 BC, no one outside his extended family was granted a full triumph, but provincial governors who had won a victory were given this distinction instead.

Ovatio (**ovation**): A lesser form of the triumph, in an ovation the general rode through the City on horseback rather than in a chariot.

Pantheon: The temple to the gods constructed by Agrippa. Although his name still appears on its inscription, the building we know today was rebuilt by Hadrian in the second century AD.

Pater patriae: The title of 'father or his country' or *pater patriae* was given to Augustus in 2 BC.

Pilum (**pl.** *pila*): The heavy javelin which was the standard equipment of the Roman legionary for much of Rome's history. Its narrow head was designed to punch through an enemy's shield, the long thin shank then giving it the reach to hit the man behind it.

Pontifex maximus: The head of the college of fifteen pontiffs, one of three major priesthoods monopolised by the Roman aristocracy. The pontiffs regulated the timing of many state festivals and events. The *pontifex maximus* was more chairman than leader, but the post was highly prestigious.

Praetor: Praetors were annually elected magistrates who under the Republic governed the less important provinces and fought Rome's smaller wars.

Praetorian cohort: The praetorians in this period were carefully selected and splendidly equipped soldiers drawn from the legions. Each general was entitled to raise a single cohort of praetorians, but in the course of the civil wars the triumvirs each came to control several of these formations, taken over from their subordinates. After Actium, Augustus established nine permanent praetorian cohorts to form his guard. At this stage they had no permanent barracks in Rome and only three cohorts were ever present in the City at any one time.

Prefect (*praefectus*): Equestrian officer with a range of duties, including the command of units of allied or auxiliary troops.

Prefect of the City (*praefectus urbis*): Archaic office revived by Augustus, and normally held by a former consul. The prefect coordinated the administration of Rome and commanded the three urban cohorts.

Principate: Modern term for the regime created by Augustus, meaning the rule of a *princeps*, sometimes less accurately referred to as an emperor.

Princeps: First citizen, and leader of the Senate, People and State, *princeps* was the term Augustus preferred for his own status. In the past the senatorial roll was headed by a *princeps senatus*, chosen by the censors supposedly as the Senate's most prestigious and respected member. In all usages the term had no particular powers, but was a mark of esteem and respect.

Princeps iuventutis (pl. *principes iuventutis*): A new title of 'leader of the youth' was given first to Caius Caesar and then extended to his brother Lucius. They became symbolic heads of the equestrian order.

Rostra: The speaker's platform in the Forum Romanum. It was remodelled by Augustus as part of Julius Caesar's planned realignment of the Curia and the surrounding area to connect with his new Forum. Another Rostra was constructed at the opposite side of the Forum Romanum, next to the Temple of the Divine Julius. The name derived from the practice of displaying the rams of captured enemy warships on the platform.

Quaestor: Magistrates whose duties were primarily financial, quaestors acted as deputies to consular governors and often held subordinate military commands.

Saepta: The voting area on the Campus Martius where the various Assemblies met to hold elections. A planned rebuilding begun by Julius Caesar was completed by Agrippa.

Scorpion: The light bolt-shooting ballista employed by the Roman army both in the field and in sieges. They possessed a long range, as well as great accuracy and the ability to penetrate any form of armour.

Secular Games (*ludi saeculares*): The 'Secular' or 'Cyclical' Games were celebrated by Augustus in 17 BC. A cycle was supposed to be longer than the life of a human being.

***Senatus consultum ultimum*:** The Senate's ultimate decree called upon magistrates to do whatever necessary to protect the state. It was employed against Catiline in 63 BC, Julius Caesar in 49 BC, and last used to suppress Egnatius Rufus in 19 BC.

***Signifer*:** The standard-bearer who carried the standard (*signum*) of the century.

Subura: The valley between the Viminal and Esquiline hills was notorious for its narrow streets and slum housing.

Talent: The actual size of this Greek measurement of weight – and by extension money – varied considerably, from *c*.57–83 pounds. It is rarely clear from our sources who employ the term which standard was in use.

Testudo: The famous tortoise formation in which Roman legionaries overlapped their long shields to provide protection to the front, sides and overhead. It was most often used during assaults on fortifications.

Tribuni aerarii: The group registered below the equestrian order in the census. Relatively little is known about them.

Tribunus militum (**military tribune**): Six military tribunes were elected or appointed to each Republican legion, one pair of these men holding command at any one time. Under Augustus the number remained at six, but of these one was pursuing a senatorial career and was senior. This man, known as the *tribunus laticlavius* from the broad stripe worn around his cuirass, was second-in-command to the legionary legate. The other five tribunes, the *tribuni angusticlavii* who wore a narrow stripe, were equestrians and had usually already served in command of an auxiliary cohort.

Tribune of the plebs: Although holding a political office without direct military responsibilities, the ten tribunes of the plebs elected each year were able to legislate on any issue. During the later years of the Republic many ambitious generals, such as Marius, Pompey and Julius Caesar, enlisted the aid of tribunes to secure important commands for themselves. Augustus was given the *sacrosanctitas* of a tribune as well as the powers of the office.

Tribunicia potestas: The powers of the tribunate, including the right to convene meetings of the Senate and present bills to the Popular Assembly, were granted to Augustus and later to Agrippa and Tiberius.

Triumph: The great celebration granted by the Senate to a successful general took the form of a procession along the Via Sacra, the ceremonial main road of Rome, displaying the spoils and captives of his victory and culminating in the ritual execution of the captured enemy leader. The commander rode in a chariot, dressed like the statue of Jupiter, a slave holding a laurel wreath of victory over his head. The slave was supposed to whisper to the general, reminding him that he was mortal.

Triumvir: In 43 BC Antony, Lepidus and Octavian were named as *triumviri rei publicae constituendae* (board of three to reconstitute the state) by the *lex Titia* proposed by a tribune and passed by the *Concilium plebis*. The triumvirate was granted dictatorial powers, initially for five years.

Urban cohorts: Three urban cohorts were raised by Augustus as a paramilitary police force for Rome itself. They were commanded by the urban prefect. It is possible that a fourth cohort was raised under Augustus to guard the imperial mint at Lugdunum in Gaul, since the unit was certainly there under Tiberius.

Vexillum: A square flag mounted crosswise on a pole, the *vexillum* was used to mark a general's position and was also the standard carried by a detachment of troops. A general's *vexillum* seems usually to have been red.

Vigiles: Formed by Augustus in AD 6, the seven cohorts of *vigiles* acted as a fire brigade and night police for the City of Rome. Each cohort was placed in control of two of the fourteen regions formed at the same time.

KEY PERSONALITIES

AGRIPPINA (*c.*14 BC–AD 33): Daughter of Agrippa and Julia, she married Germanicus and had five children with him. After his death in AD 19, she incurred the suspicion of Tiberius and she and two of her sons died in exile.

Marcus Vipsanius AGRIPPA (*c.*63–12 BC): Oldest friend and most loyal and capable subordinate of Augustus, Agrippa was with him when he heard of the assassination of Julius Caesar. His skill played a major role in the victories over Sextus Pompeius and Antony, and he also proved very effective as an administrator and builder. In 21 BC he married the widowed Julia and had three sons and two daughters with her. He was steadily advanced to become a colleague of the *princeps*.

ATIA (d. 43 BC): Daughter of Julius Caesar's sister Julia and Marcus Atius Balbus, Atia married Caius Octavius and was the mother of Augustus. Widowed, she married Lucius Marcius Philippus. Atia died not long after her son became consul for the first time, at the age of nineteen.

Titus Pomponius ATTICUS (*c.*106–32 BC): Long-time friend and correspondent of Cicero, Atticus remained an equestrian and did not enter public life, but still managed to be on good terms with almost everyone of importance in the Republic. He also corresponded with Augustus, while his daughter married Agrippa. Atticus committed suicide when he realised that he was in the advanced stages of an incurable disease.

AUGUSTUS (63 BC–AD 14): Born Caius Octavius, became Caius Julius Caesar and later Caesar Augustus. Great-nephew of Julius Caesar, he emerged victorious from the civil wars and became sole master of the Republic.

Marcus Junius BRUTUS (*c.*85–41 BC): Son of a man executed along with the father of Lepidus in 78 BC and of Servilia, long-time mistress of Julius Caesar, Brutus was considered one of the up-and-coming men in the Senate when the Civil War broke out in 49 BC. He fought against Julius Caesar at Pharsalus, but was pardoned and made praetor. This did not prevent him from leading the Liberators – the conspirators who assassinated the dictator – and he took his own life after suffering defeat at Philippi.

CAIUS CAESAR (20 BC–AD 4): Oldest son of Agrippa and Julia, Caius was adopted by Augustus in 17 BC and shown considerable favour. In 1 BC he was given major provincial commands, but in AD 3 he suffered a serious wound and died early in the next year.

Caius CASSIUS Longinus (*c.*85–41 BC): Quaestor to Crassus in 53 BC, he survived the disaster in Parthia. He also fought against Julius Caesar, but surrendered after Pharsalus and was given a praetorship by Julius Caesar. Both he and Lepidus were married to sisters of Brutus. With Brutus he led the Liberators, but killed himself after the First Battle of Philippi.

CATILINE (Lucius Sergius Catilina, *c.*108/6–62 BC): Member of an ancient, but recently obscure, patrician family, Catiline's desperate and expensive pursuit of high office eventually led him to attempt a coup. This was suppressed by Cicero.

Marcus Porcius CATO the Younger (95–46 BC): Famous for his stern virtue, Cato was a bitter opponent of Julius Caesar and killed himself rather than accept the latter's mercy. Servilia was his half-sister, and her son Brutus subsequently married Cato's widowed daughter.

Marcus Tullius CICERO (*c.*106–43 BC): One of the most successful new men of his generation, Cicero became the foremost orator in Rome. As consul in 63 BC, he outmanoeuvred Catiline, but was subsequently attacked for the legality of his conduct. In the Civil War he eventually sided against Julius Caesar, but was later pardoned. After the assassination of the dictator he encouraged the Liberators and then tried to employ Augustus to destroy Antony. When the second triumvirate was formed, he was one of the first victims of the proscriptions.

CLAUDIUS (10 BC–AD 54): Lame and suspected of mental problems, Claudius was largely kept out of public life by Augustus and Livia, and it was not until the reign of his nephew Caligula that he held office. Following Caligula's murder, he was proclaimed *princeps* by the praetorian guard.

CLEOPATRA VII (*c.*70/69–30 BC): The last member of the Macedonian Ptolemy family to rule a kingdom based around Egypt, Cleopatra was throughout her life a loyal ally of the Romans. Her misfortune was to live at a time when the Roman Republic was rent by civil war, and in the end she found herself too closely linked to the defeated Mark Antony. She took her own life once it was clear that Augustus would not permit her or any of her children to retain power.

Marcus Licinius CRASSUS *dives* (*c.*115–53 BC): Famous for his wealth, hence the nickname *dives* or 'rich', Crassus rose to prominence under Sulla and worked hard to build up political influence. Together with Pompey and Julius Caesar he formed the first triumvirate in 59 BC, and held a second consulship with Pompey in 55 BC. After this he launched an unprovoked attack on the Parthians, but was checked at Carrhae. In the subsequent retreat he was killed and most of his army massacred.

Marcus Licinius CRASSUS (consul in 30 BC, but dates otherwise unknown): Grandson of Crassus, he joined Augustus during the struggle with Antony and then as governor of Macedonia won a series of victories over the neighbouring peoples. He held a triumph in 27 BC, but is not heard of again, although his adopted son was consul in 14 BC.

DRUSUS (38–9 BC): Younger son of Livia and her first husband Tiberius Claudius Nero, Drusus was given an accelerated career and won military glory in the Alps and then campaigning in Germany, reaching as far as the Elbe. He was married to Antonia, daughter of Octavia and Mark Antony, with whom he had three children, including Germanicus and Claudius. Drusus died in 9 BC from injuries caused by a riding accident.

DRUSUS the Younger (13 BC–AD 23): Son of Tiberius and Vipsania, and grandson of Livia, the younger Drusus became Augustus' grandson when his father was adopted in AD 4.

FULVIA (d. 40 BC): Wife of Mark Antony and the mother of his two Roman sons, Antyllus and Iullus, she had already lost two husbands to violent deaths before she married him. After reluctantly supporting Lucius Antonius in his unsuccessful rebellion, Antony subsequently repudiated her and this rejection is said to have hastened her death.

GERMANICUS (15 BC–AD 19): Son of Drusus and Antonia, the popular Germanicus began to receive increasingly important commands following the rebellions in Pannonia in AD 6 and Germany in AD 9. His death in AD 19 was viewed with great suspicion.

HORACE (Quintus Horatius Flaccus, 65–8 BC): Son of a successful freedman, Horace was given a good education and fought for the Liberators at Philippi. A few years later he was accepted into the literary circle of Maecenas, and became acquainted with Augustus, who gave him a valuable estate and so permitted him to devote his time to writing. Augustus offered the poet employment as secretary, but even when he turned this down the pair remained on very familiar terms.

JULIA: Sister of Julius Caesar and grandmother of Augustus, she married Marcus Atius Balbus and with him had a daughter, Atia.

JULIA, daughter of Augustus (39 BC–AD 14): Only child of Augustus to survive birth, Julia was employed to confirm the allegiance of key supporters and was successively married to Marcellus, Agrippa and Tiberius. She had five children with Agrippa, but only a stillborn child with Tiberius. The souring of their marriage contributed to his retirement to Rhodes. In 2 BC she was condemned for adultery and sent into exile by her father.

JULIA, granddaughter of Augustus (*c.*19 BC–AD 28): Daughter of Julia and Agrippa, she was also accused of adultery and sent into exile in AD 8.

Caius JULIUS CAESAR (100–44 BC): Member of an aristocratic, but recently relatively obscure, family, Julius Caesar's early career was broadly conventional. As consul in 59 BC he joined Pompey and Crassus in a secret alliance known today as the first triumvirate. After ten years of military success in Gaul he confronted Pompey in the Civil War and became dictator. He was murdered by a conspiracy composed of former supporters and pardoned enemies.

Lucius Aemilius LEPIDUS (*c.*86–13/12 BC): Son of a consul who attempted a coup in 78 BC, Lepidus supported Julius Caesar during the Civil War and was rewarded with increasingly high office, including the post of Master of Horse (*magister equitum*) in 44 BC. This gave him command of troops and so placed him in a strong position after the assassination of the dictator. However, in the years that followed his soldiers proved unenthusiastic. He joined Mark Antony and Augustus in the second triumvirate, but over time his power waned and he was suppressed in 36 BC, remaining under virtual arrest for the remainder of his life.

LIVIA Drusilla (*c.*58 BC–AD 29): Wife of Augustus from 38 BC until his death in AD 14, the couple produced only one stillborn child. However, her two sons from an earlier marriage, Tiberius and Drusus, would play a prominent role in public life, both winning distinctions as commanders. Tiberius, Caligula, Claudius and Nero were all descendants of Livia. During Augustus' lifetime she sometimes played a significant role in public events, and was an important adviser in private.

LIVY (Titus Livius, possibly 59 BC–AD 17 or 64 BC–AD 12): Livy was the great historian of the Augustan age and his patriotic and moralistic history of Rome from its founding until the death of Drusus in 9 BC consisted of 142 books. Only a minority of these survive other than as brief summaries of contents. Although Augustus jokingly chided him as a Pompeian, there is no real trace of any hostility on Livy's part to the new regime, and in most respects he celebrated virtues dear to the heart of the *princeps*.

LUCIUS ANTONIUS (*c.*80?–40/39 BC): One of Mark Antony's two younger brothers, Lucius rebelled against Augustus in 41 BC, but was defeated at Perusia. He was spared and sent to Spain as governor, but died soon afterwards.

LUCIUS CAESAR (17 BC–AD 2): Second son of Agrippa and Julia, Lucius was adopted by Augustus and shown considerable favour like his older brother. Sent to Spain in AD 2, he fell ill and died at Massilia before reaching his province.

Caius MAECENAS (*c.*63–8 BC): A long-time friend and supporter of Augustus, Maecenas remained an equestrian and never held public office. Even so, on several occasions he was left in effective control of Rome and played a central role in politics, especially during the years of the second triumvirate. Afterwards he continued to advise Augustus, and cultivated a circle of writers, including the poets Horace and Virgil.

Caius Claudius MARCELLUS (42–23 BC): Son of Augustus' sister Octavia and the former consul Caius Claudius Marcellus, he was shown considerable favour by the *princeps* up until his sudden death.

Lucius MARCIUS PHILIPPUS (dates unknown, but consul in 56 BC and last attested in 43 BC): Second husband to Atia, he became Augustus' stepfather and seems to have helped him in the very early stages of his career.

Caius MARIUS (*c.*157–87 BC): Married to Julius Caesar's aunt, Marius was a new man who became the most celebrated Roman commander of his day, winning an unprecedented five consecutive consulships. However, his competition with Sulla led to civil war, and he died within days of capturing Rome.

MARK ANTONY (Marcus Antonius, 86/83–30 BC): Member of a successful aristocratic family, Antony inherited huge debts which he swiftly increased. He served with Julius Caesar in the last years of the Gallic Wars and supported him in the Civil War. Antony was rewarded with the consulship for 44 BC, and was thus in a position of power when the dictator was murdered. His relationship with Augustus began badly, but after a period of conflict they allied with Lepidus to form the second triumvirate. Together they beat the Liberators, but subsequent failure in a war against Parthia fatally weakened Antony, while his affair with Cleopatra damaged his image at Rome. Beaten at Actium in 31 BC, he took his own life the following year.

OCTAVIA (c.69–11 BC): Older sister of Augustus, she married Caius Claudius Marcellus and then Mark Antony to cement the alliance with her brother. She had a son, Marcellus, from her first marriage and two daughters, Antonia the elder and younger, from her second.

Caius OCTAVIUS (d. 59 BC): The father of Augustus, Octavius came from a prosperous equestrian family, but was the first of them to enter politics at Rome. He was elected praetor in 61 BC and successfully governed Macedonia as proconsul, but died at his villa in Nola on his way back from the province.

OVID (Publius Ovidius Naso, 43 BC–AD 17): From a younger generation than men like Virgil and Horace, Ovid was too young to be caught up in the civil wars and wrote all his major works under the peaceful conditions of the principate. His style was far less respectful of tradition, and his *Ars Amatoria* in particular displeased Augustus. However, it was not until he was in some way implicated in the disgrace of the Younger Julia that he was sent into exile on the Black Sea in AD 8.

POMPEY the Great (Cnaeus Pompeius Magnus, 106–48 BC): The most famous Roman general of his day, Pompey rose to prominence under Sulla, and had a spectacular career which broke most of the rules. In the fifties BC he was given command of the Spanish provinces, but stayed just outside Rome and sent subordinate legates to serve in his place. He fought Julius Caesar in the Civil War, was beaten at Pharsalus in 48 BC, and soon afterwards murdered in Egypt.

Sextus POMPEIUS (Sextus Pompeius Magnus Pius, c.67–36 BC): Younger son of Pompey the Great, Sextus raised forces against Julius Caesar just before his assassination, but only became a real power in the years that followed. Seizing Sicily as his main base, he built up a formidable fleet, allowing him to blockade Italy and rescue fugitives from the proscriptions. In spite of winning a number of battles at sea, he was eventually defeated by Augustus and his supporters.

POSTUMUS AGRIPPA (12 BC–AD 14): The youngest child of Agrippa and Julia, Postumus was given this name because he was born after his father had died. He received little public attention until his adoption by Augustus in AD 4. Even then, he received no offices and a few years later was marginalised and sent into exile. He was murdered soon after the death of Augustus, but it is unclear who gave the order.

SCRIBONIA (d. some time after AD 16): The wife of Augustus and mother of Julia, Scribonia accompanied her daughter into exile.

Titus STATILIUS TAURUS (dates unknown, but consul in 37 and 26 BC): One of Augustus' most loyal and reliable subordinates, Statilius Taurus was probably second only to Agrippa. He was made urban prefect in 16 BC, but may have died soon afterwards as he disappears from the record.

Lucius Cornelius SULLA Felix (138–78 BC): The member of an old, but recently undistinguished, patrician family, in 88 BC Sulla was the first man to turn his legions on Rome and seize power by force. He later fought a civil war against the supporters of Marius and other enemies, making himself dictator and introducing the proscription lists to legitimise the murder of opponents.

TIBERIUS (42 BC–AD 37): Older son of Livia and her first husband Tiberius Claudius Nero, Tiberius was given a succession of important offices and provincial commands at a very young age. Originally married to Agrippa's daughter Vipsania, he divorced her to marry Julia, but the match proved an unhappy one for both of them. In 6 BC he went into voluntary retirement on Rhodes and for ten years was excluded from public life. Eventually permitted to return to Italy, it was not until the deaths of Caius and Lucius that he was adopted by Augustus. In the next years he was given powers equal to those of the *princeps* and smoothly succeeded him in AD 14.

VIPSANIA (36 BC–AD 20): Daughter of Agrippa and Atticus' daughter Pomponia, Vipsania was married to Tiberius. He divorced her to marry Julia, but was said to have bitterly regretted it. She married a senator and gave him a number of children.

VIRGIL (Publius Vergilius Maro, *c.*70–19 BC): Although he appears to have suffered the loss of some family land during the confiscations organised by the second triumvirate, Virgil later became a friend of Maecenas and Augustus, producing works in tune with the new regime. His *Aeneid* was unfinished at his death, but in spite of the poet's wishes Augustus had it tidied up and released to great acclaim.

FAMILY TREES

THE FIRST TRIMVIRATE

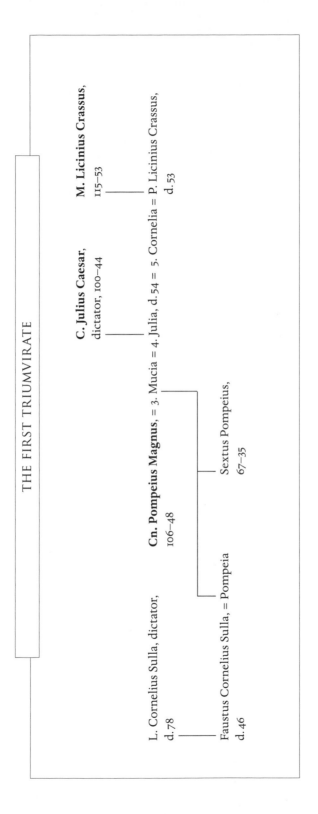

M. Licinius Crassus,
dictator, 100–44

C. Julius Caesar,
dictator, 100–44

Cn. Pompeius Magnus, = 3. Mucia = 4. Julia, d. 54 = 5. Cornelia = P. Licinius Crassus,
106–48   d. 53

Sextus Pompeius,
67–35

L. Cornelius Sulla, dictator,
d. 78

Faustus Cornelius Sulla, = Pompeia
d. 46

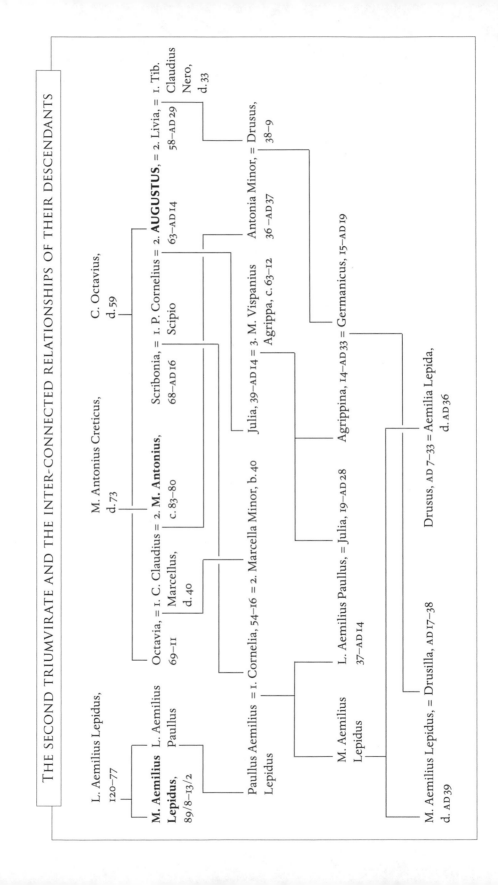

THE SECOND TRIUMVIRATE AND THE INTER-CONNECTED RELATIONSHIPS OF THEIR DESCENDANTS

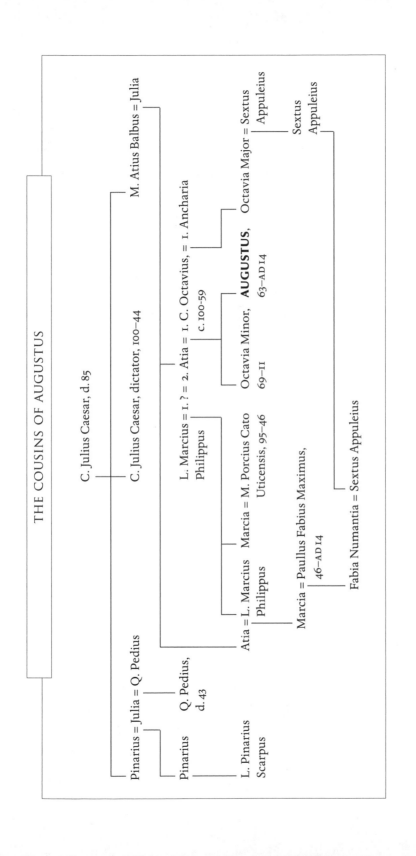

THE COUSINS OF AUGUSTUS

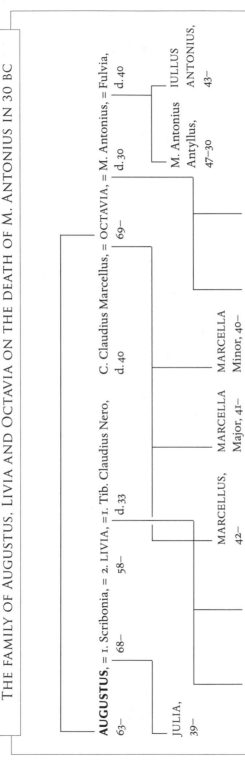

AUGUSTUS, = 1. Scribonia, = 2. LIVIA, =1. Tib. Claudius Nero,   C. Claudius Marcellus, = OCTAVIA, = M. Antonius, = Fulvia,

63–   68–   58–   d. 33   d. 40   69–   d. 30   d. 40

JULIA,   M. Antonius   IULLUS
39–   Antyllus,   ANTONIUS,
                                                                                                                           47–30   43–

TIBERIUS,   DRUSUS,   MARCELLUS,   MARCELLA   MARCELLA   ANTONIA   ANTONIA
42–   38–   42–   Major, 41–   Minor, 40–   Major, 39–   Minor, 36–

People alive and members of the imperial family at the date of the chart are in caps; people deceased or divorced are in lower case. All dates BC

THE FAMILIES AND CHILDREN OF AUGUSTUS, LIVIA AND OCTAVIA IN 19 BC

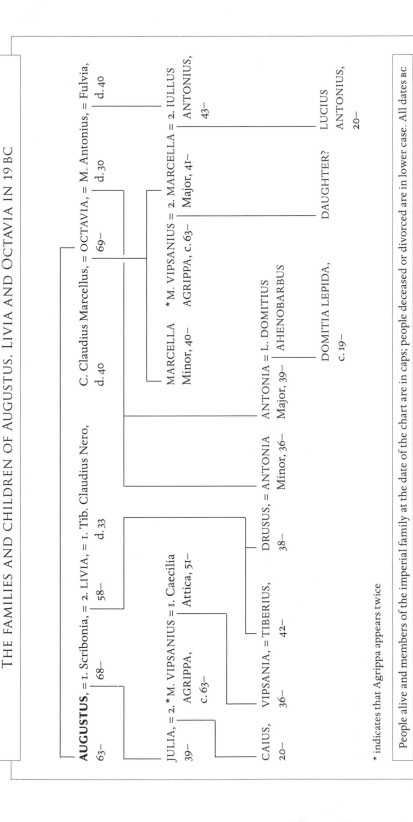

AUGUSTUS, = 1. Scribonia, = 2. LIVIA, = 1. Tib. Claudius Nero,
63–   68–   58–   d. 33

C. Claudius Marcellus, = OCTAVIA, = M. Antonius, = Fulvia,
d. 40   69–   d. 30   d. 40

JULIA, = 2. *M. VIPSANIUS = 1. Caecilia
39–   AGRIPPA,   Attica, 51–
             c. 63–

MARCELLA   *M. VIPSANIUS = 2. MARCELLA = 2. IULLUS
Minor, 40–   AGRIPPA, c. 63–   Major, 41–   ANTONIUS,
                                            43–

CAIUS,   VIPSANIA, = TIBERIUS,   DRUSUS, = ANTONIA   ANTONIA = L. DOMITIUS
20–   36–   42–   38–   Minor, 36–   Major, 39– AHENOBARBUS

                                                         DOMITIA LEPIDA,
                                                         c. 19–

DAUGHTER?   LUCIUS
             ANTONIUS,
             20–

* indicates that Agrippa appears twice

People alive and members of the imperial family at the date of the chart are in caps; people deceased or divorced are in lower case. All dates BC

THE FAMILY OF AUGUSTUS, LIVIA AND OCTAVIA IN 10 BC

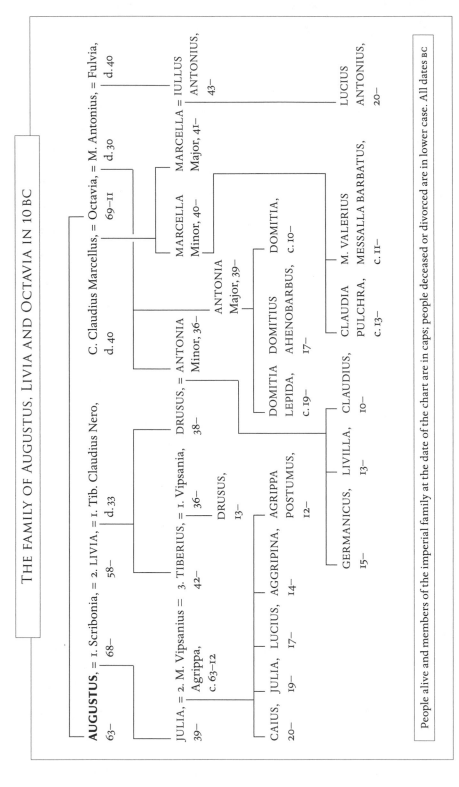

People alive and members of the imperial family at the date of the chart are in caps; people deceased or divorced are in lower case. All dates BC

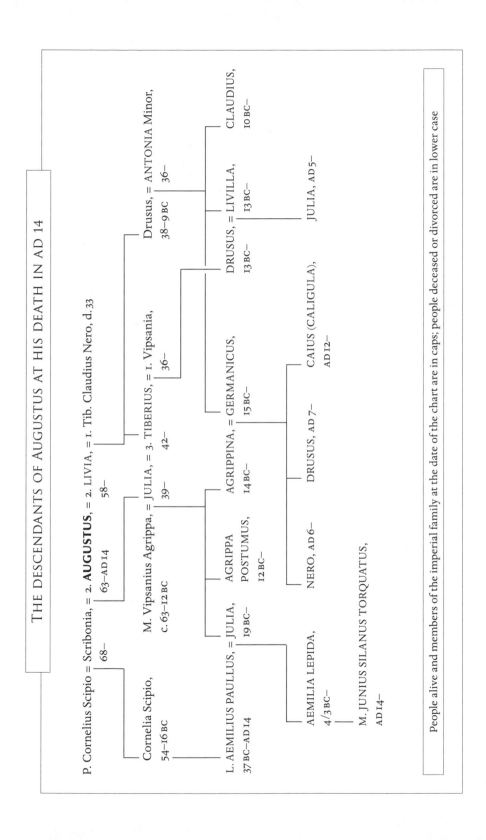

THE DESCENDANTS OF AUGUSTUS AT HIS DEATH IN AD 14

P. Cornelius Scipio = Scribonia, = 2. AUGUSTUS, = 2. LIVIA, = 1. Tib. Claudius Nero, d. 33
68–   63–AD 14   58–

Cornelia Scipio,   M. Vipsanius Agrippa, = JULIA, = 3. TIBERIUS, = 1. Vipsania,   Drusus, = ANTONIA Minor,
54–16 BC   c. 63–12 BC   39–   42–   36–   38–9 BC   36–

L. AEMILIUS PAULLUS, = JULIA,   AGRIPPA   AGRIPPINA, = GERMANICUS,   DRUSUS, = LIVILLA,   CLAUDIUS,
37 BC–AD 14   19 BC–   POSTUMUS,   14 BC–   15 BC–   13 BC–   13 BC–   10 BC–
                                 12 BC–

AEMILIA LEPIDA,   NERO, AD 6–   DRUSUS, AD 7–   CAIUS (CALIGULA),   JULIA, AD 5–
4/3 BC–   AD 12–

M. JUNIUS SILANUS TORQUATUS,
AD 14–

People alive and members of the imperial family at the date of the chart are in caps; people deceased or divorced are in lower case

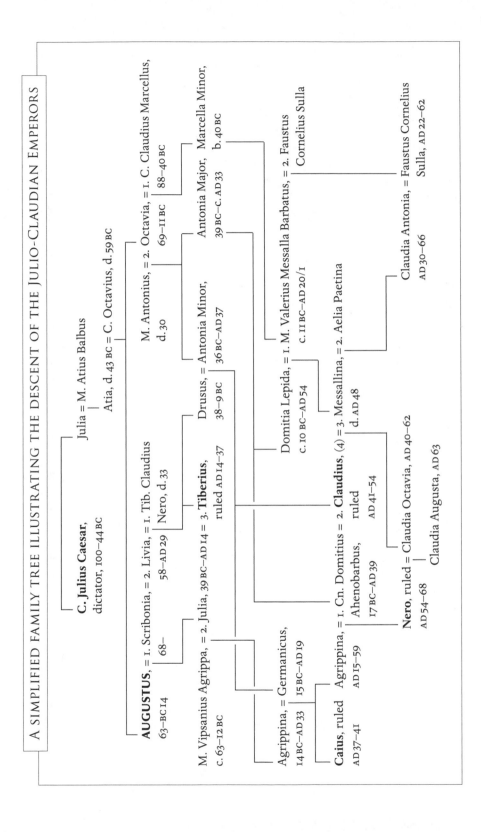

A SIMPLIFIED FAMILY TREE ILLUSTRATING THE DESCENT OF THE JULIO-CLAUDIAN EMPERORS

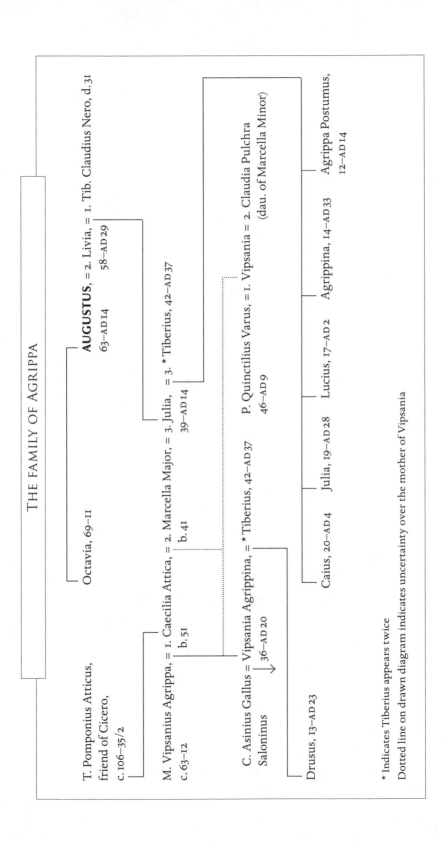

THE FAMILY OF AGRIPPA

Octavia, 69–11

AUGUSTUS, = 2. Livia, = 1. Tib. Claudius Nero, d. 31
63–AD 14   58–AD 29

T. Pomponius Atticus,
friend of Cicero,
c. 106–35/2

M. Vipsanius Agrippa, = 1. Caecilia Attica, = 2. Marcella Major, = 3. Julia, = 3. *Tiberius, 42–AD 37
c. 63–12   b. 51   b. 41   39–AD 14

P. Quinctilius Varus, = 1. Vipsania = 2. Claudia Pulchra
46–AD 9   (dau. of Marcella Minor)

C. Asinius Gallus = Vipsania Agrippina, = *Tiberius, 42–AD 37
Saloninus   36–AD 20

Drusus, 13–AD 23

Caius, 20–AD 4   Julia, 19–AD 28   Lucius, 17–AD 2   Agrippina, 14–AD 33   Agrippa Postumus,
                                                                             12–AD 14

* Indicates Tiberius appears twice
Dotted line on drawn diagram indicates uncertainty over the mother of Vipsania

BIBLIOGRAPHY

Included are all works cited in the endnotes. As is my usual practice, I have tried, where possible, to cite works published relatively recently and in English as likely to be of more use to the interested reader who develops the desire to read more. By following the references given in these works, it would be possible to extend this reading into the substantial literature in other languages.

Adcock, F., *The Roman Art of War under the Republic* (1940)

Alföldy, G., *Noricum* (1974)

Badian, E., *Publicans and Sinners* (1972)

Badian, E., '"Crisis Theories" and the beginning of the Principate', in W. Wirth, *Romanitas and Christianitas* (1982), pp. 18–41

Balsdon, J., 'Fabula Clodiana', *Historia* 15 (1966), pp. 65–73

Barnes, T., 'The victories of Augustus', *JRS* 64 (1974), pp. 21–6

Barrett, A., *Caligula. The Corruption of Power* (1989)

Barrett, A., *Livia. First Lady of Imperial Rome* (2002)

Barton, T., 'Augustus and Capricorn: Astrological polyvalency and imperial rhetoric', *JRS* 85 (1995), pp. 33–51

Billows, R., 'The religious procession of the Ara Pacis Augustae: Augustus' *supplicatio* in 13 BC', *JRA* 6 (1993), pp. 80–92

Billows, R., *Julius Caesar. The Colossus of Rome* (2009)

Bingen, J., *Hellenistic Egypt: Monarchy, Society, Economy, Culture* (2007)

Birch, R., 'The Settlement of 26 June AD 4 and its Aftermath', *Classical Quarterly* 31 (1981), pp. 443–56

Boatright, M., 'The Pomerial extension of Augustus', *Historia* 35 (1986), pp. 13–27

Bowersock, G., *Augustus and the Greek World* (1965)

Bowersock, G., 'Augustus and the East: The problem of succession', in Millar & Segal (1990), pp. 169–88

Bradley, K., 'Wet-nursing at Rome. A Study in Social Relations', in Rawson (1986), pp. 201–29

Brandon, C., 'Cement, concrete and settling barges at Sebastos: comparisons with other Roman harbour examples and the descriptions of Vitruvius', in A. Raban & K. Houm (eds), *Caesarea Maritima. A Retrospective after Two Millennia* (1996), pp. 25–40

Brunt, P., *Italian Manpower 225 BC–AD 14* (1971)

Brunt, P., 'The administrators of Roman Egypt', *JRS* 65 (1975), pp. 124–47

Brunt, P., 'Princeps and equites', *JRS* 73 (1983), pp. 42–75

Brunt, P., 'The role of the Senate in the Augustan regime', *Classical Quarterly* 34. 2 (1984), pp. 423–44

Camp, J., *The Archaeology of Athens* (2001)

Campbell, B., 'The marriage of soldiers under the Empire', *JRS* 68 (1978), pp. 153–66

Campbell, B., 'War and diplomacy: Rome and Parthia, 31 BC–AD 235', in Rich & Shipley (1993), pp. 213–40

Campbell, J., *The Emperor and the Roman Army 31 BC–AD 235* (1984)

Carson, R., 'Caesar and the monarchy', *Greece & Rome* 4 (1957), pp. 46–53

Carter, J., *The Battle of Actium: The Rise and Triumph of Augustus Caesar* (1970)

Cartledge, P., 'The second thoughts of Augustus on the res publica in 28/7 BC', *Greece and Rome* 31 (1984), pp. 30–40

Champlin, E., 'Tiberius and the Heavenly Twins', *JRS* 101 (2011), pp. 73–99

Chilver, G., 'Augustus and the Roman constitution 1939–1950', *Historia* 1 (1950), pp. 408–35

Christol, M., *Une Histoire Provinciale. La Gaule narbonnaise av. J.-C. au IIIᵉ siècle ap. J.-C.* (2010)

Clarke, J., 'Augustan domestic interiors: propaganda or fashion?' in Galinsky (2005), pp. 264–78

Collins, J., 'Caesar and the corruption of power', *Historia* 4 (1957), pp. 445–65

Conlin, D., *The Artists of the Ara Pacis. Studies in the History of Greece and Rome* (1997)

Connolly, P., *Greece and Rome at War* (1981)

Cooley, M. (ed.), *The Age of Augustus. Lactor 17* (2003)

Corbett, J., 'The Succession policy of Augustus', *Latomus* 33 (1974), pp. 87–97

Crawford, M., *Roman Republican Coinage* (1974)

Crook, J., 'Some remarks on the Augustan Constitution', *Classical Review* 3 (1953), pp. 10–12

Cunliffe, B., *Greeks, Romans and Barbarians: Spheres of Interaction* (1988)

Curchin, L., *The Romanization of Central Spain. Complexity, Diversity and Change in a Provincial Hinterland* (2004)

Delia, D., 'Fulvia Reconsidered', in S. Pomperoy (ed.), *Women's History and Ancient History* (1991), pp. 197–217

Dennison, M., *Empress of Rome. The Life of Livia* (2010)

Derks, T., *Gods, Temples and Ritual Practices: The Transformation of Religious Ideas and Values in Roman Gaul* (1998)

Dixon, S., *The Roman Mother* (1988)

Dowling, M., *Clemency and Cruelty in the Roman World* (2006)

Drinkwater, J., *Roman Gaul. The Three Provinces, 58 BC–AD 260* (1983)

Drinkwater, J., 'The Principate – lifebelt, or millstone around the neck of Empire?', in O. Hekster, G. Kleijn & D. Slootjes (eds), *Crises and the Roman Empire* (2007), pp. 67–74

Durán Cabello, R. M., 'Edificios de espectáculo', in X. Raventós (ed.), *Les capitales provinciales de Hispania 2. Merida: Colonia Augustua Emerita* (2004)

Dyson, S., 'Native Revolt Patterns in the Roman Empire', *Aufstieg und Niedergang der römischen Welt* 2. 3 (1975), pp. 38–175

Dyson, S., *The Creation of the Roman Frontier* (1985)

Dyson, S., *Rome. A Living Portrait of an Ancient City* (2010)

Eck, W., 'Senatorial Self-Representation: Developments in the Augustan Period', in Millar & Segal (eds) (1990), pp. 129–67

Eck, W., *The Age of Augustus* (2003)

Edmondson, J. (ed.), *Augustus* (2009)

Ehrenberg, V. & Jones, A., *Documents Illustrating the Reigns of Augustus and Tiberius* (2nd edn, 1975)

Everitt, A., *Cicero. A Turbulent Life* (2001)

Everitt, A., *Augustus: The Life of Rome's First Emperor* (2006)

Fantham, E., *Julia Augusti, the Emperor's Daughter* (2006)

Ferrary, J., 'The powers of Augustus', in Edmondson (2009), pp. 90–136

Ferrill, A., 'Prosopography and the Last Years of Augustus', *Historia* 20 (1971), pp. 718–31

Ferrill, A., 'Augustus and his daughter: a modern myth', in C. Deroux (ed.), *Studies in Latin Literature and Roman History* 2 (1980), pp. 332–46

Feugère, M. (ed.), *L'Équipment Militaire et L'Armement de la République, Journal of Roman Military Equipment Studies* 8 (1997)

Finley, M. I. (ed.), *Studies in Roman Property* (1976)

Fishwick, D., *The Imperial Cult in the Latin West: Studies in the Ruler Cult of the Western Roman Empire* Vol. 3 (2002)

Flory, M., '*Abducta Neroni Uxor*: The historiographic tradition on the marriage of Octavian and Livia', *Transactions of the American Philological Association* 118 (1988), pp. 343–59

Flower, H., 'The tradition of the spolia opima: M. Claudius Marcellus and Augustus', *Classical Antiquity* 19 (2000), pp. 34–64

Franzen, P., 'The Augustan legionary fortress at Nijmegen. Legionary and auxiliary soldiers', in A. Morillo, N. Hanel & E. Martín, *Limes XX: Estudios sobre la frontera romana. Roman Frontier Studies. Anejos de Gladius* 13 Vol. 1 (2009), pp. 1257–69

Gabba, E., 'The Perusine War and Triumviral Italy', *Harvard Studies in Classical Philology* 75 (1971), pp. 139–60

Gabba, E. (trans. P. Cuff), *The Roman Republic, the Army and the Allies* (1976)

Galinsky, K., *Augustan Culture* (1996)

Galinsky, K. (ed.), *The Cambridge Companion to the Age of Augustus* (2005)

Galinsky, K., *Augustus. Introduction to the Life of an Emperor* (2012)

Gardner, J., 'The Dictator', in Griffin (2009), pp. 57–71

Garnsey, P., *Famine and Food Supply in the Graeco-Roman World. Responses to Risk and Crisis* (1988)

Gelzer, M. (trans. P. Needham), *Caesar. Politician and Statesman* (1968)

Goldsworthy, A., *The Roman Army at War 100 BC–AD 200* (1996)

Goldsworthy, A., '"Instinctive genius": the depiction of Caesar the general', in Welch & Powell (1998), pp. 193–219

Goldsworthy, A., *In the Name of Rome* (2004)

Goldsworthy, A., *The Complete Roman Army* (2004)

Goldsworthy, A., *Caesar: The Life of a Colossus* (2006)

Goldsworthy, A., *Antony and Cleopatra* (2010)

Goudineau, C., *César et la Gaule* (1995)

Gowers, E., 'Augustus and "Syracuse"', *JRS* 100 (2010), pp. 69–87

Grant, M., *Cleopatra* (1972)

Green, P., *Alexander to Actium: The Historical Evolution of the Hellenistic Age* (1990)

Greenhalgh, P., *Pompey: The Roman Alexander* (1980)

Griffin, J., 'Augustus and the poets: "Caesar qui cogere posset"', in Millar & Segal (1990), pp. 189–218

Griffin, M., 'The Elder Seneca and Spain', *JRS* 62 (1972), pp. 1–19

Griffin, M. (ed.), *A Companion to Julius Caesar* (2009)

Grimal, P. (trans. A. Train), *Love in Ancient Rome* (1986)

Gruen, E., *The Last Generation of the Roman Republic* (1974)

Gruen, E., 'Cleopatra in Rome. Fact and Fantasies', in D. Braund & C. Gill (eds), *Myths, History and Culture in Republican Rome: Studies in honour of T. P. Wiseman* (2003), pp. 257–74

Gruen, E., 'Caesar as a politician', in Griffin (2009), pp. 23–36

Gwynn, A., *Roman Education* (1926)

Hallett, J., 'Perusinae Glandes and the Changing Image of Augustus', *American Journal of Ancient History* 2 (1977), pp. 151–71

Harmand, J., *L'armée et le soldat à Rome de 107 à 50 avant nôtre ère* (Paris, 1967)

Harrington, D., 'The Battle of Actium – a study in historiography', *Ancient World* 9. 1–2 (1984), pp. 59–64

Hölbl, G. (trans. T. Saavedra), *A History of the Ptolemaic Empire* (2001)

Holder, P., *The Auxilia from Augustus to Trajan* (1980)

Holland, R. , *Augustus. Godfather of Europe* (2004)

Huzar, E., 'Mark Antony: Marriages vs. careers', *The Classical Journal* 81 (1985/6), pp. 97–111

James, S., *Rome and the Sword. How Warriors and Weapons Shaped Roman History* (2011)

Johnson, J., 'The authenticity and validity of Antony's will', *L'Antiquité Classique* 47 (1978), pp. 494–503

Jones, A., 'The *Imperium* of Augustus', *JRS* 41 (1951), pp. 112–19

Jones, A., 'The elections under Augustus', *JRS* 45 (1955), pp. 9–21

Jones, R., 'The Roman Military Occupation of North-West Spain', *JRS* 66 (1976), pp. 45–66

Kennedy, D. (ed.), *The Roman Army in the East. Journal of Roman Archaeology Supplements* 18 (1996)

Kennedy, D., 'Parthia and Rome: eastern perspectives', in Kennedy (1996), pp. 67–90

Keppie, L., *Colonisation and Veteran Settlement in Italy: 47–14 BC* (1983)

Keppie, L., *The Making of the Roman Army* (1984)

Keppie, L., 'A centurion of *legio Martia* at Padova?', *Journal of Roman Military Equipment Studies* 2 (1991), pp. 115–21 = L. Keppie, *Legions and Veterans: Roman Army Papers 1971–2000* (2000), pp. 68–74

King, D., *The Elgin Marbles* (2006)

Kos, M., *Appian and Illyricum* (2005)

Lacey, W., 'Summi Fastigii Vocabulum: The story of a title', *JRS* 69 (1979), pp. 28–34

Lacey, W., *Augustus and the Principate. The Evolution of the System* (1996)

Lange, C., *Res Publica Constituta. Actium, Apollo and the Accomplishment of the Triumviral Assignment* (2009)

Lange, C., 'The Battle of Actium: A reconsideration', *Classical Quarterly* 61. 2 (2011), pp. 608–23

Last, H., 'Imperium Maius: A note', *JRS* 37 (1947), pp. 157–64

Le Bohec, Y., *The Imperial Roman Army* (1994)

Leon, E., 'Scribonia and her daughters', *Transactions and Proceedings of the American Philological Association* 82 (1951), pp. 168–75

Levick, B., 'Abdication and Agrippa Postumus', *Historia* 21 (1972), pp. 674–97

Levick, B., 'Julians and Claudians', *Greece and Rome* 22 (1975), pp. 29–38

Levick, B., *Tiberius the Politician* (1999)

Levick, B., *Augustus. Image and Substance* (2010)

Lewis, N. Reinhold, M. (eds), *Roman Civilization. Selected Readings* Vol. 1: *The Republic and the Augustan Age* (3rd edn, 1990)

Liebeschuetz, J., 'The settlement of 27 BC', in C. Deroux, *Studies in Latin Literature and Roman History* (2008), pp. 345–65

Linderski, J., 'Aphrodisias and the *Res Gestae*: The *Genera Militiae* and the Status of Octavian', *JRS* 74 (1984), pp. 74–80

Lintott, A., 'Electoral bribery in the Roman Republic', *JRS* 80 (1990), pp. 1–16

Lintott, A., *The Constitution of the Roman Republic* (1999)

Lintott, A., *Cicero as Evidence* (2008)

Lintott, A., 'The assassination', in Griffin (2009), pp. 72–82

Lo Cascio, E., 'The Size of the Roman Population: Beloch and the Meaning of the Augustan Census Figures', *JRS* 84 (1994), pp. 23–40

Lowe, B., *Roman Iberia. Economy, Society and Culture* (2009)

Luce, T., 'Livy, Augustus, and the Forum Augustum', in Edmondson (2009), pp. 399–415

MacMullen, R., *Enemies of the Roman Order. Treason, Unrest and Alienation in the Empire* (1967)

MacMullen, R., *Romanization in the Time of Augustus* (2000)

McNally, M., *Teutoburg Forest AD 9. The Destruction of Varus and his Legions.* Osprey Campaign Series 228 (2011)

Magie, D., 'Augustus' War in Spain (26–25 BC)', *Classical Philology* 15 (1920), pp. 323–39

Manley, J., *AD 43 The Roman Invasion of Britain – A Reassessment* (2002)

Marrou, H., *A History of Education in Antiquity* (1956)

Matyszak, P., *Mithridates the Great. Rome's Indomitable Enemy* (2004)

Maxfield, V., *The Military Decorations of the Roman Army* (1981)

Mayor, A., *The Poison King* (2010)

Meier, C. (trans. D. McLintock), *Caesar* (1996)

Mellor, R., *Tacitus* (1993)

Mierse, W., *Temples and Towns in Roman Iberia. The Social Dynamics of Sanctuary Designs from the Third Century BC to the Third Century AD* (1999)

Millar, F., *A Study of Cassius Dio* (1964)

Millar, F., 'Triumvirate and Principate', *JRS* 63 (1973), pp. 50–67

Millar, F., *The Emperor in the Roman World* (1977)

Millar, F., 'Empire and City, Augustus to Julian: Obligations, excuses and status', *JRS* 73 (1983), pp. 76–96

Millar, F. & Segal, E. (eds), *Caesar Augustus. Seven Aspects* (corrected paperback edn, 1990)

Millar, F., 'State and Subject: the impact of monarchy', in Millar & Segal (1990), pp. 37–60

Millar, F., *The Roman Near East 31 BC–AD 337* (1993)

Millar, F., *The Crowd in the Late Roman Republic* (1998)

Mitchell, T., *Cicero: The Ascending Years* (1979)

Mitchell, T., *Cicero the Senior Statesman* (1991)

Morillo Cerdán, A., 'The Augustean Spanish Experience: The origin of the *limes* system?', in A. Morillo, N. Hanel & E. Martín, *Limes XX: Estudios sobre la frontera romana. Roman Frontier Studies. Anejos de Gladius* 13 Vol. 1 (2009), pp. 239–51

Morrison, J. & Coates, J., *Greek and Roman Oared Warships* (1996)

Mouritsen, H., *Plebs and Politics in the Late Roman Republic* (2001)

Murdoch, A., *Rome's Greatest Defeat. Massacre in the Teutoburg Forest* (2006)

Nicolet, C., 'Augustus, Government, and the Propertied Classes', in Millar & Segal (1990), pp. 89–128

North, J., 'Caesar at the Lupercalia', *JRS* 98 (2008), pp. 144–60

Oorthuys, J. (ed.), *The Varian Disaster: The Battle of the Teutoburg Forest. Ancient Warfare* special issue (2009)

Osgood, J., *Caesar's Legacy. Civil War and the Emergence of the Roman Empire* (2006)

Paget, R., 'The ancient ports of Cumae', *JRS* 58 (1968), pp. 152–69

Paget, R., 'The Naval Battle of Cumae in 38 BC', *Latomus* 29 (1970), pp. 363–9

Parker, H., *The Roman Legions* (1957)

Patterson, J., 'The City of Rome Revisited: From Mid-Republic to Mid-Empire', *JRS* 100 (2010), pp. 210–32

Pelling, C., *Plutarch: Life of Antony* (1988)

Pelling, C., *Plutarch and History* (2002)

Pitassi, M., *The Navies of Rome* (2009)

Platner, S. & Ashby, T., *A Topographical Dictionary of Ancient Rome* (1929)

Pollini, J., 'Appuleii and Some Others on the Ara Pacis', *American Journal of Archaeology* 90 (1986), pp. 453–60

Potter, D., 'Emperors, their borders and their neighbours: the scope of imperial *mandata*', in Kennedy (1996), pp. 49–66

Powell, A., '"An island amid the flame": The Strategy and Imagery of Sextus Pompeius, 43–36 BC', in Powell & Welch (2002), pp. 103–33

Powell, A. & Welch, K. (eds), *Sextus Pompeius* (2002)

Powell, A., *Virgil the Partisan: A Study in the Re-integration of Classics* (2008)

Powell, L., *Eager for Glory. The Untold Story of Drusus the Elder, Conqueror of Germany* (2011)

Price, S., *Rituals and Power. The Roman Imperial Cult in Asia Minor* (1985)

Purcell, N., 'Livia and the Womanhood of Rome', *Proceedings of the Cambridge Philological Society* (1986), pp. 78–105 = Edmondson (2009), pp. 165–94

Queseda Sanz, F., '*Gladius hispaniensis*: an archaeological view from Iberia', *Journal of Roman Military Equipment Studies* 8 (1997), pp. 251–70

Queseda Sanz, F., *Armas de la Antigua Iberia de Tartessos a Numancia* (2010)

Raaflaub, K. & Toher, M. (eds), *Between Republic and Empire. Interpretations of Augustus and his Principate* (1990)

Raaflaub, K., 'The political significance of Augustus' military reforms', in Edmondson (2009), pp. 203–28

Ramsay, J., 'The Senate, Mark Antony, and Caesar's Legislative Legacy', *Classical Quarterly* 44 (1994), pp. 130–45

Ramsay, J. & Licht, A., *The Comet of 44 BC and Caesar's Funeral Games* (1997)

Ramsay, J., 'Did Mark Antony contemplate an alliance with his political enemies in July 44 B.C.E.?', *Classical Philology* 96. 3 (2001), pp. 253–68

Ramsay, J., 'Mark Antony's Judiciary Reform and its revival under the Triumvirs', *JRS* 95 (2005), pp. 20–37

Ramsay, J., 'The Proconsular Years: Politics at a Distance', in Griffin (2009), pp. 37–56

Rawson, B. (ed.), *The Family in Ancient Rome* (1986)

Rawson, B. (ed.), *Marriage, Divorce and Children in Ancient Rome* (1991)

Rawson, B., *Children and Childhood in Roman Italy* (2003)

Rawson, E., 'Caesar's Heritage: Hellenistic Kings and their Roman Equals', *JRS* 65 (1975), pp. 148–59

Rawson, E., 'The Ciceronian Aristocracy and its properties', in Finley (ed.) (1976), pp. 85–102

Rawson, E., *Intellectual Life in the Roman Republic* (1985)

Rea, J., 'Lease of a Red Cow called Thayris', *The Journal of Egyptian Archaeology* 68 (1982), pp. 277–82

Reinhold, M., *Marcus Agrippa: A Biography* (1933)

Reynolds, J., *Aphrodisias and Rome* (1982)

Ribera i Lacomba, A. & Calvo Galvez, M., 'La primera evidencia arqueológica de la destrucción de Valentia por Pompeyo', *Journal of Roman Archaeology* 8 (1995), pp. 19–40

Rice, E., *Cleopatra* (1999)

Rice Holmes, T., *The Roman Republic* Vols 1–3 (1923–8)

Rice Holmes, T., *The Architect of the Roman Empire* Vol. 1 (1928)

Rich, J., *Declaring War in the Roman Republic in the Period of Transmarine Expansion* (1976)

Rich, J. & Shipley, G. (eds), *War and Society in the Roman World* (1993)

Rich, J., 'Augustus and the spolia opima', *Chiron* 26 (1996), pp. 85–127

Rich, J., 'The Parthian honours', *Papers of the British School at Rome* 66 (1998), pp. 71–128

Rich, J., 'Augustus, War and Peace', in Edmondson (2009), pp. 137–64 = L. de Blois, P. Erdkamp, O. Hekster, G. de Kleijn S. Mols (eds),

The Representation and Perception of Roman Imperial Power: Proceedings of the Third Workshop of the International Network, Impact of Empire (Roman Empire c.200 BC–AD 476). Netherlands Institute in Rome, 20–23 March 2002 (2003), pp. 329–57

Rich, J., 'Cantabrian closure: Augustus' Spanish War and the ending of his memoirs', in Smith & Powell (2009), pp. 145–72

Richardson, J., 'The triumph, the praetors and the Senate in the early second century BC', *JRS* 65 (1976), pp. 50–63

Richardson, J., '*Imperium Romanum:* Empire and the Language of Power', *JRS* 81 (1991), pp. 1–9

Richardson, J., *The Romans in Spain* (1996)

Richardson, J., *Augustan Rome 44 BC TO AD 14. The Restoration of the Republic and the Establishment of Empire* (2012)

Richardson, P., *Herod. King of the Jews and Friend of the Romans* (1996)

Rickman, G., *The Corn Supply of Ancient Rome* (1980)

Rihll, T., 'Lead Slingshot (*glandes*)', *JRA* 22 (2009), pp. 149–69

Roddaz, J. M., *Marcus Agrippa* (1984)

Rogers, W., *Greek and Roman Naval Warfare* (1937)

Roller, D., *The Building Programme of Herod the Great* (1998)

Rose, C., 'Princes and barbarians on the Ara Pacis', *American Journal of Archaeology* 94 (1990), pp. 453–67

Rosenstein, N., *Imperatores Victi* (1993)

Rost, A., 'The Battle between Romans and Germans in Kalkriese: Interpreting the Archaeological Remains from an ancient battlefield', in A. Morillo, N. Hanel & E. Martín, *Limes XX: Estudios sobre la frontera romana. Roman Frontier Studies. Anejos de Gladius* 13 Vol. 3 (2009), pp. 1339–45

Roth, J., *The Logistics of the Roman Army at War (264 BC–AD 235)* (1999)

Roymans, N., *Tribal Societies in Northern Gaul: An Anthropological Perspective. Cingula* 12 (1990)

Saddington, D., *The Development of the Roman Auxiliary Forces from Caesar to Vespasian (49 BC–AD 79)* (1982)

Saller, R., 'Anecdotes as historical evidence', *Greece and Rome* 27 (1980), pp. 69–83

Salmon, E., 'The Evolution of Augustus' Principate', *Historia* 5 (1956), pp. 456–78

Salway, B., 'What's in a name? A survey of Roman onomastic practice from 700 BC–AD 700', *JRS* 84 (1994), pp. 124–45

Scheid, J., 'To honour the Princeps and venerate the gods. Public cult, neighbourhood cults, and imperial cult in Augustan Rome', in Edmondson (2009), pp. 275–99

Scheidel, W., 'Emperors, Aristocrats, and the Grim Reaper: Towards a Demographic Profile of the Roman Elite', *Classical Quarterly* 49 (1999), pp. 254–81

Schlüter, W., 'The Battle of the Teutoburg Forest: archaeological research at Kalkriese near Osnabrück', in J. Creighton & R. Wilson, *Roman Germany. Studies in Cultural Interaction. Journal of Roman Archaeology Supplementary Series* 32 (1999), pp. 125–59

Schürer, E., Vermes, G. & Millar, F., *The History of the Jewish People in the Age of Jesus Christ* Vol. 1 (1973)

Scott, K., 'The Political Propaganda of 44–30 BC', *Memoirs of the American Academy in Rome* 11 (1933), pp. 7–49

Seager, R., *Pompey the Great. A Political Biography* (2nd edn, 2002)

Seager, R., *Tiberius* (2005)

Shatzman, I., *Senatorial Wealth and Roman Politics. Collection Latomus* Vol. 142 (1975)

Sheppard, S., *Philippi 42 BC. The Death of the Roman Republic.* Osprey Campaign Series 199 (2008)

Sheppard, S., *Actium: Downfall of Antony and Cleopatra.* Osprey Campaign Series 211 (2009)

Sherk, R., *Roman Documents from the Greek East* (1969)

Sherwin-White, A., *Roman Foreign Policy in the East, 168 BC–AD 1* (1984)

Siani-Davies, M., 'Ptolemy XII Auletes and the Romans', *Historia* 46 (1997), pp. 306–40

Sidebotham, S., 'Aelius Gallus and Arabia', *Latomus* 45 (1986), pp. 590–602

Simpson, C., 'The date of the dedication of the Temple of Mars Ultor', *JRS* 67 (1977), pp. 91–4

Slater, W., 'Pueri, Turba Minuta', in Bulletin of the Institute of Classical Studies 21 (1974), pp. 133–40

Smith, C. & Powell, A. (eds), The Lost Memoirs of Augustus and the Development of Roman Autobiography (2009)

Smith, R., Service in the Post-Marian Roman Army (1958)

Spaul, J., ALA² (1994)

Spawforth, A., Greece and the Augustan Cultural Revolution. Greek Culture in the Roman World (2012)

Speidel, M., 'The Roman army in Judaea under the Procurators', in M. Speidel, Roman Army Studies Vol. 2, Mavors (1992), pp. 224–32

Stavely, E., 'The "Fasces" and "Imperium Maius"', Historia 12 (1963), pp. 458–84

Stevenson, T., 'The ideal benefactor and the father analogy in Greek and Roman thought', Classical Quarterly 42 (1992), pp. 421–36

Stockton, D., 'Primus and Murena', Historia 14 (1965), pp. 18–40

Stockton, D., Cicero. A Political Biography (1971)

Swan, M., 'The consular fasti of 23 BC and the conspiracy of Varro Murena', Harvard Studies in Classical Philology 71 (1967), pp. 235–47

Syme, R., 'Notes on the legions under Augustus', JRS 23 (1933), pp. 14–33

Syme, R., 'The Spanish War of Augustus', American Journal of Philology 55 (1934), pp. 293–317

Syme, R., 'The Allegiance of Labienus', JRS 28 (1938), pp. 113–25

Syme, R., Tacitus (2 vols, 1958)

Syme, R., 'Imperator Caesar: A study in imperial nomenclature', Historia 7 (1958), pp. 172–88 = Roman Papers Vol. 1 (1979), pp. 181–96

Syme, R., 'Livy and Augustus', Harvard Studies in Classical Philology 64 (1959), pp. 27–87

Syme, R., The Roman Revolution (paperback edn, 1960)

Syme, R., History in Ovid (1978)

Syme, R., 'The conquest of North-West Spain', Roman Papers Vol. 2 (1979), pp. 825–54

Syme, R., 'Neglected children on the Ara Pacis', American Journal of Archaeology 88 (1984), pp. 583–9

Syme, R., The Augustan Aristocracy (1986)

Talbert, R., 'Augustus and the Senate', *Greece and Rome* 31 (1984), pp. 55–63

Tatum, W., *The Patrician Tribune Publius Clodius Pulcher* (1999)

Taylor, L. Ross, *Party Politics in the Age of Caesar* (1949)

Taylor, L. Ross, 'The rise of Julius Caesar', *Greece and Rome* 4 (1957), pp. 10–18

Taylor, L. Ross, *Roman Voting Assemblies: From the Hannibalic War to the Dictatorship of Caesar* (1966)

Taylor, L. Ross, 'The dating of major legislation and elections in Caesar's first consulship', *Historia* 17 (1968), pp. 173–93

Tchernia, A., 'Italian wine in Gaul at the end of the Republic', in P. Garnsey, K. Hopkins & C. Whittaker (eds), *Trade in the Ancient Economy* (1983), pp. 87–104

Todd, M., *Roman Britain* (3rd edn, 1999)

Todd, M., *The Early Germans* (2004)

Toher, M., 'Augustus and the Evolution of Roman Historiography', in Raaflaub & Toher (1990), pp. 139–54

Torelli, M., *Typology and Structure of Roman Historical Reliefs* (1982)

Treggiari, S., *Roman Marriage* (1991)

Treggiari, S., 'Divorce Roman Style: How easy and frequent was it?' in Rawson (1991), pp. 131–46

Trillmich, W. (trans. C. Nader), *Colonia Augusta Emerita, Capital of Lusitania* in Edmondson (2009), pp. 427–67

Tyldesley, J., *Cleopatra. Last Queen of Egypt* (2009)

Tyrell, W., 'Labienus' departure from Caesar in January 49 BC', *Historia* 21 (1972), pp. 424–40

Ullman, B., 'Cleopatra's pearls', *The Classical Journal* 52. 5 (Feb. 1957), pp. 193–201

Veyne, P. (trans. B. Pearce), *Bread and Circuses* (1992)

Wallace-Hadrill, A., 'Civilis Principis: between citizen and king', *JRS* 72 (1982), pp. 32–48

Wallace-Hadrill, A., 'Image and authority in the coinage of Augustus', *JRS* 76 (1986), pp. 66–87

Wallace-Hadrill, A., *Suetonius* (2nd edn, 1995)

Wallace-Hadrill, A., 'Family inheritance in the Augustan Marriage

Laws', in Edmondson (2009), pp. 250–74 = *Proceedings of the Cambridge Philological Society* 27 (1981), pp. 58–80

Ward, A., *Marcus Crassus and the Late Roman Republic* (1977)

Wardle, D., 'Valerius Maximus on the Domus Augusta, Augustus, and Tiberius', *Classical Quarterly* 50 (2000), pp. 479–93

Wardle, D., 'A perfect send-off: Suetonius and the dying art of Augustus (Suetonius Aug. 99)', *Mnemosyne* 60 (2007), pp. 443–63

Watson, G., *The Roman Soldier* (1985)

Webster, G., *The Roman Invasion of Britain* (rev. edn, 1993)

Weigel, R., *Lepidus. The Tarnished Triumvir* (1992)

Weinstock, S., *Divus Julius* (1971)

Welch, K. & Powell, A. (eds), *Julius Caesar as Artful Reporter: The War Commentaries as Political Instruments* (1998)

Welch, K., 'Sextus Pompeius and the *Res Publica* in 42–39 BC', in Powell & Welch (2002), pp. 31–63

Wells, C., *The German Policy of Augustus. An Examination of the Archaeological Evidence* (1972)

Wells, C., 'What's new along the Lippe: Recent work in North Germany', *Britannia* 29 (1998), pp. 457–64

Wells, P., *The Barbarians Speak. How the Conquered Peoples Shaped the Roman Empire* (1999)

Wells, P., *The Battle that Stopped Rome* (2003)

White, L., 'Herod and the Jewish experience of Augustan rule', in Galinsky (2005), pp. 361–87

White, P., *Promised Verse. Poets in the Society of Augustan Rome* (1993)

Wiedermann, T., 'The political background to Ovid's *Tristia* 2', *Classical Quarterly* 25 (1975), pp. 264–71

Wilbers-Rost, S., 'The site of the Varus Battle at Kalkriese. Recent Results from Archaeological Research', in A. Morillo, N. Hanel & E. Martín, *Limes XX: Estudios sobre la frontera romana. Roman Frontier Studies. Anejos de Gladius* 13 Vol. 3 (2009), pp. 1347–52

Williams, C., *Roman Homosexuality. Ideologies of Masculinity in Classical Antiquity* (1999)

Williams, G., 'Did Maecenas "Fall from favour"? Augustan Literary Patronage', in Raaflaub & Toher (1990), pp. 258–75

Wiseman, T., 'Conspicui Postes Tectaque Digna Deo: the public image of aristocratic and imperial houses in the Late Republic and Early Empire', in L'Urbs. Espace urbain et histoire (1987), pp. 393–413

Wiseman, T., 'The House of Augustus and the Lupercal', JRA 22 (2009), pp. 527–45

Wolters, R., Die Schlacht im Teutoburger Wald (2008)

Woolf, G., 'Roman Peace', in Rich & Shipley (1993), pp. 171–94

Yakobson, A., 'Petitio et Largitio: Popular participation in the centuriate assembly of the Late Republic', JRS 8 (1992), pp. 32–52

Yavetz, Z., Plebs and Princeps (1969)

Yavetz, Z., Julius Caesar and his Public Image (1983)

Yavetz, Z., 'The Res Gestae and Augustus' public image', in Millar & Segal (1990), pp. 1–36

Yavetz, Z., 'The personality of Augustus', in Raaflaub & Toher (1990), pp. 21–41, 32

Zanker, P. (trans. A. Shapiro), The Power of Images in the Age of Augustus (1988)

Zink, S., 'Reconstructing the Palatine temple of Apollo: a case study in early Augustan temple design', JRA 21 (2008), pp. 47–63

Ziolkowski, J. & Putnam, J., The Virgilian Tradition. The First Fifteen Hundred Years (2008)

ABBREVIATIONS USED IN
THE NOTES

Ampelius, *Lib. mem* = Lucius Ampellius, *Liber memorialis*

Appian, *BC* = Appian, *Civil Wars*

Appian, *Bell. Hisp.* = Appian, *Spanish Wars*

Broughton, *MRR* 2 = Broughton, T., & Patterson, M. (1951), *The Magistrates of the Roman Republic* Vol. 2

Caesar, *BC* = Caesar, *The Civil Wars*

Caesar, *BG* = Caesar, *The Gallic Wars*

CAH² IX = Crook, J., Lintott, A., & Rawson, E. (eds), *The Cambridge Ancient History* 2nd edn Vol. IX: *The Last Age of the Roman Republic, 146–43 BC.*

CAH² X = Bowman, A., Champlin, E., & Lintott, A. (eds), *The Cambridge Ancient History* 2nd edn Vol. X: *The Augustan Empire, 43 BC–AD 69.*

Cicero, *ad Att.* = Cicero, *Letters to Atticus*

Cicero, *ad Fam.* = Cicero, *Letters to his Friends*

Cicero, *ad Quintum Fratrem* = Cicero, *Letters to his Brother Quintus*

Cicero, *Agr.* = Cicero, *Orationes de Lege Agraria*

Cicero, *Cat.* = Cicero, *Catilinarian Orations*

Cicero, *de reg. Alex F.* = Cicero, fragment from the *Oration Concerning the King of Alexandria*

Cicero, *Verrines* = Cicero, *Verrine Orations*

CIG = *Corpus Inscriptionum Graecarum*

CIL = *Corpus Inscriptionum Latinarum*

Comp. Nic. = Fragment of Nicolaus of Damascus, *History*

De vir. Ill. = the anonymous *de viris illustribus*

Dio = Cassius Dio, *Roman History*

Galen, *Comm. In Hipp. Epid., CMG* = Kühn, C., *Galenus Medicus* (1821–33), supplemented by Diels, H. *et alii* (1918–)

Gellius, *NA* = Aulus Gellius, *Attic Nights*

ILLRP = Degrassi, A. (ed.) (1963–5), *Inscriptiones Latinae Liberae Rei Republicae*

ILS = Dessau, H. (1892–1916), *Incriptiones Latinae Selectae*

Josephus, *AJ* = Josephus, *Jewish Antiquities*

Josephus, *BJ* = Josephus, *The Jewish War*

JRA = *Journal of Roman Archaeology*

JRS = *Journal of Roman Studies*

Justin = Justinus, *Epitome*

Livy, *Pers.* = Livy, *Roman History. Periochae.*

OGIS = Dittenberger, W., *Orientis Graeci Inscriptiones Selectae* (1903–5).

Pliny the Elder, *NH* = Pliny the Elder, *Natural History*

Pliny the Younger, *Epistulae* = Pliny the Younger, *Letters*

Quintilian = Quintilian, *Training in Oratory*

Sallust, *Bell. Cat.* = Sallust, *The Catilinarian War*

Sallust, *Bell. Jug.* = Sallust, *The Jugurthine War*

Sallust, *Hist.* = Sallust, *Histories*

SEG. = Roussel, P., Tod, M., Ziebarth, E. & Hondius, J. (eds), *Supplementum Epigraphicum Graecum* (1923–)

Serv. = Servius

Strabo, *Geog.* = Strabo, *Geography*

Tacitus, *Ann.* = Tacitus, *Annals*

Valerius Maximus = Valerius Maximus, *Memorable Doings and Sayings*

Velleius Paterculus = Velleius Paterculus, *Roman History*

NOTES

INTRODUCTION

1 Luke 2: 1–3.
2 The more recent HBO *Rome* (2006–07) mini-series gave the young Octavius a slightly more sympathetic character, although when a different actor took over as the older version he became colder and more calculating. His sadism was also made more than a hint, as when he tells his new bride Livia that it will give him pleasure to hurt her when they make love.
3 Shakespeare, *Julius Caesar*, 4. 1. 1.
4 Among the recent short studies of Augustus and his era, the best are D. Shotter, *Augustus Caesar* (2nd edn, 1991), W. Eck, *The Age of Augustus* (2003), K. Galinsky, *Augustus. Introduction to the Life of an Emperor* (2012), J. Richardson, *Augustan Rome 44 BC to AD 14. The Restoration of the Republic and the Establishment of the Empire* (2012); of popular accounts, R. Holland, *Augustus. Godfather of Europe* (2004) focuses mainly on the years up to Actium, while A. Everitt, *Augustus: The Life of Rome's First Emperor* (2006) is drawn to this era and the later struggle for succession.
5 Julian, *Caesars* 309 B-C; for brief discussion see K. Galinsky, *Augustan Culture* (1996), p. 373.
6 For a useful survey of historians' attitudes to Augustus see Z. Yavetz, 'The *Res Gestae* and Augustus' public image', in F. Millar & E. Segal (eds), *Caesar Augustus. Seven Aspects* (1990), pp. 1–36, esp. pp. 22–6, and also J. Edmondson (ed.) *Augustus* (2009), pp. 14–26.
7 For discussions of some of the principal sources, see F. Millar, *A Study of Cassius Dio* (1964), A. Wallace-Hadrill, *Suetonius* (2nd edn, 1995), C. Pelling, *Plutarch and History* (2002), C. Smith & A. Powell (eds), *The Lost Memoirs of Augustus and the Development of Roman Autobiography* (2009), R. Syme, *Tacitus* (2 vols,1958), and R. Mellor, *Tacitus* (1993).

CHAPTER 1

1 Suetonius, *Augustus* 94. 5.
2 For the date, see Suetonius, *Augustus* 5. 1; for this composite picture and on childbirth in general see B. Rawson, *Children and Childhood in Roman Italy* (2003), *passim*, esp. pp. 99 –113, S. Dixon, *The Roman Mother* (1988), pp. 106–8, 237–40. See also the collection of papers in B. Rawson (ed.), *Marriage, Divorce and Children in Ancient Rome* (1991); for Julius Caesar and the election to *pontifex maximus* see

A. Goldsworthy, *Caesar: The Life of a Colossus* (2006), pp. 124–6, and Suetonius, *Caesar* 59 on his lack of religious scruple; for the astrological questions posed by the date of Augustus' birth and his later adoption of the sign of the capricorn see T. Barton, 'Augustus and Capricorn: Astrological polyvalency and imperial rhetoric', *JRS* 85 (1995), pp. 33–51.

3 Suetonius, *Augustus* 94. 1–12 for a series of omens, esp. 94. 3–4; Dio 45. 1. 2–3 repeats the story of the snake, probably using Suetonius directly or a common source.

4 For detailed discussion of the consuls and other senior magistracies, see A. Lintott, *The Constitution of the Roman Republic* (1999), pp. 94–120, esp. 104–9.

5 Suetonius, *Augustus* 94. 5, where it is claimed the noted religious expert and mystic Publius Nigidius Figulus made the prediction. Other stories involved Cicero and Quintus Lutatius Catulus in probably similar attempts to make them more credible. On the question of the chronology of the Catilinarian debates see the useful discussion in D. Stockton, *Cicero. A Political Biography* (1971), pp. 336–9, esp. 337.

6 See in general Rawson (2003), pp. 105–12.

7 For a general survey of the significance of Roman names see B. Salway, 'What's in a name? A survey of Roman onomastic practice from 700 BC–AD 700', *JRS* 84 (1994), pp. 124–45, esp. 124–31. For a detailed and insightful analysis of Augustus' names and practices in this period in general see R. Syme, 'Imperator Caesar: A study in imperial nomenclature', *Historia* 7 (1958), pp. 172–88 = *Roman Papers* Vol. I (1979), pp. 181–96.

8 Plutarch, *Cato the Elder* 20. 3. For a more detailed discussion of this topic see K. Bradley, 'Wet-nursing at Rome. A Study in Social Relations', in Rawson (1986), pp. 201–29.

9 Suetonius, *Augustus* 94. 6.

10 For Mithridates see P. Matyszak, *Mithridates the Great. Rome's Indomitable Enemy* (2004), and A. Mayor, *The Poison King* (2010).

11 Suetonius, *Caesar* 13 for the comment to his mother, and see also Plutarch, *Caesar* 7, Dio 37. 1–3, Velleius Paterculus 2. 43. 3; in general see Goldsworthy (2006), pp. 124–7 = (2007), pp. 150–4.

12 For Caesar's ancestry see Goldsworthy (2006), pp. 31–4 = (2007), pp. 37–41; on Catiline see Stockton (1971), pp. 73–8, 96–8, 100–07.

13 T. Mitchell, *Cicero: The Ascending Years* (1979), pp. 149–76, 222–5, Stockton (1971), pp. 79–84.

14 In general see Sallust, *Bell. Cat.* 26–7, Stockton (1971), pp. 105–6, Mitchell (1979), pp. 226–32, T. Rice Holmes, *The Roman Republic* Vol. 1 (1928), pp. 259–72; 'resident alien' (*inquilinus civis urbis Romanam*) see Sallust, *Bell. Cat.* 31. 9; also of relevance is Cicero's *Pro Murena*, delivered in defence of one of the successful candidates who was then accused of bribery.

15 Sallust, *Bell. Cat.* 59. 3 for the eagle.

16 Cicero, *In Pisonem* 6.

17 For the narrative of the Catilinarian conspiracy see Stockton (1971), pp. 110–42, Mitchell (1979), pp. 219–40; for Caesar's role in the debate see M. Gelzer, *Caesar:*

Politician and Statesman (1968), pp. 50–52, C. Meier, *Caesar* (1996), pp. 170–72 and Goldsworthy (2006), pp. 115–42 = (2007), pp. 144–72.

CHAPTER 2

1   Velleius Paterculus 2. 59. 1–2 (Loeb translation).
2   Suetonius, *Augustus* 3, 5, Velleius Paterculus 2. 59. 1–2, Dio 45. 1. 1, Tacitus, *Ann.* 1. 9; for discussion of his wealth see I. Shatzman, *Senatorial Wealth and Roman Politics. Collection Latomus* Vol. 142 (1975), p. 387, including fns 692 and 693, and in general E. Rawson, 'The Ciceronian Aristocracy and its Properties', in M. I. Finley (ed.), *Studies in Roman Property* (1976), pp. 85–102; excavation on the north-eastern side of the Palatine has revealed an aristocratic house occupied and remodelled in the second and first centuries BC and subsequently destroyed in Nero's fire, which may possibly be the one owned by Octavius, see J. Patterson, 'The City of Rome Revisited: From Mid-Republic to Mid-Empire', *JRS* 100 (2010), pp. 210–32, esp. p. 223 fn. 112, with reference to recent Italian excavations in the area.
3   Suetonius, *Augustus* 1. 2. 2.
4   Suetonius, *Augustus* 2. 3–3. 1, Appian, *BC* 3. 23; the name C. Octavius appears on a banker's loan chit or *tessera* and is most likely associated with Caius Octavius' father. For a discussion of senators' involvement in making loans, see Shatzman (1975), pp. 75–9.
5   Livy, *Pers.* 98 gives 900,000 as the total for the census conducted in 70–69 BC, although other sources make the total 10,000 higher, see E. Lo Cascio, 'The Size of the Roman Population: Beloch and the Meaning of the Augustan Census Figures', JRS 84 (1994), pp. 23–40 for a discussion. Totals for ancient populations remain highly controversial.
6   Plutarch, *Crassus* 2 for the claim that only a man capable of supporting an army could call himself rich; for his estates see Pliny, *NH* 33. 134, although contrast slighter lower estimate in Plutarch, *Crassus* 2 with comments in Shatzman (1975), pp. 375–8, and for Pompey pp. 389–93. For their careers in general see respectively A. Ward, *Marcus Crassus and the Late Roman Republic* (1977), P. Greenhalgh, *Pompey: The Roman Alexander* (1980) and R. Seager, *Pompey the Great. A Political Biography* (2nd edn, 2002).
7   For Crassus' use of money see Plutarch, *Crassus* 2–3; for senators in debt to him see Sallust, *Bell. Cat.* 48. 5–6; on the *publicani* in general see E. Badian, *Publicans and Sinners* (1972).
8   Suetonius, *Augustus* 4. 1.
9   R. Syme, *The Roman Revolution* (1960), p. 112; relationship to Pompey, see Suetonius, *Augustus* 4. 1.
10 His age is conjectural, but based on the assumption that he held the quaestorship in 73 BC in the same year as Caius Toranius, with whom he was plebeian aedile, see *ILS* 47. However, since Toranius suffered a defeat at the hands of Spartacus (Sallust, *Hist.* 3. 46M, Florus 2. 8. 5), it is equally possible that his career slowed down, making them colleagues at a later stage. The evidence is collected in Broughton, *MRR* 2, p. 110.

11 For Caius Octavius' career see *ILS* 47; for the numbers of legions in this period see P. Brunt, *Italian Manpower 225 BC–AD 14* (1971), pp. 446–72, estimating the lowest total at thirteen legions in 80 BC, and the highest at thirty-nine to forty legions in 71–70 BC.

12 On the quaestorship see Lintott (1999), pp. 133–7, and on the dating see n. 9 above; for Toranius and Spartacus see Sallust, *Hist.* 3. 46M, Florus 2. 8. 5.

13 Lintott (1999), pp. 129–33.

14 For an excellent recent survey of Caesar's early career see E. Gruen, 'Caesar as a politician', in M. Griffin (ed.), *A Companion to Julius Caesar* (2009), pp. 23–36, and see also L. Taylor, 'The Rise of Julius Caesar', *Greece and Rome* 4 (1957), pp. 10–18, and Gelzer (1968), p. 22, and in general Goldsworthy (2006), pp. 82–151 = (2007), pp. 61–183, and R. Billows, *Julius Caesar. The Colossus of Rome* (2009), pp. 56–110, who emphasises his consistent championing of popular causes. On the *corona civica* see Gellius, *NA* 5. 6. 13–14, Pliny *NH* 16. 12–13, and discussion in V. Maxfield, *The Military Decorations of the Roman Army* (1981), pp. 70–74, 119–20.

15 For candidature and the electoral process in general see L. Taylor, *Party Politics in the Age of Caesar* (1949), esp. pp. 50–75, and *Roman Voting Assemblies: From the Hannibalic War to the Dictatorship of Caesar* (1966), esp. pp. 78–106, A. Lintott, 'Electoral Bribery in the Roman Republic', *JRS* 80 (1990), pp. 1–16, F. Millar, *The Crowd in the Late Roman Republic* (1998), H. Mouritsen, *Plebs and Politics in the Late Roman Republic* (2001), esp. pp. 63–89, A. Yakobson, '*Petitio* et *Largitio*: Popular participation in the centuriate assembly of the Late Republic', *JRS* 8 (1992), pp. 32–52

16 Q. Cicero, *Handbook on Electioneering* 35. There is a general consensus that Quintus Cicero was the author of this work. His literary output was considerable, even though little has survived. While on campaign with Julius Caesar in Gaul he told his brother that he had written four tragedies in just sixteen days, Cicero, *ad Quintum Fratrem* 3. 5/6. 8

17 Q. Cicero, *Handbook on Electioneering* 25–6 (Loeb translation).

18 See Plutarch, *Cato the Younger* 8. 2; see Q. Cicero, *Handbook on Electioneering* 41–2 on the importance of a candidate learning names and, even when reminded, of seeming natural.

19 On Caesar's stance see Goldsworthy (2006), pp. 119–45, esp. pp. 121–4 on the trial of Rabirius Postumus. For an emphasis on Caesar's consistent espousal of popular causes as a major part of his success, see the arguments in Billows (2009), pp. 56–110.

20 Sallust, *Bell. Cat.* 60. 7–61. 4.

21 For a summary of Pompey's career see A. Goldsworthy, *In the Name of Rome* (2004), pp. 152–80, for more detail see Seager (2002), pp. 20–38; his nickname, Valerius Maximus 6. 2. 8.

22 Suetonius, *Caesar* 15, Dio 37. 43. 1–4, Plutarch, *Cato the Younger* 26. 1–29. 2.

23 Q. Cicero, *Handbook on Electioneering* 45, 47–8 (Loeb translation).

24 The point is well made by Billows (2009), pp. 104–5.

25 For discussion see L. Ross Taylor, *Roman Voting Assemblies* (1966), pp. 84–106.

26 Velleius Paterculus 2. 59. 2 for coming first in the poll, with E. Gruen, *The Last Generation of the Roman Republic* (1974), pp. 118–19.

27 Cicero, *ad Quintum Fratrem* 1. 21 (Loeb translation).

28 Suetonius, *Caesar* 11, Dio 37. 10. 1–3, Plutarch, *Cato the Younger* 17. 4–5.

29 Suetonius, *Augustus* 3. 1.

30 Catullus 10; Cicero, *Verrines* 1. 40.

31 Suetonius, *Augustus* 3. 2, 94. 5, Velleius Paterculus 2. 59. 2, *ILS* 47; for the requirement for 5,000 enemy dead see Valerius Maximus 2. 8. 1 and discussion in J. Richardson, 'The triumph, the praetors and the Senate in the early second century BC', *JRS* 65 (1976), pp. 50–63, esp. 61–2.

32 Tacitus *Ann*, 1. 9, Cicero, *Philippics* 3. 15 and Gruen (1974), p. 143, fn. 96.

CHAPTER 3

1 Caelius' quote from Cicero, *ad Fam*. 8. 8. 9.

2 Suetonius, *Augustus* 8. 1, 27. 1, Nicolaus of Damascus 2, Appian, *BC* 4. 12.

3 Nicolaus of Damascus 3, and R. Syme, *The Roman Revolution* (1960), pp. 127–8 and 'Neglected children on the *Ara Pacis*', *American Journal of Archaeology* 88 (1984), pp. 583–9, 586 fn. 17.

4 Octavius' *paedogogus* see Dio 58. 33. 1, mentioning that Sphaerus was given a public funeral in 40 BC by his grateful former charge; Cicero, *Orator* 120; on childhood in general see B. Rawson (ed.), *Children and Childhood in Roman Italy* (2003), esp. pp. 99–113; on education see H. Marrou, *A History of Education in Antiquity* (1956), pp. 229–91, A. Gwynn, *Roman Education* (1926), esp. 1–32; Cicero, *de re publica* 4. 3; 'an old and wealthy equestrian family', see Suetonius, *Augustus* 2. 3.

5 Appian, *BC* 2. 9.

6 For discussion see R. Seager, *Pompey the Great. A Political Biography* (2002), pp. 72–9, and T. Wiseman in *CAH²* IX, pp. 358–67.

7 For an especially blatant illustration of the power of *auctoritas*, see Valerius Maximus 3. 7. 8.

8 Seager (2002), pp. 79–82, M. Gelzer (trans. P. Needham), *Caesar* (1968), pp. 65–8; on the pay of soldiers, it is worth noting that Julius Caesar was able to double their salary without making them rich, Suetonius, *Julius Caesar* 26, and for a wider survey of the army at this time see R. Smith, *Service in the Post-Marian Roman Army* (1958).

9 See Cicero, *ad Att*. 1. 17. 9, 18. 3, 18. 7, 2. 1. 8, with E. Badian, *Publicans and Sinners* (1972), pp. 101–4.

10 For the proconsulship in Spain and his return see in general Gelzer (1968), pp. 61–70, A. Goldsworthy, *Caesar. The Life of a Colossus* (2006), pp. 148–59 = (2007), pp. 179–95, Gruen, 'Caesar as a politician', in M. Griffin (ed.), *A Companion to Julius Caesar* (2009), pp. 23–36, esp. 29–31; for the ancient sources for Cato's filibuster see Appian, *BC* 2. 8, Dio 37. 54. 1–2, Suetonius, *Julius Caesar* 18. 2 and Plutarch, *Cato the Younger* 31. 2–3, *Caesar* 13. 1.

11 Syme (1960), pp. 34–5.

12 Cicero, *ad Att*. 2. 3, 3–4.

13 For Julius Caesar's consulship see L. Ross Taylor, 'The dating of major legislation and elections in Caesar's first consulship', *Historia* 17 (1968), pp. 173–93,

Gruen (2009), pp. 31–5, Gelzer (1968), pp. 71–101, C. Meier (trans. D. McLintock), *Caesar* (1996), pp. 204–23, Goldsworthy (2006), pp. 161–81 = (2007), pp. 196–220, R. Billows, *Julius Caesar. The Colossus of Rome* (2009), pp. 111–29, Seager (2002), pp. 86–100; the arrest of Cato, see Dio 38. 2. 1–3. 3. Suetonius, *Julius Caesar* 20. 4 and Plutarch, *Cato the Younger* 33. 1–2 give a slightly different version, apparently dating Cato's arrest to another occasion rather than the debate on the land law.

14 Suetonius, *Augustus* 4. 1 for Atius Balbus as one of the twenty land commissioners.

15 On the rioting in the Forum see Dio 38. 6. 4–7. 2, Appian, *BC* 2. 11, Plutarch, *Cato the Younger* 32. 2–6, Suetonius, *Julius Caesar* 20. 1; on Bibulus' attempts to prevent legislation, see Suetonius, *Julius Caesar* 20. 2, Dio 38. 8. 2 with comments in Taylor (1968), pp. 177–9.

16 Suetonius, *Julius Caesar* 21, 50. 1–2, Plutarch, *Pompey* 47–48, *Caesar* 14 and Dio 38. 9. 1; 'a husband to women and a wife to men', see Suetonius, *Julius Caesar* 52. 3.

17 Taylor (1968), pp. 182–8 for discussion of the *lex Vatinia* granting Julius Caesar his command.

18 Nicolaus of Damascus 3; for general discussions of Roman education see n. 4.

19 Suetonius, *Tiberius* 2–3, Cicero, *de natura deorum* 2. 7 for Claudius Pulcher in the First Punic War. For Clodius in general see W. Tatum, *The Patrician Tribune Publius Clodius Pulcher* (1999) *passim*, and on the *Bona Dea* scandal and his enmity towards Cicero see J. Balsdon, 'Fabula Clodiana', *Historia* 15 (1966), pp. 65–73; for a discussion of the family's position in the first century BC see E. Gruen, *The Last Generation of the Roman Republic* (1974), pp. 97–100.

20 Dio 38. 12. 1–3, Cicero, *de domo* 41, *ad Att.* 8. 3, Suetonius, *Julius Caesar* 20. 4, Plutarch, *Caesar* 14; see also Gelzer (1968), pp. 76–8, Seager (2002), pp. 91–9.

21 For good surveys of the politics of these years see J. Ramsay, 'The Proconsular Years: Politics at a Distance', in Griffin (2009), pp. 37–56, and Wiseman in *CAH²* IX, pp. 366–81, 385–408.

22 On the 'conference' of Luca and the confirmation of the alliance between Pompey, Crassus and Julius Caesar see Suetonius, *Caesar* 24. 1, Appian, *BC* 2. 17, Plutarch, *Pompey* 50, *Caesar* 21, *Crassus* 14; see also Gelzer (1968), pp.120–24, Seager (2002), pp. 110–19, Meier (1996), pp. 270–73 and A. Ward, *Marcus Crassus and the Late Roman Republic* (1977), pp. 262–88.

23 Julia's miscarriage, see Plutarch, *Pompey* 53; Crassus' departure from the City, see Cicero, *ad Att.* 4. 13, Plutarch, *Crassus* 16.

24 Suetonius, *Julius Caesar* 27. 1; for Carrhae and the death of Crassus the main sources are Plutarch, *Crassus* 17–33, and Dio 40. 12–30.

25 Clodius and Milo, see Gelzer (1968), pp. 145–52, Meier (1996), pp. 297–301 and Seager (2002), pp. 126–35.

26 Pompey as sole consul, see Plutarch, *Pompey* 54, *Cato* 47, Dio 40. 50. 4, Appian, *BC* 2. 23; on Pompey's position and new marriage see Syme (1960), pp. 36–40, and on Cornelia see Plutarch, *Pompey* 55.

27 For a more detailed account of the campaigns in Gaul, see Goldsworthy (2006), pp. 184–356 = (2007), pp. 222–431; for Caesar's *Commentaries* in general see the collection of papers in K. Welch & A. Powell (eds), *Julius Caesar as Artful Reporter: The War Commentaries as Political Instruments* (1998).

28 Quotations from Lucan, *Pharsalia* 1. 125–6 (Oxford translation by S. Braund), and Cicero, *ad Fam.* 8. 8. 9; for the path to the Civil War in general see Gelzer (1968), pp. 169–94, Seager (2002), pp. 138–51, Wiseman in *CAH*² IX, pp. 414–23, Goldsworthy (2006), pp. 358–79 = (2007), pp. 434–60.

29 Appian, *BC* 2. 28, with a slightly different version in Plutarch, *Pompey* 58, cf. Dio 60. 64. 1–4.

30 Plutarch, *Pompey* 59, Caesar, *BG* 8. 52. 3, Dio 40. 64. 3–4, Appian, *BC* 2. 31–2, Caesar, *BC* 1. 1–5, Suetonius, *Julius Caesar* 29. 2, Dio 41. 1. 1–3. 4.

31 Suetonius, *Caesar* 31–2, Plutarch, *Caesar* 32, Appian, *BC* 2. 35.

CHAPTER 4

1 Quoted in Suetonius, *Caesar* 30. 4.

2 Pompey's boast about stamping his foot, see Plutarch, *Pompey* 57, 60; 'Sulla did it', see Cicero, *ad Att.* 9. 10. 3; for narrative and discussion of these campaigns see A. Goldsworthy, *Caesar. The Life of a Colossus* (2006), pp. 380–471 = (2007), pp. 461–574.

3 Cicero, *ad Att.* 9. 7C.

4 For the campaigns see Goldsworthy (2006), pp. 380–431 = (2007), pp. 461–524.

5 On the behaviour of Roman commanders see N. Rosenstein, *Imperatores Victi* (1993), pp. 114–51; for a fuller account of the death of Pompey and Julius Caesar's time in Egypt see A. Goldsworthy, *Antony and Cleopatra* (2010), pp. 167–81.

6 Suetonius, *Augustus* 8. 1, Nicolaus of Damascus 3; on funerals see the famous account of Polybius 6. 53. 1–54. 6.

7 Tacitus, *Dialogues* 28. 6 (Loeb translation), p. 307.

8 Nicolaus of Damascus 3, Velleius Paterculus 2. 59. 3; for a wider discussion of attitudes to motherhood and the mother's role see S. Dixon, *The Roman Mother* (1988), pp. 104–40, esp. 129–35.

9 Nicolaus of Damascus 4; Philippus' villas are mentioned by Cicero, *ad Att.* 12. 16, 12. 18, 14. 11; for Marcellus' neutrality see R. Syme, *The Roman Revolution* (1960), p. 62.

10 Suetonius, *Augustus* 8. 1, 94. 10, Dio 45. 1. 5–6, Nicolaus of Damascus 4; on the ceremonies associated with adopting the *toga virilis* in general see B. Rawson, *Children and Childhood in Roman Italy* (2003), pp. 142–4, on the sacrifice to Iuventus see Dionysius of Halicarnassus 4. 15. 5.

11 Election as pontiff see Nicolaus of Damascus 4, Cicero, *Philippics* 5. 17. 46, Velleius Paterculus 2. 59. 3.

12 Suetonius, *Augustus* 79. 1–2.

13 Sallust, *Bell Cat.* 25.

14 Julius Caesar's appearance, see Suetonius, *Julius Caesar* 45. 1, Octavius' eyes, see Suetonius, *Augustus* 79. 2. On sexual mores and Octavius, see Nicolaus of Damascus 5, 15; the literature on sex in ancient Rome is vast, ever increasing and rather too often reflects modern preoccupations, but a reasonable introduction is provided by P. Grimal (trans. A. Train), *Love in Ancient Rome* (1986); for Antony and Cytheris see Cicero, *ad Att.* 10. 10, *Philippics* 2. 58, *ad Fam.* 9. 26. Serv. On E10; *de vir. Ill.* 82. 2, Plutarch, *Antony* 6, 9. Cicero's distaste for her only became public

in the *Philippics* 2. 58, 69, 77; in general see Grimal (1986), pp. 222–37; on the identity of Lesbia as one of Clodius' sisters see Apuleius, *Apologia*. 10.

15 Suetonius, *Augustus* 8. 1, Velleius Paterculus 2. 59. 3, Nicolaus of Damascus 10–13, 15.

16 A good survey of Julius Caesar's dictatorship is J. Gardner, 'The Dictator', in M. Griffin (ed.), *A Companion to Julius Caesar* (2009), pp. 57–71, and for more detail see M. Gelzer (trans. P. Needham), *Caesar* (1968), pp. 272–333, C. Meier (trans. D. McLintock), *Caesar* (1996), pp. 430–96.

17 See in general E. Rawson, 'Civil War and dictatorship' in *CAH*² IX, pp. 438–67, and Syme (1960), pp. 61–96 on Caesar's party and his new senators.

18 Cicero, *ad Att*. 4. 16. 3, 8, 17. 7, Suetonius, *Caesar* 26. 2, Pliny, *NH* 36. 103, with Rawson in *CAH*² IX, pp. 453–4.

19 Suetonius, *Caesar* 44. 2, Pliny, *NH* 18. 211, Plutarch, *Caesar* 59, Macrobius, *Saturnalia* 1. 14. 2–3, T. Rice Holmes, *The Roman Republic* Vol. III (1923), pp. 285–7, Gelzer (1968), p. 289, and Z. Yavetz, *Julius Caesar and his Public Image* (1983), pp. 111–14.

20 For accounts of the triumphs see Dio 43. 19. 1–21. 4, 42. 3, 44. 1–3, Appian, *BC* 2. 101–2, Plutarch, *Caesar* 55, Suetonius, *Caesar* 37, Pliny, *NH* 7. 92, Cicero, *Philippics* 14. 23; see also comments in M. Gelzer, *Caesar* (1968), pp. 284–6, Holmes (1923), pp. 279–81, and in general S. Weinstock, *Divus Julius* (1971), esp. pp. 76–7.

21 Julius Caesar's comment that he would reward even bandits if loyal to him, Suetonius, *Augustus* 72; more generally see Goldsworthy (2010), pp. 183–90 on debt and rewards to followers.

22 Suetonius, *Augustus* 8. 1, 41. 1, Nicolaus of Damascus 6–15, Dio 43. 47. 3, Tacitus, *Ann*. 11. 25. 2, and note the comments in R. Billows, *Julius Caesar: The Colossus of Rome* (2009), pp. 256–8 on his attitude to Octavius and his nephews.

23 Suetonius, *Julius Caesar* 77.

24 For discussion of Julius Caesar's plans, contrast E. Rawson, 'Caesar's Heritage: Hellenistic Kings and their Roman Equals', *JRS* 65 (1975), pp. 148–59, R. Carson, 'Caesar and the monarchy', *Greece & Rome* 4 (1957), pp. 46–53, and J. Collins, 'Caesar and the corruption of power', *Historia* 4 (1957), pp. 445–65.

25 For an excellent discussion of Cleopatra's real importance, see E. Gruen, 'Cleopatra in Rome. Fact and Fantasies', in D. Braund & C. Gill (eds), *Myths, History and Culture in Republican Rome: Studies in honour of T. P. Wiseman* (2003), pp. 257–74, and more generally Goldsworthy (2010), pp. 192–203; story of law allowing Julius Caesar to take several wives, Suetonius, *Julius Caesar* 52. 3.

26 'Not King, but Caesar', see Suetonius, *Julius Caesar* 79. 2; for the Lupercalia see Dio 44. 11. 1–3, Appian, *BC* 2. 109, Plutarch, *Caesar* 61, Antony 12, Cicero, *Philippics* 2. 84–7, *de divinatione* 1. 52, 119, Suetonius, *Caesar* 79. 2–3, and the recent survey in J. North, 'Caesar at the Lupercalia,' *JRS* 98 (2008), pp. 144–60, making a very good case that Julius Caesar cannot have staged the affair in the hope of becoming king, and so, if planned, the intention was to refuse very publicly; see also Weinstock (1971), pp. 318–41.

27 Suetonius, *Caesar* 41. 2, 76. 2, 80. 3, Dio 43. 46. 2–4, Plutarch, *Caesar* 58, Pliny *NH* 7. 181, Cicero, *ad Fam*. 7. 30. 1–2, Gelzer (1968), p. 309, 310–11, and Holmes (1923), pp. 328–30.

28 Suetonius, *Caesar* 77; for Cicero receiving unwarranted thanks from provincials, see Cicero, *ad Fam.* 9. 15. 4; behaviour at the games, Suetonius, *Augustus* 45. 1.

29 'I have lived long enough', Cicero, *pro Marcello* 8, 25; 'he hates me', Cicero, *ad Att.* 14. 1.

30 For the conspirators in general see Gelzer (1968), pp. 323–9, Syme (1960), pp. 44–5, 56–60, 64, 95, A. Lintott, 'The assassination', in Griffin (2009), pp. 72–82, and sources in Suetonius, *Caesar* 83. 2, Dio 43. 47. 3, 44. 11. 4–14. 4, Appian, *BC* 2. 111–14, 3. 98, Plutarch, *Antony* 13, *Brutus* 6–13, *Caesar* 62, Suetonius, *Caesar* 80. 1, 3–4, Velleius Paterculus 2. 58. 1–4; on Cato's suicide, see Dio 43. 10. 1–13. 4, Appian, *BC* 2. 98–9, Plutarch, *Cato the Younger* 56. 4, 59. 1–73. 1.

31 Quotation from Cicero, *ad Fam.* 15. 19. 4; the works praising Cato and Julius Caesar's *Anticato*, see Cicero, *ad Att.* 12. 21. 1, 13. 40. 1, 46, 51. 1, *Orator* 10, 35, Plutarch, *Cato the Younger* 11. 1–4, 25. 1–5, 73. 4, *Cicero* 39. 2, *Caesar* 3. 2, Suetonius, *Caesar* 56. 5, with Gelzer (1968), pp. 301–4, Holmes (1923), p. 311 and D. Stockton, *Cicero* (1971), p. 138; senators take oath to protect Julius Caesar, in Suetonius, *Julius Caesar* 84. 2; conspirators not bound by an oath, Plutarch, *Brutus* 12, unlike the Catilinarians, Sallust, *Bell. Cat.* 22. 1–2.

32 The assassination, see Plutarch, *Caesar* 66, *Brutus* 17, *Antony* 13, Dio 44. 19. 1–5, Appian, *BC* 2. 117, Suetonius, *Caesar* 82. 1–3.

33 Cicero, *ad Att.* 14. 1 for the quote from Caius Matius.

CHAPTER 5

1 Cicero, *ad Att.* 15. 12. 2.

2 Suetonius, *Augustus* 9. 2, Appian, *BC* 3. 9, Velleius Paterculus 2. 59. 4, Dio 45. 3. 1, Nicolaus of Damascus 16 for the period spent in Apollonia; examples of travelling to the Hellenic world to study rhetoric include Cicero and Julius Caesar, see Cicero, *Brutus* 316, and Suetonius, *Caesar* 4. 2, Plutarch, *Caesar* 2.

3 Appian, *BC* 3. 9 emphasises his training with the cavalry.

4 On Salvidienus and Agrippa see R. Syme, *The Roman Revolution* (1960), pp. 129, fn. 2–3.

5 On the news and reaction see in particular Nicolaus of Damascus 16, and comments in J. Osgood, *Caesar's Legacy. Civil War and the Emergence of the Roman Empire* (2006), p. 31, and comments on the legions' anticipation of plunder p. 47.

6 Nicolaus of Damascus 17–18, Appian, *BC* 3. 10–11.

7 On the aftermath of the Ides and Julius Caesar's funeral see in general Rawson in *CAH²* IX, pp. 468–70, Syme (1960), pp. 97–105, Osgood (2006), pp. 12–14, A. Goldsworthy, *Antony and Cleopatra* (2010), pp. 204–14, T. Mitchell, *Cicero the Senior Statesman* (1991), pp. 289–91; Appian, *BC* 2. 120–23, 120 on the irony of bribing the populace while proclaiming liberty.

8 On the will see Suetonius, *Julius Caesar* 83. 2, and also for a useful discussion see R. Billows, *Julius Caesar: The Colossus of Rome* (2009), pp. 256–8, and Osgood (2006), p. 31 fn. 71 with references to the debate on this subject; for Cicero's subsequent claim that Julius Caesar would not have returned from the east, see Cicero, *ad Att.* 15. 2. 3.

9 Antony refused part of his father's estate, see Cicero, *Philippics* 2. 44; powers over freedmen, see Appian, *BC* 3. 94.

10 Nicolaus of Damascus 18, Appian, BC 3. 11–13, Suetonius, Augustus 9. 2; Cicero on Philippus' campaign, see Cicero, *ad Fam.* 12. 2. 2; quoting Achilles in Appian, *BC* 3. 13, citing *Iliad* 18. 98 – 'I must die soon, then; since I was not to stand by my companion when he was killed' (Lattimore translation).

11 For emphasis on Octavius aiming at supremacy from the very start, see B. Levick, *Augustus. Image and Substance* (2010), pp. 23–4.

12 On the name see the important article by R. Syme, 'Imperator Caesar: A study in imperial nomenclature', pp. 172–88.

13 Nicolaus of Damascus 18, Appian, *BC* 3. 13–21, Cicero, *ad Att.* 14. 6. 1 and Osgood (2006), p. 31, fn. 73; Cicero, *ad Att.* 14. 5. 3 questioning Atticus about the arrival in Rome.

14 Cicero, *ad Att.* 14. 10. 3; on Balbus' background and work for Julius Caesar see Syme (1960), pp. 71–3. Cicero once defended him in court, and the speech is preserved in the *pro Balbo*; for Cicero's testimony in general see A. Lintott, *Cicero as Evidence* (2008), esp. pp. 339–73.

15 For the quote see Cicero, *ad Att.* 14. 11. 2; Marcellus on good terms with conspirators *ad Att.* 15. 12. 2; on the attitudes of the two former consuls see Syme (1960), pp. 114, 128. Syme was inclined to speak of Caesarean and Pompeian parties, but did not present these as rigid or permanent groups.

16 On Dolabella see Syme (1960), pp. 69, fn. 2, 97, 150–51; past conflict with Antony see Goldsworthy (2010), pp. 186–91.

17 Plutarch, *Antony* 4 for the aping of Hercules and stereotype of the swaggering soldier; for Antony in general see Goldsworthy (2010), *passim*.

18 For the family see Goldsworthy (2010), pp. 52–65.

19 Cicero, *Philippics* 2. 44 for refusing part of his father's estate, and 44–6 for his youth; in general see Goldsworthy (2010), pp. 81–104.

20 Cicero, *Philippics* 2. 58, *ad Att.* 10. 10, 13, *ad Fam.* 9. 26, Serv. On E10; *de vir. Ill.* 82. 2. Cicero's distaste only became public in the *Philippics* 2. 58, 69, 7; see also Plutarch, *Antony* 6, 9, Pliny, *NH* 8. 55.

21 Cicero, *Philippics* 2. 64–9, 72–4, 78, Plutarch, *Antony* 10, Dio 45. 28. 1–4; Plutarch, *Antony* 10 claims that there was a breach between Caesar and Antony. M. Gelzer (trans. P. Needham), *Caesar* (1968), pp. 261–2 is inclined to see this as serious, while Syme (1960), p. 104 doubts this; riding in the same carriage as Julius Caesar, Plutarch, *Antony* 11.

22 Plutarch, *Antony* 13.

23 See R. Weigel, *Lepidus. The Tarnished Triumvir* (1992), pp. 44–51, and Syme (1960), pp. 97–111; on Antony's attitude see the insightful discussion in J. Ramsay, 'Did Mark Antony contemplate an alliance with his political enemies in July 44 B.C.E.?', *Classical Philology* 96. 3 (2001), pp. 253–68, which although focusing more on the summer months presents a good analysis of his attitude.

24 Amatius and the altar to Julius Caesar see Appian, *BC* 3. 2–3, 36, Cicero, *ad Att.* 14. 15, Syme (1960), p. 99; his attempt to gain acceptance from the young Octavius, see Nicolaus of Damascus 14.

25 J. Ramsay, 'The Senate, Mark Antony, and Caesar's Legislative Legacy', *Classical Quarterly* 44 (1994), pp. 130–45 is rightly cautious of accepting Cicero's judgement wholesale and presents an excellent analysis of several of the most controversial measures and their context. The details do not alter the central point that bringing in such laws and grants was extremely beneficial to Antony, whether or not they were genuine decisions of the dictator.

26 Appian, *BC* 3. 27, 30, with Syme (1960), pp. 115–16, and P. Brunt, *Italian Manpower 225 BC–AD 14* (1971), pp. 477–83, Osgood (2006), pp. 33–4.

27 Cicero, *ad Att.* 16. 1, 2. 3, 4. 1, 5. 1, Appian, *BC* 3. 24, Plutarch, *Brutus* 21. 2–3; quotation from Cicero, *ad Att.* 15. 4.

28 Cicero, *ad Att.* 16. 15. 1 notes his decision to make public Dolabella's failure to repay the dowry.

CHAPTER 6

1 *Res Gestae* 1 (Brunt & Moore's translation).

2 Appian, *BC* 3. 21–2, Suetonius, *Augustus* 10. 1–2, 95, Dio 45. 3. 4–7. 2, Nicolaus of Damascus 28, see also R. Syme (1960), pp. 114–17, 116, fn. 3 citing T. Rice Holmes, *The Architect of the Roman Empire* Vol. 1 (1928), p. 191, arguing that the *ludi Ceriales* were celebrated in late May rather than April as was usual.

3 Nicolaus of Damascus 18 for Julius Caesar's war chest. For his financial backers see n. 4.

4 Appian, *BC* 3. 23–4, 28, Suetonius, *Augustus* 10. 1, Dio 45. 6. 4, Cicero, *ad Att.* 15. 2. 3, with Syme (1960), p. 131 and J. Ramsay, 'Did Mark Antony contemplate an alliance with his political enemies in July 44 B.C.E.?', *Classical Philology* 96. 3 (2001), pp. 253–68, esp. 253, fn. 3 on the length of the festival and its dates at this period. The article presents a very useful analysis of the chronology of events in the summer months of 44 BC.

5 Suetonius, *Julius Caesar* 88, Pliny, *NH* 2. 93–4, with J. Osgood, *Caesar's Legacy. Civil War and the Emergence of the Roman Empire* (2006), pp. 40–41, and for a very detailed analysis J. Ramsay & A. Licht, *The Comet of 44 BC and Caesar's Funeral Games* (1997), pp. 135–53.

6 The election to the tribunate, see Appian, *BC* 3. 31 for the fullest account, which claims he supported a candidate, but the crowd 'demanded' that he stand, but that this was blocked by Antony, and also Plutarch, *Antony* 16, Dio 45. 6. 2, Suetonius 10. 2, with Syme (1960), p. 120 and Z. Yavetz, *Plebs and Princeps* (1969), pp. 73–5 ; the comet a sign of his own future greatness, Pliny, *NH* 2. 93.

7 On the question of the jury reform see J. Ramsay, 'Mark Antony's Judiciary Reform and its revival under the Triumvirs', *JRS* 95 (2005), pp. 20–37, although note p. 31 for the dismissal of a property qualification of 40,000 or perhaps 50,000 sesterces for membership of the *prima classis* in the *Comitia centuriata* as 'an extremely paltry sum' compared to an equestrian census of eight times that size. It was still around double the very generous discharge bonus Caesar was soon to promise his soldiers. It was also a minimum qualification, and no doubt the property of individuals covered the full range up to the equestrian census.

8 Cicero, *ad Fam.* 11. 28. 6–7 for Matius' letter to Cicero explaining his financial backing for the young Caesar as a duty owed to his friendship with Julius Caesar; Appian, *BC* 3. 28–30, for reconciliation and the vote, and 32–42 for their relations and subsequent alleged plot, and see also Cicero, *ad Att.* 16. 8. 1–2, *ad Fam.* 12. 3, Dio 45. 7–3–9.5, 12. 1–6, Plutarch, *Antony* 16. For the status of Caesar's volunteers and the soldiers who subsequently joined him, see the discussion in J. Linderski, 'Aphrodisias and the *Res Gestae*: The *Genera Militiae* and the Status of Octavian,' *JRS* 74 (1984), pp. 74–80, arguing that any oath taken by Caesar's men was part of an emergency levy and so not the normal military oath or *sacramentum*, but a *coniuratio*, and discussing the implications of this for their status.

9 For Cicero's thoughts and actions during this period, see D. Stockton, *Cicero. A Political Biography* (1971), pp. 292–7, and Ramsay (2001), esp. pp. 265–7.

10 Osgood (2006), pp. 41–2, Stockton (1971), pp. 292–3, 297–9, A. Lintott, *Cicero as Evidence* (2008), pp. 375–82; Appian, *BC* 3. 5 for Antony's force of 6,000 veterans; Cicero, *ad Fam.* 12. 2. 1, 3. 1, Plutarch, *Cicero* 43 for his fears.

11 Appian, *BC* 3. 40; Cicero, *ad Att.* 16. 8, written on 4 November 44 BC reports that Caesar had 3,000 veterans and mentions the latter's hope of winning over the Macedonian legions.

12 Cicero, *ad Att.* 16. 11. 6.

13 Worries about Caesar, Cicero, *ad Att.* 16. 14. 1, Atticus' quote 16. 15. 3, cf. Plutarch, *Cicero* 44–6, with Stockton (1971), pp. 295–6.

14 Cicero, *ad Att.* 16. 15. 3 for quote, and also Appian, *BC* 3. 41–2, Dio 45. 12. 3–6.

15 Cicero, *Philippics* 3. 20 for the allegation that Antony planned to have Caesar declared a public enemy.

16 On the inevitable tail of merchants, not their presence outside Quintus Cicero's winter camp in Gaul in 53 BC, Caesar, *BG* 6. 37.

17 Julius Caesar's promotion of centurions from veteran units to higher grades in newly formed legions, e.g. Caesar, *BG* 6. 40.

18 Appian, *BC* 3. 31, 40–44, Dio 45. 12. 1–13. 5, Cicero, *Philippics* 3. 4, 6, 38–9, 4. 5–6, with Osgood (2006), pp. 47–50; for a discussion of *Legio Martia* and a possible tombstone of one of its centurions see L. Keppie, 'A centurion of *legio Martia* at Padova?', *Journal of Roman Military Equipment Studies* 2 (1991), pp. 115–21 = L. Keppie, *Legions and Veterans: Roman Army Papers 1971–2000* (2000), pp. 68–74, and A. Goldsworthy, *Antony and Cleopatra* (2010), pp. 219–21.

19 Appian, *BC* 3. 46, Dio 45. 13. 5, with Syme (1960), pp. 126–7.

20 Attack on Caesar, see Cicero, *Philippics* 3. 20, Appian, *BC* 3. 44–6, Dio 45. 13. 5; for mention of Legione Alaudarum in November, see Cicero, *ad Att.* 16. 8, although it is possible that he merely wanted to depict Antony's followers as barbarians and so chose to use the name.

21 For the Josephus quote, *BJ* 3. 75; for the army in general in this period see H. Parker, *The Roman Legions* (1957), pp. 47–71, esp. 55–6, F. Adcock, *The Roman Art of War under the Republic* (1940), P. Brunt, *Italian Manpower, 225 BC–AD 14* (1971), P. Connolly, *Greece and Rome at War* (1981), M. Feugère (ed.), *L'Équipment Militaire et L'Armement de la République*, *JRMES* 8 (1997), E. Gabba (trans. P. J. Cuff), *The*

Roman Republic, the Army and the Allies (1976), L. Keppie, *The Making of the Roman Army* (1984), Y. Le Bohec, *The Imperial Roman Army* (1994), J. Harmand, *L'armée et le soldat à Rome de 107 à 50 avant nôtre ère* (Paris, 1967); more general studies include A. Goldsworthy, *The Complete Roman Army* (2004) and the recent and excellent S. James, *Rome and the Sword. How Warriors and Weapons Shaped Roman History* (2011).

22 Quotation from Cicero, *ad Att.* 16. 5. 3, with Osgood (2006), p. 49, and Stockton (1971), pp. 299–306; Quintus' view of the consuls in *ad Att.* 16. 27. 2; Decimus Brutus in Cisalpine Gaul, Cicero, *ad Fam.* 11. 6, 6a. 2.

23 Cicero, *Philippics* 3. 2 (3, 5) (Loeb translation, slightly altered).

24 Cicero, *Philippics* 3. 3 (6) (Loeb translation, slightly altered).

25 Osgood (2006), pp. 49–51, Lintott (2008), pp. 385–8.

26 Syme (1960), pp. 162–70; the vote Appian *BC* 3. 30.

27 Suetonius, *Augustus* 2. 3–3. 1, 4. 2 preserves some of this abuse, and in general see K. Scott, 'The Political Propaganda of 44–30 BC', *Memoirs of the American Academy in Rome* 11 (1933), pp. 7–49.

28 'Boy who owes everything to a name', Cicero, *Philippics* 13. 24; flattery of Cicero by Caesar, see Plutarch, *Cicero* 45–6; on Cicero's strategy see Stockton (1971), pp. 300–02, 326–8.

29 Appian, *BC* 3. 48, 50–51, Dio 46. 29. 2–6, Cicero, *ad Brutum* 1. 12, *Philippics* 5. 3–4, 25, 31, with Rawson in *CAH*² IX, pp. 479–81.

CHAPTER 7

1 Cicero, *ad Fam.* 11. 20 (SB 401) (Loeb translation, modified).

2 Appian, *BC* 3. 27, 49. with J. Osgood, *Caesar's Legacy. Civil War and the Emergence of the Roman Empire* (2006), p. 50.

3 Appian, *BC* 3. 63, 79, with R. Syme, *The Roman Revolution* (1960), pp. 171–2, 183.

4 Caesar, *BG* 8. *praef.* which claims Balbus urged him to write, and see also Osgood (2006), p. 51, fn. 133 noting the favourable treatment of the *Seventh* and *Eighth* Legions.

5 Cicero, *ad Fam.* 10. 6. 3, cf. *Philippics* 13. 7–9, see A. Lintott, *Cicero as Evidence* (2008), p. 399.

6 Appian, *BC* 3. 50, 65, Dio 46. 35. 1–37. 3, including desertions from among Caesar's cavalry, Pliny *NH* 10. 110 for use of carrier pigeons.

7 For the twin battles of Forum Gallorum see Cicero, *ad Fam.* 10. 30 for the vivid eyewitness account of Servius Sulpicius Galba, and Appian, *BC* 66–70, Dio 46. 37. 1–7, with Osgood (2006), pp. 51–5, and L. Keppie, *The Making of the Roman Army* (1984), pp. 115–18, and A. Goldsworthy, *Antony and Cleopatra* (2010), pp. 225–7. Appian emphasises the silent, machine-like killing of the veteran legions in a dramatic piece, but this may be no more than rhetoric. It is worth remembering that the only true veterans present were the praetorian cohorts. The rank and file of the Macedonian legions had seen little active service.

8 Appian, *BC* 3. 71–2, Dio 46. 38. 1–7, Cicero, *ad Fam.* 11. 13. 2, Suetonius, *Augustus*

10. 4 on Caesar's behaviour, cf. the emphasis on his bravery and youth in Velleius
Paterculus 2. 61. 4; on challenges to battle see A. Goldsworthy, *The Roman Army
at War 100 BC–AD 200* (1996), pp. 143–5.

9 Appian, *BC* 3. 73–5, Plutarch, *Antony* 17–18; Decimus Brutus' shortage of animals,
Cicero, *ad Fam.* 11. 13. 2.

10 Cicero, *ad Brutum* 1. 6. 2 for a contemporary rumour which Brutus actually
doubted because of personal acquaintance with Pansa's physician, and Suetonius, *Augustus* 11 for later stories that Caesar was involved in the deaths of
Hirtius and Pansa, cf. Tacitus, *Ann.* 1. 10 where it is hinted that Pansa was poi-
soned and his own men persuaded to murder Hirtius; for the commander at
Forum Gallorum almost caught by the Antonians and then nearly mistakenly
killed by his own side see Cicero, *ad Fam.* 10. 30. 3.

11 Cicero, *ad Brutum* 1. 3. 4, *ad Fam.* 10. 21. 4, 11. 19. 1, 11. 21. 2, Appian, *BC* 3. 74, Dio
46. 40. 1 and Rawson in *CAH²* IX, pp. 483–5, Syme (1960), pp. 176–8 and D. Stockton, *Cicero. A Political Biography* (1971), pp. 318–23 for summaries of the Senate's
reaction and aftermath of the victory at Mutina; Pollio's letter is in Cicero, *ad
Fam.* 10. 33. 1.

12 Cicero, *ad Fam.* 11. 11. 4 for quote, *ad Fam.* 11. 19. 1 for Decimus' disappointment
in not receiving command of the *Fourth* and the *Martia*; on the defection of
Lepidus' army see Plutarch, *Antony* 18, Appian, *BC* 3. 80–84, Dio 46. 38. 6–7, with
Syme (1960), pp. 178–9, and Brunt (1971), pp. 481–4.

13 Stockton (1971), pp. 319–30.

14 Cicero, *ad Fam.* 11. 20.

15 Cicero, *Philippics* 13. 22–5.

16 Appian, *BC* 3. 82, Cicero, *ad Brutum* 1. 3. 2, 4. 3–6, *Philippics* 14. 15, Plutarch, *Cicero*
45, with Stockton (1971), pp. 325–8 , Lintott (2008), pp. 416–21; Cicero, *ad Brutum*
1. 10. 3 (Loeb translation 18.3) for relatives encouraging Caesar's desire for the
consulship.

17 Appian, *BC* 3. 88, Suetonius, *Augustus* 26. 1, Dio 46. 42. 3–43. 6; Syme (1960), p. 185,
fn. 7, expresses scepticism at the details of the story.

18 Appian, *BC* 3. 88–95, Dio 46. 44. 1–49. 5, Velleius Paterculus 2. 65. 2, *Res Gestae* 1,
with Syme (1960), pp. 185–8; on legions in this period see P. Brunt, *Italian Manpower 225 BC–AD 14* (1971), pp. 481–4.

19 J. Ramsay, 'Did Mark Antony contemplate an alliance with his political enemies
in July 44 B.C.E.?', *Classical Philology* 96. 3 (2001), pp. 253–68 argues that Antony
was only concerned to strengthen his own position and was never committed to
a permanent alliance with the conspirators.

20 On the formation of the triumvirate see Plutarch, *Antony* 19–21, Appian, *BC* 3.
96–4. 46. 50. 1–56. 4, with Syme (1960), pp. 188–91, Osgood (2006), pp. 57–61, and
Rawson in *CAH²* IX, pp. 485–6, and Goldsworthy (2010), pp. 228–31.

CHAPTER 8

1 Appian, *BC* 4. 8 (Loeb translation).
2 Velleius Paterculus 2. 67. 2 (Loeb translation)

3 Appian, *BC* 4. 6, mentioning that some sources said twelve deaths were immediately ordered and others gave the figure as seventeen.

4 On the proscriptions in general see Appian, *BC* 4. 6–31, Dio 47. 1. 1–15. 4, Plutarch,
   Cicero 46, *Antony* 19, with good surveys in J. Osgood, *Caesar's Legacy. Civil War
   and the Emergence of the Roman Empire* (2006), pp. 62–82, and R. Syme, *The Roman
   Revolution* (1960), pp. 190–94; for an interesting discussion of the impact of the
   proscriptions, their presentation and the role of the young Caesar see A. Powell,
   Virgil the Partisan: A Study in the Re-integration of Classics (2008), pp. 55–62, 68–9,
   who points out that there is a danger of forgetting the essential savagery of
   these murders because we are so used to the term 'proscriptions'; for the size
   of the force brought into Rome by each triumvir, see Appian, *BC* 4. 7; the quote
   about not writing against the triumvirs is attributed to Asinius Pollio in Macrobius, *Satires* 2. 11.1.

5 Appian, *BC* 4. 8–11 offers a version of the proscription proclamation, which may
   be authentic. Inclusion of Caius Toranius, see Suetonius, *Augustus* 27. 1.

6 Plutarch, *Antony* 19–20, Appian, *BC* 4. 5–30, 37, Dio 57. 1. 1–14. 5, with Syme (1960),
   pp. 190–96, and Osgood (2006), pp. 62–82; Plutarch, *Antony* 20 (Oxford translation, modified) for quote.

7 See Plutarch, *Cicero* 47–8, Appian, *BC* 4. 19–20, with Osgood (2006), p. 78 for discussion and the other sources, see D. Stockton, *Cicero. A Political Biography* (1971),
   pp. 331–2, T. Mitchell, *Cicero. The Senior Statesman* (1991), pp. 322–4, A. Everitt,
   Cicero. A Turbulent Life (2001), pp. 304–10.

8 Dio 47. 8. 3–4, Plutarch, *Cicero* 48–9, *Antony* 20, Appian, *BC* 4. 19, and see also Cornelius Nepos, *Atticus* 9. 3–7, with A. Goldsworthy, *Antony and Cleopatra* (2010), pp.
   245–6.

9 Suetonius, *Augustus* 27. 1–2 for emphasis on his pursuit of victims, and contrast
   with Velleius Paterculus 2. 66–7 where the blame is placed firmly on Antony and
   Lepidus, with K. Scott, 'The Political Propaganda of 44–30 BC', *Memoirs of the
   American Academy in Rome* 11 (1933), pp. 7–49, esp. 19–21, Powell (2008), pp. 63–8 on
   attitudes to and presentation of Caesar in the sources, and Goldsworthy (2010),
   pp. 246–7.

10 Corinthian vases, see Suetonius, *Augustus* 70. 2, and Antony proscribing Verres
   for his artworks see Pliny, *NH* 34. 2. 6, with Scott (1933), pp. 20–21; on Antony and
   Fulvia see Appian, *BC* 4. 40, Dio 47. 7. 4–5, 8. 5.

11 Appian, *BC* 4. 30 for youthful victims, and 4. 23–4 on stories about wives; on the
   role of women, see Osgood (2006), pp. 74–82.

12 Appian, *BC* 4. 23, with Osgood (2006), pp. 64–5, 79; the incident of the wife being
   beaten by Lepidus' attendants comes from an inscription set up as a memorial
   to her by her husband, conventionally (although probably inaccurately) known
   today as the *Laudatio Turiae*, see Osgood (2006), pp. 67–74 for discussion and
   references.

13 Dio 47. 7. 4–5.

14 Appian, *BC* 4. 31–4, Dio 47. 14. 2–3, with Osgood (2006), pp. 84–8.

15 Dio 47. 18. 3–19, with S. Weinstock, *Divus Julius* (1971), pp. 386–98.

16 Death of Atia, Suetonius, *Augustus* 61. 2, Dio 47. 17. 6; earlier betrothal and

subsequent marriage to Claudia, Suetonius, *Augustus* 62. 1, Velleius Paterculus 2. 65. 2, Plutarch, *Antony* 20; Claudia still a virgin when they divorced, Dio 48. 5. 3.

17   For discussion see R. Weigel, *Lepidus. The Tarnished Triumvir* (1992), pp. 69–70, 77–9.

18   Dio 47. 25. 3, and Appian, *BC* 4. 100–01; see also Appian, *BC* 5. 17 providing a detailed discussion of soldiers' attitudes, and Cornelius Nepos, *Eumenes* 8. 2 comparing Macedonian veterans with contemporary Roman soldiers in their greed and readiness to fight civil wars; for examples of Brutus' coinage see M. Crawford, *Roman Republican Coinage* (1974), pp. 498–508.

19   Appian, *BC* 4. 101–8, Plutarch, *Brutus* 37–40

20   Appian, *BC* 4. 106, 108, Dio 47. 37. 2–3, Suetonius, *Augustus* 13. 1.

21   For numbers see Appian, *BC* 4. 88, 108; for discussion, but generally accepting a high estimate, see P. Brunt, *Italian Manpower 225 BC–AD 14* (1971), pp. 485–8, and Goldsworthy (2010), pp. 251–3 for doubts; contrast Appian, *BC* 4. 137 who emphasises the scale of the campaign with Dio 47. 39. 1 who claims that these were not the biggest battles of the civil wars; note also Velleius Paterculus 2. 113, where the future emperor Tiberius found it too difficult to control a force of ten legions gathered in one place.

22   On challenges to battle see A. Goldsworthy, *The Roman Army at War 100 BC–AD 200* (1996), pp. 141–5.

23   For the First Battle of Philippi see Appian, *BC* 4. 109–14, Plutarch, *Brutus* 40–45, Dio 47. 42. 1–47. 1, and a well-illustrated narrative in S. Sheppard, *Philippi 42 BC. The Death of the Roman Republic* (2008); on loss of baggage causing a collapse in morale, see Caesar, *BG* 5. 33, contrasted with better discipline at *BG* 5. 43 by a different legion.

24   For the various versions of Octavian's behaviour see Plutarch, *Brutus* 41, *Antony* 22, Dio 47. 41. 3–4, 46. 2, Velleius Paterculus 2. 70. 1, Suetonius, *Augustus* 13. 1, Pliny, *NH* 7. 147, with brief discussion in Syme (1960), pp. 204–5, Osgood (2006), pp. 95–6, Stark (1933), pp. 21–2, and Powell (2008), p. 106.

25   Appian, *BC* 4. 125–31, Plutarch, *Brutus* 49–52, *Antony* 22 (who is the only source to imply that Caesar was still ill for the second battle), Dio 47. 48. 1–49. 4.

26   Appian, *BC* 4. 129–31, 135, Suetonius, *Augustus* 13. 1–2, Dio 47. 49. 2, Plutarch, *Brutus* 53. 3, *Antony* 22, *Comparison of lives of Dion and Brutus* 5. 1, with Stark (1933), pp. 22–3.

27   *Res Gestae* 2 (Loeb translation).

28   For more detail on Antony's actions in the next year and a half, see Goldsworthy (2010), pp. 261–71, with particular emphasis on the choice facing Cleopatra as a client ruler.

29   Appian, *BC* 5. 3, 12, Dio 48. 1. 2–3. 6, with Weigel (1992), pp. 79–80.

30   For detailed discussion of the land confiscations see L. Keppie, *Colonisation and Veteran Settlement in Italy: 47–14 BC* (1983), *passim* and Osgood (2006), pp. 108–51.

31   On the Perusine War see Appian, *BC* 5. 12–51, Dio 48. 5. 1–14. 6, Plutarch, *Antony* 30, Velleius Paterculus 2. 74–6, with discussions in E. Gabba, 'The Perusine War and Triumviral Italy', *Harvard Studies in Classical Philology* 75 (1971), pp. 139–60, Syme (1960), pp. 207–12, Osgood (2006), pp. 152–72, and C. Pelling in *CAH²* X, pp. 14–17.

32 On these see J. Hallett, 'Perusinae Glandes and the Changing Image of Augustus', *AJAH* 2 (1977), pp. 151–71, and see also T. Rihll, 'Lead Slingshot (*glandes*)',
JRA 22 (2009), pp. 149–69 which makes a good case that these lead shot may
have been fired from very light, possibly hand-held, artillery rather than slings.
This does not alter the significance of their messages; Caesar nearly killed by
a raiding party, see Suetonius, *Augustus* 14 claiming that the raiders were freed
gladiators, cf. Appian, *BC* 5. 33; for an escape from the siege, which later ends in
tragedy, see Propertius, *Elegies* 1. 21.

33 End of siege and treatment of prisoners, see Appian, *BC* 5. 46–9, Dio 48. 14. 3–6,
Suetonius, *Augustus* 15, and Velleius Paterculus 2. 74. 4 for the story that the fire
was started by one of the inhabitants, with Stark (1933), pp. 27–8; for Achilles'
sacrifice see *Iliad* 23. 21–2.

CHAPTER 9

1 Virgil, *Eclogues* 1. 67–72 (Loeb translation, slightly modified).

2 Virgil, *Eclogues* 4. 4–12 (Loeb translation, slightly modified).

3 Martial, *Epigrams* 11. 20. 3–8, with comments in K. Scott, 'The Political Propaganda of 44–30 BC', *Memoirs of the American Academy in Rome* 11 (1933), pp. 7–49,
esp. 24–6.

4 Appian, *BC* 5. 7, Dio 49. 32. 3 on Glaphyra, and on Manius see R. Syme, *The Roman
Revolution* (1960), pp. 208–9, and Appian, *BC* 5. 19.

5 Appian, *BC* 5. 13, and esp. 5. 15–17 with two instances of soldiers rioting against
Caesar, the second incident resulting in the murder of the centurion, Nonius,
and Dio 48. 8. 1–10. 1; Suetonius, *Augustus* 104. 12–106. 2 records his immense
conviction of his own destiny.

6 Suetonius, *Augustus* 62. 1, Dio 48. 5. 3 on Claudia. On Calenus see Dio 48. 20. 3,
Appian, *BC* 5. 51, 54, 59–61.

7 Appian, *BC* 5. 55, Velleius Paterculus 2. 76.

8 Antony's mother Julia, see Appian, *BC* 5. 52; on Labienus' father see R. Syme, 'The
Allegiance of Labienus,' *JRS* 28 (1938), pp. 113–25, and W. Tyrell, 'Labienus' departure from Caesar in January 49 BC', *Historia* 21 (1972), pp. 424–40; on the son see Dio
48. 24. 4–25. 1; on the Parthian invasion see Dio 48. 26. 5, with Syme (1960), p. 223,
and discussion of the campaign and its context in D. Kennedy, 'Parthia and Rome:
eastern perspectives', in D. Kennedy (ed.), *The Roman Army in the East. Journal of
Roman Archaeology Supplements* 18 (1996), pp. 67–90, esp. 77–81, J. Osgood, *Caesar's
Legacy. Civil War and the Emergence of the Roman Empire* (2006), pp. 185, 225–8.

9 Dio 48. 12. 1–5, Appian, *BC* 5. 20–24.

10 Appian, *BC* 5. 56–66, Dio 48. 28. 1–30. 2, with Syme (1960), pp. 129, 216–17, 242,
253–5, and Pelling in *CAH*² X, pp. 17–20; on Maecenas see Syme (1960), pp. 129,
341–2, 359.

11 On Fulvia see the scepticism concerning our sources in D. Delia, 'Fulvia Reconsidered', in S. Pomperoy (ed.), *Women's History and Ancient History* (1991), pp.
197–217, and on her death see Plutarch, *Antony* 30, Appian, *BC* 5. 59, Dio 48. 28.
3–4; on the marriage to Octavia see Plutarch, *Antony* 31, Appian, *BC* 5. 64, Dio 48.

28. 3–31. 3, Velleius Paterculus 2. 78. 1, with Osgood (2006), pp. 188–201, Syme (1960), pp. 217–20, E. Huzar, 'Mark Antony: Marriages vs. careers', *The Classical Journal* 81 (1985/6), pp. 97–111, esp. 103–11.

12 Plutarch, *Antony* 57, and in general Osgood (2006), pp. 193–200 for a good discussion of Virgil's *Fourth Eclogue* in the context of these years. There were other opinions on the identity of the child, including a claim by Pollio's son. In the Christian era the messianic tone and first-century-BC date of the poem has at times been interpreted as referring to Jesus.

13 Appian, *BC* 5. 53, Suetonius, *Augustus* 52. 2, Dio 48. 16. 3, Syme (1960), p. 213.

14 See G. Rickman, *The Corn Supply of Ancient Rome* (1980), pp. 60–61, P. Garnsey, *Famine and Food Supply in the Graeco-Roman World. Responses to Risk and Crisis* (1988), pp. 202, 206–8.

15 See K. Welch, 'Sextus Pompeius and the *Res Publica* in 42–39 BC', in A. Powell & K. Welch (eds), *Sextus Pompeius* (2002), pp. 31–63; Cassius' comments about Cnaeus Pompey, see Cicero, *ad Fam.* 15. 19. 4.

16 A. Powell, '"An island amid the flame": The Strategy and Imagery of Sextus Pompeius, 43–36 BC', in Powell & Welch (2002), pp. 103–33. esp. 105–9, 118–29, and A. Powell, *Virgil the Partisan: A Study in the Re-integration of Classics* (2008), pp. 31–83; for Lucius Antonius, see Dio 48. 5. 4.

17 Appian, *BC* 4. 25, 36, 85, 5. 143, Dio 47. 12. 1–13. 1, Velleius Paterculus 2. 72. 5, 77. 2, with Welch (2002), pp. 45–6; Caesar's formal shaving, Dio 48. 34. 3, with comments in M. Flory, '*Abducta Neroni Uxor*: The historiographic tradition on the marriage of Octavian and Livia,' *Transactions of the American Philological Association* 118 (1988), pp. 343–59, esp. 344.

18 Appian, *BC* 5. 67–8, Dio 48. 31. 1–6.

19 Appian, *BC* 5. 69–74, Dio 48. 36. 1–38. 3, Velleius Paterculus 2. 77, Plutarch, *Antony* 32, with Syme (1960), pp. 221–2, Osgood (2006), pp. 205–7, and Powell (2008), pp. 190–91; and especially Welch (2002), pp. 51–4 suggesting that the exiles may have pressured Sextus into the treaty.

20 Plutarch, *Antony* 33, Appian, *BC* 5. 76, Dio 48. 39. 2, Seneca, *Suasoriae* 1. 6, with M. Grant, *Cleopatra* (1972), pp. 129–30; on Ventidius' campaign see the brief account in A. Goldsworthy, *Antony and Cleopatra* (2010), pp. 286–8, with references to the ancient sources.

21 See Dio 54. 7. 2, Suetonius, *Tiberius* 6. 2–3, with A. Barrett, *Livia. First Lady of Imperial Rome* (2002), pp. 10–11, 16–18.

22 Barrett (2002), pp. 3–10, 15–16; death of her father, see Dio 48. 44. 1, Velleius Paterculus 2. 71. 2.

23 Suetonius, *Tiberius* 6. 1–3, *Augustus* 27. 4.

24 *Ulixes stolatus*, Suetonius *Caius* 23; in general see Flory (1988), and Barrett (2002), pp. 11–14.

25 Suetonius, *Augustus* 53. 1, 69. 1–2, with the later charges presumably dating to things Antony had seen in Rome; see also Flory (1988), pp. 352–3 and Barrett (2002), pp. 24–5 discussing the theory that the story of abducting a wife from the dining table refers to Livia, although Claudius Nero was only an ex-praetor and not an ex-consul.

26 Flory (1988), pp. 345–6 claims that 'his desire to celebrate the marriage before the birth of Livia's son suggests he stood to gain practical advantages from it on the eve of an unpopular war. Only this can explain the haste which he knew would inevitably lead to scandal about the unborn child and his prior relationship with Livia.' Yet no one can come up with any clear sign of immediate political advantage, and this probably stems from the desire to see every action of Caesar as that of a calculating and calm political schemer. It is much more straightforward and convincing to see this as the act of precocious youth.

27 Barrett (2002), pp. 11–26, Flory (1988), p. 348; on divorce in general see S. Treggiari, *Roman Marriage* (1991), pp. 435–82 and 'Divorce Roman Style: How easy and frequent was it?' in B. Rawson (ed.), *Marriage, Divorce and Children in Ancient Rome* (1991), pp. 131–46; Caesar's comment about Scribonia, see Suetonius, *Augustus* 62. 2; Suetonius, *Claudius* 1 speaks of Drusus being born three months after Caesar and Livia were married, but this must refer to the betrothal rather than the actual wedding.

28 Suetonius, *Augustus* 70. 1–2 (Loeb translation); on the wedding feast in general, see Suetonius, *Augustus* 70. 1, Dio 48. 43. 4–44. 5, with Barrett (2002), pp. 24–7, who associates the feast of the twelve gods with betrothal rather than the wedding, and Flory (1988), who makes a stronger case for this being the wedding feast; on the *deliciae*, Dio 48. 44. 3 and in general W. Slater, '*Pueri, Turba Minuta*', in *BICS* 21 (1974), pp. 133–40.

29 Dio 48. 45. 5–46. 1, and Appian, *BC* 5. 78–80, who refers to Menas as Menodorus.

30 On the campaign see Appian, *BC* 5. 81–92, Dio 48. 46. 1–48. 4, with J. Morrison & J. Coates, *Greek and Roman Oared Warships* (1996), pp. 149–52, M. Pitassi, *The Navies of Rome* (2009), pp. 186–91, W. Rogers, *Greek and Roman Naval Warfare* (1937), pp. 496–516, and R. Paget, 'The Naval Battle of Cumae in 38 BC', *Latomus* 29 (1970), pp. 363–9.

31 Suetonius, *Augustus* 16. 2 for Neptune and 70. 2 for the verse, see also Appian, *BC* 5. 100, Dio 48. 48. 6–49. 1, with Powell (2002), pp. 120–26, and (2008), pp. 97–8.

32 On the failure of Octavian to meet Antony in 38 BC, see Appian, *BC* 4. 78–80, and for the meeting in 37 BC see Appian, *BC* 5. 93–5, Plutarch, *Antony* 35, with Pelling in *CAH²* X, pp. 24–7, and P. Brunt, *Italian Manpower 225 BC–AD 14* (1971), p. 502 on the number of soldiers promised to Antony; on the ending of the first five-year term of the triumvirate see F. Millar, 'Triumvirate and Principate', *JRS* 63 (1973), pp. 50–67, esp. 51, 53, and Pelling in *CAH²* X, pp. 67–8.

33 Agrippa in Gaul, see Dio 48. 49. 2–3, Appian, *BC* 5. 92 and the discussion in J. M. Roddaz, *Marcus Agrippa* (1984), pp. 70–72, and Pelling in *CAH²* X, p. 25, Syme (1960), p. 231.

34 Appian, *BC* 5. 96–122, Dio 49. 1. 1–16. 2, Suetonius, *Augustus* 16. 1–3, Velleius Paterculus 2. 79. 1–6, Livy, *Pers.* 128–9; see also Osgood (2006), pp. 298–303, Morrison & Coates (1996), pp. 154–7, Pitassi (2009), pp. 187–91, Roddaz (1984), pp. 87–138, M. Reinhold, *Marcus Agrippa: A Biography* (1933), p. 29 noting Agrippa's lack of experience in naval warfare when given the command in 37 BC; on Agrippa's harbour see R. Paget, 'The ancient ports of Cumae,' *JRS* 58 (1968), pp. 152–69, esp. 161–9;

on the *corona navalis*, see V. Maxfield, *The Military Decorations of the Roman Army* (1981), pp. 74–6.

CHAPTER 10

1 *Res Gestae* 3 (Loeb translation).
2 Suetonius, *Augustus* 17. 1 (Loeb translation).
3 For this episode see Velleius Paterculus 2. 28. 3–4, Appian, *BC* 5. 123–6, Dio 49. 11. 1–12. 4, with discussion in R. Weigel, *Lepidus. The Tarnished Triumvir* (1992), pp. 88–92.
4 Dio 49. 17. 1–18. 7, 50. 1. 4, Appian *BC* 5. 127, 133–44, Velleius Paterculus 2. 79. 5.
5 Plutarch, *Antony* 37.
6 For a detailed description of the campaign see A. Goldsworthy, *Antony and Cleopatra* (2010), pp. 304–20; on Antony's losses see Plutarch, *Antony* 49–51, Velleius Paterculus 2. 82. 3. Dio 49. 31. 1–3, with A. Sherwin-White, *Roman Foreign Policy in the East, 168 BC–AD 1* (1984), pp. 320–21. Livy, *Pers.* 130 also claims that 8,000 men died 'in storms' during the march through Armenia, but does not give a figure for overall casualties; Antony's near-suicide, see Plutarch, *Antony* 48; modern commentators tend to be over-generous to Antony, e.g. R. Syme, *The Roman Revolution* (1960), p. 264, 'it was a defeat, but not a rout or a disaster'. C. Pelling, *Plutarch: Life of Antony* (1988), pp. 220–43 is more realistic and notes that Plutarch placed the failure of this expedition as the turning point in Antony's life.
7 Appian, *BC* 5. 130–31, *Res Gestae* 4, and 25 where it is claimed 30,000 slaves were returned to their masters; use of slaves in Octavian's fleet see Suetonius, *Augustus* 16. 1, Dio 47. 17. 4, 48. 49. 1, 49. 1. 5, the last passage implying that they were given freedom on discharge; on the honours voted to Caesar, see P. Zanker (trans. A. Shapiro), *The Power of Images in the Age of Augustus* (1988), pp. 40–42, and B. Levick, *Augustus. Image and Substance* (2010), p. 40.
8 For these campaigns in general see Appian, *Illyrian Wars* 16–29, Dio 49. 34. 2–38. 1, 43. 8, with E. Gruen in *CAH²* X, pp.172–4, and especially M. Kos, *Appian and Illyricum* (2005), pp. 393–471.
9 Appian, *Illyrian Wars* 19–21, Suetonius, *Augustus* 20.
10 Appian, *Illyrian Wars* 26, 27, Suetonius, *Augustus* 20, 24; Antony's decimation of a cohort, see Plutarch, *Antony* 39, Dio 49. 26. 1–27. 1, with Sherwin-White (1984), p. 318.
11 J. Osgood, *Caesar's Legacy. Civil War and the Emergence of the Roman Empire* (2006), pp. 325–6.
12 Dio 47. 15. 2–3, 48. 43. 2, 49. 43. 6–7, 49. 39. 1, with Osgood (2006), pp. 257–67.
13 Osgood (2006), pp. 252–3, 326–31.
14 Suetonius, *Augustus* 28. 3, Pliny *NH* 36. 121, and for discussion see N. Purcell in *CAH²* X, pp. 782–9.
15 For Cleopatra's career in general see Goldsworthy (2010), M. Grant, *Cleopatra* (1972), J. Tyldesley, *Cleopatra. Last Queen of Egypt* (2009); for a perceptive reassessment of her significance with Julius Caesar see E. Gruen, 'Cleopatra in Rome. Fact and Fantasies', in D. Braund & C. Gill (eds), *Myths, History and Culture in*

Republican Rome: Studies in honour of T. P. Wiseman (2003), pp. 257–74, and also for the history of her father's relationship with the Romans, see M. Siani-Davies, 'Ptolemy XII Auletes and the Romans', *Historia* 46 (1997), pp. 306–40; for Cicero's mentions of her see Cicero, *ad Att.* 14. 8, 15. 15, with comments in Goldsworthy (2010), p. 234, contrasting with Grant (1972), pp. 95–7; Arsinoe, see Strabo, *Geog.* 14. 6. 6, with P. Green, *Alexander to Actium: The Historical Evolution of the Hellenistic Age* (1990), p. 669, and Goldsworthy (2010), pp. 235–6; death of Ptolemy XIV, see Josephus, *AJ* 15. 39, *Against Apion* 2. 58, Porphyry, *Fragments of Greek Historians* 260.

16 Death of Arsinoe and another potential rival, see Josephus, *AJ* 15. 89, Appian, *BC* 5. 9, Dio 48. 24. 2; summoned to Lebanon, see Plutarch, *Antony* 51, Dio 49. 31. 4.

17 Plutarch, *Antony* 53–4, Appian, *BC* 5. 95, 138, Dio 49. 33. 3–4, with Grant (1972), pp. 150–53, Osgood (2006), p. 336, Syme (1960), p. 265.

18 Octavia continues to act on behalf of Antony in Rome, Plutarch, *Antony* 54; *tribunicia sacrosanctitas*, Dio 49. 15. 5–6, 38. 1, with discussion by Pelling in *CAH²* X, pp. 68–9, and A. Barrett, *Livia. First Lady of Imperial Rome* (2002), pp. 31–2; favour won by mitigating the impact of land confiscations, e.g. Virgil, *Eclogues* 1. 40–47, with Osgood (2006), pp. 121–2.

19 Plutarch, *Antony* 54, Dio 49. 40. 3–4, Velleius Paterculus 2. 82. 3–4, with comments in Grant (1972), pp. 161–2, and Pelling in *CAH²* X, p. 40.

20 Plutarch, *Antony* 54, Dio 49. 41. 1–6, with Pelling in *CAH²* X, pp. 40–41, Osgood (2006), pp. 338–9, Grant (1972), pp. 162–75, J. Bingen, *Hellenistic Egypt: Monarchy, Society, Economy, Culture* (2007), pp. 78–9, G. Hölbl, *A History of the Ptolemaic Empire* (2001), pp. 244–5; suppression of Antony's own account of this, Dio 49. 41. 4.

21 Horace, *Epodes* 9. 11–16 (Loeb translation).

22 Plutarch, *Comparison between Antony and Demetrius* 4, with Grant (1972), p. 188, and Pelling in *CAH²* X, p. 43. On Hercules and Omphale see Zanker (1988), pp. 57–65, and esp. 58–60; on magic potions see Dio 49. 34. 1, Josephus, *AJ* 15. 93.

23 Suetonius, *Augustus* 69. 2.

24 For discussions of the propaganda war, see K. Scott, 'The Political Propaganda of 44–30 BC', *Memoirs of the American Academy in Rome* 11 (1933), pp. 7–49, esp. 33–49, Osgood (2006), pp. 335–49, Pelling in *CAH²* X, pp. 40–48, and Syme (1960), pp. 276–8.

25 Suetonius, *Caesar* 52. 2 on the pamphlet written by Caius Oppius denying that Caesarion was Caesar's son; on the accusation of a marriage alliance with King Cotiso of Illyria, see Suetonius, *Augustus* 63. 2.

26 Plutarch, *Antony* 55–6, Dio 49. 44. 3, 50. 1. 1–2. 2.

27 Dio 49. 41. 4, 50. 2. 2– 7, with Osgood (2006), pp. 252–3; on the ending of the triumvirate, see the excellent summary by Pelling in *CAH²* X, pp. 67–8.

28 Velleius Paterculus 2. 83. 1–2, Pliny, *NH* 9. 119–21, cf. Horace, *Satires* 2. 3. 239–42, Valerius Maximus 9. 1. 2, Pliny, *NH* 9. 122; Suetonius, *Caligula* 37. 1, with B. Ullman, 'Cleopatra's pearls', *The Classical Journal* 52. 5 (Feb. 1957), pp. 193–201, Osgood (2006), pp. 276–80, and Goldsworthy (2010), pp. 337–9; quote in Velleius Paterculus 2. 83. 3.

29 Plutarch, *Antony* 58, Suetonius, *Augustus* 17. 1, Dio 50. 3. 1–4. 1, with J. Johnson, 'The authenticity and validity of Antony's will', *L' Antiquité Classique* 47 (1978), pp. 494–503.

30 Zanker (1988), pp. 72–7.

31 Velleius Paterculus 2. 86. 3 for Asinius Pollio. On the oath see *The Res Gestae of the Divine Augustus* 25. 2–3, Suetonius, *Augustus* 17. 2, with discussion in Osgood (2006), pp. 357–68; Syme (1960), p. 278, fn. 3 claims that more than 300 senators went to Antony, and his authority is one of the main reasons this figure is so often repeated as fact rather than inference.

32 Dio 50. 4. 1–6. 1, Livy 1. 32 for a detailed account of the ceremony written after Octavian had revived it; see also J. Rich, *Declaring War in the Roman Republic in the Period of Transmarine Expansion* (1976), pp. 56–8, 104–7.

33 Dio 50. 9. 3, Plutarch, *Antony* 56, with Pelling (1988), pp. 259–60, and *CAH²* X, pp. 52, 55, M. Grant, *Cleopatra* (1972), pp. 197–8, and R. Syme, *The Roman Revolution* (1960), pp. 294–5.

34 On the campaign in general see Goldsworthy (2010), pp. 360–64; 'sit on a ladle', see Plutarch, *Antony* 62, with Pelling (1988), pp. 271–2; on the desertions see Plutarch, *Antony 59, 63*, Velleius Paterculus 2. 84. 2, Dio 50. 13. 6, 14. 3, with Osgood (2006), pp. 372–3 and Syme (1960), p. 296.

35 For the battle see Plutarch, *Antony* 64–6, 68, Dio 50. 14. 4–35. 6, with J. Carter, *The Battle of Actium: The Rise and Triumph of Augustus Caesar* (1970), pp. 203–13, S. Sheppard, *Actium: Downfall of Antony and Cleopatra*. Osprey Campaign Series 211 (2009), Osgood (2006), pp. 374–5, 380–82, Grant (1972), pp. 206–15, and Pelling (1988), pp. 278–89, Goldsworthy (2010), pp. 364–9, D. Harrington, 'The Battle of Actium – a study in historiography', *Ancient World* 9. 1–2 (1984), pp. 59–64, and C. Lange, 'The Battle of Actium: A reconsideration', *Classical Quarterly* 61. 2 (2011), pp. 608–23, the latter arguing that scholars are mistaken to see the battle as lightly contested; on the capitulation of Antony's legions, see Plutarch, *Antony* 68, Dio 51. 1. 4–3. 1, Velleius Paterculus 2. 85. 5–6, with L. Keppie, *The Making of the Roman Army* (1984), pp. 134–6.

36 Dio 51. 3. 1–4. 8, Pelling in *CAH²* X, pp. 61–2.

37 Dio 51. 6. 4–8. 7, Plutarch, *Antony* 72–3, with Pelling (1988), pp. 297–300; apparent assistance of Caesar's invasion by Cleopatra, see Dio 51. 10. 4–5, Plutarch, *Antony* 76; see Grant (1972), pp. 222–3, doubts treachery and sees the defections as due to the hopelessness of the situation.

38 In general see Goldsworthy (2010), pp. 376–87, for Cleopatra's meeting with Caesar, see Dio 51. 11. 3, 5–13, Plutarch, *Antony* 82–3, with Pelling (1988), pp. 313–16, Florus 2. 21. 9–10; her death, Strabo, *Geog.* 17. 1. 10, Dio 51. 13. 4–14. 6, Plutarch, *Antony* 84–6, with Pelling (1988), pp. 316–22, Velleius Paterculus 2. 87. 1; see also Grant (1972), pp. 224–8, Tyldesley (2009), pp. 189–95, E. Rice, *Cleopatra* (1999), pp. 86–91, P. Green, *Alexander to Actium* (1990), pp. 679–82, and G. Hölbl (trans. T. Saavedra), *A History of the Ptolemaic Empire* (2001), pp. 248–9; Arsinoe in Julius Caesar's triumph, Dio 53. 19. 1–20. 4, Appian, *BC* 2.101.

39 Dio 51. 15. 5–6, Plutarch, *Antony* 81. Dio claims that Caesar actually delivered his speech in Greek, but may perhaps have simply ignored the use of a local orator.

CHAPTER 11

1 Tacitus, *Ann.* 1. 2 (Loeb translation, slightly modified).

2 *Res Gestae* 3, 4 (Loeb translation).

3 Horace, *Odes* 1. 37 (Loeb translation).

4 Virgil, *Aeneid* 8. 678–99 (Loeb translation, slightly modified).

5 For a good discussion of the presentation of the battle, with references to the considerable literature on the subject, see C. Lange, *Res Publica Constituta. Actium, Apollo and the Accomplishment of the Triumviral Assignment* (2009), pp. 75–90, with J. Osgood, *Caesar's Legacy. Civil War and the Emergence of the Roman Empire* (2006), pp. 370–72, 375–83.

6 Horace, *Epodes* 7. 1–10 (Loeb translation); on the popular desire for a victory over the Parthians and conquests in Britain see J. Rich, 'Augustus, War *and* Peace', in J. Edmondson (ed.), *Augustus* (2009), pp. 137–64, esp. 143–6 = L. de Blois, P. Erdkamp, G. de Kleijn and S. Mols (eds), *The Representation and Perception of Roman Imperial Power: Proceedings of the Third Workshop of the International Network, Impact of Empire (Roman Empire c.200 BC–AD 476)* (2003), pp. 329–57.

7 Horace, *Epodes* 16, quotes taken from lines 1–9 (Loeb translation).

8 Horace, *Epodes* 1 speaks of Maecenas going with Caesar's fleet and how the poet feels he must follow in spite of his own frailty, with Osgood (2006), pp. 362–3; on Horace at Philippi, see *Odes* 2. 7, which talks of fleeing the battle, cf. *Epistulae* 2. 2. 46–51.

9 Suetonius, *Augustus* 51. 1 and cf. Velleius Paterculus 2. 86. 1–3, and for a detailed discussion of Augustus' clemency to former enemies see M. Dowling, *Clemency and Cruelty in the Roman World* (2006), pp. 29–75.

10 e.g. Tacitus, *Ann.* 1. 1–2, 4, with W. Lacey, *Augustus and the Principate. The Evolution of the System* (1996), pp. 1–16.

11 Dio 51. 19. 1–7, with Lange (2009), pp. 125–48 for detailed discussion and Lacey (1996), pp. 182–3; on the longing for peace see Osgood (2006), pp. 389–98.

12 Dio 51. 20. 4–5, Suetonius, *Augustus* 22, *Res Gestae* 13, with Lange (2009), pp. 140–48 and J. Crook in *CAH*² X, pp. 74–5; Dio 51. 19. 7 for judicial rights, which he compares to the vote of Athena in Athens, allowing him to cast a vote in any court. It may be that he was allowed to act as an ultimate court of appeal, but the details are unclear; on the *augurium salutis* see Lacey (1996), p. 41, fn. 92.

13 Suetonius, *Augustus* 63. 1 for the stillborn child, and in general A. Barrett, *Livia. First Lady of Imperial Rome* (2002), pp. 28–34, 118–22, and M. Dennison, *Empress of Rome. The Life of Livia* (2010), pp. 89–96.

14 Dio 55. 7. 2–3, with quote from Loeb translation; Athenodorus from Plutarch, *Moralia* 207C. 7.

15 Suetonius, *Augustus* 85. 1–2.

16 Quote from Nepos, *Atticus* 20 (Loeb translation).

17 On the garb of the kings of Alba Longa, see Dio 43. 43. 2, with S. Weinstock, *Divus Julius* (1971), p. 324; on antiquarian interests among the nobility during this period see E. Rawson, *Intellectual Life in the Roman Republic* (1985), pp. 102–3, 233–49.

18 See Nepos, *Atticus* 20, and discussion in J. Rich, 'Augustus and the spolia opima,' *Chiron* 26 (1996), pp. 85–127, esp. 113–16.

19 Nepos, *Atticus* 22. 3–4.

20 Dio 51. 16. 3–17. 8, with A. Bowman in *CAH²* X, pp. 676–89, P. Brunt, 'The administrators of Roman Egypt', *JRS* 65 (1975), pp. 124–47 and 'Princeps and equites', *JRS* 73 (1983), pp. 42–75, esp. 62–3; on Gallus see R. Syme, *The Roman Revolution* (1960), pp. 252–3, 300.

21 Dio 51. 18. 1, Suetonius, *Augustus* 18. 2.

22 G. Hölbl (trans. T. Saavedra), *A History of the Ptolemaic Empire* (2001), pp. 14–15.

23 Suetonius, *Augustus* 18. 1, Dio 51. 16. 5; on portraits, including the period where he was made to resemble Alexander the Great, see K. Galinsky, *Augustan Culture* (1996), pp. 164–79, esp. 167–8.

24 Suetonius, *Augustus* 17. 4, Plutarch, *Antony* 86, Dio 51. 15. 1 for the burial of Antony and Cleopatra, Dio 51. 19. 3–5 on the public disgrace of Antony and his images, with Lange (2009), pp. 136–40; the story of Alexander and the Gordian knot, see Plutarch, *Alexander the Great* 18.

25 Dio 51. 18. 1–3, with Syme (1960), pp. 300–02, and F. Millar, *The Roman Near East 31 BC–AD 337* (1993), pp. 27–34.

26 Josephus, *AJ* 14. 314–16, and 14. 301–12 (quotes from Loeb translation); see also J. Osgood, *Caesar's Legacy: Civil War and the Emergence of the Roman Empire* (2006), pp. 105–6; temples and cults, see Dio 51. 20. 6–8; on the imperial cult in general see S. Price, *Rituals and Power. The Roman Imperial Cult in Asia Minor* (1985), and J. Scheid, 'To honour the Princeps and venerate the gods. Public cult, neighbourhood cults, and imperial cult in Augustan Rome', in Edmondson (2009), pp. 275–99, esp. 288–99.

27 Suetonius, *Augustus* 41. 1, Dio 51. 21. 5.

28 Josephus, *AJ* 15. 161–78, 183–236, *BJ* 1. 386–97, 431–44, with E. Schürer, G. Vermes & F. Millar, *The History of the Jewish People in the Age of Jesus Christ* Vol. 1 (1973), pp. 301–3; Josephus, *BJ* 1. 397 for bodyguard unit.

29 Dio 51. 18. 2–3, with A. Sherwin-White, *Roman Foreign Policy in the East, 168 BC–AD 1* (1984), pp. 324–41, and Rich (2009), pp. 143–8.

30 Dio 51. 19. 2–3, 20. 4 with Lacey (1996), pp. 39–41, refusal of crowns, Dio 51. 21. 4.

31 For the story of the ravens, see Macrobius 2. 4. 29.

32 Strabo, *Geog.* 12. 35 for the execution of one leader and his son.

33 For the triumphs see Dio 51. 21. 4–9, Plutarch, *Antony* 86, *Res Gestae* 4 for the royal captives, with Lange (2009), pp. 148–57, Lacey (1996), p. 41; Marcellus and Tiberius riding on the chariot horses, see Suetonius, *Tiberius* 6. 4.

34 *Res Gestae* 8.

CHAPTER 12

1 *Res Gestae* 34 (Loeb translation, slightly modified).

2 Velleius Paterculus 2. 89. 3.

3 Dio 51. 21. 3–4, *Res Gestae* 15. Dio says that Agrippa was awarded a dark blue flag. It is unclear whether or not this is the same or an additional banner to the one

awarded after the defeat of Sextus Pompey, see Suetonius, *Augustus* 25. 3; on colonisation see P. Brunt, *Italian Manpower 225 BC–AD 14* (1971), pp. 332–44, and L. Keppie, *Colonisation and Veteran Settlement in Italy 47–14 BC* (1983), esp. pp. 58–86.

4 Dio 51. 22. 1–4, Crook in *CAH*² X, pp. 75–6, and P. Zanker (trans. A. Shapiro), *The Power of Images in the Age of Augustus* (1988), pp. 79–82.

5 Dio 51. 22. 4–9, *Res Gestae* 22 for Caesar's games; Dio 51. 23. 1 for Statilius Taurus and the special honour of choosing a praetor.

6 Dio 53. 1. 1–2, with E. Stavely, 'The "Fasces" and "Imperium Maius"', *Historia* 12 (1963), pp. 458–84, esp. 466–8, F. Millar, 'Triumvirate and Principate', *JRS* 63 (1973), pp. 50–67, esp. 62.

7 Cicero, *ad Fam.* 6. 18. 1, *Philippics* 11. 5. 12, 13. 13. 27, Dio 43. 47. 3, Suetonius, *Caesar* 76. 2–3, 80. 2; for a detailed discussion of the origins of Julius Caesar's new senators, see R. Syme, *The Roman Revolution* (1960), pp. 78–96; on the period after Julius Caesar's death see J. Osgood, *Caesar's Legacy. Civil War and the Emergence of the Roman Empire* (2006), pp. 257–60, 283–8; runaway slaves discovered in office, see Dio 48. 34. 5.

8 Dio 52. 42. 1–5, Suetonius, *Augustus* 35. 1–2, *Res Gestae* 8.

9 Triumphs to Caius Calvisius Sabinus over Spain on 26 May, Caius Carrinas over Gaul on 6 July, and Lucius Autronius Paetus over Africa on 16 August.

10 Tacitus, *Ann.* 3. 28 '*non mos, non ius*'; on the role of the triumvirs to restore the state see in general C. Lange, *Res Publica Constituta. Actium, Apollo and the Accomplishment of the Triumviral Assignment* (2009), *passim*.

11 Dio 53. 2. 3, with W. Lacey, *Augustus and the Principate. The Evolution of the System* (1996), pp. 83–6, Crook in *CAH*² X, pp. 76–7. J. Liebeschuetz, 'The settlement of 27 BC', in C. Deroux, *Studies in Latin Literature and Roman History* (2008), pp. 345–65.

12 On elections see A. Jones, 'The elections under Augustus,' *JRS* 45 (1955), pp. 9–21, esp. 11; on the treasury see Dio 53. 2. 1, 3.

13 On building work, see *Res Gestae* 20, Dio 53. 2. 4–6, with Lacey (1996), pp. 83–4, and in general Zanker (1988), pp. 101–36.

14 Dio 53. 1. 4–6.

15 Dio 53. 1. 3, with Zanker (1988), pp. 65–71, 240–54, and T. Wiseman, '*Conspicui Postes Tectaque Digna Deo*: the public image of aristocratic and imperial houses in the Late Republic and Early Empire', in *L'Urbs. Espace urbain et histoire* (1987), pp. 393–413, esp. 399–407; for recent research on the Temple of Apollo see S. Zink, 'Reconstructing the Palatine temple of Apollo: a case study in early Augustan temple design', *JRA* 21 (2008), pp. 47–63.

16 Purcell in *CAH*² X, pp. 787–8, Zanker (1988), pp. 66–71; Velleius Paterculus 2. 86. 2.

17 Dio 51. 23. 2–27. 3, Livy, *Per.* 134.

18 Dio 51. 25. 2, with J. Rich, 'Augustus and the spolia opima', *Chiron* 26 (1996), pp. 85–127, esp. 95–7, and in general T. Barnes, 'The victories of Augustus', *JRS* 64 (1974), pp. 21–6.

19 Livy 4. 20. 5–7 (Loeb translation); for a good discussion of the *spolia opima* see H. Flower, 'The tradition of the spolia opima: M. Claudius Marcellus and Augustus', *Classical Antiquity* 19 (2000), pp. 34–64.

20 On the family, see Syme (1960), pp. 424, 496–7.

21 For the assumption that Crassus asked for and was refused the right to dedicate *spolia opima*, see Syme (1960), pp. 308–9 and 'Livy and Augustus', *Harvard Studies in Classical Philology* 64 (1959), pp. 27–87, esp. 43–7, Crook in *CAH²* X, p. 80, Lacey (1996), pp. 87–8, Millar (1973), p. 62, J. Richardson, '*Imperium Romanum*: Empire and the Language of Power', *JRS* 81 (1991), pp. 1–9, esp. 8; I have followed the utterly convincing arguments of E. Badian, '"Crisis Theories" and the beginning of the Principate', in W. Wirth, *Romanitas and Christianitas* (1982), pp. 18–41, esp. 24–7, and Rich (1996) on this issue.

22 Suetonius, *Augustus* 28. 1; the debate between Agrippa and Maecenas is in Dio 52. 1. 2–41. 2, with F. Millar, *A Study of Cassius Dio* (1964), pp. 102–18.

23 For the (generally assumed) contrast with Julius Caesar, e.g. P. Cartledge, 'The second thoughts of Augustus on the res publica in 28/7 BC', *Greece and Rome* 31 (1984), pp. 30–40, esp. 34–5, Syme (1960), pp. 317–18, E. Salmon, 'The Evolution of Augustus' Principate', *Historia* 5 (1956), pp. 456–78, esp. 459–62, Galinsky (2012), pp. 63, 152–3. The assumption also underlies much of the literature looking at the dictator's last days and the motives of the conspirators.

24 End of civil war, see Macrobius, *Saturnalia* 1. 12. 35, and in general Lacey (1996), pp. 81–2.

25 Suetonius, *Augustus* 84, Dio 53. 2. 7 and 11. 1 for reading the speech, and 53. 3. 1–10. 8 for Dio's version.

26 Dio 53. 8. 1–2 (Loeb translation).

27 Dio 53. 11. 1–4.

28 Dio 53. 11. 5–12. 1.

29 *Res Gestae* 34, with Lacey (1996), pp. 86–8 and Zanker (1988), pp. 91–4.

30 Dio 53. 12. 2–16. 3, with Lacey (1996), pp. 89–95, Liebeschuetz (2008), pp. 346–53, Salmon (1956), pp. 459–67, Cartledge (1984), pp. 31–8, J. Ferrary, 'The powers of Augustus', in J. Edmondson (ed.), *Augustus* (2009), pp. 90–136, esp. 90–99, A. Jones, 'The imperium of Augustus', *JRS* 41 (1951), pp. 112–19, esp. 112–14, and G. Chilver, 'Augustus and the Roman constitution 1939–1950', *Historia* 1 (1950), pp. 408–35 for a useful survey of the scholarly debate up to that point, and on the role of provinces and warfare in general for Caesar's justification of his position see J. Rich, 'Augustus, War and Peace', in Edmondson (2009), pp. 137–64, esp. 153–7; for the continuation of aristocratic competition, see W. Eck, 'Senatorial Self-Representation: Developments in the Augustan Period', in F. Millar & E. Segal (eds), *Caesar Augustus. Seven Aspects* (1990), pp. 129–67.

31 Dio 53. 11. 5, with G. Watson, *The Roman Soldier* (1985), pp. 97–8 on praetorian pay, arguing that Dio's 'double pay' must have been a rough approximation; on the control of the army in general see J. Campbell, *The Emperor and the Roman Army 31 BC–AD 235* (1984), *passim*.

32 Note Horace, *Epodes* 7. 17–20 for a contemporary claim that Rome was cursed by the fratricidal murder of Remus; on Romulus and his death see Livy 1. 16. 1–4.

33 *Res Gestae* 34, Suetonius, *Augustus* 7, Dio 53. 16. 7, Velleius Paterculus 2. 91, Lacey (1996), pp. 92–5, Zanker (1988), pp. 95–100, Syme (1959), p. 59, and 'Imperator Caesar, a study in nomenclature', *Historia* 7 (1958), pp. 172–88; for detailed

566   NOTES

discussion of the associations of the virtues on the shield and the argument that all had in the past been attributed to Julius Caesar, see S. Weinstock, *Divus Julius* (1971), pp. 228–59.

34 Suetonius, *Julius Caesar* 77.

35 Suetonius, *Augustus* 24. 1 on his reluctance to permit governors' wives to accompany them to their provinces; for Livia, see A. Barrett, *Livia. First Lady of Imperial Rome* (2002), pp. 34–7.

CHAPTER 13

1 Virgil, *Aeneid* 6. 851–3: *tu regere imperio populos, Romane, memento*
    (Hae tibi erunt artes) pacisque imponere morem,
    parcere subiectis et debellare superbos.

2 Horace, *Odes* 3. 5. 2–4 (Loeb translation, slightly modified); for the role of warfare in Augustus' public image and the popularity of attacking Parthians, Britons and Indians, see J. Rich, 'Augustus, War, *and* Peace', in L. de Blois, P. Erdkamp, O. Hekster, G. de Kleijn & S. Mols (eds), *The Representation and Perception of Roman Imperial Power: Proceedings of the Third Workshop of the International Network, Impact of Empire (Roman Empire, c.200 BC–AD 476)* (2003), pp. 329–57 = J. Edmondson (ed.), *Augustus* (2009), pp. 137–64, esp. 143–8; on Britain, see Caesar, *BG.* 4. 20 on alleged British aid to Gauls, and for these operations in general see A. Goldsworthy, *Caesar. The Life of a Colossus* (2006), pp. 278–92.

3 In general see M. Todd, *Roman Britain* (3rd edn, 1999), pp. 15–22, G. Webster, *The Roman Invasion of Britain* (rev. edn, 1993), pp. 41–74, and J. Manley, *AD 43 The Roman Invasion of Britain – A Reassessment* (2002), pp. 37–50; for the circumnavigation of Britain see Tacitus, *Agricola* 38.

4 Dio 53. 22. 5, Orosius 6. 21.1–11, Florus 2. 33. 46–59.

5 For the grim evidence from Valencia see A. Ribera i Lacomba & M. Calvo Galvez, 'La primera evidencia arqueológica de la destrucción de Valentia por Pompeyo', *Journal of Roman Archaeology* 8 (1995), pp. 19–40, and Caesar, *Spanish War* 32; for studies of the development of the Roman frontier and provinces in Spain see S. Dyson, *The Creation of the Roman Frontier* (1985), esp. pp. 199–236, and J. Richardson, *The Romans in Spain* (1996), pp. 41–126; for the origins of the *gladius hispaniensis* see F. Queseda Sanz, '*Gladius hispaniensis*: an archaeological view from Iberia', *Journal of Roman Military Equipment Studies* 8 (1997), pp. 251–70 and *Armas de la Antigua Iberia de Tartessos a Numancia* (2010) for a detailed study of Spanish equipment and warfare.

6 For Balbus see esp. Cicero, *pro Balbo*, Richardson (1996), pp. 103, 106, 117, 119, 126, citing Cicero, *ad Fam.* 10. 32. 3 where Asinius Pollio scathingly criticises the Younger Balbus' behaviour at Gades; on Spanish-born citizens seeking public careers see M. Griffin, 'The Elder Seneca and Spain', *JRS* 62 (1972), pp. 1–19; on the number of *equites* at Gades see Strabo, *Geog.* 3. 5. 3; on the economy and society in the provinces see Richardson (1996), pp. 149–78.

7 For the Celtiberians, and a very useful survey of the ongoing archaeological debate over the question of Romanisation and acculturation, see L. Curchin,

The Romanization of Central Spain. Complexity, Diversity and Change in a Provincial Hinterland (2004), esp. pp. 69–143.

8 Roman views of Spain were often simplistic, at least on the part of those who had not been there, and for this see the discussion of the out-of-date and out-landish descriptions included alongside more recent information in Strabo in Richardson (1996), pp. 150–68; note also the mention in Dio of a bandit leader eventually pardoned and rewarded by Augustus when the man gave himself up, Dio 56. 43. 3.

9 On the emperor and the army in general, see J. Campbell, *The Emperor and the Roman Army 31 BC–AD 235* (1984).

10 For Augustus' new army in general see L. Keppie, *The Making of the Roman Army* (1984), pp. 132–54, H. Parker, *The Roman Legions* (1957), pp. 72–92, and R. Syme, 'Notes on the legions under Augustus', *JRS* 23 (1933), pp. 14–33. There is some uncertainty on the date of the creation of *Legio XXI Rapax* and *Legio XXII Deiotariana*. The latter was formed from Roman-trained soldiers of the Galatian king who were given citizenship when taken into the Roman army. This may have happened on the death of the Galatian king in 25 BC.

11 For a total of 120,000 settled veterans in 29 BC see *Res Gestae* 15.

12 Suetonius, *Augustus* 38. 2.

13 Sallust, *Bell. Cat.* 24. 2, 28. 4, 30. 1, 56. 1–2, 59. 3 for the former centurion Manlius who raised an army for Catiline, and cf. 59. 6 on the opposing commander Petreius, who had served thirty years as tribune, prefect, legate, or praetor; Dio 52. 27. 4–5; see chapter 6 for Antony's recruitment of former centurions in 44 BC; and Campbell (1984), pp. 101–9 on the role of centurions, and R. Smith, *Service in the Post-Marian Roman Army* (1958), pp. 59–69.

14 See Keppie (1984), esp. pp. 134–40, 142–3.

15 For the legions in Spain see most recently A. Morillo Cerdán, 'The Augustean Spanish Experience: The origin of the *limes* system?', in A. Morillo, N. Hanel & E. Martín, *Limes XX: Estudios sobre la frontera romana. Roman Frontier Studies. Anejos de Gladius* 13 Vol. 1 (2009), pp. 239–51, 240, R. Syme, 'The Spanish War of Augustus', *American Journal of Philology* 55 (1934), pp. 293–317, 298–301, and R. Jones, 'The Roman Military Occupation of North-West Spain', JRS 66 (1976), pp. 45–66, 48–52; for *Caesar's Legio X Equestris*, see BG 1. 42 and Keppie (1984), p. 137.

16 Suetonius, *Augustus* 24. 2–25. 1; on *commilitones* and the treatment of soldiers see Campbell (1984), pp. 32–93.

17 Suetonius, *Augustus* 25. 4.

18 For discussion of Roman commanders see A. Goldsworthy, '"Instinctive genius": the depiction of Caesar the general', in K. Welch & A. Powell (eds), *Julius Caesar as Artful Reporter: The War Commentaries as Political Instruments* (1998), pp. 193–219; on responsibility for failure see Suetonius, *Augustus* 23 where failures in Gaul and Germany are seen as his defeats even though he was not in direct command.

19 Dio 53. 23. 5–7, ILS 8995, il. 4 ff., with Crook in CAH² X, pp. 80–81; seduction of Atticus' daughter Pomponia, Suetonius, *Gram.* 16.

20 Dio 53. 23. 6, 24. 1–2, and for discussion see Levick (2010), pp. 174–5.

21 Suetonius, *Augustus* 66. 2, with R. Syme, *The Roman Revolution* (1960), pp. 309–10,

who associates it with the earlier incident involving Crassus, on the basis that Gallus 'could' have been recalled from Egypt as early as 28 BC. However, there seems no reason to reject Dio's later dating.

22 For the campaigns in 26–25 BC, see the recent discussion in Morillo Cerdán (2009) with references to the archaeological evidence, and in the wider context see Gruen in *CAH²* X, pp. 163–6. Syme (1934) and 'The conquest of North-West Spain', *Roman Papers*. Vol. 2 (1979), pp. 825–54, and D. Magie, 'Augustus' War in Spain (26–25 BC), *Classical Philology* 15 (1920), pp. 323–39 remain useful discussions of the literary evidence; Suetonius, *Augustus* 85. 1 for the autobiography, with J. Rich, 'Cantabrian closure: Augustus' Spanish War and the ending of his memoirs', in C. Smith & A. Powell (eds), *The Lost Memoirs of Augustus and the Development of Roman Autobiography* (2009), pp. 145–72; Dio 53. 25. 6–7 for Augustus' illness.

23 Orosius 6. 21. 1–11, Florus 2. 33. 46–59.

24 Morillo Cerdán (2009), p. 243.

25 Florus 2. 33. 50.

26 Morillo Cerdán (2009), pp. 243–4; on the legion see Dio 54. 11. 5 with Keppie (1984), pp. 138, 157.

27 e.g. Orosius 6. 21. 19–20, Strabo, *Geog.* 12. 8. 18, with Crook in *CAH²* X, p. 82 and J. Richardson, *Augustan Rome 44 BC to AD 14. The Restoration of the Republic and the Establishment of Empire* (2012), pp. 93–4 emphasising the extent to which, for the duration of Augustus' stay, Tarraco became the centre of the Roman world.

28 For discussion of Livia's role see A. Barrett, *Livia. First Lady of Imperial Rome* (2002), pp. 127–9.

CHAPTER 14

1 Horace, *Odes* 3. 14. 1–8 (Loeb translation).

2 Dio 53. 28. 1–3, *Res Gestae* 15. 1, with Crook in *CAH²* X, pp. 83–4.

3 R. Syme, *The Roman Revolution* (1960), p. 372, citing *ILS* 7448–9 for his bodyguards.

4 Dio 53. 23. 1–4, with P. Zanker (trans. A Shapiro), *The Power of Images in the Age of Augustus* (1988), pp. 139–43.

5 Dio 53. 26. 1–5, 27. 1–2, with comments in T. Barnes, 'The Victories of Augustus', *JRS* 64 (1974), pp. 21–6.

6 For Aelius Gallus' Arabian expedition see Dio 53. 29. 3–8, Strabo, *Geog.* 16. 4. 23–4, 17. 1. 53–4, *Res Gestae* 26. 5, with S. Sidebotham, 'Aelius Gallus and Arabia', *Latomus* 45 (1986), pp. 590–602, and Gruen in *CAH²* X, pp. 148–51.

7 Tacitus, *Ann.* 6. 11 on Messalla Corvinus, with Syme (1960), p. 403 and Crook in *CAH²* X, pp. 81–2.

8 Dio 53. 22. 1–2.

9 Dio 53. 27. 5–6, 30. 1, Suetonius, *Augustus* 81. 1, with E. Badian, '"Crisis Theories" and the beginning of the Principate', in W. Wirth, *Romanitas and Christianitas* (1982), pp. 18–41, 31 for the quote.

10 Dio 53. 26. 1–2, 28. 3–4, 31. 2–3, Suetonius, *Tiberius* 8–9. 3, with B. Levick, *Tiberius the Politician* (1999), pp. 19–24, R. Seager, *Tiberius* (2005), pp. 12–13.

11 *Res Gestae* 15. 1; on Piso's reluctance to stand for office see Tacitus, *Ann.* 2. 43.

12 For grain see *Res Gestae* 15. 1.

13 Suetonius, *Augustus* 59 and 81. 1–2, Dio 53. 30. 1–3.

14 Dio 53. 31. 1.

15 For the resignation and Sestius see Dio 53. 32. 3–4, with Syme (1960), p. 335.

16 Dio 53. 32. 5–6.

17 For discussion and an ongoing scholarly debate see W. Lacey, *Augustus and the Principate. The Evolution of the System* (1996), pp. 100–16, A. Jones, 'The imperium of Augustus', *JRS* 41 (1951), pp. 112–19, E. Stavely, 'The "Fasces" and "Imperium Maius"', *Historia* 12 (1963), pp. 458–84, Salmon (1956), pp. 456–78, esp. 464–73, J. Crook, 'Some remarks on the Augustan Constitution', *Classical Review* 3 (1953), pp. 10–12, W. Lacey, 'Summi Fastigii Vocabulum: The story of a title', *JRS* 69 (1979), pp. 28–34, H. Last, 'Imperium Maius: A note', *JRS* 37 (1947), pp. 157–64, J. Ferrary, 'The powers of Augustus', in J. Edmondson (ed.), *Augustus* (2009), pp. 90–136, esp. 99–103, Syme (1960), pp. 335–8, and B. Levick, *Augustus. Image and Substance* (2010), pp. 84–7.

18 Dio 53. 32. 3.

19 For attempts to paint the events of 23 BC as a response to concerted opposition, see Syme (1960), pp. 335–6, where it is also seen as motivated by Augustus' allies, and Levick (2010), pp. 80–86 represents more balanced treatments of this; however, Badian (1982), pp. 28–38 convincingly demolishes the main arguments of this view and instead suggests that it was carefully prepared and dictated more by Augustus' illness; for the repeated attempts to elect Augustus consul see Dio 54. 6. 1–2, 10. 1, with A. Jones (1955), pp. 9–21, esp. 13.

20 Dio 53. 32. 2.

21 Tacitus, *Ann.* 3. 56, with Lacey (1979).

22 T. Wiseman, '*Conspicui Postes Tectaque Digna Deo*: the public image of aristocratic and imperial houses in the Late Republic and Early Empire', in *L'Urbs. Espace urbain et histoire* (1987), pp. 393–413, esp. 401–12

23 Dio 53. 32. 1, and see discussion of Agrippa's powers during these years in Lacey (1996), pp. 117–31, esp. 127–31.

24 Dio 53. 31. 4–32. 1, Velleius Paterculus 2. 93. 1–2, Josephus, *AJ* 15. 350, Suetonius, *Augustus* 66. 3.

25 Dio 53. 30. 4, 33. 4, Velleius Paterculus 2. 93. 1.

26 Dio mentions accusations that Livia murdered Marcellus 53. 33. 4–5, and Tacitus, *Ann.* 1. 3 for the allegation that Livia was responsible for the murder of other family members; on aristocratic mortality in general see W. Scheidel, 'Emperors, Aristocrats, and the Grim Reaper: Towards a Demographic Profile of the Roman Elite', *Classical Quarterly* 49 (1999), pp. 254–81.

27 Virgil, *Aeneid* 6. 860–65, 870–81 (Loeb translation), Propertius 3. 18.

28 Dio 54. 1. 1–3; see G. Rickman, *The Corn Supply of Ancient Rome* (1980), pp. 60–66, 179–86.

29 Dio 54. 1. 4–2. 1, *Res Gestae* 5.

30 Dio 54. 2. 1–3. 1.

31 For Julius Caesar see *BG* 4. 11–16 and Plutarch, *Cato the Younger* 51. 1–2 for attacks on him in the Senate.

32 For the trial of Primus see Dio 54. 3. 2–4; poor judgement of Marcellus Dio 53.
    31. 4.
33 For the conspiracy see Dio 54. 3. 4–8, and Syme (1960), pp. 333–4, Levick (2010),
    pp. 80–83, and D. Stockton, 'Primus and Murena', *Historia* 14 (1965), pp. 18–40
    for the emphasis on the trial and conspiracy as a major factor in shaping Au-
    gustus' reorganisation of his powers, usually backdating these incidents to 24
    or 23 BC, whereas M. Swan, 'The consular fasti of 23 BC and the conspiracy
    of Varro Murena', *Harvard Studies in Classical Philology* 71 (1967), pp. 235–47
    and Badian (1982) make clear that the conspirator was not the consul of 23 BC
    and that the trial and conspiracy occurred after Augustus' resignation from
    the consulship; Dio 53. 19 on the difficulty of understanding a period when
    all decisions were made in secret and Suetonius, *Domitian* 21 for comment on
    plots; for opposition to the emperors and the link to Brutus and Cassius see
    R. MacMullen, *Enemies of the Roman Order. Treason, Unrest and Alienation in the
    Empire* (1967), pp. 1–45.

CHAPTER 15

1 Res Gestae 29. 2 (Loeb translation)
2 Horace, *Epodes* 1. 12. 27–8 (Loeb translation).
3 On Augustus and *mandata* see F. Millar, 'State and Subject: the impact of monarchy', in F. Millar & E. Segal (eds), *Caesar Augustus. Seven Aspects* (1990), pp. 37–60,
   esp. 46–8, and on the nature of *mandata* see D. Potter, 'Emperors, their borders
   and their neighbours: the scope of imperial *mandata*', in D. Kennedy (ed.), *The
   Roman Army in the East. JRA Supplementary Series* 18 (1996), pp. 49–66.
4 Dio 54. 6. 1–4, *Res Gestae* 5.
5 Dio 54. 7. 1, Strabo, *Geog.* 6. 2. 4–5, Pliny, *NH* 3. 90, with R. Wilson in *CAH²* X, pp.
   437–9.
6 On the right for senators to travel to Sicily without formal permission see Tacitus, *Ann.* 12. 23. 1 and Dio 52. 42. 6. Dio attributes this to Augustus and both
   claim that the only similar grant was made in the case of visiting estates in Gallia
   Narbonensis.
7 See A. Wallace-Hadrill, 'Image and authority in the coinage of Augustus', *JRS* 76
   (1986), pp. 66–87.
8 Matthew 22: 20–21, with comments in Millar (1990), pp. 44–5.
9 J. Rea, 'Lease of a Red Cow called Thayris', *The Journal of Egyptian Archaeology* 68
   (1982), pp. 277–82.
10 *Inscriptiones Graecae* (1893–) II² 3173, with comments in J. Camp, *The Archaeology
    of Athens* (2001), pp. 187–8.
11 Strabo, *Geog.* 10. 5. 3.
12 Camp (2001), pp. 188–93, and for a wider discussion of Roman attitudes to Greece
    and Greek attitudes to Rome in the Augustan context see G. Bowersock, *Augus-
    tus and the Greek World* (1965), esp. pp. 42–61, 85–100, and A. Spawforth, *Greece and
    the Augustan Cultural Revolution. Greek Culture in the Roman World* (2012), *passim*
    and esp. pp. 59–86, 106–17 on Athens.

13 In general see F. Millar, 'Empire and City, Augustus to Julian: Obligations, excuses and status', *JRS* 73 (1983), pp. 76–96 and P. Veyne, *Bread and Circuses* (1992), and especially Spawforth (2012).

14 In general see B. Levick in *CAH²* X, pp. 649–50; troops for Aelius Gallus see Josephus, *AJ* 15. 317; on Herod and right to choose successor see Josephus, *AJ* 15. 343, 16. 129 and comments from Gruen in *CAH²* X, pp. 155–7.

15 Dio 54. 9. 3, Josephus, *AJ* 15. 343–8, 360, *BJ* 1. 398–400.

16 See in general D. Roller, *The Building Programme of Herod the Great* (1998), and for the harbour see C. Brandon, 'Cement, concrete and settling barges at Sebastos: comparisons with other Roman harbour examples and the descriptions of Vitruvius', in A. Raban & K. Houm (eds), *Caesarea Maritima. A Retrospective after Two Millennia* (1996), pp. 25–40.

17 For Sebasteni in the Roman army see M. Speidel, 'The Roman army in Judaea under the Procurators', in M. Speidel, *Roman Army Studies* Vol. 2, Mavors (1992), pp. 224–32.

18 For Herod's reign, E. Schürer, G. Vermes & F. Millar, *The History of the Jewish People in the Age of Jesus Christ* Vol. 1 (1973), pp. 287–329, esp. 309–15, provides an excellent introduction; on the Olympic Games see Josephus, *AJ* 16. 149, *BJ* 1. 427, and his own festival 15. 268–71; assassination attempt 15. 280–91; on Herod's gifts to Greek communities see G. Bowersock, *Augustus and the Greek World* (1965), pp. 54–6, and Spawforth (2012), pp. 84–6.

19 Josephus, *AJ* 15. 217, 17.198, *BJ* 1. 672, and Schürer (1973), p. 315.

20 Josephus, *AJ* 15. 272–9.

21 Josephus, *AJ* 15. 305–16.

22 R. MacMullen, *Romanization in the Time of Augustus* (2000), pp. 1–29.

23 L. Jalabert, R. Mouterde et al., *Inscriptiones grecques et latines de la Syrie* (1929–) 3. 718 = R. Sherk, *Roman Documents from the Greek East* (1969), no. 58, doc. iii; J. Reynolds, *Aphrodisias and Rome* (1982), no. 13.

24 Dio 54. 7. 2.

25 Dio 54. 7. 1–6; Suetonius, *Augustus* 82. 1 for his wearing a hat to protect his skin from the sun.

26 Dio 54. 7. 2, 6.

27 Dio 54. 5. 4–6, Strabo, *Geog.* 17. 1. 54 (Loeb translation); Dio 54. 6. 1 on disturbances at Rome.

28 See Velleius Paterculus 2. 91. 3–4, Suetonius, *Augustus* 19. 1, and Dio 53. 24. 4–6 who wrongly dates this incident to 26 BC, with Crook in *CAH²* X, p. 89 and R. Syme, *The Roman Revolution* (1960), pp. 371–2, W. Lacey, *Augustus and the Principate. The Evolution of the System* (1996), pp. 148–9.

29 Dio 53. 33. 1–2.

30 Dio 54. 9. 4–6, Velleius Paterculus 2. 94. 4, with Levick (1999), pp. 25–7, R. Seager, *Tiberius* (2005), pp. 13–14.

31 Dio 54. 8. 1–2, *Res Gestae* 29. 2, Velleius Paterculus 2. 91. 1, Suetonius, *Augustus* 21. 3, *Tiberius* 9. 1, Ovid, *Fasti* 5. 579–84, with D. Kennedy, 'Parthia and Rome: eastern perspectives', in Kennedy (1996), pp. 67–90, esp. 82–3, and B. Campbell, 'War and diplomacy: Rome and Parthia, 31 BC–AD 235', in J. Rich & G. Shipley (eds), *War*

and *Society in the Roman World* (1993), pp. 213–40, esp. 220–28; *dulce et decorum est pro patria mori*, Horace, *Odes* 3. 2. 13.

32 For a detailed discussion of the honours and their context see J. Rich, 'The Parthian honours', *Papers of the British School at Rome* 66 (1998), pp. 71–128; elephants and triumphs, see Plutarch, *Pompey* 14. 4, Pliny *NH* 8. 4 on Pompey's triumph and Suetonius, *Julius Caesar* 37 for elephants as torch-bearers.

33 On the arch see Rich (1998), pp. 97–115, and generally on the honours see Gruen in *CAH²* X, pp. 159–60, Levick (1996), pp. 236–7.

34 See Lacey (1996), pp. 138–40, Syme (1960), p. 367 and Crook in *CAH²* X, p. 91.

35 Dio 54. 9. 8–10, *Res Gestae* 31–2, with Rich, 'Augustus, War, and Peace', in L. de Blois, P. Erdkamp, O. Hekster, G. de Kleijn & S. Mols (eds), *The Representation and Perception of Roman Imperial Power: Proceedings of the Third Workshop of the International Network, Impact of Empire (Roman Empire, c.200 BC–AD 476)*, (2003), pp. 329–57 = J. Edmondson (ed.), *Augustus* (2009), pp. 137–64, esp. 145–6.

CHAPTER 16

1 Virgil, *Aeneid* 1. 286–94 (Loeb translation).

2 Donatus, *Life of Virgil* 31–2, 35.

3 Suetonius, *Horace* (Loeb translation).

4 'fallen on his sponge', see Suetonius, *Augustus* 85. 2, *Horace passim*; for discussion see P. White, *Promised Verse. Poets in the Society of Augustan Rome* (1993), esp. pp. 3–34, 112–55, J. Griffin, 'Augustus and the poets: "Caesar qui cogere posset",' in F. Millar & E. Segal (eds), *Caesar Augustus. Seven Aspects* (1990), pp. 189–218, and K. Galinsky, *Augustan Culture* (1996), pp. 225–79, all of which have references introducing the extensive literature on the subject of the Augustan poets.

5 Suetonius, *Horace*; Horace, *Epistulae* 2. 1. 156–7; pressed to write, e.g. Hirtius in the preface to *BG* 8; for discussion see White (1993), pp 112–42, and A. Powell, *Virgil the Partisan* (2008), esp. pp. 3–30.

6 Propertius 3. 5, 9, 12.

7 Donatus, *Life of Virgil* 20–24, 34, with Galinsky (1996), pp. 246–53.

8 Donatus, *Life of Virgil* 35–41.

9 J. Ziolkowski & J. Putnam, *The Virgilian Tradition. The First Fifteen Hundred Years* (2008), pp. 44–5.

10 Galinsky (1996), pp. 229–31, Powell (2008), pp. 11–12, 151, 153–5, 159–61.

11 Dido and a 'little Aeneas', Virgil, *Aeneid* 4. 328–9, Cleopatra 8. 685–714.

12 Virgil, *Aeneid* 10. 510–605, 12. 291–305 for battle scenes, with quote 12. 295, Dido's spirit 6. 450–76.

13 Virgil, *Aeneid* 12. 945–52.

14 For discussion of Roman attitudes to enemies see G. Woolf, 'Roman Peace', in J. Rich & G. Shipley (eds), *War and Society in the Roman World* (1993), pp. 171–94, esp. 178–85.

15 Aeneas mocking enemies as he kills them, Virgil *Aeneid* 10. 510–605.

16 Virgil, *Aeneid* 1. 286–94, which if referring to Augustus implies eventual

deification; 6. 666–70, with Powell (2008), pp. 42–3, 133; Julius Caesar and Pompey, 6. 828–35.

17 Dio 54. 10. 1–7; on the appointment of the consul see P. Brunt, 'The role of the Senate in the Augustan regime', *Classical Quarterly* 34. 2 (1984), pp. 423–44, esp. 429–30.

18 Suetonius, *Augustus* 37; B. Levick, *Augustus. Image and Substance* (2010), pp. 89–90, Salmon (1956), pp. 456–78, esp. 471–3, A. Jones, 'The *Imperium* of Augustus', *JRS* 41 (1951), pp. 112–19, esp. 117, and on the power of symbols see E. Stavely, 'The "Fasces" and "Imperium Maius"', *Historia* 12 (1963), pp. 458–84.

19 Dio 54. 13. 1–14. 5, Suetonius, *Augustus* 54, with Crook in *CAH²* X, pp. 91–3.

20 Dio 54. 15. 1–8, Suetonius, *Augustus* 35, 54, with R. Talbert, 'Augustus and the Senate', *Greece and Rome* 31 (1984), pp. 55–63, esp. 61.

21 Dio 54. 15. 1–4, 16. 1, 17. 3, Suetonius, *Augustus* 35, with Jones (1955).

22 Dio 54. 6. 4–6, 8. 5, 10. 4, 12. 4–5.

23 Dio 54. 11. 1–6 on the Cantabrian campaign.

24 Dio 54. 12. 4–5, with W. Lacey, *Augustus and the Principate. The Evolution of the System* (1996), pp. 117–31 on the province of Agrippa.

25 Suetonius, *Augustus* 55. 1 on the adoption.

26 Suetonius, *Augustus* 53. 2–3 on approachability.

27 Macrobius, *Saturnalia* 2. 4. 31.

28 Dio 54. 10. 5–7, 16. 1–2, *Res Gestae* 6. 2, with Crook in *CAH²* X, pp. 92–3.

29 Dio 54. 16. 3–5.

30 Dio 54. 16. 7.

31 Dio 54. 16. 6, and in general A. Wallace-Hadrill, 'Civilis Principis: between citizen and king', *JRS* 72 (1982), pp. 32–48.

32 Dio 54. 23, Pliny, *NH* 9. 77, Seneca, *de ira* 3. 40. 2, *de clementia* 1. 18. 2, with R. Syme, *The Roman Revolution* (1960), p. 410; on Vedius see R. Syme, 'Who was Vedius Pollio?', *Roman Papers* Vol. 2 (1979), pp. 518–29.

33 Suetonius, *Augustus* 45. 4, 55, Dio 54. 17. 4–5.

34 For the *ludi saeculares* in general see Galinsky (1996), pp. 100–06, Levick (2010), p. 152 and Price in *CAH²* X, pp. 834–7.

35 Horace, *Carmen Saeculare* 17–20, 50–52 (Loeb translation); a translation of the inscription recording the *ludi saeculares* is provided by N. Lewis & M. Reinhold (eds), *Roman Civilization. Selected Readings* Vol. 1: *The Republic and the Augustan Age* (3rd edn, 1990), pp. 612–16. The quotes, slightly modified, are taken from their translation.

36 Suetonius, *Horace, Augustus* 86. 2, Donatus, *Life of Virgil* 9, Dio 55. 7. 1–6, C. Williams, *Roman Homosexuality. Ideologies of Masculinity in Classical Antiquity* (1999), pp. 157–9.

CHAPTER 17

1 Dio 54. 19. 2 (Loeb translation).

2 *Res Gestae* 26.

3 Dio 54. 20. 4–6, Suetonius, *Augustus* 23. 1; Strabo, *Geog.* 7. 1. 4, mentions the

Sugambri led by King Melo as beginning Augustus' war with the Germans, but probably refers to a later incident.

4 Dio 54. 19. 1–2.

5 Dio 54. 19. 3; on the Temple of Quirinus see Price in *CAH²* X, p. 822.

6 R. Syme, *The Roman Revolution* (1960), p. 369.

7 Crook in *CAH²* X, pp. 94–5.

8 Dio 54. 19. 6, Suetonius, *Tiberius* 12. 2, Levick (1999), p. 27, Syme (1960), pp. 403–4.

9 Dio 53. 12. 7, 54. 4. 1; for development of Narbonensis in general see C. Goudineau in *CAH²* X, pp. 471–87, M. Christol, *Une Histoire Provinciale. La Gaule narbonnaise av. J.-C. au IIIe siècle ap. J.-C.* (2010), esp. 'La municipalisation de la Gaule narbonnaise', pp. 105–28, and J. Drinkwater, *Roman Gaul. The Three Provinces, 58 BC–AD 260* (1983), pp. 20–21.

10 For Transalpine Gaul in the last few decades of the Republic see Dyson (1985), pp. 165–73; Pliny, *NH*. 3. 31.

11 For discussion see Drinkwater (1983), pp. 17–25, and Goudineau in *CAH²* X, pp. 487–502.

12 For Julius Caesar's campaigns, see A. Goldsworthy, *Caesar. The Life of a Colossus* (2006), pp. 205–92 = (2007), pp. 248–353.

13 Dio 54. 20. 1–2, 22. 1–2, Florus 2. 22, Strabo, *Geog*. 4. 6. 7–8.

14 Dio 54. 22. 2–5, Velleius Paterculus 2. 95. 1–2, Strabo, *Geog*. 4. 6. 9, *Res Gestae* 26, Horace, *Odes* 4. 4 and 14, with Gruen in *CAH²* X, pp. 169–71, C. Wells, *The German Policy of Augustus. An Examination of the Archaeological Evidence* (1972), pp. 59–89, and G. Alföldy, *Noricum* (1974), pp. 52–61.

15 See Wolff in *CAH²* X, pp. 535–41.

16 Drinkwater (1983), pp. 12, 21, 119–40, Wells (1972), pp. 93–148.

17 On the wine trade see A. Tchernia, 'Italian wine in Gaul at the end of the Republic', in P. Garnsey, K. Hopkins & C. Whittaker (eds), *Trade in the Ancient Economy* (1983), pp. 87–104; on Gaul in general, see for a good survey of Gallic society N. Roymans, *Tribal Societies in Northern Gaul: An Anthropological Perspective. Cingula* 12 (1990), esp. pp. 17–47, and B. Cunliffe, *Greeks, Romans and Barbarians: Spheres of Interaction* (1988), esp. pp. 38–58 and 80–105.

18 R. MacMullen, *Romanization in the Time of Augustus* (2000), pp. 85–120, P. Wells, *The Barbarians Speak. How the Conquered Peoples Shaped the Roman Empire* (1999), pp. 49–78, Cunliffe (1988), pp. 48–9, 86–7, 96–7, 132–4, Dyson (1985), pp. 137–9, 154, and C. Goudineau, *César et la Gaule* (1995), pp. 141–3.

19 Drinkwater (1983), pp. 18–27, 93–118, 141–59.

20 Caesar, *BG* 6. 15, for aristocrats being judged on the number of warriors they supported; Pliny, *NH* 30. 4. 13 for the ban on citizens taking part in the druidic cult, and in general see Drinkwater (1983), pp. 38–9, 44, 179–81, 206–7, and T. Derks, *Gods, Temples and Ritual Practices: The Transformation of Religious Ideas and Values in Roman Gaul* (1998), *passim*.

21 In general see Alföldy in *CAH²* X, pp. 449–63, J. Richardson, *The Romans in Spain* (1996), pp. 41–126, and B. Lowe, *Roman Iberia. Economy, Society and Culture* (2009), esp. pp. 87–115; on the army see A. Morillo Cerdán, 'The Augustean Spanish Experience: The origin of the *limes* system?', in A. Moirillo, N. Hanel & E.

Martín, *Limes XX: Estudios sobre la frontera romana. Roman Frontier Studies.Anejos de Gladius* 13 Vol. 1 (2009), pp. 239–51, esp. 244–7.

22 See W. Mierse, *Temples and Towns in Roman Iberia. The Social Dynamics of Sanctuary Designs from the Third Century BC to the Third Century AD* (1999), pp. 54–127, Lowe (2009), pp. 87–115, and MacMullen (2000), pp. 50–84; W. Trillmich (trans. C. Nader), *Colonia Augusta Emerita, Capital of Lusitania* in J. Edmondson (ed.), *Augustus* (2009), pp. 427–67, and R. M. Durán Cabello, 'Edificios de espectáculo', in X. Raventós (ed.), *Les capitales provinciales de Hispania 2. Merida: Colonia Augustua Emerita* (2004), pp. 55–61.

23 Dio 54. 25. 5–6, with K. Raaflaub, 'The political significance of Augustus' military reforms', in Edmondson (2009), pp. 203–28.

24 For the *ala Scaevae CIL* 10. 6011 and comments in J. Spaul, *ALA²* (1994), pp. 20–21, and the auxilia more generally see D. Saddington, *The Development of the Roman Auxiliary Forces from Caesar to Vespasian (49 BC–AD 79)* (1982), pp. 15–26, 77–82, and P. Holder, *The Auxilia from Augustus to Trajan* (1980), pp. 5–13; Macrobius, *Saturnalia* 2. 4. 25 and (in less detail) Dio 55. 4. 2 for the trial; in general on the relationship with soldiers and veterans see J.Campbell, *The Emperor and the Roman Army 31 BC–AD 235* (1984), pp. 32–59, 243–81.

25 Dio 54. 15. 4–7, 27. 2–3, *Res Gestae* 10 (Loeb translation for quote), Suetonius, *Augustus* 16. 4, 31. 1, Ovid, *Fasti* 3. 415–28.

26 *Res Gestae* 10, with Price in *CAH²* X, pp. 825–7, and S. Weinstock, *Divus Iulius* (1971), pp. 276–81.

27 Dio 54. 25. 1–4, 26. 1–2.

28 Dio 54. 27. 1, and Suetonius, *Augustus* 56.

29 Dio 54. 27. 4, with Syme (1960), pp. 377, 379.

30 Dio 54. 26. 3–9, and in general R. Talbert, 'Augustus and the Senate', *Greece and Rome* 31 (1984), pp. 55–63 on the problems of creating genuinely free debate.

31 Dio 54. 28. 1.

32 For proverb *nam concordia parvae res crescunt, discordia maximae dilabuntur*, see Seneca, *Epistulae* 94. 46 (cf. Sallust, *Bell. Jug.* 10. 6 with Syme, p. 343, n. 1).

33 Dio 54. 28. 2–29. 8, Suetonius, *Augustus* 64. 1, Velleius Paterculus 2. 96, Tacitus, *Ann.* 1. 3.

CHAPTER 18

1 *Res Gestae* 12 (Loeb translation).

2 Ovid, *Fasti* 1. 709–18 (Loeb translation).

3 Dio 54. 29. 4–5, Suetonius, *Augustus* 42. 1.

4 Dio 54. 2. 5.

5 Dio 54. 25. 3, *Res Gestae* 4, 12; for the Ara Pacis see D. Conlin, *The Artists of the Ara Pacis. Studies in the History of Greece and Rome* (1997), M. Torelli, *Typology and Structure of Roman Historical Reliefs* (1982), pp. 27–61, P. Zanker (trans. A. Shapiro), *The Power of Images in the Age of Augustus* (1988), esp. pp. 158–60, 179–83, 203–4, K. Galinsky, *Augustan Culture* (1996), pp. 141–55; on the suggestion that the scene depicts the *supplicatio* in 13 BC, see R. Billows, 'The religious procession of

the Ara Pacis Augustae: Augustus' *supplicatio* in 13 BC', *JRA* 6 (1993), pp. 80–92. Torelli (1982), p. 54 is one of those who argues for an imaginary scene, a 'meeting that should have taken place' rather than a real event.

6 On the restorations see Conlin (1997), pp. 47–56.

7 For differing views of the identity of some of the children, see R. Syme, 'Neglected children on the Ara Pacis', *American Journal of Archaeology* 88 (1984), pp. 583–9, J. Pollini, 'Appuleii and Some Others on the Ara Pacis', *American Journal of Archaeology* 90 (1986), pp. 453–60, C. Rose, 'Princes and barbarians on the Ara Pacis', *American Journal of Archaeology* 94 (1990), pp. 453–67.

8 For the Parthenon friezes see D. King, *The Elgin Marbles* (2006), and esp. pp. 137–8 for the influence on the Ara Pacis and Augustus' attitude to Athens more generally.

9 Levick (1999), pp. 28–30, who argues for the succession of a series of pairs.

10 For the divorce of Vipsania and marriage to Julia, see Dio 54. 31. 1–2, 35. 4, Suetonius, *Augustus* 63. 2, *Tiberius* 7. 2, with Levick (1999), p. 31, Seager (2005), pp. 19–20.

11 Dio 54. 31. 2–4.

12 For discussion see Gruen in *CAH*² X, pp. 178–81, C. Wells, *The German Policy of Augustus* (1972), pp. 246–50, J. Rich, 'Augustus, War *and* Peace', in L. de Blois, P. Erdkamp, O. Hekster, G. de Kleijn & S. Mols (eds), *The Representation and Perception of Roman Imperial Power: Proceedings of the Third Workshop of the International Network, Impact of Empire (Roman Empire, c.200 BC–AD 476)* (2003), pp. 329–57 = J. Edmondson (ed.), *Augustus* (2009), pp. 137–64, esp. 149–62, A. Goldsworthy, *Caesar. The Life of a Colossus* (2006), pp. 205–14 = (2007), pp. 248–57.

13 Suetonius, *Augustus* 71. 3 (Loeb translation); popularity of Drusus with the crowd, Tacitus, *Ann.* 2. 41.

14 Suetonius, *Augustus* 71. 2 for the letter, and more generally A. Barrett, *Livia. First Lady of Imperial Rome* (2002), pp. 38–44.

15 Luke 2: 1, with F. Millar, 'State and subject: the impact of monarchy', in F. Millar & E. Segal (eds), *Caesar Augustus. Seven Aspects* (1990), pp. 37–60, esp. 41–2.

16 Livy, *Pers.* 137–8, Dio 54. 32. 1.

17 For Nijmegen see P. Franzen, 'The Augustan legionary fortress at Nijmegen. Legionary and auxiliary soldiers', in A. Morillo, N. Hanel & E. Martín, *Limes XX: Estudios sobre la frontera romana. Roman Frontier Studies. Anejos de Gladius* 13 Vol. I (2009), pp. 1257–69, and more generally Wells (1972), pp. 93–148, and C. Wells, 'What's new along the Lippe: Recent work in North Germany', *Britannia* 29 (1998), pp. 457–64.

18 Dio 54. 32. 1–3, Tacitus, *Agricola* 30.

19 Dio 54. 33. 1–2, Florus 2. 30. 24; L. Powell, *Eager for Glory. The Untold Story of Drusus the Elder, Conqueror of Germany* (2011), attempts to reconstruct the course of Drusus' campaigns in detail, see pp. 81–92 for this year.

20 In general see M. Todd, *The Early Germans* (2004), pp. 17–47, P. Wells, *The Barbarians Speak. How the Conquered Peoples Shaped Roman Europe* (1999), pp. 3–93.

21 On Julius Caesar in Gaul see e.g. Caesar, *BG* 1. 23 and in general J. Roth, *The Logistics of the Roman Army at War (264 BC–AD 235)* (1999), pp. 117–55.

22 Dio 54. 33. 2–4; for discussion of Germanic armies and their limitations, see A. Goldsworthy, *The Roman Army at War 100 BC–AD 200* (1996), pp. 42–53.

23 Dio 54. 33. 5–54. 4, 35. 4–5.

24 Dio 54. 32. 1, 36. 2, Suetonius, *Claudius* 2. 1, Livy, *Pers.* 139, Caesar, *BG* 6. 13 for annual meetings of the druids, with D. Fishwick, *The Imperial Cult in the Latin West: Studies in the Ruler Cult of the Western Roman Empire* Vol. 3 (2002), pp. 9–20.

25 Suetonius, *Tiberius* 50. 1, *Claudius* 1. 4, with Levick (1999), p. 34, Seager (2005), pp. 21–2.

26 Dio 54. 36. 3–55. 1. 5, Suetonius, *Claudius* 1. 2–3, Livy, *Pers.* 142, with Wells (1972), pp. 163–211 on the conquests.

27 Dio 55. 2. 1–7, Valerius Maximus 5. 5. 3, Pliny, *NH* 7. 84, Seneca, *ad Marciam* 3. 2, with Seager (2005), p. 22, and E. Champlin, 'Tiberius and the Heavenly Twins', *JRS* 101 (2011), pp. 73–99, esp. 76–81.

28 Pliny, *NH* 36. 72–73.

CHAPTER 19

1 Macrobius, *Saturnalia* 2. 5. 4.

2 Anonymous, *Consolation to Livia* 349–56. This work purports to be addressed to Livia following the death of Drusus, but may be a rhetorical exercise written several decades later during the reign of Claudius. For a good discussion of the role of Livia and dealing with this issue see N. Purcell, 'Livia and the Womanhood of Rome', *Proceedings of the Cambridge Philological Society* (1986), pp. 78–105 = J. Edmondson (ed.), *Augustus* (2009), pp. 165–94.

3 Dio 55. 2. 3, 5–7, Suetonius, *Claudius* 1. 4–5, Seneca, *de consolatione ad Marciam* 4. 3, with A. Barrett, *Livia. First Lady of Imperial Rome* (2002), pp. 44–5, 108–9.

4 Dio 58. 2. 4, Suetonius, *Augustus* 71. 1, for discussion see Barrett (2002), pp. 122–6, Purcell (2009), pp. 167–72.

5 Suetonius, *Augustus* 83, Pliny, *NH* 7. 75; Barrett (2002), pp. 103–6, 180–81, 364, n. 7 with references to many inscriptions recording members of Livia's household with very specific tasks, e.g. dressers or *ornatrices*, *CIL* 6. 3985, 4041, 4251, and a pearl-setter or *margaritarius*, *CIL* 6. 3981.

6 Dio 55. 2. 4, with Purcell (2009), pp. 165–8, 177–80.

7 Suetonius, *Tiberius* 7. 2–3, with Levick (1999), pp. 31–2, R. Seager, *Tiberius* (2005), p. 20, and E. Fantham, *Julia Augusti, the Emperor's Daughter* (2006), pp. 79–82.

8 Tacitus, *Ann.* 1. 14. 3, 53. 2, with Levick (1999), p. 37.

9 Macrobius, *Saturnalia* 2. 5. 5, 7.

10 Dio 55. 6. 2–3, cf. Caesar, *BG.* 4. 7–9 for Julius Caesar's arrest of envoys from Germanic tribes, with Plutarch, *Cato the Younger* 51. 1–2 for criticism of this breach of faith.

11 Dio 55. 6. 4–5, with Fantham (2006), pp. 97–8.

12 Dio 55. 6. 6–7, Suetonius, *Augustus* 31. 2, Macrobius *Saturnalia* 1. 12. 35, *Res Gestae* 8, with M. Boatright, 'The Pomerial extension of Augustus', *Historia* 35 (1986), pp. 13–27.

13 Dio 55. 7. 16, Suetonius, *Horace*, says that the poet died on 27 November 8 BC, fifty-nine days after the death of Maecenas; on the latter's influence, see G. Williams, 'Did Maecenas "Fall from favour"? Augustan Literary Patronage', in K. Raaflaub & M. Toher (eds), *Between Republic and Empire. Interpretations of Augustus and his Principate* (1990), pp. 258–75.

14 Dio 54. 30. 2, 55. 3. 1–4. 2, 5. 3.

15 Dio 55. 8. 1–2.

16 For discussion see E. Champlin, 'Tiberius and the Heavenly Twins', *JRS* 101 (2011), pp. 73–99.

17 Dio 55. 8. 2, with Barrett (2002), pp. 46–7, Levick (1999), pp. 36–7.

18 Dio 55. 8. 3–4, Pliny, *NH.* 16. 20.

19 Dio 55. 8. 5–6.

20 Dio 55. 8. 6–7, for the inscription see *CIL* 6. 50705 = *ILS* 3090 with Purcell in *CAH²* X, pp. 800–02.

21 Suetonius, *Tiberius* 9. 3, 11. 3, Velleius Paterculus 2. 99. 1, Tacitus, *Ann.* 56. 3, Dio 55. 9. 4, with Levick (1999), pp. 35–6.

22 Dio 55. 9. 1–5, with Levick (1999), pp. 37–8, and in general 'Julians and Claudians', *Greece and Rome* 22 (1975), pp. 29–38.

23 Dio 55. 9. 5–8, Suetonius, *Tiberius* 10. 1–2, Velleius Paterculus 2. 99. 1–4.

24 For discussion see Crook in *CAH²* X, pp. 100–01, Levick (1999), pp. 37–40 and *Augustus. Image and Substance* (2010), pp. 182–3, Seager (2005), pp. 23–7, Fantham (2006), pp. 83–4, Barrett (2002), pp. 48–9, J. Corbett, 'The Succession policy of Augustus', *Latomus* 33 (1974), pp. 87–97, esp. 87–91, and R. Syme, *The Roman Revolution* (1960), pp. 391–2, 413–14.

25 Seneca the Younger, *On the shortness of Life* 4. 2–5 on Augustus' complaints about the burden of his office.

26 Dio 55. 9. 9, 10a. 2–3, with Gruen in *CAH²* X, pp. 182–3, and Fantham (2006), p. 99.

27 Asian taxes, Dio 54. 30. 3.

28 *EJ* 312 = *SIG³* 780 (translation taken from M. Cooley [ed.], *The Age of Augustus. Lactor 17* [2003], pp. 197–8).

29 Josephus, *BJ* 1. 538–51, and in general E. Shürer, G. Vermes & F. Millar, *The History of the Jewish People in the Age of Jesus Christ* Vol. 1 (1973), pp. 320–29, Goodman in *CAH²* X, pp. 741–2 , and L. White, 'Herod and the Jewish experience of Augustan rule', in K. Galinsky (ed.), *The Cambridge Companion to the Age of Augustus* (2005), pp. 361–87, esp. 375–6 for Herod's last years.

30 Augustus' joke, see Macrobius, *Saturnalia* 2. 4. 11; executions see Josephus, *BJ* 1. 648–53, intervention of the Syrian army, *BJ* 2. 45–79.

31 See R. Sherk, *Roman Documents from the Greek East* (1969), no. 65 for the new calendar, V. Ehrenberg & A. Jones, *Documents Illustrating the Reigns of Augustus and Tiberius* (2nd edn, 1975), 311, v.

32 Suetonius, *Augustus* 58. 2, where he claims to record the exact words spoken by both Messalla and Augustus, with Crook in *CAH²* X, pp. 101–2, and Levick (2010), pp. 91–2, 204–5; for a detailed discussion of the various acclamations and the celebration of this award, see W. Lacey, *Augustus and the Principate. The Evolution of the System* (1996), pp. 193–7, and for a full discussion of the significance

of the term and the concept of a father of the state see T. Stevenson, 'The ideal benefactor and the father analogy in Greek and Roman thought', *CQ* 42 (1992), pp. 421–36, who believes that both Cicero and Julius Caesar were named *pater patriae*, and M. Gelzer (trans. P. Needham), *Caesar, Politician and Statesman* (1968), p. 315, fn. 2 for Julius Caesar.

33 *Res Gestae* 35.

34 Suetonius, *Tiberius* 7. 3 claiming that the couple ceased to sleep with each other after the loss of their child; on Julia's lifestyle in general see Fantham (2006), esp. pp. 81–4.

35 'Naso was our teacher' (*Naso magister erat*), Ovid, *Ars Amatoria* 2. 744, 3. 812, and in general see K. Galinsky, *Augustan Culture* (1996), pp. 261–9 focusing on the *Metamorphoses*, but placing Ovid in the Augustan context.

36 Macrobius, *Saturnalia* 2. 6–7, 9, Suetonius, *Augustus* 54. 2.

37 Dio 55. 9. 11–16, Suetonius, *Augustus* 65. 1, *Tiberius* 11. 4, Velleius Paterculus 2. 100. 2–5, Seneca, *Brevitate Vitae* 4. 6, *de Beneficiis* 6. 32, Pliny, *NH* 21. 8–9, Tacitus, *Ann.* 1. 53, 3. 24. 3, 4. 44; on the identities of the conspirators and their connections see A. Ferrill, 'Prosopography and the Last Years of Augustus', *Historia* 20 (1971), pp. 718–31, esp. 729, and 'Augustus and his daughter: a modern myth', in C. Deroux (ed.), *Studies in Latin Literature and Roman History* 2 (1980), pp. 332–46, and Barrett (2002), pp. 48–51.

38 Pliny, *NH* 7. 149 claims that Julia plotted her father's assassination, and Dio 55. 10.15 claims that Iullus had designs on seizing power and that other unnamed men were also put to death.

39 Tacitus, *Ann.* 3. 24, 4. 44, Dio 55. 10. 15.

40 Suetonius, *Augustus* 65. 2 for Phoebe, and for the disgrace and exile in general see Fantham (2006), pp. 84–91, and E. Leon, 'Scribonia and her daughters', *Transactions and Proceedings of the American Philological Association* 82 (1951), pp. 168–75, esp. 173–4; Ferrill (1980) presents a reasoned and sceptical analysis of the modern theories of political conspiracy; Lacey (1996), pp. 202–9 suggests that the main concern was to protect the legitimacy of Caius and Lucius.

41 Seneca, *de Beneficiis* 6. 32.

CHAPTER 20

1 Ovid, *Fasti* 5. 550–54, 567–8 (Loeb translation).

2 In general see Dio 55. 10. 6, Velleius Paterculus 2. 100. 2, Suetonius, *Augustus* 31. 5, and Ovid, *Fasti* 5. 545–98; for the date see C. Simpson, 'The date of the dedication of the Temple of Mars Ultor', *JRS* 67 (1977), pp. 91–4. An alternative date of 1 August is possible, but the arguments for 12 May are more convincing.

3 Suetonius, *Augustus* 56. 2 for his refusal to force owners of property to sell the land needed for the Forum.

4 Pliny, *NH* 36. 11, 102; on the Erechtheion see J. Camp, *The Archaeology of Athens* (2001), pp. 93–100; on the Forum of Augustus and its imagery see P. Zanker (trans. A. Shapiro), *The Power of Images in the Age of Augustus* (1988), pp. 81–2, 113–14, 193–215, S. Dyson, *Rome. A Living Portrait of an Ancient City* (2010), pp. 128–31,

and W. Lacey, *Augustus and the Principate. The Evolution of the System* (1996), pp. 193, 197–202.

5 cf. Dio 56. 34. 2–3 for a similar procession of past great men at Augustus' funeral; the term *summi viri* comes from a late source, the *Scriptores Historia Augusta, Alexander Severus* 28. 6; for discussion see T. Luce, 'Livy, Augustus, and the Forum Augustum', in J. Edmondson (ed.), *Augustus* (2009), pp. 399–415, esp. 403–6; for the fragments of the inscriptions see *CIL* I, pp. 186–202 for discussion of the *elogia*, and a useful selection translated in M. Cooley (ed.), *The Age of Augustus. Lactor 17* (2003), pp. 238–9; for Augustus' involvement in writing the *elogia* see Pliny, *NH* 22. 6. 13; for Cornelia see *CIL* I. 39.

6 Doubt over identity of Iulus, see Livy I. 3; for Marius see Luce (2009), pp. 406–7, with a translation of the text in Cooley (2003), p. 238, K25.

7 Suetonius, *Augustus* 31. 5, *Res Gestae* 35.

8 Dio 55. 10. 6–8, Suetonius, *Augustus* 43. 2. It is possible that Dio included the funeral games in honour of Agrippa as part of the wider festivities.

9 *Res Gestae* 23, Velleius Paterculus 2. 100. 1, Dio 55. 10. 7.

10 See Zanker (1988), pp. 105–6 on the magnificence of all the major Augustan temples; for claims of a change in style away from a blatantly regal form of Hellenism, see Purcell in *CAH²* X, pp. 788–90, with a more convincing view in K. Galinsky, *Augustan Culture* (1996), pp. 197–213.

11 Pliny, *NH* 34. 48, 35. 93–4.

12 Macrobius, *Saturnalia* 2. 4. 18.

13 As an example of the assumption that Augustus distanced himself from Julius Caesar, see Z. Yavetz, 'The personality of Augustus', in K. Raaflaub & M. Toher (eds), *Between Republic and Empire. Interpretations of Augustus and his Principate* (1990), pp. 21–41, 32, 'Gradually but consistently he distanced himself from the memory of Julius Caesar'; on the Temple of Mars Ultor, see Ovid, *Fasti* 570–83, and Galinsky (1996), p. 208 for deliberate evocation of Julius Caesar in the design of the Forum Augustum.

14 Tacitus, *Ann.* I. I, Suetonius, *Claudius* 41. 2; in general see M. Toher, 'Augustus and the Evolution of Roman Historiography', in Raaflaub & Toher (1990), pp. 139–54.

15 See R. Syme, 'Livy and Augustus', *Harvard Studies of Classical Philology* 64 (1959), pp. 27–87, and Galinsky (1996), pp. 280–87.

16 See Luce (2009), pp. 406–15.

17 Tacitus, *Ann.* 4. 34; Seneca, *Quaestiones Naturales* 5. 18. 4 for Livy's questioning of whether or not Julius Caesar's birth was a good thing; see Syme (1959), p. 58 for discussion and further emphasis on a supposed distancing by Augustus from Julius Caesar.

18 Suetonius, *Augustus* 51. 3 (Loeb translation for quote).

19 Seneca, *Suasoriae* 4. 22.

20 Dio 55. 10. 17–18, Ovid, *Ars Amatoria* I. 177–86, 203–4 for the quotes (Loeb translation), and more generally 177–229.

21 For Tiberius in these years see Levick (1999), pp. 39–42, 44–6, R. Seager, *Tiberius* (2005), pp. 23–9; Augustus' divorce of Julia on Tiberius' behalf, Suetonius,

Tiberius 11. 4–5; visiting the sick, Suetonius, *Tiberius* 11. 2; the philosopher, Suetonius, *Tiberius* 11. 3.

22 Dio 55. 10. 19, Velleius Paterculus 2. 101. 1, Suetonius, *Tiberius* 11. 1, 12. 2, 13. 1,
who differ over Tiberius' behaviour and where the meeting occurred; for an
interesting discussion of these years, see G. Bowersock, 'Augustus and the East:
The problem of succession', in F. Millar & E. Segal (eds), *Caesar Augustus. Seven
Aspects* (1990), pp. 169–88.

23 Bowersock (1990), p. 172.

24 Bowersock (1990), pp. 172–3, with a discussion of the debate in Camp (2001), pp.
116–17; R. Syme, *The Roman Revolution* (1960), pp. 425, 428–9 for Caius and his
advisers.

25 Gellius, *NA* 15. 7. 3 (Loeb translation, slightly emended).

26 Suetonius, *Augustus* 64. 3, 89. 2, *de grammaticus et rhetoribus* 17. 2.

27 For a useful and perceptive review of the literary evidence for Augustus' residence on the Palatine, see P. Wiseman, 'The House of Augustus and the
Lupercal', *JRA* 22 (2009), pp. 527–45, esp. 527–36.

28 Suetonius, *Augustus* 72. 1, 73, 78. 1–2, Pliny, *NH* 33. 49.

29 Suetonius, *Augustus* 72. 3 for bones, 82. 1 on sleeping with doors open or outside,
for Augustus' lifestyle in general, see Yavetz (1990), pp. 21–41, and also the cau-
tionary note in R. Saller, 'Anecdotes as historical evidence,' *Greece and Rome* 27
(1980), pp. 69–83; for wall paintings see J. Clarke, 'Augustan domestic interiors:
propaganda or fashion?' in K. Galinsky, *The Cambridge Companion to the Age of
Augustus* (2005), pp. 264–78, and Galinsky (1996), pp. 179–97; see Vitruvius, *de ar-
chitectura* 7. 5. 3–4 for one architect's criticism of the very modern fashions which
appear on the Palatine.

30 Suetonius, *Augustus* 73, 82. 1.

31 Suetonius, *Augustus* 75–77.

32 Suetonius, *Augustus* 74, noting that the only freedman ever invited to dine with
him was the turncoat admiral Menas during the war with Sextus Pompey; for
the joke, see Macrobius, *Saturnalia* 2. 4. 8.

33 Macrobius, *Saturnalia* 2. 4. 14–15.

34 Macrobius, *Saturnalia* 2. 4. 20, Suetonius, *Augustus* 53. 3; for the effectiveness of
humour see Yavetz (1990), pp. 36–38.

35 Suetonius, *Augustus* 29. 3, 86. 1–88, 95, 97. 1–2, Gellius, *NA* 10 11. 5, 24. 2.

36 Suetonius, *Augustus* 72. 2, 80–83, with E. Gowers, 'Augustus and "Syracuse"', *JRS*
100 (2010), pp. 69–87.

37 Suetonius, *Augustus* 56. 2 for recommending his relatives to voters; on Caius in
the east see Dio 55. 10. 20, 10a. 4–5, Velleius Paterculus 2. 101. 1–3, with A. Sherwin-White, *Roman Foreign Policy in the East, 168 BC to AD 1* (1984), pp. 325–41.

38 Dio 55. 10a. 5–10, Velleius Paterculus 2. 102. 1–3, Suetonius, *Augustus* 65. 1–2, Tacitus, *Ann.* 1. 3.

CHAPTER 21

1 Velleius Paterculus 2. 103. 1–2.

2 Suetonius, *Augustus* 65. 2.

3 An inscription from Pisa (*ILS* 140) makes it clear that Caius' death was known there by 2 April, and the news must have reached Rome before this; for discussion of the decisions of this year see R. Birch, 'The Settlement of 26 June AD 4 and its Aftermath', *Classical Quarterly* 31 (1981), pp. 443–56; on the name of Caesar and the associations of the family and its dwelling, see D. Wardle, 'Valerius Maximus on the Domus Augusta, Augustus, and Tiberius', *Classical Quarterly* 50 (2000), pp. 479–93.

4 Suetonius, *Caligula* 4. 1; in general see discussion in Levick (1999), pp. 47–52, R. Seager, *Tiberius* (2005), pp. 29–32; on Aemilius Paullus and his wider family see R. Syme, *The Augustan Aristocracy* (1986), pp. 104–27.

5 Suetonius, *Tiberius* 12. 2–3, 15. 1, Velleius Paterculus 2. 102, Tacitus, *Ann.* 3. 48.

6 Dio 55. 13. 1a–2, Velleius Paterculus 2. 103. 1–104. 1, Suetonius, *Tiberius* 15. 2, with discussion in Birch (1981), esp. pp. 444–8.

7 Quote from Velleius Paterculus 2. 104. 1; for discussion see Crook in *CAH²* X, p. 105, Levick (1999), pp. 49–50, Seager (2005), pp. 29–32; for letters from Augustus to Tiberius see Suetonius, *Tiberius* 21. 2–6.

8 Livia's involvement, see Dio 55. 10a. 10, Pliny, *NH* 7. 149, Tacitus, *Ann.* 1. 3, Suetonius, *Augustus* 65. 1, with A. Barrett, *Livia. First Lady of Imperial Rome* (2002), pp. 52–9, 241–2; for claims of wider rivalry between the families see B. Levick, 'Julians and Claudians', *Greece and Rome* 22 (1975), pp. 29–38.

9 Dio 55. 13. 2. Suetonius, *Tiberius* 16. 1 claims that the grant was for just three years, but in *Res Gestae* 6 Augustus makes it far more likely that the grant was for a decade.

10 Suetonius, *Tiberius* 15. 2 on the seriousness with which Tiberius viewed his adoption.

11 Dio 55. 13. 1, 14. 1–22. 2, Seneca, *de clementia* 1. 9. 1–10, with Levick (1999), p. 54, Birch (1981), p. 447, Barrett (2002), pp. 131–3, Syme (1986), p. 266.

12 Dio 55. 12. 4–5, Tacitus, *Ann.* 1. 53.

13 Dio 55. 13. 4–7, and in general see C. Nicolet, 'Augustus, Government, and the Propertied Classes', in F. Millar & E. Segal (eds), *Caesar Augustus. Seven Aspects* (1990), pp. 89–128; Hortensius Hortalus and his four sons in AD 16, see Tacitus, *Ann.* 1. 37–8, with Nicolet (1990), pp. 95–6; on elections see Levick (1999), pp. 51–4.

14 For a useful introduction see Treggiari in *CAH²* X, pp. 893–7.

15 Dio 55. 13. 1a, 29. 5–7, Velleius Paterculus 2. 104. 2–107. 3; for a summary of the finds at Lahnau-Waldgirmes see R. Wolters, *Die Schlacht im Teutoburger Wald* (2008), pp. 65–9.

16 Velleius Paterculus 2. 108. 1–109.4; on the Marcomanni and Suebi in general see Tacitus, *Germania* 38–41, Strabo, *Geog.* 7. 1. 3.

17 Velleius Paterculus 2. 109. 4–110. 2, Dio 55. 28. 6; in a highly rhetorical speech attributed to Maroboduus, it is claimed that twelve legions were deployed against him, Tacitus, *Ann.* 2. 46.

18 Dio 56. 16. 3 (Loeb translation).

19 Dio 55. 29. 1–30. 6, Velleius Paterculus 2. 110. 2–6; on the Roman army's response

to rebellion, see A. Goldsworthy, *The Roman Army at War 100 BC–AD 200* (1996), pp. 79–95.

20 Dio 55. 27. 6–28. 4, Josephus, *BJ* 2. 111–118, *AJ* 17. 314.

21 Pliny, *NH* 7. 149 for the attempted suicide.

22 Dio 55. 24. 9–25. 6, *Res Gestae* 17, with L. Keppie, *The Making of the Roman Army* (1984), pp. 147–8.

23 See Suetonius, *Augustus* 25. 2, Velleius Paterculus 2. 110. 6–111. 2, with Keppie (1984), pp. 168–9, citing V. Ehrenberg & A. Jones, *Documents Illustrating the Reigns of Augustus and Tiberius* (2nd edn, 1975), p. 368 for conscription of citizens.

24 Suetonius, *Augustus* 24. 1, and in general see Nicolet (1990), pp. 99–101.

25 The *vigiles*, see Dio 55. 26. 4–5, with G. Watson, *The Roman Soldier* (1985), pp. 19–20; on other problems see Dio 55. 26. 1–27. 3.

26 Suetonius, *Augustus* 19. 1, Dio 55. 27. 1–2, with Birch (1981), pp. 450–52, Levick (1999), pp. 55–9, and T. Wiedermann, 'The political background to Ovid's *Tristia* 2', *Classical Quarterly* 25 (1975), pp. 264–71, esp. 265–8.

27 Dio 55. 26. 2–3, 27. 3–5, Suetonius, *Claudius* 2. 2.

28 Dio 55. 32. 1–2, Suetonius, *Augustus* 51. 1, 65. 1, *Claudius* 2. 2, Velleius Paterculus 2. 112. 7, Tacitus, *Ann.* 1. 5–6, with Birch (1981), pp. 446–52, and B. Levick, 'Abdication and Agrippa Postumus', *Historia* 21 (1972), pp. 674–97, esp. 690–93.

29 Dio 55. 32. 1, with Levick (1999), pp. 51–2, A. Jones, 'The Elections under Augustus', *JRS* 45 (1955), pp. 9–21, esp. 13–17.

30 Dio 55. 32. 1, with Levick (1972), pp. 690–97, Birch (1981), pp. 448–51, 455–6, and Barrett (2002), pp. 57–65.

31 Tacitus, *Ann.* 1. 3.

32 Velleius Paterculus 2. 111. 3–4; on the war in general see Dio 55. 29. 1–32. 4, 34. 4–7, 56. 11. 1–17. 1, Velleius Paterculus 2. 110. 1–116. 5.

33 Velleius 2. 113. 1–2, Suetonius, *Tiberius* 16. 1, with Goldsworthy (1996), pp. 35–7, 116–25.

34 Dio 55. 31. 1 for the claim that Augustus believed Tiberius was not pressing the campaign quickly enough – a marked contrast to his earlier urging of caution on his generals, Suetonius, *Augustus* 25. 4.

35 Dio 55. 33. 5–34. 3.

36 Suetonius, *Augustus* 65. 1, 4, 72. 3, 101. 3, Tacitus, *Ann.* 3. 24, 4. 71, Pliny, *NH* 7. 75, with Birch (1981), pp. 452–4, R. Syme, *The Roman Revolution* (1960), pp. 432, 468, and (1986), pp. 115–27, 188–99.

37 Ovid, *Tristiae* 2. 207 speaks of 'two crimes, a song and an error'; for discussion see R. Syme, *History in Ovid* (1978), pp. 206–29.

38 Suetonius, *Augustus* 65. 4, with Levick (1999), pp. 55–62, Crook in *CAH²* X, pp. 108–9 both discussing the issue with prudent caution.

CHAPTER 22

1 Velleius Paterculus 2. 127. 3 (Loeb translation).

2 For Arminius and his early life see esp. Velleius Paterculus 2. 118. 1–3, Tacitus, *Ann.* 2. 9–10, 88, with P. Wells, *The Battle that Stopped Rome* (2003), pp. 105–10, and

A. Murdoch, *Rome's Greatest Defeat. Massacre in the Teutoburg Forest* (2006), pp. 75–97, esp. 83–6; Augustus' reluctance to grant citizenship, see Suetonius, *Augustus* 40. 3.

3 On Varus see Wells (2003), pp. 80–86, Murdoch (2006), pp. 49–74, and R. Syme, *The Roman Revolution* (1960), pp. 401, 424–5, 434, 437.

4 Tacitus, *Ann.* 1. 57–59, Velleius Paterculus 2. 118. 4.

5 Velleius Paterculus 2. 117. 2–4 including the quotes, Dio 56. 18. 1–5.

6 In general see S. Dyson, 'Native Revolt Patterns in the Roman Empire', *Aufstieg und Niedergang der römischen Welt* 2. 3 (1975), pp. 38–175.

7 For his army, see Velleius Paterculus 2. 117. 1; for the rebellion see Dio 56. 18. 5–19. 4.

8 Dio 56. 20. 1–2, and note the freedmen on the cenotaph of the centurion Marcus Caelius, *CIL* 13 8648 = *ILS* 2244; for the couch see W. Schlüter, 'The Battle of the Teutoburg Forest: archaeological research at Kalkriese near Osnabrück', in J. Creighton & R. Wilson, *Roman Germany. Studies in Cultural Interaction. Journal of Roman Archaeology Supplementary Series* 32 (1999), pp. 125–59, esp. 148–9; on soldiers' marriage see B. Campbell, 'The marriage of soldiers under the Empire', *JRS* 68 (1978), pp. 153–66.

9 Velleius Paterculus 2. 118. 4, Dio 56. 19. 2–3, Tacitus, *Ann.* 1. 58.

10 For the excavations and a range of different reconstructions of the battle, see A. Rost, 'The Battle between Romans and Germans in Kalkriese: Interpreting the Archaeological Remains from an ancient battlefield' and S. Wilbers-Rost, 'The site of the Varus Battle at Kalkriese. Recent Results from Archaeological Research', both in A. Morillo, N. Hanel & E. Martín, *Limes XX: Estudios sobre la frontera romana. Roman Frontier Studies. Anejos de Gladius* 13 Vol. 3 (2009), pp. 1339–45, 1347–52, Schlüter (1999), pp. 125–59, Wells (2003), Murdoch (2006); M. McNally, *Teutoburg Forest AD 9. The Destruction of Varus and his Legions* (2011) is well illustrated, as is the readily accessible collection of articles in J. Oorthuys (ed.), *The Varian Disaster: The Battle of the Teutoburg Forest. Ancient Warfare* special issue (2009); the main ancient sources are Dio 56. 19. 1–22. 2, Velleius Paterculus 2. 119. 1–5, Tacitus, *Ann.* 1. 61–2. The account that follows is based on all of these, and more detailed discussion may be found in the works cited.

11 Note the reaction of some of Julius Caesar's legionaries to the loss of their baggage train, see *BG* 5. 33, although contrast 5. 44.

12 On proper behaviour of commanders, see Goldsworthy (1996), pp. 163–5.

13 Tacitus, *Ann.* 1. 57–8, 71, Velleius Paterculus 2. 119. 5.

14 Velleius Paterculus 2. 117. 1.

15 Dio 56. 23. 1–4, Suetonius, *Augustus* 23. 1–2.

16 Suetonius, *Augustus* 23. 2; on the legions, see L. Keppie, *The Making of the Roman Army* (1984), pp. 163–9.

17 Dio 56. 22. 2ª–4, Velleius Paterculus 2. 120. 1–6, with Wells (2003), pp. 200–12, Murdoch (2006), pp. 121–8.

18 On *vastatio*, see J. Roth, *The Logistics of the Roman Army at War, 264 BC–AD 235* (1999), pp. 148–55, 298–305.

19 Dio 56. 25. 2–3.

20 Suetonius, *Tiberius* 21. 5–6.

21 Dio 56. 17. 1–3, 25. 1, Suetonius, *Tiberius* 17. 2, *Res Gestae* 4, with Levick (1999), pp. 61–4, and T. Barnes, 'The victories of Augustus', *JRS* 64 (1974), pp. 21–6.

22 For a good discussion of the impact of these laws see A. Wallace-Hadrill, 'Family inheritance in the Augustan Marriage Laws', in J. Edmondson (ed.), *Augustus* (2009), pp. 250–74 = *Proceedings of the Cambridge Philological Society* 27 (1981), pp. 58–80.

23 Dio 56. 1. 2–10. 3, Suetonius, *Augustus* 34. 2, 89. 2.

24 Tacitus, *Ann.* 3. 25–8 where the harshness even of the revived law is emphasised, with S. Treggiari, *Roman Marriage* (1991), esp. pp. 60–80; see also the discussion in K. Galinsky, *Augustan Culture* (1996), pp. 128–40 who places these concerns within wider fears that moral failings may lead to disasters such as the defeat of Varus. It is possible that the law was passed after news of this, but seems likely that its basic form had already been drawn up.

25 Dio 56. 25. 7–8, 27. 4, Suetonius, *Augustus* 43.3.

26 For Labienus see R. Syme, *The Roman Revolution* (1960), p. 486, and B. Levick, *Augustus. Image and Substance* (2010), pp. 190–91.

27 Dio 56. 25. 4, 27. 1, Tacitus, *Ann.* 1. 72, with Syme (1960), pp. 486–7.

28 Dio 56. 26. 1–3, 28. 2–3.

29 Dio 56. 28. 4–6; on the position of Tiberius in these years see Levick (1999), pp. 61–7.

30 Dio 56. 29. 1–6, Suetonius, *Augustus* 97. 1–3, *Res Gestae* 8.

31 Tacitus, *Ann.* 1. 5, Dio 56. 30. 1 on the journey; Suetonius, *Augustus* 101. 1–3 on the will, where he stipulates that the two Julias were not to be placed in the Mausoleum, but a similar ban on Postumus seems likely; Syme (1960), p. 433 is dismissive of the incident, whereas Levick (1999), pp. 64–5 makes a good case for the journey happening.

32 Dio 56. 29. 2. By far the most detailed account of Augustus' final days is provided by Suetonius, *Augustus* 97. 3–100. 1, supplying most of the details given below. There is a good discussion in D. Wardle, 'A perfect send-off: Suetonius and the dying art of Augustus (Suetonius Aug. 99)', *Mnemosyne* 60 (2007), pp. 443–63.

33 Suetonius, *Augustus* 98. 2 for the quote.

34 For the 'jaws' quote, Suetonius, *Tiberius* 21. 2; Dio 56. 31. 1 states that most of his sources claimed that Tiberius did not arrive until after Augustus was dead.

35 Dio 56. 30. 1–4, with A. Barrett, *Livia. First Lady of Imperial Rome* (2002), pp. 242–7.

36 Suetonius, *Augustus* 99 (Loeb translation).

37 Dio 56. 30. 4.

38 Quote from Suetonius, *Augustus* 99. 1; Dio 31. 1 for the claim that Livia concealed his death for some days.

39 Suetonius, *Augustus* 100. 2, Dio 56. 31. 2.

40 The main accounts of the funeral come from Suetonius, *Augustus* 100. 2–4, Dio 56. 34. 1–42. 4; unlike Suetonius, Dio has Drusus speak from the Rostra by the Temple of the Divine Julius and Tiberius deliver his eulogy from the old Rostra.

41 Suetonius, *Augustus* 100. 4, Dio 56. 42. 3.

CONCLUSION

1 Dio 44. 2. 1–3 (Loeb translation).
2 Tacitus, *Ann.* 1. 2.
3 Tacitus, *Ann.* 1. 8.
4 On the name, see Levick, *Tiberius the Politician* (1999), p. 247, n. 11 for references and discussion.
5 For the accession of Tiberius and the early months of his principate, see Levick (1999), pp. 68–81, and R. Seager, *Tiberius* (2005), pp. 40–59.
6 Tacitus, *Ann.* 1. 15.
7 Tacitus, *Ann.* 1. 11 for Augustus' advice.
8 For Tiberius' principate in more detail see Levick (1999) and Seager (2005).
9 Eutropius, *Breviarium* 8. 5; for an argument that Augustus' legacy was a system almost bound to fail see J. Drinkwater, 'The Principate – lifebelt, or millstone around the neck of Empire?', in O. Hekster, G. Kleijn & D. Slootjes (eds), *Crises and the Roman Empire* (2007), pp. 67–74; for the aftermath of Caligula's murder, see A. Barrett, *Caligula. The Corruption of Power* (1989), pp. 172–6.

APPENDIX TWO

1 Mentions of the execution of Jesus from early sources, see Tacitus, Ann. 15. 44, Josephus, *AJ* 18. 63–4. 20. 200, with discussion in E. Schürer, G. Vermes & F. Millar, *The History of the Jewish People in the Age of Jesus Christ* Vol. 1 (1973), pp. 430–41 as an introduction to the copious literature on the *testimonium Flavianum*, since some, but probably not all, of these passages are later interpolations; for the birth of Julius Caesar, see A. Goldsworthy, *Caesar: The Life of a Colossus* (2006), p. 30.
2 Josephus, *BJ* 2. 117–18, *AJ* 17. 355, 18. 1, 26, *ILS* 2683; for discussion see Schürer (1973), pp. 258–9, noting *ILS* 918 recording an unnamed senator who served twice as an imperial legate, at least once in Syria. This may or may not refer to Quirinius. Further complication is added by the late-second to early-third-century-AD Christian Apologist Tertullian, who dated the birth of Jesus to the time of a census held by the Syrian legate Coponius, see Tertullian, *Against Marcion* 4. 19; Strabo, *Geog.* 12. 5. 6, Tacitus, *Ann.* 3. 48 record a victory won by Quirinius on the borders of Cilicia, which probably occurred some time around 4–3 BC, perhaps during a spell as legate of Galatia and Pamphylia.
3 See Goudineau in *CAH²* X, p. 490 for the censuses in Gaul.
4 For a very useful discussion see Schürer (1973), pp. 399–427, and more briefly P. Richardson, *Herod. King of the Jews and Friend of the Romans* (1996), pp. 295–8.
5 For Egypt see A. Bowman in *CAH²* X, pp. 679–86, 689–93.
6 On the massacre see Richardson (1996), pp. 297–8 for scepticism, which can be presented as a fact even in such apparently unrelated books as A. Murdoch, *Rome's Greatest Defeat. Massacre in the Teutoburg Forest* (2006), p. 59.

INDEX